# THE FIRST AMENDMENT

AND

# THE FIFTH ESTATE

---

# REGULATION OF ELECTRONIC MASS MEDIA

By

### T. BARTON CARTER
Associate Professor of Mass Communication
College of Communication
Boston University

### MARC A. FRANKLIN
Frederick I. Richman Professor of Law
Stanford University

### JAY B. WRIGHT
Professor of Journalism
S.I. Newhouse School of Public Communications
Syracuse University

Mineola, New York
THE FOUNDATION PRESS, INC.
1986

**Library of Congress Cataloging in Publication Data**

Carter, T. Barton.
  The First Amendment and the fifth estate.

  Includes index.
  1. Broadcasting—Law and legislation—United States.
2. Cable television—Law and legislation—United
States.  3. Freedom of speech—United States.
I. Franklin, Marc A.  II. Wright, Jay B.  III. Title.
KF2805.C37  1986        343.73'0994          86–516
**ISBN** 0–88277–277–5      347.303994

C., F. & W. First Amend. Fifth Estate FP

For Alison, Jonathan, and Richard

*

# PREFACE

The shared power in the English Parliament of the three estates of the realm—the Lords Spiritual, the Lords Temporal, and the Commons—was long ago recognized as being in some ways overshadowed by the special power of the Reporters' Gallery. Journalism thus came to be known as the Fourth Estate. *Broadcasting* magazine and others have referred to the world of the electronic media as the Fifth Estate.

It is in recognition of the special importance and influence of the electronic media that we have written this book—a companion to our earlier book, *The First Amendment and the Fourth Estate.*

From the early days of radio to the current days of proliferating new communications technologies, regulation of the electronic mass media has presented difficult legal and policy issues. Technological limitations unique to the electronic media produced a level of governmental involvement previously unknown in United States media. This involvement raised serious First Amendment questions leading to new theories of the First Amendment. Constant technological development has required almost continuous reevaluation of these theories, a process that is far from over.

Those wishing to work in the electronic mass media need to know and understand not only the regulations that govern the industry, but the policies that have shaped those regulations. The entire structure of the industry is a direct result of those regulations and policies.

The goals of this book are to clarify the laws and regulations that govern the electronic mass media, examine the policies that underlie these laws and regulations, and evaluate the extent to which the laws and regulations effectuate these policies. Due to the complexity and constantly changing nature of the field of electronic media regulation, it is not sufficient to memorize some of the existing regulations along with a few slogans and phrases.

We believe that a proper understanding of this subject is possible only through examination of the opinions and decisions of those governmental bodies most directly responsible for the laws and regulations that apply to the electronic mass media: Congress, the Federal Communications Commission, and the courts.

Due in part to a major shift in the regulatory philosophy of the Federal Communications Commission, as well as numerous technological developments, the field of electronic media regulation is changing at an amazing rate. Studying the development of the field through the actual language of the courts and the Commission should help in understanding these changes and their implications.

The book is divided into three parts. Chapters I and II serve as an introduction to the legal, technological, and economic structure that has produced our system of electronic media regulation. Chapters III through X detail the laws and regulations that apply specifically to the electronic media. Finally, Chapters XI through XIV outline some of the more important laws applicable to *both* print and electronic media.

Thanks are due to the American Law Institute for excerpts from the *Restatement (Second) of Torts* and to B. M. Owen, J. H. Beebe, and W. G. Manning, Jr., for the chart from their book *Television Economics*. Our wives, Eleonore, Ruth, and Yolanda, deserve special thanks for their consideration and support.

T. Barton Carter
Marc A. Franklin
Jay B. Wright

February, 1986

# SUMMARY OF CONTENTS

## SUMMARY OF CONTENTS

*

# TABLE OF CONTENTS

## TABLE OF CONTENTS

TABLE OF CONTENTS

## APPENDIX

*

# TABLE OF CASES

The principal cases are in italic type.  Cases cited or discussed are in roman type.  References are to Pages.  Cases cited to the United States Supreme Court will be found under both plaintiff and defendant.

\*

# THE FIRST AMENDMENT

AND

# THE FIFTH ESTATE

---

## REGULATION OF ELECTRONIC MASS MEDIA

*

# Chapter I

## INTRODUCTION

For most students of electronic media, the study of the law of freedom of expression is just one part of a full professional curriculum. While some students in communications schools may decide to go on to law school and then to practice law, the vast majority will be users or consumers of law. It is primarily for the latter that this book is intended. Presumably, an intelligent professional in any aspect of communications should know enough about the law and public policy to make some on-the-spot judgments. This is particularly true in the electronic media, where deadline pressures often require quick decisions. The intelligent professional also needs to know enough to alert a superior when a potential legal problem is spotted and should know—particularly after reaching management level—when to seek the advice of an attorney.

With some experience, the consumer of legal advice learns how to take the attorney's advice. Some attorneys are much more cautious than others, and they will tend to give advice discouraging clients from airing some controversial materials that could lead to law suits. Other attorneys, particularly those who represent major media, may be much more daring and may say to a client, "Air what you need to. You're the journalist, and you know best what you think has to be aired. If you get sued, it will be my responsibility to defend you."

Newcomers are sometimes surprised to discover how unclear the law seems to be. Many questions have never been anticipated by legislators nor been answered by the courts. This is especially true with the electronic media, where technological developments are constantly raising new issues. Sometimes in two similar cases in different parts of the country, different courts have reached different conclusions. Bright attorneys disagree when they predict the outcomes of cases. Judges— even the nine justices of the Supreme Court of the United States— frequently disagree with one another and arrive at split decisions based on 5–4 or 6–3 votes. Newcomers to the law may be surprised to find, after they have read the opinion of the majority of the Court and agreed with it, that they also agree with points made in the dissenting opinion. It should not be quite so surprising that frequently there are good arguments on *both* sides of a dispute that has reached the Supreme Court.

Textbooks like this one give heavy emphasis to opinions of the Supreme Court because those opinions influence the application of the law in the courts below and they influence out-of-court settlements made on a much less formal basis. They also, of course, have an impact on rules and regulations imposed on electronic media by the Federal Com-

1

munications Commission. It should be recognized, however, that a case that reaches the Supreme Court is an unusual case rather than a typical one. If, for example, we were to examine one thousand instances in which the electronic media had aired something erroneous about individuals, we would probably find that most of the resulting "disputes" were resolved by the media's retracting the erroneous statements or by the unhappy individual's being advised that they did not have libel cases because they really suffered no reputational harm as a result of the errors, or by the individual's deciding that they did not have the time, inclination, or money to file a lawsuit. Even if 100 of those disputes resulted in lawsuits, the odds would still favor an out-of-court settlement or a decision by a trial court without getting into the appellate courts. If a single one of those 100 lawsuits reached the Supreme Court it would be surprising.

If Supreme Court cases are so relatively rare, one might ask, why not study the "ordinary" cases instead? The answer, of course, is that the way communications professionals and attorneys assess their chances of winning or losing a suit, and thereby decide whether to pursue it in court or to settle out of court, is by applying the principles from decisions in the major cases.

In this Chapter we look not just at the Supreme Court cases but at a variety of sources of law in America and at the way legal cases proceed.

## A.  THE LAW

Law has always been an important force in American life—and courts have always been at the center of our legal system. All state constitutions created state court systems. The United States Constitution established the Supreme Court of the United States and empowered Congress to create lower federal courts. Many critical national questions have been addressed and resolved in court, from sedition questions after the Revolutionary War to the treatment of blacks after the Civil War, from school desegregation beginning in the 1930's, '40's, and '50's to questions of Presidential behavior in office in the 1970's. Hindsight shows that not all judicial decisions over 200 years have been correct, nor have they all been popular. But the overall respect Americans have for the legal system, even when they may disagree with particular decisions or dislike particular judges, has allowed the country to solve most major problems without violent upheavals. In general terms, the law is a system of rules of conduct that individuals and institutions are expected to follow, rules given force by a community's decision to punish those who violate them.

## 1. Sources and Structure of Law and the Legal Process

### a. Sources of Law

In the United States, laws and sanctions for disobeying them come from four major sources: Constitutions, statutes, administrative decisions, and the judge-made law called the common law.

*Constitutions.* Although much of our legal system was borrowed from Great Britain, that country has no written constitution. This important form of law was developed in the United States. Not only is there a federal constitution, but each state has one. These documents decree governmental organization, describe the duties and responsibilities of governmental branches and officials, and frequently specify certain individual rights, such as freedom of expression.

A constitution is written to allow flexibility as social conditions change. As new questions arise courts must ascertain whether the document permits or requires certain conduct. For instance, the First Amendment to the United States Constitution reads in part: "Congress shall make no law . . . abridging the freedom of speech, or of the press . . . ." As simple as this seems, our study of electronic media law will show the complexity of these words.

*Statutes.* Another source of law is the array of statutes passed by Congress, state legislatures, and city and county governments. The law we inherited from Great Britain generally served as basic authority in the early days of the United States. After that, statutes adopted by legislative bodies began to be more important than judicially developed law. Today, statutes are the dominant form of lawmaking. Much judicial time is spent interpreting these laws and deciding how they apply to specific situations. Statutes are general in scope and prospective in operation.

Statutes are also used to create administrative agencies, specifying exactly how much authority they have. For example, the Communications Act of 1934 created the Federal Communications Commission. Today, all criminal laws in this country are statutory. Crimes must be described carefully so that people know precisely what is forbidden. Case law could rarely provide sufficient guidance.

*Administrative Regulations and Decisions.* Today, much law comes from decisions of administrative agencies. These were first developed by Congress as a way to bring expertise to bear on areas under the legislature's responsibility. The first administrative agency was the Interstate Commerce Commission, but today such agencies are numerous. The Federal Communications Commission, the Federal Trade Commission, and the Copyright Royalty Tribunal, all of which affect electronic media law, are just a few of the federal agencies. Administrative agencies also exist on the state and city levels. Much more law is created by these agencies through their delegated lawmaking powers than by all the courts in the country. We will return to administrative law and some of these agencies later in this Chapter.

*Common Law.* The term "common law" is sometimes used to distinguish the Anglo-American legal system from the "civil law" systems of continental Europe. More commonly, the term refers to those areas of law in which no statutes exist and, thus, in which courts are expected to chart their own decisional course without legislative direction. The product of this process, law based on cases alone, is called common law. It is the ever growing result of specific but principled decisions in individual disputes rather than a written body of prospective general rules set down by a legislature.

The common law came from England, where the term first was used to distinguish law made by the King's courts from that made by ecclesiastical courts. But if the law were made by courts, not following a written statute, could not each court—each judge—decide similar cases in different ways? Not only would this cause consternation among citizens who would not know how to act, but judges might totally reconsider whole areas of law as each case arose. The concept of *stare decisis* emerged from these concerns. This is the doctrine of precedent under which judges refer to previous decisions involving basically similar legal issues and facts in order to decide the case at hand. It is then possible to look at previous cases and decisions to see how a court is likely to decide future cases. However, courts are not strictly bound by *stare decisis.* They can "distinguish" a current case from previous cases and refuse to follow the guidance of the past if they find the facts sufficiently different. Or, in an unusual situation, a court can overrule precedents and explicitly embark on a new approach to the legal area. In general, though, judges work within the boundaries of *stare decisis.*

Although the common law was dominant at the time of the Revolution, the increasing complexity of our society and other factors have brought legislation in almost all areas—and a consequent reduction in the role of the common law. It still retains importance for us, however, in the areas of defamation and privacy.

### b. Hierarchy

There is a hierarchy among these four sources of law. Within a state the state constitution is dominant. If a question is not answered in the constitution, an appropriate statute, as interpreted by the courts, will be the final word. But a statute in conflict with the constitution will be struck down by the courts.

Within the spheres of their statutory authority, administrative agency rulings have the force of a statute and will be upheld by courts unless the ruling violates the constitution, the agency has violated its own rules in making the decision, or the agency is arbitrary and capricious. Courts examine decisions by zoning commissions and public utility commissions according to these criteria.

When no constitution, statute, or administrative agency ruling controls, courts will apply common law principles to decide a dispute.

### c. *Federalism*

The hierarchy just discussed applies within a single state. But the federal structure of the United States creates a second hierarchy of legal sources that must be explored. When the United States Constitution was written, most space was devoted to creating the three branches of government—Legislature in Article I, Executive in Article II, and Judiciary in Article III. Those articles dealt only with how the federal government should conduct its internal affairs. In this respect, the federal government's structure resembled that of a state government.

But the nature of federalism required that some attention be paid to the relationship between the existing state governments and the new federal government. This was addressed in Article VI, Section 2, the Supremacy Clause which provides that:

> This Constitution, and the Laws of the United States which shall be made in pursuance thereof . . . shall be the supreme Law of the Land; and the Judges in every State shall be bound thereby, any Thing in the Constitution or Laws of any State to the Contrary notwithstanding.

This aspect of federalism becomes important because some of our cases involve claims that state laws are invalid because they conflict with some federally protected right. Notice also that state court judges are obligated to declare state laws invalid if they conflict with federal provisions.

Finally, notice how important the courts are at every stage of the legal system. Although courts act only to resolve specific disputes that the parties cannot settle, the judicial power permeates every layer of the two hierarchies. When a constitutional provision is relied upon by one of the parties to the dispute, the court must interpret the provision's meaning and its application to the dispute before it. When one party relies upon a statute, the court may have to interpret it—and may also have to decide whether it is consistent with the state's constitution. When an administrative ruling is involved in the dispute, the court must decide whether the agency acted constitutionally, acted within its statutory authority, followed its own rules, and acted without being arbitrary or capricious. When none of these sources appears to have a bearing on the litigation, the court turns to common-law decisionmaking.

When federalism is involved, state and federal courts are obligated to assure that in cases of conflict proper scope is given to the federal provisions in resolving the case before them.

### d. *Litigation*

The judicial system must deal with several kinds of controversies.

The most common type we will encounter will be the administrative proceeding. A party who wishes to acquire a license to broadcast, for example, must apply to the Federal Communications Commission. Anyone who feels aggrieved by a Commission decision can appeal. The court must then determine whether the Commission acted within the limits of its authority. Commission rulemaking decisions can also be challenged in court.

Another type of controversy is the criminal case in which a government seeks to punish a party, perhaps a reporter, for illegal behavior. The defense may claim that the legal rule allegedly violated is invalid because it conflicts with the First Amendment. The court must decide whether the statute in question is constitutional.

A third form of litigation also arises from the passage of a statute. Here, however, those restricted by the statute do not wait to be prosecuted for a violation of the statute, but instead initiate a suit to have the statute or regulation declared unconstitutional. The court is asked to render a "declaratory judgment" that it would be unconstitutional for the government to enforce the statute against the complaining parties. Another way to test a statute's constitutionality without risking criminal prosecution is to seek an injunction to prohibit state officials from enforcing the statute—again on the ground that to do so would violate the constitutional rights of the plaintiff.

A fourth type of case involves "tort" litigation between two private parties for harm that one has caused the other. Examples include auto accidents and injuries caused by defective products. A tort action is usually brought for damages for alleged violation of a common law duty. We shall be concerned mainly with tort actions for damages for defamation and for invasion of privacy. In these cases it is possible for the defendant to argue that if the state court finds the defendant liable and orders it to pay damages to plaintiff, the action of the court would be "state action" that would infringe the defendant's constitutional right to freedom of expression.

Finally, we will also consider "injunctions"—court orders not to do something. Violating an injunction can lead to one's being held in contempt of court.

The courtroom drama that comes to mind in terms of litigation actually occurs primarily in criminal cases, where facts are disputed: can the victim accurately identify the defendant or is the jury persuaded by the defendant's alibi witnesses? In conventional criminal cases, the parties agree on the legal rules but they disagree about the facts—and a trial is needed to determine the facts governed by these rules.

In most of the cases in this book, and most First Amendment cases generally, the crucial questions that will determine the outcome do not depend on disputed facts. Rather, the parties usually disagree over what legal rule applies to an accepted set of facts. Such a dispute raises legal questions to be resolved by a judge, often with no need for a trial.

The dispute will be brought in one of two court systems—state or federal. Before the United States Constitution was adopted, each state had its own court system—with trial and appellate courts. These systems survived. As a result of the adoption of the United States Constitution, and early action of Congress, a second court system—the federal system—was created.

When one party sues another party in the same state, under state libel law, for example, the trial—if there is one—will take place in a state court. When the parties are individuals or corporations in different states, questions beyond our present concerns arise about whether the litigation will take place in a state or federal court. Regardless, the trial will provide the opportunity for the presentation of evidence, including testimony by witnesses. Usually a jury would hear the case, but in some instances the trial judge will decide the case alone.

If there has been a trial, or if the judge has made a legal ruling on a motion on an agreed upon set of facts, either or both of the parties may be dissatisfied. They may believe that errors were made—either errors in procedure or errors in substantive law. If they choose to appeal to a higher (appellate) court, they will submit a transcript of the lower court proceedings and a *brief,* a document explaining the alleged errors to the appellate court. Virtually every system permits the right to one appeal. But, although one is entitled to one's "day in court" and even a second day in an appellate court, higher courts often do not have to take cases for review unless they choose to do so.

Depending on the size of the state and the complexity of the state system, state judgments might be appealed to one or more levels of appellate courts before reaching the highest court in the state—typically, but not always, called the supreme court. In the federal system, decisions from the trial court, called the U.S. District Court, are appealed to a regional Court of Appeals and then to the Supreme Court of the United States. Federal administrative agency decisions are appealed directly to the Court of Appeals.

The Supreme Court performs two distinct roles. As the final appellate court for litigants who have lost cases in lower federal courts, it is the apex of the federal system of courts. Second, states and state courts have obligations imposed upon them by the United States Constitution. Some are explicit prohibitions, such as those in Article I, Section 10, that no state may adopt an *ex post facto* law or coin its own currency. Other limitations are imposed by the Supremacy Clause of Article VI, Section 2, which declares that when federal and state law conflict, the federal law is supreme—and the judges of the state courts are required to recognize that supremacy. The Supreme Court of the United States has the power to review the actions of state courts to assure that states are complying with federal obligations.

Some of the cases we consider have come to the Supreme Court from the state courts. The losing party has usually claimed that the decision of the state courts has incorrectly interpreted the First Amendment—which applies to the states because of the Fourteenth Amendment, as explained shortly. Although state courts may render decisions interpreting the First and Fourteenth Amendments, the Supreme Court is the *final* authority on the meaning of the United States Constitution.

If a case poses an important question involving the First Amendment or some other part of the United States Constitution, it can wind up in the Supreme Court whether it starts in the state courts or in the federal courts.

In most instances the Supreme Court has been given discretion by Congress to choose what cases it will hear, and of the many thousands of cases that are brought each year, the Court accepts only some 200 for hearing and decision. To seek review by the Supreme Court, the litigant who lost the case in the lower court files what is called a "petition for certiorari" stating the nature of the dispute, the decision below, and the reasons why the Court should review this case. Since a case usually reaches the Supreme Court only after several lower courts, state or federal, have considered it, it rarely suffices for the petitioner to allege that the judges below made a mistake—a better reason is necessary. A serious claim that a state law violates the First Amendment is such a reason.

After the petition for certiorari is filed, the party who won below will usually file a memorandum trying to persuade the Court either that the case is not important, that there is no conflict with other decisions, or that the decision is clearly correct in light of previous Supreme Court cases. In deciding whether or not to grant a petition for certiorari, all the justices will meet in conference and vote. The Court follows the so-called "rule of four" under which, if four justices believe the case should be heard, the petition for certiorari will be granted.

If the Supreme Court decides not to hear the case, it will usually not state its reasons and will issue an order that says simply "The petition for certiorari is denied." In this book that procedure is indicated when "certiorari denied" is part of the citation. Although this outcome favors the party that won in the lower court, the legal effect is different from having the Supreme Court listen to the case on the merits and decide to affirm the decision of the lower court. When the Supreme Court denies certiorari all that is clear is that the Court did not think the case worthy of full consideration. This does not mean that the Court believes that the case was correctly decided below. It may mean only that the Court does not think the issue is important enough to justify further attention.

When the Supreme Court decides it will listen to a case, it will generally issue an order "granting" the petition for certiorari and directing the parties to file formal briefs arguing the merits of the controversy. The losing party below, the petitioner, prepares a brief, trying to persuade the Court to decide the case on the merits in petitioner's favor. The respondent's brief seeks to persuade the Court to affirm the result reached by the lower court.

The Court will schedule oral arguments at which the attorneys representing both parties have a limited period of time before the justices of the Court to make the best arguments they can for their clients and to answer questions posed by the justices. Because new evidence is not presented at the appellate level, and witnesses are not heard, the parties to the case need not even be present. In a sense, the discussion is about whether errors have been made in the trial court below, and it is not necessary to hear from the witnesses. The witnesses' testimony and other evidence is already reflected in the transcripts of the case filed with the Court, so the oral argument should, as the name suggests, focus on the attempts to persuade the justices as to the outcome of the case.

Following the oral arguments in the case, the justices meet privately to discuss the case and to indicate how they expect to vote. In the Supreme Court, if the Chief Justice is a member of the majority, he may assign the writing of the majority opinion to himself or to any of the other justices in the majority. Similarly, the senior justice among the dissenters may assign the dissenting opinion. When the Chief Justice is dissenting, the senior justice among the majority assigns the majority opinion. Drafts of opinions, written by the justices and their clerks, are circulated privately among the justices. Agreement is reached where possible, but each of the justices reserves the right to publish his own opinion if he chooses. In the "Pentagon Papers" case (see discussion of New York Times Co. v. United States later in this Chapter), to use a most unusual example, all nine justices wrote opinions.

A single opinion that has the support of a majority of the participating justices is denominated an "opinion of the Court." As such it becomes binding on the Court, establishing a precedent for subsequent decisions (unless later overruled by the Court itself). Sometimes, however, while a majority of the Court agree on the outcome of a case, they do so for different reasons. For example, six of the nine justices might vote to affirm a lower court decision, but four could be doing so for one reason and two could be doing so for a different reason. In such a case, the opinion written by the four justices is a "plurality" opinion, not a majority opinion. Such an opinion is entitled to substantially less precedential value than an opinion of the Court. The first line of the reported decision will indicate the nature of the opinion—a named justice either delivers the "opinion of the Court" or announces "the judgment of the Court and an opinion joined by" up to three other justices. The "judgment of the Court" means the bare result, such as affirmance or reversal. The reasons for the judgment are found in the opinions.

## 2. READING THE LAW

Supreme Court decisions obviously are not written for readers who are totally unfamiliar with legal language. Typically, they refer to, or *cite*, earlier cases that you may or may not have to read. Not surprisingly, some of the justices are better writers than others. The meaning of some paragraphs may be perfectly clear, but some confuse even the best of lawyers and require subsequent cases to resolve the confusion. Although reading Supreme Court decisions may seem difficult at first, it usually becomes easier as you become more familiar with the language and gradually develop some background in reading the law.

As you read the cases, note the names. When the losing party in the lower court files a petition for certiorari, the petitioner's name comes first in the title of the case. The initial plaintiff thus may later become the *respondent* and be listed second in the title in the Supreme Court. A few other appellate courts follow the practice of putting the losing party's name first. As you read the appellate cases in this book, do not assume that the party named first in the title was the original plaintiff.

On a related point, every title of a case is followed by a group of numbers and abbreviations called a "citation." This tells which volumes in the law library contain the full report of the opinions in the case. For example, the citation to Cox Broadcasting Corp. v. Cohn, 420 U.S. 469, 95 S.Ct. 1029, 43 L.Ed.2d 328 (1975), means that the case can be found in volume 420 of the United States Reports at page 469, and also in volume 95 of the Supreme Court Reporter at page 1029, and also in volume 43 of United States Supreme Court Reports (Lawyer's Edition, 2d series) at page 328. Opinions of the United States Court of Appeals are found in the Federal Reporter Second Series (F.2d). Decisions of the United States District Courts are found in the Federal Supplement (F.Supp.). State decisions usually have two citations: one to a state reporter and one to a private service that groups state decisions in regional volumes. Thus, in Taylor v. KTVB, 96 Idaho 202, 525 P.2d 984 (1974), the first reference is to volume 96 of the official Idaho reports at page 202, and the second is to volume 525 of the Pacific Reporter, Second Series, page 984, where the Idaho case will also be found.

There are certain reporting services of special importance to electronic media regulation. The FCC's official reports are referred to by volume number, F.C.C. or F.C.C.2d, followed by page number. When the Commission proposes rules for possible adoption, formal notice of the pending action must be given to the public. This is done through the Federal Register (Fed.Reg. or F.R.). The register is organized chronologically and covers all federal agencies and departments. Regulations adopted by the Commission as well as its rules of organization and internal operation are reported and grouped together in another official publication called the Code of Federal Regulations (C.F.R.). An unofficial service reports Commission rulemaking actions and case decisions. The full name of this service, *Pike & Fischer's Radio Regulation,* is abbreviated as R.R. or R.R.2d, and sometimes as P & F Radio Reg. Note that the name *Radio Regulation* is deceptive: the service includes television decisions too. Another unofficial service reports judicial decisions in mass media law but does not include FCC decisions and covers fewer electronic cases than Pike & Fischer. This service, *Media Law Reporter,* is abbreviated as Med.L.Rptr.

The foregoing discussion of litigation and the role of the Supreme Court has necessarily been general and abstract. As we turn to actual cases you should review this information if some aspect of a case puzzles you. Any unusual matters will be discussed in the introduction to the case or in the notes that follow the opinions.

In addition to the references to reports of judicial opinions, you will note references to the *U.S. Code* (U.S.C.), which contains federal statutes, and to the *Code of Federal Regulations* (C.F.R.), which contains rules and regulations of federal regulatory agencies.

Some of the terms used in the texts, particularly the Latin ones, may be unfamiliar to you at first. While there are a variety of legal dictionaries published, some in paperback, you will probably find most of the terms defined in any good collegiate dictionary. As you see them used in the cases, they will become part of your legal vocabulary.

## B. THE FIRST AMENDMENT

In the United States, regulation of the mass media is different from the regulation of any other industry. What distinguishes it is the First Amendment to the Constitution of the United States (reproduced in Appendix A). A brief examination of the historical roots of the First Amendment and its interpretation by the courts is necessary for an understanding of electronic mass media regulation.

### 1. INTRODUCTION TO FREEDOM OF EXPRESSION

---

#### a. The English Background

In England, repression of ideas antithetical to the government was in operation by the 13th century. In 1275 and again in 1379 Parliament made it criminal to speak against the state. Later known as "seditious libel," words that questioned the crown in any way were punished by the King's Council sitting in the "starred chamber." Ecclesiastical laws forbidding heresy already existed, thus making it dangerous to say anything in opposition to the Church or the state.

With the advent of printing, around 1500, the government became even more concerned about statements that questioned the secular powers. To prevent the wider dissemination that the printing press made possible, the Crown established a system of censorship, similar to the one already used by the Church, for all publications. This repression lasted until almost 1700. The core of the censorship system was licensing. Unlicensed publication could lead to severe punishment and to charges of criminal libel.

In addition to criminal prosecutions for libel, the English government found taxation to be an effective way to control the press. The purpose of the Stamp Act of 1711 and later laws was to reduce the circulation of newspapers. Half of England's newspapers went out of business in the first year of the Act.

Despite such measures, it was possible for Great Britain still to contend that freedom of the press existed. Sir William Blackstone, the most famous compiler of the common law, wrote in the late 1760's:

> [w]here blasphemous, immoral, treasonable, schismatical, seditious, or scandalous libels are punished by the English law . . . the liberty of the press, properly understood, is by no means infringed or violated. The liberty of the press is indeed essential to the nature of a free estate; but this consists in laying no previous restraints upon publications, and not in freedom from censure for criminal matter when published. Every freeman has an undoubted right to lay what sentiments he pleases before the press: to forbid this is to destroy the freedom of the press: but if he publishes what is improper, mischievous, or illegal, he must take the consequences of his own temerity . . . .

W. Blackstone, 4 Commentaries on the Laws of England 151–52 (1765–69).

Blackstone is central to this analysis because he was a major influence on English and American legal thinking in the period when our Constitution was taking shape. His definition of freedom of the press as the absence of "previous restraints upon publications," and the distinction between liberty thus defined, and licentiousness, for which punishment was considered legitimate, made clear that freedom of expression meant, as a minimum, rejection of prior restraint. Uncertainty remains as to the legitimacy of subsequent punishment for seditious libel, and as to what types of expression constitute punishable "licentiousness."

### b. The Colonial Experience

Those who drafted and adopted the United States Constitution and the Bill of Rights were well aware of this background of repression in Great Britain. They also knew of, and had experienced, similar restrictions on freedom of expression imposed by Britain on the colonies. The British Stamp Act of 1765 was directed specifically against the colonies and was meant to offset "the expense of defending, protecting and securing" the colonies. In fact, the Act served more to anger colonists than to raise revenue. The colonists saw the Act as "taxation without representation" and rebelled against it.

Prior to that, however, laws that applied to the press in England during the 17th and 18th centuries were also applied to the emerging colonial press, and the licensing of presses in the colonies closely paralleled the English practice. The colonies saw printers jailed and their books burned for publishing without permission.

In 1734, John Peter Zenger, who printed the *Weekly Journal*, was charged with seditious libel by the Governor General of New York, whom Zenger had criticized. Zenger spent almost a year in jail awaiting trial. By the traditional common law standards he was surely guilty because he had published the articles in question and the law did not recognize truth as a defense. Zenger's lawyer, Andrew Hamilton, convinced the jury that the only question in the case involved the liberty to write the truth, and the jury, despite the judge's instructions, acquitted Zenger. Although the verdict set no precedent (because a jury verdict is not a ruling on the law), it did signal a change in the political climate.

After the American Revolution, the governments of the former colonies sought to come together to form a nation. Even before the war was ended the colonies had attempted to form a national government under the Articles of Confederation, devised in 1783. This document allowed the states to retain much power, leaving little for the central government. The Articles contained no mention of freedom of expression, but many argued such a clause was not necessary. Since the federal government had no power to interfere with citizens, there was no need to forbid it from exercising power it did not have. Additionally, most states had some form of bill of rights in their own constitutions.

The new Constitution, formulated at the Constitutional Convention of 1787, created the national government with three branches. Some states in their own constitutions had protected citizens against state government action, but the federal Constitution was not primarily concerned with that problem. The omission led some critics to oppose ratification because the new government might itself threaten the freedom of citizens of the new country.

Although the records of the Constitutional Convention are sketchy, it is known that discussion of a bill of rights did not take place until the last few days of the meeting. That short-lived debate was inconclusive. The Constitution was promulgated without a bill of rights and sent to the states for ratification.

During ratification debates there was much enthusiasm for freedom of the press but no clear idea of exactly how it should be protected or how far it should extend.

Even though 13 states ratified the Constitution, five expressed concern that a bill of rights had been omitted.

As a result of this dissatisfaction, James Madison introduced a set of amendments to the Constitution when the First Congress met. The House of Representatives approved an amendment that protected freedom of speech and press from infringement "by any state." The Senate struck the provision limiting the powers of the states and the final version provided that "Congress shall make no law . . . abridging the freedom of speech, or of the press . . . ." This was the third of 12 amendments submitted to the states for ratification. When the first two failed, this became the First Amendment to the United States Constitution.

Although it was later argued that the Bill of Rights was intended to protect citizens against invasions by the state as well as the federal government, this was rejected in Barron v. Baltimore, 32 U.S. (7 Pet.) 243

(1833) when the Supreme Court decided that the Bill of Rights applied solely against the federal government. Constraints on the states were those specified in Article I, Section 10 and in such other provisions as the Supremacy Clause.

Though on its face the First Amendment appears to bind only the Congress, it is well established today that the prohibitions of the First Amendment extend to all branches of both the federal and state governments by way of the "due process" clause of the Fourteenth Amendment. The First Amendment guarantees, the Supreme Court has held, are a fundamental element of the "liberty" protected by the Fourteenth Amendment. Gitlow v. New York, 268 U.S. 652 (1925).

As a result, what Congress may not do because of the First Amendment, a state may not do because of the Fourteenth Amendment. The Constitution restrains only governments, not private individuals from interfering with the exercise of freedom of expression.

In Free Speech in the United States (1941), Prof. Zechariah Chafee, acknowledging that very little was said at the time about the meaning of freedom of speech, reviewed some contemporary statements that suggest that in the years before the First Amendment "freedom of speech was conceived as giving a wide and genuine protection for all sorts of discussion of public matters." He argued that "such a widely recognized right must mean something," and that merely reaffirming the freedom of the press from previous censorship would have been pointless. During the 18th century, besides the narrow legal meaning of liberty of the press, there existed "a definite popular meaning: the right of unrestricted discussion of public affairs," and Chafee thought the framers were aware of basic differences between Great Britain and the former colonies.

### 2. BASES FOR FREEDOM OF COMMUNICATION

Justice Oliver Wendell Holmes observed that the First Amendment prevents all "previous restraints upon publications," but allows "the subsequent punishment of such as may be deemed contrary to the public welfare. . . . The preliminary freedom extends to the false as to the true; the subsequent punishment may extend as well to the true as to the false." Patterson v. Colorado, 205 U.S. 454, 462 (1907).

Professor Thomas I. Emerson, in The System of Freedom of Expression 6–9 (1970), asserted that "the system of freedom of expression in a democratic society" is based on four premises:

(1) freedom of expression facilitates self-fulfillment,

(2) it is an essential tool for advancing knowledge and discovering truth,

(3) it is a way to achieve a more stable and adaptable community, and

(4) it permits individuals to be involved in the democratic decision-making process.

Perhaps the most powerful judicial statement of the justifications for free expression is that of Justice Louis Brandeis, concurring in Whitney v. California, 274 U.S. 357, 375–77 (1927):

> Those who won our independence believed that the final end of the State was to make men free to develop their faculties; and that in its government the deliberative forces should prevail over the arbitrary. They valued liberty both as an end and as a means. They believed liberty to be the secret of happiness and courage to be the secret of liberty. They believed that freedom to think as you will and speak as you think are means indispensable to the discovery and spread of political truth; that without free speech and assembly discussion would be futile; that with them, discussion affords ordinarily adequate protection against the dissemination of noxious doctrine; that the greatest menace to freedom is an inert people; that public discussion is a political duty; and that this should be a fundamental principle of the American government. They recognized the risks to which all human institutions are subject. But they knew that order cannot be secured merely through fear of punishment for its infraction; that it is hazardous to discourage thought, hope and imagination; that fear breeds repression; that repression breeds hate; that hate menaces stable government; that the path of safety lies in the opportunity to discuss freely supposed grievances and proposed remedies; and that the fitting remedy for evil counsels is good ones. Believing in the power of reason as applied through public discussion, they eschewed silence coerced by law—the argument of force in its worst form. Recognizing the occasional tyrannies of governing majorities, they amended the Constitution so that free speech and assembly should be guaranteed.

How many of Emerson's premises do you find in the Brandeis view?

Each of these explanations has been used, to a greater or lesser extent, by the Supreme Court to justify the high value placed on freedom of speech in our constitutional scheme of government. Each may justify different notions of the breadth and depth of the First Amendment freedom and each may apply with peculiar force in particular contexts.

These fundamental justifications for protecting speech tend to divide into two main groups: those that stress the values to the individual and those that stress the values to the society of freedom of speech. The emphasis on value to the individual, contained in what are variously called the self-fulfillment or self-realization models, is on the importance of expression as a route to individual development and fulfillment.

### a.   For Individuals

A concept of "natural law" was actively discussed for two centuries before the Constitution was adopted. In attempting to reconcile government's role with individual rights, certain personal freedoms were seen as inviolable. They were "natural rights" of individuals, rights that

official persons or bodies had no power to affect. Among these rights
was freedom of expression.

This concept derived in large part from the 17th century English
philosopher John Locke, who contended that government's purpose was
to use its power to protect life, liberty, and property, natural rights to
which each individual was entitled. Locke's views influenced the language of the First Amendment with the notion of free speech as a
natural right, and the Fifth Amendment ("No person shall . . . be
deprived of life, liberty, or property, without due process of law.
. . .").

Locke discussed the origin of society in terms of a social contract.
He believed the pre-social status was one of freedom. Private property
was recognized, but no security existed. To achieve security, people
surrendered a certain amount of freedom to establish a government.
But the government rested on the consent of the governed, who would
control the government rather than vice versa. A government that
encroached on an individual's rights should be abolished or changed.

Several commentators believe that even with this Lockean philosophy to draw on, the framers had no clear concept of the First Amendment's purpose. No matter what the framers might have had in mind,
however, they could not have foreseen the many changes in media
technology and society generally. Thus, more expansive views of freedom of communication became necessary.


### b.  For Society

Neither disputing nor relying upon the assertion that we as individuals profit from freedom of speech, the society-centered reasons offered
for protection explain why we as a people are better for having First
Amendment freedoms.

*Marketplace of Ideas.*  The seminal view that freedom of expression
enhances the social good came from John Milton's *Areopagitica* in 1644.
Milton, an English poet and essayist, wanted a divorce and wrote an
essay he hoped would lower the strict legal barriers prohibiting it. He
was chastised for publishing without a license and wrote *Areopagitica* to
induce Parliament to allow unlicensed printing. Milton argued that
licensing was unworkable and an affront to those who had views to
express. But more, he said, it was harmful to society, since people are
better able to function as citizens if they are knowledgeable and exposed
to different points of view. Attempting to assuage official fears that the
Crown's views would be overwhelmed if unlicensed printing were allowed, Milton wrote: "And though all the winds of doctrine were let
loose to play upon the earth, so Truth be in the field, we do injuriously
by licensing and prohibiting to misdoubt her strength. Let her and
Falsehood grapple; who ever knew Truth put to the worse, in a free and
open encounter?"

English philosopher and economist John Stuart Mill, who wrote 200 years after Milton, believed more in full and free discussion than did Milton. Mill thought that society could function well only with such freedom. He saw freedom of thought, discussion, and investigation as "goods in their own right" but, more importantly, thought that society benefits from an exchange of ideas. People could trade their false notions for true ones, but only if they could hear the true ones. Such open discussion would necessarily mean that false as well as true ideas would be expressed.

The concept of the marketplace of ideas, first enunciated by Milton and later developed by Mill, was recognized in American law by Justice Holmes. In Abrams v. United States, 250 U.S. 616 (1919), Abrams and others had been accused of publishing pamphlets that criticized President Wilson's sending of troops to help counter the Russian revolution. The pamphlets also advocated a strike against American munitions plants. A majority of the Supreme Court ruled that publishing such pamphlets during wartime was not protected by the First Amendment. In dissent, Justice Holmes, joined by Justice Brandeis, argued that the pamphlets did not attack the form of the United States government, and thus did not violate the sedition statute as charged.

The marketplace of ideas approach has been criticized from several sides. In a Marxist attack, American philosopher Herbert Marcuse disagrees with the basic premise of the marketplace notion, that rational beings engage in a free interchange of opinions and information. People are not rational because government and mass media manipulate them— each for its own purposes, he says. In an essay entitled "Repressive Tolerance" in *A Critique of Pure Tolerance* (1965), he starts from the premise that "the people must be capable of deliberating and choosing on the basis of knowledge." He is appalled by the broadcaster's reporting of the momentous and the mundane in the same monotone: "It offends against humanity and truth by being calm where one should be enraged, by refraining from accusation where accusation is in the facts themselves."

Marcuse says the "concentration of economic and political power" allows "effective dissent" to be blocked where it could freely emerge, and the "monopolistic media" prejudge "right and wrong, true and false . . . wherever they affect the vital interest of the society." The situation is so dangerous that Marcuse recommends "suspension of the right of free speech and free assembly" so that "spurious objectivity" is replaced by "intolerance against movements from the Right, and toleration of movements from the Left."

Another group adopted a quite different approach. In the mid-1940's, the Commission on Freedom of the Press was organized to study the press in America. Funded primarily by Time Inc., and Encyclopedia Britannica, Inc., and chaired by Robert M. Hutchins, the Commission was composed of philosophers, historians, law professors, and others. No media professionals were included on the panel, but some were called to share their views with Commission members.  The Commission found that press freedom was not seriously threatened in mid-20th century America.  The press had, however, despite the enforcement of antitrust laws, become increasingly concentrated in the hands of fewer individuals. Media owners, in fact, were reasonably free from government interference, but the First Amendment had little direct application to most people.

One Commission member, Professor Zechariah Chafee, Jr., stated that the press could not play its proper part in society in the "mere absence of governmental restrictions."  Rather, "affirmative action by the government or others," would be needed.  Chafee started with Justice Holmes's formulation, "The best test of truth is the power of the thought to get itself accepted in the competition of the market." Abrams v. United States, 250 U.S. 616, 630 (1919).  But how, Chafee asked, could views compete in a market constricted because of a lack of media outlets?  He answered that "a free market requires regulation, just as a free market for goods needs law against monopoly.  .  .  . The government can lay down the rules of the game which will promote rather than restrict free speech."  Such laws might require "essential facilities accessible to all," methods to assure that communication channels remain open, and measures directed at particular communication industries "intended to promote freedom, improve content, or otherwise make them perform their proper function in a free society."  Z. Chafee, 2 Government and Mass Communications 471 ff. (1947).

More recently, law professor Jerome A. Barron adopted the same approach.  He believes the marketplace is an antiquated and impractical concept because of changes in the media and society since 1791.  It is difficult for a person to begin a broadcast service because of limits in spectrum allocation or to begin a newspaper because of the prohibitive cost.  Barron finds censorship by media because they limit the views they disseminate and permit few new or unpopular ideas to be heard widely.  Barron concluded that those who do not control media should be able to express their views through the mass media. "At the very minimum," Barron wrote, "the creation of two remedies is essential—(1) a nondiscriminating right to purchase editorial advertisements in daily newspapers, and (2) a right of reply for public figures and public officers defamed in newspapers."  J. Barron, Freedom of the Press for Whom? 6 (1973).  See also, Barron, Access to the Press—A New First Amendment Right, 80 Harv.L.Rev. 1641 (1967).

*Safety Valve.*  When a government permits freedom of expression it not only allows society to be exposed to a wide range of ideas, it also brings about a stable and adaptable community, according to Professor Thomas Emerson.  See T. Emerson, The System of Freedom of Expression 11–14 (1970).  Substituting force for logic, which is what happens when freedom of expression is suppressed, makes it impossible to come to rational decisions.  In addition, coercion is ineffective in changing thoughts and beliefs.  Instead, stifling expression breeds discontent that focuses not on the issues being suppressed, but on the act of suppression itself.

Emerson's argument is that freedom of expression will not cause society to become fragmented, to divide into opposing camps. Rather, suppression of communication will do that. Freedom of speech and press will allow dissidents to express their ideas "in a release of energy, a lessening of frustration and a channeling of resistance into courses consistent with law and order."

*Self-governance.* A third reason that freedom of communication is valuable in a democratic society is that such a society is based on self-governance, on an informed citizenry that will intelligently elect its representatives. James Madison believed that the people, not the government, were sovereign, and that the main purpose of freedom of speech was to allow citizens to govern themselves in a free society.

In the late 1940's, Professor Alexander Meiklejohn agreed that self-governance was the most important concern of the First Amendment. He advocated distinguishing between two kinds of expression. Speech concerning the self-governing process was "political speech" and deserved absolute protection from governmental interference. Speech that was nonpolitical in character, "private speech," was protected only by the due process clause of the Fifth Amendment, which permits the government some leeway for regulation.

Meiklejohn drew this distinction between political and private speech because he believed the central purpose of the First Amendment is to give citizens the greatest opportunity to discuss and hear about society's problems, the very information one must have to function in a self-governing society.

Meiklejohn's emphasis on self-government might have suggested that the First Amendment would protect only what we conventionally regard as political speech. His vagueness on this point in his 1948 edition was criticized by Chafee, who was concerned about what types of speech were being relegated to the Fifth Amendment's protection. Chafee observed that "there are public aspects to practically every subject." If Meiklejohn intended this broad view of the First Amendment, then Chafee wondered how there could be any limitations in such traditionally regulated areas as obscenity and libel. If, however, Meiklejohn were to place scholarship and the arts in the category of private speech, Chafee would regard it as "shocking to deprive these vital matters of the protection of the inspiring words of the First Amendment." Book Review, 62 Harv.L.Rev. 891, 900 (1949).

### 3. THE FIRST AMENDMENT AND THE INSTITUTIONAL PRESS

"Congress shall make no law . . . abridging the freedom of speech, or of the press . . . ."

The lack of a broad consensus concerning the philosophical underpinnings of the majestic words of the First Amendment does not mean that the courts and legislatures of the United States are released from the obligation to obey the Amendment's dictates. To the contrary, our Nation's lawmaking bodies have clearly acknowledged that the Amendment represents a constitutional bar to government action in numerous situations.

An appreciable and important fraction of these situations involve the institution of "the press," including the electronic press. This chapter sketches some of those elements of First Amendment doctrine that apply most directly to the press. Students interested in a more comprehensive exposition of First Amendment doctrine might consult M. Nimmer, Nimmer on Freedom of Speech (1984).

### a.    Restriction on Government Power

Liberty protected under the Fourteenth Amendment against encroachments of state governments is protected to the exact same extent that the First Amendment itself protects the freedoms of speech and press from the federal government. Lawyers and judges have developed the shorthand expression "incorporation" to express this idea. Since the First Amendment has been "incorporated" into the Fourteenth Amendment, its prohibitions are no less specific by virtue of such incorporation. This means that branches of the state governments are bound, to the same extent as the federal government, to respect the guarantees of the First Amendment.

Despite the considerable expansion of the field of operation of the First Amendment as a result of the incorporation doctrine, it is important to remember that the First Amendment is a bar only to abridgments by government. Private parties are free to "abridge" another's exercise of the speech and press clauses at will so long as they do not violate some other valid law in the process. For example, it is established that a right to distribute printed material is part and parcel of the First Amendment freedoms and the government is prohibited from interfering with such distribution. Lovell v. Griffin, 303 U.S. 444 (1938). On the other hand, the private owner of property may prohibit such a distribution from taking place on *his* property without running afoul of the First Amendment. See PruneYard Shopping Center v. Robins, 447 U.S. 74 (1980).

### b.    The Protected Sphere

*Speech v. Conduct.* More difficult than determining who is prohibited from interfering with protected expression is determining what forms of expressive activity fall within the protected category. Perhaps the most basic line between the protected and the unprotected is suggested by the distinction between "speech" and "conduct." Presumptively, at least, all oral and written communication falls within the protected sphere, and non-verbal conduct remains outside the domain of the First Amendment. Difficulties abound when verbal and non-verbal elements—"symbolic speech"—are mixed into a single expressive activity, such as labor picketing, protest marches, or the wearing of armbands.

Consider, for example, United States v. O'Brien, 391 U.S. 367 (1968). *O'Brien* resulted from the burning, on the steps of the South Boston Courthouse, of Selective Service registration certificates by David Paul O'Brien and three companions during the Vietnam War. O'Brien did not deny burning his certificate; he told the jury he did so to influence others to adopt his antiwar beliefs. Appealing his conviction ultimately to the Supreme Court, O'Brien maintained that his burning of the certificate was "symbolic speech" protected by the First Amendment.

Chief Justice Warren, in the opinion for the Court, wrote:

This Court has held that when "speech" and "nonspeech" elements are combined in the same course of conduct, a sufficiently important governmental interest in regulating the nonspeech element can justify incidental limitations on First Amendment freedoms. . . . [W]e think it clear that a governmental regulation is sufficiently justified if it is within the constitutional power of the government; if it furthers an important or substantial governmental interest; if the governmental interest is unrelated to the suppression of free expression; and if the incidental restriction on alleged First Amendment freedom is no greater than is essential to the furtherance of that interest.

Finding that the statute under which O'Brien was convicted met all of the requirements, the Court upheld O'Brien's conviction.

*O'Brien* is, of course, not a media case, but it has taken on particular importance for the electronic media because the requirements set forth in it have been used to determine the constitutionality of cable regulation in such cases as Home Box Office Inc. v. Federal Communications Commission (1977) and Quincy Cable TV, Inc. v. Federal Communications Commission (1985), both discussed in Chapter IX on cable television.

Another example of symbolic speech is found in Tinker v. Des Moines Independent School District, 393 U.S. 503 (1969), which established that public students' First Amendment rights, including the wearing of armbands, could be limited only if their exercise would cause material and substantial interference with school operations or a collision with the rights of others.

*Non-protected Speech.* Though speech *generally* is a protected activity, the Supreme Court has long placed certain categories of words outside the First Amendment's protection. In 1942, the Court asserted, in Chaplinsky v. New Hampshire, 315 U.S. 568 (1942), that certain classes of expression might be subject to legal sanctions. Chaplinsky had been arrested for calling a town marshal a "God-damned racketeer and a damned Fascist." The Supreme Court characterized the expression as "fighting words . . . likely to cause violence." The words were not protected expression because they invited a violent response by the person to whom they were directed. The Court then observed that other types of speech, including obscenity and libel, were similarly outside the protection of the First Amendment. Obscenity continues to remain outside such protection today, but most libels have been removed from the unprotected category as we will see in Chapter XII.

*Distribution.* Freedom of speech and press have been held to imply more than the freedom only to speak and write. The First Amendment guarantees include the right to disseminate the words produced after creating them. In a milestone case, a city ordinance in Griffin, Ga., prescribed criminal penalties for distributing printed material without permission. The Court found the ordinance was overly broad because it included all "literature," making no distinction between that which the First Amendment does and does not protect. Also, the ordinance gave the city manager unbridled censorship powers since he was given no criteria for decision and was not obligated to explain why he refused permission to distribute. Lovell v. Griffin, 303 U.S. 444 (1938).

*Gathering.* The "right to gather" information from willing private sources began to take shape in 1972 with two cases. In Kleindienst v. Mandel, 408 U.S. 753 (1972), American scholars sought to invite Mandel, a Belgian Marxist economist, to attend conferences and to speak at several American universities. Congress had barred visas for aliens who advocated "the economic, international and governmental doctrines of world communism or the establishment in the United States of a totalitarian dictatorship." After concluding that Mandel, as an alien, had no constitutional right of entry, the Court turned to the rights claimed by the scholars:

> The Government . . . suggests that the First Amendment is inapplicable because [the scholars] have free access to Mandel's ideas through his books and speeches, and because "technological developments," such as tapes or telephone hookups, readily supplant his physical presence. This argument overlooks what may be particular qualities inherent in sustained, face-to-face debate, discussion and questioning. . . . We are loath to hold on this record that existence of other alternatives extinguishes altogether any constitutional interest on the part of the [scholars] in this particular form of access.

The Court, however, concluded that this interest was overcome by the government's longstanding power to make rules for excluding aliens.

The second case to provide some indirect support for protection of gathering was Branzburg v. Hayes, 408 U.S. 665 (1972). Although the Court held that the reporters had no First Amendment right to refuse to testify before a grand jury, the majority acknowledged that the Court was not suggesting "that news gathering does not qualify for First Amendment protection; without some protection for seeking out the news, freedom of the press could be eviscerated." The case is discussed in Chapter XIV.

*Refusal to Speak.* Most freedom of communication questions concern whether the government can prevent a person from, or punish a person for, speaking. In Chapter III we will see that another question is whether individuals can be forced to speak against their will. In the latter situation the broadcast media and the print media are treated quite differently.

### c. Abridgment Defined

Determining whether the press is engaged in protected speech represents only half the question in evaluating whether a constitutional issue has been raised under the First Amendment. Courts must also determine whether an abridgment has taken place.

*Prior Restraints.* In the traditional view, prior restraints represented the quintessential, indeed exclusive, abridgments of speech. "Prior restraint" meant that rather than punishing the publisher by criminal or civil sanctions for what had been published, the government barred the publication from occurring in the first place. This is, of course, the essence of censorship. In English history, the censor was an administrative official, who administered the licensing system. Recall the view of Blackstone, p. 12, supra.

Although it might have been argued that only administrative or executive branch behavior could constitute a prior restraint, it has become clear in this country that judicial orders that bar publications are also analyzed as prior restraints. Nonetheless, court orders imposing prior restraints are thought somewhat less objectionable than similar administrative actions because of a perception that administrators may cut procedural corners and otherwise be unfair in executing their obligations. Even so, some administrative prior restraints are permitted even today. The most obvious example is that the Supreme Court has permitted states to license motion pictures. Under such a system, it is a crime to exhibit a film that has not been approved in advance, even if the film is totally unobjectionable on any ground. This type of licensing system was upheld in Freedman v. Maryland, 380 U.S. 51 (1965), so long as the administrative decision was subject to swift judicial review.

The deep-seated antagonism to prior restraint is seen in the Supreme Court's decision in Near v. Minnesota, 283 U.S. 697 (1931), the first case in which the Court invalidated a state law because it violated the First and Fourteenth Amendments to the United States Constitution. More specifically, *Near* involved a Minnesota statute allowing officials to stop publication of "malicious, scandalous, and defamatory" newspapers and periodicals. Once stopped, publication could be resumed only on order of a judge, who would have to approve the content before allowing continued printing. The country attorney had brought an action to stop publication of a Minneapolis newspaper, *The Saturday Press.* The newspaper had accused certain government officials of being involved in bootlegging and gambling that it said were controlled by a "Jewish gangster."

The Supreme Court of the United States reversed the state court. Chief Justice Charles Evans Hughes, writing for the 5–4 majority, noted that Blackstone's observation that "[t]he liberty of the press . . . consists in laying no *previous* restraints upon publications . . ." was too broad. Although prior restraint is presumed to be unconstitutional, "the protection . . . is not absolutely unlimited." The Court then suggested some areas in which such restraints might be upheld:

> No one would question but that a government might prevent actual obstruction to its recruiting service or to the publication of sailing dates of transports or the number and location of troops. On similar grounds, the primary requirements of decency may be enforced against obscene publications. The security of the community life may be protected against incitements to acts of violence and the overthrow by force of orderly government. The constitutional guaranty of free speech does not "protect a man from an injunction against uttering words that may have all the effect of force." [  ]

Since the defendant's charges in the Near case did not come within any of these categories, prior restraint was impermissible.

The Court similarly struck down a Rhode Island system for reviewing publications for possible obscenity in Bantam Books, Inc. v. Sullivan, 372 U.S. 58 (1963), a prior restraint on distribution of leaflets critical of a Chicago real estate agent in Organization for a Better Austin v. Keefe, 402 U.S. 415 (1971), and a restraint on publication of the Pentagon Papers in New York Times v. United States, 403 U.S. 713 (1971). In these decisions, the Court has said that "Any system of prior restraints of expression comes to this Court bearing a heavy presumption against its constitutional validity," and that the party seeking a restraint "carries a heavy burden of showing justification for the imposition of such a restraint." One of the special problems in applying the First Amendment to broadcasting is the fact that the regulatory scheme is based on a prior restraint (licensing), but the licensing system is still quite different from the sort of prior restraint which would stop the broadcast of a particular program or news story.

A federal district judge in Wisconsin issued a preliminary injunction in March, 1979, restraining *The Progressive* magazine from publishing an article by Howard Morland about the H-bomb. Some people in communications law feared that the case could become the first Supreme Court case in which a prior restraint against the news media would be upheld, but the so-called "secret of the H-bomb" was published in other media before that ever happened, and the government withdrew its request for an injunction. The government might have gone ahead with criminal proceedings but did not. *The Progressive* published its article.

In May 1980, Public Broadcasting Service broadcast a "documentary drama" portraying a love affair between a Saudi princess and a commoner, and their subsequent execution. The program also dwelt on some aspects of Saudi Arabian life that the Saudi government asserted were totally misrepresented. The program was patterned on a true story.

If the Saudi government had made a credible threat to cut off all oil shipments to the United States immediately upon the presentation of the program, and if the best evidence had been that such a cutoff would cripple the American economy, would the government have been able to obtain an injunction against the showing of the program? Is it crucial that no "secret" is involved?

A different aspect of the problem will be seen in Muir v. Alabama Educational Television Commission, discussed in Chapter VIII.

*Subsequent Sanctions.* Though far less compelling from a historical point of view, it is quite clear that sanctions imposed after publication may be like prior restraints, in that they may prevent would-be speakers and writers from publishing protected speech. Such sanctions, whether they are penal in nature, such as imprisonment or fines, or civil damage awards, or the denial of some privilege, generally raise precisely the same issues as prior restraints on publication. Recall Justice Holmes's comment in Patterson v. Colorado, p. 14, supra.

The *Virginia Pilot*, a newspaper published by Landmark Communications, Inc. was found guilty of a misdemeanor and fined $500 plus costs after it accurately reported that a named judge was under investigation by a state commission in a confidential proceeding. Chief Justice Burger delivered the opinion of the Court, reversing the decision of the Supreme Court of Virginia: "We conclude that the publication Virginia seeks to punish under its statute lies near the core of the First Amendment, and the Commonwealth's interests advanced by the imposition of criminal sanctions are insufficient to justify the actual and potential encroachments on freedom of speech and of the press which follow therefrom. [ ] Landmark Communications, Inc. v. Virginia, 435 U.S. 829, 1978.

In Smith v. Daily Mail Publishing Co., 443 U.S. 97 (1979), the Supreme Court was faced with a statute that made it a crime for a newspaper to publish a juvenile offender's name unless the paper had obtained the prior written approval of a court. The paper argued that the prior approval requirement acted in "operation and effect" like a licensing scheme. The Court decided the case in favor of the newspaper but avoided the question of whether the system had operated as a prior restraint:

> . . . [E]ven when a state attempts to punish publication after the event it must nevertheless demonstrate that its punitive action was necessary to further the state interests asserted [citing *Landmark*]. Since we conclude that this statute cannot satisfy the constitutional standards defined in *Landmark Communications, Inc.*, we need not decide whether, as argued by respondents, it operated as a prior restraint.

*Neutral Regulation.* The great proportion of government regulation of the press has never been considered to be abridgment so long as it is neutrally applied, despite the considerable costs such regulation may exact from the press. Thus, for example, one may not operate a broadcasting station without obeying local building codes, the income tax laws and other tax statutes, the antitrust laws, the Occupational Safety and Health Act, legislation dealing with labor relations or any of the myriad other bodies of general regulatory law administered by local, state, and federal governments.

### 4. APPLYING THE FIRST AMENDMENT

An "abridgment" of protected speech is not, despite the apparently unqualified language of the First Amendment, necessarily unconstitutional.

### a. Balancing

Most frequently, the Supreme Court has used a "balancing test" to determine the propriety of a restraint on freedom of expression. The test involves weighing two interests—the government's concern about protecting a particular interest, such as national security or individual reputation, and the individual's and society's interests in expression.

Professor Chafee, an early advocate of balancing, expressed the virtues of that approach in his Free Speech in the United States (1941) at 31 as follows:

> Or to put the matter another way, it is useless to define free speech by talk about rights. The agitator asserts his constitutional right to speak, the government asserts its constitutional right to wage war. The result is a deadlock. . . . To find the boundary line of any right, we must get behind rules of law to human facts. In our problem, we must regard the desires and needs of the individual human being who wants to speak and those of the great group of human beings among whom he speaks. That is, in technical language, there are individual interests and social interests, which must be balanced against each other, if they conflict, in order to determine which interest shall be sacrificed under the circumstances and which shall be protected and become the foundation of a legal right. It must never be forgotten that the balancing cannot be properly done unless all the interests involved are adequately ascertained, and the great evil of all this talk about rights is that each side is so busy denying the official's claim to rights that it entirely overlooks the human desires and needs behind that claim.

Most freedom of expression cases are decided by balancing interests. The Supreme Court, without always explaining its approach, will use one of two variations of the balancing test. Focusing on the interests at stake in the individual case is commonly characterized as "ad hoc" balancing: the specific interests applicable to the facts of the particular case are considered crucial. The court attempts to identify the state's interest in limiting or preventing the speech in question and the would-be speaker's and society's interests in having the speech permitted.

At other times, a more general process, called "definitional" or "categorical" balancing, is used. Here the interests analyzed transcend the merits of a particular case. Rather than asking, for example, whether the value of speech in a particular case outweighs the arguments for proscribing it, the Court might generalize and consider the values of that category of speech, or that category of speaker, and develop a more general analysis.  Recall *Chaplinsky,* supra.

### b.  *Preferred Position*

A basic tenet of constitutional law calls upon courts to presume that enactments of legislative bodies are constitutional.  If the legislation has a rational basis, courts will generally hold it constitutional.  In United States v. Carolene Products Co., 304 U.S. 144 (1938), involving the validity of a federal economic regulation, Justice Stone, writing for the majority, restated this generally accepted view of deference to legislatures.  But in one of the Court's most famous footnotes, Justice Stone wrote:

> There may be narrower scope for operation of the presumption of constitutionality when legislation appears on its face to be within a specific prohibition of the Constitution, such as those of the first ten amendments, which are deemed equally specific when held to be embraced within the Fourteenth.  .  .  .

> It is unnecessary to consider now whether legislation which restricts those political processes which can ordinarily be expected to bring about repeal of undesirable legislation, is to be subjected to more exacting scrutiny under the general prohibitions of the Fourteenth Amendment than are most other types of legislation.  .  .  .

Justice Stone was suggesting that legislation that inhibits political freedoms, such as freedom of communication, must survive more "exacting judicial scrutiny" than other legislative acts.  Instead of having a presumption of constitutionality, such legislation might be presumed to inhibit a basic freedom and the government might have to show an overriding need for it, not simply a rational basis.  As a result of some cases that built on this footnote, freedom of communication became a "preferred freedom," one that courts would not allow the legislature to restrict without a compelling state interest.

### c.  *Clear and Present Danger*

The balance between speech and anti-speech interests is struck in a wide variety of issues affecting mass media.  In defamation, for example, speech interests are balanced against the individual's interest in reputation.  In other cases, speech interests must be balanced against privacy interests, property interests, security interests, public safety and morals, and even countervailing speech interests, to name only a few.  The balance struck in each situation differs as the countervailing interests vary in weight and as the value of the speech interest itself changes in various contexts.

One important example of the balancing process is the evolution of the "clear and present danger" test originally framed by Justice Oliver Wendell Holmes in an important series of cases arising out of the

Espionage Act of 1917. These cases represent the struggle of the courts to accommodate both the federal government's interest in maintaining the integrity of its effort to wage war and the dissenters' free speech rights. The Espionage Act banned attempts to cause insubordination in the armed forces or to obstruct military recruiting or to conspire to achieve these results. Most of these cases, which confronted the Court from 1919 until the mid-1920's, involved radical speakers who opposed the war effort and criticized the political and economic structure of the country.

Based on his marketplace of ideas approach, Justice Holmes saw the clear and present danger test as being least intrusive on freedom of expression in a society in which absolute freedom was impractical. In Schenck v. United States, 249 U.S. 47 (1919), Justice Holmes said that expression could be punished when "the words used are used in such circumstances and are of such a nature as to create a clear and present danger that they will bring about the substantive evils that Congress has a right to prevent. It is a question of proximity and degree."

*Schenck* involved a prosecution under the Espionage Act for publishing a leaflet that interfered with recruiting by urging young men to violate the draft law. Justice Holmes, writing for the majority, found that the leaflet could be closely connected with violations of the Conscription Act (proximity) and that this was a serious danger to the country's security (degree).

In Abrams v. United States, 250 U.S. 616 (1919), the Supreme Court upheld convictions in a case involving pamphlets calling for a strike of munitions workers. And six years later the Court upheld a conviction under a New York criminal statute that barred advocating overthrow of the government by violence. Gitlow v. New York, 268 U.S. 652 (1925).

The curious case of Dennis v. United States, 341 U.S. 494 (1951), involved prosecution of 11 leading members of the Communist Party for conspiring to advocate the forcible overthrow of the government of the United States. Although a plurality of the Court recognized that the Holmes-Brandeis position had evolved to become a majority view, the plurality refused to apply it to this case. The plurality observed that each case confronting Justices Holmes and Brandeis involved "a comparatively isolated event, bearing little relation in their minds to any substantial threat to the safety of the community. . . . They were not confronted with any situation comparable to the instant one—the development of an apparatus designed and dedicated to the overthrow of the Government, in the context of world crisis after crisis."

The Court adopted the test framed by Judge Learned Hand in the lower court: "In each case [courts] must ask whether the gravity of the 'evil,' discounted by its improbability, justifies such invasion of free speech as is necessary to avoid the danger." That statement "takes into consideration those factors which we deem relevant, and relates their significances. More we cannot expect from words." The plurality found that the requisite danger existed.

The status of clear and present danger remained unclear until Brandenburg v. Ohio, 395 U.S. 444 (1969), involving prosecution of a Ku Klux Klan member for advocating racial and religious bigotry. The Court pointed out that its decisions had "fashioned the principle that the constitutional guarantees of free speech and free press do not permit a State to forbid or proscribe advocacy of the use of force or of law violation except where such advocacy is directed to inciting or producing imminent lawless action and is likely to incite or produce such action." Because the criminal syndicalism statute under which Ohio proceeded permitted punishment of advocacy with no requirement of a showing that imminent lawless action was likely to follow, the convictions could not stand.

Despite the extended period during which the clear and present danger test has been discussed in the Supreme Court, its importance and utility must not be overstated.

### d. The Literalist Interpretation of the First Amendment

Some have argued that the First Amendment allows no room for interpretation because its language is absolute: "Congress shall make no law . . . abridging the freedom of speech, or of the press . . .." They have concluded that the federal government "is without any power whatever under the Constitution to put any type of burden on speech and expression of ideas of any kind." Ginzburg v. United States, 383 U.S. 463, 476 (1966) (Black, J., dissenting). Justice Black strongly criticized the balancing approach to First Amendment questions because the test could be used to justify a judge's predilections, but he did not believe that action should be protected to the same extent as speech.

Justice Black's distinction between speech and action provided the escape hatch for his absolutist view. For instance, he would not have required states to allow public high school students to wear black arm bands to protest the Vietnam war. Recall Tinker v. Des Moines Independent School District, 393 U.S. 503, 515 (1969) (Black, J., dissenting). He called the behavior "action," not speech, and thus not protected by the First Amendment.

In his book, *The System of Freedom of Expression* 17 (1970), Professor Thomas Emerson drew a similar distinction, believing, with Justice Black, that expression should be absolutely protected by the First Amendment.

Recall Meiklejohn, too, believed in an absolute approach to the First Amendment—but only for "political speech." As with Justice Black and Emerson, his distinction narrows the types of expression to be afforded absolute protection, leaving to the courts the problem of defining "political speech" and differentiating it from unprotected or less protected expression.

### 5. "OR OF THE PRESS"

Until this point we have used the terms "freedom of speech" and "freedom of the press" interchangeably. Some have argued, however, that the speech and press guarantees have independent and distinct significance. Are some types of activity protected under the press clause not protected under the speech clause? Or are some activities, though they constitute protected speech, outside the press guarantee?

The most prominent proponent of the theory that the press clause is of different scope than the speech clause was Justice Potter Stewart, who contended that the press clause, unlike the speech guarantee, was a *structural* provision of the Constitution. Stewart relied heavily on the notion that the institutional press has a special role in our constitutional scheme as an additional check on the power of government officials. He asserted that because of this special role the institutional press in certain situations had rights of access and immunities growing out of the press clause to which the general citizenry could not lay claim.

Chief Justice Burger rejected this analysis. Concurring in First National Bank of Boston v. Bellotti, 435 U.S. 765 (1978), he contended that the press clause of the First Amendment does not give the "institutional press" a special status. The Chief Justice thought the framers did not contemplate special privileges for the press, and he foresaw difficulty in defining what was and was not included in the "institutional press" if it were to be accorded special status.

Regardless of how the issue of special protection is resolved, it is true as a practical matter that certain First Amendment issues arise in connection with the institutional press, while others are generally raised in the context of individual speech.

## C. ADMINISTRATIVE LAW

Congress usually creates administrative agencies when the task at hand requires continuing supervision, extensive technical considerations, or the development of expert skills, or all of these. The thought is that a group devoting full attention to such a problem may do a better job than Congress might do in sporadic legislative forays into an area. In 1927, Congress did not have the ability or time or desire to unravel the mess that had developed on the airwaves. The basic decision for Congress, in retrospect, was whether to decree a system of private ownership for the airwaves and to allow the courts to unravel the matters through lawsuits invoking property law, to opt for outright public ownership, or to create an administrative body to develop and enforce an allocation system that would bring order from the chaos. As we will see in Chapter II, Congress chose the last of these.

All agencies must function within the direction that the legislature gives them by statute. Here, Congress had no specific idea how the FCC should proceed. Instead, Congress provided in § 303 that "Except as otherwise provided in this Act, the Commission from time to time, as public convenience, interest, or necessity requires shall . . . ." The list that followed included powers to assign bands of frequencies to the various classes of radio stations and assign individual frequencies; decide the times each station may operate; establish areas to be served by any station; regulate the apparatus used with respect to the sharpness of the transmissions; take steps to prevent interference; suspend licenses upon a showing that the licensee violated any statute or regulation or transmitted obscene communications; make rules and regulations that are necessary to carry out the other provisions of the statute; and require licensees to keep records the FCC may deem desirable.

Notice that all these powers are conditioned on a showing that "public convenience, interest, or necessity requires" the regulation. This is a vague standard and, as we shall see, the FCC has rarely been barred from acting on the ground that Congress did not authorize the particular regulation.

An administrative agency such as the FCC usually functions in a variety of ways. Within its statutory authorization it may issue rules or regulations that have the virtual effect of statutes. At other times, it may have to choose between two applicants for a broadcasting license in what resembles a judicial proceeding. At still other times, it performs executive branch functions, as when it seeks out broadcasters or ham operators who are violating their licenses by using excessive power or using unauthorized frequencies.

This variety of regulatory patterns may not comport with traditional understandings about the separation of powers, but these multi-function agencies have been with us for so long that little concern is voiced about their structure. As we shall see, however, questions are continually raised about whether the agency followed the statutory requirements in performing its functions, whether it followed its own rules, whether its decision was arbitrary and capricious, and whether its processes met constitutional requirements.

An administrative agency like the FCC makes public announcements of possible changes in rules, through published Notices of Proposed Rule-Making, and similar announcements of inquiries, through Notices of Inquiry. The public in general—and in particular those affected by the rules or inquiries—then have opportunity to voice their opinions for or against the proposed changes. In this way, such an agency is behaving as a quasi-legislature, providing room for debate before acting.

The rules or regulations adopted by the agency are, of course, binding on the people or businesses under its regulatory jurisdiction, but Congress always has the authority to create or change statutes, thus in effect overruling the administrative agencies.

There are literally hundreds of administrative agencies. Only a few of these are important to the electronic mass media. We turn now to a brief look at those particular agencies.

### 1. The Federal Communications Commission

In 1927, Congress created a five-member Federal Radio Commission to rationalize the radio spectrum and make allocations. In 1934, the agency was expanded to seven members, given jurisdiction over telephone and telegraph communication as well, and renamed the Federal Communications Commission. In 1982, Congress voted to return to a five-member commission. Each member is appointed by the President for a seven-year term subject to Senate confirmation. No more than three members may be from the same political party. The terms are staggered so that no more than one expires in any year. If a member resigns in the middle of a term, the new appointment is only for the unexpired portion of that term. One consequence is that many of those appointed do not have the independence of beginning with a seven-year term. The Chairman, chosen by the President, is the chief executive officer and has major administrative responsibilities including the setting of the agenda. A chart showing the organization of the Commission is presented in Appendix C.

Of the agency's several offices and bureaus for its various functions, the most important for our purposes is the Mass Media Bureau, formed by the 1982 merger of the Broadcast Bureau and the Cable Bureau, which receives all applications for licenses, renewals and transfers. Under delegated authority from the Commission, the Bureau's staff is authorized to issue some licenses and renew others. In cases in which it has no such power, it may still recommend to the Commissioners which applications to grant and which to deny, thus assuming the position of an advocate within the agency. In addition, complaints of violations of the fairness doctrine or of the equal opportunities provision of § 315 are processed through the Mass Media Bureau.

When an adjudicatory hearing is required, usually in a licensing case, it is conducted by an Administrative Law Judge, formerly called a hearing examiner, who is an independent employee of the Commission. The Mass Media Bureau may also appear before the Administrative Law Judge to argue in favor of or against an applicant. The judge renders an initial decision that will become effective unless appealed. The appeal will be either to the Commission itself or to the Review Board. This Board, composed of senior employees of the Commission, sits in panels of three and reviews the initial decisions. The Commission chooses whether to accept appeals from the Review Board.

Within the Commission the Mass Media Bureau takes positions and makes recommendations. Any applicant who is unhappy with the Commission's decision may then appeal to the courts—usually to the United States Court of Appeals for the District of Columbia. But once the Commission renders a decision the Bureau's role ceases. The General Counsel then takes over to represent the Commission in any litigation that results from the Commission's decision. The General Counsel may also advise the Commission as it prepares to promulgate rules. Sometimes one part of the agency may disagree with another. For example, during reconsideration of the 1974 Fairness Report, which we will discuss in Chapter VI, the General Counsel's office proposed that complaints that a licensee had not sufficiently covered issues of public importance should be considered only at renewal time. The Bureau opposed the proposal and the Commissioners agreed with the Bureau.

## 2. THE FEDERAL TRADE COMMISSION

The Federal Trade Commission (FTC) was established by the Federal Trade Commission Act (FTCA) in 1914. The Commission was initially charged with prohibiting "unfair methods of competition in commerce." As originally conceived, this phrase was intended to allow the FTC to enforce antitrust laws, laws that courts had viewed with some hostility. The agency also concerns itself with the Clayton Act of 1914, which outlaws specific practices recognized as instruments of monopoly. Soon the FTC tried to regulate deceptive advertising as a form of "unfair competition." In 1938, Congress passed the Wheeler-Lea Amendments to the FTCA explicitly giving the FTC the authority to regulate unfair or deceptive advertising.

Overseeing advertising is just one FTC task—though the most important for the media. The agency is composed of five commissioners, including the chairman, appointed by the President for seven-year terms and confirmed by the Senate. It has a staff of more than 1,650 and an annual budget of about $70 million (compared with $90 billion spent on advertising annually). Its other responsibilities include laws concerning antitrust violations, warranties, granting of credit, and label laws.

As an administrative agency, acting quasi-judicially and quasi-legislatively, the Commission deals with trade practices on a continuing and corrective basis. The FTC has no authority to punish; its function is to "prevent," through cease-and-desist orders and other means, those practices condemned by the law of federal trade regulation. However, court-ordered civil penalties up to $10,000 may be obtained for each violation of a Commission order or trade regulation.

Cases before the Commission may originate through a complaint by a consumer or a competitor, the Congress, or from federal, state, or municipal agencies.

## 3. NATIONAL TELECOMMUNICATIONS AND INFORMATION ADMINISTRATION

The National Telecommunications and Information Administration (NTIA) was established in 1978 as part of the Commerce Department, and NTIA is headed by the Assistant Secretary for Communications and Information. The reorganization that established NTIA combined within the new unit the former Office of Telecommunications Policy, which had been part of the Executive Office of the President, and the Office of Telecommunications of the Commerce Department. There had been concern about excessive Presidential influence on the Office of Telecommunications Policy during the Nixon administration.

In essence, NTIA is the telecommunications policy research department of the government. It does long-term studies into the effects of and need for telecommunication regulation. NTIA also advises the President on telecommunications policy issues.

NTIA's role is to formulate policies to support the development and growth of telecommunications, information, and related industries; to further the efficient development and use of telecommunications and information services; to provide policy and management for federal use of the electromagnetic spectrum; and to provide telecommunications facilities grants to public service users.

In November, 1985, NTIA released staff papers giving a highly positive assessment of the pro-competitive and deregulatory policies in telecommunications. David Markey, outgoing head of NTIA, said in a cover statement that "any fair assessment of the results" of the progress toward diverse, competitive telecommunications "must conclude that the upside gains far outweigh any downside costs." The staff papers said that radio has demonstrated talent and resiliency, that cable television has a positive economic outlook, and that there is little evidence to support the notion that television is declining as a force. Broadcasting, Nov. 18, 1985 at 104.

### 4. THE COPYRIGHT ROYALTY TRIBUNAL

The Copyright Royalty Tribunal (CRT) was created by the Copyright Act of 1976, which took effect January 1, 1978. Among its duties is overseeing the compulsory licensing scheme governing cable retransmission of broadcast signals. Under this scheme money is collected from cable systems and distributed to motion picture producers, program syndicators, broadcasters, sports teams, etc. We will examine this licensing mechanism in Chapter IX.

The Tribunal also makes determinations concerning the adjustment of copyright royalty rates for records and jukeboxes. It also establishes, and makes determinations concerning, terms and rates of royalty payments for the use by public broadcasting stations of published nondramatic compositions and pictorial, graphic, and sculptural works.

Tribunal decisions take into account existing economic conditions, impact on copyright owners and users and the industry involved, and the need to maximize the availability of creative works to the public. Recognizing the right of copyright owners to receive a return, the Tribunal ensures them access to information about the use of their works.

### 5. EQUAL EMPLOYMENT OPPORTUNITY COMMISSION

The Equal Employment Opportunity Commission (EEOC), as might be imagined, is charged with enforcing the equal employment opportunity laws. Issues of illegal discrimination have become increasingly important for the electronic media, which are obligated to bear them in mind in making hiring or promotion decisions.

The EEOC was created by the Civil Rights Act of 1964 in an attempt to eliminate discrimination based on race, color, religion, sex, or national origin in hiring, promoting, firing, wages, testing, training, apprenticeship, and all other conditions of employment.

The Commission is a major publisher of data on the employment status of minorities and women.

Although the EEOC has primary responsibility for equal employment opportunities, broadcasters must also comply with requirements in this area placed on them by the FCC. Initially, the FCC required that licensees file employment reports at the time of license renewals. (We will examine the importance of equal opportunity in the licensing process in Chapter IV.) Subsequently, the FCC imposed a requirement of annual reports on full-time and part-time employees from licensees with more than four employees.

In November, 1985, the Federal Communications Commission proposed an easing of broadcasters' requirements for equal opportunity reporting. The FCC proposed to exempt licensees with no more than five employees, to change its reporting forms, and to allow lumping together of full-time and part-time employees into the same table for annual reports. Broadcasting, Nov. 18, 1985 at 42.

### 6.  NATIONAL LABOR RELATIONS BOARD

The National Labor Relations Board (NLRB) was created by the National Labor Relations Act (NLRA) of 1935 (Wagner Act), as amended by the acts of 1947 (Taft-Hartley Act), 1959 (Landrum-Griffin Act), and 1974.

The Board has two principal functions: preventing and remedying unfair labor practices by employers and labor organizations or their agents and conducting secret ballot elections among employees in appropriate collective-bargaining units to determine whether or not they desire to be represented by a labor organization.

The electronic media are heavily unionized today with most management decisions affected to at least some extent by the various union contracts in effect.

## D.  INTERNATIONAL REGULATION OF ELECTRONIC MEDIA

Radio and television signals obviously do not stop at international borders, so neighboring countries' telecommunications concerns overlap. This is true whether one is talking about Western Europe, where a country has several nearby neighbors, or the United States, where we share a very long border with Canada and a shorter one with Mexico.

The concern is not a new one. Napoleon III called a conference in Paris in 1865 to take some collective action to deal with technical standards, codes, and tariffs for telegraph. Out of that conference came the International Telegraph Union, which has been called "the first genuine international, intergovernmental organization to see the light of day." Delegates to the conference adopted the international Morse code and agreed on the interconnection of important cities, hours of reception for telegrams, and the obligation to deliver messages from abroad.

Today's International Telecommunications Union (ITU) is a direct descendant of the group formed in Paris, but its interests go far beyond the "electric telegraph." Much of the technology of today and to-morrow—communications satellites, sea cables, fiber optics, dynamic radio systems, mass data storage and processing facilities—has and will have international implications. The constitution, statutes, administrative rules and regulation, and case law of any single country obviously cannot govern the international traffic of messages, and international agreements are of increasing importance.

A reflection of that is the growth of the ITU. With more than 156 member nations today, it is headquartered in Geneva. Among its varied activities are the registration and management of frequencies and the collection and dissemination of massive amounts of information concerning telecommunications throughout the world.

The ITU Convention, which sets forth its rules of procedure, permits world and regional administrative conferences. A World Administrative Radio Conference (WARC) may have the authority to revise most of the regulations or may have jurisdiction only in a limited area. Such conferences in Geneva in 1959 and 1979 and in Atlantic City in 1974 had very broad jurisdiction. For WARC 79 in Geneva, delegates from 140 member countries met to work on 14,000 proposals that had been submitted to amend the Radio Regulations. Examples of WARCs with more limited jurisdiction include the Broadcasting Satellite WARC, the WARC on the Aeronautical Mobile, and the WARC for Space Telecommunications.

Regional Administrative Radio Conferences (RARCs) have regional jurisdiction. For the purpose of radio frequency management, the world is divided into three general regions. Region 1 includes Europe and Africa; Region 2 includes the Americas; and Region 3 includes Asia and Oceania.

The Space WARC in Geneva in 1985 left considerable work to be done in a second session scheduled for 1988. *Broadcasting* magazine reported: "In the U.S., the impressions left by the recently concluded first session of the Space WARC have grown no brighter with the passage of time. It is recalled as a session driven by politics and ideology. Conflicts that emerged in Geneva seem at least as sharp six weeks later. What's more, there is no little confusion as to what was accomplished in the session's five and a half weeks—indeed, the U.S. contributed to the uncertainty with a post-conference statement reserving the right to depart from the basic agreement reached . . . ." Broadcasting, Nov. 4, 1985 at 70.

There are quite different international implications raised by Radio Marti, a radio facility which went on the air in May, 1985, created by the Reagan administration in an attempt to break what the administration considered the Castro government's monopoly on news available to Cubans. Radio Marti was established within the Voice of America following the controversial legislation authorizing it. Voice of America's charter prohibits it from disseminating propaganda. The station is named after Cuban patriot-writer Jose Marti. Broadcasting, Oct. 8, 1984 at 78.

# Chapter II

# THE SPECTRUM AND ITS UTILIZATION

## A. THE NATURE OF THE SPECTRUM

The electromagnetic spectrum is a unique natural resource. Utilization does not use it up or wear it out. It does not require continual maintenance to remain usable. It is subject to pollution (interference), but once the interference is removed the pollution totally disappears. The value of the spectrum lies primarily in its use for conveying a wide variety of information at varying speeds over varying distances: in other words, for communication.

All electromagnetic radiation is a form of radiant energy, similar in many respects to heat, light, or X-radiation. All of these types of radiation are considered by physicists to be waves resulting from the periodic oscillations of charged subatomic particles. All radiation has a measurable frequency, or rate of oscillation, which is measured in cycles per second, or hertz. One thousand cycles per second equals one kilocycle per second (1 kHz); 1,000 kilocycles per second equals one Megacycle per second (1 MHz); and 1,000 Megacycles per second equals one Gigacycle per second (1 GHz). The frequencies of electromagnetic radiation that comprise the radio spectrum span a wide range, from 10 kHz to 3,000,000,000,000 cycles per second (3,000 GHz), all of which are nearly incomprehensibly rapid. Present technology allows use of the spectrum only up to around 40 GHz.

The radio spectrum resource itself has three dimensions: space, time and frequency. Two spectrum users can transmit on the same frequency at the same time, if they are sufficiently separate physically; the physical separation necessary will depend on the power at which each signal is transmitted. They then occupy different parts of the spectrum in the spatial sense. Similarly, the spectrum can be divided in terms of frequency, dependent on the construction of the transmitting and receiving equipment; or in a temporal sense, dependent largely on the hours of use.

The spectrum is subject to the phenomenon of interference. One radio signal interferes with another to the extent that both have the same dimensions. That is, two signals of the same frequency that occupy the same physical space at the same time will interfere with each other (co-channel interference). Signals on adjacent channels may also interfere with each other. Interference usually obscures or destroys any information that either signal is carrying: the degree to which two signals occupy the same physical space depends on the intensity of the radiated power at a given point, which in turn depends on the construction of the transmitting equipment and antenna.

The spectrum is divided into numbered bands, extending from Very Low Frequencies (VLF) to Very, Ultra, Super, and Extremely High Frequencies (EHF) and beyond. The lower frequencies of the radio spectrum are used for "point-to-point" communications and for navigational aids. AM radio is located in the range between 300 and 3,000 kHz, known as the Medium Frequency band (MF). FM radio and VHF television (channels 2–13) are in the Very High Frequency band (VHF), from 30 to 300 MHz. The Ultra High Frequency band, from 300 to 3,000 MHz, is the location of UHF television (channels 14–69). Still higher frequencies are used for microwave relays and communication satellites.

The effective limitations on use of the radio spectrum are defined by (1) the propagation characteristics of the various frequencies and (2) the level of interference. Low frequency radio waves are best suited to long distance communications. In the lowest frequency bands the radio waves propagate primarily along the ground or water and follow the curvature of the earth. The attenuation of these "ground waves" generally increases with frequency; VLF waves may be propagated for thousands of miles, which explains their value for point-to-point communication. Ground waves in the HF band below VHF can propagate no more than a few hundred miles and above that band they become unimportant. Sky wave propagation is important up to the start of the VHF band. These radio waves tend to depart from the earth's surface and are reflected by the ionosphere, an electrically charged region of the atmosphere 35 to 250 miles above the earth. The amount of reflection depends on the level of daily solar activity, the time of day, the season, geographical location, the length of the signal path, and the angle at which the waves strike the ionosphere. The reflection of sky waves is much greater at night, when they may be transmitted over great distances. Above 30 MHz, radio waves tend to pierce the ionosphere rather than to be reflected, and line-of-sight transmission becomes increasingly necessary. As frequency increases above 30 MHz, surface objects absorb radiation at an increasing rate until at 1 GHz a clear unobstructed line of sight becomes necessary. In the very highest frequencies, the waves are subject to substantial absorption by water vapor and oxygen in the atmosphere and cannot be used for communication.

Interference constitutes the second major limitation on the use of the electromagnetic spectrum. As noted above, interference results when two signals attempt to occupy the same spectrum in all three of its dimensions. Even if two users wish to transmit on the same frequency, interference can be avoided by sufficient geographical separation between transmitters, limitations of the power radiated by each transmitter, limitations on antenna height, or separation of the signals in time. The first three techniques cause spatial differentiation; the last affects the temporal dimension.

Standard (AM) broadcasting propagates its waves by "amplitude modulation." The sound waves vary in power, producing variations in the height of the waves that are transmitted. The receiving unit decodes these height variations, reproducing the original sounds. AM transmissions occur in the MF band and thus have a long range primary service through ground waves, particularly near the lower end of the band. AM also can utilize sky waves to provide a secondary service at night.

FM broadcasting utilizes "frequency modulation" rather than "amplitude modulation." In this system the height of the wave is held constant, but the frequency of the waves transmitted is varied. This type of broadcasting provides higher-quality service with less interference than does AM, but it serves smaller areas, since the waves of the VHF band do not follow the surface of the earth and are not reflected by the ionosphere. This also means that FM service is unaffected by skywave interference at night.

Television utilizes separate signals for the visual and the sound components. The picture is transmitted by amplitude modulation and the sound by frequency modulation. Since the transmissions are either in the VHF or UHF bands, the range of the signal is short and television cannot utilize either long ground waves or sky waves.

## B.  ALLOCATION OF THE SPECTRUM

The method of dividing the spectrum resource among prospective users is enormously complex and highly controversial. The general term "allocation policy" includes three separate but not always distinct processes, each of which involves both technical and nontechnical considerations. The allocation process is the division of the spectrum into blocks of frequencies to be used by specified services or users. Thus, the television service is allocated certain frequencies in the VHF and UHF bands, microwave users are allocated certain frequencies in the UHF and SHF bands, and so on. The second process, allotment, involves the distribution of spectrum rights within allocated bands to users in various geographical areas. Assignment, the third process, denotes the choice among potential individual users of allocated and allotted channels or frequency bands. We usually refer to all three processes under the general label of "allocation policy."

Perhaps the most important objective consideration in formulating an allocation policy is the technical usability of the spectrum itself. Technical usability is dependent primarily on three factors: the propagation characteristics of each frequency range, interference problems and their resolution, and limitations imposed by the communications system itself, especially the transmitting and receiving equipment. In other words, it is dependent on the physics of radio waves, other users of the spectrum, and the technical state of the electronics industry. Frequency characteristics themselves seldom pose significant problems, for although there are optimal frequency ranges for various services, these tend to be broad ranges. Consequently, there is usually considerable flexibility in the initial choice of a frequency for a given service except for whatever priority is given to those already utilizing the space.

Several forms of interference may present problems since interference can be caused by an overcrowded frequency, insufficient geographical separation, or unduly strong power levels.

The third constraint on spectrum allocation involves the technology of the communications system used, especially the antenna system and the transmitting and receiving equipment. Any major change in receivers might create economic problems for the public and thus for the industry as a whole.

The problem of crowding in the broadcasting industry began early in the 1920's. The episode is recounted by Justice Frankfurter in his opinion for the Court in National Broadcasting Co. v. United States, 319 U.S. 190 (1943), a case to which we return later:

> Federal regulation of radio begins with the Wireless Ship Act of June 24, 1910, 36 Stat. 629, which forbade any steamer carrying or licensed to carry fifty or more persons to leave any American port unless equipped with efficient apparatus for radio communication, in charge of a skilled operator. The enforcement of this legislation was entrusted to the Secretary of Commerce and Labor, who was in charge of the administration of the marine navigation laws. But it was not until 1912 when the United States ratified the first international radio treaty, 37 Stat. 1565, that the need for general regulation of radio communication became urgent. In order to fulfill our obligations under the treaty, Congress enacted the Radio Act of August 13, 1912, 37 Stat. 302. This statute forbade the operation of radio apparatus without a license from the Secretary of Commerce and Labor; it also allocated certain frequencies for the use of the Government, and imposed restrictions upon the character of wave emissions, the transmission of distress signals and the like.
>
> The enforcement of the Radio Act of 1912 presented no serious problems prior to the World War. Questions of interference arose only rarely because there were more than enough frequencies for all the stations then in existence. The war accelerated the development of the art, however, and in 1921 the first standard broadcast stations were established. They grew rapidly in number, and by 1923 there were several hundred such stations throughout the country. The Act of 1912 had not set aside any particular frequencies for the use of private broadcast stations; consequently, the Secretary of Commerce selected two frequencies, 750 and 833 kilocycles, and licensed all stations to operate upon one or the other of these channels. The number of stations increased so rapidly, however, and the situation became so chaotic, that the Secretary, upon recommendation of the National Radio Conferences which met in Washington in 1923 and 1924, established a policy of assigning specified frequencies to particular stations. The entire radio spectrum was divided into numerous bands, each allocated to a particular kind of service. The frequencies ranging from 550 to 1500 kilocycles (96 channels in all,

since the channels were separated from each other by 10 kilocycles) were assigned to the standard broadcast stations.  But the problems created by the enormously rapid development of radio were far from solved.  The increase in the number of channels was not enough to take care of the constantly growing number of stations.  Since there were more stations than available frequencies, the Secretary of Commerce attempted to find room for everybody by limiting the power and the hours of operation of stations in order that several stations might use the same channel.  The number of stations multiplied so rapidly, however, that by November, 1925, there were almost 600 stations in the country, and there were 175 applications for new stations.  Every channel in the standard broadcast band was, by that time, already occupied by at least one station, and many by several.  The new stations could be accommodated only by extending the standard broadcast band, at the expense of the other types of services, or by imposing still greater limitations upon time and power.  The National Radio Conference which met in November, 1925, opposed both of these methods and called upon Congress to remedy the situation through legislation.

[During 1926, courts held that the Secretary of Commerce lacked the power to stem the tide, and his pleas for self-regulation went unheeded by the burgeoning new industry.]

From July, 1926, to February 23, 1927, when Congress enacted the Radio Act of 1927, 44 Stat. 1162, almost 200 new stations went on the air.  These new stations used any frequencies they desired, regardless of the interference thereby caused to others.  Existing stations changed to other frequencies and increased their power and hours of operation at will.  The result was confusion and chaos.  With everybody on the air, nobody could be heard.  .  .  .

## 1.  THE FEDERAL COMMUNICATIONS COMMISSION

As we noted in Chapter I, the Radio Act of 1927 and the Communications Act of 1934 rejected the idea of a market system of spectrum allocation and of any property rights in the spectrum resource.  The Federal Communications Commission has the sole power to allocate the radio spectrum, to establish general standards of operations, and to license persons to use designated parts of the spectrum.

Many services must be placed, but some critics of Commission policies charge undue reliance on the bloc allocation concept, which calls for allocating discrete frequency bands to classes of users essentially without regard to geographical location, and maintaining a relatively strict segregation among allocations.  This can lead to such anomalous results as marine bands in Nebraska and forestry bands in New York City. These problems are exacerbated by the general administrative difficulty of changing an allocation once made: the start-up costs are so great and the capital investment is usually so heavy that there is a strong economic incentive not to move users from one frequency band to another.  Thus, as new uses develop, they are allocated higher and higher frequencies, with little consideration of which frequencies are technically best suited for which services. For example, location of radio broadcasting in the AM band (535–1605 kHz) may be inefficient. Local broadcasting might be moved to the current FM band (88–108 MHz), which is much better suited technically to local radio, and long distance broadcasting might be moved to frequencies below 500 kHz to take advantage of the long distance ground wave propagation characteristics at those frequencies.

Another claim is that area coverage by broadcasting stations would require less spectrum if the Commission were to drop its so-called "local station goal." High-power stations in major urban centers could serve the entire country in only one-third the spectrum space presently used. Yet local stations are important; they are outlets for local news and forums for local citizens to express their views, they serve local advertisers, and they provide such local services as weather reports (which might be critical in areas subject to flash flooding or sudden tornadoes or storms).

## 2. Radio Allocation

AM broadcasting occupies slightly more than 1 MHz of spectrum in the Medium Frequency band between 535 kHz and 1605 kHz. This is divided into 107 assignable channels each with a bandwidth of 10 kHz. AM stations are divided into four major classes: Class I "clear channel" stations are high-power stations designed to provide primary (groundwave) service to a metropolitan area and its environs and secondary nighttime (skywave) service to an extended rural area. Class II stations also operate on clear channels with primary service areas limited by interference from Class I stations. A Class II station must usually avoid causing interference within the normally protected service areas of Class I or other Class II stations. Class III stations are medium powered and are designed to provide service primarily to larger cities and contiguous rural areas. Class IV stations are low powered and operate on local channels to provide service to a city or town and contiguous areas.

The 1927 Act creating the Federal Radio Commission had charged the Commission to provide "fair, efficient, and equitable radio service" to all areas of the country. The Commission then proceeded by establishing general engineering constraints such as maximum interference standards, and by allocating each of the 107 frequencies to a class of stations. Within these general constraints, the Commission adopted a first-come-first-served approach. An applicant who could find a promising community could apply for a license to serve that community if it could find a channel that would satisfy the various general constraints. An applicant had to show that it would not interfere excessively with the signals of existing stations nor expose too many of its new listeners to interference beyond certain acceptable limits.

*Clear Channels.* As noted earlier, because of the skywave phenomenon, powerful AM stations can be received at great distances at night.

In the 1940's, with an estimated 20 million persons uncovered by local radio service at night, the FCC created a group of 25 powerful stations operating at 50 kw. Each station shared its daytime channel frequency with other stations around the country. But at sundown all the others left the air so that the channel was clear except for the powerful station, which could reach distant and remote areas of the country.

With the development of FM radio and a surge in interest in AM radio, some argued that the clear channel stations should have their protections reduced to allow more diversity. In response, the clear channel stations argued that their power should be increased to 750 kw so that they could provide additional service. The FCC faced the issue in 1961 but reached no conclusion. In a compromise, it ordered that 13 of the 25 frequencies be shared with one or two other stations, but left the remainder fully protected while it continued to consider the problem.

In 1980, the Commission acted decisively. The number of persons unserved by nighttime local radio was down to four million, and applicants were clamoring for space on the AM spectrum. The Commission decided to end the clear channel concept but to protect those stations from interference for a radius of 750 miles. This would still permit them to reach larger areas than ordinary stations but it would permit an additional 125 stations to broadcast at night.

The new stations will be limited in power to 1 kw except in special cases. At the same time, the FCC explicitly refused to allow the clear channel stations to raise their power above 50 kw. (In the 1930's, an experiment permitted a Cincinnati station to broadcast at 500 kw. The experiment was terminated and a limit of 50 kw imposed for all stations.) By January, 1985, more than 300 applications were already on file or designated for hearing. Broadcasting, Jan. 7, 1985 at 39.

*Expanding the Band.* A second way to increase the number of AM stations is to expand the part of the spectrum available for such broadcasting. This occurred in 1979, when the World Administrative Radio Conference at its meeting (held once every 20 years) decided to increase the AM band in the Western Hemisphere so that it will run from 525 to 1705 kHz. Part will be used exclusively for AM radio, other parts will be shared, in a manner to be decided at Regional Administrative Radio Conferences. One will be held in March, 1986, and a second sometime in 1988. Regular use of the extended part of the band is unlikely to begin before late 1989.

---

FM broadcasting, which began around 1940, is located in the VHF band. It occupies the frequencies between 88 and 108 MHz, which are excellent for aural broadcast service and allow an effective range of 30 to 75 miles. That spectrum space is divided into 100 assignable channels, each 200 kHz wide. The lowest 20 channels are reserved for noncommercial educational stations; the remaining 80 are given over to commercial use. Commercial FM channels were originally divided into three classes: A, B, and C. Class A channels are designed for use by low-power stations serving relatively small communities and the surrounding area. Class B channels are for medium-power stations intended to serve a sizable city or town or the principal city of an urbanized area. Class C channels are used by high-power stations serving a city and large surrounding areas. Noncommercial, educational FM stations operate with very low power on a fourth class or channel, Class D. Commercial FM assignments are based on a Table of Assignments, in which communities are assigned a specific number of FM stations of specified power and on specific channels. Licenses are given only for stations within the communities listed in the Table of Assignments or within a 15 mile radius—unless an application to change the table is granted.

In the late 1970's, the demand for FM licenses increased dramatically as FM outlets started to overcome the traditional dominance of AM stations. The superior quality of the FM signal and the availability of stereo were the keys to this change.

In an effort to meet the increased demand for FM stations the FCC initiated a drop-in rulemaking allowing new FM stations to be started without interfering with present broadcasters. FM Broadcast Stations (Additional Commercial Allocations), 53 R.R.2d 1550 (1983). 47 C.F.R. § 73.202 (1983). This ongoing rulemaking created three new intermediary classes of commercial licenses: B1, C1, and C2. In addition, Class A licenses will be permitted on channels previously set aside for Class B and Class C licenses. The FCC hired an outside contractor to supply the computer software that will determine the availability of these more closely spaced drop-ins. This new technology has made the FCC able to determine the coverage areas of these stations with greater accuracy. Broadcasting, Oct. 3, 1983 at 7.

In late 1984, the FCC approved a list of 689 locations, an initial step in the omnibus rulemaking process. Most of the new availabilities are Class A licenses in the southeast. The Commission initiated the application process in mid-1985, but is staggering the applications for different channels over the next three years. Broadcasting, May 13, 1985 at 105.

*Beneficiaries.* Who are the likely beneficiaries of these attempts to increase the number of broadcast outlets? In radio, daytime AM broadcasters have argued forcefully that they deserve the opportunity to obtain fulltime outlets. Meanwhile, the Commission has long been concerned that minority groups are woefully underrepresented among the owners of broadcast licenses. Although minority ownership does not necessarily mean that a station's programming will take minority tastes into special account, the FCC believes that minority ownership itself is important—and that the other may follow. Other demonstrations of the FCC's concern about minorities in broadcasting are discussed elsewhere in this and later chapters.

In the FM drop-in rulemaking, supra, the Commission voted to give preference both to AM daytime broadcasters and to minority applicants. Broadcasting, March 18, 1985 at 27.

### 3.  TELEVISION ALLOCATION

The first licensing of television stations in this country occurred in 1941 and involved 18 channels.  The first assignment plan was developed in 1945, based solely on the VHF channels.  It involved the assignment of about 400 stations to 140 major market centers.  Early comers quickly preempted the 100 choice assignments.  In 1948, because of unexpected problems with tropospheric interference and concern that the 1945 assignment plan could cause problems, the Commission ordered a freeze on channel assignments.

The freeze ended with the issuance of the Sixth Report and Order on Television Allocations, 17 Fed.Reg. 3905, 1 R.R. 91:601 (1952), creating the Table of Assignments.  The Commission rejected the idea of moving all television to the UHF band.  Instead, 12 VHF channels were retained and 70 new UHF channels were added, so that the Table provided for about 620 VHF and 1400 UHF stations.  Television uses an enormous amount of spectrum compared to radio.  One VHF channel uses six MHz—six times more than the entire AM band.

The Commission generated the Table of Assignments from its hierarchy of priorities:  (1) to provide at least one television service to every part of the United States;  (2) to provide each community with at least one television station;  (3) to provide a choice of at least two television services to all parts of the U.S.;  (4) to provide each community with at least two television stations;  and (5) to assign remaining channels to communities on the basis of population, geographical location, and the number of television services already available to that community.  Note the emphasis on "local" outlets.  Is this a sound hierarchy?

In making these assignments the Commission decided to "intermix" VHF and UHF channels as a single service in the same markets.  Many observers warned that the newer UHF channels could not survive but the Commission apparently believed that the demand for VHF would overflow into the UHF band and it also feared that failure to intermix would relegate UHF stations to markets overshadowed by VHF outlets in nearby metropolitan areas, or to remote rural areas.  In any event, the Table of Assignments called for combined VHF and UHF channels in the following pattern:  6–10 for cities with population over 1,000,000;  4–6 for cities with 250,000 to 1,000,000;  2–4 for those with populations between 50,000 and 250,000;  and 1–2 for communities under 50,000.

Because the Table tended to allot three VHF stations to most markets with only a few getting more than three, the three major networks could now program almost entirely through VHF affiliates. This gave them strong audience and advertiser support.  (In 1971, for example, 108 of the nation's 207 television markets, covering 58 percent of the nation's television households, could receive the three networks but no VHF independent stations.  R. Noll, M. Peck, and J. McGowan, Economic Aspects of Television Regulation 168 (1973) ).  Without adequate set penetration, UHF stations found it difficult if not impossible to secure advertising revenues and network affiliation.  By the end of 1956, there were 395 VHF stations and 96 UHF stations on the air. By this time Dumont, a fourth network, had collapsed. By 1960, only 75 (15 percent) of the 575 commercial stations on the air were UHF, even though 70 percent of the total channel assignments were UHF.

The Commission recognized that intermixture was not working. In 1956, while considering broader solutions such as the transfer of all television to the UHF band, the Commission adopted deintermixture as an "interim" measure in several communities, making them all-UHF. In 1961, the Commission planned to deintermix eight more communities. This time, however, the opposition from established VHF stations was formidable. After a fierce battle, Congress entered the fray and enacted a compromise: the All Channel Receiver Act of 1962. The Act, which became § 303(s) of the Communications Act, authorized the Commission to order that all sets shipped in interstate commerce be capable of receiving both VHF and UHF signals. The VHF interests gave their support for the proposal in exchange for the Commission's indefinite suspension of deintermixture proposals. The Commission did require "all-channel" receivers and declared a moratorium on most pending deintermixture proposals. The Commission's regulation came too late for many of the UHF pioneers of the 1950's. (In 1971, the Commission began steps to require detent ("click") dialing on all UHF receivers.)

The continued underutilization of UHF spots led the FCC to begin to reallocate frequencies to competing uses of the airwaves. Channels 70–83 have been reassigned for land mobile use. In some cities Channels 14 to 20 are being used by land mobile operators and are being shared elsewhere. In 1980, 63 percent of the television assignments were UHF. The vacancy rates were as follows: 61 of the 578 commercial VHFs; 266 of the 648 commercial UHFs; 23 of the 136 noncommercial VHFs; and 374 of the 570 noncommercial UHFs. In the top 100 markets, vacancies existed on 86 UHF channels but on no commercial VHF. In the top 200 markets, the comparable figures were 176 and six.

In addition to the intermixture problem, UHF stations are also more expensive to operate because it takes ten times as much power for a UHF transmitter to reach the same area as a VHF transmitter. Because of the inferior wave-propagation qualities of UHF signals compared with VHF signals, UHF stations are permitted to operate at a power of 5,000 kw compared with 100 or 316 kw for VHF stations. But the energy costs are so high that few UHF stations operate at maximum permitted power.

Since most network programs, the most popular, are on VHF stations, viewers in intermixed communities have little incentive to seek out UHF, even though by 1983, 96 percent of all homes with television could receive UHF. Until "click" dialing became common, some viewers trying to use UHF found it difficult to tune in the desired station.

In 1978, a Senate Committee observed that "the intent of the All Channel Receiver Act of 1962 has not been realized. UHF television broadcasting remains sorely disadvantaged within the national television system. The Committee directs that the Commission devise a plan for

UHF to reach comparability with VHF in as short a time as practicable. . . ." In response the FCC began studies into reducing noise in UHF reception, improving transmitting techniques, and other matters.

During 1979, the future of UHF suddenly brightened.[1] Applicants sought stations that had gone begging since 1952; existing stations were sold at increasingly higher prices, and major broadcast owners became interested in UHF for the first time. The change in climate was apparently due to a variety of independent factors coming into play at the same time. Viewers were finding "click" dialing or newer digital dialing systems more attractive; cable television was improving the reception of the UHF stations. Another temporary boost came from the introduction of Subscription Television (STV), an over-the-air pay television system in which viewers who wish to buy the service are supplied decoders that unscramble the signal being transmitted. Although little original programming was being provided, the prospect of uncut motion pictures without commercials was sufficiently attractive to make the venture appear profitable.

However, the long-term viability of STV is now in serious doubt. Hurt by increasing cable penetration, piracy of signals, and increasing interest in Multi-channel Multipoint Distribution Service (MMDS, which will be discussed in Chapter X), the STV subscriber base dropped from 1.4 million in 1981 to about 25,000 in early 1986. There are only 2 STV stations still in operation. Broadcasting, Feb. 3, 1986 at 7.

A few UHF stations have become profitable as the result of developments in cable television. Because of changes in FCC rules governing cable systems, it became possible for a single television station, in effect, to become a network by supplying its programs by satellite to cable systems throughout the country. The operation of these "superstations" is described more extensively in the discussion of cable television in Chapter IX.

*New Television Outlets.* In March, 1982, the FCC approved the start of a new television service of perhaps as many as 4,000 low-power television (LPTV) stations throughout the country. These stations operate at a power sufficient to reach viewers within a radius of 10–15 miles. It is up to the applicant to find spots on the VHF and UHF bands in which such stations will not interfere with existing stations.

LPTV operators are permitted to join together by satellite to set up networks. Neither the duopoly nor the one-to-a-market rules, which we will discuss in Chapter V, apply to LPTV. There is no limit set on the number of LPTV licenses one entity can have. Programming restrictions are also minimal. The fairness doctrine and section 315 (see Chapter VI) apply only to licensee-originated programming.

1. The press caught the change in mood. Compare "UHF's Broadcasting Struggles: F.C.C. Help for Ailing Stations," N.Y. Times, Jan. 1, 1979 at 29 with "Picture Turns Bright for UHF: Stations Draw High Prices in Heated Bidding," N.Y. Times, Dec. 20, 1979 at D1.

A lottery procedure for initial licensing of LPTV was approved by the Commission in March, 1983. Selection from Among Competing Applications Using Random Selection or Lotteries Instead of Comparative Hearings, 48 Fed.Reg. 27,182 (1983). This procedure was necessitated by the great number of applications. Despite the use of the lottery procedure, the backlog of applications was estimated at 23,000 in early 1985. Broadcasting, Jan. 7, 1985 at 46.

On the same day, the Commission, 4–3, approved four drop-ins on specific VHF channels in specific cities. These would be full-power stations that the Commission decided would provide enough new service to viewers to outweigh any loss of service to some persons in areas near existing stations on the same channel. The drop-in is required to reduce its power in the direction of existing stations, but it would be far more powerful than a low-power station.

A general VHF drop-in plan by the FCC that could add up to 140 more drop-ins is still under consideration. Fear that the plan as originally proposed would not provide sufficient protection for existing television service caused Chairman Mark Fowler to ask for a further notice of proposed rulemaking. Broadcasting, Oct. 1, 1984 at 83.

## C. A NOTE ON THE ECONOMICS OF TELEVISION

The basic unit in the broadcasting system is the individual station that receives the license from the Federal Communications Commission. As of June 30, 1985, 1,487 full-power television stations were authorized to operate in the United States. These included 680 VHF and 807 UHF. Of the total authorized, 654 VHF and 560 UHF were actually in operation, with the remainder either under construction or off the air for financial or technical reasons. Of the operating stations 915 were commercial (541 VHF and 374 UHF), and the remainder were noncommercial.

Because of multiple ownership limitations to be discussed, the ownership of the commercial stations is widely distributed. Prior to the recent relaxation of the multiple ownership rules, there were several group owners whose holdings included the maximum five VHFs. Among these group owners are the three major networks. Each owns and operates one VHF in New York City, Los Angeles, and Chicago. The fourth and fifth VHFs are located in six different cities. These 15 O & O's (owned and operated) are a major source of profit for the television networks. The O & O's realize 90 percent of their revenue from non-network sales because of their desirable frequencies in major cities. For an extended study of the economics of the industry, see Noll, Peck, and McGowan, Economic Aspects of Television Regulation 58–96 (1973) and B. Owen, Economics and Freedom of Expression 87–169 (1975).

Almost all the other commercial stations are "affiliated" with one or more networks by contractual arrangements. Of the 915 commercial stations, over 200 are affiliated with each network. A few stations hold no affiliations. As a general rule, unaffiliated VHFs—"independents"—

are located in markets that have more than three VHFs so no network affiliation is available. UHF stations generally can secure a network affiliation only in markets in which there are fewer than three commercial VHFs. Group owners, other than the networks, may produce some programs for their group or may treat their stations as individual facilities with each one affiliated with a different network or no network. According to a 1976 study, 76 percent of all VHF stations in the top 100 markets are licensed to group owners. The stations owned by each of the three networks reach many more viewers than the stations owned by any other group. The study also showed that group ownership has steadily increased over the last 20 years. Howard, The Contemporary Status of Television Group Ownership, 53 Journ.Q. 399 (1976). See also, Howard, Cox Broadcasting Corporation: A Group-Ownership Case Study, 20 J. Broadcasting 209 (1976).

The following chart, from B. Owen, J. Beebe, and W. Manning, Jr., Television Economics 7 (1974), gives an understanding of the structure and economics of the television industry and of television program procurement and production:*

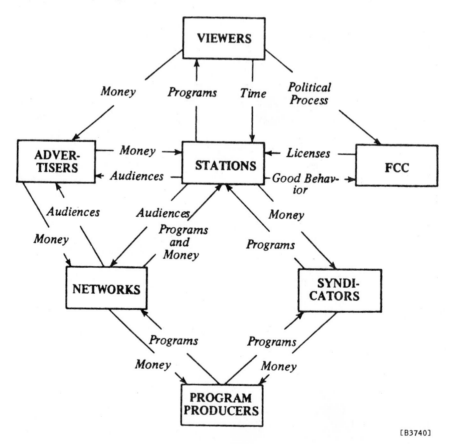

[B3740]

---

* Reprinted by permission of the author, from *Television Economics* by Bruce M. Owen, Jack H. Beebe and Willard G. Manning, Jr. (Lexington Books, D. C. Heath and Co., 1974).

The station would seem to be central and its economic relationships are complex.  Although it would have been possible for stations to develop their own programming and sell time to advertisers or to have the advertisers prepare programming and place it on individual stations, the industry has developed differently.  The most important feature from the outset has been the role of the networks.  It would have been possible for a network to own no stations and to perform no function other than as a broker between individual stations and national advertisers with no involvement in programming, or it could have arranged for the distribution of programs, often simultaneously, over common carrier interconnections.  Instead, networks emerged as group owners who each controlled stations in five of the largest cities in the country.  These have been profitable in their own right and have formed a solid base of guaranteed viewers.

To make the brokering function simpler and to maximize the audiences they can deliver, networks seek affiliates in each of the 200-odd market areas.  A station, owned individually or by a group, will eagerly seek affiliation.  The station will be relieved from having to create or purchase much of its programming because the network will supply programs to the affiliates and the profit will be more than it could make by remaining independent.  The affiliate will be able to sell advertising for some spots in and around the network programming.  Moreover, the network may pay fees to affiliates depending upon how much network programming they carry in excess of about 20 hours per week.  The result is that the station clears time for the most popular programs without charge in order to be able to sell the available commercial time for these features, and is persuaded to clear for the next tier of programs by receiving a fee.  To obtain these advantages the station turns its audience over to the network for the agreed-upon programming and gives up most of its independent efforts.  Occasionally, the relationship is discontinued.

Program production is generally thought to fall into two categories: the production of news, documentaries, and public affairs programs, and the production of entertainment programming.  Although news programming has not always been remunerative and could be left to local stations, the fact that so much of the news is national or international has led the networks themselves to undertake much of the production responsibility for these programs.  Although the networks could contract with independent producers for this programming, they have uniformly decided to develop their own news and public affairs organizations and to produce all of their own programs in this category.  Moreover, some networks will not buy documentaries from independent producers.  The probable explanation is that the networks want total editorial control over this sensitive area to protect their stations from complaints and charges that may arise.

The considerations in entertainment programming are obviously quite different.  In the earlier days of television, advertisers developed their own programming, perhaps through independent producers, and bought time to present the program and related commercials. The network simply sold time and access to the O & O's and affiliates in a single deal. As television developed, networks became more aware of the importance of continuity throughout the evening's entertainment programming, so that one show would link with the next to produce the largest loyal audiences. This required considering what the other networks were programming. Advertiser-initiated programming could aim for demographically discrete groups but could not accommodate all these concerns. By now, advertiser-prepared programs have virtually disappeared and network productions play a minor role due at least in part to the financial interest and syndication rules to be discussed in Chapter V. The independent producer pattern has become dominant. This entails interdependence of independent producers, local stations, advertisers, and the networks.

Independent stations must operate in a totally different pattern because they must provide all their own programs. Independents tend to exist in markets with more than three stations and thus compete not only with each other but also with network affiliates. If one of the networks did not have an affiliate in a market, it would make sense for the network to obtain an affiliate to increase the audience it can provide advertisers, and for the station to become an affiliate because network programming is more popular than alternatives, and affiliates are generally much more profitable than independents. If the network alternative is unavailable, the independents produce some inexpensive local programming and purchase programming from syndicators, who negotiate with individual stations rather than networks. The stations generally bargain for exclusive local rights for a period of time. Some programs are prepared by producers specially for syndication but others have previously run on networks ("off-network programs") and are now being offered to the independents—or to affiliates who want to fill open time. Occasionally, independents join together to form an impromptu network for simultaneous showing of a sporting event or other single feature, but that is unusual, and is likely to involve a program that the three networks have rejected.

Rerun syndications are generally preferred to original syndications because they are proven commodities. Station managers will be able to predict how successful a rerun of specific material will be in their viewing area. Also, off-network syndications may be less expensive because most of the original creative costs have been returned by the network runs, whereas a first-run syndication must return its costs all at once. To reduce this differential, first-run syndications must be less expensive shows that do not compete with the types of off-network programs that are most commonly and successfully syndicated; first-run syndications have moved out of the situation comedy-mystery-detective script situation into game shows and talk shows. Independent stations have "stripped" some of the syndicated programs by presenting them at the same viewing time five days each week. The original program may have been shown on the network once a week but enough backlog has been developed so that a station using syndication programming may be able to show the program daily and thereby build a loyal audience on a day-by-day basis. This will help the independent's quest for advertising.

Advertisers may deal at one of several levels. National advertisers may work through networks as well as in specific local markets through "national spot" advertising. Local advertisers will deal directly with local stations, both affiliates and independents. In all cases the rates are determined by the size and characteristics of the audience that can be delivered to the advertiser.

To keep matters in perspective, it is perhaps well to realize that television accounted for only 20 percent of advertising expenditures in 1984. By comparison, newspapers carried 26 percent of the total, magazines five percent, radio seven percent, direct mail 15 percent, and miscellaneous media accounted for the remainder.

Inevitably, the governmental regulation of broadcasting is charged with political overtones. The Commission's decisions can have an enormous impact on the political process, and conversely, the Commission and its decisions are often targets of political pressure from both the legislative and executive branches as well as those regulated. For a comprehensive look at the situation, including several case studies and a reference bibliography, see E. Krasnow, L. Longley and H. Terry, The Politics of Broadcast Regulation (3d ed. 1982).

# Chapter III

## JUSTIFICATIONS FOR GOVERNMENT REGULATION

### A. "PUBLIC INTEREST" AND GOVERNMENT REGULATION

We have just been considering the special nature of the spectrum and various actions that the FCC has taken to regulate the behavior of those who use part of the spectrum. We turn now to the legal question of what justifies the Commission in undertaking these forms of regulation, plus other types of regulation that we consider later. Although a few cases challenged this power early in the life of the FCC, the first major case to address the problem was National Broadcasting Co. v. United States, 319 U.S. 190 (1943).

After conducting a study of business practices and ownership patterns of radio networks in 1941, the Federal Communications Commission concluded that the major networks (NBC and CBS) exerted too much control over the broadcast industry through control over local station programming. To correct this situation, the Commission issued the Chain Broadcasting Regulations, which defined permissible relationships between networks and stations in terms of affiliation, network programming of affiliates' time, and network ownership of stations. These regulations were aimed at dissuading individual licensees from entering contracts that gave the networks the power to exert such control over licensees. NBC challenged the Commission's authority to adopt regulations controlling licensee behavior not related to technical and engineering matters. We will return to the substance of these regulations in Chapter V.

The first claim was that Congress had not authorized the FCC to adopt these regulations. Section 303 of the Act provided that the Commission "as public interest, convenience, or necessity requires, shall . . . have authority to make special regulations applicable to radio stations engaged in chain broadcasting. . . ." NBC argued that the "public interest" language was to be read as limited to technical and engineering aspects of broadcasting—and that these were not the basis for the FCC's regulations in this case.

The Court noted that several sections of the Act authorized the FCC in furtherance of the "public interest, convenience, or necessity" to do such things as "study new uses for radio, . . . and generally encourage the larger and more effective use of radio in the public interest" and to provide a "fair, efficient and equitable distribution [of licenses] among the states." Building from these several grants of power, the Court rejected NBC's claim:

The Act itself establishes that the Commission's powers are not limited to the engineering and technical aspects of regulation of radio communication. Yet we are asked to regard the Commission as a kind of traffic officer, policing the wave lengths to prevent stations from interfering with each other. But the Act does not restrict the Commission merely to supervision of the traffic. It puts upon the Commission the burden of determining the composition of that traffic. The facilities of radio are not large enough to accommodate all who wish to use them. Methods must be devised for choosing from among the many who apply. And since Congress itself could not do this, it committed the task to the Commission.

. . .

. . . The Commission's licensing function cannot be discharged, therefore, merely by finding that there are no technological objections to the granting of a license. If the criterion of "public interest" were limited to such matters, how could the Commission choose between two applicants for the same facilities, each of whom is financially and technically qualified to operate a station? Since the very inception of federal regulation by radio, comparative considerations as to the services to be rendered have governed the application of the standard of "public interest, convenience, or necessity."
[ ]

. . .

These provisions, individually and in the aggregate, preclude the notion that the Commission is empowered to deal only with technical and engineering impediments to the "larger and more effective use of radio in the public interest." We cannot find in the Act any such restriction of the Commission's authority. Suppose, for example, that a community can, because of physical limitations, be assigned only two stations. That community might be deprived of effective service in any one of several ways. More powerful stations in nearby cities might blanket out the signals of local stations so that they could not be heard at all. The stations might interfere with each other so that neither could be clearly heard. One station might dominate the other with the power of its signal. But the community could be deprived of good radio service in ways less crude. One man, financially and technically qualified, might apply for and obtain the licenses of both stations and present a single service over the two stations, thus wasting a frequency otherwise available to the area. The language of the Act does not withdraw such a situation from the licensing and regulatory powers of the Commission, and there is no evidence that Congress did not mean its broad language to carry the authority it expresses.

The Court then considered NBC's claims that if Congress did authorize the FCC to do this, the statute was unconstitutional. The first argument was that the phrase "public interest" was too vague a standard for delegating functions to the FCC. The Court disagreed and relied on an earlier broadcasting case in which it had said that the phrase "is as concrete as the complicated factors for judgment in such a field of delegated authority permit." The phrase is not to be interpreted as giving the FCC "unlimited power."

Next, the Court rejected NBC's First Amendment claim:

> We come, finally, to an appeal to the First Amendment. The Regulations, even if valid in all other respects, must fall because they abridge, say the appellants, their right of free speech. If that be so, it would follow that every person whose application for a license is denied by the Commission is thereby denied his constitutional right of free speech. Freedom of utterance is abridged to many who wish to use the limited facilities of radio. Unlike other modes of expression, it is subject to governmental regulation. Because it cannot be used by all, some who wish to use it must be denied. But Congress did not authorize the Commission to choose among applicants upon the basis of their political, economic or social views, or upon any other capricious basis. If it did, or if the Commission by these Regulations proposed a choice among applicants upon some such basis, the issue before us would be wholly different. The question here is simply whether the Commission, by announcing that it will refuse licenses to persons who engage in specified network practices (a basis for choice, which we hold is comprehended within the statutory criterion of "public interest"), is thereby denying such persons the constitutional right of free speech. The right of free speech does not include, however, the right to use the facilities of radio without a license. The licensing system established by Congress in the Communications Act of 1934 was a proper exercise of its power over commerce. The standard it provided for the licensing of stations was the "public interest, convenience, or necessity." Denial of a station license on that ground, if valid under the Act, is not a denial of free speech.

## Notes and Questions

1. The origin of the phrase, "public interest, convenience and necessity," § 309(a), or "public convenience, interest or necessity," § 307(a), is unclear from legislative documents. A former chairman of the Commission, Newton Minow, suggests the origin in Equal Time 8–9 (1964): Senator Clarence C. Dill, who had played a major part in the early legislation, told Minow that the drafters had reached an impasse in attempting to define a regulatory standard for this new, uncharted activity. A young lawyer who had been loaned to the Senate by the Interstate Commerce Commission proposed the words because they were used in other federal statutes.

Judge Henry Friendly, in The Federal Administrative Agencies 54–55 (1962), comments on the standard:

> The only guideline supplied by Congress in the Communications Act of 1934 was "public convenience, interest, or necessity." The

standard of public convenience and necessity introduced into the federal statute book by Transportation Act, 1920, conveyed a fair degree of meaning when the issue was whether new or duplicating railroad construction should be authorized or an existing line abandoned.  It was to convey less when, as under the Motor Carrier Act of 1935, or the Civil Aeronautics Act of 1938, there would be the added issue of selecting the applicant to render a service found to be needed; but under those statutes there would usually be some demonstrable factors, such as, in air route cases, ability to render superior one-plane or one-carrier service because of junction of the new route with existing ones, lower costs due to other operations, or historical connection with the traffic, that ought to have enabled the agency to develop intelligible criteria for selection.  The standard was almost drained of meaning under section 307 of the Communications Act, where the issue was almost never the need for broadcasting service but rather who should render it.

2.  The Radio Commission's first obligation was to clear the airwaves to avoid destructive interference.  It decided in 1928 that "as between two broadcasting stations with otherwise equal claims for privileges, the station which has the longest record of continuous service has the superior right."  Great Lakes Broadcasting Co., 3 F.R.C.Ann.Rep. 32 (1929), modified on other grounds 37 F.2d 993 (D.C.Cir.1930), certiorari dismissed 281 U.S. 706 (1930).  In that case, involving three competing stations, the Commission also stated, however, that if there was a "substantial disparity" in the services being offered by the stations, "the claim of priority must give way to the superior service."  The Commission was soon evaluating service in terms of program content.  In *Great Lakes*, the Commission contented itself with noting that stations using formats that appeal to only a "small portion" of the public were not serving the public interest because each member of the listening public is entitled to service from each station in the community.

3.  In its early years, the Radio Commission showed no hesitation in denying renewal of licenses because of the content of the speech uttered over the station.  Section 29 of the 1927 Act, reenacted as § 326 of the 1934 Act, provided in relevant part:

> Nothing in this Act shall be understood or construed to give the licensing authority the power of censorship over the radio communications or signals transmitted by any radio station, and no regulation or condition shall be promulgated or fixed by the licensing authority which shall interfere with the right of free speech by means of radio communication.  .  .  .

In 1930, the Commission denied renewal of a license to KFKB on the ground that the station was being controlled and used by Dr. J.R. Brinkley to further his personal interest.  Dr. Brinkley had three half-hour programs daily in which he answered anonymous inquiries on health and medicine and usually recommended several of his own tonics and prescriptions that were known to the public only by numerical designations. Druggists paid a fee to Dr. Brinkley for each sale they made.

In affirming the denial of renewal, KFKB Broadcasting Association v. Federal Radio Commission, 47 F.2d 670 (D.C.Cir.1931), the court rejected the station's argument that the Commission had censored in violation of § 29:

> This contention is without merit. There has been no attempt on the part of the commission to subject any part of appellant's broadcasting matter to scrutiny prior to its release. In considering the question whether the public interest, convenience, or necessity will be served by a renewal of appellant's license, the commission has merely exercised its undoubted right to take note of appellant's past conduct, which is not censorship.

In Trinity Methodist Church, South v. Federal Radio Commission, 62 F.2d 850 (D.C.Cir.1932), certiorari denied 288 U.S. 599 (1933), the controlling figure was the minister of the church, Dr. Shuler, who regularly defamed government institutions and officials, and attacked labor groups and various religions. The Commission's denial of renewal was affirmed. The court concluded that the broadcasts "without facts to sustain or to justify them" might fairly be found not to be within the public interest:

> If it be considered that one in possession of a permit to broadcast in interstate commerce may, without let or hindrance from any source, use these facilities, reaching out, as they do, from one corner of the country to the other, to obstruct the administration of justice, offend the religious susceptibilities of thousands, inspire political distrust and civic discord, or offend youth and innocence by the free use of words suggestive of sexual immorality, and be answerable for slander only at the instance of the one offended, then this great science, instead of a boon, will become a scourge and the nation a theater for the display of individual passions and the collusion of personal interests. This is neither censorship nor previous restraint, nor is it a whittling away of the rights guaranteed by the First Amendment, or an impairment of their free exercise. Appellant may continue to indulge his strictures upon the characters of men in public office. He may just as freely as ever criticize religious practices of which he does not approve. He may even indulge private malice or personal slander—subject, of course, to being required to answer for the abuse thereof—but he may not, as we think, demand, of right, the continued use of an instrumentality of commerce for such purposes, or any other, except in subordination to all reasonable rules and regulations Congress, acting through the Commission, may prescribe.

4. The Supreme Court did not again consider the FCC's power until 26 years after *NBC*. Since this case, *Red Lion*, affects everything else that follows, we consider it at the outset of our exploration of broadcasting law. The case deals fairly closely with the personal attack part of the

broader fairness doctrine.  The case also refers to the "equal opportunities" rule (sometimes incorrectly called the "equal time" rule), which applies during election campaigns.  Although we look at each of these doctrines in detail in Chapter VI, we must introduce each one now so that *Red Lion* can be fully understood.

As part of the first Communications Act, Congress passed what is now § 315, which requires any broadcaster who sells or gives time for a candidate's use to treat all other candidates for the same office equally.  This means that a broadcaster who sells a candidate for Congress 15 minutes of prime time, must be prepared to sell each opponent of that candidate the same amount of prime time at equivalent prices.

The fairness doctrine, on the other hand, was not imposed by Congress.  Developed by the Commission on its own in the 1940's, the doctrine has two separate parts.  One part requires the broadcaster to air issues that "are so critical or of such great public importance that it would be unreasonable for a licensee to ignore them completely."  Much more attention has been paid to the second part of the doctrine—that if a broadcaster does cover a "controversial issue of public importance" it must take steps to assure that important contrasting views are also presented.  These views may be presented by the licensee itself or by speakers chosen by the licensee.

The personal attack aspect of the fairness doctrine emerged in decisions in which the FCC ordered stations that had broadcast programs attacking a person's character during a discussion of a controversial issue of public importance to inform the person and offer him time to present his side.  The Red Lion case arose from such a situation.

While the Red Lion case was being litigated, the FCC decided to promulgate a formal rule to make the personal attack doctrine more precise and more readily enforceable.  The personal attack rule applied when "during the presentation of views on a controversial issue of public importance, an attack is made upon the honesty, character, integrity, or like personal qualities of an identified person or group."  Notice and an opportunity to respond were required.

At the same time, the FCC decided to promulgate a formal political editorial rule providing that when a licensee editorially endorsed a candidate for political office, other candidates for the same office were to be advised of the endorsement and offered a reasonable opportunity to respond.  The same opportunity was to be extended to any candidate who was attacked in an editorial.

As soon as these two formal rules were announced, the Radio Television News Directors Association (RTNDA) sued to declare the rules unconstitutional.  The court of appeals agreed, and held that the rules violated the First Amendment.  The Supreme Court heard both cases together and decided them in the same opinion.

## RED LION BROADCASTING CO. v. FEDERAL COMMUNICATIONS COMMISSION

Supreme Court of the United States, 1969.
395 U.S. 367, 89 S.Ct. 1794, 23 L.Ed.2d 371.

Mr. Justice White delivered the opinion of the Court.

The Federal Communications Commission has for many years imposed on radio and television broadcasters the requirement that discussion of public issues be presented on broadcast stations, and that each side of those issues must be given fair coverage. This is known as the fairness doctrine, which originated very early in the history of broadcasting and has maintained its present outlines for some time. It is an obligation whose content has been defined in a long series of FCC rulings in particular cases, and which is distinct from the statutory requirement of § 315 of the Communications Act that equal time be allotted all qualified candidates for public office. Two aspects of the fairness doctrine, relating to personal attacks in the context of controversial public issues and to political editorializing, were codified more precisely in the form of FCC regulations in 1967. The two cases before us now, which were decided separately below, challenge the constitutional and statutory bases of the doctrine and component rules. *Red Lion* involves the application of the fairness doctrine to a particular broadcast, and *RTNDA* arises as an action to review the FCC's 1967 promulgation of the personal attack and political editorializing regulations, which were laid down after the *Red Lion* litigation had begun.

### I.

### A.

The Red Lion Broadcasting Company is licensed to operate a Pennsylvania radio station, WGCB. On November 27, 1964, WGCB carried a 15-minute broadcast by the Reverend Billy James Hargis as part of a "Christian Crusade" series. A book by Fred J. Cook entitled "Goldwater—Extremist on the Right" was discussed by Hargis, who said that Cook had been fired by a newspaper for making false charges against city officials; that Cook had then worked for a Communist-affiliated publication; that he had defended Alger Hiss and attacked J. Edgar Hoover and the Central Intelligence Agency; and that he had now written a "book to smear and destroy Barry Goldwater." When Cook heard of the broadcast he concluded that he had been personally attacked and demanded free reply time, which the station refused. After an exchange of letters among Cook, Red Lion, and the FCC, the FCC declared that the Hargis broadcast constituted a personal attack on Cook; that Red Lion had failed to meet its obligation under the fairness doctrine as expressed in Times-Mirror Broadcasting Co., 24 P & F Radio Reg. 404 (1962), to send a tape, transcript, or summary of the broadcast to Cook and offer him reply time; and that the station must provide reply time whether or not Cook would pay for it. On review in the Court of Appeals for the District of Columbia Circuit, the FCC's position was upheld as constitutional and otherwise proper.  [  ]

. . .

### C.

Believing that the specific application of the fairness doctrine in *Red Lion*, and the promulgation of the regulations in *RTNDA*, are both authorized by Congress and enhance rather than abridge the freedoms of speech and press protected by the First Amendment, we hold them valid and constitutional, reversing the judgment, below in *RTNDA* and affirming the judgment below in *Red Lion*.

### II.

The history of the emergence of the fairness doctrine and of the related legislation shows that the Commission's action in the *Red Lion* case did not exceed its authority, and that in adopting the new regulations the Commission was implementing congressional policy rather than embarking on a frolic of its own.

### A.

Before 1927, the allocation of frequencies was left entirely to the private sector, and the result was chaos.  It quickly became apparent that broadcast frequencies constituted a scarce resource whose use could be regulated and rationalized only by the Government.  Without government control, the medium would be of little use because of the cacophony of competing voices, none of which could be clearly and predictably heard.  Consequently, the Federal Radio Commission was established to allocate frequencies among competing applicants in a manner responsive to the public "convenience, interest, or necessity."

Very shortly thereafter the Commission expressed its view that the "public interest requires ample play for the free and fair competition of opposing views, and the commission believes that the principle applies . . . to all discussions of issues of importance to the public."  . . . After an extended period during which the licensee was obliged not only to cover and to cover fairly the views of others, but also to refrain from expressing his own personal views, Mayflower Broadcasting Corp., 8 F.C.C. 333 (1940), the latter limitation on the licensee was abandoned and the doctrine developed into its present form.

There is a twofold duty laid down by the FCC's decisions and described by the 1949 Report on Editorializing by Broadcast Licensees, 13 F.C.C. 1246 (1949).  The broadcaster must give adequate coverage to public issues, [  ], and coverage must be fair in that it accurately reflects the opposing views.  [  ]  This must be done at the broadcaster's own expense if sponsorship is unavailable.  [  ]  Moreover, the duty must be met by programming obtained at the licensee's own initiative if available from no other source.  . . .

When a personal attack has been made on a figure involved in a public issue, both the doctrine of cases such as *Red Lion* and *Times Mirror Broadcasting Co.*, 24 P & F Radio Reg. 404 (1962), and also the 1967 regulations at issue in *RTNDA* require that the individual attacked himself be offered an opportunity to respond. Likewise, where one candidate is endorsed in a political editorial, the other candidates must themselves be offered reply time to use personally or through a spokesman. These obligations differ from the general fairness requirement that issues be presented, and presented with coverage of competing views, in that the broadcaster does not have the option of presenting the attacked party's side himself or choosing a third party to represent that side. But insofar as there is an obligation of the broadcaster to see that both sides are presented, and insofar as that is an affirmative obligation, the personal attack doctrine and regulations do not differ from the preceding fairness doctrine. The simple fact that the attacked men or unendorsed candidates may respond themselves or through agents is not a critical distinction, and indeed, it is not unreasonable for the FCC to conclude that the objective of adequate presentation of all sides may best be served by allowing those most closely affected to make the response, rather than leaving the response in the hands of the station which has attacked their candidacies, endorsed their opponents, or carried a personal attack upon them.

## B.

The statutory authority of the FCC to promulgate these regulations derives from the mandate to the "Commission from time to time, as public convenience, interest, or necessity requires" to promulgate "such rules and regulations and prescribe such restrictions and conditions . . . as may be necessary to carry out the provisions of this chapter. . . ." 47 U.S.C. § 303 and § 303(r). The Commission is specifically directed to consider the demands of the public interest in the course of granting licenses, 47 U.S.C. §§ 307(a), 309(a); renewing them, 47 U.S.C. § 307; and modifying them. Ibid. Moreover, the FCC has included among the conditions of the Red Lion license itself the requirement that operation of the station be carried out in the public interest, 47 U.S.C. § 309(h). This mandate to the FCC to assure that broadcasters operate in the public interest is a broad one, a power "not niggardly but expansive," National Broadcasting Co. v. United States, 319 U.S. 190, 219 (1943), whose validity we have long upheld. [   ] It is broad enough to encompass these regulations.

The fairness doctrine finds specific recognition in statutory form, is in part modeled on explicit statutory provisions relating to political candidates, and is approvingly reflected in legislative history.

In 1959 the Congress amended the statutory requirement of § 315 that equal time be accorded each political candidate to except certain appearances on news programs, but added that this constituted no exception *"from the obligation imposed upon them under this Act to operate in the public interest and to afford reasonable opportunity for their discussion of conflicting views on issues of public importance."* Act of September 14, 1959, § 1, 73 Stat. 557, amending 47 U.S.C. § 315(a) (emphasis added). This language makes it very plain that Congress, in 1959, announced that the phrase "public interest," which had been in the Act since 1927, imposed a duty on broadcasters to discuss both sides of controversial public issues. In other words, the amendment vindicated the FCC's general view that the fairness doctrine inhered in the public interest standard. Subsequent legislation declaring the intent of an earlier statute is entitled to great weight in statutory construction. And here this principle is given special force by the equally venerable principle that the construction of a statute by those charged with its execution should be followed unless there are compelling indications that it is wrong, especially when Congress has refused to alter the administrative construction. Here, the Congress has not just kept its silence by refusing to overturn the administrative construction, but has ratified it with positive legislation. Thirty years of consistent administrative construction left undisturbed by Congress until 1959, when that construction was expressly accepted, reinforce the natural conclusion that the public interest language of the Act authorized the Commission to require licensees to use their stations for discussion of public issues, and that the FCC is free to implement this requirement by reasonable rules and regulations which fall short of abridgment of the freedom of speech and press, and of the censorship proscribed by § 326 of the Act.

The objectives of § 315 themselves could readily be circumvented but for the complementary fairness doctrine ratified by § 315. The section applies only to campaign appearances by candidates, and not by family, friends, campaign managers, or other supporters. Without the fairness doctrine, then, a licensee could ban all campaign appearances by candidates themselves from the air and proceed to deliver over his station entirely to the supporters of one slate of candidates, to the exclusion of all others. In this way the broadcaster could have a far greater impact on the favored candidacy than he could by simply allowing a spot appearance by the candidate himself. It is the fairness doctrine as an aspect of the obligation to operate in the public interest, rather than § 315, which prohibits the broadcaster from taking such a step.

.    .    .

In light of the fact that the "public interest" in broadcasting clearly encompasses the presentation of vigorous debate of controversial issues of importance and concern to the public; the fact that the FCC has rested upon that language from its very inception a doctrine that these issues must be discussed, and fairly; and the fact that Congress has acknowledged that the analogous provisions of § 315 are not preclusive in this area, and knowingly preserved the FCC's complementary efforts, we think the fairness doctrine and its component personal attack and political editorializing regulations are a legitimate exercise of congressionally delegated authority.   .   .   .

### III.

The broadcasters challenge the fairness doctrine and its specific manifestations in the personal attack and political editorial rules on conventional First Amendment grounds, alleging that the rules abridge their freedom of speech and press.  Their contention is that the First Amendment protects their desire to use their allotted frequencies continuously to broadcast whatever they choose, and to exclude whomever they choose from ever using that frequency.  No man may be prevented from saying or publishing what he thinks, or refusing in his speech or other utterances to give equal weight to the views of his opponents. This right, they say, applies equally to broadcasters.

### A.

Although broadcasting is clearly a medium affected by a First Amendment interest, United States v. Paramount Pictures, Inc.,  334 U.S. 131, 166 (1948), differences in the characteristics of new media justify differences in the First Amendment standards applied to them. [  ]  For example, the ability of new technology to produce sounds more raucous than those of the human voice justifies restrictions on the sound level, and on the hours and places of use, of sound trucks so long as the restrictions are reasonable and applied without discrimination.  [  ]

Just as the Government may limit the use of sound-amplifying equipment potentially so noisy that it drowns out civilized private speech, so may the Government limit the use of broadcast equipment.  The right of free speech of a broadcaster, the user of a sound truck, or any other individual does not embrace a right to snuff out the free speech of others.  Associated Press v. United States, 326 U.S. 1, 20 (1945).

When two people converse face to face, both should not speak at once if either is to be clearly understood.  But the range of the human voice is so limited that there could be meaningful communications if half the people in the United States were talking and the other half listening. Just as clearly, half the people might publish and the other half read. But the reach of radio signals is incomparably greater than the range of the human voice and the problem of interference is a massive reality. The lack of know-how and equipment may keep many from the air but only a tiny fraction of those with resources and intelligence can hope to communicate by radio at the same time if intelligible communication is to be had, even if the entire radio spectrum is utilized in the present state of commercially acceptable technology.

It was this fact, and the chaos which ensued from permitting anyone to use any frequency at whatever power level he wished, which made necessary the enactment of the Radio Act of 1927 and the Communications Act of 1934, as the Court has noted at length before. National Broadcasting Co. v. United States, 319 U.S. 190, 210–214 (1943). It was this reality which at the very least necessitated first the division of the radio spectrum into portions reserved respectively for public broadcasting and for other important radio uses such as amateur operation, aircraft, police, defense, and navigation; and then the subdivision of each portion, and assignment of specific frequencies to individual users or groups of users. Beyond this, however, because the frequencies reserved for public broadcasting were limited in number, it was essential for the Government to tell some applicants that they could not broadcast at all because there was room for only a few.

Where there are substantially more individuals who want to broadcast than there are frequencies to allocate, it is idle to posit an unabridgeable First Amendment right to broadcast comparable to the right of every individual to speak, write, or publish. If 100 persons want broadcast licenses but there are only 10 frequencies to allocate, all of them may have the same "right" to a license; but if there is to be any effective communication by radio, only a few can be licensed and the rest must be barred from the airwaves. It would be strange if the First Amendment, aimed at protecting and furthering communications, prevented the Government from making radio communication possible by requiring licenses to broadcast and by limiting the number of licenses so as not to overcrowd the spectrum.

This has been the consistent view of the Court. Congress unquestionably has the power to grant and deny licenses and to eliminate existing stations. FRC v. Nelson Bros. Bond & Mortgage Co., 289 U.S. 266 (1933). No one has a First Amendment right to a license or to monopolize a radio frequency; to deny a station license because "the public interest" requires it "is not a denial of free speech." National Broadcasting Co. v. United States, 319 U.S. 190, 227 (1943).

By the same token, as far as the First Amendment is concerned those who are licensed stand no better than those to whom licenses are refused. A license permits broadcasting, but the licensee has no constitutional right to be the one who holds the license or to monopolize a radio frequency to the exclusion of his fellow citizens. There is nothing in the First Amendment which prevents the Government from requiring a licensee to share his frequency with others and to conduct himself as a proxy or fiduciary with obligations to present those views and voices which are representative of his community and which would otherwise, by necessity, be barred from the airwaves.

This is not to say that the First Amendment is irrelevant to public broadcasting. On the contrary, it has a major role to play as the

Congress itself recognized in § 326, which forbids FCC interference with "the right of free speech by means of radio communication." Because of the scarcity of radio frequencies, the Government is permitted to put restraints on licensees in favor of others whose views should be expressed on this unique medium. But the people as a whole retain their interest in free speech by radio and their collective right to have the medium function consistently with the ends and purposes of the First Amendment. It is the right of the viewers and listeners, not the right of the broadcasters, which is paramount. See FCC v. Sanders Bros. Radio Station, 309 U.S. 470, 475 (1940); FCC v. Allentown Broadcasting Corp., 349 U.S. 358, 361–362 (1955); 2 Z. Chafee, Government and Mass Communications 546 (1947). It is the purpose of the First Amendment to preserve an uninhibited marketplace of ideas in which truth will ultimately prevail, rather than to countenance monopolization of that market, whether it be by the Government itself or a private licensee. Associated Press v. United States, 326 U.S. 1, 20 (1945); New York Times Co. v. Sullivan, 376 U.S. 254, 270 (1964); Abrams v. United States, 250 U.S. 616, 630 (1919) (Holmes, J., dissenting). "[S]peech concerning public affairs is more than self-expression; it is the essence of self-government." Garrison v. Louisiana, 379 U.S. 64, 74–75 (1964). See Brennan, The Supreme Court and the Meiklejohn Interpretation of the First Amendment, 79 Harv.L.Rev. 1 (1965). It is the right of the public to receive suitable access to social, political, esthetic, moral, and other ideas and experiences which is crucial here. That right may not constitutionally be abridged either by Congress or by the FCC.

### B.

Rather than confer frequency monopolies on a relatively small number of licensees, in a Nation of 200,000,000, the Government could surely have decreed that each frequency should be shared among all or some of those who wish to use it, each being assigned a portion of the broadcast day or the broadcast week. The ruling and regulations at issue here do not go quite so far. They assert that under specified circumstances, a licensee must offer to make available a reasonable amount of broadcast time to those who have a view different from that which has already been expressed on his station. The expression of a political endorsement, or of a personal attack while dealing with a controversial public issue, simply triggers this time sharing. As we have said, the First Amendment confers no right on licensees to prevent others from broadcasting on "their" frequencies and no right to an unconditional monopoly of a scarce resource which the Government has denied others the right to use.

In terms of constitutional principle, and as enforced sharing of a scarce resource, the personal attack and political editorial rules are indistinguishable from the equal-time provision of § 315, a specific enactment of Congress requiring stations to set aside reply time under specified circumstances and to which the fairness doctrine and these constituent regulations are important complements. That provision, which has been part of the law since 1927, Radio Act of 1927, § 18, 44 Stat. 1170, has been held valid by this Court as an obligation of the licensee relieving him of any power in any way to prevent or censor the broadcast, and thus, insulating him from liability for defamation. The constitutionality of the statute under the First Amendment was unquestioned. Farmers Educ. & Coop. Union v. WDAY, 360 U.S. 525 (1959).

Nor can we say that it is inconsistent with the First Amendment goal of producing an informed public capable of conducting its own affairs to require a broadcaster to permit answers to personal attacks occurring in the course of discussing controversial issues, or to require that the political opponents of those endorsed by the station be given a chance to communicate with the public.[18] Otherwise, station owners and a few networks would have unfettered power to make time available only to the highest bidders, to communicate only their own views on public issues, people and candidates, and to permit on the air only those with whom they agreed. There is no sanctuary in the First Amendment for unlimited private censorship operating in a medium not open to all. "Freedom of the press from governmental interference under the First Amendment does not sanction repression of that freedom by private interests." Associated Press v. United States, 326 U.S. 1, 20 (1945).

## C.

It is strenuously argued, however, that if political editorials or personal attacks will trigger an obligation in broadcasters to afford the opportunity for expression to speakers who need not pay for time and whose views are unpalatable to the licensees, then broadcasters will be irresistibly forced to self-censorship and their coverage of controversial public issues will be eliminated or at least rendered wholly ineffective. Such a result would indeed be a serious matter, for should licensees actually eliminate their coverage of controversial issues, the purposes of the doctrine would be stifled.

At this point, however, as the Federal Communications Commission has indicated, that possibility is at best speculative. The communications industry, and in particular the networks, have taken pains to present controversial issues in the past, and even now they do not assert that they intend to abandon their efforts in this regard. It would be better if the FCC's encouragement were never necessary to induce the broadcast-

---

18. The expression of views opposing those which broadcasters permit to be aired in the first place need not be confined solely to the broadcasters themselves as proxies. "Nor is it enough that he should hear the arguments of adversaries from his own teachers, presented as they state them, and accompanied by what they offer as refuta- tions. That is not the way to do justice to the arguments, or bring them into real contact with his own mind. He must be able to hear them from persons who actually believe them; who defend them in earnest, and do their very utmost for them." J. Mill, On Liberty 32 (R. McCallum ed. 1947).

ers to meet their responsibility. And if experience with the administration of these doctrines indicates that they have the net effect of reducing rather than enhancing the volume and quality of coverage, there will be time enough to reconsider the constitutional implications. The fairness doctrine in the past has had no such overall effect.

That this will occur now seems unlikely, however, since if present licensees should suddenly prove timorous, the Commission is not powerless to insist that they give adequate and fair attention to public issues. It does not violate the First Amendment to treat licensees given the privilege of using scarce radio frequencies as proxies for the entire community, obligated to give suitable time and attention to matters of great public concern. To condition the granting or renewal of licenses on a willingness to present representative community views on controversial issues is consistent with the ends and purposes of those constitutional provisions forbidding the abridgment of freedom of speech and freedom of the press. Congress need not stand idly by and permit those with licenses to ignore the problems which beset the people or to exclude from the airways anything but their own views of fundamental questions. The statute, long administrative practice, and cases are to this effect.

Licenses to broadcast do not confer ownership of designated frequencies, but only the temporary privilege of using them. 47 U.S.C. § 301. Unless renewed, they expire within three years. 47 U.S.C. § 307(d). The statute mandates the issuance of licenses if the "public convenience, interest, or necessity will be served thereby." 47 U.S.C. § 307(a). In applying this standard the Commission for 40 years has been choosing licensees based in part on their program proposals. In FRC v. Nelson Bros. Bond & Mortgage Co., 289 U.S. 266, 279 (1933), the Court noted that in "view of the limited number of available broadcasting frequencies the Congress has authorized allocation and licenses." In determining how best to allocate frequencies, the Federal Radio Commission considered the needs of competing communities and the programs offered by competing stations to meet those needs; moreover, if needs or programs shifted the Commission could alter its allocations to reflect those shifts. Id., at 285. . . .

### D.

The litigants embellish their First Amendment arguments with the contention that the regulations are so vague that their duties are impossible to discern. Of this point it is enough to say that, judging the validity of the regulations on their face as they are presented here, we cannot conclude that the FCC has been left a free hand to vindicate its own idiosyncratic conception of the public interest or of the requirements of free speech. . . .

We need not and do not now ratify every past and future decision by the FCC with regard to programming.  There is no question here of the Commission's refusal to permit the broadcaster to carry a particular program or to publish his own views;  of a discriminatory refusal to require the licensee to broadcast certain views which have been denied access to the airwaves;  of government censorship of a particular program contrary to § 326;  or of the official government view dominating public broadcasting.  Such questions would raise more serious First Amendment issues.  But we do hold that the Congress and the Commission do not violate the First Amendment when they require a radio or television station to give reply time to answer personal attacks and political editorials.

E.

It is argued that even if at one time the lack of available frequencies for all who wished to use them justified the Government's choice of those who would best serve the public interest by acting as proxy for those who would present differing views, or by giving the latter access directly to broadcast facilities, this condition no longer prevails so that continuing control is not justified.  To this there are several answers.

Scarcity is not entirely a thing of the past.  Advances in technology, such as microwave transmission, have led to more efficient utilization of the frequency spectrum, but uses for that spectrum have also grown apace.  Portions of the spectrum must be reserved for vital uses unconnected with human communication, such as radio-navigational aids used by aircraft and vessels.  Conflicts have even emerged between such vital functions as defense preparedness and experimentation in methods of averting midair collisions through radio warning devices. "Land mobile services" such as police, ambulance, fire department, public utility, and other communications systems have been occupying an increasingly crowded portion of the frequency spectrum and there are, apart from the licensed amateur radio operators' equipment, 5,000,000 transmitters operated on the "citizens' band" which is also increasingly congested.  Among the various uses for radio frequency space, including marine, aviation, amateur, military, and common carrier users, there are easily enough claimants to permit use of the whole with an even smaller allocation to broadcast radio and television uses than now exists.

Comparative hearings between competing applicants for broadcast spectrum space are by no means a thing of the past.  The radio spectrum has become so congested that at times it has been necessary to suspend new applications.  The very high frequency television spectrum is, in the country's major markets, almost entirely occupied, although space reserved for ultra high frequency television transmission, which is a relatively recent development as a commercially viable alternative, has not yet been completely filled.[25]

The rapidity with which technological advances succeed one another to create more efficient use of spectrum space on the one hand, and to create new uses for that space by ever growing numbers of people on the other, makes it unwise to speculate on the future allocation of that space.  It is enough to say that the resource is one of considerable and growing importance whose scarcity impelled its regulation by an agency authorized by Congress.  Nothing in this record, or in our own researches, convinces us that the resource ·is no longer one for which there are more immediate and potential uses than can be accommodated, and for which wise planning is essential.  This does not mean, of course, that every possible wavelength must be occupied at every hour by some vital use in order to sustain the congressional judgment.  The substantial capital investment required for many uses, in addition to the potentiality for confusion and interference inherent in any scheme for continuous kaleidoscopic reallocation of all available space may make this unfeasible.  The allocation need not be made at such a breakneck pace that the objectives of the allocation are themselves imperiled.

Even where there are gaps in spectrum utilization, the fact remains that existing broadcasters have often attained their present position because of their initial government selection in competition with others before new technological advances opened new opportunities for further

**25.**  In a table prepared by the FCC on the basis of statistics current as of August 31, 1968, VHF and UHF channels allocated to and those available in the top 100 market areas for television are set forth:

**Commercial**

| Market Areas | Channels Allocated | | Channels On the Air, Authorized, or Applied for | | Available Channels | |
|---|---|---|---|---|---|---|
| | VHF | UHF | VHF | UHF | VHF | UHF |
| Top 10 | 40 | 45 | 40 | 44 | 0 | 1 |
| Top 50 | 157 | 163 | 157 | 136 | 0 | 27 |
| Top 100 | 264 | 297 | 264 | 213 | 0 | 84 |

**Noncommercial**

| Market Areas | Channels Reserved | | Channels On the Air, Authorized, or Applied for | | Available Channels | |
|---|---|---|---|---|---|---|
| | VHF | UHF | VHF | UHF | VHF | UHF |
| Top 10 | 7 | 17 | 7 | 16 | 0 | 1 |
| Top 50 | 21 | 79 | 20 | 47 | 1 | 32 |
| Top 100 | 35 | 138 | 34 | 69 | 1 | 69 |

1968 FCC Annual Report 132–135.

uses.  Long experience in broadcasting, confirmed habits of listeners and viewers, network affiliation, and other advantages in program procurement give existing broadcasters a substantial advantage over new entrants, even where new entry is technologically possible.  These advantages are the fruit of a preferred position conferred by the Government. Some present possibility for new entry by competing stations is not enough, in itself, to render unconstitutional the Government's effort to assure that a broadcaster's programming ranges widely enough to serve the public interest.

In view of the scarcity of broadcast frequencies, the Government's role in allocating those frequencies, and the legitimate claims of those unable without governmental assistance to gain access to those frequencies for expression of their views, we hold the regulations and ruling at issue here are both authorized by statute and constitutional.[28]  The judgment of the Court of Appeals in *Red Lion* is affirmed and that in *RTNDA* reversed and the causes remanded for proceedings consistent with this opinion.

It is so ordered.

Not having heard oral argument in these cases, MR. JUSTICE DOUGLAS took no part in the Court's decision.

### Notes and Questions

1.  The Court states that the differences among the technical aspects of media warrant different regulatory treatment.  Compare Jackson, J., concurring, in Kovacs v. Cooper, 336 U.S. 77, 97 (1949): "The moving picture screen, the radio, the newspaper, the handbill, the sound truck and the street corner orator have differing natures, values, abuses and dangers.  Each, in my view, is a law unto itself.  . . ."

2.  The Court states that only a tiny fraction of those who want to broadcast are able to do so "even if the entire radio spectrum is utilized. . . ."  Who decided how much of the spectrum to allocate to radio? Could a niggardly or inefficient allocation of radio space justify government exercise of its regulatory power?  The notion of "scarcity" plays a major role in the Court's analysis.  What does the term appear to mean in the opinion?

28.  We need not deal with the argument that even if there is no longer a technological scarcity of frequencies limiting the number of broadcasters, there nevertheless is an economic scarcity in the sense that the Commission could or does limit entry to the broadcasting market on economic grounds and license no more stations than the market will support.  Hence, it is said, the fairness doctrine or its equivalent is essential to satisfy the claims of those excluded and of the public generally.  A related argument, which we also put aside, is that quite apart from scarcity of frequencies, technological or economic, Congress does not abridge freedom of speech or press by legislation directly or indirectly multiplying the voices and views presented to the public through time sharing, fairness doctrines, or other devices which limit or dissipate the power of those who sit astride the channels of communication with the general public. Cf. Citizen Pub. Co. v. United States, 394 U.S. 131 (1969).

Consider whether scarcity is present in the following contexts: (a) all three radio outlets allocated to a community are being used; (b) of the five radio outlets allocated three are being used; (c) all 40 radio outlets allocated to an urban area are being used; (d) seven of the 40 outlets are vacant.

3.   Does Justice White's next-to-last paragraph suggest that the reality of scarcity in the past will be enough to justify continuing regulation even if it were determined that no scarcity exists today?

4.   Justice White says that "It is the right of the viewers and listeners, not the right of the broadcasters, which is paramount. [   ] It is the purpose of the First Amendment to preserve an uninhibited marketplace of ideas in which truth will ultimately prevail, rather than to countenance monopolization of that market, whether it be by the Government itself or a private licensee."   What philosophical strands are being brought together here?

When Justice White says that the "right" involved in the case belongs to "the public" and that this "right may not constitutionally be abridged either by Congress or by the FCC," is he suggesting that the absence of governmental control of broadcasters' programming would deny the public's constitutional right to "receive suitable access to social, political, esthetic, moral and other ideas and experiences?"

5.   There is reason to believe that Fred Cook's demand for reply time was part of a broader effort to use the fairness doctrine to soften attacks on the Kennedy administration by right-wing political commentators.   The plan was to monitor right-wing programs and then to demand balance under the general fairness doctrine.   F. Friendly, The Good Guys, The Bad Guys and the First Amendment (1976). If the result was that licensees cancelled several right-wing commentators would that affect your reaction to the *Red Lion* decision?   Did Cook misuse the doctrine?

6.   By concentrating on the scarcity issue and declaring that the rights of the listeners were paramount, the Court seemed to be agreeing with scholars like law professor Jerome Barron, who argued that the development of mass media had reduced the "marketplace of ideas" to a romantic fantasy.   Reasoning that increased concentration in media ownership had resulted in a marketplace failure, Barron contended that a government-created right of access to the media was not just allowed, but indeed required by the First Amendment.

Barron did not limit this to broadcasting, however.   Due to economic as opposed to technological scarcity, the number of daily newspapers in this country had been reduced to the point where he felt the same arguments should apply.   It was not very long before he had his chance to argue this point before the Supreme Court.   Miami Herald v. Tornillo, 418 U.S. 241 (1974), involved a Florida right-of-reply statute which provided a political candidate attacked by a newspaper space to respond.

The Court unanimously ruled the statute unconstitutional under the First Amendment. The Court argued that requiring a newspaper to print replies interfered with the editorial discretion of the publisher and had a "chilling effect" on the publisher's First Amendment rights. "Faced with the penalties that would accrue to any newspaper that published news or commentary arguably within the reach of the right-of-access statute, editors might well conclude that the safe course is to avoid controversy. Therefore, under the operation of the Florida statute, political and electoral coverage would be blunted or reduced."

What was especially interesting about the case, however, was that there were no references to *Red Lion*. Are the two cases in any way contradictory? Is it relevant that there are approximately five to six times as many radio stations in this country as there are daily newspapers? Or that there are fewer than 40 cities in the entire country with more than one daily newspaper? Is there a difference between technological and economic scarcity?

7. Aside from the spectrum scarcity arguments there are intrinsic differences between print and broadcast media. There is a physical limit to the number of words that can be uttered intelligibly over a broadcasting facility during a 24-hour day. Based on an estimate of about 200,000 words, using normal speaking patterns, one author suggests that a newspaper is the equivalent of between one and three 24-hour programs. But the reader of a newspaper can at any time go directly to what interests him and skim or ignore the rest. In broadcasting, the choice is made for the listener by the broadcaster; the speed, content, and sequence are fixed. Baxter, Regulation and Diversity in Communications Media, 64 Am.Econ.Rev. 392 (1974). Might such differences justify greater regulation of broadcasting?

On the other hand, broadcasting is an inelastic medium. In order to carry a response by the subject of a personal attack, the broadcaster must drop other programming. In contrast, a newspaper does have the option of adding pages. Does this mean that the chilling effect of forced access is greater for the broadcast media?

8. Other differences between the print and electronic media emphasize the greater impact of broadcasting in conveying certain types of information. The vivid telecasts during the Vietnam War are thought to have been a strong factor in the shift of public attitude against that war, beyond the potential of any verbal journalism. Another major difference is the role of sound in broadcasting, which makes it possible to use songs and jingles effectively in advertising. During the discussion of the broadcast advertising of cigarettes, one court observed:

> Written messages are not communicated unless they are read, and reading requires an affirmative act. Broadcast messages, in contrast, are "in the air." In an age of omnipresent radio, there scarcely breathes a citizen who does not know some part of a leading cigarette jingle by heart. Similarly, an ordinary habitual television watcher can *avoid* these commercials only by frequently leaving the

room, changing the channel, or doing some other such affirmative act.   It is difficult to calculate the subliminal impact of this pervasive propaganda, which may be heard even if not listened to, but it may reasonably be thought greater than the impact of the written word.

Banzhaf v. Federal Communications Commission, 405 F.2d 1082, 1100–01 (D.C.Cir.1968), certiorari denied 396 U.S. 842 (1969).   Does this suggest an additional basis for regulating some aspects of broadcasting?

Does the *Banzhaf* view of broadcasting imply a "captive audience" comparable to the addressees of sound trucks in residential neighborhoods or political advertisements in mass transit vehicles?   Is turning off the program like averting your eyes from offensive wording on someone's jacket?   Is it relevant to this aspect of the discussion that most television sets and radios are in private homes?   These questions are the focus of Federal Communications Commission v. Pacifica Foundation, which is discussed in Chapter VII.

9.   The Supreme Court returned to the question of forced access once again in Columbia Broadcasting System, Inc. v. Democratic National Committee, 412 U.S. 94 (1973).   The Court decided that broadcasters were not obligated to accept paid advertisements from "responsible" individuals and groups.   The majority relied upon *Red Lion.*

Justice Stewart in a separate concurring opinion stated, "I agreed with the Court in *Red Lion,* although with considerable doubt, because I thought that that much Government regulation of program content was within the outer limits of First Amendment tolerability."

In another concurring opinion, Justice Douglas stated of *Red Lion*: "I did not participate in that decision and, with all respect, would not support it.   The Fairness Doctrine has no place in our First Amendment regime."   He argued that the uniqueness of the spectrum was "due to engineering and technical problems.   But the press in a realistic sense is likewise not available to all.   Small or 'underground' papers appear and disappear; and the weekly is an established institution.   But the daily papers now established are unique in the sense that it would be virtually impossible for a competitor to enter the field due to the financial exigencies of this era.   The result is that in practical terms the newspapers and magazines, like TV and radio, are available only to a selected few."

10.   The most recent extended discussion of the bases for regulating broadcasting occurred in FCC v. League of Women Voters of California, 468 U.S. \_\_\_ (1984).   Although we will return to the fairness doctrine in Chapter VI, consider the implications of this case for its future.   The three plaintiffs were the League, which wished to persuade public noncommercial educational broadcasters to take editorial positions; a listener who wished to hear such editorials; and a noncommercial broadcaster that wished to take editorial stands.   The impediment was § 399 of the Public Broadcasting Act of 1967, as amended in 1981:

No noncommercial educational broadcasting station which receives a grant from the Corporation for Public Broadcasting under subpart C of this part may engage in editorializing. No noncommercial educational broadcasting station may support or oppose any candidate for public office.

The case in fact centered on the first sentence of the section, which most of the justices thought severable from the second sentence. The core of the decision, centering on the nature of "public broadcasting," is reprinted in Chapter VIII. Here we focus on the majority's background discussion of the bases for regulating broadcasting.

The issue arose in the context of determining the "appropriate standard of review." The trial court, whose judgment of unconstitutionality was on direct review, had held that § 399 could survive constitutional scrutiny only if it served a "compelling" governmental interest. The FCC argued that a less demanding standard was appropriate. It based this argument in part on the "special characteristic" of spectrum scarcity and in part on the unique role of noncommercial broadcasting in this country.

The response of the five-member majority follows.

## FEDERAL COMMUNICATIONS COMMISSION v. LEAGUE OF WOMEN VOTERS OF CALIFORNIA

Supreme Court of the United States, 1984.
468 U.S. \_\_, 104 S.Ct. 3106, 82 L.Ed.2d 278.

[After setting forth the facts discussed in the introduction to this case, supra, and reviewing the history of noncommercial broadcasting, Justice Brennan addressed the appropriate standard of review in the following passage:]

JUSTICE BRENNAN delivered the opinion of the Court.

.  .  .

At first glance, of course, it would appear that the District Court applied the correct standard. Section 399 plainly operates to restrict the expression of editorial opinion on matters of public importance, and, as we have repeatedly explained, communication of this kind is entitled to the most exacting degree of First Amendment protection. [ ] Were a similar ban on editorializing applied in newspapers and magazines, we would not hesitate to strike it down as violative of the First Amendment. E.g., Mills v. Alabama, 384 U.S. 214 (1966). But, as the Government correctly notes, because broadcast regulation involves unique considerations, our cases have not followed precisely the same approach that we have applied to other media and have never gone so far as to demand that such regulations serve "compelling" governmental interests. At the same time, we think the Government's argument loses sight of concerns that are important in this area and thus misapprehends the essential meaning of our prior decisions concerning the reach of Congress' authority to regulate broadcast communication.

The fundamental principles that guide our evaluation of broadcast regulation are by now well established. First we have long recognized that Congress, acting pursuant to the Commerce Clause, has power to regulate the use of this scarce and valuable national resource. The distinctive feature of Congress' efforts in this area has been to ensure through the regulatory oversight of the FCC that only those who satisfy the "public interest, convenience and necessity" are granted a license to use radio and television broadcast frequencies. 47 U.S.C. § 309(a).[11]

Second, Congress may, in the exercise of this power, seek to assure that the public receives through this medium a balanced presentation of information on issues of public importance that otherwise might not be addressed if control of the medium were left entirely in the hands of those who own and operate broadcasting stations. Although such governmental regulation has never been allowed with respect to the print media, Miami Herald Publishing Co. v. Tornillo, 418 U.S. 241 (1974), we have recognized that "differences in the characteristics of new media justify differences in the First Amendment standards applied to them." Red Lion Broadcasting Co. v. FCC, 395 U.S. 367, 386 (1969). The fundamental distinguishing characteristic of the new medium of broadcasting that, in our view, has required some adjustment in First Amendment analysis is that "[b]roadcasting frequencies are a scarce resource [that] must be portioned out among applicants." Columbia Broadcasting System, Inc. v. Democratic National Committee, 412 U.S. 94, 101 (1973). Thus, our cases have taught that, given spectrum scarcity, those who are granted a license to broadcast must serve in a sense as fiduciaries for the public by presenting "those views and voices which are representative of his community and which would otherwise, by necessity, be barred from the airwaves." Red Lion, supra, at 389. As we observed in that case, because "[i]t is the purpose of the First Amendment to preserve an uninhibited marketplace of ideas in which truth will ultimately prevail, . . . the right of the public to receive suitable access to social, political, esthetic, moral and other ideas and experiences [through the medium of broadcasting] is crucial here [and it] may not constitutionally be abridged either by the Congress or the FCC." Id., at 390.

Finally, although the government's interest in ensuring balanced coverage of public issues is plainly both important and substantial, we have, at the same time, made clear that broadcasters are engaged in a vital and independent form of communicative activity. As a result, the First Amendment must inform and give shape to the manner in which

---

**11.** [  ].

The prevailing rationale for broadcast regulation based on spectrum scarcity has come under increasing criticism in recent years. Critics, including the incumbent Chairman of the FCC, charge that with the advent of cable and satellite television technology, communities now have access to such a wide variety of stations that the scarcity doctrine is obsolete. See, e.g.,

Fowler & Brenner, A Marketplace Approach to Broadcast Regulation, 60 Tex.L. Rev. 207, 221–226 (1982). We are not prepared, however, to reconsider our longstanding approach without some signal from Congress or the FCC that technological developments have advanced so far that some revision of the system of broadcast regulation may be required.

Congress exercises its regulatory power in this area. Unlike common carriers, broadcasters are "entitled under the First Amendment to exercise 'the widest journalistic freedom consistent with their public [duties].'" Columbia Broadcasting System, Inc. v. FCC, 453 U.S. 367, 395 (1981) (quoting Columbia Broadcasting System, Inc. v. Democratic National Committee, supra, at 110). See also FCC v. Midwest Video Corp., 440 U.S. 689, 703 (1979). Indeed, if the public's interest in receiving a balanced presentation of views is to be fully served, we must necessarily rely in large part upon the editorial initiative and judgment of the broadcasters who bear the public trust. See Columbia Broadcasting System, Inc. v. Democratic National Committee, supra, at 124–127.

Our prior cases illustrate these principles. In *Red Lion*, for example, we upheld the FCC's "fairness doctrine"—which requires broadcasters to provide adequate coverage of public issues and to ensure that this coverage fairly and accurately reflects the opposing views—because the doctrine advanced the substantial governmental interest in ensuring balanced presentations of views in this limited medium and yet posed no threat that a "broadcaster [would be denied permission] to carry a particular program or to publish his own views." Id., at 396.[12] Similarly, in Columbia Broadcasting System, Inc. v. FCC, supra, the Court upheld the right of access for federal candidates imposed by § 312(a)(7) of the Communications Act both because that provision "makes a significant contribution to freedom of expression by enhancing the ability of candidates to present, and the public to receive, information necessary for the effective operation of the democratic process," id., at 396, and because it defined a sufficiently *"limited* right of 'reasonable' access" so that "the discretion of broadcasters to present their views on any issue or to carry any particular type of programming" was not impaired. Id., at 396–397 (emphasis in original). Finally, in Columbia Broadcasting System, Inc. v. Democratic National Committee, supra, the Court affirmed the FCC's refusal to require broadcast licensees to accept all paid political advertisements. Although it was argued that such a requirement would serve the public's First Amendment interest in receiving additional views on public issues, the Court rejected this approach, finding that such a requirement would tend to transform broadcasters into common carriers and would intrude unnecessarily upon the editorial discretion of broadcasters. 412 U.S., at 123–125. The FCC's ruling, therefore, helped to advance the important purposes of the Communica-

12. We note that the FCC, observing that "[i]f any substantial possibility exists that the [fairness doctrine] rules have impeded, rather than furthered, First Amendment objectives, repeal may be warranted on that ground alone," has tentatively concluded that the rules, by effectively chilling speech, do not serve the public interest, and has therefore proposed to repeal them. Notice of Proposed Rulemaking In re Repeal or Modification of the Personal Attack and Political Editorial Rules, 48 Fed.Reg. 28295, 28298, 28301 (June 21, 1983). Of course, the Commission may, in the exercise of its discretion, decide to modify or abandon these rules, and we express no view on the legality of either course. As we recognized in *Red Lion*, however, were it to be shown by the Commission that the fairness doctrine "has the effect of reducing rather than enhancing" speech, we would then be forced to reconsider the constitutional basis of our decision in that case. 395 U.S., at 393.

tions Act, grounded in the First Amendment, of preserving the right of broadcasters to exercise "the widest journalistic freedom consistent with [their] public obligations," and of guarding against "the risk of an enlargement of Government control over the broadcast discussion of public issues." 412 U.S., at 110, 127.[13]

Thus, although the broadcasting industry plainly operates under restraints not imposed upon other media, the thrust of these restrictions has generally been to secure the public's First Amendment interest in receiving a balanced presentation of views on diverse matters of public concern. As a result of these restrictions, of course, the absolute freedom to advocate one's own positions without also presenting opposing viewpoints—a freedom enjoyed, for example, by newspaper publishers and soapbox orators—is denied to broadcasters. But, as our cases attest, these restrictions have been upheld only when we were satisfied that the restriction is narrowly tailored to further a substantial governmental interest, such as ensuring adequate and balanced coverage of public issues. [ ] Making that judgment requires a critical examination of the interests of the public and broadcasters in light of the particular circumstances of each case. E.g., FCC v. Pacifica Foundation, supra.

[Justice Brennan then turned to a consideration of the specifics of this case. His discussion of this issue, and the opinions of the dissenting justices are reprinted in Chapter VIII.]

## B.  IS BROADCASTING "GOVERNMENT ACTION"?

The issues raised in *NBC*, *Red Lion*, and *League of Women Voters* revolve around the broadcaster's claim that the First Amendment protects it from government regulation. Sometimes claims in the name of the First Amendment are made by private citizens against the media. In *Tornillo*, the citizen's claim failed. But when such a claim is made against broadcast media a new element enters the picture. When government undertakes to provide a forum for discussion, or a street for parades, it must not discriminate among prospective users according to

---

**13.** This Court's decision in FCC v. Pacifica Foundation, 438 U.S. 726 (1978), upholding an exercise of the Commission's authority to regulate broadcasts containing "indecent" language as applied to a particular afternoon broadcast of a George Carlin monologue, is consistent with the approach taken in our other broadcast cases. There, the Court focused on certain physical characteristics of broadcasting—specifically, that the medium's uniquely pervasive presence renders impossible any prior warning for those listeners who may be offended by indecent language, and, second, that the ease with which children may gain access to the medium, especially during daytime hours, creates a substantial risk that they may be exposed to such offensive expression without parental supervision. Id., at 748–749. The governmental interest in reduction of those risks through Commission regulation of the timing and character of such "indecent broadcasting" was thought sufficiently substantial to outweigh the broadcaster's First Amendment interest in controlling the presentation of its programming. Id., at 750. In this case, by contrast, we are faced not with indecent expression, but rather with expression that is at the core of First Amendment protections, and no claim is made by the Government that the expression of editorial opinion by noncommercial stations will create a substantial "nuisance" of the kind addressed in FCC v. Pacifica Foundation.

their views.  Government must be neutral in such situations.  If too many want to parade or use the forum, government might develop a lottery system or queueing system; but it could not prefer those views it liked.  Some have argued that this analysis applies to broadcasters—that they are so closely related to, and regulated by, government that their actions are government action, and, thus, bound by the neutrality principle.

The Supreme Court avoided this question in Columbia Broadcasting System, Inc. v. Democratic National Committee, supra.  The DNC wanted to buy commercial time to urge financial support for the party.  Another group (BEM) sought to buy time to oppose the war in Vietnam.  The broadcasters refused to sell time to either group because the proposed commercials did not fit into the type of programming the broadcasters wanted to present.  The DNC and BEM asked the FCC to order the broadcasters to take their commercials—at least as long as they were taking commercials from other sources.  The FCC refused.  The Supreme Court upheld the FCC's refusal.

The DNC–BEM claim that the broadcasters should be treated as government fragmented the Court badly.  Three justices met it head on and rejected it.  They were concerned that the "concept of journalistic independence could not co-exist with a reading of the challenged conduct of the licensee as government action" because a government medium could not exercise editorial judgment as to what content should be carried or excluded.

The three observed, however, that even if the First Amendment applied to this case, the groups were not entitled to access.  Here, they relied on Meiklejohn's theme that the essential point was "not that everyone shall speak, but that everything worth saying shall be said."  Congress and the Commission might reasonably conclude that the "allocation of journalistic priorities should be concentrated on the licensee rather than diffused among many.  This policy gives the public some assurance that the broadcaster will be answerable if he fails to meet its legitimate needs.  No such accountability attaches to the private individual. . . ."

Three other justices agreed that even if government action were involved in the case, there was no violation of the groups' rights under the First Amendment.  They therefore refused to pass on the question of government involvement.

Justice Douglas, concurring, did not decide the question.  He noted that if a licensee were to be considered a federal agency it would "within limits of its time be bound to disseminate all views."  If a licensee was not considered a federal agency "I fail to see how constitutionally we can treat TV and radio differently than we treat newspapers."  He agreed that "The Commission has a duty to encourage a multitude of voices but only in a limited way, viz., by preventing monopolistic practices and by promoting technological developments that will open up new channels.  But censorship or editing or the screening by Government of what licensees may broadcast goes against the grain of the First Amendment."

In dissent Justice Brennan, with whom Justice Marshall concurred, disagreed:

> Thus, given the confluence of these various indicia of "governmental action"—including the public nature of the airwaves, the governmentally created preferred status of broadcasters, the extensive Government regulation of broadcast programming, and the specific governmental approval of the challenged policy—I can only conclude that the Government "has so far insinuated itself into a position" of participation in this policy that the absolute refusal of broadcast licensees to sell air time to groups or individuals wishing to speak out on controversial issues of public importance must be subjected to the restraints of the First Amendment.

The dissenters then concluded that the absolute refusal did violate the First Amendment. "The retention of such *absolute* control in the hands of a few Government licensees is inimical to the First Amendment, for vigorous, free debate can be attained only when members of the public have *some* opportunity to take the initiative and editorial control into their own hands." The emergence of broadcasting as "the public's prime source of information," has "made the soapbox orator and the leafleteer virtually obsolete."

The case, however, indicates only that the Constitution does not create a right of access to broadcasting. It does not address the question of whether Congress might enact a statute requiring broadcasters as a condition of their licenses to give a certain period of time per day or week to members of the public. How might those who wish to speak be selected? Would such a statute be valid? Might the Commission issue a rule to the same effect? Even if such a statute or rule would be constitutional, would it be sound? What does this controversy say about the "agenda-setting" role of media?

In the DNC–BEM case much of the majority's approach was based on the power to enforce the broadcaster's responsibility to program in the public interest because of the two prongs of the fairness doctrine. It is ironic that the fairness doctrine, resisted by the broadcasters in *Red Lion*, also shields them from having to give unlimited access to their broadcasting facilities. As a broadcaster, which would you find a greater interference with your freedom—the fairness doctrine or a rule requiring you to give some persons or groups access to your facilities?

# Chapter IV

# BROADCAST LICENSING

In this Chapter we consider the substantive and procedural aspects of the licensing activities of the Federal Communications Commission. As we have seen, the Commission was charged with reducing interference on the airwaves, which eventually, in the name of the public interest, involved licensing. We follow this process through from the initial stage of awarding a vacant spot to the conditions for transferring a license.

## A. INITIAL LICENSING

---

### 1. THE ADMINISTRATIVE PROCESS AT WORK

First we must examine the process by which the Commission grants licenses to applicants. To seek a license for a broadcast frequency, an applicant first asks the Commission for a construction permit to build the facility. If the construction permit is granted, the license will then follow almost automatically if the facility is constructed on schedule.

The application is filed initially with the part of the FCC called the Mass Media Bureau. Its staff reviews the papers to identify any deficiency. If the case is a routine one, the Commissioners have authorized the staff of the Mass Media Bureau to issue the license. But if the application raises any fact questions or legal questions, then a more complex procedure is required.

Section 309(a) of the Communications Act provides that if after examining an application the Commission concludes that the "public interest, convenience, and necessity" will be served it shall grant the application. But subsection (e) provides that "if a substantial and material question of fact is presented or the Commission for any reason is unable to make the finding specified in [subsection (a)], it shall formally designate the application for hearing . . . and shall forthwith notify the applicant . . . of such action and the grounds and reasons therefor, specifying with particularity the matters and things in issue. . . ."

The "hearing" mentioned in the statute is conducted by a member of the FCC's staff called an Administrative Law Judge (ALJ) (formerly called a hearing examiner), who functions much as a regular judge presiding over a trial—except that there is no jury and the issues to be explored at the hearing are prescribed, or designated, in advance by the Commission. If the application seems to raise no problem except the question of whether the applicant is adequately financed for the initial period, the Commission will order the ALJ to conduct a hearing limited to that fact question.

Does the applicant have an adversary at the hearing? The answer is that if the Mass Media Bureau has raised a question about the applicant's answers, the Mass Media Bureau itself may take part in the hearing to oppose the applicant. If the fact dispute is resolved in favor of the applicant, and the rest of the application is proper, the ALJ may grant the permit. If the Mass Media Bureau thinks the ALJ has made a mistake, it may appeal within the agency—sometimes to a "review board" that serves as an appellate decision-making body and sometimes to the Commissioners themselves. By the same token, if the judge's ruling favors the Bureau, the unhappy applicant may appeal within the agency.

If the Commission eventually decides against issuing a license or a construction permit, the unhappy applicant may then appeal to the courts—usually to the United States Court of Appeals for the District of Columbia Circuit. In this situation, the adversary is the Commission itself, represented by its general counsel's staff. However the court of appeals may decide, the losing side may seek Supreme Court review by filing a petition for a writ of certiorari.

An indication of how the court views its role in reviewing broadcast licensing is found in Greater Boston Television Corp. v. Federal Communications Commission, 444 F.2d 841, 850–53 (D.C.Cir.1970), certiorari denied 403 U.S. 923 (1971), to which we return shortly for its substantive part (footnotes citing a wealth of authorities have been excluded):

> Assuming consistency with law and the legislative mandate, the agency has latitude not merely to find facts and make judgments, but also to select the policies deemed in the public interest. The function of the court is to assure that the agency has given reasoned consideration to all the material facts and issues. This calls for insistence that the agency articulate with reasonable clarity its reasons for decision, and identify the significance of the crucial facts, a course that tends to assure that the agency's policies effectuate general standards, applied without unreasonable discrimination. . . .

> Its supervisory function calls on the court to intervene not merely in case of procedural inadequacies or bypassing of the mandate in the legislative charter, but more broadly if the court becomes aware, especially from a combination of danger signals, that the agency has not really taken a "hard look" at the salient problems, and has not genuinely engaged in reasoned decision-making. If the agency has not shirked this fundamental task, however, the court exercises restraint and affirms the agency's action even though the court would on its own account have made different findings or adopted different standards. Nor will the court upset a decision because of errors that are not material, there being room for the doctrine of harmless error. . . .

This posture of judicial self-restraint would apply to review of actions of administrative agencies generally.

This brief description assumes that it is possible for the Commission, or its Bureau, to deny an application for a vacant frequency or channel—even though no one else has applied for it. Although this may seem surprising, it does happen.

But the most complex cases before the Commission are those in which more than one applicant seeks a single vacant frequency or channel. These are called "mutually exclusive" applications because only one can be granted. These cases almost always raise serious fact questions that must be resolved in a hearing. These hearings can be very time-consuming because each of two or more parties not only attempts to present arguments showing why it should get the spot, but also may present evidence attacking each of the other applicants.

In these cases there may be specific questions, such as whether one of the applicants is an alien, or whether another is inadequately financed or proposes to use inadequate engineering equipment. But even if all the applicants meet every basic qualification, a hearing would still be needed to determine which qualified applicant should get the award.

We might note now that the same hearing process may be required at other stages in the licensing process. When a licensee applies for a renewal, if claims are made that the licensee has misbehaved in some way or should not get the license renewed, any fact questions that need to be resolved will be explored at a similar hearing conducted by an ALJ.

In the interests of simplicity, the foregoing description of the administrative process assumes that when the FCC decides to grant or renew a license to an applicant who has no competitors that is the end of the process. If the applicant has beaten out challengers they can carry the fight into the courts. But if the applicant has no challenger and the Commission decides in its favor, the Bureau—even if it has disagreed with that result—can not attack the decision of its agency.

Other parties, however, do have a right to participate ("standing"). For example, existing licensees can object to the granting of a new license on the grounds that it will cause technical interference with existing stations. A more difficult question is raised when a competitor wishes to argue that there is not enough potential advertising revenue in the community to support an additional station. Initially, the Commission was receptive to these economic injury arguments. Then, in the late 1930's, the FCC decided that economic injury was no longer a ground for denying license applications. On appeal the court of appeals held that the Commission's failure to make findings on the issue of economic injury rendered its decision arbitrary and capricious. Sanders Brothers Radio Station v. Federal Communications Commission, 106 F.2d 321 (1939). The Supreme Court disagreed and upheld the Commission's position. 309 U.S. 470 (1940). As the Court stated:

. . . . We hold that resulting economic injury to a rival station is not, in and of itself, and apart from considerations of public convenience, interest, or necessity, an element the petitioner must weigh, and as to which it must make findings, in passing on an application for a broadcasting license.

Section 307(a) of the Communications Act directs that "the Commission, if public convenience, interest, or necessity will be served thereby, subject to the limitations of this Act, shall grant to any applicant therefor a station license provided for by this Act." This mandate is given meaning and contour by the other provisions of the statute and the subject matter with which it deals. The Act contains no express command that in passing upon an application the Commission must consider the effect of competition with an existing station. Whether the Commission should consider the subject must depend upon the purpose of the Act and the specific provisions intended to effectuate the purpose.

. . . .

In contradistinction to communication by telephone and telegraph, which the Communications Act recognizes as a common carrier activity and regulates accordingly in analogy to the regulation of rail and other carriers by the Interstate Commerce Commission, the Act recognizes that broadcasters are not common carriers and are not to be dealt with as such. Thus the Act recognizes that the field of broadcasting is one of free competition. The sections dealing with broadcasting demonstrate that Congress has not, in its regulatory scheme, abandoned the principle of free competition, as it has done in the case of the railroads, in respect of which regulation involves the suppression of wasteful practices due to competition, the regulation of rates and charges, and other measures which are unnecessary if free competition is to be permitted.

An important element of public interest and convenience affecting the issue of a license is the ability of the licensee to render the best practicable service to the community reached by his broadcasts. That such ability may be assured the Act contemplates inquiry by the Commission, *inter alia,* into an applicant's financial qualifications to operate the proposed stations.

But the Act does not essay to regulate the business of the licensee. The Commission is given no supervisory control of the programs, of business management or of policy. In short, the broadcasting field is open to anyone, provided there be an available frequency over which he can broadcast without interference to others, if he shows his competency, the adequacy of his equipment, and financial ability to make good use of his assigned channel.

The policy of the Act is clear that no person is to have anything in the nature of a property right as a result of the granting of a license. Licenses are limited to a maximum of three years' duration, may be revoked, and need not be renewed. Thus the channels presently occupied remain free for a new assignment to another licensee in the interest of the listening public.

Plainly it is not the purpose of the Act to protect a licensee against competition but to protect the public. Congress intended to leave competition in the business of broadcasting where it found it, to permit a licensee who was not interfering electrically with other broadcasts to survive or succumb according to his ability to make his programs attractive to the public.

This is not to say that the question of competition between a proposed station and one operating under an existing license is to be entirely disregarded by the Commission, and, indeed, the Commission's practice shows that it does not disregard that question. It may have a vital and important bearing upon the ability of the applicant adequately to serve his public; it may indicate that both stations—the existing and the proposed—will go under, with the result that a portion of the listening public will be left without adequate service; it may indicate that, by a division of the field, both stations will be compelled to render inadequate service. These matters, however, are distinct from the consideration that, if a license be granted, competition between the licensee and any other existing station may cause economic loss to the latter. If such economic loss were a valid reason for refusing a license this would mean that the Commission's function is to grant a monopoly in the field of broadcasting, a result which the Act itself expressly negatives, which Congress would not have contemplated without granting the Commission powers of control over the rates, programs, and other activities of the business of broadcasting.

We conclude that economic injury to an existing station is not a separate and independent element to be taken into consideration by the Commission in determining whether it shall grant or withhold a license.

The FCC read *Sanders* as holding that there were no situations where economic injury arguments had to be given consideration. This overly expansive reading of *Sanders* continued until 1958, when the court of appeals announced its interpretation of *Sanders*. Carroll Broadcasting Company v. Federal Communications Commission, 258 F.2d 440 (D.C.Cir.1958):

. . . As we have just said, we think it is not incumbent upon the Commission to evaluate the probable economic results of every license grant. Of course, the public is not concerned whether it gets service from A or from B or from both combined. The public interest is not disturbed if A is destroyed by B, so long as B renders the required service. The public interest is affected when service is affected. We think the problem arises when a protestant offers to prove that the grant of a new license would be detrimental to the public interest. The Commission is equipped to receive and appraise such evidence. If the protestant fails to bear the burden of proving his point (and it is certainly a heavy burden), there may be an end to the matter. If his showing is substantial, or if there is a genuine issue posed, findings should be made.

The FCC was able to limit the number of *Carroll* doctrine complaints by ruling that when such a complaint is made and the FCC agrees that the community cannot support both stations, the existing licensee's renewal application will be heard together with the new application. As we shall see shortly, this procedure might be risky for the existing licensee.

The Commission firmly rejected all efforts of listeners or citizen groups to take a formal part in the licensing process. Formally stated, the FCC denied outsiders standing to participate.

In 1966, however, the court of appeals ordered that citizen groups be allowed to participate in these proceedings. In Office of Communications of United Church of Christ v. Federal Communications Commission, 359 F.2d 994 (D.C.Cir.1966), the opinion by then Circuit Judge Burger said in part:

> The argument that a broadcaster is not a public utility is beside the point. True it is not a public utility in the same sense as strictly regulated common carriers or purveyors of power, but neither is it a purely private enterprise like a newspaper or an automobile agency. A broadcaster has much in common with a newspaper publisher, but he is not in the same category in terms of public obligations imposed by law. A broadcaster seeks and is granted the free and exclusive use of a limited and valuable part of the public domain; when he accepts that franchise it is burdened by enforceable public obligations. A newspaper can be operated at the whim or caprice of its owners; a broadcast station cannot. After nearly five decades of operation the broadcast industry does not seem to have grasped the simple fact that a broadcast license is a public trust subject to termination for breach of duty.
>
>      .   .   .
>
> Public participation is especially important in a renewal proceeding, since the public will have been exposed for at least three years to the licensee's performance, as cannot be the case when the Commission considers an initial grant, unless the applicant has a prior record as a licensee. In a renewal proceeding, furthermore, public spokesmen, such as Appellants here, may be the only objectors. In a community served by only one outlet, the public interest focus is perhaps sharper and the need for airing complaints often greater than where, for example, several channels exist. Yet if there is only one outlet, there are no rivals at hand to assert the public interest, and reliance on opposing applicants to challenge the existing licensee for the channel would be fortuitous at best. Even when there are multiple competing stations in a locality, various factors may operate to inhibit the other broadcasters from opposing a renewal application. An imperfect rival may be thought a desira-

ble rival, or there may be a "gentleman's agreement" of deference to a fellow broadcaster in the hope he will reciprocate on a propitious occasion.

He also noted that the fears of regulatory agencies that they will be flooded with applications have rarely been borne out.

In the period since this case, the feared flood has not developed, though citizen groups are playing a more active part in the regulatory processes of the Commission than before. The role of citizen groups is extensively discussed in D. Guimary, Citizens' Groups and Broadcasting (1975). Their most common legal action is the filing of a petition to deny a renewal application on the ground that the applicant has failed to meet the required level of public service.

*Negotiation and Agreement.* Another possibility is to negotiate. In order to avoid the expense of defending against petitions to deny renewals, broadcasters have begun entering into agreements with citizen groups that challenge their license applications or renewals. In return for withdrawal of the challenge, a broadcaster typically undertakes to make certain changes in its station's operation. The broadcaster may promise to change its employment policies, to support local production of broadcast programming, or to attempt to expand certain types of programming.

The Commission generally allows broadcasters to enter into the agreements if they maintain responsibility at all times for determining how best to serve the public interest. Does recognition of these private agreements serve the public interest? Does it allow a broadcaster to "buy off" citizen groups who may be in the best position to point out programming deficiencies?

## 2. INTRODUCTION TO BASIC QUALIFICATIONS

In the 1934 Act, Congress empowered the Federal Communications Commission to grant licenses to applicants for radio stations for periods of up to three years "if public convenience, interest, or necessity will be served thereby." § 307(a). Section 307(b) requires the Commission to make "such distribution of licenses, frequencies, hours of operation, and of power among the several states and communities as to provide a fair, efficient, and equitable distribution of radio service to each of the same."

As we have seen, the Commission responded by allocating a portion of the spectrum for standard (AM) radio service and then subdividing that space further by requiring very powerful stations to use certain frequencies and weaker stations to utilize others and some stations to leave the air at sundown. The Commission used its rulemaking powers to develop these allocations and then set engineering standards of separation and interference. The 1934 Act empowered the Commission to promulgate "such rules and regulations and prescribe such restrictions and conditions, not inconsistent with law, as may be necessary to carry out the provisions of this chapter. . . ." § 303(r). The Commission did not allocate the AM frequencies to particular cities. Instead, it left it to those interested in broadcasting to determine whether they could organize an AM broadcast facility in a given location that complied with the various allocation and interference rules. With FM and television, the Commission utilized rulemaking to allocate particular frequencies to particular cities. An applicant for one of these licenses must apply for the assigned frequency in the listed, or a nearby, community or must seek to change the frequency assignments through an amendment of the rules.

In addition to requiring proof that a grant will serve the "public convenience, interest, or necessity," § 307(a), the Act also requires that each applicant demonstrate that it meets basic "citizenship, character, and financial, technical, and other qualifications," § 308(b). An applicant who fails to satisfy any one of the following "basic qualifications" is ineligible to receive a license.

a. *Legal Qualifications.* An applicant for a license must comply with the specific requirements of the Communications Act and the Commission's rules. For example, there are restrictions on permitting aliens to hold radio and broadcast licenses. § 310(b). Prior revocation of an applicant's license by a federal court for an antitrust violation precludes grant of a new application. § 313. An application will be denied if its grant would result in violation of the Commission's multiple ownership or crossownership rules or its chain broadcasting regulations. (We will discuss these in Chapter V.)

b. *Technical Qualifications.* An applicant for a broadcast station must also comply with the Commission's standards for transmission. These standards include such issues as interference with existing or allocated stations and efficiency of operation, gains or losses of service to affected populations, structure, power and location of the antenna, coverage and quality of the signal in the areas to be served, and studio location and operating equipment utilized.

c. *Financial Qualifications.* Although the applicant must show it has an adequate financial base to commence operations, it need not demonstrate that it can sustain operations indefinitely. The test applied by the Commission is that the applicant must have sufficient funds to operate a broadcast station for three months without advertising revenue. The Commission may also inquire into the applicant's estimates of the amounts that will be actually required to operate the station and the reliability of its proposed sources of funds, such as estimated advertising revenues.

d. *Character Qualifications.* Character issues that may be investigated by the Commission include past criminal convictions of the applicant, trafficking in broadcast licenses, anticompetitive business practices, lack of candor or misrepresentation to the Commission, failure to keep the Commission informed of changes in the applicant's status, and other situations that raise questions as to the integrity or reliability of the applicant in the broadcasting function. As a result of the RKO case (p. 128, infra) the FCC has decided to limit character inquiries to violations of the Communications Act or FCC regulations and policies, relevant felony convictions, and adjudicated fraud and antitrust cases.

e. The final category of basic qualifications, "other," has been interpreted to refer primarily to character issues, but it may also overlap with public interest considerations.

### 3. SUBSTANTIVE CONSIDERATIONS

Assuming an applicant has met the basic qualifications, such as citizenship and financial security, how does the Commission decide if granting the application will serve the "public interest, convenience and necessity"? In this section we will take an extensive look at the substantive considerations in the process, starting with the single applicant for the single vacancy.

As noted earlier, even though an applicant has met the basic qualifications and is the only applicant for the license, that applicant may not get the license. Since the FCC was created in large part to reduce crowding and eliminate chaos, what role may it play when only one applicant seeks an available spot? A first answer may be found in *NBC* where the Court recognized that the FCC may act beyond its policeman's role and may consider the public interest. Sometimes the public interest might be better served by leaving a vacancy that a good applicant might later fill rather than by taking the first comer.

But this, of course, requires that the FCC be able to distinguish a "good" applicant from a lesser one. From the very beginning the Commission has confronted the tension between using criteria that directly address programming considerations and the concern that too close a look at proposed programming may amount to government control.

The Commission believed that the "entire listening public within the service area of a station, or of a group of stations in one community, is entitled to service from that station or stations." Specialized stations were entitled to little or no consideration. In the Commission's opinion, "the tastes, needs, and desires of all substantial groups among the listening public should be met, in some fair proportion by a well-rounded program, in which entertainment, consisting of music of both classical and lighter grades, religion, education and instruction, important public events, discussions of public questions, weather, market reports and news, and matters of interest to all members of the family find a place." Recognizing that communities differed and that other variables were relevant, the Commission did not erect a "rigid schedule."

In 1946, the Commission issued a report entitled Public Service Responsibility of Broadcast Licensees (known generally as the "Blue Book"). The Commission stressed that although licensees bore the primary responsibility for program service, the Commission would still play a part: "In issuing and in renewing the licenses of broadcast stations, the Commission proposes to give particular consideration to four program service factors relevant to the public interest." One category was the carrying of "sustaining" (unsponsored) programs during hours "when the public is awake and listening." This would provide balance by allowing the broadcast of certain types of programs that did not lend themselves to sponsorship, including experimental programs. Second, the Commission called for local live programs to encourage local self-expression. Third, the Commission expected "programs devoted to the discussion of public issues." Finally, the Commission, expressing concern about excessive advertising, announced that "in its application forms the Commission will request the applicant to state how much time he proposes to devote to advertising matter in any one hour."

In 1960, the Commission changed direction. In Report and Statement of Policy Re: Commission En Banc Programming Inquiry, 25 Fed. Reg. 7291, 20 R.R. 1901 (1960), the FCC asserted that "the principal ingredient of the licensee's obligation to operate his station in the public interest is the diligent, positive and continuing effort . . . to discover and fulfill the tastes, needs and desires of his service area, for broadcast service." Broadcasters were advised to meet this obligation in two ways: they were to consult with members of the listening public who could receive the station's signal and with a variety of community leaders. The distinction between sustaining and sponsored programs was explicitly abandoned.

In 1971, the Commission elaborated upon and clarified the applicant's obligation. The Primer on Ascertainment of Community Problems by Broadcast Applicants, 27 F.C.C.2d 650, 21 R.R.2d 1507 (1971), standardized the Commission's policy with respect to ascertainment of, and programming for, community needs. It placed specific ascertainment requirements upon all commercial applicants for new broadcast stations, modification of existing facilities, and renewals. The Primer required that an applicant determine the economic, ethnic, and social composition of the communities it proposed to serve and that principals or management-level employees consult with leaders from each significant community group. The applicant was also to consult with a random sample of members of the general public. Finally, the applicant had to set forth in its license application, program proposals designed to meet community problems identified. The ascertainment had to take place within six months of the application.

The courts readily accepted the Commission's emphasis on the importance of the ascertainment process. In Henry v. Federal Communications Commission, 302 F.2d 191 (D.C.Cir.1962), certiorari denied 371 U.S. 821 (1962), Suburban Broadcasters filed the sole application for a permit to construct the first commercial FM station in Elizabeth, New Jersey. Although Suburban was found legally, technically, and financially qualified, the Commission found that Suburban had made no inquiry into the characteristics or programming needs of Elizabeth and was "totally without knowledge of the area." Suburban's program proposals for Elizabeth were identical to those submitted in its application for an AM station in Berwyn, Illinois, and in the application of two of its principal stockholders for an FM station in Alameda, California. Although acknowledging the community's "presumptive need" for its first FM service, the Commission denied the permit, finding that a grant would not serve the public interest.

On appeal, the Commission's denial was upheld on the ground that an applicant may be required to "demonstrate an earnest interest in serving a local community by evidencing a familiarity with its particular needs and an effort to meet them."

In 1976, the FCC amended the ascertainment regulations to require interviews "within the following [19] institutions and elements commonly found in a community." The list included agriculture, business, charities, religion, and organizations of elderly, youth, and women. "A licensee is permitted to show that one or more of these institutions or elements is not present in its community. At its option it may also utilize the 'other' category to interview leaders in its elements not found on the checklist." Other groups, particularly from the gay community, soon claimed that broadcasters were not using the "other" category to interview them, and asked to be added to the list of 19. The FCC rejected that approach because its studies did not indicate that gay (or handicapped) persons were significant elements in all or most communities. Instead, it declared that broadcasters must ascertain unlisted groups if the groups first bear the burden of getting in touch with the broadcasters to let them know of the group's needs and problems. Amendment of the Primers on Ascertainment of Community Problems, 76 F.C.C.2d 401, 47 R.R.2d 189 (1980).

The ascertainment process was designed to allow the FCC to consider proposed programming from the standpoint of the nature of the community rather than the Commission's own ideas of what is "good" programming. It was part of the Commission's continued emphasis on localism.

In January, 1981, the FCC adopted, 6–1, a set of proposals reducing the regulations affecting commercial radio licensees. Deregulation of Radio, 84 F.C.C.2d 968, 49 R.R.2d 1 (1981). The underlying rationale was that with over 8,000 radio stations on the air, the Commission could rely on competition in the market to provide appropriate service. Among the changes was the elimination of the formal ascertainment requirements. The Commission's order deleting formal ascertainment procedures for all radio broadcasters was upheld in Office of Communication of the United Church of Christ v. Federal Communications Commission, 707 F.2d 1413, 53 R.R.2d 1371 (D.C.Cir.1983).

In June, 1984, the Commission adopted a similar set of changes in the regulations for commercial television. Formal ascertainment was eliminated because, according to the Commission, the administrative costs outweighed the benefits. Deregulation of Commercial Television, 98 F.C.C.2d 1076, 56 R.R.2d 1005 (1984). We will return to the changes brought about by these proceedings in the section on renewals.

### 4. The Comparative Proceeding

If two or more applicants file for use of the same or interfering facilities the Commission must proceed by way of comparative hearing among all qualified applicants to determine which will best serve the public interest. An applicant in a comparative proceeding must not only meet minimum qualifications but must also prevail when judged on the Commission's comparative criteria. These criteria, which involve considerations other than those applied in the non-comparative proceeding, evolved through adjudication rather than rulemaking.

## POLICY STATEMENT ON COMPARATIVE BROADCAST HEARINGS

Federal Communications Commission, 1965.
1 F.C.C.2d, 5 R.R.2d 1901.

By the Commission: Commissioners HYDE and BARTLEY dissenting and issuing statements; Commissioner LEE concurring and issuing a statement.

[The Commission noted that choosing one from among several qualified applicants for a facility was one of its primary responsibilities. The process involved an extended hearing in which the various applicants were compared on a variety of subjects. The "subject does not lend itself to precise categorization or to the clear making of precedent. The various factors cannot be assigned absolute values. . . ." Moreover, the membership of the Commission is continually changing and each member has his or her own idea of what factors are important. Thus, the statement is not binding and the Commission is not obligated to deal with all cases "as it has dealt with some that seem comparable." Nonetheless, it is "important to have a high degree of consistency of decision and of clarity in our basic policies." The statement was to "serve the purpose of clarity and consistency of decision, and the further purpose of eliminating from the hearing process time-consuming elements not substantially related to the public interest." The Commission declared that this statement "does not attempt to deal with the somewhat different problems raised where an applicant is contesting with a licensee seeking renewal of license." The Commission then turned to the merits and identified "two primary objectives": "best practicable service to the public" and "maximum diffusion of control of the media of mass communications."]

Several factors are significant in the two areas of comparison mentioned above, and it is important to make clear the manner in which each will be treated.

1. *Diversification of control of the media of mass communication.*—Diversification is a factor of primary significance since, as set forth above, it constitutes a primary objective in the licensing scheme.

2. *Full-time participation in station operation by owners.*—We consider this factor to be of substantial importance. It is inherently

desirable that legal responsibility and day-to-day performance be closely associated. In addition, there is a likelihood of greater sensitivity to an area's changing needs, and of programing designed to serve these needs, to the extent that the station's proprietors actively participate in the day-to-day operation of the station. This factor is thus important in securing the best practicable service. It also frequently complements the objective of diversification, since concentrations of control are necessarily achieved at the expense of integrated ownership.

We are primarily interested in full-time participation.

Attributes of participating owners, such as their experience and local residence, will also be considered in weighing integration of ownership and management. While, for the reasons given above, integration of ownership and management is important per se, its value is increased if the participating owners are local residents and if they have experience in the field. Participation in station affairs on the basis described above by a local resident indicates a likelihood of continuing knowledge of changing local interests and needs. . . .

. . .

3. *Proposed program service.*—. . . The importance of program service is obvious. The feasibility of making a comparative evaluation is not so obvious. Hearings take considerable time and precisely formulated program plans may have to be changed not only in details but in substance, to take account of new conditions obtaining at the time a successful applicant commences operation. Thus, minor differences among applicants are apt to prove to be of no significance.

. . .

Decisional significance will be accorded only to material and substantial differences between applicants' proposed program plans. [ ] Minor differences in the proportions of time allocated to different types of programs will not be considered. Substantial differences will be considered to the extent that they go beyond ordinary differences in judgment and show a superior devotion to public service. . . .

In light of the considerations set forth above, and our experience with the similarity of the program plans of competing applicants, taken with the desirability of keeping hearing records free of immaterial clutter, no comparative issue will ordinarily be designated on program plans and policies, or on staffing plans or other program planning elements, and evidence on these matters will not be taken under the standard issues. The Commission will designate an issue where examination of the applications and other information before it makes such action appropriate, and applicants who believe they can demonstrate significant differences upon which the reception of evidence will be useful may petition to amend the issues.

No independent factor of likelihood of effectuation of proposals will be utilized. The Commission expects every licensee to carry out its proposals, subject to factors beyond its control, and subject to reasonable judgment that the public's needs and interests require a departure from original plans. If there is a substantial indication that any party will not be able to carry out its proposals to a significant degree, the proposals themselves will be considered deficient.

4. *Past broadcast record.*—This factor includes past ownership interest and significant participation in a broadcast station by one with an ownership interest in the applicant. It is a factor of substantial importance upon the terms set forth below.

A past record within the bounds of average performance will be disregarded, since average future performance is expected. Thus, we are not interested in the fact of past ownership per se, and will not give a preference because one applicant has owned stations in the past and another has not.

We are interested in records which, because either unusually good or unusually poor, give some indication of unusual performance in the future.   .   .   .

   .   .   .

5. *Efficient use of frequency.*—In comparative cases where one of two or more competing applicants proposes an operation which, for one or more engineering reasons, would be more efficient, this fact can and should be considered in determining which of the applicants should be preferred.   .   .   .

6. *Character.*—The Communications Act makes character a relevant consideration in the issuance of a license. See section 308(b), 47 U.S.C. § 308(b). Significant character deficiencies may warrant disqualification, and an issue will be designated where appropriate. Since substantial demerits may be appropriate in some cases where disqualification is not warranted, petitions to add an issue on conduct relating to character will be entertained. In the absence of a designated issue, character evidence will not be taken. Our intention here is not only to avoid unduly prolonging the hearing process, but also to avoid those situations where an applicant converts the hearing into a search for his opponents' minor blemishes, no matter how remote in the past or how insignificant.

7. *Other factors.*—As we stated at the outset, our interest in the consistency and clarity of decision and in expedition of the hearing process is not intended to preclude the full examination of any relevant and substantial factor. We will thus favorably consider petitions to add issues when, but only when, they demonstrate that significant evidence will be adduced.[13]

13. Where a narrow question is raised, for example on one aspect of financial qualification, a narrowly drawn issue will be appropriate. In other circumstances, a broader inquiry may be required. This is a matter for ad hoc determination.

### DISSENTING STATEMENT OF COMMISSIONER HYDE

. . .

The proposed fiat as to the weight which will be given to the various criteria—without sound predication of accepted data and when considered only in a vacuum and in the abstract—must necessarily result in a degree of unfairness to some applicants and in the fashioning of an unnecessary straightjacket for the Commission in its decisional process. How can we decide in advance and in a vacuum that a specific broadcaster with a satisfactory record in one community will be less likely to serve the broadcasting needs of a second community than a specific long-time resident of that second community who doesn't have broadcast experience? How can we make this decision without knowing more about each applicant? . . .

. . .

### DISSENTING STATEMENT OF COMMISSIONER ROBERT T. BARTLEY

I believe that our comparative hearings should be expedited by eliminating what has amounted to extensive bickering in the record over minutiae.

As I see it, however, the Commission majority is attempting the impossible here when it prejudges the decisional factors in future cases. My observation is that there are no two cases exactly alike. There are so many varying circumstances in each case that a factor in one may be more important than the same factor in another. Broadcasting—a dynamic force in our society—experiences constant change. I have expressed it differently on occasions by saying, "There's nothing static in radio but the noise." If we are to encourage the larger and more effective use of radio in the public interest, we must avoid becoming static ourselves.

### CONCURRING STATEMENT OF COMMISSIONER ROBERT E. LEE

Even though I recognize the policy statement adopted by the Commission to be the result of a sincere effort to clarify the historical process of selecting a winner in comparative broadcast hearings, I am concurring with considerable reluctance. . . .

Over the years I have participated in decisions in hundreds of "comparative proceedings" and candor compels me to say that our method of selection of the winning applicant has given me grave concern. I realize, of course, that where we have a number of qualified applicants in a consolidated proceeding for a single facility in a given community, it is necessary that we grant one and deny the others. The ultimate choice of the winner generally sustains the Commission's choice despite the recent rash of demands from the court. Thus, it would appear that we generally grant the "right" application. However, I am not so naive as to believe that granting the "right application" could not, in some cases, be one of several applications.

The criteria that the Commission now says will be decisive—assuming all other things are substantially equal—in choosing among qualified applicants for new broadcast facilities in comparative broadcast hearings are not new. However, the policy statement does tend to restrict the scope somewhat of existing factors and if undue delay is thus prevented, some good will have been accomplished.

I wish to make clear that my concurrence here does not bind me with respect to the weight I might see fit to put upon the various criteria in a given case.  .   .   .

Historically, a prospective applicant hires a highly skilled communications attorney, well versed in the procedures of the Commission. This counsel has a long history of Commission decisions to guide him and he puts together an application that meets all of the so-called criteria. There then follows a tortuous and expensive hearing wherein each applicant attempts to tear down his adversaries on every conceivable front, while individually presenting that which he thinks the Commission would like to hear. The examiner then makes a reasoned decision which, at first blush, generally makes a lot of sense—but comes the oral argument and all of the losers concentrate their fire on the "potential" winner and the Commission must thereupon examine the claims and counterclaims, "weigh" the criteria and pick the winner which, if my recollection serves me correctly, is a different winner in about 50 percent of the cases.

The real blow, however, comes later when the applicant that emerged as the winner on the basis of our "decisive" criteria sells the station to a multiple owner or someone else that could not possibly have prevailed over other qualified applicants under the criteria in an adversary proceeding. It may be that there is no better selection system than the one being followed. If so, it seems like a "hell of a way to run a railroad," and I hope these few comments may inspire the Commission to find that better system even if it requires changes in the Communications Act.

### Notes and Questions

1. The 1965 Policy Statement eliminated three specific criteria—staffing and related plans, likelihood of effectuation of proposals, and proposed studios and equipment—that had formerly been used for comparison.

2. Does choosing licensees on the basis of proposed programming violate either the First Amendment or § 326 of the Communications Act? How far can the Commission go in examining applicants' programming proposals? These questions were answered in Johnston Broadcasting Co. v. Federal Communications Commission, 175 F.2d 351, 359 (D.C.Cir. 1949):

As to appellant's contention that the Commission's consideration of the proposed programs was a form of censorship, it is true that the

Commission cannot choose on the basis of political, economic or social views of an applicant. But in a comparative consideration, it is well recognized that comparative service to the listening public is the vital element, and programs are the essence of that service. So, while the Commission cannot prescribe any type of program (except for prohibitions against obscenity, profanity, etc.) it can make a comparison on the basis of public interest and, therefore, of public service. Such a comparison of proposals is not a form of censorship within the meaning of the statute. . . .

3. When is a comparative hearing required? In Ashbacker Radio Corp. v. Federal Communications Commission, 326 U.S. 327 (1945), the Commission had held a hearing on an application for a construction permit while an application for license modification in a nearby community was pending. The grant of the construction permit precluded the license modification. The Court held that the second applicant was denied its § 309(e) right to a hearing by the granting of the first application. As a result the *Ashbacker* doctrine requires that whenever mutually exclusive applications are pending, the Commission must hold a single comparative hearing on all of the applications before granting any of them.

4. We consider Commissioner Lee's point about the transferability of licenses at p. 120, infra.

5. Although the Commission has emphasized localism, there has always been an undercurrent of doubt. In the early 1960's, when the Commission appeared to favor not only local programs but also live presentations, Judge Friendly observed, "I wonder also whether the Commission is really wise enough to determine that live telecasts, so much stressed in the decisions, e.g., of local cooking lessons, are always 'better' than a tape of Shakespeare's Histories." Friendly, The Federal Administrative Agencies: The Need for Better Definition of Standards, 75 Harv.L.Rev. 1055, 1071 (1962). This concern was restated in a different context by a former chairman of the Commission:

> [T]he automatic preference accorded local applicants disregards the possibility that, depending on the facts of a particular case, a competitor's proposed use of a professional employee-manager from outside the community might very well bring imagination, an appreciation of the role of journalism, and sensitivity to social issues far exceeding that of a particular local owner-manager.

Hyde, FCC Policies and Procedures Relating to Hearings on Broadcast Applications, 1975 Duke L.J. 253, 277.

In the mid-1970's, the Chairman of the House Communications Subcommittee estimated that local television averaged 80 percent nonlocal programming and "maybe that's the way the viewers want it." He was suggesting that Congress might reconsider the desirability of localism. See Broadcasting, Nov. 22, 1976 at 20.

6. *Minority Ownership.* New issues may reflect changes in licensing policy. In TV 9, Inc. v. Federal Communications Commission, 495 F.2d

929 (D.C.Cir.1973), rehearing and rehearing en banc denied (1974), Comint Corp., Mid-Florida Television Corporation, and six other applicants sought a construction permit for Channel 9 in Orlando, Florida. In making the award to Mid-Florida, the Commission rejected Comint's contention that it was entitled to special consideration because two of Comint's principals were local black residents and 25 percent of those to be served by Channel 9 were black. The Commission's position was that the Communications Act was "color blind" and did not permit considerations of color in the award of licenses. The court disagreed and ruled that the ownership interests and participation of the two black residents gave Comint an edge in providing "broader community representation and practicable service to the public by increasing diversity of content, especially of opinion and viewpoint." We will return to the issue of minority ownership in Chapter V.

7. In 1978, the Commission began granting women a preference in comparative proceedings. In 1985, the court of appeals struck down a license award based in part on such a preference. Steele v. Federal Communications Commission, 770 F.2d 1192 (D.C.Cir.1985). The court has granted a rehearing en banc.

8. The "recent rash of remands from the court" referred to by Commissioner Lee was caused by the revelation in the late 1950's that an FCC Commissioner had been bribed to vote in certain ways in licensing proceedings. Since the outcomes of these comparative hearings were not readily predictable, it was relatively easy for a Commissioner to vote one way in a particular case without being embarrassed by previous votes he might have cast in other licensing cases. The incentive to offer bribes was due to the fact that a license is awarded without charging the applicant the value of the part of the spectrum being licensed. In addition, since renewals have been virtually automatic, television channels in large cities have acquired great value—a VHF in Los Angeles was recently sold for $510 million, and a Boston VHF brought $450 million.

After the bribes came to light, the court of appeals remanded virtually every licensing decision the FCC had made for a second look by what was then an FCC with some new faces.

9. The bribery matter raises the question of whether there are better ways to decide comparative cases than through the approach developed in the Policy Statement. Is it that Congress gave the FCC a difficult, if not impossible, task?

Some critics have suggested that the Commission emphasize one or two factors, such as diversity, and use these as the major bases for decision. Others have suggested using more factors but giving each a preannounced weight, so that the result would be more predictable than it is now.

Still another suggestion is to award the license to the winner of a lottery among equally qualified applicants. The theory of this approach is that sometimes there simply is no superior applicant and it is unrealistic, if not dishonest, to announce a single winner on the merits. The lottery idea might be applied to all applicants who met the basic tests and also had offered maximum diversification or some other added criteria.

In 1980, the FCC voted, 4–3, to order its staff to prepare a decision that would award the license by lottery to one of two applicants who were both judged superior to a third but equal to each other. Two dissenters complained that one applicant should win on the merits because of the full-time participation of a black woman who was a five-percent owner. The third dissenter argued that the action was "an impermissible abdication of the Commission's statutory responsibilities and an improper denial of the hearing rights of the applicants." The FCC had an obligation to make "public-interest judgments" rather than use lotteries. Broadcasting, June 9, 1980 at 30. In early 1981, the FCC abandoned the idea of a lottery, but shortly thereafter Congress amended § 309 of the Communications Act to authorize the use of lotteries.

In response to that amendment, the Commission developed lottery procedures for some licensing proceedings including LPTV. These procedures gave preferences (additional chances) for minority ownership and diversity. Then, in 1984, the Commission decided that even though the lottery statute did not authorize the use of lotteries to resolve ties in comparative proceedings, the general public interest standard gave the FCC the authority to adopt such a system. Thus, where the Commission finds applicants who "are in true equipoise on comparative factors" it will use a lottery to decide which applicant will be awarded the license. Lottery Selection Among Applicants, 57 R.R.2d 427 (1984).

## B. RENEWAL OF LICENSES

---

### 1. INTRODUCTION

The initial license period was limited to three years by § 307(d), and the Commission considered renewal applications from about one-third of all licensees each year. In 1981, Congress changed license terms to five years for television and seven years for radio. At the outset, as it sought to unclutter the AM spectrum, the Commission frequently denied renewals, but after the initial flurry, denials were rare unless the broadcaster's behavior fell far below par. A study of denials and reasons for them is discussed at p. 103 infra. With the large number of renewal applications now filed annually, the FCC staff cannot fully investigate the performance of each applicant. Instead, the Commission has relied increasingly on informal complaints from citizens or citizen groups, and on petitions to deny renewal that became possible after the United Church of Christ case, p. 86, supra. Section 307(d) authorizes renewals only on the same terms as initial grants—public interest, convenience, and necessity.

Traditionally, members of the public who wished to challenge a station's renewal could obtain a great deal of information from the licensee itself. Broadcast licensees were required to keep detailed program logs and show them to the public on request. Commercial TV licensees were also required to submit a composite week log. (The "composite week" refers to a practice by which the Commission each year identifies one Sunday, one Monday, etc. from the prior year by which to judge whether licensees have honored their obligations. This avoids the necessity of considering an entire year's data at renewal time.)

In addition, broadcasters were required to place the results of their formal ascertainment in their public file—a collection of material available for inspection by anyone wishing to see it. Also in the public file are almost all applications filed with the FCC—including any accompanying documents, all written citizen agreements, ownership reports, network contracts, all documents relating to present or future ownership of the station, a manual on the public file prepared by the FCC, all requests for broadcast time by candidates for political office and the station's response, annual employment reports and a model EEO program, letters from the public pertaining to station operation, certification of pre- and post-filing announcements, and documents relating to sponsorship identification of political or public controversy programming.

In *Deregulation of Radio*, p. 91, supra, the Commission eliminated the requirement that commercial radio licensees keep program logs. Instead each radio station would have to list between five and ten issues of public importance in its community that it had addressed in its programming. There was no requirement that this programming be produced locally. It was this failure to require local production that brought forth the sole dissent on the Commission.

A specialized station would be able to adhere to its special focus and allow other stations in the market to serve other needs. A classical music station need no longer present national or world news, but might emphasize artistic and cultural news and events. A station presenting black programming in an urban area, might no longer need to worry about presenting programs that would be of interest to other segments of the community. The FCC expected that the array of stations would, one way or another, meet the varied needs and interests of the community's audience.

As a result of the appellate court remand of *Deregulation of Radio*, the Commission changed the annual issues/programs list to a quarterly list and specified that a minimum of five issues must be listed. The Office of Communication, United Church of Christ has again filed an appeal.

In 1981, the Commission drastically shortened and simplified the application forms that renewal applicants must use. All commercial radio renewal applicants and 95 percent of the commercial television renewal applicants would fill out short five-question forms. The other randomly chosen five percent would have to complete lónger forms similar to the old 21-page forms. This "postcard renewal" process was affirmed on appeal. The court of appeals rejected the contention that the duty to award renewals based on the public interest was violated by the absence of any questions concerning licensees' nonentertainment programming. "Although the FCC has deleted from the application many questions which previously supplied substantial information, we believe that it was not arbitrary or capricious for the Commission to conclude, in the exercise of its discretion, that it still has sufficient information to make the 'public interest' determination." Black Citizens for a Fair Media v. Federal Communications Commission, 719 F.2d 407, 54 R.R.2d 1151 (D.C.Cir.1983), certiorari denied 467 U.S. 1255 (1984).

In *Deregulation of Television*, supra, the Commission eliminated the requirement that five percent of commercial television renewal applicants fill out the longer renewal application forms. As a result, all commercial radio and television renewal applicants now use the five-question short form.

The FCC has been generally reluctant to deny renewals except in egregious cases. The reason is the size of the penalty that denial of renewal inflicts on the licensee in a world in which VHF stations may be worth $500 million or more, and even radio stations may be worth tens of millions of dollars.

*Penalties and Short Renewals.* Before 1960, the Commission had few weapons for dealing with misbehavior, since Congress assumed that denial of renewal would suffice in most cases, with revocation during the term to handle the most serious violations. But the Commission came to view denial of renewal as too harsh for all but the most serious violations of rules or other misbehavior. In the 1960 amendments to the Communications Act, Congress explicitly authorized shorter renewals by amending § 307(d), but this could not be utilized until the end of the license period. To fill this gap, Congress responded with §§ 503(b) et seq. to provide the Commission with "an effective tool in dealing with violations in situations where revocation or suspension does not appear to be appropriate." Under § 503(b), the Commission could impose a fine, called a forfeiture, against a licensee who had violated a specific rule. The maximum penalty is now "$2,000 for each violation. Each day of a continuing violation shall constitute a separate offense" but the total penalty shall not exceed $20,000 for licensees or cable operators.

The added array of sanctions reduced the likelihood that the denial of renewal would be used for what the Commission perceived to be lesser transgressions of the rules. The Commission has resorted extensively to the short-term renewal. The expectation is that if the licensee performs properly during that period it will then return to the regular renewal cycle. In addition to the probationary impact, a short renewal imposes burdens of legal expenses and administrative effort in preparing and defending the application.

Single instances of fraudulent behavior toward advertisers or conducting rigged contests, traditionally led to forfeitures or short-term renewals. Among the most common types of fraud are billing advertisers for commercials that were never actually broadcast and the practice of "double-billing." This latter involves cooperative advertising in which a national manufacturer promises to share advertising expenses with its local retailers. The retailer gets a discount for volume, but the station sends it two bills—one for the actual discounted amount due and a second based on a higher non-discounted rate to be forwarded to the national manufacturer as the basis for the sharing.

After many years of warning against the practice and punishing violators with forfeitures and other penalties, the Commission in the 1970's, began to deny license renewals to violators. The courts upheld the FCC. See White Mountain Broadcasting Co. v. Federal Communications Commission, 598 F.2d 274 (D.C.Cir.1979) (upholding denial of renewal where the practice had continued for 5½ years with full knowledge of the president and sole shareholder of licensee). In the 1980's, however, the Commission has again changed its attitude towards enforcing these regulations. In early 1985, as part of an ongoing attempt to reduce overly restrictive regulations as well as those that duplicate other federal or state law, the Commission issued an NPRM aimed at eliminating the rules on fraudulent billing. Unnecessary Broadcast Regulation, 57 R.R.2d 913 (1985). We will examine these "regulatory underbrush" proceedings in Chapter VII.

## 2. SUBSTANTIVE GROUNDS FOR NONRENEWAL

### a. *Non-speech Considerations*

Just as the Commission may deny an uncontested application for a vacant channel, it may deny renewal when no other applicant seeks the spot and even when no complaint has been made. The Mass Media Bureau may argue against renewals when it believes that they would not serve the public interest.

Lying to the Commission may be the clearest basis for denying renewal. In its early years, the FCC did not treat dishonesty toward the Commission with heavy sanctions. This led to more examples of such behavior. Finally, the Commission denied the renewal of a station whose general manager for 12 years had concealed from the Commission the fact that a vice-president of a network secretly owned 24 percent of the station's stock. The station appealed on the grounds, among others, that the harsh treatment came without warning and that there was no indication that the FCC would not have renewed the station's application even if it had known the truth.

The Supreme Court upheld the denial of renewal. The fact that the FCC had previously dealt more mildly with similar cases did not prevent it from changing course without warning. Also, the "fact of concealment may be more significant than the facts concealed. The willingness to deceive a regulatory body may be disclosed by immaterial and useless deceptions as well as by material and persuasive ones." The fact that stockholders of a majority of the shares had no knowledge of the dishonesty did not bar the FCC from acting—"the fact that there are innocent stockholders cannot immunize the corporation from the consequences of such deception." Stockholders often suffer from the misdeeds of their chosen officers. Federal Communications Commission v. WOKO, Inc., 329 U.S. 223 (1946).

Sometimes the Commission has held that the manager's deceit is the licensee's responsibility because of its failure to exercise adequate control and supervision consistent with its responsibilities as a licensee. Renewal was denied and the court affirmed in such a case. Continental Broadcasting, Inc. v. Federal Communications Commission, 439 F.2d 580 (D.C.Cir.1971), certiorari denied 403 U.S. 905 (1971).

Since the license is issued to the licensee, the licensee must meet the standards of the Communications Act and the FCC. Misbehavior of the officers may show that the licensee knew of the misbehavior or a serious failure to control the station. In an appropriate situation, either may justify denial of renewal. We will consider such a case, RKO v. Federal Communications Commission, later in this Chapter.

However, in 1980, the Commission unanimously renewed the license of a Westinghouse broadcasting station despite claims that the licensee's parent corporation had engaged in criminal misrepresentations to federal agencies. Because the licensee was "virtually autonomous," the parent's misdeeds did not reflect on the licensee's qualifications. Westinghouse Broadcasting Co., 75 F.C.C.2d 736, 46 R.R.2d 1431 (1980).

### b. *Speech Considerations*

As you will recall, p. 57, supra, in its early days the Commission was not hesitant about denying renewals when it disapproved of the speech being uttered. The potential implications of that practice were not tested because the situation eased after the famous Mayflower Broadcasting Corp. case, 8 F.C.C. 333 (1940), in which the Commission renewed a license but appeared to criticize the licensee for editorializing: "A truly free radio cannot be used to advocate the causes of the licensee. . . . In brief, the broadcaster cannot be an advocate." The case apparently deterred controversial discussion and therefore reduced the need for the Commission to judge speech directly. The situation changed after the Commission's Report on Editorializing by Broadcast Licensees, 13 F.C.C. 1246, 1 R.R. pt. 3, § 91.21 (1949), which directed licensees to devote a reasonable portion of their broadcast time to the discussion of controversial issues of public importance and to encourage the presentation of various views on these questions. This has also affected renewal cases.

One study indicates that 64 radio and television licenses were revoked or not renewed between 1970 and 1978, compared with 78 during the years from 1934 to 1969. Weiss, Ostroff & Clift, Station License Revocations and Denials of Renewal, 1970–1978, 24 J. Broadcasting 69

(1980). The authors analyzed the grounds for revocation or nonrenewal in the 64 cases. Since multiple grounds were common, 110 reasons were listed. The most common were misrepresentations to the FCC (18), failure to pursue the renewal procedure (16), fraudulent billing practices (11), departure from promised programming (11), and unauthorized transfer of control by the licensee (10).

Very few of the 64 involved speech grounds. Even those that did were commonly combined with other derelictions because the Commission has been reluctant to single out a speech basis for nonrenewal. For example, although the study shows that four licenses were lost for "news slanting," all four of these stations were also listed under "misrepresentations to the Commission," three were listed under character qualifications, and the fourth was also listed under failure to prosecute renewal. Similarly, although three cases listed "fairness" violation as grounds for nonrenewal, one of these was also one of the group of four listed above and had four separate reasons for nonrenewal. A second was also listed for misrepresentation. The third, the Brandywine case, is discussed shortly.

The situation is not surprising. First, a station that senses that it may be doing something wrong may seek to hide the matter without realizing that misrepresentation to the Commission may be much more serious than its substantive misbehavior. Recall the WOKO case. Second, misbehavior sometimes occurs because the licensee has not exerted sufficient control over management or employees. In such a case, the FCC combines the misbehavior with inadequate supervision as grounds for the denial of renewal. Third, the posture of the courts has not encouraged the FCC to deny renewals on pure speech grounds—as a few examples will make clear.

In one case, the FCC found that a disc jockey had been using vulgar and suggestive language. When the FCC began to investigate, the licensee denied all knowledge of the offending conduct. Because of the history of complaints, the Commission found that denial incredible, which raised a question about the licensee's character qualifications. After renewal was denied, the court affirmed but did so explicitly on the character ground, refusing to pass on whether the speech alone would have justified nonrenewal. Robinson v. Federal Communications Commission, 334 F.2d 534 (D.C.Cir.1964), certiorari denied 379 U.S. 843 (1964).

In Walton Broadcasting, Inc., 78 F.C.C.2d 857, 47 R.R.2d 1233 (1980), the Commission denied renewal to a station that had tried to build upon the popularity of a new disc jockey by having him disappear and reporting that he had been kidnapped. Listeners jammed telephone lines to the police and the radio station. The licensee was an absentee owner who took no steps to rectify the matter until after the FCC began investigating. The renewal was denied because the licensee failed to exercise adequate control over the station's operations:

The misconduct in this case, the hoax broadcast of news and the false announcement about the kidnapping or disappearance in a non-news context over a 4-day period, was designed to shock and alarm KIKX's listening public. The misconduct can be traced directly to the licensee's failure to require promotion formats be approved, its failure to transmit and emphasize the substance of its policies to its station manager, its failure to insure that the manager understood its policies, its failure to check to see if he transmitted the information to on-the-air personnel, and its failure to understand and inculcate the most elementary principle of public trusteeship.

The licensee was also found responsible for six technical violations of the logging rules and 12 engineering violations. Since the control was inadequate and the resulting misconduct was quite serious, the penalty of nonrenewal was justified.

Another kind of deception was attempted by a minister whose initial efforts to acquire a station for his seminary were challenged by groups who believed that his past record showed that he would not honor the fairness doctrine (see Chapter VI) or his other obligations. The prospective licensee responded by promising to provide balanced programming. Within 10 days of obtaining the license, the licensee began drastically altering its format and groups complained that the licensee was not living up to its obligations. The Commission denied renewal on two grounds: alleged violations of the fairness doctrine, and deception practiced on the Commission in obtaining the license. On appeal, the court affirmed, 2–1. Two judges agreed on the deception ground but the dissenter found that ground "too narrow a ledge" for decision. He thought that the Commission had really denied renewal because of the speech uttered on the station and he concluded that this was impermissible. Brandywine-Main Line Radio, Inc. v. Federal Communications Commission, 473 F.2d 16 (D.C.Cir.1972), certiorari denied 412 U.S. 922 (1973), Douglas, J. dissenting.

In United Television Co., 55 F.C.C.2d 416, 34 R.R.2d 1465 (1975), the Commission denied renewal to a station accused of violating 18 U.S.C. § 1304 by broadcasting information concerning lotteries. This was done by ministers who "broadcast programs offering three-digit scripture citations in return for monetary donations." The licensee conceded that the language used in the broadcasts referred to numbers games. The Commission, rejecting the claim that freedom of religion was involved, stated that it had the power to determine whether asserted beliefs are "sincerely held" and whether the ministers were in "good faith." Since the numbered references were not part of any creed and "the representations of the ministers concerning financial blessings defy belief," the Commission concluded that no First Amendment problem was involved. There was no specific reference to the speech and press parts of the First Amendment. This behavior alone was held to warrant denial and to bar United from a comparative hearing. In addition to this misbehavior, the licensee was found to have engaged in false and misleading advertising as well as violations of technical rules.

United's appeal failed.  United Broadcasting Co. v. Federal Communications Commission, 565 F.2d 699 (D.C.Cir.1977).  The court, however, refused to accept the speech ground.  It noted that the FCC's order cited several independent reasons for nonrenewal, including technical violations: "In our view, the long history of persistent violations of those rules was a sufficient reason for disqualification.  The Commission's decision is therefore affirmed on the basis of its discussion of this issue, and we reach no other question tendered by this appeal."  Certiorari was denied 434 U.S. 1046 (1978).

In Trustees of the University of Pennsylvania, 69 F.C.C.2d 1394, 44 R.R.2d 747 (1978), the Commission denied a renewal application from a university.  Listeners had complained for some time that announcers on the station had frequently used obscenity and that entire programs had been obscene.  The University took few steps to meet the problem until after the FCC began inquiries and ordered a hearing on the renewal application.  The Commission denied renewal exclusively on the ground that the licensee had totally abdicated its control over the station's management.  The Commission explicitly indicated that the ALJ had denied renewal because of lack of control "and it is that conclusion which we today affirm."  The FCC refused to accept the argument that noncommercial licensees should not be held to the same level of accountability as commercial licensees.  Finally, "corrective action taken by the licensee cannot mitigate its unsatisfactory performance . . . because remedial steps which were taken came only after months of critical deficiencies in supervision and control of the station and, moreover, they occurred after it became clear the station's license was in jeopardy."

A dissenting Commissioner argued for a short-term renewal on the ground that the FCC had been renewing university stations for years although it knew that they "were not as tightly controlled as commercially operated stations."  He was distressed that the University and the community should suffer because of the actions of a "few immature, irresponsible students" who "should have been spanked long ago and the matter ended there."

The most dramatic nonrenewal on speech grounds involved the station in Jackson, Mississippi, that was the subject of the United Church of Christ case discussed at p. 86, supra.  Strangely, the case did *not* involve a Commission decision not to renew.  Groups claimed that the station had violated the fairness doctrine, had failed to air contrasting viewpoints on racial matters, had given blacks inadequate exposure, had generally been disrespectful to blacks, had discriminated against local Catholics, and given inadequate time to public affairs.  Blacks constituted 45 percent of the population of the station's primary service area. The FCC gave the licensee a short renewal and ordered it to honor its obligations.

After the FCC had been ordered to allow the citizen groups to participate and to reconsider the case, it decided that the station deserved renewal because the allegations had not been proven.

On a second appeal, the court reversed on the ground that the FCC's decision was not supported by substantial evidence. The FCC's errors included placing the burden of proof on the citizen groups rather than on the renewal applicant and failing to accept uncontradicted testimony about the station's practices, including cutting off national programs that showed blacks in a favorable light or discussed racial issues. Sometimes the licensee falsely blamed technical difficulties for the interruptions in service. Office of Communication, United Church of Christ v. Federal Communications Commission, 425 F.2d 543 (D.C.Cir. 1969).

Rather than remand again, the court itself vacated the license and ordered the FCC to invite applications for the now vacant channel—and to provide for interim operation of the facility. Finally, the station was taken over by a different licensee.

Surely the most widescale nonrenewal occurred when the Commission refused to renew licenses for eight educational stations in Alabama as well as an application for a construction permit for a ninth. Alabama Educational Television Commission, 50 F.C.C.2d 461, 32 R.R.2d 539 (1975). The Commission found that "blacks rarely appeared on AETC programs; that no black instructors were employed in connection with locally-produced in-school programs; and that unexplained decisions or inconsistently applied policies caused the preemption of almost all black-oriented network programming." The Commission concluded that the "licensee followed a racially discriminatory policy in its overall programming practices and, by reason of its pervasive neglect of a black minority consisting of approximately 30 percent of the population of Alabama, its programming did not adequately meet the needs of the public it was licensed to serve." Although a station need not meet minority needs by special programming, the licensee "cannot with impunity ignore the problems of significant minorities in its service areas." Two dissenters argued that the improvements in the last few years should justify more lenient treatment. The majority used that improvement, which came only after the challenges to renewal, to waive its usual rule that an applicant who is denied renewal is ineligible to reapply for that same station. The state agency here was permitted to reapply but it did so on equal footing with the other applicants.

Generally, however, a licensee runs no risk of losing its license because of what it broadcasts so long as the content is not obscene or otherwise proscribed, as discussed in Chapter VII. The clearest judicial exposition of this view occurred when a petition to deny renewal was filed against a radio station that had broadcast several programs that "made offensive comments concerning persons of the Jewish faith, equating Judaism with Socialism and Socialism with Communism." The Commission granted renewal without a hearing. The court of appeals

affirmed.  Anti-Defamation League of B'nai B'rith v. Federal Communications Commission, 403 F.2d 169 (D.C.Cir.1968), certiorari denied 394
U.S. 930 (1969).

The court approvingly quoted from the Commission's opinion in the
case:

> The Commission has long held that its function is not to judge
> the merit, wisdom or accuracy of any broadcast discussion or com-
> mentary but to insure that all viewpoints are given fair and equal
> opportunity for expression and that controverted allegations are
> balanced by the presentation of opposing viewpoints.  Any other
> position would stifle discussion and destroy broadcasting as a medi-
> um of free speech.  To require every licensee to defend his decision
> to present any controversial program that has been complained of in
> a license renewal hearing would cause most—if not all—licensees to
> refuse to broadcast any program that was potentially controversial
> or offensive to any substantial group.  More often than not this
> would operate to deprive the public of the opportunity to hear
> unpopular or unorthodox views.

The court rejected the petitioner's main contention that "recurrent bigot-
ed appeals to anti-Semitic prejudice" was a basis for denial of renewal.
Here it quoted extensively from the opinion of a concurring Commissioner:

> It is not only impractical—and impossible in any ultimate
> sense—to separate an appeal to prejudice from an appeal to reason
> in this field, it is equally beyond the power or ability of authority to
> say what is religious or racial.  There are centuries of bloody strife
> to prove that man cannot agree on what is or is not "religion."
>
> .  .  .
>
> Nevertheless these subjects will and must be discussed.  But
> they cannot be freely discussed if there is to be an official ban on the
> utterance of "falsehood" or an "appeal to prejudice" as officially
> defined.  All that the government can properly do, consistently with
> the right of free speech, is to demand that the opportunity be kept
> open for the presentation of all viewpoints.  Yet this would be
> impossible under the rule espoused by the ADL.  .  .  .  If what the
> ADL calls "appeals to racial or religious prejudice" is to be classed
> with hard-core obscenity, then it has no right to be heard on the air,
> and the only views which are entitled to be broadcast on matters of
> concern to the ADL are those which the ADL holds or finds
> acceptable.  This is irreconcilable with either the Fairness Doctrine
> or the right of free speech.
>
> Talk of "responsibility" of a broadcaster in this connection is
> simply a euphemism for self-censorship.  It is an attempt to shift the
> onus of action against speech from the Commission to the broadcast-
> er, but it seeks the same result—suppression of certain views and
> arguments.  .  .  .  Attempts to impose such schemes of self-

censorship have been found as unconstitutional as more direct censorship efforts by government.  [    ]

*Promise v. Performance.*  If the Commission "encourages" promises of certain types of programs, how should the Commission treat disparities between the promises and the actual performance?  The Commission's general reluctance to deny renewals originally led it to overlook disparities.  The subject is discussed extensively in Moline Television Corp.,  31 F.C.C.2d 263, 22 R.R.2d 745 (1971), dealing with an assertion that an applicant obtained a station by lavish promises and failed to carry them out.  The Commission noted that it had "not awarded a preference to any applicant based on proposed programming. The door to a sorry episode has been firmly closed."

In 1976, the Commission adopted a quantitative guideline for the "promise versus performance" issue in renewals.  Matter of Revision of FCC Form 303, Application for Renewal of Broadcast Station Licenses, 59 F.C.C.2d 750, 37 R.R.2d 1 (1976).  The Commission's guideline was that "an actual decrease of 15% in any of the three nonentertainment program categories or a 20% decrease overall should be explained to the Commission.  This refers to decreases between the composite week performance and the amount promised in the applicant's last renewal application.  .  .  ."

In West Coast Media, Inc., 79 F.C.C.2d 610, 47 R.R.2d 1709 (1980), a petition to deny renewal was filed against a San Diego FM station for failing to comply with its promises to the FCC.  After a hearing, the FCC denied renewal.  The Commission stressed that it had not set minimum program requirements to qualify for renewal.  Instead, the licensee is obliged to comply substantially with its promises for future performance. "Insubstantial variations do not raise a question of the licensee's ability" to serve the public interest.  Here the licensee fell far below its promises.  In such cases "the Commission confines its review of programming performance to a determination of whether the licensee made reasonable and good faith efforts to effectuate its proposal. Moreover, the licensee must show that its programming has been appropriately responsive to community problems, needs and interests."

After reviewing the case, including the licensee's explanations for the substantial disparity, the Commission concluded that the record showed that the licensee failed to make "reasonable and good faith efforts to effectuate its proposal."  This order was upheld in West Coast Media, Inc. (KDIG) v. Federal Communications Commission, 695 F.2d 617, 52 R.R.2d 1295 (D.C.Cir.1982), certiorari denied 464 U.S. 816 (1983).

In *Deregulation of Television*, p. 91, supra, the Commission eliminated quantitative programming guidelines including those dealing with promise versus performance.  This action was based on studies showing that commercial television stations were carrying non-entertainment programming greatly in excess of the percentages set up by the Commission.

### 3.  COMPARATIVE RENEWAL PROCEEDINGS

In the early years of regulation of each medium, except perhaps for AM, so many vacant frequencies existed that few applicants tried to oust incumbents.  When such a challenge did occur, the Commission undertook the difficult comparison of the incumbent's actual performance and the challenger's proposed operation.  In a major case involving renewal of the license of a Baltimore AM station, the Commission's analysis included some factors favoring the incumbent and others favoring the challenger.  Hearst Radio, Inc. (WBAL), 15 F.C.C. 1149, 6 R.R. 994 (1951).  Although the incumbent had not integrated ownership and management this did not matter because its actual performance was now available for review.  Similarly, although the incumbent also controlled an FM station, a television station, and a newspaper in Baltimore, it had not abused its power so this was not a serious problem.  The Commission found little difference in programming despite the challenger's strong assertions to the contrary, and concluded:

> We have found that both of the applicants are legally, technically, and financially qualified and must therefore choose between them as their applications are mutually exclusive.  We have discussed at some length why the criteria which we may sometimes consider as determining factors when one of the applicants is not operating the facilities sought and where the applicants have not proved their abilities, are not controlling factors in the light of the record of WBAL.  The determining factor in our decision is the clear advantage of continuing the established and excellent service now furnished by WBAL and which we find to be in the public interest, when compared to the risks attendant on the execution of the proposed programming of Public Service Radio Corporation, excellent though the proposal may be.

This decision was thought to give renewal applicants such an advantage that prospective challengers began to seek entry by other means, such as buying an existing facility or seeking available, though less desirable, vacant frequencies.  In its 1965 Policy Statement on Comparative Broadcast Hearings, p. 92, supra, the Commission noted that it was not attempting to deal with "the somewhat different problems raised where an applicant is contesting with a licensee seeking renewal of a license."  Yet, later that year, in a case in which two applicants were challenging the incumbent, the Commission stated that, on further consideration, it had "concluded that the policy statement should govern the introduction of evidence in this and similar proceedings where a renewal application is contested.  .  .  .  However, we wish to make it clear that the parties will be free to urge any arguments they may deem applicable concerning the relative weights to be afforded the evidence bearing on the various comparative factors."  Seven (7) League Productions, Inc., 1 F.C.C.2d 1597 (1965).

Although the Commission might have developed a special set of standards governing renewal cases, it has found it quite difficult to do so. This was not a serious problem so long as few applicants challenged renewal applicants. But in the 1960's and early 1970's, those who wished to get into broadcasting were faced with virtually no vacancies on the spectrum (except UHF) and greatly increasing prices for existing stations. Despite the warning of *Hearst,* applicants began increasingly to challenge incumbents. Whether because the incumbents were superior—or at least equal—or because the denial of renewal imposed a serious financial penalty, the Commission continued to favor renewal applicants.

*The WHDH Case.* But in a very complex case that dragged on 15 years, the Commission rendered a decision that shocked the broadcast industry. In 1954, four mutually exclusive applicants began a contest for Channel 5 in Boston. After hearings, the FCC selected WHDH, Inc., which was wholly owned by the *Boston Herald-Traveler* newspaper. While the losers appealed, WHDH began broadcasting. During the appeals, it was learned WHDH's president, Robert Choate, had had private meetings with the FCC chairman in what was later described as a "meaningful and improper, albeit subtle, attempt to influence the Commission." * The FCC reopened the case in 1960 and WHDH again was selected—but given only a four-month license because of the misbehavior. Appeals were again taken. When WHDH filed for renewal, the FCC invited competing applications.

As a result of a new hearing in 1966, the FCC found WHDH's past record within the bounds of average performance and thus not entitled to special credit. On diversification grounds, WHDH fared badly because of its newspaper connection. In 1969, the FCC awarded BBI the license. When WHDH argued that it should benefit from the *Hearst* decision, the FCC responded that this was not an ordinary renewal case because of its "unique events and procedures." Even though WHDH had been operating for 12 years, all but four months of that had been on temporary licenses and its only permanent license had been very short because of the misbehavior.

On appeal, the court affirmed the FCC's grant of the license to BBI instead of WHDH. Greater Boston Television Corp. v. Federal Communications Commission, 444 F.2d 841 (D.C.Cir.1970), certiorari denied 403 U.S. 923 (1971). If renewal criteria had been applied, the relationship between WHDH and the newspaper would not have been considered—and WHDH would have gotten the benefits of *Hearst* and might well have gotten the license. The court recognized that the FCC had put this case into a special category and had not treated WHDH as a renewal applicant, which it found entirely appropriate given the peculiar history of the case.

* Once a proceeding is underway, parties are generally prohibited from meeting with Commission personnel outside the presence of other parties to the proceeding. The rationale for the prohibition on "ex parte" contacts is that opponents would not have the opportunity to rebut statements made at these meetings because they would be unaware of them.

The court recognized that in ordinary cases renewal expectancies "are provided in order to promote security of tenure and to induce efforts and investments, furthering the public interest, that may not be devoted by a licensee without reasonable security." But that did not apply here.

Even before the court's decision in *Greater Boston,* the industry mobilized to overturn what it saw as a retreat from *Hearst.* The FCC sought to forestall Congressional action by adopting a Policy Statement on Comparative Hearings Involving Regular Renewal Applicants. 22 F.C.C.2d 424, 18 R.R.2d 1901 (1970). Briefly, that policy stated that in any hearing between an incumbent and a challenger, the incumbent would obtain a controlling preference by demonstrating substantial past performance without serious deficiencies. The FCC would never get to consider the merits of the challenger if the incumbent's record met the non-comparative renewal standard.

The new Policy Statement was challenged in Citizens Communications Center v. Federal Communications Commission, 447 F.2d 1201 (D.C. Cir.1971). At issue was whether the Policy Statement violated § 309(e) of the Communications Act and the *Ashbacker* doctrine. Section 309(e) states in part, "If, in the case of any application to which subsection (a) of this section applies, . . . the Commission for any reason is unable to make the finding specified in such subsection, it shall formally designate the application for hearing on the ground or reasons then obtaining . . .. Any hearing subsequently held upon such application shall be a full hearing in which the applicant and all other parties in interest shall be permitted to participate . . .."

The court of appeals decided that the Policy Statement did violate § 309(e) and the *Ashbacker* doctrine despite the Commission's inclusion of all competing applicants in the renewal proceeding.

> To circumvent the *Ashbacker* strictures, however, [the Commission] adds a new twist: the Policy Statement would limit the "comparative" hearing to a single issue—whether the incumbent licensee had rendered "substantial" past performance without serious deficiencies. If the examiner finds that the licensee has rendered such service, the "comparative" hearing is at an end and, barring successful appeal, the renewal application must be granted. Challenging applicants would thus receive no hearing at all on their own applications, contrary to the express provisions of Section 309(e) which requires a full hearing.
>
> In *Ashbacker* the Commission had promised the challenging applicant a hearing on his application after the rival application was granted. The Supreme Court in *Ashbacker* said that such a promise was "an empty thing." At least the Commission here must be given credit for honesty. It does not make any empty promises. It simply denies the competing applicants the "full hearing" promised them by Section 309(e) of the Act. Unless the renewal applicant's past performance is found to be insubstantial or marred by serious deficien-

cies, the competing applications get no hearing at all. The proposition that the 1970 Policy Statement violates Section 309(e), as interpreted in *Ashbacker*, is so obvious it need not be labored.

The court did not, however, rule that superior performance by a licensee should be ignored. "At the same time, *superior* performance should be a plus of major significance in renewal proceedings. Indeed, as *Ashbacker* recognizes, in a renewal proceeding, a new applicant is under a greater burden to 'make the comparative showing necessary to displace an established licensee.'"

Thus, some renewal expectancy was clearly allowed but its exact role in the renewal process still needed clarification. *Citizens Communications Committee* stated it could never reach the level of a controlling preference. But just how much weight should renewal expectancy be given and how good did the licensee's performance have to be to earn it?

During the early 1970's, broadcasters sought legislation clarifying the position of licensees in the renewal process. Their reliance on the Commission had been shaken by their perception of the WHDH case, and the Commission's efforts to reassure them failed when the Policy Statement was upset. The pressure on Congress was aimed mainly toward obtaining a renewal standard that avoided the comparative treatment for an incumbent that had generally been acceptable during the prior period. In 1974, the broadcasters nearly succeeded. Different bills passed the House, 379–14, and the Senate, 69–2, but a conference was never held because the Chairman of the House Interstate Commerce Committee refused to name conferees. He was angry because he believed the broadcasters had reneged on a deal by maneuvering on the floor of each house to raise the term of the license to five years from the Committee's proposed four years. The concern about the length of the term was felt most strongly by smaller broadcasters who were hoping to avoid the paperwork and legal expenses that occurred every three years. These broadcasters were also not usually subject to challenges. The holders of licenses in the large urban areas cared more about the standards to be utilized in renewal cases and less about the length of the term. The result of the maneuvering was that neither group got anything at that time.

During the 1970's, the Commission continued to grant renewals except in cases of serious licensee misconduct. While the Commission purported not to be, it appeared to be giving incumbent licensees a controlling preference for "superior" or even "substantial" service. One such case involved Cowles Florida Broadcasting, Inc.'s application for renewal of the license for its Daytona Beach, Florida, television station. The administrative law judge, in recommending renewal, characterized Cowles's performance as "thoroughly acceptable." The Commission granted renewal 4–3, but the majority, after its own study of the record, concluded that the performance was "superior" and warranted renewal even though the challenger, Central Florida Enterprises, Inc., had gained advantages on several other issues, including diversification, integration, and minority participation, as well as the incumbent's having moved its main studio location in violation of an FCC regulation. The majority also chose to disregard mail fraud allegations against other subsidiaries of Cowles's parent company.

One dissenter thought that the majority had distorted the record to find "superior" service. He thought it only "solid" and would have held that enough to justify renewal but felt constrained to dissent because the court of appeals had set a higher standard. Another dissenter followed much the same path and urged alternative licensing techniques such as lotteries and auctions.

In an order "clarifying" its earlier opinion, a majority of the Commission explained that its previous use of "superior" was not meant to suggest "exceptional when compared to other broadcast stations" in the area or elsewhere. Rather, the intention was to distinguish "between the two situations—one where the licensee has served the public interest but in the least permissible fashion still sufficient to be renewed in the absence of competing applications, and the other where the licensee has done so in a solid, favorable fashion." The licensee was said to be in the second group. The majority shifted from "superior" to "substantial."

The court of appeals reversed the renewal and remanded. Central Florida Enterprises, Inc. v. Federal Communications Commission, 598 F.2d 37 (D.C.Cir.1978). The court's final position (after an original opinion, an order amending that opinion, and a supplemental opinion denying a petition for rehearing) rejected the Commission's entire approach to comparative renewal proceedings—and found inadequacies in its dealings with specific issues. The Commission purported to be following its 1965 Policy Statement in conducting a full hearing. The court observed:

> It found favorably to Central [the challenger] on each of diversification, integration, and minority participation, and adversely to Cowles on the studio move question. Then simply on the basis of a wholly noncomparative assessment of Cowles' past performance as "substantial," the Commission confirmed Cowles' "renewal expectancy." Even were we to agree (and we do not agree) with the Commission's trivialization of each of Central's advantages, we still would be unable to sustain its action here. The Commission nowhere even vaguely described how it aggregated its findings into the decisive balance; rather, we are told that the conclusion is based on "administrative 'feel.'" Such intuitional forms of decision-making, completely opaque to judicial review, fall somewhere on the distant side of arbitrary.

On remand the Commission again awarded the license to Cowles. Central Florida appealed once more.

## CENTRAL FLORIDA ENTERPRISES, INC. v. FEDERAL COMMUNICATIONS COMMISSION

United States Court of Appeals, District of Columbia Circuit, 1982.
683 F.2d 503, certiorari denied 460 U.S. 1084, 103 S.Ct. 1774,
76 L.Ed.2d 346 (1983).

Before ROBINSON, CHIEF JUDGE, WILKEY, CIRCUIT JUDGE, and FLAN-NERY, DISTRICT JUDGE for the District of Columbia.

WILKEY, CIRCUIT JUDGE:

. . .

In its decision appealed in *Central Florida I* the FCC concluded that the reasons undercutting Cowles' bid for renewal did "not outweigh the substantial service Cowles rendered to the public during the last license period." Accordingly, the license was renewed. Our reversal was rooted in a twofold finding. First, the Commission had inadequately investigated and analyzed the four factors weighing against Cowles' renewal. Second, the process by which the FCC weighed these four factors against Cowles' past record was never "even vaguely described" and, indeed, "the Commission's handling of the facts of this case [made] embarrassingly clear that the FCC [had] practically erected a presumption of renewal that is inconsistent with the full hearing requirement" of the Communications Act. We remand[ed] with instructions to the FCC to cure these deficiencies.

On remand the Commission has followed our directives and correct-ed, point by point, the inadequate investigation and analysis of the four factors cutting against Cowles' requested renewal. The Commission concluded that, indeed, three of the four merited an advantage for Central Florida, and on only one (the mail fraud issue) did it conclude that nothing needed to be added on the scale to Central's plan or removed from Cowles'. We cannot fault the Commission's actions here.

We are left, then, with evaluating the way in which the FCC weighed Cowles' main studio move violation and Central's superior diversification and integration, on the one hand, against Cowles' substan-tial record of performance on the other. This is the most difficult and important issue in this case, for the new weighing process which the FCC has adopted will presumably be employed in its renewal proceedings elsewhere. We therefore feel that it is necessary to scrutinize carefully the FCC's new approach, and discuss what we understand and expect it to entail.

For some time now the FCC has had to wrestle with the problem of how it can factor in some degree of "renewal expectancy" for a broad-caster's meritorious past record, while at the same time undertaking the required comparative evaluation of the incumbent's probable future performance versus the challenger's. As we stated in *Central Florida I*, "the incumbent's past performance is some evidence, and perhaps the best evidence, of what its future performance would be." And it has been intimated—by the Supreme Court in FCC v. National Citizen's

Committee for Broadcasting (NCCB) and by this court in Citizens Communications Center v. FCC and *Central Florida I*—that some degree of renewal expectancy is permissible. But *Citizens* and *Central Florida I* also indicated that the FCC has in the past impermissibly raised renewal expectancy to an irrebuttable presumption in favor of the incumbent.

We believe that the formulation by the FCC in its latest decision, however, is a permissible way to incorporate some renewal expectancy while still undertaking the required comparative hearing. *The new policy, as we understand it, is simply this: renewal expectancy is to be a factor weighed with all the other factors, and the better the past record, the greater the renewal expectancy "weight."*

> In our view [states the FCC], the strength of the expectancy depends on the merit of the past record. Where, as in this case, the incumbent rendered substantial but not superior service, the "expectancy" takes the form of a comparative preference weighed against [the] other factors . . .. An incumbent performing in a superior manner would receive an even stronger preference. An incumbent rendering minimal service would receive no preference.

This is to be contrasted with the Commission's *1965 Policy Statement on Comparative Broadcast Hearings*, where "[o]nly unusually good or unusually poor records have relevance."

If a stricter standard is desired by Congress, it must enact it. We cannot: the new standard is within the statute.

The reasons given by the Commission for factoring in some degree of renewal expectancy are rooted in a concern that failure to do so would hurt broadcast *consumers*.

> The justification for a renewal expectancy is three-fold. (1) There is no guarantee that a challenger's paper proposals will, in fact, match the incumbent's proven performance. Thus, not only might replacing an incumbent be entirely gratuitous, but *it might even deprive the community of an acceptable service and replace it with an inferior one.* (2) Licensees should be encouraged through the likelihood of renewal to make investments *to ensure quality service. Comparative renewal proceedings cannot function as a "competitive spur" to licensees if their dedication to the community is not rewarded.* (3) Comparing incumbents and challengers as if they were both new applicants could lead to a haphazard restructuring of the broadcast industry especially considering the large number of group owners. *We cannot readily conclude that such a restructuring could serve the public interest.*

*We are relying, then, on the FCC's commitment that renewal expectancy will be factored in for the benefit of the public, not for incumbent broadcasters.* . . . As we concluded in *Central Florida I*, "[t]he only legitimate fear which should move [incumbent] licensees is the fear of their own substandard performance, and that would be all to the good."

There is a danger, of course, that the FCC's new approach could still degenerate into precisely the sort of irrebuttable presumption in favor of renewal that we have warned against. But this did not happen in the case before us today, and our reading of the Commission's decision gives us hope that if the FCC applies the standard in the same way in future cases, it will not happen in them either. The standard is new, however, and much will depend on how the Commission applies it and fleshes it out. Of particular importance will be the definition and level of service it assigns to "substantial"—and whether that definition is ever found to be "opaque to judicial review," "wholly unintelligible," or based purely on "administrative 'feel.' "[27]

In this case, however, the Commission was painstaking and explicit in its balancing. The Commission discussed in quite specific terms, for instance, the items it found impressive in Cowles' past record. It stressed and listed numerous programs demonstrating Cowles' "local community orientation" and "responsive[ness] to community needs," discussed the percentage of Cowles' programming devoted to news, public affairs, and local topics, and said it was "impressed by [Cowles'] reputation in the community. Seven community leaders and three public officials testified that [Cowles] had made outstanding contributions to the local community. Moreover, the record shows no complaints . . .." The Commission concluded that "Cowles' record [was] more than minimal," was in fact " 'substantial,' i.e., 'sound, favorable and substantially above a level of mediocre service which might just minimally warrant renewal.' "

The Commission's inquiry in this case did not end with Cowles' record, but continued with a particularized analysis of what factors weighed against Cowles' record, and how much. The FCC investigated fully the mail fraud issue. It discussed the integration and diversification disadvantages of Cowles and conceded that Central had an edge on these issues—"slight" for integration, "clear" for diversification. But it reasoned that "structural factors such as [these]—of primary importance in a new license proceeding—should have lesser weight compared with the preference arising from substantial past service."[31] Finally, with

---

**27.** Id. at 50 (quoting earlier proceeding, 60 F.C.C.2d 372, 422 (1976)). We think it would be helpful if at some point the Commission defined and explained the distinctions, if any, among: substantial, meritorious, average, above average, not above average, not far above average, above mediocre, more than minimal, solid, sound, favorable, not superior, not exceptional, and unexceptional—all terms used by the parties to describe what the FCC found Cowles' level of performance to have been. We are especially interested to know what the standard of comparison is in each case. "Average" compared to all applicants? "Mediocre" compared to all incumbents? "Favorable" with respect to the FCC's expectations? We realize that the FCC's task

is a subjective one, but the use of imprecise terms needlessly compounds our difficulty in evaluating what the Commission has done. We think that we can discern enough to review intelligently the Commission's actions today, but if the air is not cleared or, worse, becomes foggier, the FCC's decision-making may again be adjudged "opaque to judicial review."

**31.** . . .

Here we have a caveat. We do not read the Commission's new policy as *ignoring* integration and diversification considerations in comparative renewal hearings. In its brief at page 6 the Commission states that "an incumbent's meritorious record should outweigh in the comparative renewal respect to the illegal main studio move, the FCC found that "licensee misconduct" in general "may provide a more meaningful basis for preferring an untested challenger over a proven incumbent." The Commission found, however, that here the "comparative significance of the violation" was diminished by the underlying facts . . . . The FCC concluded that "the risk to the public interest posed by the violation seems small when compared to the actuality of depriving Daytona Beach of Cowles' tested and acceptable performance."

Having listed the relevant factors and assigned them weights, the Commission concluded that Cowles' license should be renewed. We note, however, that despite the finding that Cowles' performance was " 'substantial,' i.e., 'sound, favorable and substantially above a level of mediocre service,' " the combination of Cowles' main studio rule violation and Central's diversification and integration advantages made this a "close and difficult case." Again, we trust that this is more evidence that the Commission's weighing did not, and will not, amount to automatic renewal for incumbents.

We are somewhat reassured by a recent FCC decision granting for the first time since at least 1961, on *comparative* grounds the application of the challenger for a radio station license and denying the renewal application of the incumbent licensee.[38] In that decision the Commission found that the *incumbent deserved no renewal expectancy* for his past program record and that his application was inferior to the challenger's on comparative grounds. Indeed, it was the *incumbent's* preferences on the diversification and integration factors which were overcome (there, by the challenger's superior programming proposals and longer broadcast week). The Commission found that the incumbent's "inadequate [past performance] reflects poorly on the *likelihood of future service in the public interest.*" Further, it found that the incumbent had no "legitimate renewal expectancy" because his past performance was neither "meritorious" nor "substantial."

We have, however, an important caveat. In the Commission's weighing of factors the scale mid-mark must be neither the factors themselves, nor the interests of the broadcasting industry, nor some other secondary and artificial construct, but rather the intent of Con-

context a challenging applicant's advantages under the structural factors of integration and diversification." Ceteris paribus, this may be true—depending in part, of course, on how "meritorious" is defined. But where there are weights on the scales other than a meritorious record on the one hand, and integration and diversification on the other, the Commission must afford the latter two *some* weight, since while they alone may not outweigh a meritorious record they may tip the balance if weighed with something else. See *Citizens,* 447 F.2d at 1208–09 n. 23.

That, of course, is precisely the situation here, since the main studio move violation must also be balanced against the meritorious record. The Commission may not weigh the antirenewal factors separately against the incumbent's record, eliminating them as it goes along. It must weigh them all simultaneously. . . .

38. In re Applications of Simon Geller and Grandebanke Corp., FCC Docket Nos. 21104–05 (Released 15 June 1982). We intimate no view at this time, of course, on the soundness of the Commission's decision there; we cite it only as demonstrating that the Commission's new approach may prove to be more than a paper tiger.

gress, which is to say the interests of the listening public. All other doctrine is merely a means to this end, and it should not become more. If in a given case, for instance, the factual situation is such that the denial of a license renewal would not undermine renewal expectancy *in a way harmful to the public interest*, then renewal expectancy should not be invoked.[40]

Finally, we must note that we are still troubled by the fact that the record remains that an incumbent *television* licensee has *never* been denied renewal in a comparative challenge. American television viewers will be reassured, although a trifle baffled, to learn that even the worst television stations—those which are, presumably, the ones picked out as vulnerable to a challenge[42]—are so good that they never need replacing. We suspect that somewhere, sometime, somehow, some television licensee *should* fail in a comparative renewal challenge, but the FCC has never discovered such a licensee yet. As a court we cannot say that it must be Cowles here.

We hope that the standard now embraced by the FCC will result in the protection of the public, not just incumbent licensees. And in today's case we believe the FCC's application of the new standard was not inconsistent with the Commission's mandate. Accordingly the Commission's decision is

Affirmed.

### Notes and Questions

1. Ironically, less than a year later, when the court was presented with the case alluded to in *Central Florida II* where the Commission awarded a radio license to a new applicant rather than the incumbent, the court did not approve. Simon Geller had operated a one-man classical music FM station in Gloucester, Massachusetts, since the early 1960's. In 1981, Grandebanke Corporation filed a competing application. The Commission held that because less than one percent of the station's programming was of a nonentertainment nature and the station broadcast no news, editorials, or locally produced programming, Geller was not entitled to the benefit of renewal expectancy. Simon Geller, 91 F.C.C.2d 1253, 52 R.R.2d 709 (1982).

On appeal, the FCC's action was vacated and the case remanded. The court began by characterizing it as "yet another meandering effort by the [FCC] to develop a paradigm for its license renewal hearings."

---

**40.** Thus, the justifications given by the Commission for renewal expectancy, [  ] should be remembered by the FCC in future renewal proceedings and, where these justifications are in a particular case attenuated, the Commission ought not to chant "renewal expectancy" and grant the license.

wouldn't challenge the [incumbent] they thought was exceptional or far above average." The dissent from the Commission's decision declared it a "readily apparent fact that competing applicants file against only the ne'er-do-wells of the industry." 86 F.C.C.2d at 1055 n. 99.

**42.** Counsel for the FCC conceded at oral argument, "I grant you, [competitors]

For years this court has urged the FCC to put some bite into its comparative hearings. [citing *Central Florida I*] Indeed, we have too long hungered for just one instance in which the FCC properly denied an incumbent's renewal expectancy.  Unfortunately, in the process of seeking to respond to this court's signals with regard to renewal expectancy, the FCC ignored its own precedents as to the other factors that must be considered in conducting a comparative analysis.

The court of appeals agreed that Geller was entitled to no renewal expectancy because his programming did not even attempt to respond to ascertained community needs and problems.  The FCC then properly turned to the comparative criteria.  Here, however, the court concluded that the FCC had improperly diminished the value of Geller's obvious advantages of diversification and integration of ownership and management because it tied each to its view of Geller's programming.  The FCC thus failed to accord to Geller the importance it had usually attached to diversification and integration in prior cases.  The case was remanded for further consideration.  Geller v. Federal Communications Commission, 737 F.2d 74 (D.C.Cir.1984).  In late 1985, the Commission granted Geller's application for renewal.  An appeal is expected.

2.  Is the latest Commission explanation of its comparative renewal standards clear?  Exactly how much renewal expectancy is there?  Has the Commission adequately justified the need for a strong renewal expectancy?  Some would argue that it is impossible to devise an adequate system of comparing incumbents and new applicants and that comparative renewals should be eliminated.  Wouldn't this eliminate the incentive for licensees to serve the public interest?

3.  If the purpose of renewal expectancy is to encourage licensees to serve the public interest by rewarding those who do, is there any justification for granting renewal expectancy to licensees who provide subscription television service?  This issue was forwarded to the Commission in late 1985 when the Review Board determined that it had not been previously decided.  Video 44, 58 R.R.2d 1537 (1985).

## C.  TRANSFER OF LICENSES

In part because of the Commission's renewal policies, radio and television licenses have acquired substantial value.  When a licensee decides to leave broadcasting altogether or to switch services or locations at the end of a license period, the licensee has no opportunity to reap profit.  To reap profits, the licensee must seek renewal and, during the term, sell the facilities and goodwill and assign the license to a prospective buyer.  In some ways this "transfer" procedure resembles the sale of any business, but the Commission's rules substantially affect the transaction.

Section 310(d) of the Communications Act requires the Commission to pass on all transfers and find that "the public interest, convenience, and necessity will be served thereby." But it also provides that in deciding whether the public interest would be served by the transfer the Commission "may not consider whether the public interest . . . might be served by the transfer . . . to a person other than the proposed transferee or assignee." Why might Congress have imposed this limitation?

When a transferee applies for its first full term, should it be judged as an original applicant who must compete in a comparative hearing without any advantage of incumbency or as a renewal applicant? What are the justifications for each view?

Despite the possible objections to transfer applications, most are granted, usually with little or no delay. This kind of turnover suggests a problem for the Commission. If licenses acquire substantial value a tendency may develop to build up stations and then sell them at a profit. This might be viewed as undermining the "public interest" philosophy of the licensing process. On the other hand, the public may benefit from someone's building up a station, even though that person's motive is to sell it for a profit.

In 1962, the Commission adopted a rule prohibiting licensees from transferring a broadcast license during the first three years after acquisition unless a hardship waiver—usually upon a showing of financial loss—was granted. The rationale for this rule was a belief that it took three years for a licensee to learn the needs and interests of the community and institute programming responsive to those needs and interests. Frequent changes in ownership were viewed as disruptive and thus contrary to the public interest. Applications for Voluntary Assignments or Transfer of Control, 32 F.C.C. 689 (1962).

Twenty years later, the Commission reversed its position on this issue after concluding that a willing buyer was more likely to serve the public interest than an unwilling owner prohibited from selling the station. Although the three-year rule was abolished, a one-year limitation was instituted for licenses acquired through the comparative hearing process. Applications for Voluntary Assignments or Transfer of Control, 52 R.R.2d 1081 (1982). Subsequently the one-year rule was extended to licenses obtained through the minority ownership policy. We will discuss this policy in Chapter V.

## 1.  FORMAT CHANGES

Until 1970, the foregoing summary would have covered most of the major problems related to transfers, but then the question of format change arose, plaguing the courts and the Commission for a decade until the Supreme Court decided the issue. The problem arose when a prospective transferee of a radio license proposed to change the station's distinctive programming format.

## FEDERAL COMMUNICATIONS COMMISSION v. WNCN LISTENERS GUILD

Supreme Court of the United States, 1981.
450 U.S. 582, 101 S.Ct. 1266, 67 L.Ed.2d 521.

MR. JUSTICE WHITE delivered the opinion of the Court.

Sections 309(a) and 310(d) of the Communications Act of 1934, 48 Stat. 1064, as amended, 47 U.S.C. § 151 et seq. (Act), empower the Federal Communications Commission to grant an application for license transfer or renewal only if it determines that "the public interest, convenience, and necessity" will be served thereby. The issue before us is whether there are circumstances in which the Commission must review past or anticipated changes in a station's entertainment programming when it rules on an application for renewal or transfer of a radio broadcast license. The Commission's present position is that it may rely on market forces to promote diversity in entertainment programming and thus serve the public interest.

This issue arose when, pursuant to its informal rulemaking authority, the Commission issued a "Policy Statement" concluding that the public interest is best served by promoting diversity in entertainment formats through market forces and competition among broadcasters and that a change in entertainment programming is therefore not a material factor that should be considered by the Commission in ruling on an application for license renewal or transfer. Respondents, a number of citizens groups interested in fostering and preserving particular entertainment formats, petitioned for review in the Court of Appeals for the District of Columbia Circuit. That court held that the Commission's Policy Statement violated the Act. We reverse the decision of the Court of Appeals.

I

Beginning in 1970, in a series of cases involving license transfers, the Court of Appeals for the District of Columbia Circuit gradually developed a set of criteria for determining when the "public-interest" standard requires the Commission to hold a hearing to review proposed changes in entertainment. Noting that the aim of the Act is "to secure the maximum benefits of radio to all the people of the United States, [ ], the Court of Appeals ruled in 1974 that "preservation of a format [that] would otherwise disappear, although economically and technologically viable and preferred by a significant number of listeners, is generally in the public interest." [ ] It concluded that a change in format would not present "substantial and material questions of fact" requiring a hearing if (1) notice of the change had not precipitated "significant public grumbling"; (2) the segment of the population preferring the format was too small to be accommodated by available frequencies; (3) there was an adequate substitute in the service area for the format being abandoned; or (4) the format would be economically unfeasible even if the station were managed efficiently. The court rejected the Commission's position that the choice of entertainment formats should be left to the judgment of the licensee, stating that the Commission's interpretation of the public-interest standard was contrary to the Act.

In January 1976, the Commission responded to these decisions by undertaking an inquiry into its role in reviewing format changes. In particular, the Commission sought public comment on whether the public interest would be better served by Commission scrutiny of entertainment programming or by reliance on the competitive marketplace.

Following public notice and comment, the Commission issued a Policy Statement pursuant to its rulemaking authority under the Act. The Commission concluded in the Policy Statement that review of format changes was not compelled by the language or history of the Act, would not advance the welfare of the radio-listening public, would pose substantial administrative problems, and would deter innovation in radio programming. In support of its position, the Commission quoted from FCC v. Sanders Brothers Radio Station, 309 U.S. 470, 475 (1940): "Congress intended to leave competition in the business of broadcasting where it found it, to permit a licensee . . . to survive or succumb according to his ability to make his programs attractive to the public." The Commission also emphasized that a broadcaster is not a common carrier and therefore should not be subjected to a burden similar to the common carrier's obligation to continue to provide service if abandonment of that service would conflict with public convenience or necessity.

The Commission also concluded that practical considerations as well as statutory interpretation supported its reluctance to regulate changes in formats. Such regulation would require the Commission to categorize the formats of a station's prior and subsequent programming to determine whether a change in format had occurred; to determine whether the prior format was "unique"; and to weigh the public detriment resulting from the abandonment of a unique format against the public benefit resulting from that change. The Commission emphasized the difficulty of objectively evaluating the strength of listener preferences, of comparing the desire for diversity within a particular type of programming to the desire for a broader range of program formats and of assessing the financial feasibility of a unique format.

Finally, the Commission explained why it believed that market forces were the best available means of producing diversity in entertainment formats. First, in large markets, competition among broadcasters had already produced "an almost bewildering array of diversity" in entertainment formats. Second, format allocation by market forces accommodates listeners' desires for diversity within a given format and also produces a variety of formats. Third, the market is far more flexible than governmental regulation and responds more quickly to changing public tastes. Therefore, the Commission concluded that "the market is the allocation mechanism of preference for entertainment formats, and . . . Commission supervision in this area will not be conducive either to producing program diversity [or] satisfied radio listeners."

The Court of Appeals, sitting en banc, held that the Commission's policy was contrary to the Act as construed and applied in the court's prior format decisions. [ ] The court questioned whether the Commission had rationally and impartially re-examined its position and particularly criticized the Commission's failure to disclose a staff study on the effectiveness of market allocation of formats before it issued the Policy Statement. The court then responded to the Commission's criticisms of the format doctrine. First, although conceding that market forces generally lead to diversification of formats, it concluded that the market only imperfectly reflects listener preferences[23] and that the Commission is statutorily obligated to review format changes whenever there is "strong prima facie evidence that the market has in fact broken down." [ ] Second, the court stated that the administrative problems posed by the format doctrine were not insurmountable. Hearings would only be required in a small number of cases, and the Commission could cope with problems such as classifying radio format by adopting "a rational classification schema." [ ] Third, the court observed that the Commission had not demonstrated that the format doctrine would deter innovative programming. Finally, the court explained that it had not directed the Commission to engage in censorship or to impose common carrier obligations on licensees: *WEFM* did not authorize the Commission to interfere with licensee programming choices or to force retention of an existing format; it merely stated that the Commission had the power to consider a station's format in deciding whether license renewal or transfer would be consistent with the public interest. [ ]

Although conceding that it possessed neither the expertise nor the authority to make policy decisions in this area, the Court of Appeals asserted that the format doctrine was "law," not "policy," and was of the view that the Commission had not disproved the factual assumptions underlying the format doctrine. Accordingly, the court declared that the Policy Statement was "unavailing and of no force and effect." [ ]

## II

Rejecting the Commission's reliance on market forces to develop diversity in programming as an unreasonable interpretation of the Act's public-interest standard, the Court of Appeals held that in certain circumstances the Commission is required to regard a change in entertainment format as a substantial and material fact in deciding whether a license renewal or transfer is in the public interest. With all due respect, however, we are unconvinced that the Court of Appeal's format doctrine

---

**23.** The court observed . . . that because broadcasters rely on advertising revenue they tend to serve persons with large discretionary incomes. [ ] The dissenting opinion noted that the Commission had not rejected this assumption. [ ]

is compelled by the Act and that the Commission's interpretation of the public-interest standard must therefore be set aside.

It is common ground that the Act does not define the term "public interest, convenience, and necessity." The Court has characterized the public-interest standard of the Act as "a supple instrument for the exercise of discretion by the expert body which Congress has charged to carry out its legislative policy." [  ] Although it was declared in National Broadcasting Co. v. United States, supra, that the goal of the Act is "to secure the maximum benefits of radio to all the people of the United States," [  ], it was also emphasized that Congress had granted the Commission broad discretion in determining how that goal could best be achieved. The Court accordingly declined to substitute its own views on the best method of encouraging effective use of the radio for the views of the Commission. [  ] Similarly, in FCC v. National Citizens Committee for Broadcasting, 436 U.S. 775 (1978), we deemed the policy of promoting the widest possible dissemination of information from diverse sources to be consistent with both the public-interest standard and the First Amendment, [  ], but emphasized the Commission's broad power to regulate in the public interest. We noted that the Act permits the Commission to promulgate "such rules and regulations, . . . not inconsistent with law, as may be necessary to carry out the provisions of [the Act]," and that this general rule-making authority permits the Commission to implement its view of the public-interest standard of the Act "so long as that view is based on consideration of permissible factors and is otherwise reasonable." [  ] Furthermore, we recognized that the Commission's decisions must sometimes rest on judgment and prediction rather than pure factual determinations. In such cases complete factual support for the Commission's ultimate conclusions is not required since " 'a forecast of the direction in which future public interest lies necessarily involves deductions based on the expert knowledge of the agency.' "

The Commission has provided a rational explanation for its conclusion that reliance on the market is the best method of promoting diversity in entertainment formats. . . . The Court of Appeals places great value on preserving diversity among formats, while the Commission emphasizes the value of intraformat as well as interformat diversity. Finally, the Court of Appeals is convinced that review of format changes would result in a broader range of formats, while the Commission believes that government intervention is likely to deter innovative programming.

. . .

Our opinions have repeatedly emphasized that the Commission's judgment regarding how the public interest is best served is entitled to substantial judicial deference. [  ] Furthermore, diversity is not the only policy the Commission must consider in fulfilling its responsibilities under the Act. The Commission's implementation of the public-interest standard, when based on a rational weighing of competing policies, is not to be set aside by the Court of Appeals, for "the weighing of policies under the 'public interest' standard is a task that Congress has delegated to the Commission in the first instance." [   ] The Commission's position on review of format changes reflects a reasonable accommodation of the policy of promoting diversity in programming and the policy of avoiding unnecessary restrictions on licensee discretion. As we see it, the Commission's Policy Statement is in harmony with cases recognizing that the Act seeks to preserve journalistic discretion while promoting the interests of the listening public.

.   .   .

## III

.   .   .

A major underpinning of its Policy Statement is the Commission's conviction, rooted in its experience, that renewal and transfer cases should not turn on the Commission's presuming to grasp, measure, and weigh the elusive and difficult factors involved in determining the acceptability of changes in entertainment format. To assess whether the elimination of a particular "unique" entertainment format would serve the public interest, the Commission would have to consider the benefit as well as the detriment that would result from the change. Necessarily, the Commission would take into consideration not only the number of listeners who favor the old and the new programming but also the intensity of their preferences. It would also consider the effect of the format change on diversity within formats as well as on diversity among formats. The Commission is convinced that its judgments in these respects would be subjective in large measure and would only approximately serve the public interest. It is also convinced that the market, although imperfect, would serve the public interest as well or better by responding quickly to changing preferences and by inviting experimentation with new types of programming. Those who would overturn the Commission's Policy Statement do not take adequate account of these considerations.

.   .   .

## IV

Respondents contend that the Court of Appeals' judgment should be affirmed because, even if not violative of the Act, the Policy Statement conflicts with the First Amendment rights of listeners "to receive suitable access to social, political, esthetic, moral, and other ideas and experiences." Red Lion Broadcasting Co. v. FCC, 395 U.S. 367, 390 (1969). *Red Lion* held that the Commission's "fairness doctrine" was consistent with the public-interest standard of the Communications Act and did not violate the First Amendment, but rather enhanced First Amendment values by promoting "the presentation of vigorous debate of controversial issues of importance and concern to the public." [   ] Although observing that the interests of the people as a whole were promoted by debate of public issues on the radio, we did not imply that the First

Amendment grants individual listeners the right to have the Commission review the abandonment of their favorite entertainment programs. The Commission seeks to further the interests of the listening public as a whole by relying on market forces to promote diversity in radio entertainment formats and to satisfy the entertainment preferences of radio listeners. This policy does not conflict with the First Amendment.

Contrary to the judgment of the Court of Appeals, the Commission's Policy Statement is not inconsistent with the Act. It is also a constitutionally permissible means of implementing the public-interest standard of the Act. Accordingly, the judgment of the Court of Appeals is reversed, and the case is remanded for further proceedings consistent with this opinion.

So ordered.

[JUSTICE MARSHALL joined by JUSTICE BRENNAN dissented, arguing that the Commission's failure to include a waiver provision in the Policy Statement made it too inflexible:

> The Policy Statement completely forecloses any possibility that the Commission will reexamine the validity of its general policy on format changes as it applies to particular situations. Thus, even when it can be conclusively demonstrated that a particular radio market does not function in the manner predicted by the Commission, the Policy Statement indicates that the Commission will blindly assume that a proposed format change is in the "public interest." This result would occur even where reliance on the market to ensure format diversity is shown to be misplaced, and where it thus appears that action by the Commission is necessary to promote the public interest in diversity. This outcome is not consistent with the Commission's statutory responsibilities.

JUSTICE MARSHALL argued that although the court of appeals might have gone too far in providing specific guidelines for handling unique formats, it was well within its authority when it held that the lack of any "safety valve" in the Policy Statement was a violation of the Commission's public interest obligations.]

## Notes and Questions

1. *WNCN Listeners Guild,* like many of the cases involving the Commission, revolves around the problem of defining "public interest, convenience and necessity." Is a clear definition possible? If not, how much deference should the Commission be given in applying the standard?

2. In his dissent, Justice Marshall argued that it was not impossible for the Commission to define formats. He noted two suggestions by the court of appeals for dealing with this issue. One was to develop "a format taxonomy which, even if imprecise at the margins, would be sustainable so long as not irrational." Alternatively, the Commission could avoid defining formats altogether "by simply taking the existence of significant and bona fide listener protest as sufficient evidence that

the station's endangered programming has certain unique features for which there are no ready substitutes."

Are these two suggestions in any way contradictory? The first emphasizes treating the format as a whole, and the latter focuses on individual features within a format. What are the pros and cons of each approach?

3. The Policy Statement at issue in *WNCN Listeners Guild* dealt only with renewals and transfers. Assuming that the Commission should review at least some format changes, is it practical to do so only with regard to applications for transfer or renewal? Under these restrictions review of a format change might not be possible until six years after the change takes place.

4. In 1985, a citizen group again tried to get the Commission to hold a hearing on a transfer involving a format change. The group alleged that because the station in question was simulcasting programming on its AM and FM stations 25 percent of the time and running similar formats the rest of the time, it was clear that competition in the marketplace was not producing diversity and therefore the Policy Statement should not apply. The Commission refused to hold a hearing, reaffirming its position of non-intervention in format controversies. WEAM Radio, Inc., 58 R.R.2d 141 (1985).

5. In still another format case, a Commission decision to dismiss a petition to deny and grant renewal without a hearing was reversed by the court of appeals. The petition to deny was filed by Citizens For Jazz on WRVR Inc. The court felt that there was sufficient evidence that the licensee, Viacom, Inc., misrepresented its programming intentions in its transfer application. Citizens For Jazz on WRVR Inc. v. Federal Communications Commission, 775 F.2d 392 (D.C.Cir. 1985).

## 2. THE RKO CASE

Perhaps the most complex and longest-running licensing controversy involves the stations owned by RKO General, Inc. Although most of the controversy has been tied to renewal applications for the various stations, transfer applications have also been involved. Overall, this continuing soap opera highlights many issues raised by the licensing process.

The first RKO license to be challenged was that of KHJ, Channel 9, in Los Angeles, in 1966. The examiner recommended denial of renewal and granting of the license to the challenger, Fidelity Television, Inc. He criticized KHJ's past programming, particularly its concentration on old films and its ignoring of community criticism of excessive violence in the movies. The Commission reversed the examiner and granted the renewal. In comparing the various factors, the Commission concluded that RKO's programming and community relations, though not "unusually good" or "superior," were also not "insubstantial" or "unusually poor." Thus the "record must be deemed to be within the bounds of average performance expected of all licensees" and warranted neither a merit nor a demerit. After reviewing all the factors the Commission concluded that the two applicants were essentially equal and that the outcome rested on a decision that "credit must be given in a comparative renewal proceeding, when the applicants are otherwise equal, for the value to the public in the continuation of the existing service."

The challenger's appeal was rejected, Fidelity Television, Inc. v. Federal Communications Commission, 515 F.2d 684 (D.C.Cir.1975), certiorari denied 423 U.S. 926 (1975). One ground of appeal concerned the Commission's refusal to consider programming proposals even though Fidelity proposed to offer 22 percent less entertainment and twice as much educational and news programming as KHJ. The court observed that the Commission's refusal to consider this on the ground that differences were only judgmental, might be questionable, but found that the refusal was also based on the defensible ground of the challenger's inadequate ascertainment. The court then upheld the determination that KHJ's performance was "average" because it was not "bereft of the support of substantial evidence." The court stressed that this was not a situation in which a "superior applicant is denied a license because to give it to him would work a 'forfeiture' of his opponent's investment." Rather, the incumbent's performance, was enough to "withstand the competition of a 'nothing' competitor."

While this case was progressing through the Commission and court of appeals, two other RKO General stations were challenged when they applied for license renewal. In 1969, two challengers, Community Broadcasting of Boston, Inc. and The Dudley Station Corp., filed applications for the license of WNAC–TV, channel 7, in Boston, and in 1974, Multistate Communications, Inc. filed an application for the license of WOR–TV, channel 9, in New York.

Among the issues that were raised in the WNAC–TV proceeding were allegations that RKO and its parent company, General Tire and Rubber Co., had engaged in anticompetitive practices and that RKO had violated the sponsorship identification requirements of § 317 during its broadcasts of the "Della Reese Show." (We will discuss sponsorship identification in Chapter VII.) In 1974, the ALJ awarded the license to RKO after concluding that RKO had not knowingly engaged in anticompetitive practices and that the violations that occurred with respect to the "Della Reese Show" were cause for a comparative demerit as opposed to disqualification.

In early 1975, the Securities and Exchange Commission started investigating General Tire with respect to illegal bribes of foreign public officials and illegal foreign bank accounts. Then, in late 1975, before the full FCC had heard oral argument on WNAC–TV's license renewal, Community filed a petition to reopen the record and enlarge the issues. The petition, accompanied by 640 pages of exhibits, alleged that General Tire had engaged in illegal and unethical conduct in both the United States and foreign countries and that RKO had violated the FCC's rules and "exhibited a lack of candor" by failing to disclose ongoing investigations into General Tire's conduct.

Meanwhile, the ongoing SEC investigation uncovered several examples of misconduct by General Tire. Finally, an SEC complaint was filed on May 10, 1976, covering among others, all the misconduct detailed in the 1975 Community petition. On the same day, General Tire entered into a consent decree that prohibited "the concealment of any of the misconduct alleged in the SEC complaint including, *inter alia*, unlawful political contributions, unlawful payments to foreign government officials and the overbilling of affiliates and subsidiaries." The decree also set up a Special Review Committee to further investigate General Tire's conduct and file a report with the SEC and the court. On May 14, 1976, RKO advised the FCC of the SEC inquiry and the consent decree for the first time.

On June 29, 1976, oral argument on the ALJ's renewal award to RKO was held before the FCC, en banc, and the Commission decided that any action should be delayed until the submission of the Review Committee's report. While the parties awaited the filing of the report, further issues surfaced. During the years 1972–1976, RKO had knowingly failed to properly complete the barter and trade portion of the financial report (form 324) that was required at that time. Community filed a further petition raising this issue in April, 1977.

When the Special Review Committee's report was finally filed in July, 1977, it confirmed most of Community's allegations. Among the Review Committee's findings were the following: "(a) General Tire and certain of its subsidiaries engaged in various schemes and practices that resulted in improper domestic political contributions; (b) Aerojet, an RKO subsidiary, gave gratuities to military and other government-connected personnel having dealings with Aerojet; (c) General Tire and its affiliates maintained and used improper secret and unrecorded funds designed to avoid foreign currency exchange and tax laws; (d) General Tire and its affiliates paid bribes to foreign agents and officials not only to do business in a country but also to keep competitors out; (e) through the use of secret bank accounts, General Tire systematically overbilled its foreign affiliates; and (f) RKO did not maintain adequate records concerning the amount or use of consideration resulting from its barter and trade transactions."

In April, 1978, before the FCC had taken further action on the renewal application, Community and Dudley filed another petition seeking approval of the transfer of WNAC–TV's license to New England Television Corporation—formed by the merger of Community and Dudley—for $54 million. The sale was contingent on the FCC's granting RKO's renewal application. The petition was opposed by Fidelity Television, Inc. and Multi-State Communications, Inc., challengers for RKO's Los Angeles and New York television licenses respectively. Those proceedings had by this time been conditioned on the outcome of the Boston proceeding.

In June, 1980, the Commission denied the RKO application for renewal of the WNAC–TV license:

> In general the evidence is clear and convincing that RKO has engaged in a variety of misconduct which renders it unfit to be a Commission licensee for Channel 7 in Boston. RKO has engaged in an improper reciprocal trades program that was anticompetitive, it has knowingly filed false financial statements with this Commission, and it has not been entirely honest and forthcoming in its dealings with the Commission in these proceedings. Our concern here is heightened by the misconduct engaged in by RKO's parent, General Tire. General Tire not only controls RKO as a legal matter; the record also demonstrates that General Tire has exercised practical control over RKO operations in certain respects and has involved the broadcast operations in serious misconduct. It is that close legal and practical relationship that further taints RKO's qualifications. This record thus compels the conclusion that we cannot trust RKO to operate Channel 7 in the future in a manner consistent with the public interest.

The Commission also denied RKO's renewal applications for the Los Angeles and New York stations reasoning that RKO was equally unfit to hold those licenses. However, the Commission delayed any final action on the one other TV license and 12 radio licenses held by RKO.

Commissioners Lee and Quello filed separate dissents, each arguing that the punishment—potentially the loss of all 16 licenses—was gross overkill. Commissioner Lee entitled his dissent "Capital Punishment." Commissioner Washburn dissented separately on the grounds that there was insufficient connection between General Tire's conduct and the ability of RKO to operate its stations in the public interest to justify the penalty.

### RKO v. FEDERAL COMMUNICATIONS COMMISSION

United States Court of Appeals, District of Columbia Circuit, 1981.
670 F.2d 215, certiorari denied, 457 U.S. 1119, 102 S.Ct. 2931,
73 L.Ed.2d 1331 (1982).

Before TAMM, MIKVA and EDWARDS, CIRCUIT JUDGES.

MIKVA, CIRCUIT JUDGE:

. . .

### II. INVALID BASES OF THE FCC DECISION

At the outset, we hold that the FCC has stated at least three independent grounds for its ultimate finding that RKO should be disqualified as a broadcast licensee in Boston. The Decision states that RKO's reciprocal dealings "alone" require disqualification, [ ], that RKO's "willful and repeated [financial] misrepresentation warrants disqualification by itself," [ ], and that perhaps of greatest importance, RKO has

demonstrated a persistent lack of candor with the Commission in these
proceedings.   .   .   .

   .   .   .

## A.  Reciprocal Trade Practices

There are several reasons to doubt that reciprocal trade practices
during the early 1960s can justify out-right disqualification of RKO as a
broadcast licensee in 1980.  First and foremost, the conduct of RKO at
issue has been found to be clearly improper only in retrospect.  Although
it has been understood since the 1930s that "coercive" reciprocity was
anticompetitive, it was not until the late 1960s that a series of judicial
decisions began to cast increasing doubt on the legality and propriety of
unleveraged "mutual patronage" agreements.  Even then, however,
questions remained.  As late as 1979, the FCC itself recognized that a
*per se* rule was probably inappropriate . . . .  The FCC unquestionably has the authority and even the duty to change its mind as to the
degree of anticompetitive practices that are not in the public interest.
[  ]   Such a finding may not be applied retroactively, however, to
conduct that ceased almost fifteen years ago.  [  ]

   We are particularly concerned that in retroactively applying its
"greater appreciation" for the adverse effects of reciprocal trading, the
FCC has abruptly reversed its decision to the contrary in RKO General,
Inc. (KHJ–TV), 44 F.C.C.2d 149 (1969), aff'd sub nom.  Fidelity Television, Inc. v. FCC, 515 F.2d 684.  That case held that essentially the same
conduct was neither disqualifying nor ground even for a comparative
demerit.  Failure to explain the reversal of a directly controlling precedent is unlawful.  [  ]  . . .  Although the FCC conditioned its first
decision on RKO's reciprocal dealings on the possibility that significant
new evidence might be introduced in the subsequent WNAC proceeding,
such evidence never appeared.  Additional evidence of reciprocal trading
was heard in that second proceeding, but the bulk related to nonbroadcast activities by General Tire rather than RKO, and the remainder was
merely cumulative of evidence in the first proceeding.

   Finally, we doubt the Commission's claim that it can predict RKO's
future character and performance from evidence concerning conduct that
took place between 1961 and 1964.  Only the unusual nature of these
proceedings allows the FCC to argue that such evidence is at all relevant.
FCC precedents consider a licensee's behavior during the preceding
license term relevant to renewal requests for the following term.  Central Florida Enterprises, Inc. v. FCC, 598 F.2d 37, 43 (D.C.Cir.1978), cert.
dismissed, 441 U.S. 957 (1979); Citizens Communications Center v. FCC,
447 F.2d 1201, 1208 (D.C.Cir.1971).  RKO sought renewal for the 1969–
1972 term, and the FCC has failed to allege acts of reciprocity during the
earlier term from 1966 to 1969.  But RKO's renewal application for KHJ
concerned the 1965–1968 term, thereby giving the FCC an excuse for
claiming that conduct from 1962 to 1965 "is precisely the conduct at
issue."  [  ]   Even so, the FCC acknowledges that the recency of

misconduct is an important factor for purposes of character evaluation.
[   ] The Commission has not paid sufficient heed to that principle here.

. . .

B.  *Financial Misrepresentations*

The Commission's finding that RKO submitted intentionally false
financial reports is equally insufficient to support RKO's disqualification.
The Decision states that "RKO knowingly certified to the Commission
that certain financial reports were complete and accurate when RKO
knew otherwise." [   ] The FCC's conclusion presumes that RKO's
inaccuracies were either deliberate and intentionally deceptive, [   ], or
that RKO's reports were made with such "wanton, gross, and callous"
disregard for their truth as to reflect the equivalent of such an "affirmative and deliberate intent." [   ] Despite the fact that RKO had consistently denied acting with such intent or disregard, the FCC brushed aside
proffered RKO affidavits to that effect and drew adverse inferences
without allowing RKO to defend itself in a hearing.  Such a procedure is
not lawful.

. . .

The Special Report does demonstrate a pervasive failure to maintain
adequate records at RKO stations, a failure that does nothing to recommend RKO as a broadcast licensee.  But it is a far leap from this to the
finding that RKO intentionally or knowingly misrepresented financial
information to the Commission.  Section 309 of the Communications Act,
47 U.S.C. § 309(e) (1976), requires the Commission to hold a hearing in
cases where "a substantial and material question of fact is presented,"
and to specify "with particularity the matters and things in issue but not
including issues or requirements phrased generally."  Whether RKO
submitted inaccurate reports knowingly and with intent to mislead the
Commission remains an unresolved and material question of fact, and it
was therefore error for the Commission to disqualify RKO without
following the procedures outlined by the statute.

C.  *General Tire's Nonbroadcast Misconduct*

The FCC found it unnecessary to reach the question of whether
RKO would have been disqualified had the only adverse character
evidence been that relating to General Tire's nonbroadcast misconduct.
[   ] Instead, the Commission found that General Tire's misconduct had
"an adverse effect on RKO's qualifications" and lent "substantial
weight" to the Commission's decision to disqualify RKO on each of the
other grounds. [   ] We find nothing unlawful in this approach, although it raises other questions.

As General Tire's own admissions in the Special Report illustrate, its
conduct in nonbroadcast fields hardly enhances RKO's character assessment. . . .  Were RKO's owner a single individual as opposed to a
corporation, it appears that a far lesser showing of character flaws
would support disqualification. [   ] For reasons that are far from

clear, however, the FCC seems to distinguish between misconduct by individual owners and misconduct by corporate entities. [ ]

It is difficult to discern any legitimacy for such differential treatment of individuals as opposed to corporate owners. It is to be hoped that pending FCC efforts to clarify the character standards to be applied in comparative hearings will cast more light on this point. See Policy Regarding Character Qualifications in Broadcast Licensing: Notice of Inquiry, 87 F.C.C.2d 836 (1981). In any event, the FCC has not tried in this appeal to increase the significance attached to corporate misconduct in nonbroadcast areas, [ ], nor could it have done so without first serving notice that its policy had changed. . . .

In short three of the four areas on which the FCC focused in its Decision will not serve as a basis for RKO's outright disqualification, at least on this record. It is not necessary to underscore our criticism too pointedly, however. We uphold the Commission's disqualification of RKO in the Boston proceeding because we conclude that the Decision's ultimate basis, RKO's lack of candor before the FCC, fully and independently supports that judgment.

## III. RKO's LACK OF CANDOR

The Commission found that three instances demonstrated RKO's lack of candor before the agency during a period from 1975 to 1977. First, RKO failed to inform the FCC that there was a factual basis to the allegations first made against General Tire by Community in late 1975. [ ] Second, RKO failed to report the initiation of a formal SEC investigation of General Tire in February 1976. [ ] Finally, RKO failed to concede that it had inaccurately reported trade and barter revenues when pressed to do so by Community in April 1977, despite the indication in General Tire's 1976 Annual Report that there might be some problems with these accounts. [ ]

### A. *The Merits of the FCC's Finding*

The record fully supports the Commission's finding that RKO did not display full candor before the Commission during the period from late 1975 to July 1976. Uncontroverted documentary evidence shows that General Tire responded to the initial phase of the SEC's inquiry regarding overseas operations in May 1975. [ ] As the SEC investigation progressed, RKO's competitors began pressing the FCC to reopen the Boston proceeding, alleging facts that were similar or identical to the admissions later made by General Tire in the consent decree and its Special Report. RKO's first response was to seek an extension of time in which to respond, citing the need to consult with "persons who may have knowledge of the pertinent facts." [ ] More than a month later, in January 1976, RKO clearly decided to stonewall the opposition and the FCC. This seems the only explanation for RKO's decision to file a document opposing the suggestion that the Boston proceeding be reopened on the ground that "there is no factual or legal foundation for this pyramid of charges," that "the charges, as we show below, are groundless," and that other charges were "essentially unsupported."

RKO contends that these statements were technically correct. [   ] It adds that because the burden lay on Community to establish grounds for reopening the proceeding, RKO's pleadings "in context" merely claimed that this burden had not been met. Both arguments are irrelevant, because the question before the FCC was not so much what RKO said as what it had failed to say.

Section 1.65 of the Commission's Rules requires applicants to inform the Commission within thirty days whenever "there has been a substantial change" regarding any matter that may be "of decisional significance in a Commission proceeding involving the pending application." 47 C.F.R. § 1.65 (1979). This requires that an applicant inform the Commission "of *all* facts, whether requested in [renewal] Form 303 or not, that may be of decisional significance so that the Commission can make a realistic decision based on all relevant factors." [   ] Unlike a private party haled into court, or a corporation such as General Tire facing an investigation by the SEC, RKO had an affirmative obligation to inform the Commission of the facts the FCC needed in order to license broadcasters in the public interest. As a licensing authority, the Commission is not expected to "play procedural games with those who come before it in order to ascertain the truth," [   ], and license applicants may not indulge in common-law pleading strategies of their own devise.

The Decision and the record on which it is based demonstrate irrefutably that RKO did not meet these standards, and that RKO's conduct thus threatened "the integrity of the Commission's processes." RKO General, Inc., 82 F.C.C.2d 291, 306 (1980). In spite of an SEC investigation that was rapidly gathering steam, and in spite of the fact that its qualifications as a licensee were at issue before the FCC, RKO failed to come forward with a candid statement of relevant facts. RKO did not inform the FCC that the SEC had issued a formal order of investigation in February 1976, even though this suggested the seriousness of the charges against General Tire. RKO did not advise the FCC of the SEC's preliminary findings until May 14, 1976, despite the fact that General Tire had advised its stockholders of these preliminary findings in February when it released its 1975 Annual Report. RKO did not advise the FCC until May 1976 that General Tire's own internal investigation demonstrated that many of the SEC concerns were valid, even though Community had submitted General Tire's 10–K Report the previous March. RKO never once attempted to amend or supplement its earlier pleadings with the FCC, despite a growing awareness of the facts that General Tire would later admit in its Special Report. These instances involve a lack of candor through omission. Whether or not RKO would have had an obligation to come forward with these facts under other circumstances, it could not have doubted their relevance once the filings and petitions of the intervenors put these questions before the

Commission. We need not decide whether RKO's pleadings were affirmatively misleading—it is enough to find that they did not state the facts.

. . . It is . . . unnecessary to show that RKO officials had
actual knowledge in early 1976 of the improprieties and illegalities to
which General Tire later admitted, or that RKO officials willfully intended to misrepresent these facts to the FCC. Whether RKO sought to
protect its parent, or whether the parent withheld information from the
subsidiary in order to protect itself, the result is the same. We cannot
improve on the language of FCC counsel: "It is obvious that where a
complete disclosure of facts will militate against the interests of this
organization, the Commission will be deprived of that information. It is
irrelevant where in the RKO-General Tire organizational structure this
breakdown in candor first occurs. In the end, RKO, as the public
trustee, is responsible for the reliability of the information and representations furnished by it to the Commission." [   ]

[The court next addressed the various defenses asserted by RKO.
The lack of evidence that the Commission was in fact misled by RKO's
failure to disclose was found irrelevant since it was the attempt to
mislead that indicated a lack of fitness to hold the license. A claim that
RKO's actions were on advice of counsel was dismissed since it was long
settled that "advice of counsel cannot excuse a clear breach of duty by a
licensee." Finally, the court turned to the issue of whether RKO was
denied a hearing on the "lack of candor" issue. Given that the lack of
candor was clearly proven by documents submitted by RKO in the
renewal hearing itself, the court concluded that no purpose would be
served by holding a separate hearing on that issue.]

Our decision to affirm the FCC's action should not be read to include
situations not covered by this unique record. The Commission concedes
that "this case is unprecedented," [   ], and we expect that successors if
any will be rare. Before the FCC can take action of this sort in the
future, we believe that at least three conditions must be met in order to
protect the parties. First, not only must the misconduct occur directly
before the agency, but it should be of such a blatant and unacceptable
dimension that its existence cannot be denied. The FCC has satisfied
itself that this is the case with regard to RKO, whose lack of candor "is
abundantly clear." [   ] Second, although formal notice may not always
be necessary, it should be evident that the party has some form of actual
notice of the conduct said to be at issue, and must not be prejudiced by
surprise. Finally, the party must be given an "opportunity to speak in
[its] own behalf . . .." [   ] The procedure adopted by the FCC in this
case satisfies these requirements, at least insofar as the Boston renewal
is concerned. RKO does not contend that it was prejudiced by the lack
of notice, for it undoubtedly had actual notice of the candor issue, as the
pleadings filed prior to the Commission's decision demonstrate. [   ]
. . . RKO had a full opportunity to speak on its own behalf, and
exercised it in pleadings, proffers of proof, and oral argument before the
Commission. We cannot say that the FCC abused its discretion by not

giving RKO a formal hearing on issues arising from RKO's conduct during the initial proceeding. Section 309 was not intended by Congress to reward delay and concealment that disserves the public interest. "Congress did not intend by this section of the statute to require the formality of Commission consideration of and [re]hearing on an application in which the signatory obviously fails in major material respects to abide the regulations." [  ] ("We do not think Congress intended the Commission to waste time on applications that do not state a valid basis for a hearing.") The FCC's denial of the Boston license renewal must therefore be affirmed.

## IV. THE LOS ANGELES AND NEW YORK CITY PROCEEDINGS

The narrow basis of our decision concerning RKO's Boston license illustrates why the FCC may not deny license renewals in Los Angeles and New York City simply because it happened to condition those proceedings on the Boston outcome. RKO's lack of candor during the Boston proceeding justifies its disqualification there because the misconduct took place directly before the trier of fact and has bearing on its general character, but the same cannot be said of the Los Angeles and New York City proceedings. The latter was conditioned on the Boston outcome in order to avoid making the parties "relitigate those issues" that had already been specified with regard to Boston. [  ] By contrast, the former had been conditioned on the reciprocity issue only, in order to "enable the Commission to proceed with the Los Angeles matter and bring it to a conclusion with no risk to the public interest." RKO General, Inc. (KHJ–TV), 31 F.C.C.2d 70, 74 (1971). The FCC could not have known, when it conditioned either of these proceedings as it did, that the Boston outcome would turn on a lack of candor issue that had not even been designated in the Boston proceeding. RKO's misconduct did not occur directly before the trier of fact in either the Los Angeles or New York City proceedings. Accordingly, these decisions must be remanded to the Commission for further consideration as it deems appropriate.

.  .  .

## CONCLUSION

This opinion will not close a sorry chapter in the history of American communications law. We must remand the Los Angeles and New York City proceedings because the FCC has not yet provided a principled explanation for RKO's disqualification as a licensee of those stations. The FCC's findings that RKO intentionally misrepresented financial information and engaged in unlawful reciprocal trade practices cannot stand, for one was reached without notice or hearing and the other constitutes an ex post facto application of new standards to conduct that is long past.

We affirm the Commission's decision in the Boston proceeding, however, because the Commission's finding that RKO displayed an egregious lack of candor in that proceeding does not suffer from either of these infirmities. During an administrative review that had already lasted for years, the FCC suddenly was confronted by documentary evidence establishing beyond doubt that RKO had been less than candid with the Commission in the very proceeding under way. The FCC could observe all material facts for itself, simply by comparing the documents that had already been submitted with those that were now before it.

The denial of a license renewal to a major licensee in a major market is of manifest moment and financial impact. The FCC's decision has not been reviewed callously, and we have tried not to lose sight of the difficult issues in this case by sweeping the reasoning of the Commission under a rug of agency expertise or administrative convenience. The record presented to this court shows irrefutably that the licensee was playing the dodger to serious charges involving it and its parent company. The Commission was entitled to ask whether such conduct, however convenient for corporate purposes, was consistent with the candor required of an applicant for a license to the public airwaves. We believe the Commission's answer is not open to doubt. The disqualification of RKO as a licensee of WNAC in Boston is affirmed.

It is so ordered.

### Notes and Questions

1. While the New York proceeding was pending, Congress amended the Communications Act (adding § 331) to require that the Commission renew the license of any VHF licensee willing to relocate to a state with no commercial television stations. After RKO notified the FCC in September, 1982, that it would move WOR–TV from New York City to Secaucus, New Jersey, its license was renewed. RKO General, Inc. (WOR–TV), 53 R.R.2d 469 (1983). In addition, RKO was granted a temporary waiver of the main studio rule, which permitted the use of the station's existing New York studio facilities while the Commission's renewal order was on appeal. Otherwise, RKO would have been required to expend large sums of money on studio construction in New Jersey during a period when the station's relocation was uncertain. RKO General, Inc., 54 R.R.2d 853 (1983). The grant of the five-year license to RKO without a hearing, pursuant to § 331, was unanimously affirmed in Multi-State Communications, Inc. v. Federal Communications Commission, 728 F.2d 1519, 55 R.R.2d 911 (D.C.Cir.1984), certiorari denied, 469 U.S. ___ (1984).

2. In addition to WOR and KHJ, RKO owns one other TV station and twelve radio stations. In February, 1983, acting under an order from the court of appeals, the Commission started accepting competing applications for the other 13 RKO stations. Over 160 applications were filed. Initially, no action on these applications was to be taken until the character issue in the KHJ case was decided. In early 1985, however,

the Commission decided to start comparative proceedings among the applicants. As a result, by the time the character issue is resolved, there may be only one competing applicant for each license. Broadcasting, Mar. 4, 1985 at 75.

3. Compounding RKO's difficulties are allegations of fraud and over-billing by the two RKO radio networks. In 1984, RKO announced that there was truth to some of these allegations. Despite the subsequent sale of the networks to United Stations, the question of network fraud has been designated as an issue in the KHJ case.

4. In late 1985, Westinghouse Broadcast and Cable (Group W) agreed to purchase KHJ–TV from RKO for $313 million. Technically, the proposal calls for RKO to dismiss its application for renewal and sell KHJ's physical assets to Group W for $215 million. As a result of RKO's withdrawal of its application, Fidelity would be awarded the license. Fidelity would then sell its stock to Group W for $95 million. Group W would also pay Fidelity's current liabilities, approximately $3.25 million. Whether or not the transaction is approved, the hearings into RKO's qualifications to be a licensee are expected to continue. Broadcasting, Nov. 11, 1985 at 39.

### 3. HOSTILE TAKEOVERS OF CORPORATIONS

Up until now we have been looking at cases where the incumbent licensee wishes to transfer the license. Recently, the Commission has found itself faced with a different sort of problem: hostile takeovers of corporations with broadcast properties. The leading example was Ted Turner's unsuccessful attempt in early 1985 to take over CBS. How should the Commission treat cases like this?

What if existing shareholders wish to replace a corporation's board of directors? Does this constitute a transfer of control and, if so, is it the same as an attempt by outsiders to take over a corporation? The Commission faced this issue for the first time in Committee for Full Value of Storer Communications, Inc., 57 R.R.2d 1651 (1985). The Committee for Full Value of Storer Communications, Inc. was a group of dissident Storer stockholders who wished to sell all the assets of Storer and distribute the proceeds to the stockholders. Since the incumbent board of directors opposed this plan, the dissidents announced that they would stage a proxy contest to elect a board of directors that would implement their plan. The scheme raised several important questions for the Commission.

Under § 309(b) of the Communications Act, applications for a trans-fer of control of a broadcast licensee are subject to a public notice requirement and a 30-day waiting period. The purpose of these require-ments is to give members of the public who feel that the proposed transfer is not in the public interest an opportunity to file a petition to deny. However, § 309(c) contains an exception to these requirements for cases where the transfer of control is not substantial. Thus, the Commission had to determine whether election of a new board of directors, absent any significant change in stock ownership, constitutes a transfer of control, and if so is it a substantial transfer of control.

The Mass Media Bureau concluded that ownership of the corporation resides in the stockholders, and thus there is no transfer of control, substantial or otherwise. The Commission disagreed, holding that electing a new board of directors is a transfer of control, but since the ultimate control of any corporation rests with the stockholders, the transfer of control is not a substantial one. The practical effect of this decision was that the Committee did have to file an application for transfer of control, but the application was not subject to the public notice and 30-day waiting period requirements.

The Commission's decision was affirmed on appeal. The court of appeals reasoned that the Commission had not abused its discretion in resolving a case with competing policy considerations. Although a change in directors might indeed result in a major change in the working control of the corporation, determining what constitutes a "substantial" change was a complex task best resolved by the Commission. Also, there was the danger that requiring public notice and a 30-day waiting period in any such proxy fight would allow incumbent boards of directors to use the Commission to insulate them from challenges since the added delay and cost that would occur might well discourage such challenges. Storer Communications, Inc. v. Federal Communications Commission, 58 R.R.2d 244 (D.C.Cir.1985).

Despite the favorable ruling, the Committee for Full Value of Storer Communications, Inc. was unable to elect a majority of the board of directors.

In January, 1986, the Commission decided to affirm its previous policies with regard to takeovers. When a proxy fight involves a majority of the seats on the board of directors, an application must be filed with the Commission, but the notice and 30-day waiting period requirements will not apply. In the case of hostile takeover attempts, notice and a 30-day waiting period prior to approval will be required. However, a special temporary authorization will be issued allowing the takeover attempt to proceed subject to a subsequent full review.

# Chapter V

## MEDIA CONCENTRATION

As we saw when considering the NBC case, the Commission has long been concerned about excessive concentration of control over the process of deciding what programs to present. There are several ways to attack the problem. One, utilized in that case, is to prevent the networks from imposing their power on the licensees. Another is to order licensees to obtain their programs from non-network sources for certain periods of the day. Still another, which gets at this problem indirectly but also attacks other problems, is to attempt to diversify the ownership of broadcast facilities. In this Chapter we consider these various methods of limiting concentration of control.

The Commission has used its rulemaking powers primarily to handle technical and engineering matters, which can be addressed in quantitative terms—and which are more likely to lend themselves to uniform treatment without the need for exceptions.

The Commission has also used rulemaking to achieve diversity of control—again perhaps because the material lends itself to quantitative expression, such as how many stations a person should be allowed to control in a particular area. It is important to realize, however, that even though the Commission may choose to adopt specific rules to meet a problem, it must always consider requests for waivers of that rule if the public interest would be furthered by the waiver. The 1934 Act grants the Commission powers to act in the public interest and, although a rule may operate in the public interest most of the time, some exceptions may be in the public interest.

In 1980, for example, a radio station licensee in Alaska sought a license for a vacant television channel in the same community. A rule barred the same licensee from controlling radio and VHF stations in the same community. The community had three vacant VHF frequencies. If the FCC adhered to its rule, the community might not get any television service for several years. The Commission granted a waiver of its rule to meet the needs of the situation.

Note, however, that the Commission might be able to argue in some situations that the overriding public interest may be better served by rigorous adherence to a firm rule that all know will be followed, than by granting waivers that seriously undercut the thrust of a vitally important main rule.

## A.  LOCAL CONCENTRATION

---

### 1.  DUOPOLY

Local concentration of control of mass media facilities has been a problem for the Commission at least since 1938, when it received an application for a standard broadcasting station in Flint, Michigan, from applicants who already controlled another corporation that operated a standard broadcasting station in the same area.  Although there were no rival applicants, the Commission refused to grant the second facility without a compelling showing that the public interest would be served in such a situation.

This was the beginning of the so-called "duopoly" rule, which the Commission formalized in a general rule that it would not grant a license to any applicant who already held a similar facility or license so located that the service areas of the two would overlap.

In the 1960's, the Commission returned to this subject and recognized that the dwindling number of American newspapers made the impact of individual broadcasting stations "significantly greater."  This reinforced the need for diversity in the broadcast media and led the Commission to announce that it would never again grant a duopoly.

During this period, however, the Commission was granting to the same applicant one AM, one FM and one television station in the same locality because this was not a duplication of facilities in the same service area.  In 1970, the Commission moved the next step and proposed the "one-to-a-customer" rule.  In the Matter of the Rules Relating to Multiple Ownership, 22 F.C.C.2d 306, 18 R.R.2d 1735 (1970).  Under this rule licensees would be limited to one broadcast station in any given market, regardless of the type of broadcast service involved.  The Commission viewed this as a logical extension of its earlier diversification rules:

> 21.  Application of the principles set forth above dictates that one person should not be licensed to operate more than one broadcast station in the same place, and serving substantially the same public, unless some other relevant public interest consideration is found to outweigh the importance of diversifying control.  It is elementary that the number of frequencies available for licensing is limited.  In any particular area there may be many voices that would like to be heard, but not all can be licensed.  A proper objective is the maximum diversity of ownership that technology permits in each area.  We are of the view that 60 different licensees are more desirable than 50, and even that 51 are more desirable than 50.  In a rapidly changing social climate, communication of ideas is vital.  If a city has 60 frequencies available but they are licensed to only 50 different licensees, the number of sources for ideas is not maximized.  It might be the 51st licensee that would become the communication channel for a solution to a severe social crisis.  No one can

say that present licensees are broadcasting everything worthwhile that can be communicated. We see no existing public interest reason for being wedded to our present policy that permits a licensee to acquire more than one station in the same area.

The Commission rejected an argument "that the good profit position of a multiple owner in the same market results in more in-depth informational programs being broadcast and thus, in more meaningful diversity. We do not doubt that some multiple owners may have a greater capacity to so program, but the record does not demonstrate that they generally do so. The citations and honors for exceptional programming appear to be continually awarded to a very few licensees—perhaps a dozen or so multiple owners out of a total of hundreds of such owners."

The Commission was persuaded, however, that UHF stations presented a special problem in that they were still weak competitively and few would go on the air unless affiliated with an established radio station. Therefore, the Commission refused to adopt a firm rule against radio-UHF combinations but again indicated that it would review those on a case-by-case basis. Finally, the Commission announced that the rules would be prospective only and no divestitures would be required, due to the large number of existing combinations and a sense that ordering divestiture for such a large group might very well create instability.

The rules as originally adopted would have banned not only VHF-radio combinations, but also AM–FM combinations, even though traditionally FM had been weak as a competitive force and indeed the Commission during the 1950's had encouraged AM stations to acquire FM stations. On reconsideration the Commission decided that although FM stations were becoming more powerful competitors and increasingly profitable, most AM–FM combinations might still be "economically and/or technically interdependent." Concerned that the rules as originally adopted might hinder the development of FM service, the FCC modified them to permit the formation of new AM–FM combinations. Multiple Ownership of Standard, FM and TV Broadcast Stations, 28 F.C.C.2d 662, 21 R.R.2d 1551 (1971). Thus, only VHF-radio combinations were banned by the new rules.

## 2. CROSSOWNERSHIP

When the Commission adopted its one-to-a-customer rules, it also proposed the adoption of another set of rules that would proscribe common ownership of newspapers and broadcast facilities serving the same area, and require divestiture of prohibited combinations. Although the Commission had flirted with such a regulation in the early 1940's, it had abandoned the attempt. The basis for the Commission movement in 1970 was an awareness that 94 television stations were affiliated through common control with newspapers in the same city. In addition, of course, "some newspapers own television stations in other cities, which also serve the city in which the newspaper is located." The

Commission thought this situation was very similar to the joint ownership of two television stations in the same community, something the
Commission has never permitted. "The functions of newspapers and
television stations as journalists are so similar that their joint ownership
is, in this respect, essentially the same as the joint ownership of two
television stations." After extensive consideration, the Commission
adopted rules in 1975 that prohibit granting a license for a television or
radio station to any applicant who already controls, owns, or operates a
daily newspaper serving part of the same area.

## FEDERAL COMMUNICATIONS COMMISSION v. NATIONAL CITIZENS COMMITTEE FOR BROADCASTING

Supreme Court of the United States, 1978.
436 U.S. 775, 98 S.Ct. 2096, 56 L.Ed.2d 697.

MR. JUSTICE MARSHALL delivered the opinion of the Court.

. . .

### I

### A

. . .

In setting its licensing policies, the Commission has long acted on
the theory that diversification of mass media ownership serves the public
interest by promoting diversity of program and service viewpoints, as
well as by preventing undue concentration of economic power. See, *e.g.,*
*Multiple Ownership of Standard, FM and Television Broadcast Sta-
tions,* 45 F.C.C. 1476, 1476–1477 (1964). . . .

. . .

Diversification of ownership has not been the sole consideration
thought relevant to the public interest, however. The Commission's
other, and sometimes conflicting, goal has been to ensure "the best
practicable service to the public." [ ] To achieve this goal, the
Commission has weighed factors such as the anticipated contribution of
the owner to station operations, the proposed program service, and the
past broadcast record of the applicant—in addition to diversification of
ownership—in making initial comparative licensing decisions. [ ]
Moreover, the Commission has given considerable weight to a policy of
avoiding undue disruption of existing service. As a result, newspaper
owners in many instances have been able to acquire broadcast licenses
for stations serving the same communities as their newspapers, and the
Commission has repeatedly renewed such licenses on findings that continuation of the service offered by the common owner would serve the
public interest. [ ]

### B

Against this background, the Commission began the instant
rulemaking proceeding in 1970 to consider the need for a more restrictive

policy toward newspaper ownership of radio and television broadcast stations. [ ] Citing studies showing the dominant role of television stations and daily newspapers as sources of local news and other information, [ ], the notice of rulemaking proposed adoption of regulations that would eliminate all newspaper-broadcast combinations serving the same market, by prospectively banning formation or transfer of such combinations and requiring dissolution of all existing combinations within five years, [ ]. The Commission suggested that the proposed regulations would serve "the purpose of promoting competition among the mass media involved, and maximizing diversification of service sources and viewpoints." [ ] At the same time, however, the Commission expressed "substantial concern" about the disruption of service that might result from divestiture of existing combinations. [ ] . . .
. . .

. . . While recognizing the pioneering contributions of newspaper owners to the broadcast industry, the Commission concluded that changed circumstances made it possible, and necessary, for all new licensing of broadcast stations to "be expected to add to local diversity." [ ] In reaching this conclusion, the Commission did not find that existing co-located newspaper-broadcast combinations had not served the public interest, or that such combinations necessarily "spea[k] with one voice" or are harmful to competition. [ ] In the Commission's view, the conflicting studies submitted by the parties concerning the effects of newspaper ownership on competition and station performance were inconclusive, and no pattern of specific abuses by existing cross-owners was demonstrated. [ ] The prospective rules were justified, instead, by reference to the Commission's policy of promoting diversification of ownership: Increases of diversification of ownership would possibly result in enhanced diversity of viewpoints, and, given the absence of persuasive countervailing considerations, "even a small gain in diversity" was "worth pursuing." [ ]

With respect to the proposed across-the-board divestiture requirement, however, the Commission concluded that "a mere hoped-for gain in diversity" was not a sufficient justification, [ ]. Characterizing the divestiture issues as "the most difficult" presented in the proceeding, the Order explained that the proposed rules, while correctly recognizing the central importance of diversity considerations, "may have given too little weight to the consequences which could be expected to attend a focus on the abstract goal alone." [ ] Forced dissolution would promote diversity, but it would also cause "disruption for the industry and hardship for individual owners," "resulting in losses or diminution of service to the public." [ ]

The Commission concluded that in light of these countervailing considerations divestiture was warranted only in "the most egregious cases," which it identified as those in which a newspaper-broadcast combination has an "effective monopoly" in the local "marketplace of ideas as well as economically." [ ] The Commission recognized that any standards for defining which combinations fell within that category would necessarily be arbitrary to some degree, but "[a] choice had to be made." [   ] It thus decided to require divestiture only where there was common ownership of the sole daily newspaper published in a community and either (1) the sole broadcast station providing that entire community with a clear signal, or (2) the sole television station encompassing the entire community with a clear signal. [   ]

The Order identified 8 television-newspaper and 10 radio-newspaper combinations meeting the divestiture criteria. [   ] Waivers of the divestiture requirement were granted *sua sponte* to 1 television and 1 radio combination, leaving a total of 16 stations subject to divestiture. The Commission explained that waiver requests would be entertained in the latter cases, but, absent waiver, either the newspaper or the broadcast station would have to be divested by January 1, 1980, [   ].

. . .

## C

. . .

. . . the Court of Appeals affirmed the prospective ban on new licensing of co-located newspaper-broadcast combinations, but vacated the limited divestiture rules, and ordered the Commission to adopt regulations requiring dissolution of all existing combinations that did not qualify for a waiver under the procedure outlined in the order. [The court concluded that the Commission had no rational basis for banning prospective combinations while grandfathering most existing combinations. The court was also unable to find a rational basis for distinguishing between the 16 egregious cases that had to be divested and the remaining grandfathered combinations. The Commission, NAB, ANPA and some of the cross-owners who had been grandfathered under the Commission's order petitioned the Supreme Court for review.]

## II

. . .

## A

Section 303(r) of the Communications Act, [   ], provides that "the Commission from time to time, as public convenience, interest, or necessity requires, shall . . . [m]ake such rules and regulations and prescribe such restrictions and conditions, not inconsistent with law, as may be necessary to carry out the provisions of [the Act]." [   ] As the Court of Appeals recognized, [   ], it is now well established that this general rulemaking authority supplies a statutory basis for the Commission to enact regulations codifying its view of the public interest licensing standard, so long as that view is based on consideration of permissible factors and is otherwise reasonable. If a license applicant does not qualify under standards set forth in such regulations, and does not proffer sufficient grounds for waiver or change of those standards, the Commission may deny the application without further inquiry. [  ]

This Court has specifically upheld this rulemaking authority in the context of regulations based on the Commission's policy of promoting diversification of ownership. In United States v. Storer Broadcasting Co., [  ], we sustained the portion of the Commission's multiple owner-ship rules placing limitations on the total number of stations in each broadcast service a person may own or control. [  ] And in National Broadcasting Co. v. United States, [  ], we affirmed regulations that, *inter alia*, prohibited broadcast networks from owning more than one AM radio station in the same community, and from owning " 'any standard broadcast station in any locality where the existing standard broadcast stations are so few or of such unequal desirability . . . that competition would be substantially restrained by such licensing.' " [  ]

Petitioner NAB attempts to distinguish these cases on the ground that they involved efforts to increase diversification within the bounda-ries of the broadcasting industry itself, whereas the instant regulations are concerned with diversification of ownership in the mass communica-tions media as a whole. NAB contends that, since the Act confers jurisdiction on the Commission only to regulate "communication by wire or radio," 47 U.S.C. § 152(a), it is impermissible for the Commission to use its licensing authority with respect to broadcasting to promote diversity in an overall communications market which includes, but is not limited to, the broadcasting industry.

This argument undersells the Commission's power to regulate broad-casting in the "public interest." In making initial licensing decisions between competing applicants, the Commission has long given "primary significance" to "diversification of control of the media of mass commu-nications," and has denied licenses to newspaper owners on the basis of this policy in appropriate cases. [  ] As we have discussed on several occasions, [  ], the physical scarcity of broadcast frequencies, as well as problems of interference between broadcast signals, led Congress to delegate broad authority to the Commission to allocate broadcast licenses in the "public interest." And "[t]he avowed aim of the Communications Act of 1934 was to secure the maximum benefits of radio to all the people of the United States." [  ] It was not inconsistent with the statutory scheme, therefore, for the Commission to conclude that the maximum benefit to the "public interest" would follow from allocation of broadcast licenses so as to promote diversification of the mass media as a whole.

Our past decisions have recognized, moreover, that the First Amend-ment and antitrust values underlying the Commission's diversification policy may properly be considered by the Commission in determining where the public interest lies. "[T]he 'public interest' standard necessar-ily invites reference to First Amendment principles," Columbia Broad-casting System, Inc. v. Democratic National Committee, 412 U.S. 94, 122 (1973), and, in particular, to the First Amendment goal of achieving "the

widest possible dissemination of information from diverse and antagonistic sources," Associated Press v. United States, supra, 326 U.S., at 20.
See Red Lion Broadcasting Co. v. FCC, supra, at 385, 390. See also
United States v. Midwest Video Corp., 406 U.S. 649, 667–669, and n. 27
(1972) (plurality opinion). And, while the Commission does not have
power to enforce the antitrust laws as such, it is permitted to take
antitrust policies into account in making licensing decisions pursuant to
the public interest standard. See, e.g., United States v. Radio Corp. of
America, 358 U.S. 334, 351 (1959); National Broadcasting Co. v. United
States, supra, at 222–224. . . .

### (2)

It is thus clear that the regulations at issue are based on permissible
public interest goals and, so long as the regulations are not an unreasonable means for seeking to achieve these goals, they fall within the
general rulemaking authority recognized in the *Storer Broadcasting* and
*National Broadcasting* cases. Petitioner ANPA contends that the
prospective rules are unreasonable in two respects: first, the rulemaking
record did not conclusively establish that prohibiting common ownership
of co-located newspapers and broadcast stations would in fact lead to
increases in the diversity of viewpoints among local communications
media; and second, the regulations were based on the diversification
factor to the exclusion of other service factors considered in the past by
the Commission in making initial licensing decisions regarding newspaper owners, [  ]. With respect to the first point we agree with the Court
of Appeals that, notwithstanding the inconclusiveness of the rulemaking
record, the Commission acted rationally in finding that diversification of
ownership would enhance the possibility of achieving greater diversity of
viewpoints. As the Court of Appeals observed, "[d]iversity and its
effects are . . . elusive concepts, not easily defined let alone measured
without making qualitative judgments objectionable on both policy and
First Amendment grounds." [  ] Moreover, evidence of specific abuses
by common owners is difficult to compile; "the possible benefits of
competition do not lend themselves to specific forecast." [  ] In these
circumstances, the Commission was entitled to rely on its judgment,
based on experience, that "it is unrealistic to expect true diversity from a
commonly owned station-newspaper combination. The divergency of
their viewpoints cannot be expected to be the same as if they were
antagonistically run." [  ]

As to the Commission's decision to give controlling weight to its
diversification goal in shaping the prospective rules, the Order makes
clear that this change in policy was a reasonable administrative response
to changed circumstances in the broadcasting industry. [  ] The Order
explained that, although newspaper owners had previously been allowed,
and even encouraged to acquire licenses for co-located broadcast stations
because of the shortage of qualified license applicants, a sufficient
number of qualified and experienced applicants other than newspaper
owners was now readily available. In addition, the number of channels

open for new licensing had diminished substantially. It had thus become both feasible and more urgent for the Commission to take steps to increase diversification of ownership, and a change in the Commission's policy toward new licensing offered the possibility of increasing diversity without causing any disruption of existing service. In light of these considerations, the Commission clearly did not take an irrational view of the public interest when it decided to impose a prospective ban on new licensing of co-located newspaper-broadcast combinations.

### B

Petitioners NAB and ANPA also argue that the regulations, though designed to further the First Amendment goal of achieving "the widest possible dissemination of information from diverse and antagonistic sources," Associated Press v. United States, supra, 326 U.S. at 20, nevertheless violate the First Amendment rights of newspaper owners. We cannot agree, for this argument ignores the fundamental proposition that there is no "unabridgeable First Amendment right to broadcast comparable to the right of every individual to speak, write, or publish." Red Lion Broadcasting Co. v. FCC, supra, 395 U.S. at 388.

. . .

In the instant case, far from seeking to limit the flow of information, the Commission has acted, in the Court of Appeals' words, "to enhance the diversity of information heard by the public without ongoing government surveillance of the content of speech." [ ] The regulations are a reasonable means of promoting the public interest in diversified mass communications; thus they do not violate the First Amendment rights of those who will be denied broadcast licenses pursuant to them. Being forced to "choose among applicants for the same facilities," the Commission has chosen on a "sensible basis," one designed to further, rather than contravene, "the system of freedom of expression." T. Emerson, The System of Freedom of Expression 663 (1970).

### III

After upholding the prospective aspect of the Commission's regulations, the Court of Appeals concluded that the Commission's decision to limit divestiture to 16 "egregious cases" of "effective monopoly" was arbitrary and capricious within the meaning of the Administrative Procedure Act (APA), § 10(e), 5 U.S.C. § 706(2)(A). We agree with the Court of Appeals that regulations promulgated after informal rulemaking . . . may be invalidated by a reviewing court under the "arbitrary or capricious" standard if they are not rational and based on consideration of the relevant factors. [ ] Although this review "is to be searching and careful, [t]he court is not empowered to substitute its judgment for that of the agency." [ ]

In the view of the Court of Appeals, the Commission lacked a rational basis, first, for treating existing newspaper-broadcast combinations more leniently than combinations that might seek licenses in the future; and, new combinations had been justified, for requiring divestiture in the "egregious cases" while allowing all other existing combinations to continue in operation. We believe that the limited divestiture requirement reflects a rational weighing of competing policies, and we therefore reinstate the portion of the Commission's order that was invalidated by the Court of Appeals.

A

(1)

The Commission was well aware that separating existing newspaper-broadcast combinations would promote diversification of ownership. It concluded, however, that ordering widespread divestiture would not result in "the best practicable service to the American public," [ ], a goal that the Commission has always taken into account and that has been specifically approved by this Court, FCC v. Sanders Bros. Radio Station, 309 U.S. 470, 475 (1940); [ ]. In particular, the Commission expressed concern that divestiture would cause "disruption for the industry" and "hardship to individual owners," both of which would result in harm to the public interest. Order, at 1078. Especially in light of the fact that the number of co-located newspaper-broadcast combinations was already on the decline as a result of the prospective rules, the Commission decided that across-the-board divestiture was not warranted. [ ]

The Order identified several specific respects in which the public interest would or might be harmed if a sweeping divestiture requirement were imposed: the stability and continuity of meritorious service provided by the newspaper owners as a group would be lost; owners who had provided meritorious service would unfairly be denied the opportunity to continue in operation; "economic dislocations" might prevent new owners from obtaining sufficient working capital to maintain the quality of local programming; and local ownership of broadcast stations would probably decrease. [ ] We cannot say that the Commission acted irrationally in concluding that these public interest harms outweighed the potential gains that would follow from increasing diversification of ownership.

In the past, the Commission has consistently acted on the theory that preserving continuity of meritorious service furthers the public interest, both in its direct consequence of bringing proven broadcast service to the public, and in its indirect consequence of rewarding—and avoiding losses to—licensees who have invested the money and effort necessary to produce quality performance. Thus, although a broadcast license must be renewed every three years, and the licensee must satisfy the Commission that renewal will serve the public interest, both the Commission and the courts have recognized that a licensee who has given meritorious service has a "legitimate renewal expectanc[y]" and should not be destroyed absent good cause. [ ] Accordingly, while diversification of ownership is a relevant factor in the context of license renewal as well as initial licensing, the Commission has long considered the past performance of the incumbent as the most important factor in deciding whether to grant license renewal and thereby to allow the existing owner to continue in operation. Even where an incumbent is challenged by a competing applicant who offers greater potential in terms of diversification, the Commission's general practice has been to go with the "proven product" and grant renewal if the incumbent has rendered meritorious service. [　] In the instant proceeding, the Commission specifically noted that the existing newspaper-broadcast cross-owners as a group had a "long record of service" from the outset. [　] Notwithstanding the Commission's diversification policy, all were granted initial licenses upon findings that the public interest would be served thereby, and those that had been in existence for more than three years had also had their licenses renewed on the ground that the public interest would be furthered. The Commission noted, moreover, that in terms of percentage of time devoted to several categories of local programming, these stations had displayed "an undramatic but nonetheless statistically significant superiority" over other television stations. [　] An across-the-board divestiture requirement would result in loss of the services of these superior licensees, and—whether divestiture caused actual losses to existing owners, or just denial of reasonably anticipated gains—the result would be that future licensees would be discouraged from investing the resources necessary to produce quality service.

At the same time, there was no guarantee that the licensees who replaced the existing cross-owners would be able to provide the same level of service or demonstrate the same longterm commitment to broadcasting. And even if the new owners were able in the long run to provide similar or better service, the Commission found that divestiture would cause serious disruption in the transition period. Thus, the Commission observed that new owners "would lack the long knowledge of the community and would have to begin raw," and—because of high interest rates—might not be able to obtain sufficient working capital to maintain the quality of local programming. [　]

The Commission's fear that local ownership would decline was grounded in a rational prediction, based on its knowledge of the broadcasting industry and supported by comments in the record, [　], that many of the existing newspaper-broadcast combinations owned by local interests would respond to the divestiture requirement by trading stations with out-of-town owners. It is undisputed that roughly 75% of the existing co-located newspaper-television combinations are locally owned, [　], and these owners' knowledge of their local communities and concern for local affairs, built over a period of years, would be lost if they were replaced with outside interests. Local ownership in and of itself has been recognized to be a factor of some—if relatively slight—significance even in the context of initial licensing decisions. [　] It was not unreasonable, therefore, for the Commission to consider it as one of several factors militating against divestiture of combinations that have been in existence for many years.

In light of these countervailing considerations, we cannot agree with the Court of Appeals that it was arbitrary and capricious for the Commission to "grandfather" most existing combinations, and to leave opponents of these combinations to their remedies in individual renewal proceedings. In the latter connection we note that, while individual renewal proceedings are unlikely to accomplish any "overall restructuring" of the existing ownership patterns, the Order does make clear that existing combinations will be subject to challenge by competing applicants in renewal proceedings, to the same extent as they were prior to the instant rulemaking proceedings. [  ]  That is, diversification of ownership will be a relevant but somewhat secondary factor. And, even in the absence of a competing applicant, license renewal may be denied if, *inter alia*, a challenger can show that a common owner has engaged in specific economic or programming abuses. [  ]

(2)

In concluding that the Commission acted unreasonably in not extending its divestiture requirement across-the-board, the Court of Appeals apparently placed heavy reliance on a "presumption" that existing newspaper-broadcast combinations "do not serve the public interest." [  ] The Court derived this presumption primarily from the Commission's own diversification policy, as "reaffirmed" by adoption of the prospective rules in this proceeding, and secondarily from "[t]he policies of the First Amendment," [  ], and the Commission's statutory duty to "encourage the larger and more effective use of radio in the public interest." 47 U.S.C. § 303(g). As explained in Part II above, we agree that diversification of ownership furthers statutory and constitutional policies, and, as the Commission recognized, separating existing newspaper-broadcast combinations would promote diversification. But the weighing of policies under the "public interest" standard is a task that Congress has delegated to the Commission in the first instance, and we are unable to find anything in the Communications Act, the First Amendment, or the Commission's past or present practices that would require the Commission to "presume" that its diversification policy should be given controlling weight in all circumstances.

Such a "presumption" would seem to be inconsistent with the Commission's long-standing and judicially approved practice of giving controlling weight in some circumstances to its more general goal of achieving "the best practicable service to the public." Certainly, as discussed in Part III–A(1) above, the Commission through its license renewal policy has made clear that it considers diversification of ownership to be a factor of less significance when deciding whether to allow an existing licensee to continue in operation than when evaluating applicants seeking initial licensing. Nothing in the language or the legislative history of § 303(g) indicates that Congress intended to foreclose all differences in treatment between new and existing licensees, and indeed, in amending § 307(d) of the Act in 1952, Congress appears to have lent its approval to the Commission's policy of evaluating existing licensees on a somewhat different basis than new applicants. Moreover, if enactment of the prospective rules in this proceeding itself were deemed to create a "presumption" in favor of divestiture, the Commission's ability to experiment with new policies would be severely hampered. One of the most significant advantages of the administrative process is its ability to adapt to new circumstances in a flexible manner, [ ], and we are unwilling to presume that the Commission acts unreasonably when it decides to try out a change in licensing policy primarily on a prospective basis.

The Court of Appeals also relied on its perception that the policies militating against divestiture were "lesser policies" to which the Commission had not given as much weight in the past as its divestiture policy. [ ] This perception is subject to much the same criticism as the "presumption" that existing co-located newspaper-broadcast combinations do not serve the public interest. The Commission's past concern with avoiding disruption of existing service is amply illustrated by its license renewal policies. In addition, it is worth noting that in the past when the Commission has changed its multiple ownership rules it has almost invariably tailored the changes so as to operate wholly or primarily on a prospective basis. . . .

The Court of Appeals apparently reasoned that the Commission's concerns with respect to disruption of existing service, economic dislocations, and decreases in local ownership necessarily could not be very weighty since the Commission has a practice of routinely approving voluntary transfers and assignments of licenses. [ ] But the question of whether the Commission should compel proven licensees to divest their stations is a different question from whether the public interest is served by allowing transfers by licensees who no longer wish to continue in the business. . . .

The Court of Appeals' final basis for concluding that the Commission acted arbitrarily in not giving controlling weight to its divestiture policy was the Court's finding that the rulemaking record did not adequately "disclose the extent to which divestiture would actually threaten" the competing policies relied upon by the Commission, [ ]. However, to the extent that factual determinations were involved in the Commission's decision to grandfather most existing combinations, they were primarily of a judgmental or predictive nature—e.g., whether a divestiture requirement would result in trading of stations with out-of-town owners; whether new owners would perform as well as existing cross-owners, either in the short run or in the long run; whether losses to existing owners would result from forced sales; whether such losses would discourage future investment in quality programming; and whether new owners would have sufficient working capital to finance local programming. In such circumstances complete factual support in the record for the Commission's judgment or prediction is not possible or required; "a forecast of the direction in which future public interest lies necessarily involves deductions based on the expert knowledge of the agency." [    ]

B

We also must conclude that the Court of Appeals erred in holding that it was arbitrary to order divestiture in the 16 "egregious cases" while allowing other existing combinations to continue in operation. The Commission's decision was based not—as the Court of Appeals may have believed, [    ]—on a conclusion that divestiture would be more harmful in the grandfathered markets than in the 16 affected markets, but rather on a judgment that the need for diversification was especially great in cases of local monopoly. This policy judgment was certainly not irrational, [    ], and indeed was founded on the very same assumption that underpinned the diversification policy itself and the prospective rules upheld by the Court of Appeals and now by this Court—that the greater the number of owners in a market, the greater the possibility of achieving diversity of program and service viewpoints.

As to the Commission's criteria for determining which existing newspaper-broadcast combinations have an "effective monopoly" in the "local marketplace of ideas as well as economically," we think the standards settled upon by the Commission reflect a rational legislative-type judgment. Some line had to be drawn, and it was hardly unreasonable for the Commission to confine divestiture to communities in which there is common ownership of the only daily newspaper and either the only television station or the only broadcast station of any kind encompassing the entire community with a clear signal. [    ] It was not irrational, moreover, for the Commission to disregard media sources other than newspapers and broadcast stations in setting its divestiture standards. The studies cited by the Commission in its notice of rulemaking unanimously concluded that newspapers and television are the two most widely utilized media sources for local news and discussion of public affairs; and, as the Commission noted in its Order, [    ], "aside from the fact that [magazines and other periodicals] often had only a tiny fraction in the market, they were not given real weight since they often dealt exclusively with regional or national issues and ignored local issues." Moreover, the differences in treatment between radio and television stations, [    ], were certainly justified in light of the far greater influence of television than radio as a source for local news. [    ]

The judgment of the Court of Appeals is affirmed in part and reversed in part.

It is so ordered.

MR. JUSTICE BRENNAN took no part in the consideration or decision of these cases.

## Notes and Questions

1. As in *WNCN Listeners Guild*, the primary issue in this case is the scope of the appellate court's power to review Commission decisions.

How does the Supreme Court's view of this differ from the appellate court's?

2. During the time between the appellate court decision and the Supreme Court decision, *The Washington Post* and the *Detroit Evening News* exchanged their locally-owned television stations to achieve compliance with the crossownership rule. If most crossowners had engaged in similar swaps, would divestiture have accomplished its goals? As the Supreme Court noted, one obvious effect of such transactions would be to reduce local ownership of broadcast stations.

3. The Commission has also established limitations on broadcast-cable crossownership. We will discuss these in Chapter IX.

## B. NATIONAL CONCENTRATION

The Commission has proven equally concerned about the effects of concentration of ownership across different markets. Are the issues raised by national concentration different from those presented by local concentration? How is the marketplace of ideas in one city affected by a company's media holdings in other cities? Are there any potential benefits of a company owning stations in other communities?

### 1. MULTIPLE OWNERSHIP RULES

Beginning in 1940, the Commission adopted rules limiting the number of stations that might be held by a single owner. In 1953, the Commission resolved that the rules should prohibit the ownership or control, directly or indirectly, by any party of more than seven AM stations, seven FM stations, and seven television stations of which not more than five could be VHF. The Commission explained its position as follows:

> The vitality of our system of broadcasting depends in large part on the introduction into this field of licensees who are prepared and qualified to serve the varied and divergent needs of the public for radio service. Simply stated, the fundamental purpose of this facet of the multiple ownership rules is to promote diversification of ownership in order to maximize diversification of program and service viewpoints as well as to prevent any undue concentration of economic power contrary to the public interest. In this connection, we wish to emphasize that by such rules diversification of program services is furthered without any governmental encroachment on what we recognize to be the prime responsibility of the broadcast licensee. (See Section 326 of the Communications Act.) . . .

The Commission chose an equal number of AM and FM stations because at that time 538 of the 600 FM stations were owned by AM licensees, the result of a conscious Commission policy to encourage AM stations to put FM stations on the air since most of those operating FM stations alone were finding it extremely unprofitable. The number seven was chosen "in order that present holdings of such stations be not unduly disrupted." Very few owners had holdings in excess of seven, and the Commission planned to hold a divestiture hearing for each of them. Rules and Regulations Relating to Multiple Ownership, 18 F.C.C. 288 (1953).

This limitation rule was challenged immediately by a group owner who claimed that the Commission was illegally using the rulemaking procedure to foreclose the right of an applicant to a hearing as to whether the license would be in the public interest, by making a categorical judgment linking the public interest with a given maximum concentration of holdings. The rules were upheld in United States v. Storer Broadcasting Co., 351 U.S. 192 (1956). The Court rejected Storer's argument that § 309 of the Communications Act always requires a full hearing to determine whether granting additional licenses to the applicant would be in the public interest:

> We do not read the hearing requirement, however, as withdrawing from the power of the Commission the rule-making authority necessary for the orderly conduct of its business. As conceded by Storer, "Section 309(b) does not require the Commission to hold a hearing before denying a license to operate a station in ways contrary to those that the Congress has determined are in the public interest." The challenged Rules contain limitations against licensing not specifically authorized by statute. But that is not the limit of the Commission's rulemaking authority.
>
> This Commission, like other agencies, deals with the public interest. [  ] Its authority covers new and rapidly developing fields. Congress sought to create regulation for public protection with careful provision to assure fair opportunity for open competition in the use of broadcasting facilities. Accordingly, we cannot interpret § 309(b) as barring rules that declare a present intent to limit the number of stations consistent with a permissible "concentration of control." It is but a rule that announces the Commission's attitude on public protection against such concentration. . . .

The opinion did state, however, that the Commission's responsibility to behave in the public interest required it to grant a hearing to an applicant who had already reached the maximum number of stations but nonetheless asserted sufficient reasons why the rule should be waived in its particular case.

In early 1984, the Commission voted to expand the limits on multiple ownership from 7–7–7 to 12–12–12 with a six-year sunsetting provision (eliminating the rules entirely at the end of six years). The new rule made no distinction between VHF and UHF television. Faced with mounting criticism of the new rule and threatened Congressional action, the Commission delayed implementation of the television portion of the order and reconsidered it. The revised order contained several new provisions:

> 33. After reviewing the petitions for reconsideration filed in this proceeding, we now find it appropriate to modify certain aspects

of our Report and Order.  In this regard, we now find our modification of the rule should be revised to better account for the effect that this relaxation will have on population penetration.  We also find that the Report and Order should be revised to take cognizance of the limitations inherent in UHF broadcasting and to promote our traditional policy of facilitating minority ownership.  In addition, we find that a more appropriate approach is to eliminate the automatic sunset provision contained in our previous decision.

.  .  .

36.  On reconsideration, we have become increasingly aware of the limitations of proceeding solely with a numerical multiple ownership limit in the event that there is a rapid expansion of group ownership in the wake of our relaxing of the national multiple ownership rules.  As various parties have argued throughout this proceeding, a numerical approach may not give appropriate consideration to wide discrepancies in population coverage because a station in the largest market is deemed equivalent to a station in the smallest market for purposes of ownership regulation.  As a consequence, relaxing the numerical cap from seven stations to twelve stations may provide an opportunity for a single group owner to increase its audience base substantially, particularly if acquisitions are made in the largest markets.  A numerical cap does not affect this type of restructuring.  While there is no evidence in the record that would lead us to believe that such an eventuality would necessarily have an adverse result, we now believe that the potential for this type of restructuring warrants a more cautious approach.  To this extent, we now believe it is advisable to adopt an additional ownership limit based on audience reach.

The Commission settled on a 25-percent limit on audience reach. This limited the growth of the largest group owners without requiring any divestiture or grandfathering. (Metromedia had the largest combined reach at 23.89 percent.)

The FCC then turned to requests for special treatment for both UHF's and minorities.  Due to the physical limitations inherent in the UHF band, UHF stations cannot compete on an equal basis.  The original rules' stricter limitation on VHF ownership was part of the Commission's longstanding efforts to foster the development of UHF. There were no incentives for minorities in the original rules, but the Commission has adopted several other policies designed to increase minority ownership:

44.  While we agree with the petitioners' assessment as to the need for a UHF incentive within the context of the audience reach limit, we do not believe that the incentive should be structured so as to merely increase the reach cap.  Such an approach would not accurately represent the physical handicaps confronting UHF television.  Consistent with the diversity objectives expressed in our ownership rules, we believe that a more appropriate indicator of the

reach handicap of UHF stations is one that measures the actual coverage limitation inherent in the UHF signal. Therefore, with respect to the audience reach limit adopted herein, we believe that owners of UHF stations should be attributed with only 50 percent of an ADI market's theoretical audience reach to account for this disparity. For example, the theoretical ADI audience reach of the New York market comprises 7.72 percent of all television households. Under the system adopted today, the owner of a UHF station in the New York market would be attributed with an audience reach of only 50 percent of this amount which equals 3.86 percentage points. We find that the discount system adopted herein properly reflects the Commission's historical concern with UHF television. Furthermore, the discount approach provides a measure of the actual voice handicap and is therefore consistent with our traditional diversity objectives.

### (b) Minority Incentives

45. In the Report and Order, we observed that the national multiple ownership rules were not primarily intended to function as a vehicle for promoting minority ownership in broadcasting. In this regard, we noted that the Commission has instituted various policies such as tax certificates, distress sale benefits and lottery preferences to promote minority ownership in communications. We continue to believe that these policies, as opposed to our multiple ownership rules, should serve as the primary mechanisms to promote minority ownership in television and radio broadcasting. We recognize, however, that our national multiple ownership rules may, in some circumstances, play a role in fostering minority, ownership. Thus, while it would be inappropriate to retain multiple ownership regulations for the sole purpose of promoting minority ownership, we now believe that a minority incentive should be included in the rules adopted by our action today. Accordingly, we are adopting rules today which permit group owners of television and radio stations to utilize a maximum numerical cap of 14 stations provided that at least two of the stations in which they hold cognizable interests are minority controlled. Group owners having a cognizable interest in at least one minority controlled television or radio station may utilize a maximum numerical cap of 13 stations. Extending this policy to the audience reach limit for television, we believe that a group owner having cognizable interests in minority controlled television stations should be allowed to reach a maximum of 30 percent of the national audience, provided that at least five percent of the aggregate reach of its stations is contributed by minority controlled stations.

Commissioners Dawson and Patrick each wrote a separate statement to express disagreement with using the multiple ownership rules to promote minority ownership. Commissioner Dawson stated that she did not see how national "concentration is in any way ameliorated by the race of [an] entity's owners." Commissioner Patrick similarly observed, "If the public interest is threatened by concentrating ownership of 14 stations in a single owner, how is that threat obviated by the race of that owner?"

Both Commissioners seem to be taking the position that any specific rule must serve only one interest. But remember the newspaper-broadcast crossownership case. Isn't the Commission allowed to apply rules differently to various groups as long as it can provide a rational basis for the unequal treatment?

## 2. CONGLOMERATES IN BROADCASTING

Occasionally the problem has been raised, not in terms of multiple ownership of competing media, but concern about other businesses in which a prospective licensee is engaged. The prime example is a merger that was proposed between ABC, which in its capacity as group owner, owned 17 broadcasting stations, and International Telephone and Tele-graph, a vast conglomerate with manufacturing facilities, telecommuni-cation operations and other activities in 66 countries throughout the world.

Critics were concerned that ITT would use the broadcasting facilities to further the interests of the parent corporation in ways that might include distorting the news and making editorial decisions on grounds other than professional journalism criteria. The Commission rejected these concerns on the ground that "it is too late in the day to argue that such outside business interests are disqualifying. . . . We cannot in this case adopt standards which when applied to other cases would require us to restructure the industry unless we are prepared to under-take that task. We could not, in good conscience, forbid ABC to merge with ITT without instituting proceedings to separate NBC from RCA, both of which are bigger than the respective principals in this case." The Commission granted the application for transferring of the 17 licenses by a 4 to 3 vote. Memorandum Opinion and Order 7 F.C.C.2d 245, 9 R.R.2d 12 (1966).

While an appeal by the Justice Department on antitrust grounds was pending, the parties abandoned their proposed merger. Would there be any problem if, for example, General Motors sought to acquire a televi-sion station in Detroit? Are different questions raised if a book publish-er or motion picture producer seeks a television license?

*The Gannett-Combined Communications Merger.* In 1979, the FCC approved what was at that time the largest deal in broadcasting history. The parties were Gannett, which at the time published 77 daily and 32 weekly newspapers and owned WHEC–TV in Rochester, New York, and Combined Communications Corp. which at the time owned newspapers in Cincinnati and Oakland, plus five VHF, two UHF, six AM and six FM stations. In addition, Gannett owned Louis Harris and Associates, the polling firm, and Combined was a major supplier of outdoor advertising. The deal called for $370 million in Gannett stock to go to Combined. After spin-offs to meet the FCC's cross-ownership policies, Gannett had 79 daily newspapers, seven television stations, and 12 radio stations.

The final result, because of the spin-offs, violated no concentration rule. Nonetheless, the Commission considered whether granting the applications to transfer ownership of the stations would be in the "public interest." The majority concluded that the deal was not likely to affect competition adversely or raise antitrust concerns.

The First Amendment issue, however, raised harder questions. The FCC noted that Gannett had represented that "local autonomy will be the touchstone for the operation of each newspaper and broadcast property" and that the newspapers would operate separately from the broadcast properties. For example, Gannett asserted that in 1976, of its 35 papers that made endorsements, 22 endorsed Gerald Ford and 13 endorsed Jimmy Carter. Decentralized operation was the goal, although everyone recognized that under § 310 of the 1934 Act, Gannett had to retain ultimate control of its stations.

Some were concerned about the possibility that the size of the combination would lead advertisers and stock market investors to exercise more control over management than would occur with less centralized control. They feared that a large communications entity might "harm diversity of information and opinion through its institutional pressures rather than by any intentional acts of its corporate leadership."

The FCC stressed countervailing considerations: "Media chains may have more freedom and might be inclined to take more risks in their reporting of news and opinion because their financial health allows a degree of independence from the political views of their major advertisers." The size of the organization might permit more coverage of national news in competition with the wire services, the television networks, and the largest newspapers and magazines.

Since all of these newspapers and stations face "substantial local mixed-media competition," even if a "Gannett" view entered a new market it was not eliminating other views available in that market. Affirmatively, the Commission noted that the deal had resulted in the break-up of cross-ownership interests in Phoenix and St. Louis, as well as sale of WHEC–TV to a buyer controlled by a minority group. This made WHEC–TV the first network-affiliated major market television station controlled by a minority group. The merger was approved 5–1.

The dissenter was greatly concerned by the "trend" toward placing "organs of information and news and opinion in this country in fewer and fewer hands. This is an unhealthy thing for a democracy: absentee ownership, on a vast scale, of newspapers and broadcasting stations. . . . Where are the William Allen Whites of 1979? Too many of them have been bought out, one by one, by the chains. They've been made offers they could not refuse."

In 1985, Gannett reached an agreement to purchase the Evening News Association, expanding both its newspaper and its broadcast holdings.  As a result of the purchase, the audience reach of Gannett's television stations will be increased from six to ten percent.

*The Capital Cities Communications-American Broadcasting Companies Merger.*  In March, 1985, Capital Cities Communications (CCC) announced plans to acquire American Broadcasting Companies, Inc. (ABC) for $3.5 billion.  This transaction, larger by far than any previous broadcast sale or merger, resulted in the formation of a new company, Capital Cities/ABC, Inc. (CC/ABC).

To meet the various FCC ownership rules, CC/ABC had to sell over $1 billion worth of properties.  Although CCC and ABC owned only 12 AM stations, 12 FM stations and 12 TV stations between them, the total reach of the TV stations was 28.59%.  To bring that figure down to the 25% maximum allowed by the new multiple ownership rules, CCC sold WKBW–TV, Buffalo, and WTNH(TV), New Haven.

The latter was also necessary because of a signal overlap between WTNH and WABC–TV, New York.  A similar overlap between WABC–TV and WPVI–TV in Philadelphia did not necessitate selling one of those stations because the Commission granted them a waiver of the duopoly rule.  However, a number of radio stations had to be sold to comply with the duopoly rule.  Record prices were paid for many of these properties.

Several CCC newspapers were also subject to divestiture requirements.  *The Oakland Press* and *The Daily Register* are published in suburbs of cities in which ABC broadcast outlets are located.

Finally, CC/ABC had to sell all the cable properties owned by CCC.  Another FCC media concentration rule prohibits network ownership of cable.  *The Washington Post* purchased the cable properties.

The Commission approved the merger in late 1985.  There was not much concern with the more general media concentration issues addressed in the Gannett case.  (The Commission also approved the purchase of six Metromedia television stations by Rupert Murdoch and granted him a two-year waiver of the cross-ownership rules as applied to his properties in New York and Chicago.)

In late 1985, General Electric (G.E.) announced the purchase of RCA for more than $6 billion.  Among RCA's various subsidiaries is NBC.  These sales and mergers may herald a new wave of acquisitions and mergers, further concentrating the ownership of the nation's media in the hands of a few large corporations.

### 3.  MINORITY OWNERSHIP

*Distress Sales and Minority Broadcasters.*  One of the FCC's concerns in recent years has been the dearth of minority broadcasters.  In 1978, in an effort to meet two concerns at once, the Commission announced steps to allow licensees whose renewals might be in jeopardy to sell their stations to minority groups for more than the value of the

buildings and equipment but less than the going concern value. Statement of Policy on Minority Ownership of Broadcast Facilities, 68
F.C.C.2d 979, 42 R.R.2d 1689 (1978). The Commission announced that it
would permit "licensees whose licenses have been designated for revocation hearings, or whose renewal applications have been designated for
hearing on basic qualification issues .  .  . to transfer or assign their
licenses at a 'distress sale' price to applicants with a significant minority
ownership interest, assuming the proposed assignee or transferee meets
our other qualifications." The distress price was expected to be "somewhat greater than the value of the unlicensed equipment, which could be
realized even in the event of revocation."

In a clarifying statement, the Commission stated that the opportunity for distress sales applied only when no competing applicant was
involved in the hearing.

The distress sale option has been attractive to licensees who are
ordered to hearings. The fact that allegations have been thought serious
enough to warrant a hearing is a dangerous warning. To litigate and
lose the renewal would leave the licensee with nothing except the
buildings and equipment that it owns. The distress sale may yield the
owner as much as 75 percent of the fair appraised value of a viable
business.

The immediate social result of the distress sale policy has been to
allow minority groups to enter the broadcasting industry in greater
numbers. If the FCC's efforts to develop new stations, discussed in
Chapter II, work as expected, many minority broadcasters will use that
route and the relatively limited distress sale route will become less
important.

The distress sale policy explicitly limited "minority" to specific
ethnic groups but indicated that "other clearly definable groups, such as
women, may be able to demonstrate that they are eligible for similar
treatment." But in Petition for Issuance of Policy Statement or Notice
of Inquiry, 69 F.C.C.2d 1591, 44 R.R.2d 1051 (1978), the Commission
ruled that although it had on occasion recognized female involvement as
a merit in comparative proceedings, it would not extend the minority
policy to women because it had "not concluded that the historical and
contemporary disadvantagement suffered by women is of the same
order, or has the same contemporary consequences" as those involving
groups covered in the original policy statement.

In 1985, the Commission similarly refused to extend the minority
preference in lottery proceedings. The FCC concluded that it did not
have the authority and that, furthermore, extending it to women was
inappropriate. Lottery Selection (Preference for Women), 58 R.R.2d
1077 (1985).

The FCC has developed other techniques for encouraging minority
entry into broadcasting. In the 1978 Policy Statement, the Commission
also announced that it would grant tax certificates, permitting a seller to
defer payment of capital gains taxes, to owners who sell their stations to

groups controlled by members of minority groups. Recall also the preference awarded minorities applying for the new FM licenses recently created by the Commission.

## C. NETWORKS

Concentration of control problems are not limited, however, to ownership issues. Because broadcast networks supply much of the programming in the country, their influence extends far beyond the stations they own. The two primary legal avenues available to control or limit the actions of the networks are application of the antitrust laws and FCC regulation.

### 1. ANTITRUST LAW

In its discussions of the various media concentration rules, the Commission often makes reference to antitrust concerns. The goals of American antitrust law were set in 1890, with the enactment of the Sherman Antitrust Act, 15 U.S.C.A. §§ 1 and 2. Section 1 states a desire to "protect trade and commerce against unlawful restraints and monopolies," and then declares illegal "every contract, combination in the form of trust or otherwise, or conspiracy, in restraint of trade, or commerce." Section 2 provides that "Every person who shall monopolize, or attempt to monopolize, or combine or conspire with any other person or persons, to monopolize any part of the trade or commerce . . . shall be guilty of a misdemeanor."

The quoted provisions of the Sherman Act have been applied against business enterprises engaged in manufacturing or marketing tangible products. In the early 1940's, the Supreme Court decided that the First Amendment did not bar antitrust actions against media organizations. Associated Press v. United States, 326 U.S. 1 (1945). However, the special regulatory status of broadcasting under the Communications Act of 1934 raised two other important questions, both dealing with jurisdiction.

Since the antitrust laws are enforced by the Justice Department and the Federal Trade Commission, the first question was whether the Federal Communications Commission was barred from issuing regulations based on antitrust principles. In *NBC*, which we first considered in Chapter III and which we will examine further in this Chapter, the Supreme Court concluded that the FCC was entitled to use antitrust principles in determining what constitutes the public interest.

The second jurisdictional question, whether an FCC ruling in a specific case barred action by other agencies, was raised in United States v. Radio Corporation of America, 358 U.S. 334 (1959). NBC, a wholly owned subsidiary of RCA, reached an agreement with Westinghouse to exchange NBC's Cleveland VHF television station plus three million dollars for Westinghouse's Philadelphia VHF television station. Despite allegations that NBC had forced the transaction by threatening to withhold network affiliation from all Westinghouse stations, the FCC approved the transfer.

The Justice Department then filed an antitrust action against RCA and NBC asking among other things that NBC be forced to divest itself of the Philadelphia station. RCA argued that the FCC's approval of the sale had decided the antitrust questions, barring the government from bringing a separate antitrust action. The Supreme Court disagreed:

> . . . Appellees, like unregulated business concerns, made a business judgment as to the desirability of the exchange. Like unregulated concerns, they had to make this judgment with knowledge that the exchange might run afoul of the antitrust laws. Their decision varied from that of unregulated concern only in that they also had to obtain the approval of a federal agency. But [the] scope of that approval in the case of the FCC was limited to the statutory standard, "public interest, convenience, and necessity." . . . The monetary terms of the exchange were set by the parties, and were of concern to the Commission only as they might have affected the ability of the parties to serve the public. Even after approval, the parties were free to complete or not to complete the exchange as their sound business judgment dictated. In every sense, the question faced by the parties was solely one of business judgment (as opposed to regulatory coercion), save only that the Commission must have found that the "public interest" would be served by their decision to make the exchange. . . .

> This is not to imply that federal antitrust policy may not be considered in determining whether the "public interest, convenience, and necessity" will be served by proposed action of the broadcaster, for this Court has held to the contrary. National Broadcasting Co. v. United States, 319 U.S. 190, 222–224. Moreover, in a given case the Commission might find that antitrust considerations alone would keep the statutory standard from being met, as when the publisher of the sole newspaper in an area applies for a license for the only available radio and television facilities, which, if granted, would give him a monopoly of that area's major media of mass communication.
> [  ]

In 1972, the Justice Department, concerned with excessive network control over the market for television prime-time programming, filed antitrust suits against the three major networks. Six years later, NBC entered into a consent decree that prohibited acquisition of syndication rights from independent producers and reciprocal dealings with the other networks and placed other limitations on dealings with independent producers. Subsequently, the other networks signed similar consent decrees.

## 2. THE CHAIN BROADCASTING RULES

By the late 1930's, the three national network companies (NBC, CBS and Mutual) had almost half of the entire broadcast business in the country. In 1938, deeply concerned by this concentration of control the Commission began an inquiry into the need for special regulations to curb the power of the networks by prohibiting certain common network practices. In 1941, after extensive public hearings at which nearly 100 witnesses testified, the Commission adopted a series of regulations pertaining to chain broadcasting.

The networks then brought suit to enjoin enforcement of the chain broadcasting rules. We examined the arguments concerning the Commission's authority to regulate broadcasting at p. 54, supra. We now turn to the Court's consideration of the rules themselves.

## NATIONAL BROADCASTING COMPANY v. UNITED STATES

Supreme Court of the United States, 1943.
319 U.S. 190, 63 S.Ct. 997, 87 L.Ed. 1344.

MR. JUSTICE FRANKFURTER delivered the opinion of the Court.

. . .

The Commission recognized that network broadcasting had played and was continuing to play an important part in the development of radio. "The growth and development of chain broadcasting," it stated, "found its impetus in the desire to give widespread coverage to programs which otherwise would not be heard beyond the reception area of a single station. Chain broadcasting makes possible a wider reception for expensive entertainment and cultural programs and also for programs of national or regional significance which would otherwise have coverage only in the locality of origin. Furthermore, the access to greatly enlarged audiences made possible by chain broadcasting has been a strong incentive to advertisers to finance the production of expensive programs. . . . But the fact that the chain broadcasting method brings benefits and advantages to both the listening public and to broadcast station licensees does not mean that the prevailing practices and policies of the networks and their outlets are sound in all respects, or that they should not be altered. The Commission's duty under the Communications Act of 1934 is not only to see that the public receives the advantages and benefits of chain broadcasting, but also, so far as its powers enable it, to see that practices which adversely affect the ability of licensees to operate in the public interest are eliminated." [ ]

The Commission found that eight network abuses were amenable to correction within the powers granted it by Congress:

*Regulation 3.101—Exclusive affiliation of station.* The Commission found that the network affiliation agreements of NBC and CBS customarily contained a provision which prevented the station from broadcasting the programs of any other network. The effect of this provision was to hinder the growth of new networks, to deprive the listening public in many areas of service to which they were entitled, and to prevent station licensees from exercising their statutory duty of determining which programs would best serve the needs of their community. The Commission observed that in areas where all the stations were under exclusive contract to either NBC or CBS, the public was deprived of the opportunity to hear programs presented by Mutual. To take a case cited in the Report: In the fall of 1939 Mutual obtained the exclusive right to broadcast the World Series baseball games. It offered this program of outstanding national interest to stations throughout the country, including NBC and CBS affiliates in communities having no other stations. CBS and NBC immediately invoked the "exclusive affiliation" clauses of their agreements with these stations, and as a result thousands of persons in many sections of the country were unable to hear the broadcasts of the games.

"Restraints having this effect," the Commission observed, "are to be condemned as contrary to the public interest irrespective of whether it be assumed that Mutual programs are of equal, superior, or inferior quality. The important consideration is that station licensees are denied freedom to choose the programs which they believe best suited to their needs; in this manner the duty of a station licensee to operate in the public interest is defeated. . . . Our conclusion is that the disadvantages resulting from these exclusive arrangements far outweigh any advantages. A licensee station does not operate in the public interest when it enters into exclusive arrangements which prevent it from giving the public the best service of which it is capable, and which, by closing the door of opportunity in the network field, adversely affects the program structure of the entire industry." [  ] . . .

*Regulation 3.102—Territorial exclusivity.* The Commission found another type of "exclusivity" provision in network affiliation agreements whereby the network bound itself not to sell programs to any other station in the same area. The effect of this provision, designed to protect the affiliate from the competition of other stations serving the same territory, was to deprive the listening public of many programs that might otherwise be available. If an affiliated station rejected a network program, the "territorial exclusivity" clause of its affiliation agreement prevented the network from offering the program to other stations in the area. For example, Mutual presented a popular program, known as "The American Forum of the Air," in which prominent persons discussed topics of general interest. None of the Mutual stations in the Buffalo area decided to carry the program, and a Buffalo station not affiliated with Mutual attempted to obtain the program for its listeners. These efforts failed, however, on account of the "territorial exclusivity" provision in Mutual's agreements with its outlets. The result was that this program was not available to the people of Buffalo.

The Commission concluded that "It is not in the public interest for the listening audience in an area to be deprived of network programs not carried by one station where other stations in that area are ready and willing to broadcast the programs. It is as much against the public interest for a network affiliate to enter into a contractual arrangement which prevents another station from carrying a network program as it would be to drown out that program by electrical interference." [  ]

Recognizing that the "territorial exclusivity" clause was unobjectionable in so far as it sought to prevent duplication of programs in the same area, the Commission limited itself to the situations in which the clause impaired the ability of the licensee to broadcast available programs. . . .

*Regulation 3.103—Term of affiliation.* The standard NBC and CBS affiliation contracts bound the station for a period of five years, with the network having the exclusive right to terminate the contracts upon one year's notice. The Commission, relying upon § 307(d) of the Communications Act of 1934, under which no license to operate a broadcast station can be granted for a longer term than three years, found the five-year affiliation term to be contrary to the policy of the Act: "Regardless of any changes that may occur in the economic, political, or social life of the Nation or of the community in which the station is located, CBS and NBC affiliates are bound by contract to continue broadcasting the network programs of only one network for 5 years. The licensee is so bound even though the policy and caliber of programs of the network may deteriorate greatly. The future necessities of the station and of the community are not considered. The station licensee is unable to follow his conception of the public interest until the end of the 5-year contract." [  ] The Commission concluded that under contracts binding the affiliates for five years, "stations become parties to arrangements which deprive the public of the improved service it might otherwise derive from competition in the network field; and that a station is not operating in the public interest when it so limits its freedom of action." [  ] . . .

*Regulation 3.104—Option time.* The Commission found that network affiliation contracts usually contained so-called network optional time clauses. Under these provisions the network could upon 28 days' notice call upon its affiliates to carry a commercial program during any of the hours specified in the agreement as "network optional time." For CBS affiliates "network optional time" meant the entire broadcast day. For 29 outlets of NBC on the Pacific Coast, it also covered the entire broadcast day; for substantially all of the other NBC affiliates, it included, 8½ hours on weekdays and 8 hours on Sundays. Mutual's contracts with about half of its affiliates contained such a provision, giving the network optional time for 3 or 4 hours on weekdays and 6 hours on Sundays.

In the Commission's judgment these optional time provisions, in addition to imposing serious obstacles in the path of new networks, hindered stations in developing a local program service. The exercise by the networks of their options over the station's time tended to prevent regular scheduling of local programs at desirable hours. The Commission found that "shifting a local commercial program may seriously interfere with the efforts of a [local] sponsor to build up a regular listening audience at a definite hour, and the long-term advertising contract becomes a highly dubious project. This hampers the efforts of the station to develop local commercial programs and affects adversely its ability to give the public good program service. . . . A station licensee must retain sufficient freedom of action to supply the program and advertising needs of the local community. Local program service is a vital part of community life. A station should be ready, able, and willing to serve the needs of the local community by broadcasting such outstanding local events as community concerts, civic meetings, local sports events, and other programs of local consumer and social interest. We conclude that national network time options have restricted the freedom of station licensees and hampered their efforts to broadcast local commercial programs, the programs of other national networks, and national spot transcriptions. We believe that these considerations far outweigh any supposed advantages from 'stability' of network operations under time options. We find that the optioning of time by licensee stations has operated against the public interest." [   ]

. . .

*Regulation 3.105—Right to reject programs.* The Commission found that most network affiliation contracts contained a clause defining the right of the station to reject network commercial programs. The NBC contracts provided simply that the station "may reject a network program the broadcasting of which would not be in the public interest, convenience, and necessity." NBC required a licensee who rejected a program to "be able to support his contention that what he has done has been more in the public interest than had he carried on the network program." Similarly, the CBS contracts provided that if the station had "reasonable objection to any sponsored program or the product advertised thereon as not being in the public interest, the station may, on 3 weeks' prior notice thereof to Columbia, refuse to broadcast such program, unless during such notice period such reasonable objection of the station shall be satisfied."

While seeming in the abstract to be fair, these provisions, according to the Commission's finding, did not sufficiently protect the "public interest." As a practical matter, the licensee could not determine in advance whether the broadcasting of any particular network program would or would not be in the public interest. "It is obvious that from such skeletal information [as the networks submitted to the stations prior to the broadcasts] the station cannot determine in advance whether the program is in the public interest, nor can it ascertain whether or not parts of the program are in one way or another offensive. In practice, if not in theory, stations affiliated with networks have delegated to the networks a large part of their programming functions. In many instances, moreover, the network further delegates the actual production of programs to advertising agencies. These agencies are far more than mere brokers or intermediaries between the network and the advertiser. To an ever-increasing extent, these agencies actually exercise the function of program production. Thus it is frequently neither the station nor the network, but rather the advertising agency, which determines what broadcast programs shall contain. Under such circumstances, it is especially important that individual stations, if they are to operate in the public interest, should have the practical opportunity as well as the contractual right to reject network programs.　.　.　.

"It is the station, not the network, which is licensed to serve the public interest. The licensee has the duty of determining what programs shall be broadcast over his station's facilities, and cannot lawfully delegate this duty or transfer the control of his station directly to the network or indirectly to an advertising agency. He cannot lawfully bind himself to accept programs in every case where he cannot sustain the burden of proof that he has a better program. The licensee is obliged to reserve to himself the final decision as to what programs will best serve the public interest. We conclude that a licensee is not fulfilling his obligations to operate in the public interest, and is not operating in accordance with the express requirements of the Communications Act, if he agrees to accept programs on any basis other than his own reasonable decision that the programs are satisfactory." [　]

.　.　.

*Regulation 3.106—Network ownership of stations.* The Commission found that NBC, in addition to its network operations, was the licensee of 10 stations, 2 each in New York, Chicago, Washington, and San Francisco, 1 in Denver, and 1 in Cleveland. CBS was the licensee of 8 stations, 1 in each of these cities: New York, Chicago, Washington, Boston, Minneapolis, St. Louis, Charlotte, and Los Angeles. These 18 stations owned by NBC and CBS, the Commission observed, were among the most powerful and desirable in the country, and were permanently inaccessible to competing networks. "Competition among networks for these facilities is nonexistent, as they are completely removed from the network-station market. It gives the network complete control over its policies. This 'bottling-up' of the best facilities has undoubtedly had a discouraging effect upon the creation and growth of new networks. Furthermore, common ownership of network and station places the network in a position where its interest as the owner of certain stations may conflict with its interest as a network organization serving affiliated stations. In dealings with advertisers, the network represents its own stations in a proprietary capacity and the affiliated stations in something akin to an agency capacity. The danger is present that the network organization will give preference to its own stations at the expense of its affiliates." [　]

The Commission stated that if the question had arisen as an original matter, it might well have concluded that the public interest required severance of the business of station ownership from that of network operation. But since substantial business interests have been formed on the basis of the Commission's continued tolerance of the situation, it was found inadvisable to take such a drastic step. The Commission concluded, however, that "the licensing of two stations in the same area to a single network organization is basically unsound and contrary to the public interest," and that it was also against the "public interest" for network organizations to own stations in areas where the available facilities were so few or of such unequal coverage that competition would thereby be substantially restricted. Recognizing that these considerations called for flexibility in their application to particular situations, the Commission provided that "networks will be given full opportunity, on proper application for new facilities or renewal of existing licenses, to call to our attention any reasons why the principle should be modified or held inapplicable." [ ] . . .

*Regulation 3.107—Dual network operation.* [Since the Commission had indefinitely suspended this regulation, the Court did not consider it.]

*Regulation 3.108—Control by networks of station rates.* The Commission found that NBC's affiliation contracts contained a provision empowering the network to reduce the station's network rate, and thereby to reduce the compensation received by the station, if the station set a lower rate for non-network national advertising than the rate established by the contract for the network programs. Under this provision the station could not sell time to a national advertiser for less than it would cost the advertiser if he bought the time from NBC. In the words of NBC's vice-president, "This means simply that a national advertiser should pay the same price for the station whether he buys it through one source or another source. It means that we do not believe that our stations should go into competition with ourselves." [ ]

The Commission concluded that "it is against the public interest for a station licensee to enter into a contract with a network which has the effect of decreasing its ability to compete for national business. We believe that the public interest will best be served and listeners supplied with the best programs if stations bargain freely with national advertisers." [ ] . . .

. . .

In essence the Chain Broadcasting Regulations represent a particularization of the Commission's conception of the "public interest" sought to be safeguarded by Congress in enacting the Communications Act of 1934. The basic consideration of policy underlying the Regulations is succinctly stated in its Report: "With the number of radio channels limited by natural factors, the public interest demands that those who are entrusted with the available channels shall make the fullest and most effective use of them. If a licensee enters into a contract with a network organization which limits his ability to make the best use of the radio facility assigned him, he is not serving the public interest. . . . The net effect [of the practices disclosed by the investigation] has been that broadcasting service has been maintained at a level below that possible under a system of free competition. Having so found, we would be remiss in our statutory duty of encouraging 'the larger and more effective use of radio in the public interest' if we were to grant licenses to persons who persist in these practices."

We would be asserting our personal views regarding the effective utilization of radio were we to deny that the Commission was entitled to find that the large public aims of the Communications Act of 1934 comprehend the considerations which moved the Commission in promulgating the Chain Broadcasting Regulations. True enough, the Act does not explicitly say that the Commission shall have power to deal with network practices found inimical to the public interest. But Congress was acting in a field of regulation which was both new and dynamic. "Congress moved under the spur of a widespread fear that in the absence of governmental control the public interest might be subordinated to monopolistic domination in the broadcasting field." [ ] In the context of the developing problems to which it was directed, the Act gave the Commission not niggardly but expansive powers. It was given a comprehensive mandate to "encourage the larger and more effective use of radio in the public interest," if need be, by making "special regulations applicable to radio stations engaged in chain broadcasting." § 303(g)(i).

. . .

A totally different source of attack upon the Regulations is found in § 311 of the Act, which authorizes the Commission to withhold licenses from persons convicted of having violated the anti-trust laws. Two contentions are made—first, that this provision puts considerations relating to competition outside the Commission's concern before an applicant has been convicted of monopoly or other restraints of trade, and second, that, in any event, the Commission misconceived the scope of its powers under § 311 in issuing the Regulations. Both of these contentions are unfounded. Section 311 derives from § 13 of the Radio Act of 1927, which expressly commanded, rather than merely authorized, the Commission to refuse a license to any person judicially found guilty of having violated the anti-trust laws. . . . The Commission was thus permitted to exercise its judgment as to whether violation of the anti-trust laws disqualified an applicant from operating a station in the "public interest." We agree with the District Court that "The necessary implication from this [amendment in 1934] was that the Commission might infer from the fact that the applicant had in the past tried to monopolize radio, or had engaged in unfair methods of competition, that the disposition so manifested would continue and that if it did it would make him an unfit licensee." [ ]

That the Commission may refuse to grant a license to persons adjudged guilty in a court of law of conduct in violation of the anti-trust laws certainly does not render irrelevant consideration by the Commission of the effect of such conduct upon the "public interest, convenience, or necessity." A licensee charged with practices in contravention of this standard cannot continue to hold his license merely because his conduct is also in violation of the anti-trust laws and he has not yet been proceeded against and convicted. By clarifying in § 311 the scope of the Commission's authority in dealing with persons convicted of violating the anti-trust laws, Congress can hardly be deemed to have limited the concept of "public interest" so as to exclude all considerations relating to monopoly and unreasonable restraints upon commerce. Nothing in the provisions or history of the Act lends support to the inference that the Commission was denied the power to refuse a license to a station not operating in the "public interest," merely because its misconduct happened to be an unconvicted violation of the anti-trust laws.

Alternatively, it is urged that the Regulations constitute an *ultra vires* attempt by the Commission to enforce the anti-trust laws, and that the enforcement of the anti-trust laws is the province not of the Commission but of the Attorney General and the courts. This contention misconceives the basis of the Commission's action. The Commission's Report indicates plainly enough that the Commission was not attempting to administer the anti-trust laws:

"The prohibitions of the Sherman Act apply to broadcasting. This Commission, although not charged with the duty of enforcing that law, should administer its regulatory powers with respect to broadcasting in the light of the purposes which the Sherman Act was designed to achieve. . . . While many of the network practices raise serious questions under the antitrust laws, our jurisdiction does not depend on a showing that they do in fact constitute a violation of the antitrust laws. It is not our function to apply the antitrust laws as such. It is our duty, however, to refuse licenses or renewals to any person who engages or proposes to engage in practices which will prevent either himself or other licensees or both from making the fullest use of radio facilities. This is the standard of public interest, convenience or necessity which we must apply to all applications for licenses and renewals. . . . We do not predicate our jurisdiction to issue the regulations on the ground that the network practices violate the antitrust laws. We are issuing these regulations because we have found that the network practices prevent the maximum utilization of radio facilities in the public interest." [   ]

We conclude, therefore, that the Communications Act of 1934 authorized the Commission to promulgate regulations designed to correct the abuses disclosed by its investigation of chain broadcasting. There remains for consideration the claim that the Commission's exercise of such authority was unlawful.

The Regulations are assailed as "arbitrary and capricious." If this contention means that the Regulations are unwise, that they are not likely to succeed in accomplishing what the Commission intended, we can say only that the appellants have selected the wrong forum for such a plea. What was said in Board of Trade v. United States, 314 U.S. 534, 548, is relevant here: "We certainly have neither technical competence nor legal authority to pronounce upon the wisdom of the course taken by the Commission." Our duty is at an end when we find that the action of the Commission was based upon findings supported by evidence, and was made pursuant to authority granted by Congress. It is not for us to say that the "public interest" will be furthered or retarded by the Chain Broadcasting Regulations. The responsibility belongs to the Congress for the grant of valid legislative authority and to the Commission for its exercise.

. . .

Affirmed

MR. JUSTICE BLACK and MR. JUSTICE RUTLEDGE took no part in the consideration or decision of these cases.

[Mr. Justice Murphy dissented on the grounds that the regulations went beyond the authority delegated to the Commission by Congress.]

### Notes and Questions

1. The reason that the dual network provision was suspended was that NBC had sold its Blue Network, thus obviating the need for that provision. The Blue Network subsequently became ABC.

2. In 1977, the Commission re-examined the application of the Chain Broadcasting Regulations to radio and concluded that due to the high degree of competition that now existed, most of the Regulations were no longer necessary. Consequently, they eliminated all but a modified version of the territorial exclusivity regulation for both AM and FM stations.

> § 73.132 Territorial exclusivity. No licensee of an AM broadcast station shall have any arrangement with a network organization which prevents or hinders another station serving substantially the same area from broadcasting the network's programs not taken by the former station, or which prevents or hinders another station serving a substantially different area from broadcasting any program of the network organization: provided, however, that this section does not prohibit arrangements under which the station is granted first call within its primary service area upon the network's programs. The term 'network organization' means any organization originating program material, with or without commercial messages, and furnishing the same to stations interconnected so as to permit simultaneous broadcast by all or some of them. However, arrangements involving only stations under common ownership, or only the rebroadcast by one station of programming from another with no compensation other than a lump-sum payment by the station rebroadcasting, are not considered arrangements with a network organization. The term 'arrangement' means any contract, arrangement or understanding, express or implied.

Section 73.232 applies the same restrictions to FM stations. 47 C.F.R. § 73.232.

As a result of the elimination of these rules several companies now operate more than one radio network. For example, ABC operates the Contemporary, Direction, Entertainment, FM, Information, Rock and Talkradio networks.

3. In 1965, the Commission issued a notice of proposed rulemaking in which it sought, among other things, to limit the networks' control over

programming during prime time. After extensive comments and hearings, the Commission decided in 1970 to adopt a rule providing that after Sept. 1, 1971,

> . . . no television station, assigned to any of the top 50 markets in which there are three or more operating commercial television stations, shall broadcast network programs offered by any television network or networks for a total of more than 3 hours per day between the hours of 7 p.m. and 11 p.m. local time, except that in the Central time zone the relevant period shall be between the hours of 6 p.m. and 10 p.m.

Competition and Responsibility in Network Television Broadcasting, 23 F.C.C.2d 382, 18 R.R.2d 1825 (1970). This prime time access rule (PTAR I) exempted fast-breaking news events, on-the-spot coverage of news events, and political broadcasts by candidates.

The Commission presented several reasons for its action. Primarily, it was concerned that during the 1960's the number of first-run syndicated entertainment series had fallen. The role of "off-network" entertainment series (programs that had been on the networks earlier and were now being syndicated to other stations) had grown enormously, as had the role of the networks in preparing new programs. Even among independent stations, "which should be the backbone of the syndication market," first-run syndications were being replaced by off-network programs. Only 14 of the top 50 markets had at least one independent VHF station.

Finally, the financial involvement of the networks in evening programming had doubled during the 1960's, and the independently produced programs had fallen by 90 percent. The Commission deplored this "unhealthy situation" and asserted that the new rule would provide a "healthy impetus to the development of independent program sources, with concomitant benefits in an increased supply of programs for independent (and, indeed, affiliated) stations. The entire development of UHF should be benefitted."

A constitutional and statutory challenge to the rules was rejected in Mt. Mansfield Television, Inc. v. Federal Communications Commission, 442 F.2d 470 (2d Cir.1970). The court relied on *Red Lion's* observations that the peculiar qualities of each medium must be considered in deciding the application of the First Amendment. It also quoted from cases, such as *Associated Press*, that stressed the virtues of "the widest possible dissemination of information from diverse and antagonistic sources," and observed:

> When viewed in the light of these principles, the prime time access rule, far from violating the First Amendment, appears to be a reasonable step toward fulfillment of its fundamental precepts, for it is the stated purpose of that rule to encourage the "[d]iversity of programs and development of diverse and antagonistic sources of program service" and to correct a situation where "[o]nly three organizations control access to the crucial prime time evening sched-

ule." The specific arguments raised by the petitions reflect basic misconceptions of that purpose and of the First Amendment principles outlined above.

For example, petitioner Columbia Broadcasting System, Inc. attempts an analogy between the prime time access rule and an imaginary governmental edict prohibiting newspapers in the 50 largest cities from devoting more than a given portion of their news space to items taken from national news services. This analogy completely overlooks the essential fact that "[w]here there are substantially more individuals who want to broadcast than there are frequencies to allocate, it is idle to posit an unabridgeable First Amendment right to broadcast comparable to the right of every individual to speak, write, or publish." Red Lion Broadcasting Co., supra, 395 U.S. at 388.

To argue that the freedom of networks to distribute and licensees to select programming is limited by the prime time access rule, and that the First Amendment is thereby violated, is to reverse the mandated priorities which subordinate these interests to the public's right of access. The licensee is in many ways a "trustee" for the public in the operation of his channel. . . .

The Court found statutory authority to promulgate PTAR I in the power of the Commission to regulate in the public interest, citing *National Broadcasting Co.*, p. 54, supra. It also upheld the Commission's adoption of the syndication and financial interest rules, the first direct regulation of networks (rather than regulating licensees of stations), as within the Commission's statutory power because they were "reasonably ancillary to the effective performance of the Commission's various responsibilities for the regulation of television broadcasting." 442 F.2d at 481.

The Commission considered requests for waiver of the off-network programs to be presented during prime time without being counted toward the permissible three hours of network and off-network material each evening. What considerations might lead the Commission to grant waivers for "Wild Kingdom," "National Geographic," "Six Wives of Henry VIII," and "Animal World," but to deny waivers to "Lassie" and "Hogan's Heroes"?

4. Less than two years later, the Commission issued a Notice of Inquiry and a Notice of Proposed Rulemaking in which it announced its intention to consider whether to modify or repeal PTAR I. In November, 1973, the Commission adopted PTAR II, which modified PTAR I in several ways. The major change was to eliminate access time altogether on Sunday evenings and to reduce it to one half-hour other evenings. However, PTAR II was successfully challenged in court because the effective date did not allow sufficient time for independent producers to withdraw programs being produced in reliance on PTAR I. National Association of Independent Television Producers & Distributors v. Federal Communications Commission, 502 F.2d 249 (2d Cir.1974).

As a result, in January, 1975, the Commission adopted PTAR III, effective September, 1975. The provisions were similar to PTAR I, covering one hour per night, except for certain exemptions that reflected waivers regularly granted under PTAR I and new provisions for the use of feature films. Exemptions covered network or off-network "public affairs" progamming, documentaries, and programs designed for children. The Commission also noted that it expected "that stations subject to the rule will devote an appropriate portion of 'cleared time' or at least of total prime time to material particularly directed to the needs or problems of the station's community . . ., including programming addressed to the special needs of minority groups." 50 F.C.C.2d at 852, 32 R.R.2d at 722.

It reaffirmed its view that the rule lessened network dominance by releasing a portion of prime time for licensees of individual stations to use to respond to their respective communities and by encouraging a new body of syndicated programming. It also denied that the rule led to a lack of diversity and to low quality programs, arguing that the rule had not yet been fully tested. Although the Justice Department argued that to assure stability the Commission should guarantee that PTAR III would remain in effect at least five years, the Commission refused to do so.

Another challenge followed. In National Association of Independent Television Producers & Distributors v. Federal Communications Commission, 516 F.2d 526 (2d Cir.1975), the court generally upheld PTAR III, but remanded to the Commission for reconsideration of several aspects of the rule. The Commission responded and PTAR III became effective in September, 1975. The court recognized that the rule's results had been mixed at best:

> The result has been, as could have been expected to some degree, that it is largely the cheaper productions, daytime fare, that have been put into cleared prime time slots. What was not anticipated by the Commission was the monotony of the product. A kind of Gresham's law seems to operate in first-run syndication—the cheaper tending to drive the dearer out of circulation. The fact is, as the Commission concedes, that the degree of diversity in programming for access time has been disappointing. In the entertainment area, the emphasis has largely been on game shows and animal shows, game shows constituting 41.9% of the 2,100 access half hours on 150 stations in one season. [ ] Comedies, dramas, and Westerns in access time have dropped significantly. Comedy has been virtually eliminated. The Commission notes a similar lack of diversity, however, with respect to the three networks themselves which all show a crime drama at the same hour in prime time, also giving the viewer no choice.

> On the other hand, as the Commission found, and as the public *amici* stress, programs of local interest, on matters of concern to the people served by local stations, have begun to obtain a foothold

on commercial stations in the access time period.  One may assume that in the long run game shows will pall to some extent and that independent producers will have to turn to more variegated fare if they wish to survive, but any prophecy on public taste, certainly by judges, would be hazardous indeed.

Under PTAR I, the Commission had to pass upon waivers for specific network programs, said to be in the public interest, that would preempt access time.  As noted, these *ad hoc* decisions gave rise to contentions that the Commission was regulating program content in violation of the First Amendment.  In PTAR III the Commission exempted public affairs, documentary, and children's programs.  This led to a major constitutional challenge to PTAR III.  The court considered the problem at some length (516 F.2d at 536–38):

> This is said to be in violation of the First Amendment.  It is true that the Commission has never before considered what types of program may be played at particular times.  And it may be that *mandatory* programming by the Commission even in categories would raise serious First Amendment questions.  On the other hand, the general power of the F.C.C. to interest itself in the kinds of programs broadcast by licensees has consistently been sustained by the courts against arguments that the supervisory power violates the First Amendment.

> .   .   .

> The only way that broadcasters can operate in the "public interest" is by broadcasting programs that meet somebody's view of what is in the "public interest."  That can scarcely be determined by the broadcaster himself, for it is an obvious conflict of interest. "There is no sanctuary in the First Amendment for unlimited private censorship operating in a medium not open to all."  Red Lion, supra, 395 U.S. at 392.  "It is the right of the viewers and listeners, not the right of the broadcasters, which is paramount."  Id. at 390.

> Since the public cannot through a million stifled yawns convey that their television fare, as a whole, is not in their interest, the Congress has made the F.C.C. the guardian of that public interest. All that the Commission can do about it is to encourage competitive fare.  If a large segment of the public prefers game shows to documentaries, the Commission can hardly do more than admit paradoxically that taste *is* a matter for dispute.  The Commission surely cannot do its job, however, without interesting itself in general program format and the kinds of programs broadcast by licensees.   .   .   .

> The Commission by this amendment of the rule is not ordering any program or even any type of program to be broadcast in access time.  It has simply lifted a restriction on network programs if the licensee chooses to avail himself of such network programs in specified categories of programming.   .   .   .

> .   .   .

It is suggested that the Commission should have elected to force the stations to carve out *network* prime time for these programs. Whether or not the Commission could have done this—a course that would doubtless have evoked constitutional protests from the networks—it is not for this court to say. Nor is it for this court to say that the Commission had, in any event, no right to choose between reasonable alternatives.

5.   In 1980, as part of a study of network power, the FCC staff reported that the prime time access rule had not increased local programming. Many major stations were "stripping" syndicated programs five nights per week. (Four NBC O & O's were running "Family Feud" five nights each week at 7:30 p.m.) A few creative local programs, particularly "Evening Magazine" on Westinghouse stations (syndicated as "PM Magazine" to non-Westinghouse stations), had emerged, but these were the rare exceptions. The staff suggested that if the Commissioners wanted local programming they should order it directly.

There are, however, other justifications for the prime time access rule. In the top 50 markets, the network affiliates are banned from using off-network programs during the access period. This has allowed independent stations, primarily UHFs, to offer these popular programs as competition to the network affiliate offerings. As a result the viability of the UHF stations has been strengthened considerably.

At the same time the network affiliates have come to appreciate the rule because they can make more money selling all the commercial availabilities in syndicated programming in contrast to the limited availabilities in network programming. Most affiliates now oppose any proposals to eliminate the prime time access rule.

6.   At the same time it adopted PTAR I, the Commission adopted rules "designed to eliminate the networks from distribution and profit-sharing in domestic syndication and to restrict their activities in foreign markets to distribution of programs of which they are the sole producers." These rules were defended on the ground that networks had a conflict of interest in choosing programs. Independent producers who sought to exhibit their products on a network had to bargain with the networks, who were their "principal competitors in syndication and foreign sales." The Commission concluded that "networks do not normally accept new, untried packager-licensed programs for network exhibition unless the producer/packager is willing to cede a large part of the valuable rights and interests in subsidiary rights to the program to the network." There were also allegations of "warehousing," purchasing programs with no intention of showing them in order to keep them out of the marketplace.

In 1981, acting on a petition by CBS, Inc., the Commission ruled that the financial interest and syndication rules do not apply to nonbroadcast rights to television programs. The decision opened the way for the networks to enter the cable, video cassette and video disc markets. An appeal by Viacom International, Inc., a major program syndicator, was denied. Viacom International, Inc. v. Federal Communications Commission, 672 F.2d 1034 (2d Cir.1982).

In 1982, the Commission issued a Notice of Proposed Rulemaking (NPRM) aimed at eliminating the financial interest and syndication rules. The NPRM was based on a 1980 report by the FCC Network Inquiry Special Staff that concluded the rules were unnecessary and ineffective. A year later, the Commission issued a Tentative Decision proposing the deletion of the financial interest rule and modifying the syndication rule. 54 R.R.2d 457 (1983). The reaction in Congress to the Tentative Decision was extremely negative. Congress barred the Commission from expending any funds to repeal or modify the rules prior to May 31, 1984. Meanwhile, Senator Pete Wilson (R–Cal.) introduced a bill calling for a five-year moratorium.

Bowing to Presidential, as well as legislative, pressure, Chairman Fowler indicated that he would not bring the matter before the Commission. Meanwhile, negotiations between the networks and syndicators have been unable to resolve the issue.

7. The following are the current Chain Broadcasting Regulations for television:

§ 73.658 Affiliation agreements and network program practices; territorial exclusivity in non-network program arrangements.—(a) Exclusive affiliation of station. No license shall be granted to a television broadcast station having any contract, arrangement, or understanding, express or implied, with a network organization under which the station is prevented or hindered from, or penalized for, broadcasting the programs of any other network organization. (The term "network organization" as used in this section includes national and regional network organizations. [ ])

(b) Territorial exclusivity. No license shall be granted to a television broadcast station having any contract, arrangement, or understanding, express or implied, with a network organization which prevents or hinders another broadcast station located in the same community from broadcasting the network's programs not taken by the former station, or which prevents or hinders another broadcast station located in a different community from broadcasting any program of the network organization. This regulation shall not be construed to prohibit any contract, arrangement, or understanding between a station and a network organization pursuant to which the station is granted the first call in its community upon the programs of the network organization. As employed in this paragraph, the term "community" is defined as the community specified in the instrument of authorization as the location of the station.

(c) Term of affiliation. No license shall be granted to a television broadcast station having any contract, arrangement, or understanding, express or implied, with a network organization which provides, by original terms, provisions for renewal, or otherwise, for the affiliation of the station with the network organization for a period longer than two years: provided, that a contract, arrangement, or understanding for a period up to two years may be entered into within six months prior to the commencement of such period.

(d) Station commitment of broadcast time.  No license shall be granted to a television broadcast station having any contract, arrangement, or understanding, express or implied, with any network organization which provides for optioning of the station's time to the network organization, or which has the same restraining effect as time optioning. As used in this section, time optioning is any contract, arrangement, or understanding, express or implied, between a station and a network organization which prevents or hinders the station from scheduling programs before the network agrees to utilize the time during which such programs are scheduled, or which requires the station to clear time already scheduled when the network organization seeks to utilize the time.

(e) Right to reject programs.  No license shall be granted to a television broadcast station having any contract, arrangement, or understanding, express or implied, with a network organization which, with respect to programs offered or already contracted for, pursuant to an affiliation contract, prevents or hinders the station from (1) rejecting or refusing network programs which the station reasonably believes to be unsatisfactory or unsuitable, or contrary to the public interest, or (2) substituting a program which, in the station's opinion, is of a greater local or national importance.

(f) Network ownership of stations.  No license shall be granted to a network organization, or to any person directly or indirectly controlled by or under common control of a network organization, for a television broadcast station in any locality where the existing television broadcast stations are so few or of such unequal desirability (in terms of coverage, power, frequency, or other related matters) that competition would be substantially restrained by such licensing. (The word "control", as used in this section, is not limited to full control but includes such a measure of control as would substantially affect the availability of the station to other networks.)

(g) Dual network operation.  No license shall be issued to a television broadcast station affiliated with a network organization which maintains more than one network of television broadcast stations:  provided, that this section shall not be applicable if such networks are not operated simultaneously, or if there is no substantial overlap in the territory served by the group of stations comprising each such network.

(h) Control by networks of station rates.  No license shall be granted to a television broadcast station having any contract, arrangement, or understanding, express or implied, with a network organization under which the station is prevented or hindered from, or penalized for, fixing or altering its rates for the sale of broadcast time for other than the network's programs.

(i) No license shall be granted to a television broadcast station which is represented for the sale of non-network time by a network organization or by an organization directly or indirectly controlled by or under common control with a network organization, if the station has any contract, arrangement, or understanding, express or implied, which provides for the affiliation of the station with such network organization: provided, however, that this rule shall not be applicable to stations licensed to a network organization or to a subsidiary of a network organization.

(j) Network syndication and program practices.

(1) Except as provided in subparagraph (3) of this paragraph, no television network shall:

(i) After June 1, 1973, sell, license, or distribute television programs to television station licensees within the United States for non-network television exhibition or otherwise engage in the business commonly known as "syndication" within the United States; or sell, license, or distribute television programs of which it is not the sole producer for exhibition outside the United States; or reserve any option or right to share in revenues or profits in connection with such domestic and/or foreign sale, license, or distribution; or

(ii) After August 1, 1972, acquire any financial or proprietary right or interest in the exhibition, distribution, or other commercial use of any television program produced wholly or in part by a person other than such television network, except the license or other exclusive right to network exhibition within the United States and on foreign stations regularly included within such television network; provided that if such network does not timely avail itself of such license or other exclusive right to network exhibition within the United States, the grantor of such license or right to network exhibition may, upon making a timely offer reasonably to compensate the network, re-acquire such license or other exclusive right to exhibition of the program.

(2) Nothing contained in subparagraphs (1) and (2) of this paragraph shall prevent any television network from selling or distributing programs of which it is the sole producer for television exhibition outside the United States, or from selling or otherwise disposing of any program rights not acquired from another person, including the right to distribute programs for non-network exhibition (as in syndication) within the United States as long as it does not itself engage in such distribution within the United States or retain the right to share the revenues or profits therefrom.

(3) Nothing contained in this paragraph shall be construed to include any television network formed for the purpose of producing, distributing, or syndicating program materials for educational, non-commercial, or public broadcasting exhibition or uses.

(4) For the purposes of this paragraph and paragraphs (k) and (l) of this section the term network means any person, entity or corporation which offers an interconnected program service on a regular basis for fifteen or more hours per week to at least twenty-five affiliated television licensees in ten or more states; and/or any person, entity or corporation controlling, controlled by or under common control with such person, entity or corporation.

(k) Effective September 8, 1975, commercial television stations owned by or affiliated with a national television network in the 50 largest television markets . . . shall devote, during the four hours of prime time (7–11 p.m. E.T. and P.T., 6–10 p.m. C.T. and M.T.), no more than three hours to the presentation of programs from a national network, programs formerly on a national network (off-network programs) other than feature films, or, on Saturdays, feature films; provided, however, that the following categories of programs need not be counted toward the three-hour limitations:

(1) On nights other than Saturdays, network or off-network programs designed for children, public affairs programs or documentary programs (see NOTE 2 to this paragraph for definitions).

(2) Special news programs dealing with fast-breaking news events, on-the-spot coverage of news events or other material related to such coverage, and political broadcasts by or on behalf of legally qualified candidates for public office.

(3) Regular network news broadcasts up to a half hour, when immediately adjacent to a full hour of continuous locally produced news or locally produced public affairs programming.

(4) Runovers of live network broadcasts of sporting events, where the event has been reasonably scheduled to conclude before prime time or occupy only a certain amount of prime time, but the event has gone beyond its expected duration due to circumstances not reasonably foreseeable by the networks or under their control. This exemption does not apply to post-game material.

(5) In the case of stations in the Mountain and Pacific time zones, on evenings when network prime time programming consists of a sports event or other program broadcast live and simultaneously throughout the contiguous 48 states, such stations may assume that the network's schedule that evening occupies no more of prime time in these time zones than it does in the Eastern and Central time zones.

(6) Network broadcasts of an international sports event (such as the Olympic Games), New Year's Day college football games, or any other network programming of a special nature other than motion pictures or other sports events, when the network devotes all of its time on the same evening to the same programming, except brief incidental fill material.

.  .  .

NOTE 2.  As used in this paragraph, the term "programs designed for children" means programs primarily designed for children aged 2 through 12.  The term "documentary programs" means programs which are nonfictional and educational or informational, but not including programs where the information is used as part of a contest among participants in the program, and not including programs relating to the visual entertainment arts (stage, motion pictures or television) where more than 50% of the program is devoted to the presentation of entertainment material itself.  The term "public affairs programs" means talks, commentaries, discussions, speeches, editorials, political programs, documentaries, forums, panels, roundtables, and similar programs primarily concerning local, national, and international public affairs.

## Chapter VI

# LEGAL CONTROL OF BROADCAST
# PROGRAMMING: POLITICAL SPEECH

In this Chapter we consider direct regulation of content but not necessarily prohibitions on speech. We begin, for example, with Congressional legislation to provide access and fairness in the electoral process. No speech is prohibited. Rather, broadcasters are told that they must allow certain candidates to use the station's facilities. In addition, if a candidate for an office is allowed to use the facilities, all other candidates for that office must be allowed equal opportunities.

We then turn to doctrines developed by the Commission itself that require broadcasters who have allowed certain types of comments to be made over their facilities to expose their listeners to contrasting viewpoints on that subject.

In each case consider whether the regulations, although not prohibitory, may nonetheless indirectly influence broadcasters to air or not to air certain types of content.

## A. EQUAL OPPORTUNITIES AND ACCESS IN POLITICAL CAMPAIGNS

### 1. EQUAL OPPORTUNITIES—SECTION 315

In the Radio Act of 1927, § 18 provided:

> If any licensee shall permit any person who is a legally qualified candidate for any public office to use a broadcasting station, he shall afford equal opportunities to all other such candidates for that office in the use of such broadcasting station; . . . *Provided,* That such licensee shall have no power of censorship over the material broadcast under the provisions of this paragraph. No obligation is hereby imposed upon any licensee to allow the use of its station by any such candidate.

This became § 315 of the 1934 Act. Although the Commission has explicit rulemaking power to carry out the provisions of § 315(a), few rules have been promulgated. Most of the problems involve requests in the heat of an election campaign, and for this reason few decisions have been reviewed by the courts until recently.

### a. *General Application*

One major limitation on the applicability of § 315 was defined in 1951 when it was held that the section did not apply to uses of a broadcast facility on behalf of a candidate unless the candidate appeared personally during the program. This meant that friends and campaign committees could purchase time without triggering § 315. Felix v. Westinghouse Broadcasting Co., 186 F.2d 1 (3d Cir.1951). This raised a separate set of problems discussed at p. 237, infra.

Section 315 applies only to "legally qualified" candidates for public office. According to § 73.1940(a) of the Commission's rules, a legally qualified candidate is one who:

> (i) has publicly announced his or her intention to run for nomination or office;

> (ii) is qualified under the applicable local, state or federal law to hold the office for which he or she is a candidate; and

> (iii) has met the qualifications set forth in either paragraphs (a)(2), (3), or (4) below.

In essence, these other subparagraphs require the candidate either to have qualified for a place on the ballot or to have made a public commitment to seeking election by the write-in method as well as a substantial showing of being a bona-fide candidate for the office. Ways of making a substantial showing include "making campaign speeches, distributing campaign literature, issuing press releases, maintaining a campaign committee, and establishing campaign headquarters (even though the headquarters in some instances might be the residence of the candidate or his campaign manager)." 47 C.F.R. § 73.1940(a)(1–5).

Another basic question regarding § 315 was resolved in Farmers Educational & Cooperative Union v. WDAY, Inc., 360 U.S. 525 (1959), when the Court unanimously held that a licensee was barred from censoring the comments of a speaker exercising rights under § 315. The Court also held, 5–4, that the section preempted state defamation law and created an absolute privilege that protected the licensee from liability for statements made by such a candidate. Are these rulings sound? Because of the way the litigation arose, neither party challenged the constitutionality of § 315. Note, however, that although the station is protected from liability for defamation, the person who utters the statements is subject to liability under the general rules of defamation. We will examine these rules in Chapter XII.

Other content problems under § 315 are rare, but do arise. Among the candidates running in 1972 for the Democratic nomination for Senator from Georgia, one was broadcasting the following spot announcement:

> I am J.B. Stoner. I am the only candidate for U.S. Senator who is for the white people. I am the only candidate who is against integration. All of the other candidates are race mixers, to one degree or another. I say we must repeal Gambrell's civil rights law. Gambrell's law takes jobs from us whites and gives those jobs to the niggers. The main reason why niggers want integration is because the niggers want our white women. I am for law and order with the knowledge that you cannot have law and order and niggers too.

Vote white. This time vote your convictions by voting white racist J.B. Stoner into the run-off election for U.S. Senator. Thank you.

Several groups asked the Commission to rule that a licensee may, and has the responsibility to, withhold announcements under § 315 if they "pose an imminent and immediate threat to the safety and security of the public it serves." The groups alleged that the spot had created racial tension and that the Mayor of Atlanta had urged broadcasters not to air the advertisement. Letter to Lonnie King, 36 F.C.C.2d 635, 25 R.R.2d 54 (1972). The Commission refused to issue the requested order:

> The relief requested in your letter would amount to an advance approval by the Commission of licensee censorship of a candidate's remarks. By way of background, we note that Constitutional guarantees do not permit the proscription of even the advocacy of force or of law violation "except where such advocacy is directed to inciting or producing imminent lawless action and is likely to incite or produce such action." Brandenburg v. Ohio, 395 U.S. 444, 447 (1969). And a prior restraint bears a heavy presumption against its constitutional validity. Carroll v. Princess Anne, 393 U.S. 175, 181 (1968). While there may be situations where speech is "so interlaced with burgeoning violence that it is not protected," Carroll v. Princess Anne, 393 U.S. at 180 and while a similar approach might warrant overriding the no-censorship command of Section 315, we need not resolve that difficult issue here, for we conclude on the basis of the information before us that there is no factual basis for the relief you request. Despite your report of threats of bombing and violence, there does not appear to be that clear and present danger of imminent violence which might warrant interfering with speech which does not contain any direct incitement to violence. A contrary conclusion here would permit anyone to prevent a candidate from exercising his rights under Section 315 by threatening a violent reaction. In view of the precise commands of Sections 315 and 326, we are constrained to deny your requests.

The FCC has also received occasional complaints about political announcements that contain indecent language. The problem of indecent and obscene political announcements will be discussed in Chapter VII.

### b. Exemptions

During its early years the statute apparently caused few serious problems. The advent of television, however, changed matters dramatically. In 1956, the Commission issued two major rulings during the presidential campaign. In one it ruled that presentation of President Eisenhower's appearance in a two-to-three minute appeal on behalf of the annual drive of the United Community Funds would be a "use" of the facility by a candidate that would trigger the equal opportunities provision. The section carried no exception for "public service" nor did it require the appearance to be "political." Columbia Broadcasting System (United Fund), 14 R.R. 524 (F.C.C.1956). One week before the election,

President Eisenhower requested and received 15 minutes of free time from the three networks to discuss the sudden eruption of war in the Middle East. His Democratic opponent's request for equal time was rejected by the networks. One day before the election, the Commission, without opinion and with one dissent, upheld the networks' position. Columbia Broadcasting System (Suez Crisis), 14 R.R. 720 (F.C.C.1956).

This response to an incumbent speaking as President rather than as candidate was unusual for the Commission, which had interpreted "use" very broadly. It did so, again, in 1959 when a third-party candidate for mayor of Chicago, Lar Daly, requested equal time on the basis of two series of television clips of his opponents, incumbent Mayor Daley and the Republican challenger. One group of clips showed the two major candidates filing their papers (46 seconds); Mayor Daley accepting the nomination (22 seconds); and a one-minute clip asking the Republican why he was running. A second group of clips included "nonpolitical" activities such as a 29-second clip of Mayor Daley on a March of Dimes appeal and 21 seconds of his greeting President Frondizi of Argentina at a Chicago airport. The Commission, in a long opinion, ruled that both groups required equal time. Columbia Broadcasting System, Inc. (Lar Daly), 26 F.C.C. 715 (1959). It relied on the words "use" and "all" in the statute and thought the issue of who initiated the appearance (such as the March of Dimes asking the Mayor to appear) to be irrelevant. Although formal campaigning was the most obvious way of putting forward a candidacy, "of no less importance is the candidate's appearance as a public servant, as an incumbent office holder, or as a private citizen in a nonpolitical role." Such "appearances and uses of a nonpolitical nature may confer substantial benefits on a candidate who is favored."

Congressional response was swift—and negative. Hearings began within days after the decision and the result was an amended version of § 315:

> Sec. 315. (a) If any licensee shall permit any person who is a legally qualified candidate for any public office to use a broadcasting station, he shall afford equal opportunities to all other such candidates for that office in the use of such broadcasting station: *Provided,* That such licensee shall have no power of censorship over the material broadcast under the provisions of this section. No obligation is hereby imposed upon any licensee to allow the use of its station by any such candidate.\* Appearance by a legally qualified candidate on any—
>
> (1) bona fide newscast,
>
> (2) bona fide news interview,
>
> (3) bona fide news documentary (if the appearance of the candidate is incidental to the presentation of the subject or subjects covered by the news documentary), or

---

\* In 1971 Congress amended this sentence by adding "under this subsection" after the word "imposed." The reason for this is given when we consider § 312(a)(7) shortly.

(4) on-the-spot coverage of bona fide news events (including but not limited to political conventions and activities incidental thereto), shall not be deemed to be use of a broadcasting station within the meaning of this subsection.  Nothing in the foregoing sentence shall be construed as relieving broadcasters, in connection with the presentation of newscasts, news interviews, news documentaries, and on-the-spot coverage of news events, from the obligation imposed upon them under this chapter to operate in the public interest and to afford reasonable opportunity for the discussion of conflicting views on issues of public importance.

Recall the significance of this episode to the Court in *Red Lion*, p. 60, supra.

In 1960, Congress suspended the operation of § 315 so that the stations could give time to national candidates without creating a § 315 obligation.  This permitted the Kennedy-Nixon debates to be held without need to provide free time for the many minority candidates.  There was no incumbent and no major third party candidate—two factors that made the debates politically possible.

Presidential election problems returned in 1964.  First, the Commission ruled that coverage of an incumbent President's press conferences were not exempt under either § 315(a)(2) or (4).  Nor were those of his main challenger.  Columbia Broadcasting System (Presidential Press Conference), 3 R.R.2d 623 (F.C.C.1964).  Then, two weeks before the election, the three networks granted President Johnson time to comment on two events that had just occurred: a sudden change of leadership was announced in Moscow, and China exploded a nuclear device.  The Commission adhered to its 1956 ruling that this was not a "use."  It also upheld a network claim that this program came within § 315(a)(4) as a bona fide news event.  Republican National Committee (Dean Burch), 3 R.R.2d 647 (F.C.C.1964).  An appeal of this ruling to the court of appeals led to an affirmance on a divided vote, 3–3, without opinion.  A petition for certiorari was denied, Goldwater v. Federal Communications Commission, 379 U.S. 893 (1964), with Justice Goldberg, joined by Justice Black, dissenting with opinion.  They argued that the case presented substantial questions and that the Commission seemed not to be consistent in its own decisions.

In 1968, Senator Eugene McCarthy announced early that he was a candidate for the Democratic nomination for President against the incumbent, Lyndon Johnson.  During a traditional year-end interview with television reporters, President Johnson criticized Senator McCarthy and made several political statements.  McCarthy sought "equal time" but the Commission denied the request on the ground that the President had not announced that he was a candidate for re-election and thus did not come within the statute or the Commission's rules on who is a "legally qualified candidate" for office.  Eugene McCarthy, 11 F.C.C.2d 511, 12 R.R.2d 106 (1968).  On appeal, the Commission's position was affirmed.  McCarthy v. Federal Communications Commission, 390 F.2d 471 (D.C.Cir.

1968). Shortly thereafter, President Johnson abruptly announced that he would not seek reelection.

In 1972, the problems centered around the Democratic nomination. Just before the crucial California primary, CBS held a joint session of "Face the Nation," expanded from its regular half-hour to one hour, featuring Senators Humphrey and McGovern, the two leading candidates in the primary and for the nomination. The network claimed that this was a bona fide news interview and thus exempt under § 315(a)(2) from time requests by other Democratic candidates. Similar programs on other networks raised similar questions. The Commission found the changes did not deprive the programs of their bona fide character as interviews, and perceived and intended its opinion to accord "with the remedial purpose of the 1959 amendments to accord leeway to licensee journalistic decisions." Hon. Sam Yorty and Hon. Shirley Chisholm, 35 F.C.C.2d 572, 24 R.R.2d 447 (1972). On Chisholm's appeal, the FCC's ruling was vacated. Chisholm v. Federal Communications Commission, 24 R.R.2d 2061 (D.C.Cir.1972). The court thought the program more a debate than an interview. On remand, the Commission begrudgingly complied and ordered the networks to grant Chisholm one half-hour of prime time before the election. 35 F.C.C.2d 579, 24 R.R.2d 720 (1972).

Through the 1960's and 1970's, various proposals were made in Congress to amend or repeal § 315. Nothing came of any of them. But in 1975, the Commission responded dramatically to two petitions. It overruled its 1962 decisions that coverage of a debate did not come within the exemption for on-the-spot coverage of bona fide news events. The Commission said that it had misinterpreted legislative history when it required the appearance of the candidate to be incidental to the coverage of a separate news event. The Commission now concluded that in 1959 Congress intended to run the risks of political favoritism among broadcasters in an effort to allow broadcasters to "cover the political news to the fullest degree." Debates were exempt if controlled by someone other than the candidates or the broadcaster, and if judged to be bona fide news events under § 315(a)(4).

In a companion ruling, the Commission overruled its 1964 decision on press conference coverage. It decided that full coverage of a press conference by any incumbent or candidate would come within the exemption for on-the-spot coverage of a bona fide news event if it "may be considered newsworthy and subject to on-the-spot coverage." But the Commission refused to bring a press conference within the exemption for bona fide news interviews because the licensee did not "control" the format and the event was not "regularly scheduled." Petitions of Aspen Institute and CBS, Inc., 55 F.C.C.2d 697, 35 R.R.2d 49 (1975).

Appeals were taken against both parts of the Commission's 1975 rulings. The main contentions were that the Commission had not followed the Congressional mandate when it permitted the candidate to "become the event" under the (a)(4) exemption, and that the statute did not allow the Commission to uphold licensee decisions as long as they are in "good faith"—that it is for the Commission to make these judgments. By a vote of 2–1, the court affirmed both rulings, Chisholm v. Federal Communications Commission, 538 F.2d 349 (D.C.Cir.1976). The opinions differed as to the significance of the complex legislative history, with the majority concluding that the Commission's interpretation was "reasonable." Rehearing en banc was denied. A petition for certiorari was denied, 429 U.S. 890 (1976), White, J., dissenting.

Seizing on the Commission's rulings, the League of Women Voters set up "debates" between the two major Presidential candidates in 1976. They were held in auditoriums before invited audiences. The candidates were questioned by panelists selected by the League after consultation with the participants. Television was allowed to cover the events—but the League imposed restrictions against showing the audience or any audience reactions. Although the networks complained about the restrictions and about the way the panelists were selected, they did carry the programs live and in full.

Again in 1980, the League took steps to sponsor debates among the major candidates. It decided that John Anderson's showing in public opinion polls was sufficiently strong to warrant his inclusion in a three-way debate. When President Carter refused to participate in a debate with Anderson, the League went ahead anyway and staged an Anderson-Reagan debate. If networks decided to cover the event, as CBS and NBC did, the coverage would be exempt under (a)(4) because the networks and licensees were making the judgment it was a bona fide news event even without the President.

After Anderson's ratings fell to around 10 percent, the League invited Carter and Reagan to debate. Both accepted the invitation and held a single head-to-head debate a week before the election.

In 1980, just before the primaries began, President Carter, seeking renomination as Democratic candidate for President in a contest against Senator Edward M. Kennedy, held a press conference that was carried live in prime time by the three commercial networks and the Public Broadcasting Service. Senator Kennedy, claiming that President Carter had used more than five minutes on that occasion to attack him and to misstate several of his positions, sought relief from the FCC.

In Kennedy for President Committee v. Federal Communications Commission, 636 F.2d 432 (D.C.Cir.1980) (*Kennedy I*), the Senator asked for equal opportunities under § 315 to respond to the "calculated and damaging statements" and to "provide contrasting viewpoints." The FCC denied the request. On appeal, the court affirmed.

The press conference was exempt under § 315(a)(4) so long as the broadcasters reasonably believed that the conference was a "bona fide news event." The Commission said, in a passage approved by the court, that an incumbent President "may well have an advantage over his opponent in attracting media coverage" but "absent strong evidence that broadcasters were not exercising their bona fide news judgment, the Commission will not interfere with such judgments." The Senator was free to hold a press conference the next day to rebut the charges. Indeed, generally, Senator Kennedy was getting substantial media coverage.

The court traced the history of the exemptions to § 315 and adhered to its decision in *Chisholm* upholding the Commission's new approach to § 315. "The only inquiry now in order is whether there was anything so peculiar about the February 13 presidential press conference as to remove it from the ambit of *Aspen* and *Chisholm.* " The court found no reason to doubt the broadcasters' good faith. It also concluded that the actual content of the event could not control the question of exemption. Not only would the Commission and the courts have to make difficult judgments about content, context, and impact, but also the goal of the exemptions would be defeated if broadcasters could not know until after an event whether it was exempt.

Senator Kennedy then argued that the First Amendment required that he be granted time to respond, even if the statute did not. The court rejected that contention on the basis of CBS v. DNC, p. 79, supra:

> From its inception more than a half-century ago, federal regulation of broadcasting has largely entrusted protection of that public right to short-term station licensees functioning under Commission supervision, and with liberty as well as responsibility to determine who may get on the air and when. The history of this era portrays Congress' consistent refusal to mandate access to the air waves on a non-selective basis and, contrariwise, its decision "to permit private broadcasting to develop with the widest journalistic experience consistent with its public obligations." [CBS v. DNC] The Commission has honored that policy in a series of rulings establishing that a private right to utilize the broadcaster's facilities exists only when specially conferred. The net of these many years of legislative and administrative oversight of broadcasting is that "[o]nly when the interests of the public are found to outweigh the private journalistic interests of the broadcasters will government power be asserted within the framework of the Act."

The First Amendment permits Congress to enforce the public's primary interests by using broadcasters as public trustees, and CBS v. DNC shows that no one has a constitutional right to broadcast his own views on any matter.

In Petitions of Henry Geller et al., 54 R.R.2d 1246 (1983), the FCC reversed long-standing administrative decisions by permitting broadcasters themselves to sponsor debates between political candidates without having to provide uninvited candidates with equal broadcasting opportunities. Such debates may still fall within the § 315(a)(4) exemption. The Commission concluded that its previous interpretations neither represented the outer bounds of its legislated authority under the statute nor met the overriding Congressional mandate to encourage broadcast coverage of electoral issues. Third-party sponsorship was not the *sine qua non* of impartiality. For example, the risks of favoritism in the news interview format (§ 315(a)(2)) were thought to be no different from those in the debate format and therefore disparate treatment was not justified. The League of Women Voters' argument that this approach creates too great a risk of favoritism was rejected. The risks inherent in broadcaster-sponsored debates were no greater than the *Chisholm* court had understood the 1959 amendments to be willing to accept.

The Commission also noted that in many cases a broadcaster may be "the ideal, and perhaps the only, entity interested in promoting a debate between candidates for a particular office, especially at the state or local level." Exempting broadcaster-sponsored debates would therefore increase the number of debates and ultimately benefit the public. Finally, a debate's exempt status "should not be contingent upon whether a broadcaster is the sponsoring or controlling entity—for such control generally would not affect the program's news value." The Commission also made clear that this new interpretation of § 315(a)(4) did not authorize licensees to favor or disfavor any candidate.

The League's expedited appeal was rejected without opinion. League of Women Voters v. FCC, 731 F.2d 995 (D.C.Cir.1984).

The "on the spot" language of § 315(a)(4) also has produced litigation. Groups afraid that an exempt program, such as a debate, might be recorded and replayed several times to the detriment of excluded candidates, have argued that the statute permits only one showing—and that it must be live. The FCC rejected this and allowed the broadcaster to tape the live event and to present it once during the next 24 hours. When that ruling was challenged, the court affirmed the Commission. The agency had authority to develop a balance between rigidly equal opportunities and the new freedom provided by the 1959 exemptions. There was no showing that the FCC had misconstrued the law, and it had fully explained what it was doing. Office of Communication of the United Church of Christ v. Federal Communications Commission, 590 F.2d 1062 (D.C.Cir.1978).

The one-day rule was eliminated in *Henry Geller*, supra. The reasonableness of a delayed broadcast will now be left to the broadcaster's good faith determination that the delay of more than one day after the occurrence of the exempt debate will better serve the community. Such delay, however, must be motivated by concerns of informing the public, and not in order to favor or disfavor any candidate.

The other subdivisions, (a)(1) and (a)(3), have given rise to fewer problems. In 1976, supporters of Ronald Reagan complained when a Miami television station broadcast six-minute interviews with President Ford on five consecutive evening newscasts. The complaint asserted that the segments were from a single half-hour interview that had been broken up into five parts. The Commission held that even if the 30-minute interview would not have been exempt under § 315, inclusion of the segments within newscasts would not preclude "exempt status pursuant to § 315(a)(1) unless it has been shown that such a decision is clearly unreasonable or in bad faith." Even though this was broadcast during the last week of a primary campaign and might benefit President Ford, the complainants "have not shown that the licensee in deciding to air them, considered anything other than their newsworthiness." Citizens for Reagan, 58 F.C.C.2d 925, 36 R.R.2d 885 (1976). Does the statute's use of "bona fide" support the Commission's decision to leave the decision in the first instance with the licensee?

If a program is exempt, that status is not lost simply because its timing may help one candidate more than another. The day before the Iowa caucus vote in 1980, President Carter was the guest on NBC's "Meet the Press," a program normally exempt under (a)(2) as a bona fide news interview program. One of his opponents argued that the program lost its exemption because of the impact just before the critical first voting of the 1980 primary process.

The FCC rejected the complaint. So long as the format remains the same and is controlled by the broadcaster, and the choice of guest is based on newsworthiness, the FCC would not intervene. The spirit of the Aspen decision was to leave judgments of newsworthiness to the professionals. In this case, since there was no showing that the incumbent's appearance would not be newsworthy, the timing was not controlling.

The FCC has granted general exemptions under (a)(1) to such programs as "Today" and "Good Morning America." In each case, the FCC was influenced by the fact that the program was regularly scheduled and involved regular coverage of current news supplemented by interviews, commentary, and discussions. The determinations of what to cover are made in the exercise of news judgment and not to further a particular candidate's advantage. On the other hand, the Commission denied such a general exemption to "Donahue" because both Phil Donahue, the host, and the audience can, and often do, give their personal opinions about the subjects being discussed. Also, "Tonight" has been held to be a variety show and thus not entitled to exemption.

In 1984, the Commission unanimously overruled its earlier ruling denying an exemption to "Donahue." Multimedia Entertainment, Inc., 56 R.R.2d 143 (1984). The Commission concluded that it "would appear immaterial" that some parts of the show have nothing to do with elections or politics. Also, the Commission now accepted the claim that Donahue would be able to control the audience to prevent anyone from using the show for partisan purposes. It noted that tickets are distributed months before any particular program. The Commission concluded that it would be unwise to bar exemptions to any program that did not rigidly adhere to a traditional news interview format.

### c. *Nonpolitical Appearances*

The Commission appears to be holding firm to its earlier decisions broadly defining "use" in cases of "nonpolitical" appearances. Thus, in United Way of America, 35 R.R.2d 137 (F.C.C.1975), which was decided at about the same time as the Aspen-CBS petitions, the Commission, 4–3, adhered to its earlier rulings that an appearance by candidate Ford opening an annual charity fund drive came within § 315. The Commission has also adhered to its view that appearances by television personalities or film stars after they have announced their candidacy for office constitute a "use" under § 315. In Adrian Weiss, 58 F.C.C.2d 342, 36 R.R.2d 292 (1976), the Broadcast Bureau ruled that the showing of old Ronald Reagan films on television would require the offering of equal opportunities to other Republican presidential aspirants. The Bureau relied heavily on the claim that nonpolitical uses can be very effective. The Commission refused to review the Bureau's decision, with two Commissioners concurring separately and two dissenting. These four all thought that common sense dictated exempting movies made before Reagan actively entered politics, but the two concurring Commissioners thought that any change should be made by Congress.

In Pat Paulsen, 33 F.C.C.2d 297, affirmed 33 F.C.C.2d 835, 23 R.R.2d 861 (1972), affirmed 491 F.2d 887 (9th Cir.1974), the Commission rejected a comedian's argument that applying § 315 would deprive him of due process and equal protection by forcing him to give up his livelihood in order to run for public office. Their interpretation was held permissible "to achieve the important and legitimate objectives of encouraging political discussion and preventing unfair and unequal use of the broadcast media." In mid-1985, the Commission turned down a petition by a California TV reporter asking for a ruling that appearing on the air as a journalist would not trigger § 315. The Commission also refused his request to declare § 315 a violation of the First Amendment.

### d. Lowest Unit Rate

In 1971, as part of legislation concerning election campaigning, Congress passed two statutes that affect broadcasting during political campaigns. One requires that candidates using broadcast facilities during the 45 days before a primary and the 60 days before a general election be charged rates not to exceed "the lowest unit charge of the station for the same class and amount of time for the same period. . . ." At all other times, the rates charged candidates are not to exceed "the charges made for comparable use of such station by other users thereof." 47 U.S.C. § 315(b). The major difference between the two quoted passages is that during the 45- and 60-day periods, the candidate pays the rate that the highest-volume advertiser would pay for that time. At other times, the candidate pays the rates charged to those who advertise as little or as much as the candidate does.

The lowest unit rate provision has caused great confusion among broadcasters. Most often a broadcaster will charge a candidate the lowest commercial rate for the number of spots he buys when the rule requires giving the candidate all volume and frequency discounts offered to any advertiser regardless of the number of spots the candidate purchases. However, this is not necessarily the lowest overall spot rate since the rule applies only to spots of the same class or type. Thus, a candidate buying prime time spots does not get the benefit of non-prime-time rates.   Barter and per-inquiry spots are not applicable to the calculation of lowest unit rate.

Broadcasters are allowed to set certain conditions for political advertising—broadcast quality, prepayment, etc., but any discrimination in the application of these conditions to different candidates is strictly prohibited.   For a recent example of the application of § 315(b), see Alpha Broadcasting Corporation, 57 R.R.2d 469 (1984).

### 2.   REASONABLE ACCESS—SECTION 312(a)(7)

In 1971, at the same time it passed the lowest unit rate provision, Congress adopted § 312(a)(7), providing that the Commission may revoke a license:

> (7) for willful or repeated failure to allow reasonable access to or to permit purchase of reasonable amounts of time for the use of a broadcasting station by a legally qualified candidate for Federal elective office on behalf of his candidacy.

The legislative history indicates that one purpose of the overall legislation was to "give candidates for public office greater access to the media so that they may better explain their stand on the issues and thereby more fully and completely inform the voters."

It was only in 1980 that cases involving the section began to reach the courts.

The first case raised the questions of when the campaign had begun and how requests should be treated.   The Carter-Mondale Committee asked each major network to sell it 30 minutes of prime time in December, 1979 (just after the formal announcement that President Carter was seeking renomination), in order to show a documentary on President Carter's first term.   CBS offered two five-minute segments, one of which would be in prime time.   ABC indicated that it would make time available beginning in January, 1980.   NBC said that it was "too early in the political season for nationwide broadcast time to be made available for paid political purposes."   The Committee complained to the FCC, which found the stations in violation of § 312(a)(7), by a vote of 4–3.   The court of appeals affirmed.

### CBS, INC. v. FEDERAL COMMUNICATIONS COMMISSION

Supreme Court of the United States, 1981.
453 U.S. 367, 101 S.Ct. 2813, 69 L.Ed.2d 706.

CHIEF JUSTICE BURGER delivered the opinion of the Court.

[The Court agreed with the FCC that the section had "created an affirmative, promptly enforceable right of reasonable access to the use of broadcast stations for individual candidates seeking federal elective office" rather than simply codifying prior policies that the FCC had developed under the general public interest standard.   The Court relied on the specific language of the statute itself, the legislative history, and what the Court found to be the FCC's consistent administrative interpretation of the language since the statute's enactment. Perhaps the "most telling evidence" of Congressional intent was the contemporaneous change in § 315 from a statement that "No obligation is imposed upon any licensee to allow the use of its station by" a candidate to the statement that no such obligation "is imposed under this subsection [§ 315(a) ]."]

## III

### A

Although Congress provided in § 312(a)(7) for greater use of broadcasting stations by federal candidates, it did not give guidance on how the Commission should implement the statute's access requirement. Essentially, Congress adopted a "rule of reason" and charged the Commission with its enforcement. . . . The Commission has issued some general interpretative statements, but its standards implementing § 312(a)(7) have evolved principally on a case-by-case basis and are not embodied in formalized rules. . . .

Broadcasters are free to deny the sale of air time prior to the commencement of a campaign, but once a campaign has begun, they must give reasonable and good faith attention to access requests from "legally qualified" candidates for federal elective office. Such requests must be considered on an individualized basis, and broadcasters are required to tailor their responses to accommodate, as much as reasonably possible, a candidate's stated purposes in seeking air time. In responding to access requests, however, broadcasters may also give weight to such factors as the amount of time previously sold to the candidate, the disruptive impact on regular programming, and the likelihood of requests for time by rival candidates under the equal opportunities provision of § 315(a). These considerations may not be invoked as pretexts for denying access; to justify a negative response, broadcasters must cite a realistic danger of substantial program disruption—perhaps caused by insufficient notice to allow adjustments in the schedule—or of an excessive number of equal time requests. Further, in order to facilitate review by the Commission, broadcasters must explain their reasons for refusing time or making a more limited counteroffer. If broadcasters take the appropriate factors into account and act reasonably and in good faith, their decisions will be entitled to deference even if the Commission's analysis would have differed in the first instance. But if broadcasters adopt "across-the-board policies" and do not attempt to respond to the individualized situation of a particular candidate, the Commission is not compelled to sustain their denial of access. [ ] Petitioners argue that certain of these standards are contrary to the statutory objectives of § 312(a)(7).

### (1)

The Commission has concluded that, as a threshold matter, it will independently determine whether a campaign has begun and the obligations imposed by § 312(a)(7) have attached. [ ] Petitioners assert that, in undertaking such a task, the Commission becomes improperly involved in the electoral process and seriously impairs broadcaster discretion.

However, petitioners fail to recognize that the Commission does not set the starting date for a campaign. Rather, on review of a complaint alleging denial of "reasonable access," it examines objective evidence to find whether the campaign has already commenced, "taking into account the position of the candidate *and the networks* as well as other factors." . . . Such a decision is not, and cannot be, purely one of editorial judgment.

. . .

### (2)

Petitioners also challenge the Commission's requirement that broadcasters evaluate and respond to access requests on an individualized basis. In petitioners' view, the agency has attached inordinate significance to candidates' needs, thereby precluding fair assessment of broadcasters' concerns and prohibiting the adoption of uniform policies regarding requests for access.

While admonishing broadcasters not to " 'second guess' the 'political' wisdom or . . . effectiveness" of the particular format sought by a candidate, the Commission has clearly acknowledged that "the candidate's . . . request is by no means conclusive of the question of how much time, if any, is appropriate. Other . . . factors, such as the disruption or displacement of regular programming (particularly as affected by a reasonable probability of requests by other candidates), must be considered in the balance." [ ] Thus, the Commission mandates careful consideration of, not blind assent to, candidates' desires for air time.

Petitioners are correct that the Commission's standards proscribe blanket rules concerning access; each request must be examined on its own merits. While the adoption of uniform policies might well prove more convenient for broadcasters, such an approach would allow personal campaign strategies and the exigencies of the political process to be ignored. A broadcaster's "evenhanded" response of granting only time spots of a fixed duration to candidates may be "unreasonable" where a particular candidate desires less time for an advertisement or a longer format to discuss substantive issues. . . . § 312(a)(7) assures a right of reasonable access to *individual* candidates for federal elective office, and the Commission's requirement that their requests be considered on an *individualized* basis is consistent with that guarantee.

[The Court concluded that the Commission's actions were a "reasoned attempt to effectuate the statute's access requirement, giving broadcasters room to exercise their discretion but demanding that they act in good faith." These ground rules were sufficiently clear in late 1979 to permit the FCC to rule that the networks had violated the statute by failing to grant "reasonable access."]

IV

Finally, petitioners assert that § 312(a)(7) as implemented by the Commission violates the First Amendment rights of broadcasters by unduly circumscribing their editorial discretion. . . .

. . .

The First Amendment interests of candidates and voters, as well as broadcasters, are implicated by § 312(a)(7). We have recognized that "it is of particular importance that candidates have the . . . opportunity to make their views known so that the electorate may intelligently evaluate the candidates' personal qualities and their positions on vital public issues before choosing among them on election day." [Buckley v. Valeo]. [ ] Indeed, "speech concerning public affairs is . . . the essence of self-government." [Garrison v. Louisiana]. The First Amendment "has its fullest and most urgent application precisely to the conduct of campaigns for public office." [Monitor Patriot Co. v. Roy]. Section 312(a)(7) thus makes a significant contribution to freedom of expression by enhancing the ability of candidates to present, and the public to receive, information necessary for the effective operation of the democratic process.

Petitioners are correct that the Court has never approved a *general* right of access to the media. [ ] Nor do we do so today. Section 312(a)(7) creates a *limited* right to "reasonable" access that pertains only to legally qualified federal candidates and may be invoked by them only for the purpose of advancing their candidacies once a campaign has commenced. The Commission has stated that, in enforcing the statute, it will "provide leeway to broadcasters and not merely attempt *de novo* to determine the reasonableness of their judgments. . . ." If broadcasters have considered the relevant factors in good faith, the Commission will uphold their decisions. See 629 F.2d, at 25. Further, § 312(a)(7) does not impair the discretion of broadcasters to present their views on any issue or to carry any particular type of programming.

Section 312(a)(7) represents an effort by Congress to assure that an important resource—the airwaves—will be used in the public interest. We hold that the statutory right of access, as defined by the Commission and applied in these cases, properly balances the First Amendment rights of federal candidates, the public, and broadcasters.

The judgment of the Court of Appeals is

Affirmed.

[Justice White, joined by Justices Rehnquist and Stevens, dissented on the grounds that the decision negated "the long-standing statutory policy of deferring to editorial judgments that are not destructive of the goals of the Act." Justice White also argued that the Commission had misinterpreted § 312(a)(7). His reading of the legislative history led him to believe that Congress intended only "to codify what it conceived to be the pre-existing duty of the broadcasters to serve the public interest by presenting political broadcasts."]

JUSTICE STEVENS, dissenting.

. . . The approach the Federal Communications Commission has taken in this case, now adopted by the Court, creates an impermissible risk that the Commission's evaluation of a given refusal by a licensee will be biased—or will appear to be biased—by the character of the office held by the candidate making the request.* Indeed, anyone who listened to the campaign rhetoric that was broadcast in 1980 must wonder how an impartial administrator could conclude that any presidential candidate was denied "reasonable access" to the electronic media. That wonderment is not dispelled by anything said in the opinions for the majority of the Commission in this case.

### Notes and Questions

1. The relationship between § 312(a)(7) and § 315 was central to Kennedy for President Committee v. Federal Communications Commission, 636 F.2d 417 (D.C.Cir.1980) (*Kennedy II*). On March 14, 1980, President Carter made a 30-minute speech in the afternoon and held a press conference from 9:00 to 9:30 p.m. that night. The three major commercial networks carried both programs live, except that ABC delayed the press conference for three hours. Senator Kennedy charged that these programs saturated the public with the President's views on the economy only four days before the Illinois primary. He asked for free time to reply under § 312(a)(7). The networks denied the request, the Commission refused to order that time be granted, and the court affirmed.

The court began by noting that Congress, in 1971, enacted § 312(a) (7) and § 315(b)(1), requiring lowest charges to candidates using broadcast facilities, because Congress was concerned about the rising cost of candidates' televised appearances:

> It was believed that the informational and educational aspects of political broadcasting would be greatly enhanced by ensuring that more time would be made available to candidates at lower rates. This expectably would encourage less dependence on thirty- to sixty-second "spots"—necessarily little more than slogans—in favor of longer, more illuminating presentations; it would also enable more candidates to afford the television appearances so instrumental to present-day electioneering.

The court concluded that the "most straightforward reading" of § 312(a)(7) "is that broadcasters may fulfill their obligation thereunder either by allotting free time to a candidate *or* by selling the candidate time at the rates prescribed by Section 315(b)." Considering the legisla-

---

* The possibility that Commission decisions under § 312(a)(7) may appear to be biased is well illustrated by this case. In its initial decision and its decision on the networks' petitions for reconsideration, the Commission voted 4–3 in favor of the Cart-er-Mondale Presidential Committee. [ ] In both instances, the four Democratic Commissioners concluded that the networks had violated the statute by denying the Committee's request for access; the three Republican Commissioners disagreed. [ ]

tive history, the FCC's consistent administrative interpretations, and the apparent statutory scheme of the various provisions, the court concluded that § 312(a)(7), although seeking to assure federal candidates access to broadcasting, did not "confer the privilege of using the broadcaster's facilities without charge." The choice of giving or selling time is for the broadcaster:

> Should Section 312(a)(7) be construed as automatically entitling a candidate to responsive broadcast access whenever and for whatever reason his opponent has appeared on the air, Section 315(a)'s exemptions would soon become meaningless. Statutes are to be interpreted, if possible, to give operation to all of their parts, and to maintain them in harmonious working relationship.

Since Kennedy never claimed that he had not been given an opportunity to buy time, he could not invoke § 312(a)(7). Nor had he sought relief under § 315.

2. In 1981, the National Conservative Political Action Committee (NCPAC) petitioned the Commission for a ruling that an independent political action committee (PAC) had a right of reasonable access similar to that granted candidates for federal office by § 312(a)(7). The Broadcast Bureau rejected NCPAC's request, finding nothing in either the language of § 312(a)(7) or its legislative history that would support a right of access for anyone other than a candidate for federal office. The Commission upheld the Bureau's action, citing CBS v. DNC. National Conservative Political Action Committee (NCPAC), 89 F.C.C.2d 626, 51 R.R.2d 233 (1982).

3. In June, 1985, Senators Jack Danforth (R–Mo.) and Ernest Hollings (D–S.C.) introduced the Clean Campaign Act of 1985. The bill would require candidates attacking their opponents in radio, television or cable advertisements to appear personnally in the advertisements. Any broadcaster airing an advertisement that violates that requirement would have to provide free response time to the opponent who was attacked. In addition, the bill would require provision of free, equal response time to any candidate who is attacked by a political action committee or whose opponent is endorsed by a political action committee. In hearings held in September, 1985, a number of people spoke in favor of the bill, arguing that negative political ads are undermining the political process. The ACLU, on the other hand, claimed that the bill raises serious First Amendment problems.

## B. THE FAIRNESS DOCTRINE

------

### 1. IN GENERAL

While equal opportunities originated in the Communications Act, the fairness doctrine was created by the Commission itself. The Commission has been concerned with fairness and the exposure of varying views since its earliest days. Indeed, the Radio Commission in 1928 indicated as much in a discussion of the implications of the limited spectrum. It observed that there was not room "for every school of thought, religious, political, social, and economic, each to have its separate broadcasting station, its mouthpiece in the ether." Such ideas "must find their way into the market of ideas by the existing public-service stations, and if they are of sufficient importance to the listening public, the microphone will undoubtedly be available. If it is not, a well-founded complaint will receive the careful consideration of the commission in its future action with reference to the station complained of." Great Lakes Broadcasting Co., 3 F.R.C.Ann.Rep. 32 (1929), modified on other grounds 37 F.2d 993 (D.C.Cir.1930), certiorari dismissed 281 U.S. 706 (1930).

The doctrine evolved through case law until it became the subject of a major report in 1949. The doctrine has two separate parts. One part requires the broadcaster to air issues that "are so critical or of such great public importance that it would be unreasonable for a licensee to ignore them completely." Much more attention has been paid to the second part of the doctrine—that if a broadcaster does cover a "controversial issue of public importance" it must take steps to assure that important contrasting views are also presented. These views may be presented by the licensee itself or by speakers chosen by the licensee.

In 1959, when § 315 was amended, p. 187, supra, many people interpreted the phrase, "nothing in the foregoing sentence shall be construed as relieving broadcasters . . . from the obligation under this chapter to operate in the public interest and to afford reasonable opportunity for the discussion of conflicting views on issues of public importance" as codifying the fairness doctrine in the Communications Act.

## IN THE MATTER OF THE HANDLING OF PUBLIC ISSUES UNDER THE FAIRNESS DOCTRINE AND THE PUBLIC INTEREST STANDARDS OF THE COMMUNICATIONS ACT

### (1974 FAIRNESS REPORT)

Federal Communications Commission, 1974.
48 F.C.C.2d 1, 30 R.R.2d 1261.

By the Commission: COMMISSIONER HOOKS concurring in part and dissenting in part and issuing a separate statement.

[The Commission first restated its commitment to the goal of "uninhibited, robust, wide open" debate on public issues and the need to recognize that achievement of this goal must be compatible with the public interest in "the larger and more effective use of radio" § 303(g). This included the fact that "ours is a commercially-based broadcast system" and that the Commission's policies "should be consistent with the maintenance and growth of that system." The Commission then quoted a critical passage from its Report on Editorializing, 13 F.C.C. 1246, 1249 (1949), in which the fairness doctrine was formally announced:

> It is axiomatic that one of the most vital questions of mass communication in a democracy is the development of an informed public opinion through the public dissemination of news and ideas concerning the vital public issues of the day. . . . The Commission has consequently recognized the necessity for licensees to devote a reasonable percentage of their broadcast time to the presentation of news and programs devoted to the consideration and discussion of public issues of interest in the community served by the particular station. And we have recognized, with respect to such programs, the paramount right of the public in a free society to be informed and to have presented to it for acceptance or rejection the different attitudes and viewpoints concerning these vital and often controversial issues which are held by the various groups which make up the community. It is this right of the public to be informed, rather than any right on the part of the Government, any broadcast licensee or any individual member of the public to broadcast his own particular views on any matter, which is the foundation stone of the American system of broadcasting.

The 1974 Report stressed that two basic duties were involved: "(1) the broadcaster must devote a reasonable percentage of time to coverage of public issues; and (2) his coverage of these issues must be fair in the sense that it provides an opportunity for the presentation of contrasting points of view." The Commission also noted that in 1970 it had described the two parts of the fairness doctrine "as the single most important requirement of operation in the public interest—the *sine qua non* for grant of a renewal of license." The Commission denied that imposition of these two duties could be inhibiting:

> 18. In evaluating the possible inhibitory effect of the fairness doctrine, it is appropriate to consider the specifics of the doctrine and the procedures employed by the Commission in implementing it. When a licensee presents one side of a controversial issue, he is not required to provide a forum for opposing views on that same program or series of programs. He is simply expected to make provision for the opposing views in his *overall programming.* Further, there is no requirement that any precisely equal balance of views be achieved, and all matters concerning the particular opposing views to be presented and the appropriate spokesmen and format for their presentation are left to the licensee's discretion subject only to a standard of reasonableness and good faith.

> 19. As a matter of general procedure, we do not monitor broadcasts for possible violations, but act on the basis of complaints received from interested citizens. These complaints are not forwarded to the licensee for his comments unless they present *prima facie* evidence of a violation. Allen C. Phelps, 21 F.C.C.2d 12 (1969). Thus, broadcasters are not burdened with the task of answering idle

or capricious complaints. By way of illustration, the Commission received some 2,400 fairness complaints in fiscal 1973, only 94 of which were forwarded to licensees for their comments.

20. While there may be occasional exceptions, we find it difficult to believe that these policies add significantly to the overall administrative burdens involved in operating a broadcast station. . . . The Supreme Court has made it clear and it should be reemphasized here that "if present licensees should suddenly prove timorous, the Commission is not powerless to insist that they give adequate and fair attention to public issues." Red Lion Broadcasting Co. v. FCC, 395 U.S. at 393.

As to the first duty imposed, the Commission noted:

We have, in the past, indicated that some issues are so critical or of such great public importance that it would be unreasonable for a licensee to ignore them completely. [ ] But such statements on our part are the rare exception, not the rule, and we have no intention of becoming involved in the selection of issues to be discussed, nor do we expect a broadcaster to cover each and every important issue which may arise in his community.

26. We wish to emphasize that the responsibility for the selection of program material is that of the individual licensee. That responsibility "can neither be delegated by the licensee to any network or other person or group, or be unduly fettered by contractual arrangements restricting the licensee in his free exercise of his independent judgments." Report on Editorializing, 13 FCC at 1248. We believe that stations, in carrying out this responsibility, should be alert to the opportunity to complement network offerings with local programming on these issues, or with syndicated programming.

The Commission then turned to the second, and more frequently litigated, aspect of the fairness doctrine.]

## 2. *A Reasonable Opportunity for Opposing Viewpoints*

. . .

28. It has frequently been suggested that individual stations should not be expected to present opposing points of view and that it should be sufficient for the licensee to demonstrate that the opposing viewpoint has been adequately presented on another station in the market or in the print media. See WSOC Broadcasting Co., 17 P & F Radio Reg. 548, 550 (1958). While we recognize that citizens receive information on public issues from a variety of sources, other considerations require the rejection of this suggestion. First, in amending section 315(a) of the Communications Act in 1959, Congress gave statutory approval to the fairness doctrine, including the requirement that broadcasters themselves provide an opportunity for opposing viewpoints. See BEM, 412 U.S. at 110, note 8. Second, it would be an administrative nightmare for this Commission to attempt to review the overall coverage of an issue in all of the

broadcast stations and publications in a given market. Third, and perhaps most importantly, we believe that the requirement that *each* station provide for contrasting views greatly increases the likelihood that individual members of the public will be exposed to varying points of view.  .  .  .

### a.   What is a "controversial issue of public importance"?

29.  It has frequently been suggested that the Commission set forth comprehensive guidelines to aid interested parties in recognizing whether an issue is "controversial" and of "public importance." However, given the limitless number of potential controversial issues and the varying circumstances in which they might arise, we have not been able to develop detailed criteria which would be appropriate in all cases. For this very practical reason, and for the reason that our role must and should be limited to one of review, we will continue to rely heavily on the reasonable, good faith judgments of our licensees in this area.

30.  Some general observations, however, are in order. First of all, it is obvious that an issue is not necessarily a matter of significant "public importance" merely because it has received broadcast or newspaper coverage. "Our daily papers and television broadcasts alike are filled with news items which good journalistic judgment would classify as newsworthy, but which the same editors would not characterize as containing important controversial public issues." Healey v. FCC, 460 F.2d 917, 922 (D.C.Cir.1972). Nevertheless, the degree of media coverage is one factor which clearly should be taken into account in determining an issue's importance. It is also appropriate to consider the degree of attention the issue has received from government officials and other community leaders. The principal test of public importance, however, is not the extent of media or governmental attention, but rather a subjective evaluation of the impact that the issue is likely to have on the community at large. If the issue involves a social or political choice, the licensee might well ask himself whether the outcome of that choice will have a significant impact on society or its institutions. It appears to us that these judgments can be made only on a case-by-case basis.

31.  The question of whether an issue is "controversial" may be determined in a somewhat more objective manner. Here, it is highly relevant to measure the degree of attention paid to an issue by government officials, community leaders, and the media. The licensee should be able to tell, with a reasonable degree of objectivity, whether an issue is the subject of vigorous debate with substantial elements of the community in opposition to one another. It is possible, of course, that "programs initiated with no thought on the part of the licensee of their possible controversial nature .  .  . will merit presentation of opposing views." Report on Editorializing, 13 FCC at 1251. In such circumstances, it would be appropriate to make provision for opposing views when the opposition becomes manifest.

### b.    *What specific issue has been raised?*

32.　One of the most difficult problems involved in the administration of the fairness doctrine is the determination of the specific issue or issues raised by a particular program.　This would seem to be a simple task, but in many cases it is not.　.　.　.

.　.　.

### c.    *What is a "reasonable opportunity" for contrasting viewpoints?*

.　.　.

37.　The first point to be made with regard to the obligation to present contrasting views is that it cannot be met "merely through the adoption of a general policy of not refusing to broadcast opposing views where a demand is made of the station for broadcast time."　Report on Editorializing, 13 FCC at 1251.　The licensee has a duty to play a conscious and positive role in encouraging the presentation of opposing viewpoints.[13]　.　.　.

38.　In making provision for the airing of contrasting viewpoints, the broadcaster should be alert to the possibility that a particular issue may involve more than two opposing viewpoints.　Indeed, there may be several important viewpoints or shades of opinion which warrant broadcast coverage.

.　.　.

41.　In providing for the coverage of opposing points of view, we believe that the licensee must make a reasonable allowance for presentations by genuine partisans who actually believe in what they are saying. The fairness doctrine does not permit the broadcaster "to preside over a 'paternalistic' regime," BEM, 412 U.S. at 130, and it would clearly not be acceptable for the licensee to adopt a "policy of excluding partisan voices and always itself presenting views in a bland, inoffensive manner. .　.　."　.　.　.

42.　This does not mean, however, that the Commission intends to dictate the selection of a particular spokesman or a particular format, or indeed that partisan spokesmen must be presented in every instance. We do not believe that it is either appropriate or feasible for a governmental agency to make decisions as to what is desirable in each situation. In cases involving personal attacks and political campaigns, the natural opposing spokesmen are relatively easy to identify.　This is not the case, however, with the majority of public controversies.　Ordinarily, there are

---

**13.** This duty includes the obligation defined in Cullman Broadcasting Co., 40 FCC 576, 577 (1963) .　.　.　.

We do not believe that the passage of time since *Cullman* was decided has in any way since diminished the importance and necessity of this principle.　If the public's right to be informed of the contrasting views on controversial issues is to be truly honored, broadcasters must provide the forum for the expression of those viewpoints at their own expense if paid sponsorship is unavailable.

a variety of spokesmen and formats which could reasonably be deemed to be appropriate. We believe that the public is best served by a system which allows individual broadcasters considerable discretion in selecting the manner of coverage, the appropriate spokesmen, and the techniques of production and presentation.

43. Frequently, the question of the reasonableness of the opportunity provided for contrasting viewpoints comes down to weighing the *time* allocated to each side. Aside from the field of political broadcasting, the licensee is not required to provide equal time for the various opposing points of view. Indeed, we have long felt that the basic goal of creating an informed citizenry would be frustrated if for every controversial item or presentation on a newscast or other broadcast the licensee had to offer equal time to the other side. . . . Similarly, we do not believe that it would be appropriate for the Commission to establish any other mathematical ratio, such as 3 to 1 or 4 to 1, to be applied in all cases. We believe that such an approach is much too mechanical in nature and that in many cases our preconceived ratios would prove to be far from reasonable. In the case of a 10-second personal attack, for example, fairness may dictate that more time be afforded to answer the attack than was given the attack itself.

.   .   .

## E.  *Fairness and Accurate News Reporting*

58. In our 1949 Report on Editorializing, we alluded to a licensee's obligation to present the news in an accurate manner:

> It must be recognized, however, that the licensee's opportunity to express his own views . . . does not justify or empower any licensee to exercise his authority over the selection of program material to distort or suppress the basic factual information upon which any truly fair and free discussion of public issues must necessarily depend. . . . A licensee would be abusing his position as public trustee of these important means of mass communication were he to withhold from expression over his facilities relevant news or facts concerning a controversy or to slant or distort the presentation of such news. No discussion of the issues involved in any controversy can be fair or in the public interest where such discussion must take place in a climate of false or misleading information concerning the basic facts of the controversy, 13 FCC at 1254–55.

It is a matter of critical importance to the public that the basic facts or elements of a controversy should not be deliberately suppressed or misstated by a licensee. But we must recognize that such distortions are "so continually done in perfect good faith, by persons who are not considered . . . ignorant or incompetent, that it is rarely possible on adequate grounds, conscientiously to stamp the misrepresentations as morally culpable. . . ." J.S. Mill, On Liberty 31 (People's ed. 1921). Accordingly, we do not believe that it would be either useful or appropriate for us to investigate charges of news misrepresentations in the absence of substantial extrinsic evidence or documents that on their face reflect deliberate distortion. See The Selling of the Pentagon, 30 FCC2d 150 (1971).

### Notes and Questions

1. In 1976, the Commission denied reconsideration of the 1974 Fairness Report. 58 F.C.C.2d 691, 36 R.R.2d 1021 (1976). Commissioner Robinson dissented because he doubted the value of the efforts involved and was concerned about the intrusion into editorial decisions. He noted that in 1973 and 1974, of 4,280 formal fairness complaints, only 19 resulted in findings adverse to the licensee. These included seven in the political editorial area, seven cases of personal attack, and five general fairness complaints. Of the 19 violations, only eight resulted in tangible penalty to the licensee—seven political editorializing cases and one personal attack case involved forfeitures under § 503. Since this sanction is available only for violations of formal rules, it is not available for violations of the uncodified general doctrine.

2. Commissioner Robinson asserted that so long as *Red Lion* was the law the Commission could not eliminate the fairness doctrine completely. He favored the suggestion made by the Committee for Open Media, under which a licensee might choose to meet its obligations under the fairness doctrine by allowing access to its facilities. The proposal was to allow 35 one-minute messages per week scheduled at different times, including prime time. Half the spots would be allocated on a first-come, first-served basis and the other half would use "a representative spokesperson" system. If an excessive number wanted to speak, Commissioner Robinson suggested that speakers might be chosen by lot or by queueing so as to minimize licensee bias. Efforts would be made to prevent monopolization by one outside group. Commissioner Robinson thought few licensees would choose to relinquish control in this way, but he thought it offered the Commission an opportunity to avoid judging content and he urged offering this alternative to licensees. For a study of the operation of Free Speech Messages in San Francisco, see Harris, Free Speech Messages: When the Public Gets Access, What Does It Say?, Access 34 at 20 (1976).

    In a separate statement, Chairman Wiley attacked the access proposal on the grounds that it encouraged licensees to abdicate editorial control and emphasized a single programming technique: the access announcement. "In my opinion a more varied, interesting and informative coverage would be possible if professional journalists played a conscious and positive role in the process."

3. After the Commission's denial of reconsideration of the Fairness Report, the court of appeals generally affirmed that ruling. National Citizens Committee for Broadcasting v. Federal Communications Commission, 567 F.2d 1095 (D.C.Cir.1977). The court upheld the Commission's decision to discontinue applying the fairness doctrine to most

commercial advertisements—a result already reached in the snowmobile case, infra. The court did remand two issues to the Commission for additional consideration. One was the COM proposal, discussed supra. The other was a proposal that the Commission order each licensee to "list annually the ten controversial issues of public importance, local and national, which it chose for the most coverage in the prior year, set out the offers for response made, and note representative programming that was presented on each issue."

The parties who were dissatisfied with the commercial advertisement part of the decision sought Supreme Court review, but certiorari was denied. 436 U.S. 926 (1978).

On the remand, the Commission adhered to its earlier views. 74 F.C.C.2d 163, 46 R.R.2d 999 (1979). It rejected the COM proposal on the ground that "any system which has its emphasis on speakers rather than on ideas is at cross-purposes to that of the Fairness Doctrine. Since the goal of the Fairness Doctrine is to inform the public, any substitute means of compliance must do this." Studies of access usage in various cities provided no assurances that important and timely public issues would be discussed, that presentations on issues would be balanced, or that they would be informative and comprehensible. Even time assigned to spokespersons for issue-oriented groups might not be devoted to the discussion of important public issues.

Despite the acknowledged attractions of the access proposal, such as the opportunity for "true partisans" to express their views and the use of spot announcements "to reach larger and more diverse audiences than through program-length public affairs broadcasts," the defects were held to outweigh the potential gains.

Licensees who might choose to institute an access program must still comply with the fairness doctrine. "How the licensee achieves this mandate depends, as we have always stated, upon the journalistic discretion of each participating station."

The Commission again rejected the Geller proposal that television licensees be required to list annually the 10 community and national controversial issues of public importance that they chose for the most coverage in the prior year. The licensees would have been required to keep a record of their offers to the public for response, the representative programming that was devoted to each issue, the partisan speakers presented, and the sources and times of the broadcasts. Routine news coverage would have been excluded.

The Commission concluded that the added record keeping would not "necessarily enhance coverage" of controversial issues. The existing rules already required television licensees "to keep in their public inspection file a listing of no more than ten significant problems of the area served by the station during the preceding twelve months and to indicate typical and illustrative programming broadcast in response to those problems and needs." At renewal time, the listings for the three prior years were sent to the Commission as part of the renewal process. In the absence of any showing that television licensees were not already covering controversial issues, the added burden was unwarranted.

Moreover, Geller's proposal was inconsistent with the goal of reviewing fairness doctrine complaints as they arose rather than waiting until renewal when the issues might have become stale.

4. In September, 1984, during "ABC World News Tonight," ABC broadcast allegations that the Central Intelligence Agency had participated in various illegal activities including a plot to assassinate an American citizen. Two months later, ABC reported that efforts to substantiate the allegations had failed and that there was "no reason to doubt" the CIA's denials.

Both the CIA and the American Legal Foundation (ALF) filed complaints claiming deliberate news distortion and violations of the fairness doctrine and the personal attack rule. The Commission held that there was insufficient proof of deliberate news distortion. "The Commission will initiate action in this area *only* when furnished with direct extrinsic evidence that a broadcaster possessed a deliberate intent to distort the news." Central Intelligence Agency, 58 R.R.2d 1544, 1549 [1985].

Turning to the fairness and personal attack complaints, the Commission found that the broadcasts did not deal with a controversial issue of public importance. The FCC rejected the CIA's contention that the controversial issue was, "Does the Central Intelligence Agency adhere to the mandate of American Law generally, and more particularly, does the CIA participate in or condone murder as a practice?" The Commission distinguished between an allegation of specific CIA misconduct and a statement that the CIA generally violates the law. "Under the Fairness Doctrine an issue must be addressed in an obvious and meaningful fashion so as to amount to advocacy on that particular issue. [ ] The Commission does not expect its licensees to present contrasting viewpoints on every statement or shade of opinion, or every possible inference to be drawn from individual statements or presentations." ALF has filed an appeal.

While the Commission rejected the substance of the complaints, it did hold that governmental agencies do have the right to file fairness complaints. In essence, this means that the government has the right to determine whether the government has been treated fairly by the press. Is such a possibility disturbing? How can the broadcast press function as a critic of government under these circumstances?

5. *The Affirmative Duty to Raise Issues.* The Commission refers to the fairness doctrine as having two parts. Virtually all the litigation and discussion have involved the second part: the requirement that a licensee who has presented one side of a controversial issue of public importance must present contrasting views.

In 1976, for the first time, the Commission applied the first part. A Congresswoman sent an 11-minute tape opposing strip mining to West

Virginia radio stations to counter a presentation in favor of strip mining that had been distributed to many stations by the U.S. Chamber of Commerce. One station, WHAR, refused to play the tape because it had not presented the first program. Indeed, it had presented nothing on the issue except items on regular newscasts taken from the AP news service. Several persons and groups complained to the Commission contending that in this part of West Virginia at this time the question of strip mining was of primary importance. In its renewal application, WHAR had cited "development of new industry" and "air and water pollution" as issues of great concern to its listeners. In addition, bills on the subject were pending in Congress at the time, and local newspapers were extensively discussing the question. (Presentation of a five-minute tape by an outspoken foe of strip mining was not relevant because he did not discuss the economic or ecological aspects of strip mining or the pending legislation.)

The Commission asserted that although a violation of the first part "would be an exceptional situation and would not counter our intention to stay out of decisions concerning the selection of specific programming matter," this was such a case and demonstrated an "unreasonable exercise" of discretion. The Commission quoted the passage from *Red Lion* that "if the present licensees should suddenly prove timorous, the Commission is not powerless to insist that they give adequate and fair attention to public issues." The lack of any prior request to program on this subject was irrelevant because "it is the station's obligation to make an affirmative effort to program on issues of concern to its community." The role of the AP news items was minimal because it was not even clear which ones were aired. "Where, as in the present case, an issue has significant and possibly unique impact on the licensee's service area, it will not be sufficient for the licensee as an indication of compliance with the fairness doctrine to show that it may have broadcast an unknown amount of news touching on a general topic related to the issue cited in a complaint." The station was ordered to tell the Commission within 20 days how it intended to meet its fairness obligations. Rep. Patsy Mink, 59 F.C.C.2d 987, 37 R.R.2d 744 (1976).

What is the difference between saying (1) a station has an obligation to present programs on the need for good dental hygiene, even though the subject may not be controversial, and (2) a station must present programs on a controversial issue in the community? Are both covered by the fairness doctrine?

What is the justification for requiring each station in a community to present a range of views on controversial issues of public importance? Why is it not enough if the spectrum as a whole provides contrasting viewpoints? Is there more or less reason to require a station to raise important subjects when other stations in the community are doing so? Thus, in the strip mining case, should it matter that other broadcasters are devoting extensive coverage to the subject? What has this obligation to do with "fairness"?

6. *The Duty to Present Contrasting Views.* At one point the Commission quotes a court to the effect that not everything that is thought newsworthy by journalists necessarily presents a controversial issue of public importance. What are some examples of divergence between the two?

The Commission has never declared the fairness doctrine "applicable to issues involving the interpretation of religious doctrine." When a group complained that the program "In Search of Noah's Ark" presented one side of the issue of whether the Ark exists, and gave mistaken impressions about the attitudes of historians, archaeologists, and scholars, the Broadcast Bureau responded: "While such issues may be widely and vigorously disputed in the religious community, they generally do not rise to the level of a controversial issue of public importance. . . . Although the issue has received media coverage in that the film itself was broadcast, you have not shown that government and community leaders have taken positions on the issue. Nor have you demonstrated that the issue has any particular impact on the community at large." The network's determination that the fairness doctrine did not apply was not unreasonable. Religion and Ethics Institute, Inc., 42 R.R.2d 1657 (Bd.Bur.1978).

7. *Defining the "Issue."* In American Sec. Council Educational Foundation v. Federal Communications Commission, 607 F.2d 438 (D.C.Cir. 1979), ASCEF analyzed a full year's news programming of CBS. It transcribed all CBS news reports, broke them into sentences, and then determined whether each was relevant to four topics: "United States military and foreign affairs; Soviet Union military and foreign affairs; China military and foreign affairs; and Vietnam affairs." Each relevant sentence was put into one of three categories: Viewpoint A was that the "threat to U.S. security is more serious than perceived by the government or that the United States ought to *increase* its national security efforts." Viewpoint B was that the government's perception is essentially correct, and viewpoint C was that the threat is less serious than perceived and national security efforts should be decreased. The ASCEF analysis put 3.54 percent of the content into viewpoint A; 34.63 percent into viewpoint B, and 61.83 percent into viewpoint C. Based on these results and claimed similar disparities for later years, ASCEF filed a fairness complaint with the FCC asking that CBS be ordered to provide a reasonable opportunity for the expression of "A" viewpoints.

The FCC dismissed the complaint without calling for any response from CBS on the ground that the complaint did not identify "the particular issue of a controversial nature" that was involved. The court, 6–3, affirmed:

> We affirm the Commission's decision that ASCEF failed to base its complaint on a particular well-defined issue because (1) the indirect relationships among the issues aggregated by ASCEF under the umbrella of "national security" do not provide a basis for determining whether the public received a reasonable balance of conflicting

views, and (2) a contrary result would unduly burden broadcasters without a countervailing benefit to the public's right to be informed.

Since the fairness doctrine is issue-oriented, it is essential that the "issue" be clearly identified. Here "national security" was an umbrella that held within it too many issues that were only tangentially related, such as detente with China, America's commitment to NATO, SALT, and response to the Soviet Union's role in the Middle East.

The court suggested that a fairness complaint could be based on an issue that consists of separately identifiable subissues only if the main issue was well defined. If ASCEF had used single issues, it could have analyzed actual views "instead of superimposing artificial A, B, and C viewpoints on the broadcasts studied." Then the FCC could have determined the question of balance and, if necessary, framed a specific remedy.

Acceptance of ASCEF's approach would also burden broadcasters. "CBS could have had to review all of its news programming relevant to national security over at least a year's time. . . . It would have been virtually impossible to know which broadcasts should be included as relevant to national security, or how views discussed . . . should be tallied to measure 'balance' under the fairness doctrine."

Further burdens would fall on editors: "An editor preparing an evening newscast would be required to decide whether any of the day's newsworthy events is tied, even tangentially, to events covered in the past, and whether a report on today's lead story, in some remote way, balances yesterday's, last week's or last year's." Certiorari was denied, 444 U.S. 1013 (1980).

8. A potentially significant case involved a complaint that a network documentary about the failure of some private pension plans had been unfairly one-sided. The network responded that the program was about "some problems in some pension plans." The Commission concluded that the network had presented a one-sided program on the operation of the overall pension system and must provide balance. On appeal, the court, 2–1, reversed the Commission on the ground that the Commission was wrong in thinking that it was the proper body to decide the subject of the program. Instead, the court held that it was for the network to decide what the program was about and the Commission could reject the network's characterization only if it was found to be unreasonable. Since that was not the case here, the Commission's order could not stand.

The entire court voted to review the panel's decision en banc. But at that stage the Commission asked that the case be remanded to be dismissed. That occasioned another round of judicial opinions, but finally the case was remanded to the Commission and all decisions were vacated. All the action is reported in National Broadcasting Co. v. Federal Communications Commission, 516 F.2d 1101 (D.C.Cir.1974–75). An effort by the complainant, Accuracy in Media (AIM), to get the Supreme Court to reinstate the case failed when the Court denied AIM's petition for certiorari. 424 U.S. 910 (1976).

Although the Pensions case was mooted, subsequent cases have reiterated the court's finding that licensee discretion is central to fairness doctrine questions. The Commission is limited to judging the reasonableness of a licensee's determination. Thus, the Commission refused even to review a Broadcast Bureau ruling denying a fairness doctrine complaint in which the controversial issue of public importance was alleged to be whether or not the FBI was responsible for some of actress Jean Seberg's problems. The Bureau had accepted the licensee's assertion that the broadcasts did not concern a controversial issue of public importance. Accuracy in Media, Inc. v. CBS Television Network, 94 F.C.C.2d 501, 54 R.R.2d 518 (1983).

9. However, a San Francisco licensee's determination that programs advocating defeat of gay rights legislation elsewhere did not present a controversial question of public importance, was rejected by the Commission as unreasonable. The Commission stated that although the discussion was of "primary importance to the homosexual community . . ., the issue has had and continues to have a significant impact on the public at large." Council on Religion and the Homosexual, 68 F.C.C.2d 1500, 43 R.R.2d 1580 (1978).

The licensee had presented eight hours of programs (half original and half rebroadcasts) featuring Anita Bryant and others arguing against the proposed Dade County, Florida, ordinance barring discrimination on grounds of sexual preference. These programs were presented over a period of four months, with one and a half hours in prime time. The licensee presented a one-hour tape supporting gay rights, nine times over a period of four days, never in prime time. The complainants argued that this did not afford a reasonable opportunity for the presentation of opposing viewpoints. The Commission disagreed. It noted that the gay rights position had received more total time than the other side. Also, the licensee had advertised only the pro-gay talks in local newspapers.

When complainants objected to equating a single one-hour tape with more varied presentations on the other side, and four months on one side with four days on the other, the Commission noted that its role was "not to substitute our judgment for that of the licensee but merely to review that judgment for reasonableness." The Commission could not, and would not, "make the subjective determination of the relative impact of the pro or anti-gay rights programming presented on the station." The licensee's judgment could not be deemed unreasonable.

10. In December, 1983, a rare successful fairness complaint was filed against a Syracuse television licensee for a series of commercials discussing a proposed nuclear power plant. Syracuse Peace Council, 57 R.R.2d 519 (1984). According to the Syracuse Peace Council (SPC), the controversial issue of public importance was "whether the Nine Mile II plant is a sound investment for New York." The station, WTVH, contended that the issues discussed in the advertisement were "the need to eliminate dependence on foreign oil" and "the need for electricity." WTVH

further argued that "[t]he advertisements [were] institutional in nature and merely [sought] to portray a favorable image of the new Nine Mile Point nuclear energy plant." As such they did not take a position on a controversial issue of public importance. The Commission rejected WTVH's definition of the issue.

15. . . . To determine whether the licensee was reasonable in its determination as to what issue was actually discussed during the advertisement, we carefully examined the texts of the advertisements. It is noteworthy that U.S. dependence on foreign oil was mentioned only in the first two advertisements while only the last advertisement mentioned "needed electricity." On the other hand, all three advertisements ended with the tag line "Nine Mile Point . . . a *sound investment* for New York's future." (Emphasis added.) All three advertisements are framed in terms of problems facing New York—unemployment, dependence on foreign oil, and the need for electricity—and a solution to these problems—the Nine Mile II plant. In this regard, the plain thrust of each of the advertisements is whether continued construction of Nine Mile II is desirable; the need for electricity and the elimination of foreign oil dependency are the reasons given by the Energy Association as to why this question should be answered affirmatively. Under these circumstances, we cannot find that the licensee's definition of the issue was reasonable. We recognize that different parties may reach different conclusions concerning the issue addressed by a broadcast, and that, unless the facts are so clear that reasonable people could not differ as to the issue in question, a licensee's characterization of a broadcast will govern. However, we cannot find that reasonable people could differ on the conclusion that the issue discussed and the point to be made by each of these ads is that the Nine Mile II plant is an economically sound investment and, therefore, an answer to New York's economic and energy problems. In this instance, licensee's characterization of the issues simply falls beyond the bounds of a licensee's wide zone of discretion.

The Commission then turned to the question of the reasonableness of WTVH's determination that "whether the Nine Mile II plant is a sound investment for New York" was neither controversial nor of public importance. "The key issue here is whether the issue is the subject of vigorous debate with substantial elements of the community in opposition to one another." Based on newspaper articles submitted with the complaint, the Commission found that the ads did present one side of a controversial issue of public importance. As a result the FCC then had to determine if WTVH's overall programming had been fair.

23. As noted above, there is no mathematical formula or mechanical requirement for achieving fairness. [ ] However, there are a number of factors that are relevant considerations in determining whether a "reasonable opportunity" has been afforded for the presentation of contrasting viewpoints on the subject contro-

versial issue of public importance. We have stated that in order to determine whether an unreasonable imbalance exists, three factors must be considered—(1) the total amount of time afforded to each side, (2) the frequency with which each side is presented, and (3) the size of the listening audience during the various broadcasts. By applying these to the facts of a particular case, we determine "whether the public has been left uninformed." An unreasonable imbalance in the presentation of contrasting views results "from the sheer weight on one side as against the other." We will not apply formulae so specific and detailed that they can lead to excessive intrusion into licensee judgment. . . .

Finding a 9:1 ratio in total time allotted to the two points of view and a 13:1 ratio in terms of frequency of presentation, the Commission found an unreasonable imbalance in the presentation of the contrasting points of view. In so doing the Commission rejected an argument by WTVH that most of the pro-Nine Mile II programming was commercial and should thus be discounted because " '[a]s a general principle, the public is more likely to place credibility in the information it receives from news stories and public affairs programming than it does in commercial.' " The Commission reiterated its long-standing position that it would not distinguish between news and other programming in fairness controversies.

Commissioner Dawson dissented, claiming that the decision was "a departure from consistent Commission precedent." In Dawson's opinion the issue raised by the commercials was anything but clear and thus, she believed, the licensee's determination should have been accepted. She also argued that there was insufficient proof to override the licensee's determination that the issue was not a controversial issue of public importance and that the proof that was offered was not sufficiently "contemporaneous with the broadcast." As she pointed out, more than half the articles submitted were published more than six months after the commercials had been aired.

The Commission denied a petition for reconsideration by Meredith Broadcasting, licensee for WTVH. Meredith Broadcasting has filed an appeal.

11. How helpful is the Commission's test for determining balance? While it provides great flexibility, does it provide sufficient guidance? The absence of more specific guidelines has proved troubling for the Court of Appeals, District of Columbia Circuit, when it has been called upon to review Commission rulings on fairness complaints. For an extensive discussion of this problem, see Public Media Center v. Federal Communications Commission, 587 F.2d 1322 (D.C.Cir.1978).

12. Occasionally, entertainment programming may raise problems under the fairness doctrine. One typical example would be a story in which a character considers whether to seek an abortion. See Diocesan Union of Holy Name Societies, 41 F.C.C.2d 297, 28 R.R.2d 545 (1973) (involving a pro-abortion theme). Must contrasting views be presented? If so,

must it be by other entertainment programming or will an interview program suffice? What about implicit presentations, such as a series featuring a happily married couple of different faiths? Must the licensee provide for contrasting views against interfaith marriages?

13. The owner of a station in the same county as WXUR, which was denied renewal in *Brandywine-Main Line*, p. 105, supra, wrote that his station presented two guests on a call-in show on consecutive days. The first day, Dr. McIntire, the principal figure behind WXUR, appeared. Every question called in was favorable to his position. The next day, the guest was an opponent, who believed strongly in the fairness doctrine and who attacked the operation of WXUR. He did not receive a single supportive call. The owner's point was that "liberal intellectuals" are most comfortable with each other and shy away from the less educated. When the "average liberal-intellectual" listens to radio he seeks out classical music or an all-news or educational station. "If he should tune in to a talk station and listen to some of the 'drivel' broadcast, he would become furious and switch to a station with which he is more at home." The conclusion was that if the liberal hopes to convert others to his viewpoint he must become a proselytizer, and call-in shows are an easy way to reach large numbers of voters. Tannen, Liberals and the Media, The Progressive, April, 1974 at 11. Is this report an accurate picture of "liberal" attitudes? If so, does that affect your view of the fairness doctrine?

14. *Commercials.* In the 1960's, the Commission decided that advertisements for cigarettes required stations to present some programming on the dangers of smoking. This ruling was upheld in Banzhaf v. Federal Communications Commission, 405 F.2d 1082 (D.C.Cir.1968), certiorari denied 396 U.S. 842 (1969). Although the licensee could decide how to meet this requirement, most licensees presented material that had been prepared by the American Cancer Society and similar organizations. We trace the future of cigarette advertising in the next note.

The Commission attempted to treat the cigarette case as unique. Thus, when opponents of high-powered automobiles wanted the FCC to require licensees to present contrasting views on the value of such cars, the FCC refused. On appeal, the court of appeals could not distinguish the cigarette situation from the high-powered car situation and ordered the FCC to be consistent. Friends of the Earth v. Federal Communications Commission, 449 F.2d 1164 (D.C.Cir.1971).

In 1974, the Commission, in an omitted portion of its Fairness Report, rethought the question of applying the fairness doctrine to commercials. It finally decided to divide commercials into those that simply try to sell products and those that present a "meaningful statement which obviously addresses, and advocates a point of view on, a controversial issue of public importance." The latter, also called "editorial" or "advocacy" advertisements, gave rise to obligations under the fairness doctrine. If an advertisement is false or misleading, it might give rise to some action by the Federal Trade Commission or by competitors, but the fairness doctrine is not the appropriate way to handle commercials that do not address public issues.

This position was quickly challenged in the courts in a case involving a commercial for snowmobiles. Environmental groups complained that the commercials showed only one side of the controversial issue of the desirability of snowmobiles. The FCC rejected the complaint on the ground that, although the environmental effects of snowmobiles might involve a controversial issue of public importance, the commercials themselves were not devoted to an obvious or meaningful discussion of that issue.

The court of appeals affirmed. Public Interest Research Group v. Federal Communications Commission, 522 F.2d 1060 (1st Cir.1975), certiorari denied 424 U.S. 965 (1976). The appellants argued that the FCC had no authority to retreat from its earlier rulings that selling commercials might invoke the fairness doctrine. The court disagreed. "In the absence of statutory or constitutional barriers, an agency may abandon earlier precedents and frame new policies." Congress had not frozen the fairness doctrine in any particular form. Nor was there any reason to require the FCC to apply the doctrine to all commercials or to none.

Finally, the appellants argued that the First Amendment itself required that the fairness doctrine be rigorously enforced so that the airwaves would be true public forums for the presentation of divergent views. The court rejected this argument. Although the *Red Lion* approach might be furthered by extending the fairness doctrine to all advertising, the court did "not view that question, in the short and long run, as so free from doubt that courts should impose an inflexible response as a matter of constitutional law. We believe that the first amendment permitted the Commission not only to experiment with full-scale application of the fairness doctrine to advertising but also to retreat from its experiment when it determined from experience that the extension was unworkable."

15. *Cigarettes.* After the *Banzhaf* decision, Congress moved into the picture. In 1969, it adopted 15 U.S.C. § 1335: "After January 1, 1971, it shall be unlawful to advertise cigarettes on any medium of electronic communication subject to the jurisdiction of the Federal Communications Commission."

The statute was challenged by broadcasters—but not by cigarette manufacturers. It was upheld by a three judge court in Capital Broadcasting Co. v. Mitchell, 333 F.Supp. 582 (D.D.C.1971), affirmed without opinion 415 U.S. 1000 (1972). The dissenting opinion in the lower court suggested that the cigarette manufacturers were not at all unhappy to be ordered to stop advertising on radio and television because it had become unprofitable.

The court rejected the argument that this amounted to censorship in violation of § 326 because licensees were still free to present pro-smoking messages—except to the extent that Congress had forbidden commercial messages. The Commission was leaving that decision to the licensees. Moreover, some aspects of anti-smoking messages might still be found to invoke the fairness doctrine—but health danger was not one of them. Also, it was permissible to consider at renewal time whether a licensee carried programs on the dangers of smoking—not because it was a controversial issue, but because one aspect of meeting the public interest is to warn about dangers to health and safety, even if they are obvious and non-controversial. What might the Commission do at renewal time if it found a licensee had presented several debates on cigarette smoking in which half the speakers argued that there was no health hazard in smoking? Is there a tension between saying that licensees are free to program pro-smoking material if they wish and that they will be judged at renewal time on how they have programmed on matters of health and safety?

16. Recently, the fairness doctrine has come under renewed attack. In May, 1984, the FCC released a notice of inquiry on the fairness doctrine stating that "continuance of these obligations now or in the future may be at odds not only with the very same First Amendment goals underlying their foundation but with other First Amendment principles in other areas of speech and expression. . . . [Q]uestions exist over the need for continued government interference into the private journalistic discretion that the fairness doctrine occasions." The notice sought comments as to whether the doctrine was essential, desirable, or required by § 315.

In August, 1985, the Commission issued its report on the fairness doctrine, concluding that the fairness doctrine was no longer essential or even desirable. However, the Commission stopped short of abolishing the fairness doctrine, suggesting, instead, that Congress should examine the question.

## IN THE MATTER OF INQUIRY INTO SECTION 73.1910 OF THE COMMISSION'S RULES AND REGULATIONS CONCERNING THE GENERAL FAIRNESS DOCTRINE OBLIGATIONS OF BROADCAST LICENSEES

### (1985 FAIRNESS REPORT)

Federal Communications Commission, 1985.
___ F.C.C.2d ___, 58 R.R.2d 1137.

By the Commission: Chairman Fowler issuing a separate statement; Commissioner Quello concurring and issuing a statement; Commissioner Rivera not participating.

### I. INTRODUCTION

. . .

4. Our past judgment that the fairness doctrine comports with the public interest was predicated upon three factors. First, in light of the limited availability of broadcast frequencies and the resultant need for government licensing, we concluded that the licensee is a public fiduciary, obligated to present diverse viewpoints representative of the community at large. We determined that the need to effectuate the right of the

viewing and listening public to suitable access to the marketplace of ideas justifies restrictions on the rights of broadcasters. Second, we presumed that a governmentally imposed restriction on the content of programming is a viable—indeed the best mechanism—by which to vindicate this public interest. Third, we determined, as a factual matter, that the fairness doctrine, in operation, has the effect of enhancing the flow of diverse viewpoints to the public.

5. On the basis of the voluminous factual record compiled in this proceeding, our experience in administering the doctrine and our general expertise in broadcast regulation, we no longer believe that the fairness doctrine, as a matter of policy, serves the public interest. In making this determination, we do not question the interest of the listening and viewing public in obtaining access to diverse and antagonistic sources of information. Rather, we conclude that the fairness doctrine is no longer a necessary or appropriate means by which to effectuate this interest. We believe that the interest of the public in viewpoint diversity is fully served by the multiplicity of voices in the marketplace today and that the intrusion by government into the content of programming occasioned by the enforcement of the doctrine unnecessarily restricts the journalistic freedom of broadcasters. Furthermore, we find that the fairness doctrine, in operation, actually inhibits the presentation of controversial issues of public importance to the detriment of the public and in degradation of the editorial prerogatives of broadcast journalists.

6. We believe that the same factors which demonstrate that the fairness doctrine is no longer appropriate as a matter of policy also suggest that the doctrine may no longer be permissible as a matter of constitutional law. We recognize that the United States Supreme Court, in *Red Lion Broadcasting Co. v. FCC*, upheld the constitutionality of the fairness doctrine. But in the intervening sixteen years the information services marketplace has expanded markedly, thereby making it unnecessary to rely upon intrusive government regulation in order to assure that the public has access to the marketplace of ideas. In addition, the compelling evidence adduced in this proceeding demonstrates that the fairness doctrine, in operation, inhibits the presentation of controversial issues of public importance; this fact impels the dual conclusion that the doctrine impedes the public's access to the marketplace of ideas and poses an unwarranted intrusion upon the journalistic freedom of broadcasters.

.  .  .

## II. THE CONSTITUTIONALITY OF THE FAIRNESS DOCTRINE IS SUSPECT

[After reviewing the purpose of the First Amendment and relevant cases including *Red Lion, Miami Herald,* and *League of Women Voters,* the Commission noted that it was not the responsibility of an administrative agency to adjudicate the constitutionality of a federal statute. Nevertheless, the Commission asserted that its opinion on the issue is important because the First Amendment issues are an integral part of the public interest standard, because, as the agency that oversees broadcasting, the FCC has a unique perspective on the issue, and finally, because the Supreme Court in *Red Lion* had relied so heavily on the Commission's assertion that the fairness doctrine did not inhibit coverage of controversial issues—a position no longer held by the Commission.]

19.    We believe that there are serious questions raised with respect to the constitutionality of the fairness doctrine whether or not the Supreme Court chooses to continue to apply the less exacting standard which it has traditionally employed in assessing the constitutionality of broadcast regulation.    As demonstrated infra, the compelling evidence in this proceeding demonstrates that the fairness doctrine, in operation, inhibits the presentation of controversial issues of public importance.    As a consequence, even under a standard of review short of the strict scrutiny standard applied to test the constitutionality of restraints on the press, we believe that the fairness doctrine can no longer be justified on the grounds that it is necessary to promote the First Amendment rights of the viewing and listening public.    Indeed, the chilling effect on the presentation of controversial issues of public importance resulting from our regulatory policies affirmatively disserves the interest of the public in obtaining access to diverse viewpoints.    In addition, we believe that the artificial mechanism of interjecting the government into an affirmative role of overseeing the content of speech is unnecessary to vindicate the interest of the public in obtaining access to the marketplace of ideas. Were the balance ours alone to strike, the fairness doctrine would thus fall short of promoting those interests necessary to uphold its constitutionality.    And because the constitutionality of the fairness doctrine, in our view, is suspect under the less searching broadcast standard of review, *a fortiori*, it would prove constitutionally infirm under the more stringent First Amendment standard applicable in cases involving the print media.

.    .    .

21.    In sum, while we recognize that the United States Supreme Court found that the fairness doctrine was constitutionally permissible sixteen years ago, we believe that the transformation of the broadcast marketplace and the compelling documentation of the "chilling effect" undermine the factual predicate of that decision.    We will now specifically address the factors which, in our view, mandate a reassessment of our historical position that the fairness doctrine is consistent with the public interest.

### III. A NUMBER OF FACTORS JUSTIFY A REASSESSMENT OF THE FAIRNESS DOCTRINE

#### A.    The Need for and Costs of the Fairness Doctrine and its Actual Effect on the Coverage of Controversial Issues of Public Importance

22.    As we stated in our *Notice,* the purpose in instituting this inquiry was to undertake a "searching and comprehensive reexamination

of the fairness doctrine. . . ." This reappraisal will consist of three parts: an exploration as to whether the doctrine furthers or impedes the regulatory and constitutional objectives it seeks to promote, an assessment of the potential costs and other detriments which may arise from the operation of the doctrine and an evaluation as to whether or not the communications marketplace has undergone such a transformation that the doctrine is no longer warranted or supportable.

. . .

### B. The Fairness Doctrine in Operation Lessens the Amount of Diverse Views Available to the Public

#### 1. *Broadcasters Perceive That the Fairness Doctrine Involves Significant Burdens*

26. A licensee may be inhibited from presenting controversial issues of public importance by operation of the fairness doctrine even though the first prong of that doctrine affirmatively requires the licensee to broadcast such issues. The reason underlying this apparent paradox is that the two parts of the fairness doctrine differ markedly in the scope of the controversial issues that they encompass, the ease by which a licensee can meet the requirements embodied in the two prongs and the degree to which the Commission, in the past, has taken affirmative action to enforce compliance with them.

27. It is well-established that a licensee, in complying with the first prong of the fairness doctrine, has broad discretion in determining the specific controversial issues of public importance that it chooses to present. Indeed, in our *1974 Fairness Report,* we stated that "we have no intention of becoming involved in the selection of issues to be discussed, nor do we expect a broadcaster to cover each and every important issue which may arise in his community." Rather, with respect to the affirmative obligation to cover controversial issues of public importance, "[a] presumption of compliance exists" and only "in *rare instances,* where a licensee has failed to give coverage to an issue found to be of critical importance to its particular community, would questions be raised as to whether a licensee had fulfilled its fairness obligations." Indeed, the United States Court of Appeals has characterized this requirement as one which is "not extensive and [can be] met by presenting a minimum of controversial subject matter."

28. In contrast to the paucity of challenges under the first part of the fairness doctrine, "[t]he usual fairness complaint . . . concerns a claim that the licensee has presented one viewpoint on a 'controversial issue of public importance' and has failed to afford a 'reasonable opportunity for the presentation of contrasting viewpoints.' "[57] The responsive programming obligation embodied in the second prong of the fairness doctrine arises whenever the licensee airs any controversial issue of public importance, even in situations where the issue broadcast is not "so

---

57. 1974 Fairness Report, 48 F.C.C.2d at 10.

critical or of such great public importance" to trigger a requirement under the first part of the fairness doctrine. An overwhelming majority of the complaints we receive and virtually all our orders directing licensees to take corrective action to conform to the requirements of the fairness doctrine involve the second prong of that doctrine.

29. As a result of the asymmetry between its two components, the fairness doctrine in its operation encourages broadcasters to air only the minimal amount of controversial issue programming sufficient to comply with the first prong. By restricting the amount and type of controversial programming aired, a broadcaster minimizes the potentially substantial burdens associated with the second prong of the doctrine while remaining in compliance with the strict letter of its regulatory obligations. Therefore, despite the first prong obligation, in net effect the fairness doctrine often discourages the presentation of controversial issue programming.[66]

30. There are a variety of reasons why a broadcaster might be inhibited from providing comprehensive coverage of controversial issues of public importance by operation of the fairness doctrine. One reason is the fear of government sanction. Under our regulatory scheme, a broadcaster must obtain a license from the Commission prior to entry into the broadcast field. Because broadcast licenses are granted only for limited periods of time, all broadcasters must periodically renew that license if they wish to remain in business. Compliance with the fairness doctrine is an important consideration in our determination as to whether renewal of a broadcast license is in the public interest. Indeed, we have characterized the "strict adherence to the fairness doctrine . . . as the *sine qua non* for grant of a renewal of license."

31. Because a decision by this Commission to deny the renewal of a broadcast license is "a sanction of tremendous potency" which can be triggered by a finding by this Commission that the licensee failed to comply with the fairness doctrine, a licensee has the incentive to avoid even the potential for such a determination. Therefore, in order to attenuate the possibility that opponents, in a renewal proceeding, will challenge the manner in which a licensee provides balance with respect to the controversial issues it chooses to cover, a broadcaster may be inhibited from presenting controversial issue programming in excess of the minimum required to satisfy the first prong of the fairness doctrine. As Chief Judge David Bazelon has stated, "[w]hen the right to continue

**66.** We do not believe that more stringent enforcement of the first prong would be an appropriate remedial response to the existence of a "chilling effect." Indeed, such an approach increases the severity of major detriments associated with the fairness doctrine. For example, contrary to the principles of the First Amendment, a stricter regulatory approach would increase the government's intrusion into the editorial decisionmaking process of broadcast journalists. It would enlarge the opportunity for governmental officials to abuse the doctrine for partisan political purposes. Were the chilling effect of the government sanction removed, the result might well be greater coverage of issues and thus, more satisfaction of the policy behind the fairness doctrine's first prong. Moreover, a more stringent enforcement of first prong obligations would merely increase the economic costs that are borne both by broadcasters and the Commission.

to operate a lucrative broadcast facility turns on periodic government approval, even a governmental 'raised eyebrow' can send otherwise intrepid entrepreneurs running for the cover of conformity."

32.   While denial of a license renewal is the most severe sanction we can impose for failure to abide by the fairness doctrine, it is not the only sanction.   Typically, upon a finding that a licensee has violated the fairness doctrine, we order the broadcaster to provide additional programming in order to redress the imbalance in time and frequency given to one side of a controversial issue.   Since broadcast time is a valuable resource, such a requirement imposes costs upon the licensee.   In order to avoid these costs, a broadcaster may be inhibited from presenting more than a minimal amount of controversial issue programming.

33.   The potential of a "chilling effect," however, is not restricted to the fear by a broadcaster that the Commission will find a violation of the fairness doctrine and impose sanctions on the licensee.   A licensee may also be inhibited from presenting controversial issue programming by the fear of incurring the various expenses and other burdens which may arise in the context of fairness doctrine litigation regardless of whether or not it is ultimately found to be in violation of the doctrine.

34.   As one broadcaster noted, licensees are "conscious of the probability that coverage of a highly controversial issue will trigger an avalanche of protests" demanding air time for the presentation of opposing viewpoints.   While most requests may be made in good faith, there is evidence that some complainants invoke a licensee's fairness doctrine obligations in an attempt either to pressure a broadcaster to censor specific programming or to harass licensees into presenting a particular spokesman or broadcast.   Whether or not the requests are legitimate, a station nonetheless may incur additional personnel costs in negotiating with the group seeking responsive programming.

35.   Broadcasters can also be deterred by the financial costs involved in defending a fairness doctrine complaint.   The record reflects that such costs can be substantial.   .   .   .

[The Commission then cited examples of unsuccessful, but costly, fairness complaints.   A Spokane, Washington, television station spent more than $20,000 in legal fees alone to defend successfully a single fairness complaint.   NBC incurred expenses of more than $100,000 in the Pensions case.]

### 2.   *The Record Demonstrates that The Fairness Doctrine Causes Broadcasters to Restrict Their Coverage of Controversial Issues*

53.   Further evidence of the demonstrable inhibiting effect of the fairness doctrine is documented by our own administrative decisions. Except in extremely rare situations, a licensee is not challenged under the fairness doctrine for a failure to air a specific controversial issue of importance to the community; rather, the typical fairness doctrine case addresses whether the licensee provided overall balanced coverage with

respect to those issues which, in its discretion, it chose to present. As a consequence, in those instances in which we determined that the licensee failed to broadcast a sufficient amount of responsive programming which is mandated under the second prong of the fairness doctrine, we have imposed sanctions—including the ultimate penalty of non-renewal—upon broadcasters who have actually provided large amounts of controversial issue programming. With respect to these broadcasters, the anomalous result of enforcing the second prong of the fairness doctrine is to inhibit or silence licensees who make significant contributions to the market-place of ideas.

54. *Brandywine-Main Line Radio Inc.*, a case involving the license renewal of WXUR, is a vivid illustration of the way in which application of the fairness doctrine has operated to stifle controversial issue programming. The uncontroverted evidence of that case demonstrated that "controversial issue programming was a substantial part of WXUR's total programming" during its term of license. The Commission also found that the station did provide some coverage of opposing viewpoints, but the Commission determined that the station did not satisfy the requirement of overall balance in its public issue programming, as "those holding viewpoints contrary to those of the moderator were forced to give their views in an antagonistic setting." As a consequence, the Commission refused to renew the license of WXUR.

55. The Commission's decision in that case had the direct result of reducing the amount of controversial issue programming available to the public. Chief Judge David Bazelon, in dissent to the Court of Appeals' affirmance, stated that WXUR was:

> a radio station devoted to speaking out and stirring debate on controversial issues. The station . . . propagate[d] a viewpoint which was not being heard in the greater Philadelphia area. The record is clear that through its interview and call-in shows it did offer a variety of opinions on a broad range of public issues, and that it never refused to lend its broadcast facilities to spokesmen of conflicting viewpoints. . . .
>
> The Commission's . . . decision, has removed WXUR from the air. This has deprived the listening public not only of a viewpoint but also of robust debate on innumerable controversial issues. It is beyond dispute that the public has lost access to information and ideas. This is not a loss to be taken lightly, however unpopular or disruptive we might judge these ideas to be.
>
> . . .

68. In sum, we find that the evidence, derived from the record as a whole, leads us to conclude that the fairness doctrine chills speech. As a result of this finding alone we no longer believe that the fairness doctrine, as a matter of policy, furthers the public interest and we have substantial doubts that the fairness doctrine comports with the strictures of the First Amendment. Because the fairness doctrine inhibits the presentation of controversial and important issues, in operation, it actual-

ly disserves the purpose it was designed to achieve. In our view, an elimination of the doctrine would result in greater discussion of controversial and important public issues on broadcast facilities. While we believe that the existence of a "chilling effect" is sufficient to support our policy conclusion, it is not the only basis upon which we make this determination. In the following sections we shall discuss other detriments attributable to the fairness doctrine.

## C. The Administration of the Fairness Doctrine Operates to Inhibit the Expression of Unorthodox Opinions

69. While the fairness doctrine has the laudatory purpose of encouraging the presentation of diverse viewpoints, we fear that in operation it may have the paradoxical effect of actually inhibiting the expression of a wide spectrum of opinion on controversial issues of public importance. In this regard, our concern is that the administration of the fairness doctrine has unintentionally resulted in stifling viewpoints which may be unorthodox, unpopular or unestablished.

70. First, the requirement to present balanced programming under the second prong of the fairness doctrine is in itself a government regulation that inexorably favors orthodox viewpoints. As we stated in our *1974 Fairness Report*, it is only "major" or "significant" opinions which are within the scope of the regulatory obligation to provide contrasting viewpoints. As a consequence, the fairness doctrine makes a regulatory distinction between two different categories of opinions: those which are "significant enough to warrant broadcast coverage [under the fairness doctrine]" and opinions which do not rise to the level of a major viewpoint of sufficient public importance that triggers responsive programming obligations. While the broadcaster in the first instance is responsible for evaluating the "viewpoints and shades of opinion which are to be presented," we are obligated to review the reasonableness of the broadcaster's evaluation. As a consequence, the fairness doctrine in operation inextricably involves the Commission in the dangerous task of evaluating the merits of particular viewpoints. This evaluation has serious First Amendment ramifications. As the Supreme Court has stated:

> If there is any fixed star in our constitutional constellation, it is that no official, high or petty, can prescribe what shall be orthodox in politics, nationalism, religion, or other matters of opinion. . . .

71. Second, as Chief Judge David Bazelon has stated, our own administrative enforcement of the doctrine provides some support for the contention that some "controversial viewpoint[s] [are] being screened out in favor of the dreary blandness of a more acceptable opinion." Broadcasters who have been denied or threatened with a denial of the renewal of their licenses due to fairness doctrine violations have generally not been those which have provided only minimal coverage of controversial and important public issues. Indeed, some licensees that we have not renewed or threatened with non-renewal have presented controversial

issue programming far in excess of that aired by the typical licensee. In a number of situations it was the licenses of broadcasters who aired opinions which many in society found to be abhorrent or extreme which were placed in jeopardy due to allegations of fairness doctrine violations. In conclusion, we are extremely concerned over the potential of the fairness doctrine, in operation, to interject the government, even unintentionally, into the position of favoring one type of opinion over another. To the extent that the doctrine has this effect it both disserves the interest of the public in an unencumbered marketplace of ideas and contravenes the fundamental purposes of the First Amendment.

### D. In Operation the Fairness Doctrine Places the Government into the Intrusive and Constitutionally Disfavored Role of Scrutinizing Program Content

72. Although we have traditionally attempted to minimize our role in evaluating program content in administering the fairness doctrine, the doctrine has the inexorable effect of interjecting the Commission into the editorial decisionmaking process. In evaluating whether or not a broadcaster has met his or her balanced programming obligations under the fairness doctrine, we are obligated to determine whether or not the broadcaster made a reasonable determination as to whether or not the programming presented controversial issues of public importance, and if so, we must assess whether or not the broadcaster provided reasonable opportunities for the presentation of contrasting viewpoints. In evaluating the adequacy of the responsive programming, we have had to draw conclusions as to the reasonableness of the selected program formats and spokespersons.

73. Moreover, in making these assessments, we must necessarily take into account the amount of time in which a specific viewpoint was broadcast. Our staff often performs this task by mechanistically weighing the minutes and even the seconds of time devoted to each expression of opinion. In addition, we must assess the frequency of the broadcast and the degree of audience exposure. Further, because the opportunity to present responsive programming may lose its utility if the controversial issue of public importance triggering the obligation subsequently becomes moot, we must also make judgments as to the timeliness of the opportunity for the discussion of contrasting viewpoints. The minute and subjective scrutiny of program content resulting from the enforcement of the fairness doctrine is at odds with First Amendment principles. For example, in *Miami Herald,* the United States Supreme Court expressed concern that a governmentally mandated right of reply statute applicable to newspapers constituted an unwarranted intrusion on the editorial freedoms of journalists

> because of its intrusion into the function of editors. A newspaper is more than a passive receptacle or conduit for news, comment and advertising. The choice of material to go into a newspaper, and the decisions made as to the limitations on the size and content of the

paper, and treatment of public issues and public officials—whether fair or unfair—constitute the exercise of editorial control and judgment. It has yet to be demonstrated how governmental regulation of this crucial process can be exercised consistent with First Amendment guarantees of free press as they have evolved to this time.

### E.  The Fairness Doctrine Creates the Opportunity For Intimidation of Broadcasters by Governmental Officials

74.  Notwithstanding our recent efforts to reduce unnecessary regulatory burdens on licensees, the broadcast industry is one which is characterized by pervasive regulation.  The fact of this pervasive regulatory authority, including the intrusive power over program content occasioned by the fairness doctrine, provides governmental officials with the dangerous opportunity to abuse their position of power in an attempt either to stifle opinion with which they disagree or to coerce broadcasters to favor particular viewpoints which further partisan political objectives. In this regard, Chief Judge Bazelon has observed that "the potential to subject the 'fairness' theory to political abuse is inherent in the operation of the doctrine."

75.  Political officials have not been loath to criticize the manner in which broadcasters have aired controversial matters of public concern and at times the criticism has been accompanied by overt pressure to influence the manner in which these issues are covered.  For example, a White House official during the Nixon Administration suggested to the President's Chief of Staff that the Administration respond to the alleged "unfair coverage" of the broadcast media by showing "favorites within the media," establishing "an official monitoring system through the FCC" and making "official complaints from the FCC."  The attempts to coerce broadcast journalists, moreover, have not been restricted to specific partisan viewpoints or politicians of a particular political party. As described in the *Notice*, a government official in another administration was reported to state that the:

> massive strategy [of the Administration] was to use the fairness doctrine to challenge and harass the right-wing broadcasters and hope that the challenges would be so costly to them that they would be inhibited, and decide that it was too expensive to continue.

We believe that the potential for the fairness doctrine to be abused in order to further partisan political purposes has dangerous policy ramifications.  As Justice William O. Douglas has stated:

> the regime of federal supervision under the Fairness Doctrine is contrary to our constitutional mandate and makes the broadcast licensee an easy victim of political pressures and reduces him to a timid or submissive segment of the press whose measure of the public interest will now be echoes of the dominant political voice that emerges after every election.

76.  Several parties contend that we should not be concerned that the fairness doctrine has the potential to be used as a vehicle for

governmental officials to improperly affect the viewpoints aired over broadcast frequencies because such governmental officials have other means, such as the license renewal process and Internal Revenue Service audits, by which to improperly attempt to exert control over broadcasters. We disagree. While the commenters are correct in their assertion that governmental abuse may be effectuated by other mechanisms, we do not have plenary power to safeguard against all types of potential governmental abuse. Certainly the mere fact that alternative means of intimidation may be available does not provide justification for us to blithely ignore the fact that the fairness doctrine provides the dangerous potential for governmental abuse. As Chief Judge Bazelon has stated, "[w]ithout the FCC lever to manipulate, we could hope that there would be less chance that the licensees would be forced to kowtow to the wishes of an incumbent politician."

### F.   The Fairness Doctrine Imposes Unnecessary Economic Costs Upon Broadcasters and the Commission

77.   In addition to the detriments described above, a further consequence of the fairness doctrine is the economic burdens imposed upon broadcasters and the Commission. As described above, the doctrine places significant economic costs upon a licensee. Such costs are incurred, for example, in negotiating with the public regarding responsive programming obligations, in defending fairness doctrine challenges in both administrative and judicial forums, in complying with the requirement to broadcast controversial issues of public importance, and in airing alternative viewpoints of these controversial issues.

78.   In addition to these economic burdens, the administration and enforcement of the doctrine imposes regulatory costs upon the Commission. We receive thousands of inquiries and complaints concerning the fairness doctrine annually,[188] each of which requires an individualized evaluation or response by our staff. In the course of assessing the merits of a complaint, the Commission's staff may seek further information from the complainant. If it determines that the complainant has established a *prima facie* case, the staff may request justification from the licensee, thereby precipitating potentially costly administrative litigation, which, when terminated, is subject to judicial review, with its attendant costs. Contrary to the position of some commenters, therefore, we do not believe that the economic burdens incurred by the Commission in administering the fairness doctrine are *de minimis*.

79.   In evaluating the propriety of a policy, the costs associated with the rule are to be balanced against its benefits. As a consequence, the significant economic costs associated with the administration of the fairness doctrine are a necessary factor in a considered evaluation of whether or not retention of the fairness doctrine comports with the

188.   For example, in 1984 our staff received 6,787 inquiries and complaints regarding the fairness doctrine.

public interest. By this assertion we do not imply that the administrative costs standing alone would be sufficient to justify the elimination of the doctrine. To the contrary, these costs might be justified were it demonstrated that the doctrine increased the amount of controversial issue programming and that its retention was necessary to assure that the public had access to the marketplace of ideas. In a situation in which there are no countervailing justifications, however, we believe that even a moderate amount of administrative costs may constitute substantial justification for the elimination of regulation. For example, we have recently stated that regulatory costs are a significant criterion in justifying repeal of a rule "especially when the other factors considered indicate that the need for the rule has been effectively eliminated and that the rule imposes significant costs on both the public and the broadcast industry." We find that these factors are applicable with respect to the fairness doctrine because, as discussed, the doctrine "chills" the broadcast of controversial issue programming and, as explained below, is not required to assure that the public has access to diverse viewpoints.

80. For the reasons set forth above, we find that the fairness doctrine, in operation, has the effect of inhibiting the presentation of controversial issues of public importance. We also believe that the doctrine operates to favor the expression of orthodox viewpoints and to require unwarranted scrutiny by the Commission into program content. In addition, we find it provides a vehicle by which governmental officials can intimidate broadcasters for partisan political purposes. Moreover, we determine that the doctrine, in operation, imposes significant economic costs upon the Commission and the broadcasting industry. As a consequence, on the basis of the record in this proceeding, we conclude that there are a number of significant detriments associated with the fairness doctrine. In the following section we will evaluate, in light of the current communications marketplace, whether or not there is any need for us to retain the doctrine.

### G. Need for the Fairness Doctrine In Light of the Increase in the Amount and Type of Information Sources in the Marketplace

81. Our conclusions regarding the disutility of the fairness doctrine find further support by examining the current amount of diverse and antagonistic sources of information available in the marketplace. As we observed in the *Notice*, significant increases in the number and variety of information sources attenuate the need for a system of government imposed "fairness" with its corollary duty to discover and present controversial issues of public importance. The Commission's last assessment of the information marketplace, and its necessary relationship to the legal and policy underpinnings of the fairness doctrine, occurred in 1974. At that time the Commission concluded:

The effective development of an electronic medium with an abundance of channels through the use of cable or otherwise is still very much a thing of the future. *For the present,* we do not believe that it would be appropriate—or even permissible—for a government agency charged with the allocation of the *channels now available* to ignore the legitimate First Amendment interests of the public. *(emphasis added)*

82.   More than a decade has passed since this examination.  During this time, we have witnessed explosive growth in various communications technologies.  We find the information marketplace of today different from that which existed in 1974, as many of the "future" electronic technologies have now become contributors to the marketplace of ideas. . . .  [T]he growth of traditional broadcast facilities, as well as the development of new electronic information technologies, provides the public with suitable access to the marketplace of ideas so as to render the fairness doctrine unnecessary.  Moreover, we find that the dynamics of the information services marketplace overall insures that the public will be sufficiently exposed to controversial issues of public importance. Accordingly, we no longer believe it appropriate to continue a system of government imposed obligations requiring licensees to discover and "fairly" address controversial issues of public importance.  We believe that elimination of the fairness doctrine would not only promote discussion of such issues, but also pay greater fidelity to fundamental First Amendment values.

. . .

## 1.   *Nature and Scope of the Information Services Marketplace*

84.   The Commission has previously addressed this specific issue in the context of a television station licensee's programming obligations. In our decision deregulating the programming guidelines for commercial television, we noted that the relevant information marketplace includes a variety of information sources such as cable television, Lower Power Television (LPTV), Multipoint Distribution Service (MDS), Multichannel Multipoint Distribution Service (MMDS), Satellite Master Antenna Service (SMATV), and other electronic technologies.  . . .

85.   The Commission has also addressed the issue of determining the relevant information marketplace in fashioning its rules regarding concentration of ownership.  . . .   More recently, the Commission addressed this issue in a proceeding revising its national multiple ownership rules.  In this context the Commission noted:

The record in this proceeding supports the conclusion that the information market relevant to diversity includes not only TV and radio outlets, but cable, other video media and numerous print media as well.  In the *Notice,* we took account of the fact that these other media compete with broadcast outlets for the time that citizens devote to acquiring the information they desire.  That is, cable, newspapers, magazines and periodicals are substitutes in the provision of such information.

That the various media are in fact information substitutes in the marketplace of ideas is further reflected in our local cable and television, newspaper and broadcast, radio and television cross-ownership rules.

86.  Against this background, the issue in this proceeding is whether or not there are inherent differences among various media outlets so as to prevent substitutability with respect to the presentation of controversial issues of public importance.  We find nothing in this record which would cause us to arrive at a conclusion different from these prior decisions.  Accordingly, for the purpose of analyzing the fairness doctrine, we believe it is appropriate to consider traditional broadcast services, new electronic media and print as all part of the information services marketplace.

[The Commission went on to reject arguments that because studies have shown television to be the primary and most believed news source, other media are not adequate alternatives.  Similarly, the Commission was not persuaded by a claim that print is different from broadcast because it must be read.  Availability of information sources was the issue as far as the Commission was concerned.

The Commission then turned to the status of the information services marketplace and cited statistics regarding the growth of information services since *Red Lion*.  There has been a 48 percent increase in radio stations and a 44.3 percent increase in television outlets during that time period.  As of 1984, 96 percent of television households received five or more television signals.  Meanwhile, the networks' share of the market has declined from 90 percent to 76 percent, and the number of independent television stations has grown from 90 to 214.

The Commission also cited the development of other electronic distribution systems such as cable and MMDS, noting their tremendous growth in the past decade, the continued availability of more than 1,700 daily newspapers and the increase in the number of periodicals from 6,960 in 1950 to 10,688 in 1982.]

### H.  The Fairness Doctrine Can Not Be Justified on the Basis that It Protects Either Broadcasters or the Public from Undue Influence

132.  As noted above, the Commission historically justified the retention of the fairness doctrine on the sole basis that affirmative regulatory intervention was necessary to vindicate the interest of the public in obtaining access to diverse viewpoints on controversial issues of public importance.  Our evaluation of the fairness doctrine both in terms of its efficacy and its continued need in the communications marketplace today is based upon this expressed regulatory objective.  Several participants in this proceeding, however, have argued that the retention of the doctrine furthers other regulatory goals.  Specifically, these parties argue that there are legitimate "protective" functions which are promot-

ed by the continued existence of the doctrine. In this section we will assess the merits of these arguments.

133. Several commenters contend that retention of the fairness doctrine is useful as a "protection against outside pressures" by groups within the community which would otherwise exert undue influence on the editorial decisionmaking of broadcasters. Absent the fairness doctrine, these parties contend that broadcasters will simply "cave-in" to the pressures of advertisers, political action committees, or other powerful groups in the community who do not wish to have particular controversial viewpoints expressed.

134. We take issue with the assumption that intrusive governmental regulation is necessary to "protect" broadcasters from groups which allegedly attempt to influence their programming decisions. The First Amendment forbids governmental intervention in order to "protect" print journalists and we believe that broadcast journalists are in no greater need of "protection" than their counterparts in the print media. We think it telling, in this regard, that broadcasters themselves are not seeking this protection. Moreover, the framework of broadcast regulation is predicated in large part upon reliance on the editorial discretion of broadcast journalists. As the Supreme Court has stated, the Communications Act "manifest[s] the intention of Congress to maintain a substantial measure of journalistic independence for the broadcast licensee." Consequently, consistent with their public interest responsibilities, broadcasters are accorded wide discretion under the Communications Act with respect to their programming decisions. We are not convinced that broadcasters have been unduly pressured by groups within the community in the past. Moreover, in our view, the speculative notion that, absent the fairness doctrine, they will be unable to resist undue pressure in the future is a wholly inadequate basis upon which to justify the continued existence of rules which intervene in the editorial decisionmaking process of broadcast journalists. Rather, we deem it appropriate to rely, as we have in the past, upon the good faith judgment of the licensee regarding the selection of programming material.

135. In addition, several commenters, in support of the fairness doctrine, argue that the doctrine serves to safeguard the public against unwarranted influence by what they perceive as biased broadcast reporting. Although the commenting parties differ among themselves in their perception of the bias to which they object, they believe that retention of the fairness doctrine is appropriate to prevent broadcasters from presenting biased or one-sided programming. The argument apparently is predicated upon the presumption that the requirement to provide "balanced" controversial issue programming is not merely a means to assure access to the marketplace of ideas but is itself a valid regulatory objective.

136. Balance may be a laudable editorial goal, but there are grave dangers when the government tries to strike that balance. First, as we have just noted above, determining what constitutes balanced program-

ming is a very subjective endeavor. Second, as we have described, having the government attempt to achieve balance by means of enforcing the fairness doctrine results in a chilling effect to the ultimate detriment of the listening public. Third, there are the inherent dangers of an arm of the federal government influencing the content of programming in an attempt to guarantee balance. Further, the First Amendment does not require and may well not permit a neat apportionment, dictated by the government, in the marketplace of ideas, with equal space assigned to every viewpoint. As the Supreme Court noted in *First National Bank v. Bellotti:*

> [T]he people in our democracy are entrusted with the responsibility for judging and evaluating the relative merits of conflicting arguments. They may consider, in making their judgment, the source and credibility of the advocate. But if there be any danger that the people can not evaluate the information and arguments advanced by appellants, it is a danger contemplated by the Framers of the First Amendment.

The fact that a particular viewpoint may have the capability to be extremely influential or offensive does not mean that it is accorded a lesser degree of First Amendment protection than the expression of less influential or more reasonable opinions. Therefore, we do not believe that the "protection" of the viewing and listening public against even allegedly one-sided presentations affords a justifiable basis for the retention of the fairness doctrine.

[After examining all the evidence regarding the Commission's authority to eliminate the fairness doctrine, the FCC decided that it was unnecessary to reach a definitive conclusion in light of its decision to defer further action on the fairness doctrine until Congress could be given an opportunity to review the Commission's report. The Commission ordered the proceeding terminated and a copy of the report forwarded to Congress.]

[Chairman Fowler's concurrence emphasized his belief that the fairness doctrine is a misguided policy that should be abolished. Commissioner Quello concurred separately to state his belief that the fairness doctrine was indeed codified by the 1959 amendments to § 315.]

**Notes and Questions**

1. What effect might the Commission's conclusion that the fairness doctrine reduces rather than enhances speech have on a constitutional challenge to the doctrine? Could it lead the Supreme Court to overrule *Red Lion?* This possibility was raised in n. 12 of *League of Women Voters*, p. 77, supra. A challenge based on the Commission's report is almost inevitable, whether in the context of a specific fairness decision (*Syracuse Peace Council*, p. 213, supra, and *Central Intelligence Agency*, p. 209, supra, are both possibilities) or a suit challenging the entire doctrine.

2. Similarly, what is the possible effect of the Commission's finding that the scarcity rationale is no longer viable in the face of the expanded

information services marketplace? Recall in n. 11 of *League of Women Voters* the Court noted the possible obsolescence of the scarcity rationale, but stated it would not review the matter without some signal from Congress or the FCC. If the scarcity rationale is no longer valid, how much revision of the broadcast regulatory scheme would be required?

3. On more than one occasion, Senator Packwood (R.-Ore.) has introduced legislation in Congress to among other things, repeal the fairness doctrine and §§ 315 and 312(a)(7). Freedom of Expression Act of 1983, S.1917, 2d Sess. (1983). So far these bills have met strong resistance. If the fairness doctrine is to be eliminated, it will almost certainly be the result of judicial, as opposed to legislative, action.

## 2. PERSONAL ATTACK RULES

As we saw in *Red Lion*, p. 60, supra, the personal attack part of the general fairness doctrine has been crystallized into a rule, 47 C.F.R. § 73.123:

> (a) When, during the presentation of views on a controversial issue of public importance, an attack is made upon the honesty, character, integrity or like personal qualities of an identified person or group, the licensee shall, within a reasonable time and in no event later than 1 week after the attack, transmit to the person or group attacked (1) notification of the date, time and identification of the broadcast; (2) a script or tape (or an accurate summary if a script or tape is not available) of the attack; and (3) an offer of a reasonable opportunity to respond over the licensee's facilities.

> (b) The provisions of paragraph (a) of this section shall not be applicable (1) to attacks on foreign groups or foreign public figures; (2) to personal attacks which are made by legally qualified candidates, their authorized spokesmen, or those associated with them in the campaign, on other such candidates, their authorized spokesmen, or persons associated with the candidates in the campaign; and (3) to bona fide newscasts, bona fide news interviews, and on-the-spot coverage of a bona fide news event (including commentary or analysis contained in the foregoing programs, but the provisions of paragraph (a) of this section shall be applicable to editorials of the licensee).

The first point to note is that the episode must occur "during the presentation of views on a controversial issue of public importance." This limitation means that personal attacks unrelated to such a discussion do not invoke the rule—and presumably are left exclusively to defamation suits. Why is this distinction drawn?

Sometimes it is difficult to determine what constitutes "during the presentation of views on a controversial issue of public importance." In Straus Communications, Inc. v. Federal Communications Commission, 530 F.2d 1001 (D.C.Cir.1976), a licensee's argument that time for reply was not justified because the attack did not take place during such a discussion was rejected by the Commission. On appeal, the court ruled that the Commission had used the wrong standard when stating that it "believed" that the comment was sufficiently related to an earlier discussion of a meat boycott to justify the conclusion that the personal attack occurred during a continuation of that discussion. The court concluded that the proper approach was for the Commission to judge "the objective reasonableness of the licensee's determination" that the meat boycott discussion had long since ended.

See also Polish American Congress v. Federal Communications Commission, 520 F.2d 1248 (7th Cir.1975), certiorari denied 424 U.S. 927 (1976), in which the complainants had claimed that a skit of Polish jokes on television violated the personal attack part of the fairness doctrine. The Commission rejected the complaint. On appeal, the court stated that the order must be upheld "if the Commission properly determined that ABC's conclusion that the broadcast did not involve a controversial issue of public importance was not unreasonable or in bad faith." The court concluded that "the Commission was correct in ruling that ABC did not overstep its discretion in failing to find a controversial issue of public importance." This was true whether the issue was stated to be (1) whether "Polish Americans are inferior to other human beings in terms of intelligence, personal hygiene, etc." or (2) whether "promulgating" Polish jokes by broadcasting them is desirable. If the former, ABC could reasonably conclude that even if some people felt that way they had not generated enough support to raise a controversial issue of public importance. Even if they had, ABC could conclude that the skit presented did not constitute a "discussion" of this issue. If the issue was the latter, no controversy was shown.

Another issue raised in *Polish American Congress* (although it was not addressed due to the lack of a controversial issue of public importance) was the size of the group attacked. In defamation law, when a group is very large there is no identification (one of the requisite elements), and the individual plaintiff would have difficulty showing that his own personal reputation was harmed. Should the same analysis apply to the personal attack rule when the target is a large group rather than an individual or a small group? In Diocese of Rockville Centre, 50 F.C.C.2d 330, 32 R.R.2d 376 (1973), a licensee had broadcast a statement that perhaps an earlier writer was correct when he stated, "The Roman Church is filled with men who were led into it merely by ambition, who though they might have been useful and respectful as laymen, are hypocritical and immoral." The Commission ruled that the group is not sufficiently "identified" unless the licensee "could reasonably be expected to know exactly who or what finite group" is best able to inform the public of the contrasting viewpoint. The reference to "men" who fill the "Roman Church" was found too vague.

Similarly, a personal attack claim was rejected where the complainant organization was one of several organizations discussed during a program. The program noted there were many differences among the groups and made no explicit allegations against complainant's church. The Commission concluded that the claimant had not met the burden of showing an attack on an identified person or group.  Disciples of the Lord Jesus, 93 F.C.C.2d 7, 53 R.R.2d 319 (1983).

The Commission has also employed a very narrow definition of what constitutes a personal attack.  In *Straus,* the FCC decided that calling a Congressman a coward did not constitute a personal attack.  Similarly, the rule was held inapplicable to remarks reflecting on a journalist's personal competence.  41 R.R.2d 573 (1977).

The Commission has made clear that attacks during discussions of controversial issues of public importance are not misbehavior, and wide-open debate is encouraged so long as the rules are followed.

---

The FCC has begun rulemaking to modify or eliminate the personal attack and political editorializing rules, questioning whether they have enhanced diversity of expression.  The National Association of Broadcasters has contended that the personal attack rule has been misused by people more intent upon vindicating their reputations than in providing the public with information about their positions, and that the political editorializing rule has discouraged broadcasters from making political endorsements.  Chairman Fowler has characterized the personal attack rule as mainly a "quasi-defamation" action because it is not being used to enlighten public debate.

Representatives Timothy Wirth (D.-Colo.) and John Dingell (D.-Mich.) opposed repeal in a letter to Fowler in June, 1983.  They said the proposals represent "yet another disturbing step in the Commission's pattern of systematic retreat from the principles of public service and accountability that form the cornerstone of a broadcaster's responsibilities under the Communications Act."  Broadcasting, June 27, 1983 at 86. This view was joined by Accuracy in Media, the Conservative Caucus, the American Business Media Council, and the Telecommunications Research and Action Center, creating an alliance of the right and left.  Broadcasting, Aug. 22, 1983 at 48.

### 3.  Fairness in Political Campaigns

The fairness doctrine enters into political issues in two ways.  The first involves the use of broadcasting by the party in power, particularly the President, between political campaigns.  The courts have taken the view that when the President speaks on an issue of national concern, the party out of power has no automatic right to reply.  The only exception occurred when the President delivered five uninterrupted speeches during a seven-month period about the war in Indochina.  Since broadcast coverage of that dispute had otherwise been roughly in balance, the FCC decided that the networks were obligated to provide free time for a spokesman from the other side of the issue.

But that instance aside, the courts have considered the speeches of a President just one factor to weigh in deciding whether the required rough balance in the presentation of contrasting views has been achieved. As usual, the FCC will generally defer to the views of the licensees, and the courts will generally defer to the views of the FCC. The subject is explored extensively in Democratic National Committee v. Federal Communications Commission, 481 F.2d 543 (D.C.Cir.1973) (unsuccessful attempt to obtain free reply time to counter President's speeches on economic policy). The official use of television and the response of the networks to official requests are discussed in N. Minow, J.B. Martin, and L.M. Mitchell, Presidential Television (1973).

The second role of the fairness doctrine in politics involves the campaign itself. Since § 315 was construed not to cover appearances by anyone other than candidates, and since the section also does not cover ballot propositions, many important political campaign broadcasts must be regulated under provisions much less precise than § 315. Not surprisingly, as television has become increasingly important in election campaigns, questions not covered by § 315 have arisen more frequently.

*Uses by Supporters.* Turning first to a close parallel situation, what are the controlling principles when Candidate A's friends or campaign committee purchase time to further his candidacy or to attack B, his opponent? In its Letter to Nicholas Zapple, 23 F.C.C.2d 707, 19 R.R.2d 421 (1970), the Commission stated that the 1959 amendment to § 315 had explicitly recognized the operation of the fairness doctrine when the candidate's own appearance was exempted from § 315. The doctrine was thought equally applicable here. Moreover, when a candidate is supported or his opponent attacked, although the licensee has the responsibility of identifying suitable speakers for opposing views, "barring unusual circumstances, it would not be reasonable for a licensee to refuse to sell time to spokesmen for or supporters of candidate B comparable to that previously bought on behalf of candidate A." But there was no obligation to provide B's supporters with free time. Although usually requiring that time be given away, if necessary, to get contrasting views before the public, the Commission thought this unsound in the political arena. To hold otherwise would require licensees, or other advertisers, to subsidize B's campaign. The rejection of subsidization meant that even if A's friends mounted a personal attack on B, B would not get free time. The Commission has adhered closely to the *Zapple* ruling, which is sometimes referred to as the "quasi equal opportunities" or "political party" corollary to the fairness doctrine.

In 1979, the Commission decided that Congress intended that "uses" under § 315 and *Zapple* were to be mutually exclusive of the fairness doctrine. The Commission concluded that licensees should not be responsible for "uses" since they have no control over them. As a result, the personal attack rule was rewritten to provide that it did not apply to personal attacks occurring during uses under § 315 or those occurring under *Zapple* situations.

More generally, the fairness doctrine was declared not to apply to issues raised during "uses." The Commission believed that issues raised during "uses" were likely to be of such public interest that other views would be aired in due course without the goad of the fairness doctrine. Personal Attacks and Applicability of the Fairness Doctrine to Section 315 "Uses," 78 F.C.C.2d 457, 45 R.R.2d 1635 (1979).

Recall that § 315 itself explicitly provides that the fairness doctrine applies to programs that are exempted from the equal opportunities provision of § 315.

A new problem emerged in 1980 involving groups organized by friends of Ronald Reagan but not controlled by the candidate. These groups are not bound by spending limits that may bind the candidates themselves. When these groups began to buy time on broadcast stations, the Carter campaign committee complained to the FCC that the stations selling time to these "independent expenditure groups" should be required to make equal, and free, opportunities available to the Carter campaign (and presumably to all other campaigns). These should be free, the Carter committee asserted, because it and the Reagan campaign were each limited to $29.4 million for campaigning because they agreed to accept federal funds. As a result, they could not match both the money Reagan was spending and that being spent by the independent groups.

The FCC rejected the claim on the ground that friends of Carter could start comparable groups to match the expenditures being made by the Reagan groups. To allow the Carter campaign free time would put the Commission in the position of benefitting one of the candidates at the expense of the other, whose friends had been required to pay for his time.

In an effort to apply the *Zapple* ruling outside campaign periods, CBS and others asked the FCC to declare that "when a licensee sells broadcast time for political advertisements by a political party, independent political committee or other supporters of a candidate, whether during or outside a campaign period, the *Cullman* doctrine does not apply and thus, the licensee has no obligation to provide free time to opposing groups." The FCC refused on the ground that Congress had shown that § 315 was to apply only during campaign periods and that *Zapple* was designed to supplement the statute only during the same periods. At other times, *Cullman* applied. CBS, Inc., 95 F.C.C.2d 1152 (1983). As a result many licensees simply refuse to sell time for these political advertisements. Remember that Political Action Committees have no right of access under § 312(a)(7), *National Conservative Political Action Committee*, p. 200, supra.

In *Kennedy II*, p. 199, supra, after rejecting the candidate's claims under § 312 and § 315, the court turned to the role of the fairness doctrine in political campaigns. The Broadcast Bureau and the Commission had found three fatal flaws in Senator Edward M. Kennedy's reliance on the fairness doctrine in this case—and the court agreed.

First, he had failed to define the particular controversial issue involved with sufficient specificity. Second, there was no showing that the networks had failed to present contrasting viewpoints on the national economy in their overall programming. The fairness doctrine "does not operate with the dissective focus of" § 315(a). "Intelligent assessment of the nature and caliber of a broadcaster's overall programming obviously cannot be confined to one program, or even to one day's presentations, so a failure to show some fairness deficiency on the whole is necessarily fatal."

Even if imbalance were established, the third flaw was that Senator Kennedy had no "individual right to broadcast his views on the current economic crisis." Kennedy did not show that he was "uniquely and singularly qualified to represent those who dispute the President's economic leadership or strategies."

Finally, the fairness doctrine extends to political campaigns since the question of which candidate should be elected may be considered a "controversial issue of public importance." This means that even if no requests for time are made under § 315 or § 312, a broadcaster might be required to introduce the issue under the first part of the fairness doctrine. If some views are expressed about the forthcoming campaign during non-uses, the licensee would be obligated under the second part of the doctrine to provide coverage of contrasting views. In determining what views should get how much time, the licensee must make good faith judgments about the importance of the race and the significance of each candidate.

The Commission's dismissal of a fairness complaint alleging unbalanced coverage of economic matters was upheld in DNC v. Federal Communications Commission, 717 F.2d 1471, 54 R.R.2d 941 (D.C.Cir. 1983). Disparities approximating 3:1 and 4:1 in favor of the pro-Administration economic view occurred on the networks. Compliance with fairness doctrine obligations was to be measured by a standard of good faith and reasonableness, not by reference to "rough approximations of equality." Since the disparities were not "glaring," and the audiences were not shown to be very different in size, the Commission's dismissal of the complaint was reasonable. Although the court cited data showing that fairness complainants prevail in roughly 1 in 1,000 cases, the court rejected Commission statements that fairness complaints will inevitably be futile.

Putting § 315, § 312, *Zapple*, and the general fairness doctrine together, do you have a coherent package? What changes would you advocate?

*Political Editorials.* In a section of the personal attack rules, 47 C.F.R. § 73.123(c), the Commission covered political editorials:

> Where a licensee, in an editorial (i) endorses or (ii) opposes a legally qualified candidate or candidates, the licensee shall, within 24 hours after the editorial, transmit to respectively (i) the other qualified candidate or candidates for the same office or (ii) the

candidate opposed in the editorial (1) notification of the date and the time of the editorial; (2) a script or tape of the editorial; and (3) an offer of a reasonable opportunity for a candidate or a spokesman of the candidate to respond over the licensee's facilities: *Provided, however,* That where such editorials are broadcast within 72 hours prior to the day of the election, the licensee shall comply with the provisions of this paragraph sufficiently far in advance of the broadcast to enable the candidate or candidates to have a reasonable opportunity to prepare a response and to present it in a timely fashion.

Be sure to note that a single editorial on behalf of one candidate creates an opportunity to respond for *each* opposing candidate. This is true regardless of the number of opposing candidates. Friends of Howard Miller, 72 F.C.C.2d 508, 45 R.R.2d 1142 (1979).

*Ballot Propositions.* In an omitted part of the 1974 Fairness Report, the Commission reached the conclusion that such matters as referenda, initiative and recall propositions, bond proposals, and constitutional amendments were to be regulated under the fairness doctrine. The area was thought closer to general political discussion not involving elections than it was to the election of individuals to office. Thus, the *Cullman* doctrine requiring the licensee to present contrasting views, by the use of free time if necessary, was applicable. One argument against the *Cullman* doctrine was that some groups might spend their available money on non-broadcast media, wait for the other side to buy broadcast time, and then insist on free time under *Cullman* to counter their adversary. The Commission was not persuaded. First, this concern can always be raised against *Cullman*, but the Commission thought it most important that the public have access to contrasting views. On the tactical level, the Commission noted that the fairness doctrine does not guarantee equality of exposure of views nor who will be chosen as speakers. Those who rely solely on *Cullman* "have no assurance of obtaining equality by such means." Fairness Report, 48 F.C.C.2d 1, 33, 30 R.R.2d 1261, 1302 (1974).

# Chapter VII

# LEGAL CONTROL OF BROADCAST PROGRAMMING: NONPOLITICAL SPEECH

In Chapter VI we examined legal controls on broadcast programming that were concerned primarily with political speech. We now turn to other content regulation of broadcasting. Here, the restrictions often take the form of direct bans on speech. As we examine each case ask yourself whether these restrictions are more, or less, justifiable than those covered in the previous Chapter.

## A. DRUGS

### YALE BROADCASTING CO. v. FEDERAL COMMUNICATIONS COMMISSION

United States Court of Appeals, District of Columbia Circuit, 1973.
478 F.2d 594, certiorari denied 414 U.S. 914, 94 S.Ct. 211, 38 L.Ed.2d 152
(1973).

Before DANAHER, SENIOR CIRCUIT JUDGE, and ROBINSON and WILKEY, CIRCUIT JUDGES.

WILKEY, CIRCUIT JUDGE:

The source of this controversy is a Notice issued by the Federal Communications Commission regarding "drug oriented" music allegedly played by some radio stations. This Notice and a subsequent Order, the stated purposes of which were to remind broadcasters of a pre-existing duty, required licensees to have knowledge of the content of their programming and on the basis of this knowledge to evaluate the desirability of broadcasting music dealing with drug use. Appellant, a radio station licensee, argues first that the Notice and the Order are an unconstitutional infringement of its First Amendment right to free speech. . . .

   . . .

Despite all its attempts to assuage broadcasters' fears, the Commission realized that if an Order can be misunderstood, it will be misunderstood—at least by some licensees. To remove any excuse for misunderstanding, the Commission specified examples of how a broadcaster could obtain the requisite knowledge. A licensee could fulfill its obligation through (1) pre-screening by a responsible station employee, (2) monitoring selections while they were being played, or (3) considering and responding to complaints made by members of the public. The Order made clear that these procedures were merely suggestions, and were not to be regarded as either absolute requirements or the exclusive means for fulfilling a station's public interest obligation.

Having made clear our understanding of what the Commission has done, we now take up appellant's arguments seriatim.

## III. AN UNCONSTITUTIONAL BURDEN ON FREEDOM OF SPEECH

Appellant's first argument is that the Commission's action imposes an unconstitutional burden on a broadcaster's freedom of speech. This contention rests primarily on the Supreme Court's opinion in Smith v. California,[12] in which a bookseller was convicted of possessing and selling obscene literature. The Supreme Court reversed the conviction. Although the State had a legitimate purpose in seeking to ban the distribution of obscene materials, it could not accomplish this goal by placing on the bookseller the procedural burden of examining every book in his store. To make a bookseller criminally liable for all the books sold would necessarily "tend to restrict the books he sells to those he has inspected; and thus the State will have imposed a restriction upon the distribution of constitutionally protected as well as obscene literature. . . ."

Appellant compares its own situation to that of the bookseller in *Smith* and argues that the Order imposes an unconstitutional burden on a broadcaster's freedom of speech. The two situations are easily distinguishable.

Most obviously, a radio station can only broadcast for a finite period of twenty-four hours each day; at any one time a bookstore may contain thousands of hours' worth of readable material. Even if the Commission had ordered that stations pre-screen all materials broadcast, the burden would not be nearly so great as the burden imposed on the bookseller in *Smith*. As it is, broadcasters are not even required to pre-screen their maximum twenty-four hours of daily programming. Broadcasters have specifically been told that they may gain "knowledge" of what they broadcast in other ways.

A more subtle but no less compelling answer to the appellant's argument rests upon *why* knowledge of drug oriented music is required by the Commission. In *Smith*, knowledge was imputed to the purveyor in order that a criminal sanction might be imposed and the dissemination halted. Here the goal is to assure the broadcaster has adequate knowledge. . . .

We say that the licensee must have *knowledge* of what it is broadcasting; the precise *understanding* which may be required of the licensee is only that which is reasonable. No radio licensee faces any realistic possibility of a penalty for misinterpreting the lyrics it has chosen or permitted to be broadcast. If the lyrics are completely obscure, the station is not put on notice that it is in fact broadcasting material which would encourage drug abuse. If the lyrics are meaningless, incoherent, the same conclusion follows. The argument of the

---

12.   361 U.S. 147 (1959).

appellant licensee, that so many of these lyrics are obscure and ambiguous, really is a circumstance available to some degree in his defense for permitting their broadcast, at least until their meaning is clarified. Some lyrics or sounds are virtually unintelligible. To the extent they are completely meaningless gibberish and approach the equivalent of machinery operating or the din of traffic, they, of course, do not communicate with respect to drugs or anything else, and are not within the ambit of the Commission's order. Speech is an expression of sound or visual symbols which is intelligible to some other human beings. At some point along the scale of human intelligibility the sounds produced may slide over from characteristics of free speech, which should be protected, to those of noise pollution, which the Commission has ample authority to abate.[15]

We not only think appellant's argument invalid, we express our astonishment that the licensee would argue that before the broadcast it has no knowledge, and cannot be required to have any knowledge, of material it puts over the airwaves. We can understand that the individual radio licensees would not be expected to know in advance the content or the quality of a network program, or a free flowing panel discussion of public issues, or other audience participation program, and certainly not a political broadcast. But with reference to the broadcast of that which is frequently termed "canned music," we think the Commission may require that the purveyors of this to the public make a reasonable effort to know what is in the "can." No producer of pork and beans is allowed to put out on a grocery shelf a can without knowing what is in it and standing back of both its content and quality. The Commission is not required to allow radio licensees, being freely granted the use of limited air channels, to spew out to the listening public canned music, whose content and quality before broadcast is totally unknown.

Supposedly a radio licensee is performing a public service—that is the raison d'etre of the license. If the licensee does not have specific knowledge of what it is broadcasting, how can it claim to be operating in the public interest? Far from constituting any threat to freedom of speech of the licensee, we conclude that for the Commission to have been less insistent on licensees discharging their obligations would have verged on an evasion of the Commission's own responsibilities.

By the expression of the above views we have no desire whatsoever to express a value judgment on different types of music, poetry, sound, instrumentation, etc., which may appeal to different classes of our most diverse public. "De gustibus non est disputandum." But what we are saying is that whatever the style, whatever the expression put out over the air by the radio station, for the licensee to claim that it has no responsibility to evaluate its product is for the radio station to abnegate completely what we had always considered its responsibility as a licensee. All in all, and quite unintentionally, the appellant-licensee in its free

15. Cf. Noise Control Act of 1972, Pub. L. No. 92–574, 86 Stat. (1972).

speech argument here has told us a great deal about quality in this particular medium of our culture.

. . .

For the reasons given above, the action of the Federal Communications Commission is

Affirmed.

### Notes and Questions

1.   A motion for a rehearing en banc was denied over the objection of Chief Judge Bazelon, who commented that

> . . . the Order restated its basic threat: "the broadcaster could jeopardize his license by failing to exercise licensee responsibility in this area." As we have recognized, "licensee responsibility" is a nebulous concept. It could be taken to mean—as the panel opinion takes it—only that "a broadcaster must 'know' what it is broadcasting." On the other hand, in light of the earlier Notice, and in light of the renewed warnings in the Order about the dangers of "drug-oriented" popular songs, broadcasters might have concluded that "responsibility" meant "prohibition."
>
> . . .

> This case presents several other questions of considerable significance: Is the popular song a constitutionally protected form of speech?[23] Do the particular songs at which these directives were aimed have a demonstrable connection with illegal activities? If so, is the proper remedy to "discourage or eliminate" the playing of such songs? Can the FCC assert regulatory authority over material that could not constitutionally be regulated in the printed media?[25]

Clearly, the impact of the Commission's order is ripe for judicial review. And, on that review, it would be well to heed Lord Devlin's recent warning:

> If freedom of the press . . . [or freedom of speech] perishes, it will not be by a sudden death. . . . It will be a long time dying from a debilitating disease caused by a series of erosive measures, each of which, if examined singly, would have a good deal to be said for it.

23.   Popular songs might be considered mere entertainment, or even noise pollution. Yale Broadcasting Co. v. FCC, at 598, 599. On the other hand, historians and sociologists have noted that the popular song has been an important medium of political, moral, and aesthetic expression in American life.

25.   See Brandywine-Main Line Radio, Inc. v. FCC, 473 F.2d 16 (1972) (Chief Judge Bazelon, dissenting) (application of the Fairness Doctrine). Unlike the "Fairness Doctrine" cases, there can be no assertion here that the chilling effect is incidental to providing access to the media for viewpoints that would contribute to a fuller debate on public issues. The question is thus presented whether the rationale of the "Fairness Doctrine," or any other realities of the electronic media, warrant intrusion on broadcasters' free speech rights in this case.

2. The Supreme Court denied certiorari, 414 U.S. 914 (1973). Justice Brennan would have granted the writ and set the case for argument. Justice Douglas dissented along the lines sketched by Chief Judge Bazelon. He noted that the Commission majority apparently had intended to ban drug-related lyrics from the air and that at a Congressional hearing the Chairman testified that if a licensee were playing songs that the Commission thought promoted the use of "hard drugs," "I know what I would do, I would probably vote to take the license away." Even though drug lyrics might not cause great concern if banned, "next year it may apply to comedy programs, and the following year to news broadcasts." He concluded that:

> The Government cannot, consistent with the First Amendment, require a broadcaster to censor its music any more than it can require a newspaper to censor the stories of its reporters. Under our system the Government is not to decide what messages, spoken or in music, are of the proper "social value" to reach the people.

3. Could Congress ban pro-drug broadcasts—whether of songs or of normal speech? Are your views here consistent with your views about Congressional power to ban cigarette commercials, p. 217, supra?

4. Could Congress ban pro-drug messages in the print media? What about pro-cigarette messages? In late 1985, the American Medical Association recommended extending the ban on cigarette commercials to all media.

5. In mid-1985, the Parents Music Resource Center proposed that record companies place warning labels on records with lyrics that contain "explicit sexual language, profanity, violence, the occult and the glorification of drugs and alcohol." Broadcasting, Sept. 26, 1985 at 28. What if the Commission were to ban the playing of records with warning labels? What if the Commission merely indicated a belief that playing records with those labels was against the public interest?

## B. OBSCENITY AND INDECENCY

Obscenity as a class of speech has long been viewed as unprotected by the First Amendment, even though the Supreme Court did not address the issue until 1957. In Roth v. United States, 354 U.S. 476 (1957), the Court held that even though it was "expression," obscenity was outside the protection of the First and Fourteenth Amendments.

The current definition of obscenity, the *Miller* standard, was handed down by the Supreme Court in 1973, Miller v. California, 413 U.S. 15 (1973):

> (a) whether "the average person, applying contemporary community standards" would find that the work, taken as a whole, appeals to the prurient interest, [ ]; (b) whether the work depicts or describes, in a patently offensive way, sexual conduct specifically defined by the applicable state law; and (c) whether the work, taken as a whole, lacks serious literary, artistic, political, or scientific value.

In order for something to be declared legally obscene, all three parts of the test must be met.

Since obscenity is beyond the protection of the First Amendment, both state and federal government are free to regulate it. However, statutes that are not limited to material covered by the *Miller* standard are usually considered unconstitutionally overbroad. For example, in Erznoznik v. Jacksonville, 422 U.S. 205 (1975), the Court struck down an ordinance forbidding the showing of nudity on drive-in theatre screens visible from the public streets. When its captive audience justification proved unsuccessful, the city also asserted that the ordinance was justified as a protection of children. This also failed because the restriction was "broader than permissible. The ordinance is not directed against sexually explicit nudity, nor is it otherwise limited. Rather, it sweepingly forbids display of films containing any uncovered buttocks or breasts, irrespective of contexts or pervasiveness. Thus, it would bar a film containing a picture of a baby's buttocks, the nude body of a war victim, or scenes from a culture in which nudity is indigenous. . . . Clearly all nudity cannot be deemed obscene even as to minors." In appropriately drafted statutes, it is possible to protect minors from obscenity even though such a statute could not apply to the general public. See Ginsberg v. New York, 390 U.S. 629 (1968) for a discussion of the states' power to regulate minors' access to obscene material.

The subject of obscenity did not become a problem on radio and television until recently. In the earlier years of these media, the licensees apparently had no practical reason to want to test the limits of permissible communication and were unsure what the Commission might legally do to licensees who stepped over the line.

In the 1934 Act, § 326, the prohibition on censorship, also contained a passage forbidding the use of obscene or indecent speech in broadcasting. In 1948, that ban was removed from § 326 and added to the general criminal law in 18 U.S.C.A. § 1464:

> Whoever utters any obscene, indecent, or profane language by means of radio communication shall be fined not more than $10,000 or imprisoned not more than two years, or both.

Several other sections empower the Commission to impose sanctions for violation of § 1464.

In 1964, the Commission considered renewal of stations belonging to the Pacifica Foundation. Five programs had provoked complaints: two poets reading their own works; one author reading from his novel; a recording of Edward Albee's "Zoo Story"; and a program "in which eight homosexuals discussed their attitudes and problems." All were late at night except one of the poetry readings. The Commission indicated that it was "not concerned with individual programs" but with whether there had been a pattern of programming inconsistent with the public interest. Although it found nothing to bar renewal, the Commission discussed the five programs, claiming it would be "useful" to the "industry and the public."

The Commission found three of the programs were well within the licensee's judgment under the public interest standard. The Commission recognized that provocative programming might offend some listeners. To rule such programs off the air, however, would mean that "only the wholly inoffensive, the bland, could gain access to the radio microphone or TV camera." The remedy for offended listeners was to turn off the program. The two poetry readings raised different questions. One did not measure up to the licensee's standards for presentation but it had not been carefully screened because it had come from a reputable source. The other reading, involving 28 poems, was broadcast at 7:15 p.m. because the station's editor admitted he had been lulled by the poet's "rather flat, monotonous voice" and did not catch unidentified "offensive words" in the 19th poem. The errors were isolated and thus caused no renewal problem. Pacifica Foundation, 36 F.C.C. 147, 1 R.R.2d 747 (1964). For a history of Pacifica's struggle in 1964, including the fact that no broadcaster came to its defense, see Barton, The Lingering Legacy of Pacifica: Broadcasters' Freedom of Silence, 53 Journ.Q. 429 (1976).

Another episode involved a taped interview on a noncommercial FM station with Jerry Garcia, leader of a musical group known as the Grateful Dead. Garcia apparently used "various patently offensive words as adjectives, introductory expletives, and as substitutes for 'et cetera.'" The Commission imposed a forfeiture of $100 for "indecency" and apparently hoped for a court test of its powers. Eastern Educational Radio (WUHY–FM), 24 F.C.C.2d 408, 18 R.R.2d 860 (1970). The licensee paid the fine and the case was over.

Next came charges of obscenity leveled at "topless radio," midday programs consisting of "call-in talk shows in which masters of ceremonies discuss intimate sexual topics with listeners, usually women." The format quickly became very popular. The Commission responded to complaints by ordering its staff to tape several of the shows and to present a condensed tape of some of the most offensive comments. The next day, Chairman Burch spoke to the National Association of Broadcasters condemning the format. Two weeks later, the Commission issued a Notice of Apparent Liability proposing a forfeiture of $2,000 against one licensee. Sonderling Broadcasting Corp. (WGLD–FM), 27 R.R.2d 285 (F.C.C.1973). The most troublesome language was apparently:

> Female Listener: . . . of course I had a few hangups at first about—in regard to this, but you know what we did—I have a craving for peanut butter all that [sic] time so I used to spread this on my husband's privates and after a while, I mean, I didn't even need the peanut butter anymore.
>
> Announcer: (Laughs) Peanut butter, huh?
>
> Listener: Right. Oh, we can try anything—you know—any, any of these women that have called and they have, you know,

hangups about this, I mean they should try their favorite—you know like—uh.  .  .  .

Announcer: Whipped cream, marshmallow .  .  .  .

In addition, the host's conversation with a complaining listener was thought to be suffused with "leering innuendo." The Commission thought this program ran afoul of both the "indecency" and "obscenity" standards of § 1464. On the other hand, the Commission disclaimed any intention to ban the discussion of sex entirely:

> We are emphatically not saying that sex *per se* is a forbidden subject on the broadcast medium. We are well aware that sex is a vital human relationship which has concerned humanity over the centuries, and that sex and obscenity are not the same thing. In this area as in others, we recognize the licensee's right to present provocative or unpopular programming which may offend some listeners, Pacifica Foundation, 36 FCC 147, 149 (1964). Second, we note that we are not dealing with works of dramatic or literary art as we were in *Pacifica*. We are rather confronted with the talk or interview show where clearly the interviewer can readily moderate his handling of the subject matter so as to conform to the basic statutory standards which, as we point out, allow much leeway for provocative material. .  .  .  The standards here are strictly defined by the law: The broadcaster must eschew the "obscene or indecent."

Again the Commission sought a test: "we welcome and urge judicial consideration of our action." Commissioner Johnson dissented on several grounds, including the view that the Commission had no duty to act in these cases and should leave the matter to possible prosecution by Justice Department. Sonderling denied liability but paid the fine. Two citizen groups asked the Commission to reconsider on the grounds that listeners' rights to hear such programs had been disregarded by the Commission's action. The Commission reaffirmed its action. 41 F.C.C.2d 777, 27 R.R.2d 1508 (1973). It indicated that it had based its order "on the pervasive and intrusive nature of broadcast radio, even if children were left completely out of the picture." It went on, however, to point out that children were in the audience in these afternoon programs and there was some evidence that the program was not intended solely for adults. "The obvious intent of this reference to children was to convey the conclusion that this material was unlawful, and that it was even more clearly unlawful when presented to an audience which included children."

The citizen groups appealed but lost. Illinois Citizens Committee for Broadcasting v. Federal Communications Commission, 515 F.2d 397 (D.C. Cir.1974). The court refused to allow the petitioners to make certain procedural arguments that it thought were open only to the licensee itself. On the merits:

> The excerpts cited by the Commission contain repeated and explicit descriptions of the techniques of oral sex. And these are

presented, not for educational and scientific purposes, but in a context that was fairly described by the FCC as "titillating and pandering." The principles of Ginzburg v. United States, 383 U.S. 463 (1966) are applicable, for commercial exploitation of interests in titillation is the broadcaster's sole end. It is not a material difference that here the tone is set by the continuity provided by the announcer rather than, as in *Ginzburg*, by the presentation of the material in advertising and sale to solicit an audience. We cannot ignore what the Commission took into account—that the announcer's response to a complaint by an offended listener and his presentation of advertising for auto insurance are suffused with leering innuendo. Moreover, and significantly, "Femme Forum" is broadcast from 10 a.m. to 3 p.m. during daytime hours when the radio audience may include children—perhaps home from school for lunch, or because of staggered school hours or illness. Given this combination of factors, we do not think that the FCC's evaluation of this material infringes upon rights protected by the First Amendment.

The FCC found Sonderling's broadcasts obscene . . . .

. . .

Petitioners object that the Commission's determination was based on a brief condensation of offensive material and did not take into account the broadcast as a whole, as would seem to be required by certain elements of both the *Memoirs* and the *Miller* tests. The Commission's approach is not inappropriate in evaluating a broadcasting program that is episodic in nature—a cluster of individual and typically disconnected commentaries, rather than an integrated presentation. It is commonplace for members of the radio audience to listen only to short snatches of a broadcast, and programs like "Femme Forum" are designed to attract such listeners.

We conclude that, where a radio call-in show during daytime hours broadcasts explicit discussions of ultimate sexual acts in a titillating context, the Commission does not unconstitutionally infringe upon the public's right to listening alternatives when it determines that the broadcast is obscene.

The court explicitly did not rely upon the Commission's argument that it had latitude to hold things "indecent" that are not obscene.

A motion for rehearing en banc was denied over the lengthy dissent of Chief Judge Bazelon. He was much concerned about the ability of the Commission, by "raised eyebrow" and the Chairman's speech, to virtually end a very popular format. He saw this as "flagrant and illegal censorship." He also found four areas of error committed by the panel.

## INTRODUCTION TO THE PACIFICA CASE

Two points should be made before reading the following case. The first involves the notion of "nuisance" in law. Activities that may be socially desirable are often called nuisances if located in the wrong place.

This might include a factory that emits smoke in an amount that would be acceptable in a factory district but is unacceptable in a residential district. The legal goal is to encourage the factory either to conform to the needs of its surroundings or to relocate to a factory area.

The second point involves a conflict within the Court about the legitimacy of regulations based on the content of the communication. In Police Department of Chicago v. Mosley, 408 U.S. 92 (1972), the Court invalidated an ordinance that barred picketing outside schools unless the picketing was related to a labor-management dispute concerning the school. "Once a forum is opened up to assembly or speaking by some groups, government may not prohibit others from assembling or speaking on the basis of what they intend to say."

In Young v. American Mini Theatres, Inc., 427 U.S. 50 (1976), Detroit adopted a zoning ordinance requiring that theaters that specialized in showing sexually explicit movies had to be separated from one another by a minimum distance. The Court upheld the ordinance 5–4, but there was no majority opinion. Justice Stevens, for the plurality of four, said that the *Mosley* statement must be kept in context. Even though the First Amendment did not permit "total suppression of erotic materials that have some arguably artistic value, it is manifest that society's interest in protecting this type of expression is of a wholly different, and lesser, magnitude than the interest in untrammeled political debate . . . . [F]ew of us would march our sons and daughters off to war to preserve the citizen's right to see 'Specified Sexual Activities' exhibited in the theaters of our choice."

The plurality then concluded that the record supported the city council's conclusion that unfortunate effects followed from the clustering of such enterprises in one area.

Justice Powell provided the crucial fifth vote on the ground that this case involved "an example of innovative land-use regulation, implicating First Amendment concerns only incidentally and to a limited extent." The ordinance did not "restrict in any significant way the viewing of these movies by those who desire to see them."

The four dissenters considered the decision "a drastic departure from established principles of First Amendment law." These principles require that regulations concerning the time, place, and manner of communicating "be content-neutral except in the limited context of a captive or juvenile audience."

As we will see, this conflict reappears in *Pacifica.*

### FEDERAL COMMUNICATIONS COMMISSION v. PACIFICA FOUNDATION

Supreme Court of the United States, 1978.
438 U.S. 726, 98 S.Ct. 3026, 57 L.Ed.2d 1073.

[George Carlin, a "satiric humorist," recorded a 12-minute monologue entitled "Filthy Words" before a live audience in a California theater. The theme was "the words you couldn't say on the public, ah, airwaves. . . ." Carlin then proposed a basic list: "The original seven words were shit, piss, fuck, cunt, cocksucker, motherfucker, and tits. Those are the ones that will curve your spine, grow hair on your hands and (laughter) maybe, even bring us, God help us, peace without honor (laughter) um, and a bourbon." Carlin then discussed "shit" and "fuck" at length, including the various phrases that use each word. The following passage gives some idea of the format:

> Now the word shit is okay for the man. At work you can say it like crazy. Mostly figuratively. Get that shit out of here, will ya? I don't want to see that shit anymore. I can't *cut* that shit, buddy. I've had that shit up to here. I think you're full of shit myself. (laughter) He don't know shit from Shinola. (laughter) You know that? (laughter) Always wondered how the Shinola people felt about that? (laughter) Hi, I'm the new man from Shinola. (laughter) Hi, how are ya? Nice to see ya. (laughter) How are ya? (laughter) Boy, I don't know, whether to shit or wind my watch. (laughter) Guess I'll shit on my watch. (laughter) Oh, *the* shit is going to hit *de* fan. (laughter) Built like a brick shit-house. (laughter) Up, he's up shit's creek. (laughter) He's had it. (laughter) He hit me, I'm sorry. (laughter) Hot shit, holy shit, tough shit, eat shit. (laughter) Shit-eating grin. Uh, whoever thought of that was ill. (murmur laughter) He had a shit-eating grin! He had a what? (laughter) Shit on a stick. (laughter) Shit in a handbag. I always like that.

One Tuesday afternoon at 2:00 p.m., Pacifica's FM station in New York City played the monologue during a discussion about society's attitude toward language. The station warned that the monologue included language that might offend some listeners. A man who apparently did not hear the warning heard the broadcast while driving with his young son, and complained to the Commission. In response to an inquiry from the Commission, Pacifica responded that Carlin was a "significant social satirist" who "like Twain and Sahl before him, examines the language of ordinary people. . . ." Apparently, no one else complained about the broadcast.

The Commission ruled that Pacifica's action was subject to administrative sanction. Instead of imposing a formal sanction, it put the order in the file for possible use if subsequent complaints were received. The Commission asserted four reasons for treating broadcasting differently from other media: access by unsupervised children; since radio receivers are in the home, privacy interests are entitled to extra deference; unconsenting adults may tune in without a warning that offensive language is being used; and scarcity of spectrum space requires government to license in the public interest. Further facts are stated in the opinions.]

MR. JUSTICE STEVENS delivered the opinion of the Court (Parts I, II, III, and IV-C) and an opinion in which THE CHIEF JUSTICE and MR. JUSTICE REHNQUIST joined (Parts IV-A and IV-B).

This case requires that we decide whether the Federal Communications Commission has any power to regulate a radio broadcast that is indecent but not obscene.

. . .

. . . [T]he Commission found a power to regulate indecent broadcasting in two statutes: 18 U.S.C. § 1464, which forbids the use of "any obscene, indecent, or profane language by means of radio communications," and 47 U.S.C. § 303(g), which requires the Commission to "encourage the larger and more effective use of radio in the public interest."

The Commission characterized the language used in the Carlin monologue as "patently offensive," though not necessarily obscene, and expressed the opinion that it should be regulated by principles analogous to those found in the law of nuisance where the "law generally speaks to *channeling* behavior more than prohibiting it. . . . [T]he concept of 'indecent' is intimately connected with the exposure of children to language that describes, in terms patently offensive as measured by contemporary community standards for the broadcast medium, sexual or excretory activities and organs, at times of the day when there is a reasonable risk that children may be in the audience." 56 F.C.C.2d, at 98.[5]

. . . In summary, the Commission stated: "We therefore hold that the language as broadcast was indecent and prohibited by 18 U.S.C. 1464."

After the order issued, the Commission was asked to clarify its opinion by ruling that the broadcast of indecent words as part of a live newscast would not be prohibited. . . . The Commission noted that its "declaratory order was issued in a specific factual context," and declined to comment on various hypothetical situations presented by the petition.[7] . . .

The United States Court of Appeals for the District of Columbia reversed, with each of the three judges on the panel writing separately.

Having granted the Commission's petition for certiorari, 434 U.S. 1007, we must decide: (1) whether the scope of judicial review encompasses more than the Commission's determination that the monologue was indecent "as broadcast"; (2) whether the Commission's order was a form of censorship forbidden by § 326; (3) whether the broadcast was indecent within the meaning of § 1464; and (4) whether the order violates the First Amendment of the United States Constitution.

---

5. Thus, the Commission suggested, if an offensive broadcast had literary, artistic, political, or scientific value, and were preceded by warnings, it might not be indecent in the late evening, but would be so during the day, when children are in the audience.

7. The Commission did, however, comment that:

" '[I]n some cases, public events likely to produce offensive speech are covered live,

and there is no opportunity for journalistic editing.' Under these circumstances we believe that it would be inequitable for us to hold a licensee responsible for indecent language . . . . We trust that under such circumstances a licensee will exercise judgment, responsibility, and sensitivity to the community's needs, interests, and tastes." [ ]

## I

The general statements in the Commission's memorandum opinion do not change the character of its order. Its action was an adjudication. . . . The specific holding was carefully confined to the monologue "as broadcast."

. . . Accordingly, the focus of our review must be on the Commission's determination that the Carlin monologue was indecent as broadcast.

## II

The relevant, statutory questions are whether the Commission's action is forbidden "censorship" within the meaning of 47 U.S.C. § 326 and whether speech that concededly is not obscene may be restricted as "indecent" under the authority of 18 U.S.C. § 1464. The questions are not unrelated, for the two statutory provisions have a common origin. . . .

The prohibition against censorship unequivocally denies the Commission any power to edit proposed broadcasts in advance and to excise material considered inappropriate for the airwaves. The prohibition, however, has never been construed to deny the Commission the power to review the content of completed broadcasts in the performance of its regulatory duties.[9]

During the period between the original enactment of the provision in 1927 and its re-enactment in the Communications Act of 1934, the courts and the Federal Radio Commission held that the section deprived the Commission of the power to subject "broadcasting matter to scrutiny prior to its release," but they concluded that the Commission's "undoubted right" to take note of past program content when considering a licensee's renewal application "is not censorship."

Not only did the Federal Radio Commission so construe the statute prior to 1934; its successor, the Federal Communications Commission, has consistently interpreted the provision in the same way ever since. [ ]   And, until this case, the Court of Appeals for the District of Columbia has consistently agreed with this construction. . . .

Entirely apart from the fact that the subsequent review of program content is not the sort of censorship at which the statute was directed, its history makes it perfectly clear that it was not intended to limit the Commission's power to regulate the broadcast of obscene, indecent, or profane language. . . .

9.  Zechariah Chafee, defending the Commission's authority to take into account program service in granting licenses, interpreted the restriction on "censorship" narrowly: "This means, I feel sure, the sort of censorship which went on in the seventeenth century in England—the deletion of specific items and dictation as to what should go into particular programs." 2 Z. Chafee, Government and Mass Communications 641 (1947).

There is nothing in the legislative history to contradict this conclusion. . . .

We conclude, therefore, that § 326 does not limit the Commission's authority to impose sanctions on licensees who engage in obscene, indecent, or profane broadcasting.

### III

The only other statutory question presented by this case is whether the afternoon broadcast of the "Filthy Words" monologue was indecent within the meaning of § 1464.[13] Even that question is narrowly confined by the arguments of the parties.

The Commission identified several words that referred to excretory or sexual activities or organs, stated that the repetitive, deliberate use of those words in an afternoon broadcast when children are in the audience was patently offensive, and held that the broadcast was indecent. Pacifica takes issue with the Commission's definition of indecency, but does not dispute the Commission's preliminary determination that each of the components of its definition was present. Specifically, Pacifica does not quarrel with the conclusion that this afternoon broadcast was patently offensive. Pacifica's claim that the broadcast was not indecent within the meaning of the statute rests entirely on the absence of prurient appeal.

The plain language of the statute does not support Pacifica's argument. The words "obscene, indecent, or profane" are written in the disjunctive, implying that each has a separate meaning. Prurient appeal is an element of the obscene, but the normal definition of "indecent" merely refers to nonconformance with accepted standards of morality.

Pacifica argues, however, that this Court has construed the term "indecent" in related statutes to mean "obscene" as that term was defined in Miller v. California, 413 U.S. 15 (1973). Pacifica relies most heavily on the construction this Court gave to 18 U.S.C. § 1461 in Hamling v. United States, 418 U.S. 87 (1974). See also United States v. Twelve 200–foot Reels of Film, 413 U.S. 123, 130 n. 7 (1973) (18 U.S.C. § 1462) (dicta). . . .

The reasons supporting *Hamling*'s construction of § 1461 do not apply to § 1464. Although the history of the former revealed a primary concern with the prurient, the Commission has long interpreted § 1464 as encompassing more than the obscene. The former statute deals primarily with printed matter enclosed in sealed envelopes mailed from one individual to another; the latter deals with the content of public broadcasts. It is unrealistic to assume that Congress intended to impose

---

**13.** In addition to § 1464, the Commission also relied on its power to regulate in the public interest under 47 U.S.C. § 303(g). We do not need to consider whether § 303 may have independent significance in a case such as this. The statutes authorizing civil penalties incorporate § 1464, a criminal statute. See 47 U.S.C. §§ 312(a)(6), 312(b)(2), and 503(b)(1)(E). But the validity of the civil sanctions is not linked to the validity of the criminal penalty. The legislative history of the provisions establishes their independence. . . .

precisely the same limitations on the dissemination of patently offensive matter by such different means.[17]

Because neither our prior decisions nor the language or history of § 1464 supports the conclusion that prurient appeal is an essential component of indecent language, we reject Pacifica's construction of the statute. When that construction is put to one side, there is no basis for disagreeing with the Commission's conclusion that indecent language was used in this broadcast.

## IV

Pacifica makes two constitutional attacks on the Commission's order. First, it argues that the Commission's construction of the statutory language broadly encompasses so much constitutionally protected speech that reversal is required even if Pacifica's broadcast of the "Filthy Words" monologue is not itself protected by the First Amendment. Second, Pacifica argues that inasmuch as the recording is not obscene, the Constitution forbids any abridgment of the right to broadcast it on the radio.

## A

The first argument fails because our review is limited to the question whether the Commission has the authority to proscribe this particular broadcast. As the Commission itself has emphasized, its order was "issued in a specific factual context." 59 F.C.C.2d, at 893. That approach is appropriate for courts as well as the Commission when regulation of indecency is at stake, for indecency is largely a function of context—it cannot be adequately judged in the abstract.

The approach is also consistent with Red Lion Broadcasting Co., Inc. v. FCC, 395 U.S. 367 (1969). . . .

It is true that the Commission's order may lead some broadcasters to censor themselves. At most, however, the Commission's definition of indecency will deter only the broadcasting of patently offensive references to excretory and sexual organs and activities.[18] While some of these references may be protected, they surely lie at the periphery of First Amendment concern. Cf. Bates v. State Bar, 433 U.S. 350, 380–381

17. This conclusion is re-enforced by noting the different constitutional limits on Congress' power to regulate the two different subjects. Use of the postal power to regulate material that is not fraudulent or obscene raises "grave constitutional questions." Hannegan v. Esquire, Inc., 327 U.S. 146, 156 (1946). But it is well settled that the First Amendment has a special meaning in the broadcasting context. See, e.g., FCC v. National Citizens Committee for Broadcasting, 436 U.S. 775 (1978); Red Lion Broadcasting Co., Inc. v. FCC, 395 U.S. 367 (1969); Columbia Broadcasting System, Inc. v. Democratic National Committee, 412 U.S. 94 (1973). For this reason, the presumption that Congress never intends to exceed constitutional limits, which supported *Hamling's* narrow reading of § 1461, does not support a comparable reading of § 1464.

18. A requirement that indecent language be avoided will have its primary effect on the form, rather than the content, of serious communication. There are few, if any, thoughts that cannot be expressed by the use of less offensive language.

(1977). Young v. American Mini Theatres, Inc., 427 U.S. 50, 61 (1976). The danger dismissed so summarily in *Red Lion*, in contrast, was that the broadcasters would respond to the vagueness of the regulations by refusing to present programs dealing with important social and political controversies. Invalidating any rule on the basis of its hypothetical application to situations not before the Court is "strong medicine" to be applied "sparingly and only as a last resort." Broadrick v. Oklahoma, 413 U.S. 601, 613 (1973). We decline to administer that medicine to preserve the vigor of patently offensive and excretory speech.

B

When the issue is narrowed to the facts of this case, the question is whether the First Amendment denies government any power to restrict the public broadcast of indecent language in any circumstances.[19] For if the government has any such power, this was an appropriate occasion for its exercise.

The words of the Carlin monologue are unquestionably "speech" within the meaning of the First Amendment. It is equally clear that the Commission's objections to the broadcast were based in part on its content. The order must therefore fall if, as Pacifica argues, the First Amendment prohibits all governmental regulation that depends on the content of speech. Our past cases demonstrate, however, that no such absolute rule is mandated by the Constitution.

The classic exposition of the proposition that both the content and the context of speech are critical elements of First Amendment analysis is Mr. Justice Holmes' statement for the Court in Schenck v. United States:

> "We admit that in many places and in ordinary times the defendants in saying all that was said in the circular would have been within their constitutional rights. But the character of every act depends upon the circumstances in which it is done. . . . The most stringent protection of free speech would not protect a man in falsely shouting fire in a theatre and causing a panic. It does not even protect a man from an injunction against uttering words that may have all the effect of force. . . . The question in every case is whether the words used are used in such circumstances and are of such a nature as to create a clear and present danger that they will bring about the substantive evils that Congress has a right to prevent." 249 U.S. 47, 52.

**19.** Pacifica's position would of course deprive the Commission of any power to regulate erotic telecasts unless they were obscene under Miller v. California, 413 U.S. 15 (1973). Anything that could be sold at a newsstand for private examination could be publicly displayed on television.

We are assured by Pacifica that the free play of market forces will discourage inde-cent programming. "Smut may," as Judge Leventhal put it, "drive itself from the market and confound Gresham," 556 F.2d at 35; the prosperity of those who traffic in pornographic literature and films would appear to justify his skepticism.

Other distinctions based on content have been approved in the years since *Schenck*. The government may forbid speech calculated to provoke a fight. See Chaplinsky v. New Hampshire, 315 U.S. 568 (1942). It may pay heed to the " 'commonsense differences' between commercial speech and other varieties." Bates v. State Bar, 433 U.S. 350, 381 (1977). It may treat libels against private citizens more severely than libels against public officials. See Gertz v. Robert Welch, Inc., 418 U.S. 323 (1974). Obscenity may be wholly prohibited. Miller v. California, 413 U.S. 15 (1973). And only two Terms ago we refused to hold that a "statutory classification is unconstitutional because it is based on the content of communication protected by the First Amendment." Young v. American Mini Theatres, 427 U.S. 50, 52 (1976).

The question in this case is whether a broadcast of patently offensive words dealing with sex and excretion may be regulated because of its content. Obscene materials have been denied the protection of the First Amendment because their content is so offensive to contemporary moral standards. Roth v. United States, 354 U.S. 476 (1957). But the fact that society may find speech offensive is not a sufficient reason for suppressing it. Indeed, if it is the speaker's opinion that gives offense, that consequence is a reason for according it constitutional protection. For it is a central tenet of the First Amendment that the government must remain neutral in the marketplace of ideas. If there were any reason to believe that the Commission's characterization of the Carlin monologue as offensive could be traced to its political content—or even to the fact that it satirized contemporary attitudes about four-letter words[22]—First Amendment protection might be required. But that is simply not this case. These words offend for the same reasons that obscenity offends.[23] Their place in the hierarchy of First Amendment values was aptly sketched by Mr. Justice Murphy when he said, "such utterances are no essential part of any exposition of ideas, and are of such slight social value as a step to truth that any benefit that may be derived from them is clearly outweighed by the social interest in order and morality." Chaplinsky v. New Hampshire, 315 U.S. 568, 572 (1942).

Although these words ordinarily lack literary, political, or scientific value, they are not entirely outside the protection of the First Amendment. Some uses of even the most offensive words are unquestionably protected. See, e.g., Hess v. Indiana, 414 U.S. 105 (1973). Indeed, we

22. The monologue does present a point of view; it attempts to show that the words it uses are "harmless" and that our attitudes toward them are "essentially silly." [ ] The Commission objects, not to this point of view, but to the way in which it is expressed. The belief that these words are harmless does not necessarily confer a First Amendment privilege to use them while proselytizing, just as the conviction that obscenity is harmless does not license one to communicate that conviction by the indiscriminate distribution of an obscene leaflet.

23. The Commission stated: "Obnoxious, gutter language describing these matters has the effect of debasing and brutalizing human beings by reducing them to their mere bodily functions . . . ." 56 F.C.C. 2d, at 98. Our society has a tradition of performing certain bodily functions in private, and of severely limiting the public exposure or discussion of such matters. Verbal or physical acts exposing those intimacies are offensive irrespective of any message that may accompany the exposure.

may assume, *arguendo*, that this monologue would be protected in other contexts. Nonetheless, the constitutional protection accorded to a communication containing such patently offensive sexual and excretory language need not be the same in every context. It is a characteristic of speech such as this that both its capacity to offend and its "social value," to use Mr. Justice Murphy's term, vary with the circumstances. Words that are commonplace in one setting are shocking in another. To paraphrase Mr. Justice Harlan, one occasion's lyric is another's vulgarity. Cf. Cohen v. California, 403 U.S. 15, 25.

In this case it is undisputed that the content of Pacifica's broadcast was "vulgar," "offensive," and "shocking." Because content of that character is not entitled to absolute constitutional protection under all circumstances, we must consider its context in order to determine whether the Commission's action was constitutionally permissible.

## C

We have long recognized that each medium of expression presents special First Amendment problems. Joseph Burstyn, Inc. v. Wilson, 343 U.S. 495, 502–503 (1952). And of all forms of communication, it is broadcasting that has received the most limited First Amendment protection. Thus, although other speakers cannot be licensed except under laws that carefully define and narrow official discretion, a broadcaster may be deprived of his license and his forum if the Commission decides that such an action would serve "the public interest, convenience, and necessity." Similarly, although the First Amendment protects newspaper publishers from being required to print the replies of those whom they criticize, Miami Herald Publishing Co. v. Tornillo, 418 U.S. 241, it affords no such protection to broadcasters; on the contrary, they must give free time to the victims of their criticism. Red Lion Broadcasting Co. v. FCC, 395 U.S. 367 (1969).

The reasons for these distinctions are complex, but two have relevance to the present case. First, the broadcast media have established a uniquely pervasive presence in the lives of all Americans. Patently offensive, indecent material presented over the airwaves confronts the citizen, not only in public, but also in the privacy of the home, where the individual's right to be let alone plainly outweighs the First Amendment rights of an intruder. Rowan v. Post Office Department, 397 U.S. 728 (1970). Because the broadcast audience is constantly tuning in and out, prior warnings cannot completely protect the listener or viewer from unexpected program content. To say that one may avoid further offense by turning off the radio when he hears indecent language is like saying that the remedy for an assault is to run away after the first blow. One may hang up on an indecent phone call, but that option does not give the caller a constitutional immunity or avoid a harm that has already taken place.[27]

27. Outside the home, the balance between the offensive speaker and the unwilling audience may sometimes tip in favor of the speaker, requiring the offended listener

Second, broadcasting is uniquely accessible to children, even those too young to read. Although Cohen's written message might have been incomprehensible to a first grader, Pacifica's broadcast could have enlarged a child's vocabulary in an instant. Other forms of offensive expression may be withheld from the young without restricting the expression at its source. Bookstores and motion picture theaters, for example, may be prohibited from making indecent material available to children. We held in Ginsberg v. New York, 390 U.S. 629 (1968), that the government's interest in the "well being of its youth" and in supporting "parents' claim to authority in their own household" justified the regulation of otherwise protected expression. Id., at 640 and 639.[28] The ease with which children may obtain access to broadcast material, coupled with the concerns recognized in *Ginsberg*, amply justify special treatment of indecent broadcasting.

It is appropriate, in conclusion, to emphasize the narrowness of our holding. This case does not involve a two-way radio conversation between a cab driver and a dispatcher, or a telecast of an Elizabethan comedy. We have not decided that an occasional expletive in either setting would justify any sanction or, indeed, that this broadcast would justify a criminal prosecution. The Commission's decision rested entirely on a nuisance rationale under which context is all-important. The concept requires consideration of a host of variables. The time of day was emphasized by the Commission. The content of the program in which the language is used will also affect the composition of the audience,[29] and differences between radio, television, and perhaps closed-circuit transmissions, may also be relevant. As Mr. Justice Sutherland wrote, a "nuisance may be merely a right thing in the wrong place—like a pig in the parlor instead of the barnyard." Euclid v. Ambler Realty Co., 272 U.S. 365, 388 (1926). We simply hold that when the Commission finds that a pig has entered the parlor, the exercise of its regulatory power does not depend on proof that the pig is obscene.

The judgment of the Court of Appeals is reversed.

MR. JUSTICE POWELL, with whom MR. JUSTICE BLACKMUN joins, concurring.

I join Parts I, II, III, and IV(C) of Mr. Justice Stevens' opinion, and with its conclusion that the Commission's holding in this case does not violate the First Amendment. . . .

to turn away. See Erznoznik v. Jacksonville, 422 U.S. 205 (1975).

**28.** The Commission's action does not by any means reduce adults to hearing only what is fit for children. Cf. Butler v. Michigan, 352 U.S. 380, 383 (1957). Adults who feel the need may purchase tapes and records or go to theatres and nightclubs to hear these words. In fact, the Commission has not unequivocally closed even broadcasting to speech of this sort; whether broadcast audiences in the late evening contain so few children that playing this monologue would be permissible is an issue neither the Commission nor this Court has decided.

**29.** Even a prime-time recitation of Chaucer's Miller's Tale would not be likely to command the attention of many children who are both old enough to understand and young enough to be adversely affected by passages such as "And prively he caughte hire by the queynte." G. Chaucer, *The Miller's Tale* 1.3276 (c. 1386).

. . .  Because I do not subscribe to all that is said in Part IV, however, I state my views separately.

## I

It is conceded that the monologue at issue here is not obscene in the constitutional sense.  See 56 F.C.C.2d 94, 98 (1975); Brief for Petitioner 18.  Nor, in this context, does its language constitute "fighting words" within the meaning of Chaplinsky v. New Hampshire, 315 U.S. 568 (1942).  Some of the words used have been held protected by the First Amendment in other cases and contexts. [  ] I do not think Carlin, consistently with the First Amendment, could be punished for delivering the same monologue to a live audience composed of adults who, knowing what to expect, chose to attend his performance.  See Brown v. Oklahoma, 408 U.S. 914 (1972) (Powell, J., concurring in result).  And I would assume that an adult could not constitutionally be prohibited from purchasing a recording or transcript of the monologue and playing or reading it. in the privacy of his own home.  Cf. Stanley v. Georgia, 394 U.S. 557 (1969).

But it also is true that the language employed is, to most people, vulgar and offensive.  It was chosen specifically for this quality, and it was repeated over and over as a sort of verbal shock treatment.  The Commission did not err in characterizing the narrow category of language used here as "patently offensive" to most people regardless of age.

The issue, however, is whether the Commission may impose civil sanctions on a licensee radio station for broadcasting the monologue at two o'clock in the afternoon.  The Commission's primary concern was to prevent the broadcast from reaching the ears of unsupervised children who were likely to be in the audience at that hour.  In essence, the Commission sought to "channel" the monologue to hours when the fewest unsupervised children would be exposed to it.  See 56 F.C.C.2d at 98.  In my view, this consideration provides strong support for the Commission's holding.

The Court has recognized society's right to "adopt more stringent controls on communicative materials available to youths than on those available to adults."  Erznoznik v. City of Jacksonville, [  ].  This recognition stems in large part from the fact that "a child . . . is not possessed of that full capacity for individual choice which is the presupposition of First Amendment guarantees."  Ginsberg v. New York, supra, at 649–650 (Stewart, J., concurring in result).  Thus, children may not be able to protect themselves from speech which, although shocking to most adults, generally may be avoided by the unwilling through the exercise of choice.  At the same time, such speech may have a deeper and more lasting negative effect on a child than an adult.  For these reasons, society may prevent the general dissemination of such speech to children, leaving to parents the decision as to what speech of this kind their children shall hear and repeat:

"[C]onstitutional interpretation has consistently recognized that the parents' claim to authority in their own household to direct the rearing of children is basic in the structure of our society. 'It is cardinal with us that the custody, care and nurture of the child reside first in the parents, whose primary function and freedom include preparation for obligations the state can neither supply nor hinder.' Prince v. Massachusetts, [321 U.S. 158, 166 (1944)]. The legislature could properly conclude that parents and others, teachers for example, who have this primary responsibility for children's well-being are entitled to the support of laws designed to aid discharge of that responsibility." Ginsberg v. New York, supra, at 639.

The Commission properly held that the speech from which society may attempt to shield its children is not limited to that which appeals to the youthful prurient interest. The language involved in this case is as potentially degrading and harmful to children as representations of many erotic acts.

In most instances, the dissemination of this kind of speech to children may be limited without also limiting willing adults' access to it. Sellers of printed and recorded matter and exhibitors of motion pictures and live performances may be required to shut their doors to children, but such a requirement has no effect on adults' access. See Ginsberg v. New York, supra, at 634–635. The difficulty is that such a physical separation of the audience cannot be accomplished in the broadcast media. During most of the broadcast hours, both adults and un-supervised children are likely to be in the broadcast audience, and the broadcaster cannot reach willing adults without also reaching children. This, as the Court emphasizes, is one of the distinctions between the broadcast and other media to which we often have adverted as justifying a different treatment of the broadcast media for First Amendment purposes. [ ] In my view, the Commission was entitled to give substantial weight to this difference in reaching its decision in this case.

A second difference, not without relevance, is that broadcasting—unlike most other forms of communication—comes directly into the home, the one place where people ordinarily have the right not to be assaulted by uninvited and offensive sights and sounds. . . . The Commission also was entitled to give this factor appropriate weight in the circumstances of the instant case. This is not to say, however, that the Commission has an unrestricted license to decide what speech, protected in other media, may be banned from the airwaves in order to protect unwilling adults from momentary exposure to it in their homes.[2] Making the sensitive judgments required in these cases is not easy. But

2. It is true that the radio listener quickly may tune out speech that is offensive to him. In addition, broadcasters may preface potentially offensive programs with warnings. But such warnings do not help the unsuspecting listener who tunes in at the middle of the program. In this respect, too, broadcasting appears to differ from books and records, which may carry warnings on their faces, and from motion pictures and live performances, which may carry warnings on their marquees.

this responsibility has been reposed initially in the Commission, and its judgment is entitled to respect.

## II

As the foregoing demonstrates, my views are generally in accord with what is said in Part IV(C) of Mr. Justice Stevens' opinion. I therefore join that portion of his opinion. I do not join Part IV(B), however, because I do not subscribe to the theory that the Justices of this Court are free generally to decide on the basis of its content which speech protected by the First Amendment is most "valuable" and hence deserving of the most protection, and which is less "valuable" and hence deserving of less protection. Compare ante, at 15–19; Young v. American Mini Theatres, 427 U.S. 50, 63–73 (1976) (opinion of Stevens, J.), with id., at 73 n. 1 (Powell, J., concurring).[3] In my view, the result in this case does not turn on whether Carlin's monologue, viewed as a whole, or the words that comprise it, have more or less "value" than a candidate's campaign speech. This is a judgment for each person to make, not one for judges to impose upon him.[4]

The result turns instead on the unique characteristics of the broadcast media, combined with society's right to protect its children from speech generally agreed to be inappropriate for their years, and with the interest of unwilling adults in not being assaulted by such offensive speech in their homes. Moreover, I doubt whether today's decision will prevent any adult who wishes to receive Carlin's message in Carlin's own words from doing so, and from making for himself a value judgment as to the merit of the message and words. . . .

MR. JUSTICE BRENNAN, with whom MR. JUSTICE MARSHALL joins, dissenting.

I agree with Mr. Justice Stewart that, under Hamling v. United States, 418 U.S. 87 (1974) and United States v. 12 200-ft. Reels of Film, 413 U.S. 123 (1973), the word "indecent" in 18 U.S.C. § 1464 must be construed to prohibit only obscene speech. . . .

## I

For the second time in two years, see Young v. American Mini Theatres, 427 U.S. 50 (1976), the Court refuses to embrace the notion, completely antithetical to basic First Amendment values, that the degree of protection the First Amendment affords protected speech varies with the social value ascribed to that speech by five Members of this Court. See opinion of Mr. Justice Powell . . . . Yet despite the Court's refusal to create a sliding scale of First Amendment protection calibrated

---

**3.** The Court has, however, created a limited exception to this rule in order to bring commercial speech within the protection of the First Amendment. See Ohralik v. Ohio State Bar Association, 436 U.S. 447 (1978).

**4.** For much the same reason, I also do not join IV(A). I had not thought that the application *vel non* of overbreadth analysis should depend on the Court's judgment as to the value of the protected speech that might be deterred. . . .

to the Court's perception of the worth of a communication's content, and despite our unanimous agreement that the Carlin monologue is protected speech, a majority of the Court nevertheless finds that, on the facts of this case, the FCC is not constitutionally barred from imposing sanctions on Pacifica for its airing of the Carlin monologue. This majority apparently believes that the FCC's disapproval of Pacifica's afternoon broadcast of Carlin's "Dirty Words" recording is a permissible time, place, and manner regulation. . . .

### A

Without question, the privacy interests of an individual in his home are substantial and deserving of significant protection. In finding these interests sufficient to justify the content regulation of protected speech, however, the Court commits two errors. First, it misconceives the nature of the privacy interests involved where an individual voluntarily chooses to admit radio communications into his home. Second, it ignores the constitutionally protected interests of both those who wish to transmit and those who desire to receive broadcasts that many—including the FCC and this Court—might find offensive.

. . . I believe that an individual's actions in switching on and listening to communications transmitted over the public airways and directed to the public at-large do not implicate fundamental privacy interests, even when engaged within the home. Instead, because the radio is undeniably a public medium, these actions are more properly viewed as a decision to take part, if only as a listener, in an ongoing public discourse. See Note, Filthy Words, the FCC, and the First Amendment: Regulating Broadcast Obscenity, 61 Va.L.Rev. 579, 618 (1975). Although an individual's decision to allow public radio communications into his home undoubtedly does not abrogate all of his privacy interests, the residual privacy interests he retains vis-a-vis the communication he voluntarily admits into his home are surely no greater than those of the people present in the corridor of the Los Angeles courthouse in *Cohen* who bore witness to the words "Fuck the Draft" emblazoned across Cohen's jacket. Their privacy interests were held insufficient to justify punishing Cohen for his offensive communication.

Even if an individual who voluntarily opens his home to radio communications retains privacy interests of sufficient moment to justify a ban on protected speech if those interests are "invaded in an essentially intolerable manner," Cohen v. California, supra, at 21, the very fact that those interests are threatened only by a radio broadcast precludes any intolerable invasion of privacy; for unlike other intrusive modes of communication, such as sound trucks, "[t]he radio can be turned off," Lehman v. City of Shaker Heights, 418 U.S. 298, 302 (1974)—and with a minimum of effort. . . . Whatever the minimal discomfort suffered by a listener who inadvertently tunes into a program he finds offensive during the brief interval before he can simply extend his arm and switch stations or flick the "off" button, it is surely worth the candle to

preserve the broadcaster's right to send, and the right of those interested to receive, a message entitled to full First Amendment protection.
. . .

The Court's balance, of necessity, fails to accord proper weight to the interests of listeners who wish to hear broadcasts the FCC deems offensive. It permits majoritarian tastes completely to preclude a protected message from entering the homes of a receptive, unoffended minority. No decision of this Court supports such a result. Where the individuals comprising the offended majority may freely choose to reject the material being offered, we have never found their privacy interest of such moment to warrant the suppression of speech on privacy grounds.
. . .

### B

Most parents will undoubtedly find understandable as well as commendable the Court's sympathy with the FCC's desire to prevent offensive broadcasts from reaching the ears of unsupervised children. Unfortunately, the facial appeal of this justification for radio censorship masks its constitutional insufficiency.

Because the Carlin monologue is obviously not an erotic appeal to the prurient interests of children, the Court, for the first time, allows the government to prevent minors from gaining access to materials that are not obscene, and are therefore protected, as to them. It thus ignores our recent admission that "[s]peech that is neither obscene as to youths nor subject to some other legitimate proscription cannot be suppressed solely to protect the young from ideas or images that a legislative body thinks unsuitable for them." [*Erznoznik* ][3] The Court's refusal to follow its own pronouncements is especially lamentable since it has the anomalous subsidiary effect, at least in the radio context at issue here, of making completely unavailable to adults material which may not constitutionally be kept even from children.  .  .  .

In concluding that the presence of children in the listening audience provides an adequate basis for the FCC to impose sanctions for Pacifica's broadcast of the Carlin monologue, the opinions of my Brother Powell and my Brother Stevens both stress the time-honored right of a parent to raise his child as he sees fit—a right this Court has consistently been vigilant to protect. See Wisconsin v. Yoder, 406 U.S. 205 (1972); Pierce

---

3. It may be that a narrowly drawn regulation prohibiting the use of offensive language on broadcasts directed specifically at younger children constitutes one of the "other legitimate proscription[s]" alluded to in *Erznoznik.* This is so both because of the difficulties inherent in adapting the *Miller* formulation to communications received by young children, and because such children are "not possessed of that full capacity for individual choice which is the presupposition of the First Amendment guarantees." Ginsberg v. New York, 390 U.S. 629, 649–650 (1968) (Stewart, J., concurring). I doubt, as my Brother Stevens suggests, ante, at 17 n. 20, that such a limited regulation amounts to a regulation of speech based on its content, since, by hypothesis, the only persons at whom the regulated communication is directed are incapable of evaluating its content. To the extent that such a regulation is viewed as a regulation based on content, it marks the outermost limits to which content regulation is permissible.

v. Society of Sisters, 268 U.S. 510 (1925).   Yet this principle supports a result directly contrary to that reached by the Court.   *Yoder* and *Pierce* hold that parents, *not* the government, have the right to make certain decisions regarding the upbringing of their children.   As surprising as it may be to the individual Members of the Court, some parents may actually find Mr. Carlin's unabashed attitude toward the seven "dirty words" healthy, and deem it desirable to expose their children to the manner in which Mr. Carlin defuses the taboo surrounding the words. Such parents may constitute a minority of the American public, but the absence of great numbers willing to exercise the right to raise children in this fashion does not alter the right's nature or its existence.   Only the Court's regrettable decision does that.[4]

## C

As demonstrated above, neither of the factors relied on by both the opinion of my Brother Powell and the opinion of my Brother Stevens— the intrusive nature of radio and the presence of children in the listening audience—can, when taken on its own terms, support the FCC's disapproval of the Carlin monologue.   These two asserted justifications are further plagued by a common failing:  the lack of principled limits on their use as a basis for FCC censorship.   No such limits come readily to mind, and neither of the opinions constituting the Court serve to clarify the extent to which the FCC may assert the privacy and children-in-the-audience rationales as justification for expunging from the airways protected communications the Commission finds offensive.  .  .  .

.  .  . The opinions of both my Brother Powell and my Brother Stevens take the FCC at its word, and consequently do no more than permit the Commission to censor the afternoon broadcast of the "sort of verbal shock treatment," opinion of Mr. Justice Powell, involved here. To insure that the FCC's regulation of protected speech does not exceed these bounds, my Brother Powell is content to rely upon the judgment of the Commission while my Brother Stevens deems it prudent to rely on this Court's ability accurately to assess the worth of various kinds of speech.[6]   For my own part, even accepting that this case is limited to its facts, I would place the responsibility and the right to weed worthless and offensive communications from the public airways where it belongs and where, until today, it resided:  in a public free to choose those

4. The opinions of my Brothers Powell and Stevens rightly refrain from relying on the notion of "spectrum scarcity" to support their result.   As Chief Judge Bazelon noted below, "although scarcity has justified *increasing* the diversity of speakers and speech, it has never been held to justify censorship."   See Red Lion Broadcasting Co. v. FCC, 395 U.S. 367, 396 (1969).

6. Although ultimately dependent upon the outcome of review in this Court, the approach taken by my Brother Stevens would not appear to tolerate the FCC's suppression of any speech, such as political speech, falling within the core area of First Amendment concern.   The same, however, cannot be said of the approach taken by my Brother Powell, which, on its face, permits the Commission to censor even political speech if it is sufficiently offensive to community standards.   A result more contrary to rudimentary First Amendment principles is difficult to imagine.

communications worthy of its attention from a marketplace unsullied by the censor's hand.

## II

    . . .

    . . . The idea that the content of a message and its potential impact on any who might receive it can be divorced from the words that are the vehicle for its expression is transparently fallacious. A given word may have a unique capacity to capsule an idea, evoke an emotion, or conjure up an image. Indeed, for those of us who place an appropriately high value on our cherished First Amendment rights, the word "censor" is such a word. Mr. Justice Harlan, speaking for the Court, recognized the truism that a speaker's choice of words cannot surgically be separated from the ideas he desires to express when he warned that "we cannot indulge the facile assumption that one can forbid particular words without also running a substantial risk of suppressing ideas in the process." Cohen v. California, 403 U.S., at 26. Moreover, even if an alternative phrasing may communicate a speaker's abstract ideas as effectively as those words he is forbidden to use, it is doubtful that the sterilized message will convey the emotion that is an essential part of so many communications.

    . . .

    The Court apparently believes that the FCC's actions here can be analogized to the zoning ordinances upheld in Young v. American Mini Theatres, supra. For two reasons, it is wrong. First, the zoning ordinances found to pass constitutional muster in *Young* had valid goals other than the channeling of protected speech. [ ] No such goals are present here. Second, . . . the ordinances do not restrict the access of distributors or exhibitors to the market or impair the viewing public's access to the regulated material. [ ] Again, this is not the situation here. Both those desiring to receive Carlin's message over the radio and those wishing to send it to them are prevented from doing so by the Commission's actions. Although, as my Brethren point out, Carlin's message may be disseminated or received by other means, this is of little consolation to those broadcasters and listeners who, for a host of reasons, not least among them financial, do not have access to, or cannot take advantage of, these other means.

    . . .

## III

    It is quite evident that I find the Court's attempt to unstitch the warp and woof of First Amendment law in an effort to reshape its fabric to cover the patently wrong result the Court reaches in this case dangerous as well as lamentable. Yet there runs throughout the opinions of my Brothers Powell and Stevens another vein I find equally disturbing: a depressing inability to appreciate that in our land of cultural pluralism, there are many who think, act, and talk differently from the Members of this Court, and who do not share their fragile sensibilities. It is only an acute ethnocentric myopia that enables the Court to approve the censorship of communications solely because of the words they contain.

. . . The words that the Court and the Commission find so unpalatable may be the stuff of everyday conversations in some, if not many, of the innumerable subcultures that comprise this Nation. Academic research indicates that this is indeed the case. [ ] As one researcher concluded, "[w]ords generally considered obscene like 'bullshit' and 'fuck' are considered neither obscene nor derogatory in the [black] vernacular except in particular contextual situations and when used with certain intonations." [ ] Cf. Keefe v. Geanakos, 418 F.2d 359, 361 (1st Cir.1969) (finding the use of the word "motherfucker" commonplace among young radicals and protestors).

Today's decision will thus have its greatest impact on broadcasters desiring to reach, and listening audiences comprised of, persons who do not share the Court's view as to which words or expressions are acceptable and who, for a variety of reasons, including a conscious desire to flout majoritarian conventions, express themselves using words that may be regarded as offensive by those from different socio-economic backgrounds.[8] . . .

MR. JUSTICE STEWART, with whom MR. JUSTICE BRENNAN, MR. JUSTICE WHITE, and MR. JUSTICE MARSHALL join, dissenting.

. . .

The statute pursuant to which the Commission acted, 18 U.S.C. § 1464, makes it a federal offense to utter "any obscene, indecent, or profane language by means of radio communication." The Commission held, and the Court today agrees, that "indecent" is a broader concept than "obscene" as the latter term was defined in Miller v. California, 413 U.S. 15, because language can be "indecent" although it has social, political, or artistic value and lacks prurient appeal. 56 F.C.C.2d, at 97–98. But this construction of § 1464, while perhaps plausible, is by no means compelled. To the contrary, I think that "indecent" should properly be read as meaning no more than "obscene." Since the Carlin monologue concededly was not "obscene," I believe that the Commission lacked statutory authority to ban it. Under this construction of the statute, it is unnecessary to address the difficult and important issue of the Commission's constitutional power to prohibit speech that would be constitutionally protected outside the context of electronic broadcasting.

. . .

8. Under the approach taken by my Brother Powell, the availability of broadcasts *about* groups whose members comprise such audiences might also be affected. Both news broadcasts about activities involving these groups and public affairs broadcasts about their concerns are apt to contain interviews, statements, or remarks by group leaders and members which may contain offensive language to an extent my Brother Powell finds unacceptable.

**Notes and Questions**

1.　There are now products available to control what programs can be seen on a television set.　Using a weekly schedule, a parent can enter the day, time, channel number, and duration of time of each program the parent wishes a child to be able to see.　If the set is turned to a channel that is not cleared for that day and time, no picture or sound will appear. A key permits changes to be made.　If this were standard equipment on all television sets (and radios), might it meet some of the concerns in *Pacifica*?

2.　Is the "risk" of tuning in an offensive program on radio or television any greater than the risk of encountering offensive language on a person's clothing in a public place, as in Cohen v. California, 403 U.S. 15 (1971)?　Or offensive films visible from the street while being shown at an outdoor movie theatre, Erznoznik v. City of Jacksonville, 422 U.S. 205 (1975)?　If averting your eyes is an adequate remedy in these cases why is turning off the radio or television set not adequate here?　Is the fact that one may occur in the home relevant?

3.　It is easier to warn viewers that an adult, or possibly offensive, program is being presented when television is involved.　In some countries such programs carry a white dot in a corner of the picture so that a viewer can know the nature of the programming instantly.　Would this solve our problems so far as television is concerned?　Is there a similar technique that can be used for radio?　Is it enough that certain stations become known as likely to present certain kinds of material offensive to some?　What more could the licensee have done here to warn adult listeners?　See Glasser and Jassem, Indecent Broadcasts and the Listener's Right of Privacy, 24 J. Broadcasting 285 (1980).

4.　It has long been agreed that Congress has preempted the matter of obscenity on radio and television—both of which are within "radio communication."　Thus, a state may not impose its movie censorship scheme on films shown on television.

5.　In a clarification sought by the Radio Television News Directors Association (RTNDA), the Commission announced that its decision in the Pacifica case was not meant to impinge on the coverage of news events in which offensive speech is sometimes uttered without a chance for editing: "Under these circumstances we believe that it would be inequitable for us to hold a licensee responsible for indecent language." Pacifica Foundation, 59 F.C.C.2d 892, 36 R.R.2d 1008 (1976).　What if there is time for editing the dialogue but to do so would change the impact of the event?　Can this be handled by an announcer who says "At this point the speaker launched into a stream of obscenities"?

　　　Vice President Nelson Rockefeller used a finger gesture generally considered "obscene" when replying in kind to a heckler during a campaign rally.　Most newspapers ran the photograph, but some did not. Would the decision be different for television stations?　Are the considerations different for the 6 p.m. and the 11 p.m. news?　Does the fact that it was in the course of a live news event make a difference?

6. Shortly after *Pacifica*, the Commission rejected a petition to deny renewal to a television station. The petitioners had contended that the station had broadcast programs in which obscenities had been used, and also carried programs with unacceptable themes, such as a Masterpiece Theatre episode that was said to approve of adultery. The Commission stated that its role in reviewing programs at renewal time "is and must be limited to determining whether the licensee's *overall* programming has served its service area, and not whether a particular program is 'appropriate' for broadcast." Nor can the subjective views of groups of listeners be considered.

Turning to the relevance of *Pacifica*, the Commission stated that it "affords no general prerogative to intervene in any case where words similar or identical to those in *Pacifica* are broadcast over a licensed radio or television station. We intend strictly to observe the narrowness of the *Pacifica* holding." The FCC noted that in *Pacifica*, the Commission had stressed the "repetitive occurrence" of the words and that Justice Powell had stressed the same feature in his opinion. "It was certainly not our intent . . . to inhibit coverage of diverse and controversial subjects by licensees, whether in news and public affairs or in dramatic or other programming contexts." WGBH Educational Foundation, 69 F.C.C.2d 1250, 43 R.R.2d 1436 (1978).

7. Shortly after *Pacifica*, a primary election for governor was held in Georgia. J.B. Stoner, a legally qualified candidate, speaking under § 315, made broadcast messages using the word "nigger." Black groups asked the Commission to bar such language as indecent under the *Pacifica* principle. The Broadcast Bureau rejected the request. First, it ruled that the word was not "language that describes in the broadcast medium, sexual or excretory activities and organs, at times of the day when there is reasonable risk that children may be in the audience," quoting the Commission's language in *Pacifica*. Also, the Commission had already announced that "we intend strictly to observe the narrowness of the Pacifica holding." Even if the Commission were to find the word obscene or indecent, under § 315 the candidate could not be prevented from using the word during his "use" of the licensee's facilities. Julian Bond, 69 F.C.C.2d 943, 43 R.R.2d 1015 (Bd.Bur.1978).

8. During the 1980 Presidential campaign, one radio commercial began as follows: A man says "Bullshit!" After a woman says "What?", the man's voice replies: "Carter, Reagan, and Anderson. It's all Bullshit! Bullshit!" Then the party's candidate says "Too bad people have to use such strong language, but isn't that what you think too? That's why we started an entirely new political party, the Citizens Party." The FCC, which received many complaints and inquiries, responded that the precedents were quite clear that no censorship was possible—at least unless a candidate created a clear and present danger of riot or violence.

The campaign director said that for six months the media had been covering only the three major candidates "despite the fact that they have little to say of substance about the problems of the nation." He observed that "It's a sad commentary on the media that we received more attention as a result of using that word than we've received in the last six months combined."

9.   In 1983, *Hustler* magazine publisher Larry Flynt was reported to be intending to use clips from X-rated films in television ads supporting his presidential candidacy.   This caused Senator Jeremiah Denton (R–Ala.) to introduce legislation to allow broadcasters to refuse to air pornographic political announcements despite the no-censorship provision of § 315. Subsequently, the FCC indicated that it would not apply the no-censorship provision to obscene or indecent political announcements.   The issue never arose as Flynt chose not to run.

## C.   SAFETY—VIOLENCE AND PANIC

Although the Surgeon General has issued reports on the relationship between violence and television, and other academic studies have addressed the same issue primarily in connection with children, the Commission has never attempted to regulate the area in any substantive way. It has been asked several times but each time has refused.

In 1972, for example, the Commission was asked to analogize the area to cigarette smoking because of the actions of the Surgeon General in the two areas.   George Corey, 37 F.C.C.2d 641, 25 R.R.2d 437 (1972). The complainant sought to have three Boston stations carry a public service notice at appropriate times: "Warning: Viewing of violent television programming by children can be hazardous to their mental health and well being."   The Commission rejected the request on two grounds. First, it stated any action should come by rule rather than moving against a few stations.   Second, the Commission rejected the contention that the fairness doctrine was applicable to violent programming.   The cigarette episode was discussed:

> However, it could not reasonably or logically be concluded that the mere viewing of a person smoking a cigarette during a movie being broadcast on television constitutes a discussion of a controversial issue of public importance thus raising a fairness doctrine obligation.  Similarly, we cannot agree that the broadcast of violent episodes during entertainment programs necessarily constitutes the presentation of one side of a controversial issue of public importance.  It is simply not an appropriate application of the fairness doctrine to say that an entertainment program—whether it be Shakespeare or an action-adventure show—raises a controversial issue if it contains a violent scene and has a significant audience of children.  Were we to adopt your construction that the depiction of a violent scene is a discussion of one side of a controversial issue of public importance, the number of controversial issues presented on entertainment shows would be virtually endless (e.g., a scene with a high-powered car; or one showing a person taking an alcoholic drink or cigarette; depicting women in a soft, feminine, or light romantic role).  Finally, we note that there are marked differences in the

conclusiveness of the hazard established in this area as against cigarette smoking.  [   ]

The real thrust of your complaint would appear to be not fairness in the discussion of controversial issues but the elimination of violent TV children's programming because of its effect on children.  That issue is being considered particularly by appropriate Congressional committees and agencies such as HEW.  [   ]  It is a difficult, complex, and sensitive matter.  But whatever its resolution, there is no basis for the action along the line proposed by you.

In its Report on the Broadcast of Violent, Indecent, and Obscene Material, 51 F.C.C.2d 418, 32 R.R.2d 1367 (1975), the Commission explained to Congress that the violence area was unlike the obscenity area because of the totally different statutory framework involved.  In the absence of any prohibitions on violence in programming, "industry self-regulation is preferable to the adoption of rigid governmental standards."  The Commission took this position for two reasons.  First, it feared the constitutional questions that would emerge from such an intrusion into program content.  Second, the judgments concerning the suitability of certain programming for children are "highly subjective."  A speech by Chairman Wiley was quoted to the effect that slapstick comedy, an episode in Peter Pan when Captain Hook is eaten by a crocodile, and the poisoning of Snow White by the witch, all raise judgmental questions for which there is no objective standard.

One surge of interest has been concentrated on advertisers.  A pilot study indicated that 10 percent of those surveyed had considered not buying a product because it was advertised on a program they thought excessively violent.  The president of a leading advertising agency announced that it counsels clients to consider the negative aspects of placing commercials in violent programs.  Editor & Publisher, June 12, 1976 at 5. The FCC chairman also suggested that advertisers consider the commercial implications of such programs.  See also Broadcasting, June 14, 1976 at 32, 42.

––––––

Recently, lawsuits have asserted that mass media are legally liable for personal injuries that can be traced in one way or another to a broadcast.  These cases, which have not yet produced definitive results, raise some of the most hotly disputed questions in all of media liability.  The examples that follow suggest the range of situations that might give rise to controversy.  The cases tend to fall into two main categories— those in which the content of the program has an immediate impact on the recipient and those in which the recipient engages in conduct that hurts third parties.  Both types of cases raise questions about tort law and the First Amendment.

The most extensive suit raising this question arose out of a television drama entitled "Born Innocent."

## OLIVIA N. v. NATIONAL BROADCASTING CO.

California Court of Appeal, First District, 1981.
126 Cal.App.3d 488, 178 Cal.Rptr. 888.

Before: CALDECOTT, P.J., CHRISTIAN and POCHE, JJ.

CHRISTIAN, J.:

Olivia N. appeals from a judgment of nonsuit terminating her action against the National Broadcasting Company and the Chronicle Broadcasting Company. Appellant sought damages for physical and emotional injury inflicted by assailants who had seen a television broadcast of a film drama.

[The case was originally dismissed before trial, but the appellate court held that improper procedure below had deprived the plaintiff of her right to a jury trial. After a jury was empaneled on the remand and plaintiff had made an opening statement, the trial judge dismissed the case on the ground that the only basis for recovery would be a showing that NBC intended that violence follow its presentation of the drama. Since plaintiff did not make that claim, the case was dismissed.]

At 8 p.m. on September 10, 1974, NBC telecast nationwide, and Chronicle Broadcasting Company broadcast locally, a film entitled "Born Innocent."

> The subject matter of the television film was the harmful effect of a state-run home upon an adolescent girl who had become a ward of the state. In one scene of the film, the young girl enters the community bathroom of the facility to take a shower. She is then shown taking off her clothes and stepping into the shower, where she bathes for a few moments. Suddenly, the water stops and a look of fear comes across her face. Four adolescent girls are standing across from her in the shower room. One of the girls is carrying a "plumber's helper," waving it suggestively by her side. The four girls violently attack the younger girl, wrestling her to the floor. The young girl is shown naked from the waist up, struggling as the older girls force her legs apart. Then the television film shows the girl with the plumber's helper making intense thrusting motions with the handle of the plunger until one of the four says "That's enough." The young girl is left sobbing and naked on the floor. [ ]

It is alleged that on September 14, 1974, appellant, aged 9, was attacked and forcibly "artificially raped" with a bottle by minors at a San Francisco beach. [ ] The assailants had viewed and discussed the "artificial rape" scene in "Born Innocent," and the film allegedly caused the assailants to decide to commit a similar act on appellant. Appellant offered to show that NBC had knowledge of studies on child violence and should have known that susceptible persons might imitate the crime enacted in the film. Appellants alleged that "Born Innocent" was particularly likely to cause imitation and that NBC televised the film without proper warning in an effort to obtain the largest possible viewing audience. Appellant alleged that as a proximate result of respondents' telecast, she suffered physical and psychological damage.

Appellant contends that where there is negligence liability could constitutionally be imposed despite the absence of proof of incitement as defined in Brandenburg v. Ohio, 395 U.S. 444, 447 (1969). Appellant argues in the alternative that a different definition of "incitement" should be applied to the present circumstances.

"Analysis of this appeal commences with recognition of the overriding constitutional principle that material communicated by the public media, including fictional material such as the television drama here at issue, is generally to be accorded protection under the First Amendment to the Constitution of the United States. [ ]" First Amendment rights are accorded a preferred place in our democratic society. [ ] First Amendment protection extends to a communication, to its source and to its recipients. [ ] "[A]bove all else, the First Amendment means that government has no power to restrict expression because of its message, its ideas, its subject matter, or its content." . . .

. . .

The electronic media are also entitled to First Amendment protection. . . .

Appellant does not seek to impose a prior restraint on speech; rather, she asserts civil liability premised on traditional negligence actions for a television broadcast is obvious. "The fear of damage awards . . . may be markedly more inhibiting than the fear of prosecution under a criminal statute." New York Times Co. v. Sullivan, 376 U.S. 254, 277 (1964). Realistically, television networks would become significantly more inhibited in the selection of controversial materials if liability were to be imposed on a simple negligence theory. "[T]he pall of fear and timidity imposed upon those who would give voice to public criticism is an atmosphere in which the First Amendment cannot survive." New York Times v. Sullivan [ ]. . . .

Although the First Amendment is not absolute, the television broadcast of "Born Innocent" does not, on the basis of the opening statement of appellant's attorney, fall within the scope of unprotected speech. Appellant concedes that the film did not constitute an "incitement" within the meaning of [*Brandenburg*]. Notwithstanding the pervasive effect of the broadcasting media (see FCC v. Pacifica Foundation (1978) 438 U.S. 726, 748; Note, The Future of Content Regulation in Broadcasting (1981) 69 Cal.L.Rev. 555, 580–581) and the unique access afforded children [*Pacifica*], the effect of the imposition of liability could reduce the U.S. adult population to viewing only what is fit for children. [ ] Incitement is the proper test here. [ ] In areas outside of obscenity the United States Supreme Court has "consistently held that the fact that protected speech may be offensive to some does not justify its suppression. See, e.g., Cohen v. California, 403 U.S. 15 (1971)." [ ] . . . the television broadcast which is the subject of this action concededly did not fulfill the incitement requirements of *Brandenburg.* Thus it is constitutionally protected.

Appellant would distinguish between the fictional presentation of "Born Innocent" and news programs and documentaries. But that distinction is too blurred to protect adequately First Amendment values. "Everyone is familiar with instances of propaganda through fiction. What is one man's amusement, teaches another's doctrine." [ ] If a negligence theory is recognized, a television network or local station could be liable when a child imitates activities portrayed in a news program or documentary. Thus, the distinction urged by appellant cannot be accepted. [ ] . . . "Among free men, the deterrents ordinarily to be applied to prevent crime are education and punishment for violations of the law, not abridgment of the rights of free speech . . . ." [ ] The trial court's determination that the First Amendment bars appellant's claim where no incitement is alleged must be upheld.

[*Pacifica* was held inapplicable to anything other than regulation of indecency.]

**Notes and Questions**

1. Is there any possible showing that should entitle plaintiff to a judgment against NBC? What if the plaintiff could show that NBC officials had been warned by psychologists that the program was likely to provoke imitation? Is it significant that there has been only one reported case of imitation? What if plaintiff could show only that the attackers heard about the program from friends but that none of them saw it? Is it relevant that the show was presented at 8:00 p.m.?

2. Is there a difference between the "Born Innocent" program and a news broadcast that reports the details of a recent case of torture in the city—which is then imitated by persons unknown?

3. *Direct Harm.* During a 1979 broadcast of "The Tonight Show," a Hollywood stunt man showed how to stage a hanging that appeared real but was not. A few hours after the program, a 14-year-old boy was found hanging in front of his television set, which was on, and tuned to the local outlet that had carried that show. The plaintiff's attorney alleged that "the entire tenor of the scene was such as to challenge a teenaged boy to imitate the hanging." DeFilippo v. NBC. The trial judge dismissed the complaint in mid-1980.

The dismissal was affirmed in DeFilippo v. National Broadcasting Co., __ R.I. __, 446 A.2d 1036 (1982). The court concluded that "incitement" was required and that it could not be shown here. Plaintiff was apparently the only viewer who tried the stunt and those on the program had warned viewers that this was not something to try at home. To permit recovery here "would invariably lead to self-censorship by broadcasters in order to remove any matter that may be emulated and lead to a law suit."

4. *Indirect Harm.* *Olivia N.* is only one of a number of cases in which a victim has claimed that a broadcast caused listeners or viewers to engage in conduct that led to plaintiff's injury.

In one such case later relied on by the plaintiff in *Olivia N.*, a radio station catering to teenagers broadcast clues as to the whereabouts of a disc jockey and offered a cash prize to the first listener to reach him. Two teenagers reached the correct location but were not the first to arrive. While following the disc jockey to his next stop, the two drivers vied for position on the freeway and thereby caused a fatal accident. The court held that the station owed the decedent a duty of care and had violated it. Weirum v. RKO General, Inc., 15 Cal.3d 40, 123 Cal.Rptr. 468, 539 P.2d 36 (1975). Without relying on the fact that the contest was a boost for the station, the court easily rejected the station's First Amendment claim as "clearly without merit. The issue here is civil accountability for the foreseeable results of a broadcast which created an undue risk of harm to decedent. The First Amendment does not sanction the infliction of physical injury merely because achieved by word, rather than act." Is this sound? The court in *Olivia N.* distinguished *Weirum* on the ground that the station in that case actively encouraged the conduct leading to the accident. No such encouragement was present in "Born Innocent."

5. *The Zamora Case.* In Florida, 15-year-old Ronald Zamora was convicted of murdering his 83-year-old neighbor and was sentenced to a long prison term. He sued all three networks claiming that between the ages of 5 and 15 he had become involuntarily addicted to, and "completely subliminally intoxicated" by, extensive viewing of television violence. He claimed that the networks had "impermissibly stimulated, incited and instigated" him to duplicate the atrocities he viewed on television. He alleged further that he had developed a sociopathic personality, had become desensitized to violent behavior, and had become a danger to himself and others. The trial judge dismissed the complaint. Zamora v. Columbia Broadcasting System, 480 F.Supp. 199 (S.D.Fla.1979).

The judge refused to impose any tort obligation on the networks because he concluded that courts lack "the legal and institutional capacity to identify isolated depictions of violence, let alone the ability to set the standard for media dissemination of items containing 'violence' in one form or the other. Airway dissemination is, and to some extent should be, regulated but not on the basis or by the [tort] procedure suggested by the plaintiffs."

To the extent plaintiff was arguing for the regulation of programming that would adversely affect "susceptible" viewers, the judge indicated that the "imposition of such a generally undefined and undefinable duty would be an unconstitutional exercise by this Court in any event." Plaintiffs "would place broadcasters in jeopardy for televising Hamlet, Julius Caesar, Grimm's Fairy Tales; more contemporary offerings such as All Quiet On The Western Front, and even The Holocaust, and indeed would render John Wayne a risk not acceptable by any but the boldest broadcasters."

The judge observed, however, that "One day, medical or other sciences with or without the cooperation of programmers may convince the F.C.C. or the Courts that the delicate balance of First Amendment rights should be altered to permit some additional limitations in programming." But this case did not present such an occasion.

The judge implied that the plaintiff's approach in the "Born Innocent" case was stronger because of its claim that a specific program stimulated the harmful conduct. Is that a sound distinction? Note that the *Zamora* suit involves direct harm because the viewer is the one claiming that his life has been ruined by the programming. There is no reason, however, to think that the judge would have been any more receptive to a suit by the heirs of the dead neighbor against the networks.

6. Is the plaintiff's case stronger in general if more recipients are affected? If half the viewers faint in front of their screens after viewing a particularly gory shot of a murder victim presented during a news program, is the case any different from one in which a few "susceptible" viewers faint? Is there any reason to distinguish the cases in which direct harm occurs from those in which indirect harm occurs? Can you imagine a case in which the "average" viewer would be induced to engage in antisocial behavior that harmed others?

7. *Mass Hysteria.* Another substantive problem involves programs that frighten the listening public. At 11:00 p.m. on Oct. 30, 1974, a radio station in Rhode Island presented a contemporary version of the famous H.G. Wells's "War of the Worlds," that had been presented on the same night in 1938. A meteorite was reported to have fallen in a sparsely populated community killing several people; later "black-eyed, V-shaped mouthed, glistening creatures dripping saliva" were reported to have emerged from what turned out to be a capsule, and other landings were reported. What steps would you expect the licensee to take before presenting such a program—or is it inappropriate to present such material at any time? Telephone calls from frightened, and later from angry, listeners flooded the station, police, and other public service departments.

The licensee had taken several steps before the program to inform state public safety officials in the listening area of the station. The state police in turn sent notices to all their stations in the area alerting them to the program. Approximately once an hour from noon until 10:00 p.m. the licensee broadcast the following promotional announcement: "Tonight at 11:00 p.m., WPRO invites you to listen to a spoof of the 1930's a special Halloween classic presentation. . . ." The last was made about an hour before the program. Three announcements were made during the program—after 47, 48, and 56 minutes. The reason for the timing was said to be that the first 30 to 35 minutes of the show involved what appeared to be a meteor crashing in a remote spot and the arrival of creatures was not reported until 30 minutes into the program.

The Commission told the licensee that it had not met its responsibility to operate in a manner consistent with the public interest. The warnings were inadequate because "it is a well known fact that the radio audience is constantly changing. The only way to assure adequately that the public would not be alarmed in this case would be an introductory statement repeated at frequent intervals throughout the program." One Commissioner dissented because intrusion into presentations of drama should be made with "utmost caution" and the licensee's precautions "were not in my opinion unreasonable." Capital Cities Communications, Inc., 54 F.C.C.2d 1035, 34 R.R.2d 1016 (1975).

Would the Commission's suggestions impinge on the dramatic effect sought by the licensee? Is that relevant? Can you think of other ways to meet the Commission's concern? Recall the greater ease of warning an unwilling audience about possibly offensive programs over television as opposed to radio. Is that distinction applicable here?

8. On April 1, 1980, a Boston television station's local news program was interrupted by a bulletin that a 635-foot mound in suburban Milton had just blown its top and erupted. The reporter indicated that the disaster was traceable to a chain reaction set off by the earlier eruption of Mt. St. Helens in Washington. After 98 seconds, the reporter held up a sign saying "April Fool."

"But by then it was too late. Local police and civil-defense officials were deluged with calls from more than a hundred frantic Milton residents trying to find out the best evacuation routes." Newsweek, April 14, 1980 at 35. The executive producer of the program was fired.

## D.  CHILDREN'S PROGRAMMING

Over the years, groups have expressed special concern about programs aimed at children. Some have been concerned primarily with commercials and others have been concerned about the content of the programs themselves. Still others have been concerned that there is too little children's programming. All of these concerns and conflicts became more heated in the late 1970's. As we consider each situation, note the different approaches being considered. Sometimes it is prohibiting certain content; sometimes it involves mandatory programming; and sometimes it is conditional in the sense that if a broadcaster presents one kind of content it may be obligated to present other types of programs. Also note that occasionally the FCC invokes the aid of private groups such as the National Association of Broadcasters (NAB) to alter a practice within the industry.

### 1.  PROGRAM CONTENT

Most of the concern about the impact of television on children has stressed the role of violence and sexual innuendo. Although some groups have been concerned about these matters so far as adults are concerned, more seem concerned about their impact on children. Under Butler v. Michigan, 352 U.S. 380 (1957), it is unlawful for government to impose a complete ban on printed matter that is legally protected as to adults, simply to keep the material from children. Might that rule be different with television or radio? Does *Pacifica* suggest differences?

Several detailed studies of the impact of television on children are collected in 20 J. Broadcasting 1—68 (1976). See also, D. Cater and S. Strickland, TV Violence and the Child—The Evolution and Fate of the Surgeon General's Report, (1975).

The NAB is a private voluntary organization whose membership includes the three major networks, well over half the television stations in the country, and some 3,000 radio broadcasters. The NAB promulgated codes and standards that members had to follow if they wished to retain membership. The codes addressed such matters as how many minutes of commercials were appropriate in an hour; what types of commercials should not be accepted; what material should not be shown on the screen; and how subjects such as suicide or astrology or religion should be treated. We shall see examples from the NAB Code shortly.

A broadcaster that adhered to the code could display the NAB seal. The NAB maintained a staff that advised members about the propriety of their behavior under the codes.

In 1975, the result of the interaction of the network officials, the FCC chairman, and the NAB was the promulgation of the "family viewing policy" as an amendment to the NAB's Television Code. Under the policy, programs of a violent or sexually-oriented nature were wholly barred from the time slots before 9:00 p.m. (8:00 p.m. Central Time). This required moving some programs that had been popular in earlier prime-time slots and also involved decisions about which programs were affected in the first place. The entire story of the development and early enforcement of the family viewing policy is traced at length in G. Cowan, See No Evil: The Backstage Battle over Sex and Violence on Television (1979). The policy was challenged in court as being the result of illegal government pressure. Writers Guild of America v. Federal Communications Commission, 609 F.2d 355 (9th Cir.1979), certiorari denied 449 U.S. 824 (1980). After years of litigation complicated by jurisdictional issues, all parties in the case agreed to a settlement in 1984. The Family Viewing Policy had not been enforced for years.

## 2. TOO FEW PROGRAMS FOR CHILDREN

There has long been concern that too few programs are written expressly for children. Although the prime time access rule was motivated in part by hopes that this type of programming would result, the rule had no such effect. Following a petition in 1970 from Action for Children's Television (ACT) to require children's programming, the FCC spent much of the 1970's trying to decide how to react. In 1974, it issued a Policy Statement asking licensees to "make a meaningful effort" to increase overall programming for children; to air "a reasonable amount" of programming designed to educate and inform children, not simply to entertain them; to address the needs of both preschool and school-age children; and to air these programs on weekdays as well as weekends.

The Commission, in 1979, concluded that over a five-year period, the amount of children's programming per station had increased less than one hour per week (from 10.5 to 11.3 hours) and that this was totally accounted for by new programming from independent stations. Network affiliates had not increased their programming at all. No significant increase in education or informational programs was detected. Few licensees sought to develop age-specific programs for children. Finally, although only eight percent of children's television viewing occurred on weekends, almost half the programs for children were presented on weekends.

The staff concluded that "the small numbers of children and their limited appeal to advertisers, combined with the small outlets in most markets, create incentives for the commercial television system to neglect the specific needs of the child audience." Age-specific programming would be even less attractive to broadcasters because of the further splitting of an already small market.

In Children's Television Programming and Advertising Practices, 75 F.C.C.2d 138 (1979), the FCC announced a proposed rulemaking in which it listed five options. These were to rescind the 1974 Policy Statement and rely on program sources other than commercial broadcasting; to maintain or modify the policy statement; to institute mandatory programming requirements; to develop renewal guidelines; or to increase the number of video outlets.

The Commission completed the proceeding in late 1983. Mandatory children's programming obligations for television stations were rejected. The FCC found that the amount and variety of children's programming available was substantial and diverse. It noted that establishment of quotas might be impermissible content-based regulation and would create difficult definitional problems. Such quotas would also preclude the establishment of experimental children's services and efforts at specialization. Although no quotas were created, each licensee has the obligation to consider the needs of all significant elements of the community. A licensee at renewal time must demonstrate the attention devoted to the needs of children in its viewing audience, but may consider the alternative program sources available to children in its area. Children's Television Programming, 55 R.R.2d 199 (1984). On appeal, the D.C. Circuit affirmed the Commission's position that alternatives such as public broadcasting and cable could be considered in assessing the need for children's programming. "To be sure, Congress did not intend noncommercial broadcasting to 'relieve commercial broadcasters of their responsibilities to present public affairs and public service programs, and in general to program their stations in the public interest,' [   ]. But that does not mean that the Commission must require commercial broadcasters to pursue those responsibilities in disregard of the fact that some gaps in the public interest may have been filled by that source while other needs remain entirely unmet." The court did not read the Commission's Order as relieving broadcasters of the obligation, under the public interest standard, to present age-specific programming. Action for Children's Television v. Federal Communications Commission, 57 R.R.2d 1406 (1985).

In addition, ACT and other groups are pursuing mandatory children's programming quotas in Congress. In July, 1985, Congressman Tim Wirth (D-Colo.) introduced a bill that would require commercial television stations to offer a minimum of seven hours of children's programming each week. Broadcasting, Aug. 5, 1985 at 28.

An effort by citizen groups to deny license renewals to television stations that had no regularly scheduled children's programming failed in Washington Association for Television and Children v. Federal Communications Commission, 712 F.2d 677, 54 R.R.2d 293 (D.C.Cir.1983). The Commission's policy statement did not require regular scheduling, and the Commission did not have to prefer a station that presented regularly scheduled cartoons to one that presented educational specials.

### 3.   COMMERCIALS IN CHILDREN'S PROGRAMS

Efforts to eliminate all sponsorship of children's programs have been rejected by the Commission. The court of appeals affirmed on the ground that the FCC's refusal to adopt the ban "was a reasoned exercise of its broad discretion." The Commission had taken some steps, such as ordering a clear separation between programming and advertising on children's programs and prohibiting "host selling"—program hosts, personalities or characters endorsing products—and this could not be held insufficient as a matter of law. Action for Children's Television v. Federal Communications Commission, 564 F.2d 458 (D.C.Cir.1977).

Another innovative attempt to address the question of commercials in children's programming occurred when Public Advocates, Inc. and ACT petitioned the Commission to require television licensees and cable companies to insert an inaudible electronic signal at the beginning and end of every advertisement aimed at children. The signal would allow parents to attach a device to their television sets which would blank out the advertisements. After a rulemaking proceeding, the Commission decided against such a requirement. The obvious effect of such a requirement would be to reduce the value of the advertising that in turn would diminish the economic base for children's programming. In essence it would be a milder form of the ban on advertising aimed at children that the Commission had rejected several years earlier. Children's Advertising Detector Signal, 57 R.R.2d 935 (1985). Is advertising the only effective way to finance children's programming?

The Commission has also declined to require the networks to provide instructional programs to educate children about television advertising. The Commission was concerned about the impact of the First Amendment and § 326 on an order requiring programs with certain content. The issue was not so critical that, under the first part of the fairness doctrine, a licensee who ignored the issue would be acting unreasonably. Finally, since commercials being shown did not meaningfully discuss the issue it did not come within the second part of the fairness doctrine. Council on Children, Media and Merchandising, 65 F.C.C.2d 421, 40 R.R.2d 1718 (1977).

In 1983, ACT and the National Association for Better Broadcasting (NABB) filed complaints against various licensees alleging violations of the Commission policy against "program length commercials." These complaints focused on a new marketing strategy for children's television, basing shows on toys that were already on the market. Among the shows at issue were "He Man and the Masters of the Universe," "G.I. Joe: A Real American Hero," "Dungeons and Dragons," "Rubik the Amazing Cube," "Monchhichi's," "The Shirt Tales," "Strawberry Short-cake and Care Bears Family TV Fun Festival," and "Pac-Man."

According to ACT and NABB, these shows were created for the sole purpose of selling the toys that were featured in the show. As further evidence of this allegation, ACT cited an arrangement offered by Telepictures Corporation whereby broadcasters could receive a share of the profits derived from the sale of "Thunder Cats" toys in return for carrying the "Thunder Cats" cartoon show.

The Commission rejected the complaints. "[O]nly when the program segment is 'so interwoven with, and in essence auxiliary to the sponsor's advertising . . . to the point that the entire program constitutes a single, commercial promotion for the sponsor's products or services'" will an entire program be considered a commercial. Since the toys featured in the shows were not being advertised during those shows, the Commission did not find an interweaving of commercials and program content sufficient to constitute a program length commercial.

> The fact that programming may serve commercial goals, however, in and of itself, is not controlling. If the existence of commercial rewards from associated products were the criteria for imposing restrictions upon children's programming, then no program-related product licensing would be possible and even popular educational programs such as "Sesame Street" and critically acclaimed commercial television programs like those in the "Peanuts" series would have to be eliminated from broadcast station schedules. We see no sensible or administratively practical method of making distinctions among programs based on the subjective intentions of the program producers or on the product licensing/program production sequence. Considering that ACT's, NABB's, and the Commission's primary intention is to prevent harm to children, we must consider what, if any, possible harm might result from product-based programming. There is, however, no evidence before us to demonstrate that exposure to programming based on products harms the child audience. Action for Children's Television, 58 R.R.2d 61 (F.C.C.1985).

In a related proceeding the Commission rejected ACT's petition for rule making pertaining to profit-sharing arrangements in the broadcasting of children's programming.  ACT asserted that profit-sharing arrangements such as that offered by Telepictures for "Thunder Cats" would induce licensees to select programs for financial as opposed to public interest reasons.  The Commission concluded that such a danger was extremely speculative and did not warrant an NOI or NPRM, but stressed that licensees should not allow profit sharing or product tie-ins to detract from the " 'bedrock obligation of every broadcaster to be responsive to the needs and interests of its community, including the specialized needs of children in that community.' "  Commissioner Rivera dissented, believing that profit sharing and product tie-ins raised enough questions to justify further study.  Children's Programming (Profit-Sharing Arrangements), 58 R.R.2d 90 (F.C.C.1985).

The latest children's advertising controversy involves television advertisements for recorded telephone announcements.  These messages, which cost between 50 cents and two dollars per call, provide anything from sports scores to messages from Santa Claus.  As a result of television advertisements, many children have been calling these services without their parents' knowledge or permission, sometimes running up hundreds of dollars in charges.  In August, 1985, ACT filed a petition with the Federal Trade Commission asking the FTC to declare the ads unfair and deceptive.

## E.  MISCELLANEOUS CONSTRAINTS

---

### 1.  LOTTERIES

Another specific substantive limitation has been 18 U.S.C. § 1304, prohibiting broadcast of "any advertisement of or information concerning any lottery . . . ."  What is the basis for this statute?  As with the specific obscenity statute, the Commission has taken the view that it has responsibility for enforcement.  This has been bolstered by the provisions in the Communications Act that provide for revocation of license and for forfeitures against those who violate § 1304: §§ 312(a) (6), 312(b), 503(b)(1)(E).  Remember the United Television case discussed in Chapter IV.

A lottery is defined as anything containing three elements: chance, consideration, and a prize.  If all three are present, the broadcaster cannot air any information either as an advertisement or public service announcement concerning the lottery, and even news coverage is limited to situations where the lottery is truly newsworthy.  Whether the beneficiary of the lottery is a commercial enterprise or non-profit is irrelevant.  The fact that a lottery is being run by or on behalf of a charitable institution does not exempt it from the prohibition.  Technically, a licensee can be punished for announcing that a church bingo game will still be held despite bad weather.

What constitutes chance as opposed to skill is up to the interpretation of the Commission.  Guessing the number of beans in a jar has been held to be chance, but betting on horse races is viewed as skill. A golf tournament would be viewed as skill, but a hole-in-one contest would be chance. The distinction is supposed to be whether some difference in ability significantly improves a contestant's chances of winning. Where elements of both chance and skill are present—for example, a tie among all those who correctly answer contest questions is broken by a coin flip—then, assuming there is consideration and a prize, the contest is a lottery.

Consideration exists when an entrant must provide something of value to enter the contest. The most obvious examples of consideration are entry fees or purchase requirements. Sometimes, however, a significant expenditure of effort will be viewed as "shoe-leather" consideration. Thus, having to visit an automobile showroom is not consideration, but being required to take a test drive is. Similarly, having to be present at a drawing is not consideration as long as the drawing is held at a previously announced time. If, however, one must be present for a long period of time, then it is consideration.

The most common method of circumventing this lottery element is to allow people who have not provided consideration also to enter the contest. This is why so many giveaways advertise no purchase necessary or allow contestants to submit facsimiles of proofs of purchase. However, in order to avoid having the contest declared a lottery, those who do not provide consideration must have an equal chance of winning. Sometimes the question of what constitutes an equal chance presents a difficult problem. For example, in contests where people have to match the insides of soft drink bottle caps, the Commission has determined that a non-purchaser who sends in a self-addressed, stamped envelope must receive six bottle caps because people usually buy soft drinks in six-packs.

If the consideration does not go to the promoter, it is not a lottery. Thus, in the soft drink example above, the postage required to obtain the caps does not constitute consideration because the money goes to the Post Office, not the soft drink company. Similarly, a broadcaster could hold a contest inside a county fair without the admission fee constituting consideration, as long as the broadcaster did not receive any of the admissions proceeds.

The easiest element of a lottery to ascertain is the prize. If any contestant receives a benefit as a result of entering the contest, then there is a prize. Prizes usually take the form of money, merchandise, services, or discounts.

As a number of Washington, D.C., area radio stations discovered, licensees can be held responsible under § 1304 even in cases where they don't know they are promoting a lottery. A 1975 "Dial-a-Discount" promotion for Allyn's Pants Ranch allowed customers to spin a wheel to determine how much of a discount would be applied to a pants purchase. The licensees were under the impression that the spin occurred prior to purchase, which meant there was no consideration. In support of this position they submitted written "procedure rules" for the promotion and affidavits from various store personnel that no purchase was necessary. However, Commission investigators who visited the stores were told that a purchase was required. Also, the original broadcast announcements contained the statement, "After you purchase any pair of pants . . . you get to dial your own discount." The Commission determined that the promotion required, at the very least, an agreement to purchase. The agreement alone was sufficient to supply the element of consideration.

With regard to the argument that § 1304 requires "knowingly" broadcasting lottery information, the Commission construed that to mean the announcements were knowingly broadcast, not that the licensee knew it was a lottery. Rather, the licensee is required to exercise reasonable diligence in determining whether any promotion is a lottery. Relying on the assurances of the store or advertising agency is not considered reasonable diligence. Metromedia, Inc., 38 R.R.2d 785 (1976).

When states began running their own lotteries, new questions arose concerning the ban on lottery information. After an early case that somewhat limited the scope of § 1304, New York State Broadcasters Association v. United States, 414 F.2d 990 (2d Cir.1969), the issue came to a head in New Jersey. During three consecutive news broadcasts each Thursday, the day of the drawing in the state lottery, a licensee wanted to announce: "The winning state lottery number drawn today is . . . ." The Commission in a declaratory ruling concluded that such a statement would violate § 1304, even though it was presented as a news item. A main argument was that this was "news" only to those who held tickets. Experience had shown that the lottery's telephone lines were greatly overloaded on Thursdays as people called to learn the winning number. On a typical Thursday, there were 2,750,000 ticketholders. On appeal, the court, sitting en banc, unanimously reversed the Commission's ban on such broadcasts. New Jersey State Lottery Commission v. United States, 491 F.2d 219 (3d Cir.1974). The court concluded that the Commission had misconstrued § 1304 by interpreting it to ban "news." Although the information here was of transitory value, the court noted that on Thursdays more people in New Jersey care about this information than care about any given stock market quotation. Thus, the size of the interested group could not be the test of news. Broadcasters should be free to decide what is news and what news will serve the public unless their decision is beyond the realm of reason. The court was also influenced by the no-censorship language of § 326, which reinforced its view that § 1304 should be limited to advertising and information meant to make a particular lottery more attractive to participants.

The government's petition for certiorari was granted to resolve the apparent conflict between the decisions of the Second and Third Circuits. After argument, but before decision, Congress passed a statute providing that § 1304 shall not apply to "an advertisement, list of prizes, or information concerning a lottery conducted by a State acting under the authority of State law . . . broadcast by a radio or television station licensed to a location in that State or an adjacent State which conducts such a lottery." 18 U.S.C. § 1307(a)(2). On the government's motion, the Court, over a dissent by Justice Douglas, vacated the judgment of the Third Circuit and remanded for its consideration of whether the case had become moot. United States v. New Jersey State Lottery Commission, 420 U.S. 371 (F.C.C.1975).

On remand, the court noted that states adjacent to New Jersey (and to intervenor New Hampshire) did not have state lotteries, so that broadcasters in those states were not permitted by § 1307 to broadcast information about the New Jersey (or New Hampshire) lottery. The concern about limited dissemination of "news" still existed and the case was not moot. The court reaffirmed its earlier decision rejecting the Commission's interpretation of § 1304. The result is reported in New Jersey State Lottery Commission v. United States, 519 F.2d 1398 (3d Cir. 1975). The opinion is reported in 34 R.R.2d 825 (1975).

Could a statute constitutionally ban the type of statement the licensee wanted to make?

The only other significant case in this area involved whether so-called "give-away" programs on radio and television ran afoul of § 1304 as lotteries. The Supreme Court construed the statute narrowly and held that requiring contestants to listen to the program did not constitute a "valuable consideration." Thus, the Commission had no basis for prohibiting the programs. Federal Communications Commission v. American Broadcasting Co., 347 U.S. 284 (1954).

## 2.  CONTESTS

The stations themselves, however, are permitted to run their own contests so long as they are not fraudulent, are not broadcast only during rating periods to increase the figures ("hypoing"), and do not disturb public safety. The Commission has rejected an effort to ban contests that involve no skill, such as those in which listeners tune in to know how much money is in the jackpot in case they are telephoned. The complaint was that this type of contest "bribed" listeners and tended to force other stations to compete by imitation rather than by making improvements in programming. The Commission refused to act because it was not convinced that the problem required attention or that it was empowered to deal with such a situation. Broadcast of Station Contests, 37 R.R.2d 260 (F.C.C.1976). Does this kind of situation warrant action? Under what authority?

Although contests are not prohibited, they are subject to strict standards of honesty. Section 73.1216 of the Code of Federal Regulations provides:

A licensee that broadcasts or advertises information about a contest it conducts shall fully and accurately disclose the material terms of the contest, and shall conduct the contest substantially as announced or advertised. No contest description shall be false, misleading, or deceptive with respect to any material terms.

When determining whether or not a contest is deceptive, the Commission is not limited to considering the promotional announcements as a complete package but can also look at individual announcements or even misleading phrases. For example, referring to a prize as a "$479 cash prize jackpot" when it consisted of $30 in cash and $449 in non-cash prizes was held deceptive even though other promotional announcements made it clear that the jackpot was not all cash. Musical Heights, Inc., 40 R.R.2d 1016 (F.C.C.1977).

Note that the § 73.1216 requires that disclosure be full as well as accurate. Omission of relevant details can be viewed as seriously as deceptive statements. This applies to both the rules of the contest and the prizes to be awarded. Any ambiguity is decided against the licensee. Consider the following promotional announcement:

> THIS SOUND COULD MEAN 4 DAYS AND 3 NIGHTS FOR YOU AND YOUR COMPANION IN YOUR CHOICE OF *LAS VEGAS, SAN JUAN, FT. LAUDERDALE OR ACAPULCO, MEXI-CO. SECRET SOUNDS* ARE COMING THIS FRIDAY TO 99 WIBZ. EACH DAY FOR FIFTEEN DAYS WIBZ WILL BROAD-CAST A *SECRET SOUND* . . . LISTEN EACH DAY AND IDENTIFY EACH SOUND, THEN ON MAY 7TH SEND IN A LIST OF THE *SECRET SOUNDS* AS YOU HAVE IDENTIFIED THEM. WE WILL SELECT THE 25 ENTRIES THAT COME THE CLOS-EST TO BEING CORRECT THEN THOSE 25 PEOPLE WILL RECEIVE *4* DAYS AND *3* NIGHTS IN YOUR CHOICE OF *LAS VEGAS, SAN JUAN, FT. LAUDERDALE OR ACAPULCO. SE-CRET SOUNDS* STARTS THIS FRIDAY ON *WIBZ.* THE SOUNDS WILL BE BROADCAST NUMEROUS TIMES DURING THE DAY WITH A DIFFERENT SOUND EACH DAY FOR 15 DAYS. IT'S EASY . . . SIMPLY LISTEN AND WIN ON *WIBZ 99—STILL THE BEST ROCK!* (SORRY ONLY THOSE OVER 23 YEARS OF AGE ELIGIBLE.)

The Commission held that the above announcement was deceptive and misleading because it created the impression that transportation was included when in fact it was not. An official admonishment was placed in the station's files for consideration with the next renewal application. Randy Jay B/casting Co., 39 R.R.2d 937 (1977).

Often, where there has been deception as to the prizes to be awarded, stations have been required to provide the promised prizes. More serious violations—a "find the disc jockey" contest where the disc jockey was in another part of the country, a contest requiring winners to call during a specified time period when the phone was left off the hook, or a treasure hunt where the treasure was not hidden until the last day of the contest—have led to forfeitures and revocations.

In 1966, the Commission issued a Policy Statement entitled "Contests and Promotions Which Adversely Affect the Public Interest." 2 F.C.C.2d 464, 6 R.R.2d 671 (1966). Among the specific examples cited as contests that "adversely affect the public interest" were the following.

A contest which resulted in a vast accumulation of scrap metal in a certain location, blocking access to nearby commercial establishments.

A contest which led listeners to choose names at random from the telephone directory and to call the persons listed at all hours of the day and night causing great annoyance and effectively blocking use of their telephones for normal purposes.

Contests which, by requiring the participants to travel to a specified place in a very short time, have caused traffic violations and endangered life.

The broadcast of "scare" announcements or headlines which either are untrue or are worded in such a way as to mislead and frighten the public; e.g., a sudden announcement delivered in a tone of excitement to the effect that "amoebas" were invading a certain city, implying that the amoebas were dangerous creatures.

In 1985, as part of its ongoing attempt to remove "regulatory underbrush," the Commission rescinded the 1966 Policy Statement. "[M]ost important by far in our conclusion to delete the policy is that it is simply unwarranted and unnecessary—the raison d'etre of this 'underbrush' proceeding. While the stated purposes for the policy of public safety, etc. are important, the examples cited therefor and the resultant policy constitute regulatory overkill. To issue a Public Notice cautioning all broadcast licensees against engaging in such an obvious hoax as 'amoebas' invading a city is simply an overreaction." The Commission concluded that alternative remedies were adequate to protect the public interest in these areas. These alternative remedies include civil suits (remember *Weirum*, supra) and criminal statutes prohibiting disturbing the peace, maintaining a public nuisance, and making harassing phone calls. The Commission did note, however, that despite the elimination of the 1966 Policy Statement, a broadcast of something similar to "War of the Worlds" without adequate cautionary language would still be a violation of the general duty to program in the public interest. Unnecessary Broadcast Regulation, 57 R.R.2d 939 (1985).

*Broadcasts of Telephone Conversations.* Some of the most common promotional contests involve telephoning a viewer or listener and broadcasting the conversation. Section 73.1206 of the Commission's rules sets very strict guidelines for broadcasting phone conversations. If the conversation is live, the party answering the phone must give consent *before* the licensee can start to broadcast it. If the conversation is to be recorded for later broadcast, consent must be given before the recording can start. In response to broadcaster complaints that this rule destroys all spontaneity, the Commission has issued an NPRM proposing to either modify or delete § 73.1206. 50 Fed.Reg. 7931 (February 19,

1985).  At issue is whether § 73.1206 is necessary to protect individual privacy interests.  Broadcasting telephone conversations may also raise invasion of privacy questions.  We will discuss these issues in Chapter XIII.

### 3.  PAYOLA AND PLUGOLA

Perhaps the biggest scandal ever to occur in broadcasting was the quiz show scandal of the late 1950's.  At that time big money quiz shows such as "The $64,000 Question," "Tic Tac Dough," and "Twenty One" constituted one of the most popular forms of prime-time programming.  However, in November, 1959, the nation was shocked when Charles Van Doren, a popular contestant and leading money winner on "Twenty One," testified before a House subcommittee that the shows were fixed.  At approximately the same time, evidence also surfaced that many disc jockeys and program directors were accepting bribes to play specific records on their stations.  This latter practice became known as "payola."

Congressional and Commission reaction was swift.  Section 317 of the Communications Act was amended and two new sections, 508 and 509, were added to the Communications Act.

### Section 317

(a)(1) All matter broadcast by any radio station for which any money, service or other valuable consideration is directly or indirectly paid, or promised to or charged or accepted by, the station so broadcasting, from any person, shall, at the time the same is so broadcast, be announced as paid for or furnished, as the case may be, by such person: *Provided,* That "service or other valuable consideration" shall not include any service or property furnished without charge or at a nominal charge for use on, or in connection with, a broadcast unless it is so furnished in consideration for an identification in a broadcast of any person, product, service, trademark, or brand name beyond an identification which is reasonably related to the use of such service or property on the broadcast.

Section 508 requires employees, program producers and program suppliers to notify broadcasters of any payments given or received for the purpose of inducing the inclusion of specific material in broadcast programming.

### Section 509

(a) It shall be unlawful for any person, with intent to deceive the listening or viewing public—

(1) To supply to any contestant in a purportedly bona fide contest of intellectual knowledge or intellectual skill any special and secret assistance whereby the outcome of such contest will be in whole or in part prearranged or predetermined.

(2) By means of persuasion, bribery, intimidation, or otherwise, to induce or cause any contestant in a purportedly bona fide contest of intellectual knowledge or intellectual skill to refrain in any manner from using or displaying his knowledge or skill in such contest, whereby the outcome thereof will be in whole or in part prearranged or predetermined.

After the passage of these new provisions, the Commission issued notices that they would be strictly enforced.

Technically, payola is accepting or receiving money or other valuable consideration for the inclusion of material in a broadcast *without* disclosing that fact to the audience, while plugola is promoting goods or services in which someone responsible for selecting the material broadcast has a financial interest. The Commission has adopted several rules governing payola and plugola. In essence, these rules are aimed at preventing the public from being deceived as to the commercial nature of sponsored material. We will return to the most important of these rules, the sponsorship identification requirement, shortly.

The structure of the radio industry has changed dramatically since the original payola scandal. In the late 1950's, most radio programming was done by the individual stations. Now many stations have their music programmed by syndicated programmers who supply the music on record or tape as well as directions as to the order of play. Even more control of programming exists with the hundreds of stations that are carrying satellite-delivered programming. How can the Commission control potential payola problems with these syndicators?

In 1980, after lengthy proceedings, the Commission concluded that plugola was best handled on a case-by-case basis and that "it would be difficult to frame a rule that covered the important elements of this complex subject without either going too far in regulating licensees or leaving important loopholes in the effectiveness of the rule." The Commission also noted that relatively few plugola complaints had been filed in the the late 1970's. Plugola Practices, 46 R.R.2d 1421 (F.C.C.1980).

### 4. ADVERTISING AND COMMERCIAL PRACTICES

Broadcasters are of course subject to advertising regulation aimed at the mass media in general. However, as we saw in our discussion of cigarette advertising, p. 217, supra, broadcast advertising is also subject to special restrictions not applicable to other media.

#### a. *Sponsorship Identification*

One such restriction is the sponsorship identification requirement that is part of the measures taken in response to the payola scandal. The Commission has interpreted § 317 to require that every advertisement must contain material specifying that it was paid for, and by whom. 47 C.F.R. § 73.1212. This information is obvious in most cases—a commercial for a specific brand of automobile is assumed to have been purchased by the manufacturer or dealers association promoted in the commercial. But it does restrict one specific form of advertising, "teasers." A teaser is an advertisement that withholds specific information to arouse the public's interest, e.g., "On August 2, automotive history will be made." Obviously ads of this nature violate the sponsorship identification rules.

### b.  Commercial Speech Doctrine

Traditionally, special restrictions on broadcast advertising were not seen as raising serious constitutional problems. While the special status of broadcasting contributed to the lack of constitutional protection, the primary reason was that commercial speech was viewed as outside the protection of the First Amendment. However, as a result of a series of Supreme Court decisions during the past decade, commercial speech now enjoys considerable First Amendment protection.

Thus far, the effect of the new commercial speech doctrine on broadcast advertising restrictions has not yet been fully determined. In addition, to the inevitable reliance on *Red Lion* and the scarcity rationale, several arguments for allowing more extensive restrictions on the broadcast media have been advanced. Relying on *Pacifica*, advocates of regulation argue that the greater impact of broadcasting, its unique accessibility to children and its intrusion into the home all mandate less constitutional protection for broadcast advertising. Others contend that the restricted format of broadcast advertising—thirty- or sixty-second commercials—makes it inherently deceptive and misleading.

Recently, there has been a lot of pressure for a ban on alcoholic beverages on electronic media similar to the cigarette advertising ban. Due to the changes in the commercial speech doctrine, the constitutionality of such a ban is in doubt. The test that would have to be applied to any such restriction originated in Central Hudson Gas & Electric Corp. v. Public Service Commission of New York, 447 U.S. 557 (1980).

> In commercial speech cases, then, a four-part analysis has developed. At the outset, we must determine whether the expression is protected by the First Amendment. For commercial speech to come within that provision, it at least must concern lawful activity and not be misleading. Next, we ask whether the asserted governmental interest is substantial. If both inquiries yield positive answers, we must determine whether the regulation directly advances the governmental interest asserted, and whether it is not more extensive than is necessary to serve that interest.

Would a ban on alcoholic beverage advertising be constitutional under the *Central Hudson* four-part test? Would *Capital Broadcasting*, p. 217, supra, be decided differently today? Faced with a state ban on cable advertising of electronic beverages, the Court invalidated the statute on other grounds and did not address the commercial speech issue. Capital Cities Cable v. Crisp, 467 U.S. 691 (1984).

What about a requirement of equal time for messages aimed at discouraging the consumption of alcoholic beverages? In May, 1985, Congressman John Seiberling (D–Oh.) introduced the "Fairness in Alcohol Advertising Act of 1985." It would mandate response time for alcohol-related health messages in direct proportion to beer and wine advertisements that are broadcast. Meanwhile, Congressman Howard Nielson (R–Vt.) introduced a bill to direct the Bureau of Alcohol, Tobacco and Firearms to investigate the relationship between beer and wine advertising, and alcohol abuse. Broadcasting May 20, 1985 at 46.

### c.  The NAB Codes

As we have seen, indirect regulation of the content of broadcast programs was possible through the NAB Codes. The adherence was even greater because of the membership of the three major networks. Since they abided by the Television Code, even affiliates that did not themselves belong would be carrying only material acceptable under the Code whenever they carried network programming.

Among the provisions of the code were several restrictions on advertising. Advertising of products such as hard liquor and contraceptives were prohibited. Limits on the total number of advertising minutes per hour were part of the code as was a ban on single 30-second advertisements for two or more unrelated products ("split 30's"). In 1979, the Justice Department brought an action against the NAB charging that certain of the commercial time restrictions violated the antitrust laws. In 1982, Judge Greene declared the prohibition against split-30's to be an antitrust violation. As a result the NAB negotiated a consent decree with the Justice Department that prohibited the NAB from adopting any rule respecting the quantity, placement, or format of advertising or other nonprogram material. In addition, although not as a requirement of the settlement, the NAB cancelled the advertising standards of the Television and Radio Codes and dissolved the Code Boards of Directors. Broadcasting and Government, Jan. 1, 1985 at 138–139.

In late 1983, Alberto-Culver filed an action against NAB, CBS, Inc., and several group owners alleging that they were still conspiring to prevent the broadcast of multiple product ads. Alberto-Culver negotiated a settlement with each of the broadcasters named in the case and the suit was dismissed.

### d.  Commercial Practices

The Commission has long taken an interest in the commercial practices of broadcast licensees. Recall the White Mountain Broadcasting case where renewal was denied for "double billing." In 1985, as part of another "regulatory underbrush" proceeding, the Commission eliminated many of these rules and issued an NPRM proposing deletion of others. Among the regulations deleted were those covering distortion of audience ratings, selection of sports announcers, conflicts of interest, promotion of nonbroadcast business of a station, concert promotion announcements, and false, misleading, or deceptive advertisements. The regulations proposed for deletion apply to fraudulent billing practices, network clipping, and joint sales practices. As in the other "underbrush" proceedings the Commission argued that the policies eliminated "either relate to areas which often are not within this Commission's area of expertise and where either alternate remedies exist to deter the activity addressed by the particular policy or where marketplace forces will correct the particular abuse." Unnecessary Broadcast Regulation, 57 R.R.2d 913 (1985).

In addition, the Commission will no longer hear complaints regarding distortion of a station's ratings or inaccurate signal coverage maps. It did state that the filing of a misleading coverage map would imply unacceptable character and could place a station's renewal at risk. Unnecessary Broadcast Regulation (Advertising Misrepresentations), 54 R.R.2d 705 (F.C.C.1983).

### 5.   OTHER CONSTRAINTS

#### a.   *Sports Blackouts*

In 1973, Congress passed a statute to resolve the clamor raised by the refusal of professional football teams to permit televising of a home game that was being televised to other parts of the country (47 U.S.C. § 331). It provided that professional sports telecasts could not be barred if all the tickets had been sold 72 hours before game time, and spelled out the conditions under which the rights to telecast could be made available. The statute expired by its own terms in 1975. A permanent anti-blackout statute was blocked in 1976, but the National Football League agreed to follow the expired statute.

#### b.   *Other Underbrush*

We considered some of the policies eliminated in the regulatory underbrush proceedings earlier in this Chapter. Policies aimed at discouraging liquor advertisements in dry areas, restrictions on broadcasts of foreign language programs, broadcast of astrology information, music format service agreements, repetitious broadcasts, call-in polls, private interest broadcasts, the use of sirens and sound effects, and rules regarding harassing and threatening phone calls resulting from broadcasts were all eliminated. Unnecessary Broadcast Regulation, 54 R.R.2d 1043 (F.C.C.1983). The FCC also eliminated restrictions on horse racing programming and advertising. Unnecessary Broadcast Regulation, 56 R.R.2d 976 (F.C.C.1984).

# Chapter VIII

# NONCOMMERCIAL BROADCASTING

## A. DEVELOPMENT OF PUBLIC BROADCASTING

Virtually all of our attention so far has been devoted to commercial broadcasting. Most of the litigation and regulation has involved commercial broadcasters, and, in terms of viewers, commercial broadcasting is the preeminent part of the picture. But it is not the only part. AM broadcasting developed too early for the Commission to be able to consider reserving spots for noncommercial educational stations. In allocating FM and television, however, the Commission was able to plan in advance and reserved certain spots for educational broadcasters. These are usually operated by academic institutions, by governmental groups, or by groups organized by private citizens. Although an academic institution may operate a station only in a community where it operates a bona fide fulltime school, a private or governmental organization may qualify for a station in any community as long as it demonstrates an educational goal and a commitment to the advancement of an educational program. A station run by a sectarian academic institution may be eligible for a reserved educational spot in the community in which the school is located. If an organization's central purpose is religious, it is not eligible for a reserved channel. We will return to the issue of religious broadcasting later in this Chapter.

While many of the Commission's rules apply equally to commercial and noncommercial licensees, there are some differences. For example, the duopoly and multiple ownership rules are not applicable to noncommercial licensees.

The development of public broadcasting and several questions it raises are considered in the following case.

### ACCURACY IN MEDIA, INC. v. FEDERAL COMMUNICATIONS COMMISSION

United States Court of Appeals, District of Columbia Circuit, 1975.
521 F.2d 288, certiorari denied 425 U.S. 934 (1976).

Before BAZELON, CHIEF JUDGE, LEVENTHAL, CIRCUIT JUDGE and WEIGEL, UNITED STATES DISTRICT JUDGE for the Northern District of California.

BAZELON, CHIEF JUDGE.

Accuracy in Media, Inc. (AIM) filed two complaints with the FCC against the Public Broadcasting Service (PBS) concerning two programs distributed by PBS to its member stations. AIM alleged that the programs, dealing with sex education and the American system of criminal justice, were not a balanced or objective presentation of each

293

subject and requested the FCC to order PBS to rectify the situation. The legal basis for AIM's complaints was the Fairness Doctrine and 47 U.S.C. § 396(g)(1)(A) (1970). On its initial hearing of the matter, the FCC concluded that the PBS had not violated the Fairness Doctrine and invited comments from interested parties on its authority to enforce whatever standard of program regulation was contained in § 396(g)(1) (A). AIM does not seek the review of the Commission's decision on the Fairness Doctrine issue.

Section 396(g)(1)(A) is part of the Public Broadcasting Act of 1967, an act which created the Corporation for Public Broadcasting (CPB) and authorized it to fund various programming activities of local, non-commercial broadcasting licensees. Section 396(g)(1)(A) qualifies that authorization in the following language:

> In order to achieve the objectives and to carry out the purposes of this subpart, as set out in subsection (a) of this section, the Corporation is authorized to—
>
>> (A) facilitate the full development of educational broadcasting in which programs of high quality, obtained from diverse sources, will be made available to noncommercial educational television or radio broadcast stations, with strict adherence to objectivity and balance in all programs or series of programs of a controversial nature. . . .

AIM contends that since the above-mentioned PBS programs were funded by the CPB, pursuant to this authorization, the programs must contain "strict adherence to authorization and balance," a requirement AIM contends is more stringent than the standard of balance and fairness in overall programming contained in the Fairness Doctrine. AIM alleges that the two relevant programs did not meet this more stringent standard of objectivity and balance.

After consideration of the comments received on the matter, invited in its preliminary decision discussed above, the Commission concluded that it had no jurisdiction to enforce the mandate of § 396(g)(1)(A) against CPB. . . .

## I. THE ORGANIZATION OF PUBLIC BROADCASTING IN THE UNITED STATES

Resolution of the issues raised by AIM's petition requires an understanding of the operation of the public broadcasting system. There are three tiers to this operation, each reflecting a different scheme of governmental regulation. The basic level is comprised of the local, noncommercial broadcasting stations that are licensed by the FCC and, with a few exceptions, subject to the same regulations as commercial licenses. Through the efforts of former Commissioner Frieda Hennock, the FCC has reserved exclusive space in its allocation of frequencies for such noncommercial broadcasters. Other than this specific reservation, noncommercial licensees are still subject to the same renewal process and potential challenges as their commercial counterparts.

Such was the state of the public broadcasting system until the passage of the Educational Television Facilities Act in 1962. The Act added the element of government funding to public broadcasting by establishing a grant program for noncommercial facilities. This second level of the system was reorganized and expanded by the Public Broadcasting Act of 1967 which created the Corporation for Public Broadcasting (CPB). The Corporation, the product of a study made by the Carnegie Commission on Educational Television, was established as a funding mechanism for virtually all activities of noncommercial broadcasting. In setting up this nonprofit, private corporation, the Act specifically prohibited CPB from engaging in any form of "communication by wire or radio."

The third level of the public broadcasting system was added in 1970 when CPB and a group of noncommercial licensees formed the Public Broadcasting Service (PBS) and National Public Radio. The Public Broadcasting Service operates as the distributive arm of the public television system. As a nonprofit membership corporation, it distributes national programming to approximately 150 educational licensees via common carrier facilities. This interconnection service is funded by the Corporation (CPB) under a contract with PBS; in addition, much of the programming carried by PBS is either wholly or partially funded by CPB. National Public Radio provides similar services for noncommercial radio. In 1974, CPB and the member licensees of PBS agreed upon a station program cooperative plan[14] to insure local control and origination of noncommercial broadcasting funded by CPB. Though PBS is the national coordinator under this scheme, it is not a "network" in the commercial broadcasting sense, and does not engage in "communication by wire or radio," except to the extent that it contracts for interconnection services.

## II. FCC JURISDICTION OVER THE CORPORATION FOR PUBLIC BROADCASTING

With the structure of the public broadcasting system in view, we turn to AIM's contention that the FCC should enforce the mandate of § 396(g)(1)(A) against the CPB. Since the Section is clearly directed to the Corporation and its programming activities, we have no doubt that the Corporation must respect the mandate of the Section. However, we conclude that nothing in the language and legislative history of the

14. The Station Program Cooperative (SPC) is a unique concept in program selection and financing for public television stations. Though the idea of public broadcasting as a "fourth network" had been proposed at various times, the 1974 plan reversed this trend toward centralization. Under the SPC, certain programming will be produced only if the individual local stations decide together to fund the production. The local licensees will be financed through the CPB and other sources; the funding of specific programs will be by a 4 to 5 ratio (station funds to national cooperative funds). The aim of this cooperative is to reinforce the existing licensee responsibility for programming discretion. Through this plan the local stations will eventually assume the responsibility for support of the cooperative and the Corporation will concentrate on new programming development. [ ]

Federal Communications Act or the Public Broadcasting Act of 1967 authorizes the FCC to enforce that mandate against the CPB.

Section 398 of the Communications Act expresses the clear intent of Congress that there shall be no direct jurisdiction of the FCC over the Corporation. That section states that nothing in the 1962 or 1967 Acts "shall be deemed (1) to amend any other provision of, or requirement under this Act; or (2) to authorize any department, agency, officer, or employee of the United States to exercise any direction, supervision or control over educational television or radio broadcasting, or over the Corporation or any of its grantees or contractors . . . ." Since the FCC is obviously an "agency . . . of the United States" and since any enforcement of § 396(g)(1)(A) would necessarily entail "supervision" of the Corporation, the plain words of subsection (2) preclude FCC jurisdiction. . . .

Congress desired to establish a program funding agency which would be free from governmental influence or control in its operations. Yet, the lawmakers feared that such complete autonomy might lead to biases and abuses of its own. The unique position of the Corporation is the synthesis of these competing influences. Reference to the legislative history of the 1967 Act shows a deep concern that governmental regulation or control over the Corporation might turn the CPB into a Government spokesman. Congress thus sought to insulate CPB by removing its "programming activity from governmental supervision." . . .

. . .

AIM maintains that this view of FCC jurisdiction to enforce § 396(g) (1)(A) renders the section nugatory and hence ignores the Congressional sentiment that biases and abuses within the public broadcasting system should be controlled. We do not view our holding on the FCC's jurisdiction as having that effect. Rather, we take notice of the carefully balanced framework designed by Congress for the control of CPB activities.

The Corporation was established as nonprofit and non-political in nature and is prohibited from owning or operating "any television or radio broadcast station, system or network, community antenna system, or interconnection, or production facility." Numerous statutory safeguards were created to insure against partisan abuses.[28] Ultimately, Congress may show its disapproval of any activity of the Corporation through the appropriation process.[29] This supervision of CPB through its funding is buttressed by an annual reporting requirement.[30] Through

---

**28.** Other statutory checks on the Corporation include: restricting the Board membership to no more than eight out of fifteen members from the same political party, § 396(c)(1). The composition of the Board was an important issue during debate and the decision to make the Board bipartisan was a significant addition to the original Carnegie Commission proposal. The Act also requires that the CPB's accounts be audited annually by an independent accountant, § 396($l$)(1)(A), and *may* be audited by the General Accounting Office, § 396($l$)(2)(A).

**29.** Section 396(k) assures that most of the CPB's operating budget be derived through the Congressional appropriation process.

**30.** 47 U.S.C. § 396(i) (1970).

these statutory requirements and control over the "purse-strings," Congress reserved for itself the oversight responsibility for the Corporation.

A further element of this carefully balanced framework of regulation is the accountability of the local noncommercial licensees under established FCC practice, including the Fairness Doctrine in particular. This existing system of accountability was clearly recognized in the 1967 legislative debates as a crucial check on the power of the CPB. . . .

. . .

The framework of regulation of the Corporation for Public Broadcasting we have described—maximum freedom from interference with programming coupled with existing public accountability requirements—is sensitive to the delicate constitutional balance between First Amendment rights of the broadcast journalist and the concerns of the viewing public struck in Columbia Broadcasting System, Inc. v. Democratic National Committee, 412 U.S. 94 (1973). There the Supreme Court warned that "only when the interests of the public are found to outweigh the private journalistic interests of the broadcasters" will governmental interference with broadcast journalism be allowed. The Court on the basis of this rule rejected a right of access to broadcast air time greater than that mandated by the Fairness Doctrine as constituting too great a "risk of an enlargement of Governmental control over the content of broadcast discussion of public issues."

It is certainly arguable that FCC application of the standard—whatever that standard may be—of § 396(g)(1)(A) could "risk [an] enlargement of Government control over the content of broadcast discussion of public issues" in the following two ways: whereas the existing Fairness Doctrine requires only that the presentation of a controversial issue of public importance be balanced in *overall* programming, § 396(g)(1)(A) might be argued to require balance of controversial issues within each individual program. Administration of such a standard would certainly require a more active role by the FCC in oversight of programming. Furthermore, whereas the FCC has at present carefully avoided anything but the most limited inquiry into the factual accuracy of programming, § 396(g)(1)(A) by use of the term "objective" could be read to expand that inquiry and thereby expand FCC oversight of programming. Both of these potential enlargements of government control of programming, whether directed against the CPB, PBS or individual noncommercial licensees, threaten to upset the constitutional balance struck in *CBS*. We will not presume that Congress meant to thrust upon us the substantial constitutional questions such a result would raise. We thus construe § 396(g)(1)(A) and the scheme of regulation for public broadcasting as a whole to avoid such questions.

. . . We hold today only that the FCC has no function in this scheme of accountability established by § 396(g)(1)(A) and the 1967 Act in general other than that assigned to it by the Fairness Doctrine. Therefore, we deny the petition for review and affirm the Commission's decision rejecting jurisdiction over the Corporation for Public Broadcasting.

So ordered.

## Notes and Questions

1. What is the difference between the Fairness Doctrine and AIM's reading of § 396(g)(1)(A)? Why does the court think that one would call for more Commission intervention in programming than the other?

2. The court suggests that PBS, although thought of by many as a "fourth network," does not properly fit such a description. Why not?

3. Since many of these stations are run by state and local governments, which also provide some of the financing, an additional set of problems has emerged with regard to the power of the state to impose restrictions more stringent than those imposed by Congress. In State of Maine v. University of Maine, 266 A.2d 863 (Me.1970), the state-run educational television system was partially financed from state funds. A statute ordered that no facilities "supported in whole or in part by state funds shall be used directly or indirectly for the promotion, advertisement or advancement of any political candidate . . . or for the purpose of advocating or opposing any specific program, existing or proposed, of governmental action which shall include, but shall not be limited to, constitutional amendments, tax referendums or bond issues."

The court concluded that the limitations ran counter to federal demands that a licensee operating in the public interest may not flatly ban all such programming. The role of state funding gave the state no added power in this area. Although the state "has a valid surviving power to protect its citizens in matters involving their health and safety or to protect them from fraud and deception, it has no such valid interest in protecting them from the dissemination of ideas as to which they may be called upon to make an informed choice."

4. Despite the ruling in the AIM case, the Commission retains several controls over public noncommercial broadcasters. The primary power is to be found in the licensing process. Recall the denial of renewal to the eight Alabama stations, p. 107, supra. A fundamental dispute over the proper role of educational stations emerged when WNET in New York was challenged on its application for renewal: Commissioner Hooks dissented from the approval on the ground that the station was programming for a very small elite minority and essentially neglecting the needs of larger groups in the community that would benefit from language, vocational, and remedial programs. Elite programming is defended on the ground that the noncommercial stations do not get enough money from public sources and must solicit funds from their communities. It is thought that a station that presents culturally high-level programs for the wealthier segments of the community will have better success at raising the funds necessary to keep the station going. Is this a problem? How might the situation be changed?

5. Concern about adequate funding for public broadcasting has increased during the past few years because of decreases in federal funding. In 1981, Congress created the Temporary Commission on Alternative Financing for Public Telecommunications (TCAF). Chaired by Commissioner Quello of the FCC, TCAF was directed as part of its investigation of alternative funding to oversee an 18-month experiment allowing some public broadcasters to sell advertising. Nine public television stations participated in the experiment. Although the advertising experiment generated significant income for the participants, it was not extended.

TCAF has recommended to Congress that advertising not be allowed but that enhanced underwriting (allowing identification of contributors to include product identifications and slogans) be given explicit approval. What are the risks of allowing advertising on noncommercial stations? What other funding mechanisms should be considered?

6. In keeping with these recommendations and the Public Broadcasting Amendments Act of 1981, the Commission reconsidered its 1982 ruling prohibiting the inclusion of brand names in donor acknowledgements. Under the new rules "donor acknowledgements utilized by public broadcasters may include (1) logograms or slogans which identify and do *not* promote, (2) location, (3) value neutral descriptions of a product line or service, (4) brand and trade names and product or service listings." Noncommercial Educational Broadcasting Stations, 55 R.R.2d 1190 (1984).

7. Another approach to helping public television stations raise badly needed funds is contained in an NPRM released in March, 1985. The Commission proposes to permit noncommercial and commercial licensees in the same community to exchange channels and amend the TV Table of Assignments accordingly without allowing third parties to apply for the channels in question. In essence, this would allow commercial licensees to exchange less desirable channels for more attractive noncommercial channels, e.g. a UHF for a VHF. The commercial licensees would pay the noncommercial licensees for this exchange. 50 Fed.Reg. 11909 (March 8, 1985). So far, the general reaction to this proposal has been negative.

8. Section 399(b) required public broadcasters to make and retain for 60 days (to allow inspection by government or public) audio tapes for all programs "in which any issue of public importance is discussed." It has been declared unconstitutional in an en banc decision, 5–4. Community-Service Broadcasting of Mid-America, Inc. v. Federal Communications Commission, 593 F.2d 1102 (D.C.Cir.1978). The majority relied on equal protection grounds—that no similar burden was imposed on commercial broadcasters. Several members of the majority also expressed varying degrees of certainty that such a provision imposed on all broadcasters would violate the First Amendment. The dissenters thought that the statutory requirement of "objectivity and balance" justified the special obligation of § 399(b).

## B.  CONTENT REGULATION OF PUBLIC BROADCASTING

One of the more troublesome questions in the 1967 Act involved § 399 restrictions on editorializing, p. 75, supra.  What arguments might be made against such a provision?  What arguments to sustain it?

In late 1982, a district judge declared unconstitutional the ban on editorializing by stations accepting CPB grants.  The Supreme Court, 5–4, affirmed.

### FEDERAL COMMUNICATIONS COMMISSION v. LEAGUE OF WOMEN VOTERS OF CALIFORNIA

Supreme Court of the United States, 1984.
468 U.S. ___, 104 S.Ct. 3106, 82 L.Ed.2d 278.

JUSTICE BRENNAN delivered the opinion of the Court.

[The background of the case and an excerpt from an earlier part of Justice Brennan's opinion appear at page 75.]

### III

We turn now to consider whether the restraint imposed by § 399 satisfies the requirements established by our prior cases for permissible broadcast regulation.  Before assessing the government's proffered justifications for the statute, however, two central features of the ban against editorializing must be examined, since they help to illuminate the importance of the First Amendment interests at stake in this case.

### A

First, the restriction imposed by § 399 is specifically directed at a form of speech—namely, the expression of editorial opinion—that lies at the heart of First Amendment protection.  In construing the reach of the statute, the FCC has explained that "although the use of noncommercial educational broadcast facilities by licensees, their management or those speaking on their behalf for the propagation of the licensee's own views on public issues is not permitted, such prohibition should not be construed to inhibit any *other* presentations on controversial issues of public importance."  As we recently reiterated in NAACP v. Claiborne Hardware Co., 458 U.S. 886 (1982), "expression on public issues 'has always rested on the highest rung of the hierarchy of First Amendment values.'"  Id., at 913 (quoting Carey v. Brown, 447 U.S. 455, 467 (1980)).  And we have emphasized that:

> "The freedom of speech and of the press guaranteed by the Constitution embraces at least the liberty to discuss publicly and truthfully all matters of public concern without previous restraint or fear of subsequent punishment. . . . Freedom of discussion, if it would fulfill its historic function in this nation, must embrace all issues about which information is needed or appropriate to enable the

members of society to cope with the exigencies of their period."
Thornhill v. Alabama, 310 U.S. 88, 101–102 (1940).

The editorial has traditionally played precisely this role by informing
and arousing the public, and by criticizing and cajoling those who hold
government office in order to help launch new solutions to the problems
of the time.  Preserving the free expression of editorial opinion, therefore, is part and parcel of "our profound national commitment . . .
that debate on public issues should be uninhibited, robust, and wide-
open."  New York Times v. Sullivan, 376 U.S. 254, 270 (1964).  As we
recognized in Mills v. Alabama, supra, the special place of the editorial in
our First Amendment jurisprudence simply reflects the fact that the
press, of which the broadcasting industry is indisputably a part, United
States v. Paramount Pictures, Inc., 334 U.S. 131, 166 (1948), carries out a
historic, dual responsibility in our society of reporting information and of
bringing critical judgment to bear on public affairs.  Indeed, the pivotal
importance of editorializing as a means of satisfying the public's interest
in receiving a wide variety of ideas and views through the medium of
broadcasting has long been recognized by the FCC; the Commission has
for the past 35 years actively encouraged commercial broadcast licensees
to include editorials on public affairs in their programming.  Because
§ 399 appears to restrict precisely that form of speech which the
Framers of the Bill of Rights were most anxious to protect—speech that
is "indispensable to the discovery and spread of political truth"—we
must be especially careful in weighing the interests that are asserted in
support of this restriction and in assessing the precision with which the
ban is crafted.  Whitney v. California, 274 U.S. 357, 375 (1927) (Brandeis,
J., concurring).

Second, the scope of § 399's ban is defined solely on the basis of the
content of the suppressed speech.  A wide variety of non-editorial speech
"by licensees, their management or those speaking on their behalf," In
re Complaint of Accuracy in Media, Inc., supra, 45 F.C.C.2d, at 302, is
plainly not prohibited by § 399.  Examples of such permissible forms of
speech include daily announcements of the station's program schedule or
over-the-air appeals for contributions from listeners.  Consequently, in
order to determine whether a particular statement by station management constitutes an "editorial" proscribed by § 399, enforcement authorities must necessarily examine the content of the message that is
conveyed to determine whether the views expressed concern "controversial issues of public importance."  Ibid.

As Justice Stevens observed in Consolidated Edison Co. v. Public
Service Commission, 447 U.S. 530 (1980), however, "[a] regulation of
speech that is motivated by nothing more than a desire to curtail
expression of a particular point of view on controversial issues of general
interest in the purest example of a 'law . . . . abridging the freedom of
speech, or of the press.'  A regulation that denies a group of persons the
right to address a selected audience on 'controversial issues of public
policy' is plainly such a regulation."  Id., at 546 (concurring opinion);

accord id., at 537–540 (majority opinion). Section 399 is just such a regulation, for it singles out noncommercial broadcasters and denies them the right to address their chosen audience on matters of public importance.  .   .   .

### B

In seeking to defend the prohibition on editorializing imposed by § 399, the Government urges that the statute was aimed at preventing two principal threats to the overall success of the Public Broadcasting Act of 1967. According to this argument, the ban was necessary, first, to protect noncommercial educational broadcasting stations from being coerced, as a result of federal financing, into becoming vehicles for government propagandizing or the objects of governmental influence; and, second, to keep these stations from becoming convenient targets for capture by private interest groups wishing to express their own partisan viewpoints.[16] By seeking to safeguard the public's right to a balanced presentation of public issues through the prevention of either governmental or private bias, these objectives are, of course, broadly consistent with the goals identified in our earlier broadcast regulation cases. But, in sharp contrast to the restrictions upheld in *Red Lion* or in Columbia Broadcasting System, Inc. v. FCC, which left room for editorial discretion and simply required broadcast editors to grant others access to the microphone, § 399 directly prohibits the broadcaster from speaking out on public issues even in a balanced and fair manner. The Government insists, however, that the hazards posed in the "special" circumstances of noncommercial educational broadcasting are so great that § 399 is an indispensable means of preserving the public's First Amendment interests. We disagree.

### (1)

When Congress first decided to provide financial support for the expansion and development of noncommercial educational stations, all concerned agreed that this step posed some risk that these traditionally independent stations might be pressured into becoming forums devoted solely to programming and views that were acceptable to the Federal government. That Congress was alert to these dangers cannot be doubted. It sought through the Public Broadcasting Act to fashion a system that would provide local stations with sufficient funds to foster their growth and development while preserving their tradition of autonomy and community-orientation.  .   .   .

---

**16.** The Government also contends that § 399 is intended to prevent the use of taxpayer monies to promote private views with which taxpayers may disagree. This argument is readily answered by our decision in Buckley v. Valeo, 424 U.S. 1, 90–93 (1976) (per curiam). As we explained in that case, virtually every congressional appropriation will to some extent involve a use of public money as to which some taxpayers may object. Id., at 91–92. Nevertheless, this does not mean that those taxpayers have a constitutionally protected right to enjoin such expenditures. Nor can this interest be invoked to justify a congressional decision to suppress speech.

The intended role of § 399 in achieving these purposes, however, is not as clear. The provision finds no antecedent in the Carnegie Report, which generally provided the model for most other aspects of the Act. It was not part of the Administration's original legislative proposal. And it was not included in the original version of the Act passed by the Senate. The provision found its way into the Act only as a result of an amendment in the House. Indeed, it appears that, as the House Committee Report frankly admits, § 399 was added not because Congress thought it was essential to preserving the autonomy and vitality of local stations, but rather "out of an abundance of caution." H.R.Rep. No. 572, 90th Cong., 1st Sess. 20 (1967). [　][18]

More importantly, an examination of both the overall legislative scheme established by the 1967 Act and the character of public broadcasting demonstrates that the interest asserted by the Government is not substantially advanced by § 399. First, to the extent that federal financial support creates a risk that stations will lose their independence through the bewitching power of governmental largesse, the elaborate structure established by the Public Broadcasting Act already operates to insulate local stations from governmental interference. Congress not only mandated that the new Corporation for Public Broadcasting would have a private, bipartisan structure, see §§ 396(c)–(f), but also imposed a variety of important limitations on its powers. The Corporation was prohibited from owning or operating any station, § 396(g)(3), it was required to adhere strictly to a standard of "objectivity and balance" in disbursing federal funds to local stations, § 396(g)(1)(A), and it was prohibited from contributing to or otherwise supporting any candidate for office, § 396(f)(3).

The Act also established a second layer of protections which serve to protect the stations from governmental coercion and interference. Thus, in addition to requiring the Corporation to operate so as to "assure the maximum freedom [of local stations] from interference with or control of program content or other activities," § 396(g)(1)(D), the Act expressly forbids "any department, agency, officer, or employee of the United States [from] exercis[ing] any direction, supervision, or control over educational television or radio broadcasting, or over the Corporation or any of its grantees or contractors . . . ," § 398(a). . . . The principal thrust of the amendments, therefore, has been to assure long-term appropriations for the Corporation and, more importantly, to insist that it pass specified portions of these funds directly through to local stations to give them greater autonomy in defining the uses to which those funds

18. Of course, as the Government points out, Congress has consistently retained the basic proscription on editorializing in § 399, despite periodic reconsiderations and modifications of the Act in 1973, 1978, and 1981. Brief for the United States 25–27; see also n. 7, supra. A reviewing court may not easily set aside such a considered congressional judgment. At the same time, "[d]eference to a legislative finding cannot limit judicial inquiry when First Amendment rights are at stake. . . . Were it otherwise, the scope of freedom of speech and of the press would be subject to legislative definition and the function of the First Amendment as a check on legislative power would be nullified." Landmark Communications, Inc. v. Virginia, 435 U.S. 829, 843–844 (1978).

should be put. Thus, in sharp contrast to § 399, the unifying theme of these various statutory provisions is that they substantially reduce the risk of governmental interference with the editorial judgments of local stations without restricting those stations' ability to speak on matters of public concern.[19]

Even if these statutory protections were thought insufficient to the task, however, suppressing the particular category of speech restricted by § 399 is simply not likely, given the character of the public broadcasting system, to reduce substantially the risk that the Federal Government will seek to influence or put pressure on local stations. An underlying supposition of the Government's argument in this regard is that individual noncommercial stations are likely to speak so forcefully on particular issues that Congress, the ultimate source of the stations' Federal funding, will be tempted to retaliate against these individual stations by restricting appropriations for all of public broadcasting. But, as the District Court recognized, the character of public broadcasting suggests that such a risk is speculative at best. There are literally hundreds of public radio and television stations in communitees scattered throughout the United States and its territories, see CPB, 1983–84 public Broadcasting Directory 20–50, 66–86 (Sept. 1983). Given that central fact, it seems reasonable to infer that the editorial voices of these stations will prove to be as distinctive, varied, and idiosyncratic as the various communities they represent. More importantly, the editorial focus of any particular station can fairly be expected to focus largely on issues affecting only its community.[20] Accordingly, absent some showing by the Government to the contrary, the risk that local editorializing will place all of public broadcasting in jeopardy is not sufficiently pressing to warrant § 399's broad suppression of speech.

Indeed, what is far more likely than local station editorials to pose the kinds of dangers hypothesized by the Government are the wide variety of programs addressing controversial issues produced, often with substantial CPB funding, for national distribution to local stations. . . .

**19.** Furthermore, the risk that federal coercion or influence will be brought to bear against local stations as a result of federal financing is considerably attenuated by the fact that CPB grants account for only a portion of total public broadcasting income. CPB, Public Broadcasting Income: Fiscal Year 1982, at Table 2 (Final Report, Dec. 1983) (noting that federal funds account for 23.4% of total income for all public broadcasting stations). The vast majority of financial support comes from state and local governments, as well as a variety of private sources, including foundations, businesses, and individual contributions; indeed, as the CPB recently noted, "[t]he diversity of support in America for public broadcasting is remarkable," CPB, 1982 Annual Report 2 (1982). Given this diversity of funding sources and the decentralized manner in which funds are secured, the threat that improper federal influence will be exerted over local stations is not so pressing as to require the total suppression of editorial speech by these stations.

**20.** This likelihood is enhanced with respect to public stations because they are required to establish community advisory boards which must reasonably reflect the "diverse needs and interests of the communities served by such station[s]." § 396(k)(9)(A). . . .

Furthermore, the manifest imprecision of the ban imposed by § 399 reveals that its proscription is not sufficiently tailored to the harms it seeks to prevent to justify its substantial interference with broadcasters' speech. Section 399 includes within its grip a potentially infinite variety of speech, most of which would not be related in any way to governmental affairs, political candidacies or elections. Indeed, the breadth of editorial commentary is as wide as human imagination permits. But the Government never explains how, say, an editorial by local station management urging improvements in a town's parks or museums will so infuriate Congress or other Federal officials that the future of public broadcasting will be imperiled unless such editorials are suppressed. Nor is it explained how the suppression of editorials alone serves to reduce the risk of governmental retaliation and interference when it is clear that station management is fully able to broadcast controversial views so long as such views are not labelled as its own. [  ]

The Government appears to recognize these flaws in § 399, because it focuses instead on the suggestion that the source of governmental influence may well be state and local governments, many of which have established public broadcasting commissions that own and operate local noncommercial educational stations.[22] The ban on editorializing is all the more necessary with respect to these stations, the argument runs, because the management of such stations will be especially likely to broadcast only editorials that are favorable to the state or local authorities that hold the purse strings. The Government's argument, however, proves too much. First, § 399's ban applies to the many private noncommercial community organizations that own and operate stations that are not controlled in any way by state or local government. Second, the legislative history of the Public Broadcasting Act clearly indicates that Congress was concerned with "assur[ing] complete freedom from any *Federal Government influence.*" [  ] Consistently with this concern, Congress refused to create any federally owned stations and it expressly forbid the CPB to own or operate any television or radio stations, § 396(g)(3). By contrast, although Congress was clearly aware in 1967 that many noncommercial educational stations were owned by state and local governments, it did not hesitate to extend Federal assistance to such stations, it imposed no special requirements to restrict state or local control over these stations, and, indeed, it ensured through the structure of the Act that these stations would be as insulated from Federal interference as the wholly private stations.

Finally, although the Government certainly has a substantial interest in ensuring that the audiences of noncommercial stations will not be led to think that the broadcaster's editorials reflect the official view of the government, this interest can be fully satisfied by less restrictive

---

**22.** As the Government points out in its Brief, at least two-thirds of the public television broadcasting stations in operation are licensed to (a) state public broadcasting authorities or commissions, in which commission members are often appointed by the governor with the advice and consent of the state legislature, (b) state universities or educational commissions, or (c) local school boards or municipal authorities. [  ]

means that are readily available. To address this important concern, Congress could simply require public broadcasting stations to broadcast a disclaimer every time they editorialize which would state that the editorial represents only the view of the station's management and does not in any way represent the views of the Federal Government or any of the station's other sources of funding. Such a disclaimer—similar to those often used in commercial and noncommercial programming of a controversial nature—would effectively and directly communicate to the audience that the editorial reflected only the views of the station rather than those of the government. . . .

In sum, § 399's broad ban on all editorializing by every station that receives CPB funds far exceeds what is necessary to protect against the risk of governmental interference or to prevent the public from assuming that editorials by public broadcasting stations represent the official view of government. The regulation impermissibly sweeps within its prohibition a wide range of speech by wholly private stations on topics that do not take a directly partisan stand or that have nothing whatever to do with federal, state, or local government.

(2)

Assuming that the Government's second asserted interest in preventing noncommercial stations from becoming a "privileged outlet for the political and ideological opinions of station owners and management," Brief at 34, is legitimate, the substantiality of this asserted interest is dubious. The patent over- and underinclusiveness of § 399's ban "undermines the likelihood of a genuine [governmental] interest" in preventing private groups from propagating their own views via public broadcasting. First National Bank of Boston v. Bellotti, supra, 435 U.S., at 793. If it is true, as the government contends, that noncommercial stations remain free, despite § 399, to broadcast a wide variety of controversial views through their power to control program selection, to select which persons will be interviewed, and to determine how news reports will be presented, Brief at 41, then it seems doubtful that § 399 can fairly be said to advance any genuinely substantial governmental interest in keeping controversial or partisan opinions from being aired by noncommercial stations. . . .

In short, § 399 does not prevent the use of noncommercial stations for the presentation of partisan views on controversial matters; instead, it merely bars a station from specifically communicating such views on its own behalf or on behalf of its management. If the vigorous expression of controversial opinions is, as the Government assures us, affirmatively encouraged by the Act, and if local licensees are permitted under the Act to exercise editorial control over the selection of programs, controversial or otherwise, that are aired on their stations, then § 399 accomplishes only one thing—the suppression of editorial speech by station management. It does virtually nothing, however, to reduce the risk that public stations will serve solely as outlets for expression of narrow partisan views. What we said in Columbia Broadcasting System,

Inc. v. Democratic National Committee, supra, applies, therefore, with equal force here: the "sacrifice [of] First Amendment protections for so speculative a gain is not warranted. . . ." 412 U.S., at 127.

Finally, the public's interest in preventing public broadcasting from becoming forums for lopsided presentations of narrow partisan positions is already secured by a variety of other regulatory means that intrude far less drastically upon the "journalistic freedom" of noncommercial broadcasters. [ ] The requirements of the FCC's fairness doctrine, for instance, which apply to commercial and noncommercial stations alike, ensure that such editorializing would maintain a reasonably balanced and fair presentation of controversial issues. Thus, even if the management of a noncommercial educational station were inclined to seek to further only its own partisan views when editorializing, it simply could not do so. . . . Since the breadth of § 399 extends so far beyond what is necessary to accomplish the goals identified by the Government, it fails to satisfy the First Amendment standards that we have applied to this area.

We therefore hold that even if some of the hazards at which § 399 was aimed are sufficiently substantial, the restriction is not crafted with sufficient precision to remedy those dangers that may exist to justify the significant abridgement of speech worked by the provision's broad ban on editorializing. The statute is not narrowly tailored to address any of the government's suggested goals. Moreover, the public's "paramount right" to be fully and broadly informed on matters of public importance through the medium of noncommercial educational broadcasting is not well served by the restriction, for its effect is plainly to diminish rather than augment "the volume and quality of coverage" of controversial issues. *Red Lion*, supra, at 393. Nor do we see any reason to deny noncommercial broadcasters the right to address matters of public concern on the basis of merely speculative fears of adverse public or governmental reactions to such speech.

## IV

Although the Government did not present the argument in any form to the District Court, it now seeks belatedly to justify § 399 on the basis of Congress' Spending Power. Relying upon our recent decision in Regan v. Taxation With Representation, 461 U.S. 540 (1983), the Government argues that by prohibiting noncommercial educational stations that receive CPB grants from editorializing, Congress has, in the proper exercise of its Spending Power, simply determined that it "will not subsidize public broadcasting station editorials." Brief of the United States 42. In *Taxation With Representation*, the Court found that Congress could, in the exercise of its Spending Power, reasonably refuse to subsidize the lobbying activities of tax-exempt charitable organizations by prohibiting such organizations from using tax-deductible contributions to support their lobbying efforts. . . .

. . .

Of course, if Congress were to adopt a revised version of § 399 that permitted noncommercial educational broadcasting stations to establish "affiliate" organizations which could then use the station's facilities to editorialize with non-federal funds, such a statutory mechanism would plainly be valid under the reasoning of *Taxation With Representation*. Under such a statute, public broadcasting stations would be free, in the same way that the charitable organization in *Taxation With Representation* was free, to make known its views on matters of public importance through its non-federally funded, editorializing affiliate without losing federal grants for its non-editorializing broadcast activities. [ ] But in the absence of such authority, we must reject the Government's contention that our decision in *Taxation With Representation* is controlling here.

## V

In conclusion, we emphasize that our disposition of this case rests upon a narrow proposition. We do not hold that the Congress or the FCC are without power to regulate the content, timing, or character of speech by noncommercial educational broadcasting stations. Rather, we hold only that the specific interests sought to be advanced by § 399's ban on editorializing are either not sufficiently substantial or are not served in a sufficiently limited manner to justify the substantial abridgement of important journalistic freedoms which the First Amendment jealously protects. Accordingly, the judgment of the District Court is affirmed.

JUSTICE REHNQUIST, with whom THE CHIEF JUSTICE and JUSTICE WHITE join, dissenting.

All but three paragraphs of the Court's lengthy opinion in this case are devoted to the development of a scenario in which the government appears as the "Big Bad Wolf" and appellee Pacifica as "Little Red Riding Hood." In the Court's scenario the Big Bad Wolf cruelly forbids Little Red Riding Hood from taking to her grandmother some of the food that she is carrying in her basket. Only three paragraphs are used to delineate a truer picture of the litigants, wherein it appears that some of the food in the basket was given to Little Red Riding Hood by the Big Bad Wolf himself, and that the Big Bad Wolf had told Little Red Riding Hood in advance that if she accepted his food she would have to abide by his conditions. Congress in enacting § 399 of the Public Broadcasting Act, 47 U.S.C. (Supp. V) § 399, has simply determined that public funds shall not be used to subsidize noncommercial, educational broadcasting stations which engage in "editorializing" or which support or oppose any political candidate. I do not believe that anything in the First Amendment to the United States Constitution prevents Congress from choosing to spend public monies in that manner. Perhaps a more appropriate analogy than that of Little Red Riding Hood and the Big Bad Wolf is that of Faust and Mephistopheles; Pacifica, well aware of § 399's condition on its receipt of public money, nonetheless accepted the public money and now seeks to avoid the conditions which Congress legitimately has attached to receipt of that funding.

. . .

The Court's three-paragraph discussion of why § 399, repeatedly reexamined and retained by Congress, violates the First Amendment is to me utterly unpersuasive. Congress has rationally determined that the bulk of the taxpayers whose monies provide the funds for grants by the CPB would prefer not to see the management of local educational stations promulgate its own private views on the air at taxpayer expense. Accordingly Congress simply has decided not to subsidize stations which engage in that activity.

. . .

This is not to say that the government may attach *any* condition to its largess; it is only to say that when the government is simply exercising its power to allocate its own public funds, we need only find that the condition imposed has a rational relationship to Congress' purpose in providing the subsidy and that it is not primarily "aimed at the suppression of dangerous ideas." Cammarano v. United States, 358 U.S. 498, 513 (1959), quoting Speiser v. Randall, 357 U.S. 513, 519 (1958). In this case Congress' prohibition is directly related to its purpose in providing subsidies for public broadcasting, and is plainly rational for Congress to have determined that taxpayer monies should not be used to subsidize management's views or to pay for management's exercise of partisan politics. Indeed, it is entirely rational for Congress to have wished to avoid the appearance of government sponsorship of a particular view or a particular political candidate. Furthermore, Congress' prohibition is strictly neutral. In no sense can it be said that Congress has prohibited only editorial views of one particular ideological bent. Nor has it prevented public stations from airing programs, documentaries, interviews, etc. dealing with controversial subjects, so long as management itself does not expressly endorse a particular viewpoint. And Congress has not prevented station management from communicating its own views on those subjects through any medium other than subsidized public broadcasting.

For the foregoing reasons I find this case entirely different from the so-called "unconstitutional condition" cases, wherein the Court has stated that the government "may not deny a benefit to a person on a basis that infringes his constitutionally protected interests—especially his interest in freedom of speech." Perry v. Sinderman, 408 U.S. 593, 597 (1972). In those cases the suppressed speech was not content-neutral in the same sense as here, and in those cases, there is at best only a strained argument that the legislative purpose of the condition imposed was to avoid *subsidizing* the prohibited speech. Speiser v. Randall, supra, is illustrative of the difference. In that case California's decision to deny its property tax exemption to veterans who would not declare that they would not work to overthrow the government was plainly directed at suppressing what California regarded as speech of a dangerous content. And the condition imposed was so unrelated to the benefit to be conferred that it is difficult to argue that California's property tax exemption actually subsidized the dangerous speech.

Here, in my view, Congress has rationally concluded that the bulk of taxpayers whose monies provide the funds for grants by the CPB would prefer not to see the management of public stations engage in editorializing or the endorsing or opposing of political candidates. Because Congress' decision to enact § 399 is a rational exercise of its spending powers and strictly neutral, I would hold that nothing in the First Amendment makes it unconstitutional. Accordingly, I would reverse the judgment of the District Court.

JUSTICE WHITE: Believing that the editorializing and candidate endorsement proscription stand or fall together and being confident that Congress may condition use of its funds on abstaining from political endorsements, I join JUSTICE REHNQUIST's dissenting opinion.

JUSTICE STEVENS, dissenting.

The court jester who mocks the King must choose his words with great care. An artist is likely to paint a flattering portrait of his patron. The child who wants a new toy does not preface his request with a comment on how fat his mother is. Newspaper publishers have been known to listen to their advertising managers. Elected officials may remember how their elections were financed. By enacting the statutory provision that the Court invalidates today, a sophisticated group of legislators expressed a concern about the potential impact of government funds on pervasive and powerful organs of mass communication. One need not have heard the raucous voice of Adolph Hitler over Radio Berlin to appreciate the importance of that concern.

As Justice White correctly notes, the statutory prohibitions against editorializing and candidate endorsements rest on the same foundation. In my opinion that foundation is far stronger than merely "a rational basis" and it is not weakened by the fact that it is buttressed by other provisions that are also designed to avoid the insidious evils of government propaganda favoring particular points of view. The quality of the interest in maintaining government neutrality in the free market of ideas—of avoiding subtle forms of censorship and propaganda—outweigh the impact on expression that results from this statute. Indeed, by simply terminating or reducing funding, Congress could curtail much more expression with no risk whatever of a constitutional transgression.

·  ·  ·

Although appellees originally challenged the validity of the entire statute, in their amended complaint they limited their attack to the prohibition against editorializing. In its analysis of the case, the Court assumes that the ban on political endorsements is severable from the first section and that it may be constitutional.[3] In view of the fact that

3. The Court actually raises the wrong severability issue. The serious question in this regard is whether the entire public funding scheme is severable from the prohibition on editorializing and political endorsements. The legislative history of the stat-

the major difference between [the restrictions on editorializing and] the ban on political endorsements is based on the content of the speech, it is apparent that the entire rationale of the Court's opinion rests on the premise that it may be permissible to predicate a statutory restriction on candidate endorsements on the difference between the content of that kind of speech and the content of other expressions of editorial opinion.

The Court does not tell us whether speech that endorses political candidates is more or less worthy of protection than other forms of editorializing, but it does iterate and reiterate the point that "the expression of editorial opinion" is a special kind of communication that "is entitled to the most exacting degree of First Amendment protection." [   ].[4]

Neither the fact that the statute regulates only one kind of speech, nor the fact that editorial opinion has traditionally been an important kind of speech, is sufficient to identify the character or the significance of the statute's impact on speech. Three additional points are relevant. First, the statute does not prohibit Pacifica from expressing its opinion through any avenue except the radio stations for which it receives federal financial support. It eliminates the subsidized channel of communication as a forum for Pacifica itself, and thereby deprives Pacifica of an advantage it would otherwise have over other speakers, but it does not exclude Pacifica from the marketplace for ideas. Second, the statute does not curtail the expression of opinion by individual commentators who participate in Pacifica's programs. Third, and of greatest significance for me, the statutory restriction is completely neutral in its operation—it prohibits all editorials without any distinction being drawn concerning the subject matter or the point of view that might be expressed.[5]

ute indicates the strength of the congressional aversion to these practices.
. . .

4. Thus, once again the Court embraces the obvious proposition that some speech is more worthy of protection than other speech—that the right to express editorial opinion may be worth fighting to preserve even though the right to hear less worthy speech may not—a proposition that several members of today's majority could only interpret "as an aberration" in Young v. American Mini Theaters, 427 U.S. 50, 87 (1976) (dissenting opinion) ("The fact that the 'offensive' speech here may not address 'important' topics—'ideas of social and political significance,' in the Court's terminology, *ante*, does not mean that it is less worthy of constitutional protection." Ibid.)

5. Section 399's ban on editorializing is a content based restriction on speech, but not in the sense that the majority implies. The majority speaks of "editorial opinion" as if it were some sort of special species of opinion, limited to issues of public importance.

The majority confuses the typical content of editorials with the meaning of editorial itself. An editorial is, of course, a statement of the *management's* opinion on any topic imaginable. The Court asserts that what the statute "forecloses is the expression of editorial opinion on 'controversial issues of public importance.'" The statute is not so limited. The content which is prohibited is that the station is not permitted to state its opinion with respect to any matter. In short, it may not be an on-the-air advocate if it accepts government funds for its broadcasts. The prohibition on editorializing is not directed at any particular message a station might wish to convey,. . . .

Paradoxically, section 399 is later attacked by the majority as essentially being underinclusive because it does not prohibit "controversial" national programming that is often aired with substantial federal funding. . . . Next, § 399's ban on editorializing is attacked by the majority on overinclusive grounds—because it is content-neutral—since it prohibits a "potentially in-

## II

The statute does not violate the fundamental principle that the citizen's right to speak may not be conditioned upon the sovereign's agreement with what the speaker intends to say.  On the contrary, the statute was enacted in order to protect that very principle—to avoid the risk that some speakers will be rewarded or penalized for saying things that appeal to—or are offensive to—the sovereign.[7]  The interests the statute is designed to protect are interests that underlie the First Amendment itself.

In my judgment the interest in keeping the Federal Government out of the propaganda arena is of overriding importance.  That interest is of special importance in the field of electronic communication, not only because that medium is so powerful and persuasive, but also because it is the one form of communication that is licensed by the Federal Government.[8]  When the government already has great potential power over the electronic media, it is surely legitimate to enact statutory safeguards to make sure that it does not cross the threshold that separates neutral regulation from the subsidy of partisan opinion.

The Court does not question the validity of the basic interests served by § 399.  Instead, it suggests that the statute does not substantially serve those interests because the Public Broadcasting Act operates in many other respects to insulate local stations from governmental interference.  In my view, that is an indication of nothing more than the strength of the governmental interest involved here—Congress enacted many safeguards because the evil to be avoided was so grave.  Organs of official propaganda are antithetical to this nation's heritage and Congress understandably acted with great caution in this area.  It is no answer to say that the other statutory provisions "substantially reduce the risk of government interference with the editorial judgments of the local stations without restricting the stations' ability to speak out on matters of public concern."  [ ]  The other safeguards protect the stations from interference with judgments that they will necessarily make in selecting programming, but those judgments are relatively amorphous.  No safeguard is foolproof; and the fact that funds are dispensed according to largely "objective" criteria certainly is no guaran-

---

finite variety of speech, most of which would not be related in any way to governmental affairs, political candidacies or elections." . . .

7.  . . .

Moreover, the statute will also protect the listener's interest in not having his tax payments used to finance the advocacy of causes he opposes.  The majority gives extremely short shrift to the Government's interest in minimizing the use of taxpayer monies to promote private views with which the taxpayers may disagree.  The Court briefly observes that the taxpayers do not

have a constitutionally protected right to enjoin such expenditures and then leaps to the conclusion that given the fact that the funding scheme itself is not unconstitutional, this interest cannot be used to support the statute at issue.  The conclusion manifestly does not follow from the premise, and this interest is plainly legitimate and significant.

8.  We have consistently adhered to the following guiding principles applicable to First Amendment claims in the area of broadcasting, and they bear repeating at some length: [quoting from *Red Lion* ].

tee. Individuals must always make judgments in allocating funds, and pressure can be exerted in subtle ways as well as through outright fund-cutoffs.

Members of Congress, not members of the Judiciary, live in the world of politics. When they conclude that there is a real danger of political considerations influencing the dispensing of this money and that this provision is necessary to insulate grantees from political pressures in addition to the other safeguards, that judgment is entitled to our respect.

The magnitude of the present danger that the statute is designed to avoid is admittedly a matter about which reasonable judges may disagree.[10] Moreover, I would agree that the risk would be greater if other statutory safeguards were removed. It remains true, however, that Congress has the power to prevent the use of public funds to subsidize the expression of partisan points of view, or to suppress the propagation of dissenting opinions. No matter how great or how small the immediate risk may be, there surely is more than a theoretical possibility that future grantees might be influenced by the ever present tie of the political purse strings, even if those strings are never actually pulled.

. . .

## III

The Court describes the scope of § 399's ban as being "defined solely on the basis of the content of the suppressed speech," [  ], at 18, and analogizes this case to the regulation of speech we condemned in Consolidated Edison Co. v. Public Serv. Comm'n, 447 U.S. 530 (1980). This description reveals how the Court manipulates labels without perceiving the critical differences behind the two cases.

In *Consolidated Edison* the class of speakers that was affected by New York's prohibition consisted of regulated public utilities that had been expressing their opinion on the issue of nuclear power by means of written statements inserted in their customers' monthly bills. Although the scope of the prohibition was phrased in general terms and applied to a select group of speakers, it was obviously directed at spokesmen for a particular point of view. The justification for the restriction was phrased in terms of the potential offensiveness of the utilities' messages to their audiences. It was a classic case of a viewpoint-based prohibition.

In this case, however, although the regulation applies only to a defined class of noncommercial broadcast licensees, it is common ground

---

**10.** The majority argues that the Government's concededly substantial interest in ensuring that audiences of educational stations will not perceive the station to be a government propaganda organ can be fully satisfied by requiring such stations to broadcast a disclaimer each time they editorialize stating that the editorial "does not in any way represent the views of the Federal Government. . . ." [  ]. This solution would be laughable were it not so Orwellian: the answer to the fact that there is a real danger that the editorials are really government propaganda is for the government to require the station to tell the audience that it is not propaganda at all!

that these licensees represent heterogenous points of view.[12]   There is simply no sensible basis for considering this regulation a viewpoint restriction—or, to use the Court's favorite phrase, to condemn it as "content-based"—because it applies equally to station owners of all shades of opinion.   Moreover, the justification for the prohibition is not based on the "offensiveness" of the messages in the sense that that term was used in *Consolidated Edison*.   Here, it is true that taxpayers might find it offensive if their tax monies were being used to subsidize the expression of editorial opinion with which they disagree, but it is the fact of the subsidy—not just the expression of the opinion—that legitimates this justification.   Furthermore, and of greater importance, the principal justification for this prohibition is the overriding interest in forestalling the creation of propaganda organs for the Government.

I respectfully dissent.

### Notes and Questions

1.   How realistic are the fears of the dissenting justices?   President Nixon once vetoed the CPB budget because of dissatisfaction with CPB programming.   Are noncommercial licensees likely to be influenced by the "power of the purse?"   If, indeed, prohibitions on specific forms of speech are unconstitutional, how can noncommercial licensees be insulated from government control?

2.   In response to a complaint by Senator James F. Buckley, the Commission held that § 312(a)(7) was equally applicable to commercial and noncommercial stations.   However, only those noncommercial stations using channels specifically reserved for noncommercial broadcasting are prohibited from charging for the time they must make available.   Senator James F. Buckley, 63 F.C.C.2d 952, 38 R.R.2d 1255 (1976).

3.   From a First Amendment perspective, the crucial difference between commercial and noncommercial broadcasting involves the question of the licensee's ability to control content and to reject programming.   In *League of Women Voters* the Court was faced with the problem of indirect control of PBS stations through the CPB funding mechanism. Consider, however, that more than 140 PBS stations are under some form of government ownership.   What effect should that have on the ability of those licensees to control content and reject programming? Consider the following case.

### MUIR v. ALABAMA EDUCATIONAL TELEVISION COMMISSION

United States Court of Appeals, Fifth Circuit, en banc, 1982.
688 F.2d 1033, 52 R.R.2d 935, certiorari denied 460 U.S. 1023 (1983).

[In this case, decided by the old Fifth Circuit before it was split, 22 judges participated in the decision.   Judge Hill's opinion, referred to by

---

12. That does not necessarily mean, however, "that the editorial voices of these stations will prove to be as distinctive, va- ried, and idiosyncratic as the various communities they represent," [   ] given the potential effects of government funding, [   ].

all as the majority opinion, has the implicit support of 10 judges. Judge Garwood states that he concurs in the majority opinion and then adds some thoughts of his own. Judge Rubin and the three judges who join him say that they join only the result reached by the majority because they reach their conclusion on a different basis. Yet, they join in the views expressed by Judge Garwood (who says that he joins the majority opinion). That makes 15. The seven dissenters write three opinions. Judge Garwood's opinion is placed earlier in the sequence to make matters easier to understand. The opinions in this case offer enough food for thought to match the size of the bench.]

Before BROWN, CHARLES CLARK, RONEY, GEE, TJOFLAT, HILL, FAY, RUBIN, VANCE, KRAVITCH, FRANK M. JOHNSON, HENDERSON, REAVLEY, POLITZ, HATCHETT, ANDERSON, RANDALL, TATE, SAM D. JOHNSON, THOMAS A. CLARK, WILLIAMS and GARWOOD, CIRCUIT JUDGES.

JAMES C. HILL, CIRCUIT JUDGE:

## I. *Introduction*

The two appeals before this Court on consolidated rehearing raise the important and novel question of whether individual viewers of public television stations, licensed by the Federal Communications Commission to state instrumentalities, have a First Amendment right to compel the licensees to broadcast a previously scheduled program which the licensees have decided to cancel. For the reasons below we find that the viewers do not have such a right.

Both cases before us concern the decisions of the licensees not to broadcast the program "Death of a Princess." In Muir v. Alabama Educational Television Commission, 656 F.2d 1012 (5th Cir.1981), the District Court for the Northern District of Alabama denied the plaintiff viewers' motion for a preliminary injunction requiring the defendant licensee, Alabama Educational Television Commission (AETC), to broadcast the program. The district court found (1) that the likelihood of success on the merits criterion for an injunction had not been shown; (2) that the First Amendment protects the right of broadcasters, private and public, to make programming decisions free of interference; and (3) that viewers have no First Amendment right of access to the Alabama educational television network sufficient to compel the showing of "Death of a Princess." The court granted summary judgment for AETC.

In Barnstone v. University of Houston, 514 F.Supp. 670 (S.D.Tex. 1980), the District Court for the Southern District of Texas reached a different conclusion and granted the injunction requested by the plaintiff viewers and ordered the defendant licensee, University of Houston, to broadcast the program. The court held that KUHT–TV, the television station operated by the university, was a public forum and as such it could not deny access to speakers—here, the producers of "Death of a Princess"—who wished to be heard in the public forum, unless its reasons for doing so could withstand the rigorous scrutiny to which "prior restraints" are traditionally subjected.

On appeal a panel of this court affirmed the District Court's decision in *Muir*. The panel held that the plaintiffs had no constitutional right to compel the broadcast of "Death of a Princess," and that AETC's refusal to broadcast the program was a legitimate exercise of its statutory authority as a broadcast licensee and was protected by the First Amendment. In *Barnstone* another panel of this court found that the decision in *Muir* required that the panel reverse the judgment of the District Court for the Southern District of Texas and dissolve the injunctive relief which had been granted the plaintiffs.

We directed both cases be consolidated and reheard en banc. We now affirm the judgment of the District Court for the Northern District of Alabama in *Muir* and reverse the judgment of the District Court for the Southern District of Texas in *Barnstone*.

## II.  *Factual Background*

The *Muir* case arose when AETC decided not to broadcast "Death of a Princess," which had been scheduled for broadcast on May 12, 1980 at 8:00 p.m. The program, one of thirteen in the series "World," is a dramatization of the investigation by the program's director, producer, and co-author into the motivations and circumstances which were said to have led to the July 1977 execution for adultery of a Saudi Arabian princess and her commoner lover.

AETC, organized under Ala.Code 1975, § 16–7–1, is responsible for "making the benefits of educational television available to and promoting its use by inhabitants of Alabama" and has "the duty of controlling and supervising the use of channels reserved by the Federal Communications Commission to Alabama for noncommercial, educational use." Ala.Code 1975, § 16–7–5. AETC operates a statewide network of nine noncommercial, educational television stations licensed by the Federal Communications Commission under the Communications Act of 1934 (47 U.S.C. §§ 151, et seq.). AETC is funded through state legislative appropriations from the Special Education Trust Fund, matching federal grants through the Corporation for Public Broadcasting (CPB), and private contributions.

AETC is a member of the Public Broadcasting Service (PBS), a non-profit corporation distributing public, non-commercial television programs to its members by satellite. AETC is also a member of the Station Program Cooperative (SPC), a program funding and acquisition mechanism operated by PBS. Membership in SPC entitles licensees to participate in the selection and funding of national public television programs distributed by PBS. Only those licensees who contribute to a program's cost have a right to broadcast it. Those who contribute are free to broadcast or not to broadcast the program.

PBS's acquisition of the program series "World" was funded by 144 public television licensees, including AETC, through the SPC. During the week prior to the scheduled broadcast of "Death of a Princess" AETC received numerous communications from Alabama residents protesting the showing of the program. The protests expressed fear for the personal safety and well-being of Alabama citizens working in the Middle East if the program was shown. On May 10 AETC announced its decision not to broadcast the film as scheduled.

Appellants Muir, Buttram, and Faircloth, residents of Alabama who had planned to watch "Death of a Princess," brought this action on May 12, 1980 under the First and Fourteenth Amendments and 42 U.S.C. § 1983, seeking to compel AETC to broadcast the film, and preliminary and permanent injunctions against AETC's making "political" decisions on programming. The *Barnstone* case arose in a factual context similar to that of *Muir.* The University of Houston is a co-educational institution of higher learning funded and operated by the State of Texas. See Tex.Educ.Code Ann. §§ 111.01 et seq. The university funds and operates KUHT–TV, a public television station licensed to the university by the F.C.C. As a member of the SPC, KUHT–TV contributed to the funding of the "World" program series. KUHT–TV scheduled "Death of a Princess" for broadcast on May 12, 1980 at 8:00 p.m.

On May 1, 1980 KUHT–TV announced that it had decided not to broadcast the program. This decision was made by Dr. Patrick J. Nicholson, University of Houston Vice-President for Public Information and University Relations. Dr. Nicholson had never previously made a programming decision such as this, though as the university official charged with the responsibility of operating KUHT–TV he had the power to do so. In a press release announcing the cancellation Dr. Nicholson gave the basis of his decision as "strong and understandable objections by the government of Saudi Arabia at a time when mounting crisis in the Middle East, our long friendship with the Saudi government and U.S. national interest all point to the need to avoid exacerbating the situation." Dr. Nicholson also expressed a belief that the program was not balanced in a "responsible manner."[5]

Upon learning of Dr. Nicholson's decision, on May 8, 1980, plaintiff Barnstone brought a suit to require KUHT–TV to air "Death of a Princess." Ms. Barnstone argued that as a subscriber to and regular viewer of KUHT–TV her First and Fourteenth Amendment rights were violated by the decision to cancel the program.

5. In addition to the reasons cited in the press release, the District Court, upon consideration of Dr. Nicholson's testimony, found four other reasons why the cancellation decision may have been made. First, Dr. Nicholson testified that he considered the program to be "in bad taste." Second, Dr. Nicholson expressed concern that some members of the public might believe that the "docu-drama" was a true documentary. Third, Dr. Nicholson testified that the University of Houston had previously entered into a contract with the Saudi Arabian royal family to instruct a particular princess. Finally, Dr. Nicholson testified that he had been in charge of fund raising activities for the university from 1957–1978 and that a significant percentage of the university's private contributions came from major oil companies and from individuals in oil related companies.

### III. *The First Amendment Does Not Prohibit Governmental Expression*

The central argument advanced by the plaintiffs on appeal is that their First Amendment rights were violated when the defendants, as state actors, denied the plaintiffs an opportunity to view "Death of a Princess" on the public television stations operated by the defendants. We are thus called upon to determine whether the First Amendment rights of viewers impose limits on the programming discretion of public television stations licensed to state instrumentalities.

The First Amendment operates to protect private expression from infringement by government. Such protection applies both to the right to speak and the right to hear and is operative in a variety of contexts. The amendment prohibits government from controlling or penalizing expression which has been singled out by government because of the expression's viewpoint. The First Amendment also prohibits government from taking certain actions which impermissibly constrict the flow of information or ideas.

The plaintiffs emphasize that the protection of the First Amendment extends only to private expression and not to governmental expression. They assert that the amendment serves only to confer duties on government—not rights. While this argument of the plaintiffs may be essentially correct it in no way resolves the issue before us. To find that the government is without First Amendment protection is not to find that the government is prohibited from speaking or that private individuals have the right to limit or control the expression of government. Even without First Amendment protection government may "participate in the marketplace of ideas," and "contribute its own views to those of other speakers." Community Service Broadcasting v. F.C.C., 593 F.2d 1102, 1110 n. 17 (D.C.Cir.1978). As Justice Stewart aptly noted in Columbia Broadcasting Systems, Inc. v. Democratic National Committee, 412 U.S. 94, 139, n. 7 (1973) (Stewart, J., concurring) (hereinafter CBS), "[g]overnment is not restrained by the First Amendment from controlling its own expression . . . '[t]he purpose of the First Amendment is to protect the private expression and nothing in the guarantee precludes the government from controlling its own expression or that of its agents.' "[12]

Our essential task thus does not center on determining whether AETC and the University of Houston are vested with a First Amendment right to make the programming decisions which they make regarding "Death of a Princess." In the absence of a violation of constitutional

---

12. Government expression, being unprotected by the First Amendment, may be subject to legislative limitation which would be impermissible if sought to be applied to private expression. Yet there is nothing to suggest that, absent such limitation, government is restrained from speaking any more than are the citizens. Freedom of expression is the norm in our society, for government (if not restrained) and for the people. Freedom of speech is not good government because it is in the First Amendment; it is in the First Amendment because it is good government.

right inhering in the plaintiffs, AETC and the University of Houston are free to make whatever programming decisions they choose, consistent with statutory and regulatory requirements. The fundamental question before us is whether in making the programming decisions at issue here, the defendants violated the First Amendment rights of the plaintiffs.

## IV. *The Regulatory Framework Enacted by Congress*

Our inquiry into the constitutional issue at hand is aided by a brief review of the broadcast legislation enacted by Congress.  .  .  .
. . .

The picture which emerges from the regulatory scheme adopted by Congress is one which clearly shows broadcast licensees endowed with the privilege and responsibility of exercising free programming control of their broadcasts, yet also charged with the obligation of making programming decisions which protect the legitimate interests of the public. The right to the free exercise of programming discretion is, for private licensees, not only statutorily conferred but also constitutionally protected. *CBS.* Under the existing statutes public licensees such as AETC and the University of Houston possess the same rights and obligations to make free programming decisions as their private counterparts; however, as state instrumentalities, these public licensees are without the protection of the First Amendment. This lack of constitutional protection implies only that government could possibly impose restrictions on these licensees which it could not impose on private licensees. The lack of First Amendment protection does not result in the lessening of any of the statutory rights and duties held by the public licensees. It also does not result in individual viewers gaining any greater right to influence the programming discretion of the public licensees.

## V.  *KUHT-TV and AETC Are Not Public Forums*

It is clear that Congress did not deem it necessary for viewers to be accorded a right of access to television broadcast stations in order for the public's First Amendment interests in this medium to be fully realized. Indeed it is clear that Congress concluded that the First Amendment rights of public television viewers are adequately protected under a system where the broadcast licensee has sole programming discretion but is under an obligation to serve the public interest. In spite of this Congressional scheme the District Court in *Barnstone* found that KUHT–TV was a public forum because it was operated by the government for public communication of views on issues of political and social significance. The court held that as a public forum the station could not deny access to speakers who wished to be heard in the forum, unless the requirements for prior restraint were satisfied. 514 F.Supp. at 689–91.

The plaintiffs now urge that we affirm the District Court's ruling that public television stations are public forums. The plaintiffs, unlike the District Court, however, do not argue for a public right of access to the stations. Instead the plaintiffs contend that as public forums the stations are prohibited by the First Amendment from making programming decisions motivated by hostility to the communicative impact of a program's message and stemming from a specific viewpoint of the broadcaster.

We find both the holding of the District Court and the argument of the plaintiffs to be incorrect. The Supreme Court has recently rejected the theory adopted by the District Court that because a government facility is "specifically used for the communication of information and ideas" it is *ipso facto* a public forum. United States Postal Service v. Council of Greenburgh Civic Ass'ns, 453 U.S. 114 (1981).[22] A facility is a public forum only if it is designed to provide a general public right of access to its use, or if such public access has historically existed and is not incompatible with the facility's primary activity.

.   .   .

In the cases in which a public facility has been deemed a public forum the speakers have been found to have a right of access because they were attempting to use the facility in a manner fully consistent with the "pattern of usual activity" and "the general invitation extended." The pattern of usual activity for public television stations is the statutorily mandated practice of the broadcast licensee exercising sole programming authority. The general invitation extended to the public is not to schedule programs, but to watch or decline to watch what is offered.[25] It is thus clear that the public television stations involved in the cases before us are not public forums. The plaintiffs have no right of access to compel the broadcast of any particular program.

Our holding today is consistent with the Supreme Court's ruling in *CBS* that television stations operated by private broadcast licensees provide no public right of access.   .   .   .

The plaintiffs stress that they do not argue for the creation of a public right of access to public television stations. They contend that, even without a public right of access, the stations are public forums and as such cannot make programming decisions based on communicative impact of a program. We find this contention to be untenable. It is the right of public access which is the essential characteristic of a public forum and the basis which allows a speaker to challenge the state's regulation of the forum. The gravamen of a speaker's public forum complaint is the invalid and discriminatory denial of his right of access to the forum. If a speaker does not have a right of access to a facility, that

**22.** The Court in *United States Postal Service* ruled that mailboxes are not public forums.

**25.** Similarly producers of television programs are extended no invitation to air their programs on the public television stations. Producers are, of course, free to submit their programs to the stations with a request that they be broadcast, but they have no right to compel the broadcast. The decision whether to broadcast a program remains entirely with the licensee. The District Court for the Southern District of Texas thus erred in finding that the producers of "Death of a Princess" had a right of access to station KUHT–TV to broadcast the film.

facility by definition is not a "public forum" and the speaker is without grounds for challenge under the public forum doctrine.

## VI. *The Decision to Cancel Death of a Princess Was Not Governmental Censorship*

The plaintiffs argue that even if we decline to characterize KUHT-TV and AETC as public forums we should nonetheless find that the defendants violated the plaintiffs' First Amendment rights by "censoring" "Death of a Princess." The plaintiffs contend that censorship, in violation of the First Amendment, occurs when state officials in charge of state operated public television stations decide to cancel a scheduled program because of the officials' opposition to the program's political content.

There is no question that "the First Amendment means that government has no power to restrict expression because of its message, its ideas, its subject matter, or its content. . . . The essence of this forbidden censorship is content control." Police Dept. of Chicago v. Mosley, 408 U.S. 92, 95–96 (1972). . . .

We are not convinced that editorial decisions of public television stations owned and operated by the state must, or should, be viewed in the same manner and subjected to the same restrictions as state regulatory activity affecting speech in other areas. Standard First Amendment doctrine condemns content control by governmental bodies where the government sponsors and financially supports certain facilities through the use of which others are allowed to communicate and to exercise their own right of expression. Government is allowed to impose restrictions only as to "time, place, or manner" in the use of such public access facilities—public forums. As we observed earlier, however, the First Amendment does not prohibit the government, itself, from speaking, nor require the government to speak. Similarly, the First Amendment does not preclude the government from exercising editorial control over its own medium of expression. [ ]

The plaintiffs concede that state officials operating public television stations can exercise some editorial discretion. They contend, however, that in exercising this discretion the officials must be "carefully neutral as to which speakers or viewpoints are to prevail in the marketplace of ideas." The plaintiffs further contend that if the officials restrict a program due to the political content of the program then the restriction is presumptively unconstitutional. The plaintiffs suggest that we adopt the evidentiary standard established by the Supreme Court in Mt. Healthy City School Dist. v. Doyle, 429 U.S. 274 (1977). Under this standard the initial burden would be on the plaintiffs to show that unconstitutional motivations were a "substantial" or "motivating" factor in the defendants' decisions to cancel "Death of a Princess." Once this burden is met by the plaintiffs the duty shifts to the defendants to show that the decisions would have been the same if the improper factor had not been considered.

The plaintiffs' analysis fails to recognize a number of essential differences between typical state regulation of private expressive activity and the exercise of editorial discretion by state officials responsible for the operation of public television stations.   When state officials operate a public television station they must necessarily make discriminating choices.   As the Supreme Court pointed out in CBS, 412 U.S. at 124, "[f]or better or worse, editing is what editors are for; and editing is selection and choice of material."   In exercising their editorial discretion state officials will unavoidably make programming decisions which can be characterized as "politically motivated."   All television broadcast licensees are required, under the public interest standard, to cover political events and to provide news and public affairs programs dealing with the political, social, economic and other issues which concern their community.   [   ]   The licensees are thus required to make the inherently subjective determination that their programming decisions are responsive to the needs, problems and interests of the residents of the area they serve.   Red Lion, 395 U.S. at 380.   A general proscription against political programming decisions would clearly be contrary to the licensees' statutory obligations, and would render virtually every programming decision subject to judicial challenge.

The plaintiffs seek to draw a distinction between a decision not to show a program and a decision to cancel a previously scheduled program. They suggest that while it is a proper exercise of editorial discretion for a licensee initially to decide not to schedule a program, it is constitutionally improper for the licensee to decide to cancel a scheduled program because of its political content.   In support of their view the plaintiffs cited decisions holding that school officials may be free initially to decide which books to place in their school libraries but that a decision to remove any particular book may be subject to constitutional challenge. We are not persuaded, however, that the distinction urged upon us is valid or that the school library cases are applicable.

The decision to cancel a scheduled program is no less editorial in nature than an initial decision to schedule the program.   [   ]   Both decisions require the licensee to determine what will best serve the public interest, and, as we noted earlier, such a determination is inherently subjective and involves judgments which could be termed "political."

School libraries are distinguishable from broadcast stations in a number of important ways.   There are limited hours in a day for broadcasting, and broadcast licensees are constantly required to make sensitive choices between available programs.   Cf. Board of Education v. Pico, 457 U.S. 853, 875, n. 1, (1982) ("The school's finite resources—as well as the limited number of hours in the day—require that educational officials make sensitive choices between subjects to be offered. . . .") (Blackmun, J., concurring in part).   The maintenance of one volume on a library shelf does not (absent space limitations) preempt another.   In broadcast, only one transmission of information, entertainment, or other message can occur at any one time.   A library constantly and simultaneously proffers a myriad of written materials.   As discussed in Part IV, hereinabove, the Congress has undertaken its careful analysis and balancing of conflicting interests involved in broadcasting and in public broadcasting, and the judicial branch should pay careful attention. [ ] There have been no comparable deliberations or enactments by that branch with respect to libraries. More specifically, there is no counterpart, vis-a-vis libraries, to the Federal Communications Commission's "Fairness Doctrine." When a television broadcaster finds that it has scheduled a program espousing one view, it may have unwittingly encumbered its limited broadcast hours with a requirement that equal time be devoted to other viewpoints which might touch upon an issue of limited interest in its viewing area. But the maintenance of one volume espousing one side of an issue does not invoke government regulation requiring that shelf space be made available for all other views. Finally, a school would be expected to furnish only one library for its student population. The residents of a state may expect a choice of a number of television stations, often with the publicly owned facility attracting the smallest number of viewers.

The right to cancel a program is, furthermore, far more integral a part of the operation of a television station than the decision to remove a book from a school library. Libraries typically have at least the opportunity to review a book before acquiring it, therefore, there may be "few legitimate reasons why a book, once acquired, should be removed from a library not filled to capacity." [ ] In comparison, television stations frequently do not have the chance to see a program until after the station's schedule has been printed, and there are numerous legitimate reasons why a station may decide to cancel a program it has initially scheduled. Indeed FCC regulations specifically require that licensees retain the power to reject any program which the licensee has already contracted for if the licensee determines that the program is "unsatisfactory or unsuitable or contrary to the public interest." 47 C.F.R. § 73.658.

We conclude that the defendants' editorial decisions to cancel "Death of a Princess" cannot be properly characterized as "censorship." Had the states of Alabama and Texas sought to prohibit the exhibition of the film by another party then indeed a question of censorship would have arisen. Such is not the case before us. The states have not sought to forbid or curtail the right of any person to show or view the film. In fact plaintiff Barnstone has already viewed the film at an exhibition at Rice University in Houston. The state officials in charge of AETC and KUHT–TV have simply exercised their statutorily mandated discretion and decided not to show a particular program at a particular time. There is a clear distinction between a state's exercise of editorial discretion over its own expression and a state's prohibition or suppression of the speech of another.

## VII. *The Plaintiffs Can Seek Remedial Relief From the FCC*

Our holding that the defendants did not violate the plaintiffs' First Amendment rights does not preclude the plaintiffs from challenging the propriety of the defendants' programming decision with the FCC. Our decision is limited to the constitutional issue presented. We offer no opinion as to whether or not the actions of AETC and the University of Houston comport with their statutory and regulatory obligation.

.  .  .

## VIII. *Conclusion*

The decisions of AETC and the University of Houston to cancel "Death of a Princess" did not violate the First Amendment rights of the plaintiffs. The plaintiffs have no constitutional right to compel the broadcast of the program. Accordingly, we find that the District Court for the Northern District of Alabama properly awarded summary judgment to AETC. We also find that the District Court for the Southern District of Texas erred in issuing its order requiring KUHT–TV to broadcast the program.

.  .  .

GARWOOD, CIRCUIT JUDGE, concurring.

I concur in the majority opinion, and append these remarks only to point up two additional interrelated matters I believe significant.

First, plaintiffs are not attacking governmental "public" broadcasting as such. Nor do they seek to require its operation to be on a pure "open forum" basis—like an empty stage available to all comers—where each citizen can cause the broadcast of his or her program of choice, with their inevitable selectivity determined by completely content neutral factors such as lot, or first come first served or the like. Rather, plaintiffs seek to become a *part* of governmental "public" broadcasting essentially as it is, except they want it to broadcast this particular program of their choice. However, there is simply no way for them— together with all others who might wish to assert similar rights for their favorite "dramatization"—to become a part of *such* "conventional" (as distinguished from pure "open forum") governmental broadcasting *except* on the basis of governmental selection of the individual programs.

As the majority opinion convincingly demonstrates, in television broadcasting not only is selection inevitable, but it is likewise inevitable that in numerous instances it will be largely based on factors that are not content neutral and on considerations that involve sympathy for or hostility to the program's "message" on the part of the party having the power of selection. This is *not* to say that program selection influenced by "message" sympathy or hostility on the part of governmental television stations is a desirable phenomenon, or even one which is wholly consistent with the values underlying the First Amendment. But such a characteristic is part and parcel of the operation of the conventional (not pure "open forum") governmental television stations of which plaintiffs seek to avail themselves. They are not entitled to have a special exception made in their favor so that for this particular program *they* are entitled to make the selection and require that these conventionally operated governmental stations broadcast it.

. . .

In the second place, plaintiffs do not assert that the stations in question have, on the basis of their agreement or disagreement with the different points of view involved or for similar "political" type reasons, structured their programming so that it constitutes a one-sided or slanted presentation of any matter of public concern, importance or controversy, whether relevant to the "message" of plaintiffs' desired program or otherwise.[3] So far as any such matters are concerned, plaintiffs' complaint is made essentially in a vacuum—they claim that merely because on one particular occasion a "political" type decision was made *not* to air one specific program plaintiffs wished to see, they therefore have a right to a court order directing these conventionally operated government stations to promptly air this precise program. We have rejected this claim. This is not to say, however, that no private citizen has a right to question the programming of governmental "public" television stations under any circumstances, or that the remedy of complaint to the F.C.C. will always be adequate.

A private citizen has no constitutional right to force a conventionally operated governmental "public" television station to enter with its broadcasting a particular propaganda war by showing a specific program selected by the citizen. Whether it is proper for such a governmental station to enter that kind of a war at all, or whether if it does so it may nevertheless present only one side while refusing, for reasons of a "political" nature, to broadcast any competing view, are questions of a different nature that are not now before us.

RUBIN, CIRCUIT JUDGE, with whom POLITZ, RANDALL and WILLIAMS, CIRCUIT JUDGES, join, specially concurring.

While I join in the result reached by the majority, I reach my conclusion on a different basis. Therefore, I join in the views expressed by Judge Garwood and add:

The sensitive and important issues in these cases cannot be resolved simply by attempting to decide whether a television station operated by a state agency is, or is not, a public forum. That term is but a label, developed to describe a location the use of which is open to the public. It does not express a definition but a conclusion. . . .

The issue directly presented can be stated simply: whether an individual viewer has a right to compel a television station operated by a state agency to broadcast a single program previously scheduled by an employee of the agency that a higher-ranking state official has decided, because of its content, to cancel. This pretermits the factual questions whether the program was canceled for what the dissent calls "legitimate reasons" and whether the official's objection to the content of the program and to its political implications was in either of these cases the sole reason for canceling "Death of a Princess" or merely the decisive

---

3. And plaintiffs do not contend their particular (or some similar) program must be shown to fairly balance the presentation on this subject matter which the stations have improperly slanted by showing some other program or programs.

one. Although these are not unimportant inquiries, they do not focus on the crucial issue: how does the first amendment control state action when the state is operating a television station?

Determination of the constitutional limitations that result because a television licensee is a state agency rather than a private agency must take into account not only the rights of viewers but a number of other considerations. The license is federally bestowed. The state agency licensee has both a statutory duty to comply with the rules and regulations governing the use of its license and, like other licensees, the statutory right to determine the way in which it shall fulfill that duty. Those state employees who are charged with operation of the station, whether high or low in the managerial hierarchy, may have some right to free expression, which may be stronger if, for example, they function in an academic environment devoted to freedom of inquiry. Those who want access to the medium in order not to view and listen but to disseminate a message must also be considered. Viewers also have an interest in the content of programs, not only because of their "right to see" but also because the state agency is financed at least in part by viewers as taxpayers.

These interests are all entitled to consideration and some or all of them may be accorded constitutional protection. . . .

Even the fact that the state is engaged in television broadcasting does not fully define the constitutional limitations on its actions, for such broadcasting might be designed to serve differing purposes. Licensing is not destiny. That the state is the licensee does not predetermine the station's function. The state may elect the station's mission, so long as this mission is consistent with the station's license and the Constitution. The prerogatives of managers, editors, and programmers, the rights of access of those who seek exposure, and the rights of viewers, as well as the prerogatives of the licensee itself as a state agency, are at least in part determined by this mission.

All, or in other instances a part, of a station's programs might be devoted to providing a medium for the communication of competing views. Some channels on cable television networks and some viewer or listener call-in programs on television and radio stations are of this kind. Some television stations are devoted entirely to educational purposes, designed solely for pedagogy. Others may be operated to furnish a varied menu of entertainment having greater cultural and educational value than the programs available on commercial stations. While the record is not clear, it appears that the two stations involved in these cases were of this sort. Neither station has been shown to have been a magazine of the air, a forum for all views, or a dispassionate communicator on issues of the day. Each appears to serve instead a diet that differs from commercial television primarily in appeal to a somewhat more sophisticated audience, the absence of commercials, and efforts to raise funds from viewers.

The function of a state agency operating an informational medium is significant in determining first amendment restrictions on its actions. State agencies publish alumni bulletins, newsletters devoted to better farming practices, and law reviews; they operate or subsidize art museums and theater companies and student newspapers. The federal government operates the Voice of America and Radio Free Europe and Radio Liberty, publishes "journals, magazines, periodicals, and similar publications" that are "necessary in the transaction of the public business," including newspapers for branches of the Armed Forces, and pays the salaries of many federal officials who, like the President's Press Secretary, communicate with the public through the media. The first amendment does not dictate that what will be said or performed or published or broadcast in these activities will be entirely content-neutral. In those activities that, like television broadcasting to the general public, depend in part on audience interest, appraisal of audience interest and suitability for publication or broadcast inevitably involves judgment of content.

If the state is conducting an activity that functions as a marketplace of ideas, the Constitution requires content neutrality. Thus, a state university may not override editorial freedom for student newspapers. If, however, the state's activity is devoted to a specific function rather than general news dissemination or free exposition of ideas, the state may regulate content in order to prevent hampering the primary function of the activity, just as it may to some degree restrict the content of material distributed or displayed on military establishments, in prisons, on public buses, or in public hospitals.

All of the opinions in Board of Educ. v. Pico, 457 U.S. 853 (1982) recognize such a distinction either implicitly or expressly.[18] . . .

. . .

While the Mobile and Houston television stations are operated by state agencies, neither station is designed to function as a marketplace of ideas, a medium open to all who have a message, whatever its nature. The staff of each station had made an initial programming decision based in part on their assessment of the content of "Death of a Princess." Had the initial decision been not to use the program, the argument might have been made that this too was censorship and violated the potential viewers' right to see. If a decision is initially made at one level to use a program and is then reversed at a higher level, the content assessment involved is more apparent, but it is not necessarily converted thereby from legitimate programming into forbidden censorship.

Judicial reassessment of the propriety of a programming decision made in operating a television station involves not only interference with station management but also reevaluation of all the content-quality-

---

18. Seven justices filed opinions in *Pico*. The Court divided four-four on the constitutional issue of the extent to which the first amendment limits the discretion of a school board to remove books from a school library. Justice White concurred in the judgment of the Court but did not reach this issue. [ ]

audience reaction factors that enter into a decision to use or not to use a program by a medium that cannot possibly, by its very nature, accommodate everything that every viewer might desire. With deference to the dicta observations made in the *Pico* plurality opinion, our reexamination of such a decision cannot logically be confined to occasions when higher officials overrule subordinates. If it is forbidden censorship for the higher official to cancel a program, it is equally censorship for the lower officials to decide initially to reject a program.

The Constitution is categoric but it does not command the theoretical. The state's discretion is confined by the functions it may perform as a broadcast licensee, and the purpose to which it has dedicated its license. Moreover, these cases involve only one program, not a licensee policy or practice of, for example, favoring only one political party, or of broadcasting racially or religiously discriminatory views. Neither complaint even alleges that either station has a policy of curtailing access to ideas. Each seeks only to compel the defendant station to show a single program. Judicial intervention might be required if these or other licensees should adopt or follow policies or practices that transgress constitutional rights. But, one call, even if it is ill-advised, does not constitute a policy or practice, and judicial intervention does not appear required or warranted for a single programming decision.

For these reasons, although I cannot agree with all of the majority opinion, particularly its discussion of the application of the public forum doctrine, I concur in the result.

KRAVITCH, CIRCUIT JUDGE, dissenting:

I agree with the analysis in Judge Johnson's thorough and well-reasoned dissent, with one exception: his statement that the government's decision to withdraw a program becomes presumptively unconstitutional once a plaintiff has shown that the decision was made because of the program's "substantive content." In my view, in addition to "substantive content," there must be shown an improper motivation, an intent to "restrict[] access to the political ideas or social perspectives discussed. . . ." Board of Education v. Pico, 457 U.S. 853, 879 (1982) (Blackmun, J., concurring). In this regard I agree with Judge Reavley. I do not join Judge Reavley's dissent, however, because his standard suggests that intent to suppress must be the *sole* factor before the withdrawal violates the First Amendment. The *Pico* plurality explicitly stated that an improper motive is a "decisive factor" and makes the withdrawal unconstitutional if it is a "substantial factor." Id. at ___ & n. 22 (plurality opinion of Brennan, J., Marshall, J., and Stevens, J.). The improper motivation need not be the only factor in the withdrawal decision. For these reasons I write separately.

FRANK M. JOHNSON, Jr., CIRCUIT JUDGE, with whom HATCHETT, ANDERSON, TATE and THOMAS A. CLARK, CIRCUIT JUDGES, join, dissenting.

I dissent because I am convinced that the majority has committed a serious error in applying the law to these cases. The clearly defined issue in these appeals is whether the executive officers of a state operated public television station may cancel a previously scheduled program because it presents a point of view disagreeable to the religious and political regime of a foreign country. The majority opinion permitting cancellation on these grounds flies completely in the face of the First Amendment and our tradition of vigilance against governmental censorship of political and religious expression.

.　.　.

The majority of the Court . . . has affirmed *Muir* and reversed *Barnstone* in an opinion which grants state authorities unlimited discretion to regulate the content of public television within their control. Because state law and FCC licensing grant defendants full broadcasting authority over these stations in their respective areas, the majority's decision confers unrestricted control over a monopoly market. [  ] By finding no other restriction on state operated television than that imposed by federal regulation, the Court has elevated "the Communications Act above the Constitution." [  ] Moreover, the Court has abdicated its duty in an area in which the plaintiffs have no comparable remedy.

The freedom of expression protected by the First Amendment encompasses the rights of both speakers and listeners . . .. The proper inquiry for this Court, then, should not be whether the Communications Act grants state broadcasters editorial discretion, but whether the action of state officials in these cases abridged free expression protected by the First Amendment. [  ]

Our system of constitutional protection clearly reflects the free discussion of public issues on the basis of the political, religious, or ideological content of the message. Freedom of expression concerning public issues "is at the heart of the First Amendment's protection." [  ] Self-government suffers when those in power suppress competing views on public issues. [  ] As a result, federal courts have consistently struck down content-based restrictions on the discussion of public issues. [  ]

.　.　.

The majority opinion completely ignores the critical issue in these cases by concluding that "[t]he state officials in charge of AETC and KUHT–TV have simply exercised their statutorily mandated discretion and decided not to show a particular program at a particular time." The very simple answer to that position is that FCC regulation is designed neither to preempt judicial scrutiny nor to redress state censorship as alleged in these cases.

Federal regulation of the broadcast media, for the most part, reflects the government's attempt to balance the allocation of a scarce resource with the First Amendment interests of private broadcasters and the public. [  ] The fact that state operated television stations are entitled to exercise editorial discretion, however, does not absolve them of their First Amendment responsibilities. "The First Amendment protects the press *from* governmental interference; it confers no analogous protection *on* the Government." CBS, Inc. v. FCC, 395 U.S. at 390 (First Amendment protects against governmental monopolization of the free marketplace of ideas). The majority commits fundamental error when it permits state broadcasters to ride on the coattails of their private counterparts. Even when the majority admits that state broadcasters "are without the protection of the First Amendment," it offers no principled reason why this "implies only that government could possibly impose restrictions on these licensees which it could not impose on private licensees."

In addition, while it is true that the FCC hears complaints similar to those raised in these cases, it is also true that the FCC routinely denies relief. A brief review of the cases cited by the majority reveals that the FCC steadfastly refuses to depart from its "longstanding policy of deferring to licensee discretion." . . .

Complaints regarding individual cancellation decisions are regularly denied. [  ]

Thus it is clear that the majority's deference to the FCC in these cases that present important constitutional questions amounts to nothing more than ". . . a promise to the ear . . ." which will most certainly be broken "to the hope." [  ] Relying on the system of FCC regulation, the majority has granted state broadcasters immunity from constitutional scrutiny. . . . Because the FCC does not distinguish between private and public broadcasters in its regulation of the airwaves, [  ] it provides no protection from the kind of state censorship alleged in these cases.

The concurring opinions of Judges Rubin and Garwood erroneously suggest that official censorship may only be found when the state operates a medium which is "content neutral," [  ], or which is a "public forum." [  ] In all other cases, the concurrences suppose, the state must be given unbridled authority to discriminate among different viewpoints, even if the state chooses to suppress a particular point of view solely on the basis of the political content of the message. Otherwise, the opinions caution, any citizen would have the "right" to force the state operated televisions in this case to broadcast any program of his choosing.

These suppositions erroneously ignore the proper considerations a Court may give the editorial process.

In the recent case of Board of Educ. v. Pico, 457 U.S. 853 (1982), both the plurality and Justice Blackmun recognized the presence of enforceable First Amendment rights, even within the context of a highly discretionary state function. As Justice Blackmun wrote, concurring: "In my view, we strike a proper balance here by holding that school officials may not remove books for the *purpose* of restricting access to the political ideas or social perspectives discussed in them, when that action is motivated simply by the officials' disapproval of the ideas involved." Id. at 899–80, (Blackmun, J., concurring). Unlike Judges Hill and Rubin, I find allegations of censorship in the context of state operated television broadcasting entitled to much greater scrutiny than similar allegations involving school board regulation of students' reading material. Public television stations "provide educational, cultural, and discussion programs which serve the general community." [ ] AETC is specifically charged with the duty "of making the benefits of educational television available to and promoting its use by inhabitants of Alabama . . .." Ala.Code 1975, § 16–7–5. Viewed in the context of these stations' purposes and the framework of existing regulation, the editorial discretion of a state broadcaster is more circumscribed than that of a school board member. Moreover, the facts of both *Muir* and *Barnstone* reveal dramatic departures from established editorial practice in direct response to the urgings or implied threats of a foreign government.

Finally, the concurring opinions would appear to recognize official censorship by state television broadcasters when that censorship is conducted as a "policy or practice" of the state. Neither opinion, however, advances a principled distinction between censorship which is a "policy or practice" and that which is an individual overt act of suppression. It is clear to me that the First Amendment does not prohibit censorship only when it reaches the level of state "policy." To do so would be to allow the state to abrogate the fundamental concept of individual civil liberty. [ ]

It is the judiciary which is the ultimate arbiter of the fundamental rights involved in these cases. Courts may not abdicate their duty by reference to a system of administrative regulation, or because they would prefer that the plaintiffs take their complaints elsewhere. We must review the allegations of state censorship in the context of television broadcasting according to applicable legal standards. The standard for evaluating the allegations of abridgment in these cases must be that which was articulated in Mt. Healthy School Dist. v. Doyle, 429 U.S. 274, 287 (1977). Once the plaintiff demonstrates that the government has silenced a message because of its substantive content, the government's decision becomes presumptively unconstitutional. The government should then be allowed to demonstrate that it would have taken the same action on the basis of legitimate reasons. Finally, the plaintiff should be given a full opportunity to refute the government's assertion.

. . .

REAVLEY, CIRCUIT JUDGE, dissenting:

I cannot join the majority or concurring opinions for the reason that each of these television stations does far more than transmit expressions of the state. Our desire to free non-profit public broadcasting from judicial interference is no justification for pretending that the state is not relaying messages into the idea marketplace. I must conclude that the state encounters the First Amendment requirement of neutrality for reasons generally discussed in my original panel concurrence. Barnstone v. University of Houston, KUHT–TV, 660 F.2d 137, 138 (5th Cir. 1981).

On the other hand, I would not go so far as Judge Johnson does to make the state's decision presumptively unconstitutional whenever a program is not shown "because of its substantive content." State operated television stations should be given more latitude, even to choose on the basis of substantive content, in their program selection. They should be entitled to pursue excellence, to build viewing audiences, to respond to what viewers want, and to consider the effect of their programs upon that audience. Bona fide programming decisions would not, for me, violate First Amendment neutrality. Only if the decision to show or not to show were based upon viewpoint alone, in juxtaposition to the personal viewpoint of the programming authority or state superiors, entirely aside from any opinion as to program value or effect, would I regard neutrality abused and court action justifiable.

### Notes and Questions

1.   Judge Garwood points out that the plaintiffs did not "attack governmental 'public' broadcasting as such." Are there any grounds for such an attack? What are the justifications for allowing government organizations, such as AETC or the University of Houston, to be broadcast licensees?

2.   Given the difficulty of finding alternative funding and the difficulty of insulating recipients of government funding from interference—either direct or indirect—in their programming policies, what changes should be made in the public broadcasting scheme?

3.   In both *League of Women Voters* and *Muir* the majority relied in part on the protection against one-sided programming afforded by the fairness doctrine. How much protection against pro-government bias can necessarily be expected from the FCC when its members are political appointees? What if the fairness doctrine is abolished, as the Commission has suggested? Are there stronger arguments for retaining it with respect to noncommercial broadcasting?

## C.  RELIGIOUS BROADCASTING

As noted earlier, religious institutions may be eligible for reserved educational channels. The test used by the Commission to decide whether an institution is eligible for a reserved spot is "whether the primary thrust is educational, albeit with a religious aspect to the educational activity. Recognizing that some overlap in purposes is, or can be, involved, we look to the application as a whole to determine which is the essential purpose and which is incidental." Bible Moravian Church, Inc., 28 F.C.C.2d 1, 21 R.R.2d 492 (1971) (rejecting an application for a reserved educational spot).

Religious institutions that do not meet the educational qualifications are able to apply for other spots as noncommercial licensees. In such instances, the rules applicable to other broadcasters are applicable to religious broadcasters as well. In addition, the Commission will apply the 'fair break' doctrine by inquiring as to "whether the applicant, whatever his own views, is likely to give a 'fair break' to others who do not share them." Noe v. Federal Communications Commission, 260 F.2d

739, 742 (D.C.Cir.1958). The Commission has made one major exception to its general rules in allowing a religious broadcaster to consider an applicant's religion for employment, but only to "those persons hired to espouse a particular religious philosophy over the air."

In its early days of reallocating frequencies, when there were no spots reserved for educational broadcasting, the Radio Commission had occasion to consider the value of a station emphasizing religious programming. It decided that such programming was usually aimed at too narrow a base of listeners and this "discriminated against" the rest of the listeners. "In rare cases it is possible to combine a general public-service station and a high-class religious station in a division of time which will approximate a well-rounded program. In other cases religious stations must accept part time on inferior channels or daylight assignments . . . ." Great Lakes Broadcasting Co., 3 F.R.C.Ann.Rep. 32 (1929), modified on other grounds 37 F.2d 993 (D.C.Cir.1930), certiorari dismissed 281 U.S. 706 (1930). As the spectrum has expanded, religious broadcasting has gained a more secure footing.

Some have argued that religious programming provides too narrow a base to justify the allocation of a license. An effort to persuade the Commission of this failed in 1975. Multiple and Religious Ownership of Educational Stations, 54 F.C.C.2d 941, 34 R.R.2d 1217 (1975). Two persons requested a "freeze" on all grants of reserved educational FM and television channels to religious institutions pending a study of their value. The Commission thought this would violate its obligation of "neutrality" toward sectarian applicants. The Commission concluded that no new policies were needed and decided to continue ad hoc enforcement of its existing policies such as the fairness doctrine and "the principle that a broadcast station may not be used solely to promote the personal or partisan objectives of the broadcaster."

One effect of this petition was to demonstrate the support for religious stations. Periodically, a rumor surfaces that this petition—incorrectly attributed to famous atheist Madalyn Murray O'Hair—is again being considered by the Commission. Each time this happens, the Commission is flooded with calls and letters opposing the petition.

As we saw in Chapter VI with the fairness complaint against the program "In Search of Noah's Ark," the Commission has never declared the fairness doctrine "applicable to issues involving the interpretation of religious doctrine." This position was challenged in 1965 by Madalyn Murray O'Hair, who requested time on several Hawaiian radio stations to discuss "freethought." She argued that the various church services carried by these stations entitled her to time to discuss her contrasting views. The Commission rejected her complaint on the grounds that "mere broadcast of church services, devotionals and prayers is not the presentation of a controversial issue within the meaning of the Fairness Doctrine." Madalyn Murray, 40 F.C.C. 647 (1965).

At what point do religious statements become statements on issues of public controversy? Would a sermon against abortion shown as part of a televised church service raise a fairness doctrine problem? What about references to the need for eliminating "smut" from the airwaves, or a suggestion that viewers should boycott companies that advertise on shows that do not reflect traditional Christian values? Traditionally, the Commission has tended to avoid these questions by deferring to the licensee's determination of whether it was a presentation on an issue of public importance. With the growing number of religious programs and even networks for broadcasting and cable, these issues assume greater importance.

# Chapter IX

# CABLE TELEVISION

Our discussion until this point has been addressed solely to broadcasting. Some programs reached the public through radios and others through television sets. In this Chapter and the next we will examine other forms of communication that do not necessarily involve broadcasting—though the end product does emerge through the television set. It is important to recognize at the outset that although broadcasting and the television set have been joined, new technology permits the television set to be used for communications that have not been broadcast. The most obvious example is the use of video cassette players and recorders, which permit the owner of a television set to buy or rent a video cassette at a store and play it on a television set at home—all without any use of the spectrum. That activity much more closely resembles the showing of movies at home than anything else.

## A. DEVELOPMENT

Cable television, the first of the "new" communication technologies, involves the transmission of electrical signals over wires to television sets in homes or elsewhere. The technique involves a studio, called the "head-end," and coaxial cables that physically connect the head-end with every television set in the system. The cable is capable of carrying such a wide range of electrical signals that it can simultaneously carry signals sufficient for 55 or more television channels. (As the signals are carried along the cable they become weaker and must be amplified along the way.)

It is possible to transmit certain signals in scrambled forms that require decoders, but others can be received by all users. It is also possible, as Warner Communications first showed with QUBE in Columbus, Ohio, to run a system in which the users are able to send signals back to the head-end: voting on a question asked on a program, ordering merchandise, or telling a quarterback what plays to call in a semiprofessional football game.

The programming sent out from the head-end can come from many sources. The system owner might send out a variety of motion pictures he has bought or rented; he might send a camera crew out to cover the local high school football game; he might present live programs from his own studio; he might carry programs prepared by others specially for cable that he receives by wire or by satellite; or he might seek to transmit over his system the signals and programs broadcast by television stations. This last source of programming raises serious questions of the relationship between cable and over-the-air television. So long as the cable system carries only programming from other sources, cable television is simply another competitor of broadcasting, along with movies, phonograph records, books and other communications sources. In fact, however, cable has been intimately involved with broadcasting since its inception—and that has produced substantial conflict.

Cable transmission was first used in the 1950's to provide television reception in remote locations that otherwise would have received none. For example, a community in the mountains of West Virginia could construct an antenna on high ground to receive the signals of nearby television stations and transmit them through cable to households in the community. Such systems were called CATV for "community antenna television." Since cable was the only means of bringing television service to these remote areas, television broadcasters welcomed the additional viewers.

It was soon realized, however, that cable could do more than merely provide television service to remote areas. In 1961, a cable operator began serving San Diego, a city already served by three VHF network affiliates. The cable operator erected an antenna capable of picking up signals from Los Angeles, 100 miles away. In addition to the three networks received locally, cable offered four independent stations that served Los Angeles with sports, old motion pictures, and reruns of network shows. The San Diego experience demonstrated that the three channels offered by over-the-air signals were not enough to satisfy an ordinary audience and that viewers were willing to pay for more diversified programming through importation of distant signals. In effect, cable television service filled in the uneven pattern of FCC station allocation. Since cable offered a service alternative to that offered by local, over-the-air stations, television broadcasters began to view cable transmission as a competitive threat.

The spread of color television also provided a new impetus to cable development. VHF signals tend to bounce off large obstacles rather than bend around them. Hence a tall building can act like a weak transmitter, rebroadcasting the television signal at the same frequency as the station from which the signal originates. The result is interference, barely noticeable on a black-and-white set, but more pronounced on a color set. Cable provides the residents of large cities something that an over-the-air television signal cannot—a high-quality color picture. Thus, cable television invaded large cities, despite the presence of a full complement of VHF signals.

Finally, cable began to originate programming not available to viewers of network or independent television. Cable systems offered entertainment programming, sports events, and special programs designed to meet the interests of discrete groups. Communication satellites made nationwide distribution of this programming economically feasible. The discovery that viewers were willing to pay a few dollars more per month for programming not available on over-the-air television led to the development of pay cable service.

Pay cable involves the cable distribution of non-broadcast programming for which the subscriber is charged an additional program or channel fee beyond the regular monthly fee for the system's television signal reception service. The systems for distributing pay cable vary technically. The simplest method is to distribute the programming on one or more channels of a cable television system in garbled form. System subscribers who wish to receive the additional programming are supplied with a device that converts the programming transmission so that it can be understood. It is technically possible, but more expensive, to use systems that permit a separate charge to be made for each program viewed. These either require the subscriber to purchase a ticket for each program in advance, which when inserted into a decoding device in the subscriber's home provides access to the programming, or to utilize the return communications capacity of a cable system or a telephone connection to activate a central computer facility that releases the programming through the subscriber's decoding device (an addressable converter) and performs the billing functions.

Most cable systems utilize a fee structure known as "tiering." A relatively low monthly fee gives the subscriber access to the local over-the-air television stations as well as any community access or local origination channels. Access channels carry programming produced by citizens or community groups, and local origination consists of local news, sports and public affairs programming produced by the cable operator. Sometimes advertiser-supported services such as the Entertainment and Sports Programming Network (ESPN), the Cable News Network (CNN), and over-the-air signals imported from other parts of the country are included.

An additional monthly fee gives the subscriber access to other specialized programming services ranging from children's programs to adult entertainment. These services are usually bundled together in groups called "tiers." Thus, the subscriber must often take several unwanted program services to obtain one desired service. Usually a higher tier includes all the programming available in lower tiers.

The range of programming available via cable has grown greatly. In the New York area, for example, cable companies include more than 10 services in the basic monthly fee, such as programming directed to racial and religious groups, all-news and all-sports channels, live coverage of the House of Representatives, children's programming, and "superstations" (discussed infra). For an extra monthly charge, subscribers may obtain an equal number of additional services, such as movie and entertainment channels, adult movies, and cultural programming.

In the late 1970's and early 1980's, new programming services were constantly beginning, but recently, a shakeout in the industry has begun. CBS shut down CBS Cable after losing $30 million on the new service in its first year. The RCA and Rockefeller Center entry, The Entertainment Channel, was discontinued after posting a $35 million loss after nine months.

In 1983, Ted Turner agreed to pay ABC and Westinghouse $12.5 million each to shut down Satellite News Channel, which was the main competitor to Turner's Cable News Network and CNN Headline News. Group W and ABC promised not to compete in the cable news business for at least three years.

Thus, cable has provided a variety of services. It began as a way of bringing to a community programming that would have been available but for geographical barriers. Then, it imported programs from communities beyond the reach of normal reception. Later, it became a service for those who wished to improve reception of their local signals. These features have been combined with each other as well as with the origination of new programming on cable. Now it is possible to obtain the origination without any of the other features—and this origination may be local or part of a network that programs specially for cable subscribers.

By 1985, cable systems had been installed in 36.1 million (42.9 percent) of the nation's 84 million television homes. Systems varied in size from a few hundred homes to some in larger cities with hundreds of thousands of subscribers. The largest multiple system operators (MSOs) owned hundreds of systems. Pay cable reached 25 million of these subscribers. The pay systems ranged from Home Box Office with 14.5 million subscribers to specialized services with only a few thousand subscribers.

## B. FCC JURISDICTION

When the first CATV systems emerged in the late 1950's, rural television stations became concerned about their local dominance. Their requests that the FCC assume jurisdiction over the activities of these new enterprises were rejected on the ground that the problem was trivial and no different from a request for protection against motion picture theaters or publishers, who also compete with broadcasting.

In 1962, however, the FCC changed direction and began to deny cable systems permission to carry broadcast signals that might adversely affect local television. The Commission had two main concerns. First, it believed that if cable systems were allowed to import distant signals, this would fragment the audience available to local stations, erode their revenue bases, affect their programming, and perhaps cause the stations to leave the air—to the public's detriment.

The second concern was that a cable system's use of retransmitted broadcast programming, for which the cable system had paid nothing, gave it an unfair competitive advantage over local television stations since the latter had to pay considerable sums to those who held the copyrights on particular programs. We will discuss the copyright decisions allowing cable to retransmit free of charge later in this Chapter.

These two concerns—for fragmentation and program costs—led the FCC to embark on a series of regulations designed to keep cable systems subservient to over-the-air broadcasting. Recall that this was the period of weak UHF stations, for whom audience fragmentation might well have been fatal.

One of the restrictions imposed was a ban on importing distant signals (those from outside the market area) into a top-100 market unless the cable system could prove that the importation would not hurt UHF development in that market. This restriction resulted in the first court challenge to the FCC's authority to regulate cable. United States v. Southwestern Cable Co., 392 U.S. 157 (1968). The Commission relied on § 152(a) of the Communications Act: "The provisions of this Act shall apply to all interstate and foreign communication by wire or radio . . . ." 47 U.S.C. § 152(a). Southwestern argued that "§ 152(a) does not independently confer regulatory authority upon the Commission, but instead merely prescribes the forms of communication to which the Act's other provisions may separately be made applicable." Since there were no specific cable provisions in the Act, Southwestern contended the Commission had no authority to regulate cable.

The Court rejected that argument as an overly restrictive reading of the Act. Relying on *National Broadcasting Co.*, the case involving the chain broadcasting rules, the Court held that Congress had delegated "not niggardly but expansive powers" over electronic media to the Commission and that a broad reading of the Act was required:

> Moreover, the Commission has reasonably concluded that regulatory authority over CATV is imperative if it is to perform with appropriate effectiveness certain of its other responsibilities. Congress has imposed upon the Commission the "obligation of providing a widely dispersed radio and television service," with a fair, efficient, and equitable distribution" of service among the "several States and communities." 47 U.S.C. § 307(b). . . . The Commission has concluded, and Congress has agreed, that these obligations require for their satisfaction the creation of a system of local broadcasting stations, such that "all communities of appreciable size [will] have at least one television station as an outlet for local self-expression." In turn the Commission has held that an appropriate system of local broadcasting may be created only if two subsidiary goals are realized. First, significantly wider use must be made of the available ultra-high-frequency channels. Second, communities must be encouraged "to launch sound and adequate programs to utilize the television channels now reserved for educational purposes." These subsidiary goals have received the endorsement of Congress.

> The Commission has reasonably found that the achievement of each of these purposes is "placed in jeopardy by the unregulated explosive growth of CATV." [ ] Although CATV may in some circumstances make possible "the realization of some of the [Commission's] most important goals," [ ], its importation of distant

signals into the service areas of local stations may also "destroy or seriously degrade the service offered by a television broadcaster," [ ], and thus ultimately deprive the public of the various benefits of a system of local broadcasting stations. In particular, the Commission feared that CATV might, by dividing the available audiences and revenues, significantly magnify the characteristically serious financial difficulties of UHF and educational television broadcasters. The Commission acknowledged that it could not predict with certainty the consequences of unregulated CATV, but reasoned that its statutory responsibilities demand that it "plan in advance of foreseeable events, instead of waiting to react to them." [ ] We are aware that these consequences have been variously estimated, but must conclude that there is substantial evidence that the Commission cannot "discharge its overall responsibilities without authority over this important aspect of television service." [ ]

The Commission has been charged with broad responsibilities for the orderly development of an appropriate system of local television broadcasting. The significance of its efforts can scarcely be exaggerated, for broadcasting is demonstrably a principal source of information and entertainment for a great part of the Nation's population. The Commission has reasonably found that the successful performance of these duties demands prompt and efficacious regulation of community antenna television systems. We have elsewhere held that we may not, "in the absence of compelling evidence that such was Congress' intention . . . prohibit administrative action imperative for the achievement of an agency's ultimate purposes." [ ] There is no such evidence here, and we therefore hold that the Commission's authority over "all interstate . . . communication by wire or radio" permits the regulation of CATV systems.

There is no need here to determine in detail the limits of the Commission's authority to regulate CATV. It is enough to emphasize that the authority which we recognize today under § 152(a) is restricted to that reasonably ancillary to the effective performance of the Commission's various responsibilities for the regulation of television broadcasting. The Commission may, for these purposes, issue "such rules and regulations and prescribe such restrictions and conditions, not inconsistent with law," as "public convenience, interest, or necessity requires." 47 U.S.C. § 303(r). We express no views as to the Commission's authority, if any, to regulate CATV under any other circumstances or for any other purposes.

Although *Southwestern Cable* established that the Commission did have jurisdiction over cable, it left unanswered the boundaries of that jurisdiction. The next challenge arose from the promulgation in the late 1960's of rules requiring larger cable systems to originate a certain amount of programming from their own resources. This requirement was upheld, 5-4, by the Supreme Court in United States v. Midwest

Video Corp. (Midwest Video I), 406 U.S. 649 (1972), on the ground that the regulation was "reasonably ancillary" to the FCC's obligations to regulate over-the-air television. Since cable operators had become enmeshed with television broadcasting, the FCC could require them to engage in the functional equivalent of broadcasting. Chief Justice Burger concurred but noted that the FCC's regulations "strain[ed] the outer limits of even the open-ended and pervasive jurisdiction that has evolved by decisions of the Commission and the Courts." Ironically, less than two years later, the FCC eliminated the origination requirement because it concluded that quality local programming could not be obtained by government mandate.

Instead, the Commission issued rules requiring new cable systems to allocate four of their 20 channels to public, educational, local government and leased access. The systems had to make equipment available for studio use by the public and could not control who might use the facilities or what they might say. Charges for use of the facilities were controlled. The court of appeals invalidated the regulations. Once again the Court was asked to define the limits of the Commission's jurisdiction in the case that has come to be called Midwest Video II.

## FEDERAL COMMUNICATIONS COMMISSION v. MIDWEST VIDEO CORPORATION

Supreme Court of the United States, 1979.
440 U.S. 689, 99 S.Ct. 1435, 59 L.Ed.2d 692.

MR. JUSTICE WHITE delivered the opinion of the Court.

In May 1976, the Federal Communications Commission promulgated rules requiring cable television systems that have 3,500 or more subscribers and carry broadcast signals to develop, at a minimum, a 20-channel capacity by 1986, to make available certain channels for access by third parties, and to furnish equipment and facilities for access purposes. [ ] The issue here is whether these rules are "reasonably ancillary to the effective performance of the Commission's various responsibilities for the regulation of television broadcasting," United States v. Southwestern Cable Co., 392 U.S. 157, 178 (1968), and hence within the Commission's statutory authority.

. . .

II

. . .

B

Because its access and capacity rules promote the long-established regulatory goals of maximization of outlets for local expression and diversification of programming—the objectives promoted by the rule sustained in *Midwest Video*—the Commission maintains that it plainly had jurisdiction to promulgate them. Respondents, in opposition, view the access regulations as an intrusion on cable system operations that is qualitatively different from the impact of the rule upheld in *Midwest Video*. Specifically, it is urged that by requiring the allocation of access channels to categories of users specified by the regulations and by depriving the cable operator of the power to select individual users or to control the programming on such channels, the regulations wrest a considerable degree of editorial control from the cable operator and in effect compel the cable system to provide a kind of common-carrier service. Respondents contend, therefore, that the regulations are not only qualitatively different from those heretofore approved by the courts, but also contravene statutory limitations designed to safeguard the journalistic freedom of broadcasters, particularly the command of § 3(h) of the Act that "a person engaged in . . . broadcasting shall not . . . be deemed a common carrier." 47 U.S.C. § 153(h).

We agree with respondents that recognition of agency jurisdiction to promulgate the access rules would require an extension of this Court's prior decisions. Our holding in *Midwest Video* sustained the Commission's authority to regulate cable television with a purpose affirmatively to promote goals pursued in the regulation of television broadcasting; and the plurality's analysis of the origination requirement stressed the requirement's nexus to such goals. But the origination rule did not abrogate the cable operators' control over the composition of their programming, as do the access rules. It compelled operators only to assume a more positive role in that regard, one comparable to that fulfilled by television broadcasters. Cable operators had become enmeshed in the field of television broadcasting, and, by requiring them to engage in the functional equivalent of broadcasting, the Commission had sought "only to ensure that [they] satisfactorily [met] community needs within the context of their undertaking." 406 U.S., at 670 (opinion of BRENNAN, J.).

With its access rules, however, the Commission has transferred control of the content of access cable channels from cable operators to members of the public who wish to communicate by the cable medium. Effectively, the Commission has relegated cable systems, *pro tanto*, to common-carrier status. A common-carrier service in the communications context is one that "makes a public offering to provide [communications facilities] whereby all members of the public who choose to employ such facilities may communicate or transmit intelligence of their own design and choosing. . . ." [ ] A common carrier does not "make individualized decisions, in particular cases, whether and on what terms to deal." [ ]

The access rules plainly impose common-carrier obligations on cable operators. . . . Indeed, in its early consideration of access obligations—whereby "CATV operators [would] furnish studio facilities and technical assistance [but] have no control over program content except as may be required by the Commission's rules and applicable law"—the Commission acknowledged that the result would be the operation of cable systems "as common carriers on some channels." . . . But the

Commission continues to insist that this characterization of the obligation imposed by the rules is immaterial to the question of its power to issue them; its authority to promulgate the rules is assured, in the Commission's view, so long as the rules promote statutory objectives.

Congress, however, did not regard the character of regulatory obligations as irrelevant to the determination of whether they might permissibly be imposed in the context of broadcasting itself. The Commission is directed explicitly by § 3(h) of the Act not to treat persons engaged in broadcasting as common carriers. . . .

. . .

"Congress' flat refusal to impose a 'common carrier' right of access for all persons wishing to speak out on public issues," [　], was perceived as consistent with other provisions of the 1934 Act evincing "a legislative desire to preserve values of private journalism." [　] Notable among them was § 326 of the Act, which enjoins the Commission from exercising " 'the power of censorship over the radio communications or signals transmitted by any radio station,' " and commands that " 'no regulation or condition shall be promulgated or fixed by the Commission which shall interfere with the right of free speech by means of radio communication.' " [　]

. . . The language of § 3(h) is unequivocal; it stipulates that broadcasters shall not be treated as common carriers. As we see it, § 3(h), consistently with the policy of the Act to preserve editorial control of programming in the licensee, forecloses any discretion in the Commission to impose access requirements amounting to common-carrier obligations on broadcast systems. The provision's background manifests a congressional belief that the intrusion worked by such regulation on the journalistic integrity of broadcasters would overshadow any benefits associated with the resulting public access. It is difficult to deny, then, that forcing broadcasters to develop a "nondiscriminatory system for controlling access . . . is precisely what Congress intended to avoid through § 3(h) of the Act." [　]

Of course, § 3(h) does not explicitly limit the regulation of cable systems. But without reference to the provisions of the Act directly governing broadcasting, the Commission's jurisdiction under § 2(a) would be unbounded. [　] Though afforded wide latitude in its supervision over communication by wire, the Commission was not delegated unrestrained authority. The Court regarded the Commission's regulatory effort at issue in *Southwestern* as consistent with the Act because it had been found necessary to ensure the achievement of the Commission's statutory responsibilities. Specifically, regulation was imperative to prevent interference with the Commission's work in the broadcast area. And in *Midwest Video* the Commission had endeavored to promote long-established goals of broadcasting regulation. Petitioners do not deny that statutory objectives pertinent to broadcasting bear on what the Commission might require cable systems to do. Indeed, they argue that the Commission's authority to promulgate the access rules derives from the relationship of those rules to the objectives discussed in *Midwest Video*. But they overlook the fact that Congress has restricted the Commission's ability to advance objectives associated with public access at the expense of the journalistic freedom of persons engaged in broadcasting.

That limitation is not one having peculiar applicability to television broadcasting. Its force is not diminished by the variant technology involved in cable transmissions. Cable operators now share with broadcasters a significant amount of editorial discretion regarding what their programming will include. As the Commission, itself, has observed, "both in their signal carriage decisions and in connection with their origination function, cable television systems are afforded considerable control over the content of the programming they provide." [  ]

In determining, then, whether the Commission's assertion of jurisdiction is "reasonably ancillary to the effective performance of [its] various responsibilities for the regulation of television broadcasting," United States v. Southwestern Cable Co., 392 U.S., at 178, we are unable to ignore Congress' stern disapproval—evidenced in § 3(h)—of negation of the editorial discretion otherwise enjoyed by broadcasters and cable operators alike. Though the lack of congressional guidance has in the past led us to defer—albeit cautiously—to the Commission's judgment regarding the scope of its authority, here there are strong indications that agency flexibility was to be sharply delimited.

The exercise of jurisdiction in *Midwest Video*, it has been said, "strain[ed] the outer limits" of Commission authority. [  ] In light of the hesitancy with which Congress approached the access issue in the broadcast area, and in view of its outright rejection of a broad right of public access on a common-carrier basis, we are constrained to hold that the Commission exceeded those limits in promulgating its access rules. The Commission may not regulate cable systems as common carriers, just as it may not impose such obligations on television broadcasters. We think authority to compel cable operators to provide common carriage of public-originated transmissions must come specifically from Congress.[19]

Affirmed.

### Notes and Questions

1.  In the early 1980's there were no serious challenges to the Commission's jurisdiction over cable, perhaps because the Commission changed its regulatory posture towards cable. As we will discuss later in this Chapter, the Commission began to eliminate its regulations governing cable in the late 1970's.

19. The court below suggested that the Commission's rules might violate the First Amendment rights of cable operators. Because our decision rests on statutory grounds, we express no view on that question, save to acknowledge that it is not frivolous and to make clear that the asserted constitutional issue did not determine or sharply influence our construction of the statute. . . . .

2.  In October, 1984, the jurisdictional question was settled when Congress passed the Cable Communications Policy Act of 1984. One of the provisions of the Cable Act amended § 152 of the Communications Act of 1934 to include within the FCC's jurisdiction "cable service to all persons engaged within the United States in providing such service, and to the facilities of cable operators which relate to such service, as provided in Title VI." 47 U.S.C. § 152. In addition, Title VI, Cable Communications, has been added to the Communications Act of 1934. 47 U.S.C. §§ 601–639. We will consider many of these provisions later in this Chapter. Thus, the Commission no longer has to derive its jurisdiction over cable from its jurisdiction over broadcasting, and courts will no longer have to determine whether a Commission rule is reasonably ancillary to its jurisdiction over broadcasting.

3.  The elimination of the Commission's mandatory access channels did not eliminate access channel requirements. Filling the vacuum were state and municipal requirements. Most cities demanded access channels and studios as a prerequisite for obtaining a cable franchise. Often these demands were more extensive than the FCC's had been.

In the Cable Communications Policy Act of 1984, Congress provided express authorization for access channel requirements. Section 611 states that access channels for public, educational, and governmental use can be required as part of a franchise proposal or a proposal for renewal. 47 U.S.C. § 611. Furthermore, a federal requirement to set aside some channels for commercial use by persons unaffiliated with the operator is imposed on all systems with 36 or more activated channels. The number of channels that must be set aside varies according to the size of the system. 47 U.S.C. § 612.

4.  The Court in *Midwest Video II* chose not to address the question of whether mandatory access channels violated the First Amendment. In 1983, a Rhode Island Public Utility Commission requirement that cable operators set aside at least seven channels for public access withstood a First Amendment challenge. Berkshire Cablevision of Rhode Island, Inc. v. Burke, 571 F.Supp. 976 (D.R.I.1983). The judge likened cable more to broadcasting than to newspapers. Berkshire's appeal was dismissed as moot. It had not been awarded any franchises and thus, was not affected by the regulations. More First Amendment challenges to access channel requirements are likely, especially now that Congress has authorized the imposition of access channel requirements.

## C.  SIGNAL CARRIAGE RULES AND COPYRIGHT PROBLEMS

All of the major challenges to the Commission's jurisdiction over cable resulted from the Commission's various signal carriage rules. Each of these rules was designed to protect local broadcasting from cable competition. We have already discussed the mandatory access requirements in great detail. We now turn to the other signal carriage rules.

## 1. Leapfrogging and Superstations

One of the earliest restrictions, called the anti-leap-frogging rule, provided that when it was permissible to import distant signals, the system had to select from among those nearest to the city in which the system was operating. The FCC deleted this rule in 1976. One result was the emergence of the so-called "superstation"—an independent television station that makes its programs available to cable systems throughout the country, via satellite transmission.

The most famous superstation is Ted Turner's Channel 17 in Atlanta, which has access to 200 live sporting events each year. By early 1985, the station was distributing its programs nationwide to 7,798 cable systems with 31.6 million subscribers. The satellite company charged the cable systems 10 cents per subscriber per month. The cable systems made the programs available as part of their basic monthly charge to attract subscribers.

Channel 17 prospered by increased charges for advertising on its programs that are now reaching up to 30 million more viewers than previously. In addition, Turner has begun substituting national commercials for local commercials in the feed he sends Southern Satellite Systems, Inc., the company that distributes Channel 17 nationally. Thus, there are now two versions of Channel 17. One is broadcast in Atlanta; the other is distributed to cable systems throughout the country. Current estimates are that 40 percent of the local commercials are replaced. Program suppliers have increased charges to Channel 17 because the program is reaching a much larger audience than it did before and cable distribution may result in reduced licensing fees or even preclude sales to local stations in cities receiving the cable program.

Other superstations have followed, but they lag behind the Atlanta enterprise, which had a two-year head start. Some, using wires instead of satellites, have become regional stations.

## 2. Exclusivity

### a. *Network Exclusivity*

To protect the local station when it was carrying network programs, the FCC promulgated exclusivity rules (formerly called non-duplication rules) to prevent cable from carrying an imported distant signal that was offering the same network program as the local network affiliate. First, the FCC required the cable system to black out the distant signal if the program was being broadcast on the same day as it was being presented by the local affiliate. Later, the FCC changed the rule to require blackout only if the two showings were at the same hour.

In the mid-1970's the Commission modified the black-out requirement, permitting cable systems to show the local station's signal (and its commercials) simultaneously on both the local channel and the channel that normally carries the distant signal, even though the local station might suffer if the local audience stays with the distant station after the program is over. This more limited protection survives.

### b.  Syndication Exclusivity

Another regulation protecting local stations had provided that cable systems in large markets could not carry distant signals showing programs to which a local station had acquired exclusive future local rights. The obvious concern underlying the syndicated program exclusivity rule was that the increased availability of the program would fragment the audience for the show. This was repealed in 1980, see p. 349, infra.

### 3.  COPYRIGHT PROBLEMS

One of the major factors influencing the Commission in its decisions governing signal carriage has been the application of copyright law to the retransmission of broadcast signals by cable operators. The question has always been whether or not cable operators should have to compensate either the broadcasters or the program producers for retransmission and, if so, how the compensation should be determined.

The issue first reached the Supreme Court in Fortnightly Corp. v. United Artists Television, Inc., 392 U.S. 390 (1968). The case involved a West Virginia cable operator who was retransmitting the signals of five broadcast television stations. The stations were all located between 50 and 85 miles from the cable system. Fortnightly provided no other service.

United Artists, which owned the copyright to various shows that were aired over the five broadcast stations, claimed that the retransmission constituted infringement of its copyrights. The Court held that retransmission was not a "performance," and thus, there was no infringement. The Court was unable to find a real distinction between a viewer's antenna system and the cable company's equipment. Both were designed to improve reception of the broadcast signals.

When cable systems started using microwaves to import signals from around the country, there was some question whether this would change the copyright issue. The Supreme Court decided that the fact that there was no way a non-cable subscriber could receive these signals using existing technology did not make a difference. "When a television broadcaster transmits a program, it has made public for simultaneous viewing and hearing the contents of that program. The privilege of receiving the broadcast electronic signals and of converting them into the sights and sounds of the program inheres in all members of the public who have the means of doing so. The reception and rechanneling of these signals for simultaneous viewing is essentially a viewer function, irrespective of the distance between the broadcast station and the ultimate viewer." Teleprompter Corporation v. Columbia Broadcasting System, 415 U.S. 394 (1974).

These copyright rulings greatly increased the importance to local broadcasters of the FCC signal carriage rules. The increased coverage afforded the imported signals was of minimal value to them, since their local advertisers had little or no interest in reaching consumers in other parts of the country. Meanwhile, the imported signals fragmented the local audiences, reducing the number of viewers they could offer to local advertisers.

There also was an apparent inequity in the system. Broadcasters had to pay royalties or license fees for much of their programming. Cable operators were paying nothing to distribute the exact same programming and were collecting a fee for doing so. The Copyright Act of 1976 attempted to remedy this seemingly unfair situation.

In the 1976 copyright statute, retransmission of broadcast signals by cable systems is defined as copyright infringement. However, the simultaneous retransmission, "secondary transmission," of broadcast signals is governed by a complex compulsory licensing scheme. Section 111 provides, in effect, that cablecasters need pay no royalties for programs on "local" (or "must-carry") stations that they were required to carry until September, 1985. (We will discuss the must-carry rules later in this Chapter.) Cablecasters are permitted to carry the copyrighted programs of "distant" (or "may-carry") stations without the owner's consent in return for the payment of a compulsory royalty fee. This fee is fixed by statute and depends on the size of the cable system and whether the distant station is commercial or educational.

The Act represented a compromise between the interests of broadcasters and cable operators. Although cable operators now had to pay for the right to retransmit broadcast programming, broadcasters were still unable to withhold the right to carry the programming.

Because of this inability to refuse transmission consent, certain stations found themselves unwilling superstations. As previously noted, the added audience resulting from the cable distribution is of little value to the broadcaster. The only way to benefit is to sell to national advertisers as opposed to local or regional advertisers. Meanwhile, there are several disadvantages to being a superstation, although Turner for one found them outweighed by the advantages. Program acquisition costs increase as a result of the increased audience. In addition, certain sports programming is unavailable because the importation of that programming into other areas of the country will violate agreements between the syndicator and the league or conference. For example, WTBS was unable to carry baseball playoff games involving the Atlanta Braves, even though the station that carries a team during the regular season is normally entitled to carry that team's playoff games. Importation of the games on WTBS into other markets would have conflicted with an agreement between the networks and professional baseball giving the networks exclusivity outside the markets of the teams participating in the playoffs.

A second controversy involves distribution of the royalties collected each year. Demands from the various claimants, such as program producers and syndicators, sports leagues, music groups, broadcast licensees themselves, and others, greatly exceed 100 percent. In September, 1980, the Tribunal allocated the 1978 revenues, giving 75 percent to program producers and syndicators, and 3.25 percent to commercial television broadcasters. This means that total copyright payments to all commercial television for programs carried during 1978 by cable systems amounted to $476,000.

The enactment of the Copyright Act of 1976 was soon followed by a change in the Commission's attitude toward cable. In 1980, the FCC repealed the distant signal limitations and syndicated program exclusivity rule. The Commission argued that there was no real evidence that repeal of the rules would seriously harm broadcasters. Furthermore, the new copyright act now provided compensation for the retransmission of those programs. Finally, with regard to syndicated program exclusivity, the viewers' interest in "time-diversity"—seeing programs when they wanted—was more compelling than the local station's interest in the exclusive programming. Deletion of the old rule would not reduce the supply of programs for television. The deletion of the rules was upheld in Malrite T.V. of New York v. Federal Communications Commission, 652 F.2d 1140 (2d Cir.1981), certiorari denied 454 U.S. 1143 (1982).

As a result of the FCC's repeal of the distant signal rules, the Tribunal raised the rates cable operators must pay for distant signals effective March 15, 1983. Large cable systems became liable for a compulsory license fee of 3.75 percent of their basic revenues for each distant signal added since June 24, 1981. This increase was upheld in National Cable Television Association v. Copyright Royalty Tribunal, 724 F.2d 176, 55 R.R.2d 387 (D.C.Cir.1983). In response, some cable operators dropped distant signals to reduce their copyright liability. Superstations were the major casualties.

As a result of these changes, fee distribution has also become more complicated. There are now three funds at stake: the basic royalties, the 3.75 percent fund which contains the fees for distant signals added after June 24, 1981, and the syndex fund which contains a surcharge adopted as a result of the repeal of the syndicated program exclusivity rules.

In mid-1985, proceedings were held to allocate the 1983 royalties. Broadcasters have requested 97 percent of the syndex fund and 19.4 percent of the other two funds. MPAA has requested 80 percent of the basic fund, 85 percent of the 3.75 percent fund and all of the syndex fund. Meanwhile, joint sports applicants have requested 20 percent of the basic fund and 30 percent of the 3.75 percent and PBS has requested 8 percent of each fund. As in previous years, several parties will obviously be disappointed. Broadcasting, July 29, 1985 at 51.

Broadcasters maintain that cable's contribution to the fund is tiny when compared with the fact that commercial television broadcasters spend some 35 percent of their budgets on program acquisition. Cable operators claim the current fees, after the recent rate hikes, are already prohibitive. Meanwhile, the FCC has asserted that any economic problem for the broadcasters derives from the Copyright Act or the Tribunal's allocation—and relief must come from those sources.

For years, the compulsory license and royalty provision has been under attack in Congress. The recent decision in the Quincy Cable case, p. 353, infra, has only intensified the pressure. The problem is that the 1976 Act did not contemplate the changes in FCC rules that have permitted the growth of superstations and increased carriage of distant signals. The result is that an increasing amount of cable programming is coming from distant sources, leaving the program suppliers with less control over geographical distribution of their products. Complaints are also being heard from major sports leagues because, for example, an Atlanta baseball game may be shown on a Boston area cable system at the same time another game is being played in Boston. In early 1985, the Atlanta Braves and New York Yankees agreed to pay the other major league teams a special annual fee based on the subscriber base of the superstations that carry their games. The New York Mets and Chicago Cubs, whose games are also carried by superstations, were expected to follow suit. Cablevision, Feb. 4, 1985 at 12.

Broadcasters have argued that the compulsory license should be abolished and replaced by a negotiated agreement between the cable system and the originating broadcaster (who, under contract, would need the consent of the copyright owner). This need not lead to individual negotiations—the matter could be handled the way song writers grant licenses and collect royalties, through such groups as ASCAP and BMI that grant bulk licenses for a fee and then distribute the proceeds according to a formula.

———

One of the requirements for coverage by the compulsory copyright license for secondary transmissions is that the signal be transmitted unaltered. In late 1985, the court of appeals upheld a ruling that Ted Turner's practice of substituting national commercials for local ones, p. 346, supra, does not cause Southern Satellite Systems, Inc. (SSS) to forfeit the compulsory license. The court held that Turner's microwave feed to SSS, which already contains the national commercials, is a primary transmission. Because SSS transmits this signal unaltered, it is covered by the compulsory license. Hubbard Broadcasting, Inc., which brought the suit has indicated that it will either petition the court of appeals for a rehearing or petition the Supreme Court for certiorari. Hubbard Broadcasting, Inc. v. Southern Satellite Systems, Inc., 777 F.2d 393 (8th Cir.1985).

### 4. THE ANTI-SIPHONING RULES

After an erratic early history, the Commission began to regulate pay systems' programs. The first major challenge of these regulations involved subscription television (STV).  In defending the regulations, the Commission noted that they were the result of a two-year test in Hartford, Connecticut.  The rules generally barred STV from showing any sports that were regularly carried on conventional television and also restricted showing of feature films that were more than three but less than 10 years old.  Also, commercials were barred, and no more than 90 percent of the programming could be movies and sports.  The Commission decided that although it had the authority to allocate scarce channels to a pay service, such a service would not be justifiable unless it presented programs that were not readily available on conventional television.  A second concern was that revenues from subscription operations might be sufficient to permit pay systems to bid away the most popular programs on conventional television, thus reducing the quality of conventional programming.  These regulations were upheld in National Ass'n of Theater Owners v. Federal Communications Commission, 420 F.2d 194 (D.C.Cir.1969), certiorari denied 397 U.S. 922 (1970).

The next major development was the promulgation of similar restrictions for pay cable origination.  These regulations, similar to those just mentioned for STV, were overturned in a lengthy opinion in Home Box Office Inc. v. Federal Communications Commission, 567 F.2d 9 (D.C.Cir. 1977), certiorari denied 434 U.S. 829 (1977).  In the consolidated proceeding, involving 15 cases, the Commission's pay cable regulations, previously aimed at preventing cable from "siphoning" programs from "free" commercial television, were now said to be intended to prevent the "migration" of such programs from "free" television to cable.

The Court in *Home Box Office* found that the connection between the perceived threat to broadcasting and the anti-siphoning rules was insufficient to justify them under the "reasonably ancillary to broadcasting" standard.  Therefore, they held the rules were beyond the Commission's jurisdiction.

Although the lack of jurisdiction alone would necessitate rejection of the Commission's action, the court decided to consider the merits of the rules.

Here the court found insufficient evidence to support the claim that pay cable would bar popular programs to the conventional audience. Rather, the court assumed that pay cable would sell these programs for use by conventional broadcasters.  The court was more concerned about the problem of the poor since pay cable would demand exclusive rights— at least for first presentation.  But the court concluded that it was not clear that the popularity of films declined "with an increase in the interval between first theater exhibition and first television broadcast." The conclusion was that as to movies, at least, migration would not hurt the poor "very much."  Also, the court noted that the Commission's exclusion of advertising on pay cable hurt the poor because it prevented cablecasters from experimenting with a combined revenue system that allowed lower program fees together with some advertising.  But all this was speculation; the record was silent and could not support these restrictions on cable.

Addressing the constitutional question, the court started by rejecting the contention that cable's First Amendment rights were governed by *Red Lion,* supra. This left the question of what constituted permissible restrictions on cable. "The absence in cable television of the physical restraints of the electromagnetic spectrum does not, however, automatically lead to the conclusion that no regulation of cable television is valid."

The court drew a distinction between regulation aimed at suppression of free speech and regulation where the restriction on speech is incidental to the purpose of the regulation. Cases involving the latter situation are governed by a test first set out in United States v. O'Brien, p. 21, supra: "If such regulations '[1] further an important or substantial governmental interest; . . . and [2] if the incidental restriction on alleged First Amendment freedoms is no greater than is essential to the furtherance of that interest,' [  ] (bracketed numbers added), then the regulations are valid."

Applying the test to the anti-siphoning rules, the court found them "grossly overbroad." For example, the rules restricted the exhibition on cable of many films that were clearly unsuitable for broadcast television. Furthermore, there was no real evidence that siphoning was a serious threat to broadcasting. "Where the First Amendment is concerned, creation of such a rebuttable presumption of siphoning without clear record support is simply impermissible."

### 5.   MUST-CARRY RULES

One of the earliest signal carriage rules was a requirement that cable systems retransmit the signal of any local television station or "significantly viewed" station that requested carriage. Cable systems were allowed to request a waiver of the rule where it created hardship, but the process was a slow one, and few waivers were granted. The "must-carry" rules imposed a special hardship on the smaller systems as most of the channels could be occupied by must-carry channels. Due to overlapping signals, some systems were forced to carry several affiliates of the same network or similarly duplicative stations to the exclusion of other non-duplicative services.

As with the other rules, the purpose was to protect local broadcasters, especially UHF stations, whose picture quality was noticeably inferior to that provided by cable. There was also concern that people would remove their television antennas upon subscribing to cable, or at the very least fail to maintain them, putting broadcasters not carried by the cable system at a great competitive disadvantage.

After the compulsory scheme was enacted in the Copyright Act of 1976, many believed that it was a trade-off for the must-carry rules. Although the legislative history on this issue is inconclusive, many cable operators were reluctant to challenge the must-carry rules for fear of losing the compulsory license.

However, in 1980, Turner Broadcasting System petitioned the Commission to institute rulemaking proceedings to delete the must-carry rules. TBS argued that the rules violated the First Amendment rights of cable operators and furthermore, that at the very least extensive changes in the broadcast and cable industries since the promulgation of the rules required a re-examination of the rules. The Commission denied the TBS petition.

Meanwhile, the FCC ordered Quincy Cable Television Inc., operator of a cable system in Quincy, Washington, to carry the signals of various Spokane, Washington television stations and fined it $5,000 for failing to do so. Quincy Cable's appeal of the order and the fine was consolidated with TBS's appeal resulting in what may be one of the most important decisions involving cable television.

## QUINCY CABLE TV, INC. v. FEDERAL COMMUNICATIONS COMMISSION

United States Court of Appeals, District of Columbia Circuit, 1985.
768 F.2d 1434, 58 R.R.2d 977.

Before WRIGHT, GINSBURG, and BORK, CIRCUIT JUDGES.

WRIGHT, CIRCUIT JUDGE:

FCC regulations require cable television operators, upon request and without compensation, to transmit to their subscribers every over-the-air television broadcast signal that is "significantly viewed in the community" or otherwise considered local under the Commission's rules. 47 C.F.R. §§ 76.57–76.61 (1984). Alleging that these mandatory carriage or "must-carry" rules violate the First Amendment rights of cable programmers, cable operators, and the viewing public, Turner Broadcasting Systems, Inc. (TBS), the owner of a variety of cable services, petitioned the FCC to institute rulemaking procedures to delete the offending regulations. Although acknowledging that the challenged rules deprive cable programmers of access to some audiences and "compel carriage of broadcast signals in place of alternate programming that subscribers, if given a choice, might otherwise choose," the Commission denied TBS's petition. [ ] TBS now petitions for review of that denial. In a separate action, Quincy Cable Television, Inc. (Quincy), the operator of a cable system in Quincy, Washington, petitions for review of an FCC order requiring it to carry the signals of several local broadcast stations and imposing a $5,000 "forfeiture" for its failure to do so.

In the course of reviewing those petitions, we have concluded and now hold that the must-carry rules are fundamentally at odds with the First Amendment and, as currently drafted, can no longer be permitted to stand.

## I. BACKGROUND

The Supreme Court has repeatedly stressed that "[e]ach medium of expression . . . must be assessed for First Amendment purposes by standards suited to it, for each may present its own problems." [   ] Mindful that in applying the broad principles of the First Amendment to new media we must remain sensitive to the "differing natures, values, abuses and dangers" of each method of expression, [   ], we examine in detail the nature of cable television technology, the history and purposes of the FCC's regulation of that technology, and prior judicial assessments of the constitutionality of that regulation.

### A. *Cable Television Regulation and the Origins and Purposes of the Must-Carry Rules*

#### 1.

[The court started by distinguishing cable television from broadcasting on both technological and economic grounds. The court then turned to the evolution of the FCC's signal carriage rules.]

The Commission's objective was not merely to protect an established industry from the encroachment of an upstart young competitor, although such a result was clearly the byproduct of the regulatory posture that developed. Rather, the Commission took the position that without the power to regulate cable it could not discharge its statutory obligation to provide for "fair, efficient, and equitable" distribution of service among "the several States and communities." 47 U.S.C. § 307(b) (1982). [   ] If permitted to grow unfettered, the Commission feared, cable might well supplant ordinary broadcast television. A necessary consequence of such displacement would be to undermine the FCC's mandate to allocate the broadcast spectrum in a manner that best served the public interest. In particular, if an unregulated, unlicensed cable industry were to threaten the economic viability of broadcast television, the Commission would be powerless to effect what it saw (and continues to see) as one of its cardinal objectives: the development of a "system of [free] local broadcasting stations, such that 'all communities of appreciable size [will] have at least one television station as an outlet for local self-expression.' " [   ]

#### 2.

Almost from the beginning, the must-carry rules were a centerpiece of the FCC's efforts to actively oversee the growth of cable television. Then, as now, the applicability of the rules varied according to such factors as the quality of the broadcast signal available in the community. In general, however, the rules required cable operators, upon request, to carry any broadcast signal considered local under the Commission's complex formula. Affected parties could petition for a waiver from their must-carry obligations, but the rules themselves drew few lines. They required carriage of every local or significantly viewed signal irrespective of the number of must-carry channels already being transmitted, the degree of programming duplication, or the channel capacity of a cable system.

Although the economic analysis initially advanced in support of the must-carry rules was somewhat complicated, the Commission's general objective was straightforward: to assure that the advent of cable technology not undermine the financial viability of free, community-oriented television. If cable were to "drive out television broadcasting service," the Commission reasoned, "the public as a whole would lose far more—in free service, in service to outlying areas, and in local service with local control and selection of programs—than it would gain." [ ] The must-carry rules, together with a comprehensive body of related regulations, would channel the development of the nascent cable industry to limit the risks it might pose to conventional broadcasting, "society's chosen instrument for the provision of video services." [ ]

At the time of the initial promulgation of the rules, the Commission acknowledged that it had insufficient data to "predict with reliability" the extent of the risk posed by cable. [ ] But the economic analysis posited by the broadcasting industry (and now espoused by the Commission) painted a dire picture. [ ] The profitability of local commercial television is dependent on the number of viewers in the audience. Self-evidently, an advertiser will pay less per unit of air time as viewership decreases. If a significant percentage of viewers subscribe to cable *and* if subscribers view cable to the exclusion of broadcast television, the audience will become fragmented. "A gain of a subscriber to the [cable] system will in most cases mean the effective loss of a potential viewer for the local station." [ ] With access to a smaller (often less affluent) market, advertisers will pay less for air time and profits will decline, a consequence that both discourages others from seeking a broadcast license and, in the extreme case, might even result in financial failure of some existing stations. Only if local broadcasters were assured access to the whole of their allocated audience, the FCC believed, could the risk of audience fragmentation and the concomitant threat to free, local television be forestalled.

A central premise of this analysis was that a significant proportion of cable subscribers would cease to view local television unless such signals were carried by the cable system. At first blush, as the cable industry vigorously pointed out, this assumption was somewhat counter-intuitive. Almost without exception, the must-carry rules only mandate carriage of signals that can already be picked up off the air. . . . Thus, in principle, a cable subscriber with little or no effort could still view local broadcasts even without the benefit of the must-carry rules. If that were the case, cable's gain would not necessarily mean broadcast television's loss, and the Commission's reasoning would be deprived of its major premise.

But, as the FCC pointed out when it first enacted the rules, the technical availability of off-air signals does not necessarily defeat the assumption that without the must-carry rules a significant number of cable subscribers might curtail their viewing of local broadcast television. . . . [L]ocal signals are available to the subscriber only if the antenna remains attached. Yet, the Commission observed, one of the main selling points of cable is the prospect of dispensing with unsightly or expensive antennas. [ ] Finally, even if the antenna remains in place, cable retransmission of UHF signals usually provides a far clearer picture than is available off-air. Thus, the Commission suggested, without the benefit of must-carry UHF stations would be at a significant competitive disadvantage. [ ]

In sum, at the time of their original promulgation the Commission viewed the must-carry rules as critical stones in the regulatory bulwark erected to guard against destruction of free, community-oriented television. By forcing cable systems to carry local and significantly viewed broadcast signals, the Commission sought to channel the growth of cable in a manner consistent with the public's interest in the preservation of local broadcasting.

3.

When it first promulgated the must-carry rules in the mid–1960's, the Commission recognized that it could not prove the factual predicates of its analysis. Although frankly relying on its "collective instinct" and "intuition," [ ], it concluded that it would be inconsistent with its responsibilities to "withhold action until indisputable proof of irreparable damage to the public interest in television broadcasting has been compiled—i.e., by waiting 'until the bodies pile up' before conceding that the problem exists." [ ]

In the ensuing years the Commission has repeatedly repromulgated and fine-tuned the must-carry rules. [ ] It has, however, never reconsidered or seriously questioned the elaborate and concededly speculative premises on which its economic defense of the rules rests.

This approach is in sharp contrast to the Commission's treatment of several components of the regulatory framework imposed in the early years of its regulation of cable television. After conducting a comprehensive economic analysis based on a detailed and highly sophisticated examination of a number of discrete television markets, the Commission eliminated the distant-signal-carriage and syndicated-exclusivity rules. Like the must-carry rules, the deleted regulations were originally promulgated to protect broadcast television from competition from the expanding cable industry. [ ]

In the context of this wide-ranging deregulatory effort, the Commission acknowledged a radical shift in its perception of the role of cable in the array of viewing options available in a given community. Abandoning its initial view of cable as an auxiliary service that merely supplemented broadcasting by improving reception in outlying areas, the

Commission now recognized cable as a legitimate, independent vehicle for providing alternative video services to the public. [ ] With respect to the specific question of the continued value of the distant-signal and syndicated-exclusivity rules, the Commission found that its general economic analysis had failed to substantiate the intuitive fears on which the rules had been premised since the mid-1960's.

.  .  .

Stating that the comprehensive nature of its analysis enabled it to speak "with a clarity which is uncommon in matters of public policy," the Commission found that "continued regulatory intervention is not merely unnecessary, it is counterproductive." [ ]

.  .  .

## II.  THE FIRST AMENDMENT: STANDARD OF REVIEW

.  .  .

### A.  *The Scarcity Rationale*

It has become something of a truism to observe that "differences in the characteristics of new media justify differences in the First Amendment standards applied to them." Red Lion Broadcasting Co. v. FCC, 395 U.S. at 386. [ ] The suggestion is not that traditional First Amendment doctrine falls by the wayside when evaluating the protection due novel modes of communication. For the core values of the First Amendment clearly transcend the particular details of the various vehicles through which messages are conveyed. Rather, the objective is to recognize that those values are best served by paying close attention to the distinctive features that differentiate the increasingly diverse mechanisms through which a speaker may express his view.

.  .  .

As this and other courts have recognized, the "scarcity rationale" has no place in evaluating government regulation of cable television.

> The First Amendment theory espoused in *National Broadcasting Co.* and reaffirmed in *Red Lion Broadcasting Co.* cannot be directly applied to cable television since an essential precondition of that theory—physical interference and scarcity requiring an umpiring role for government—is absent.  .  .  .

Home Box Office, Inc. v. FCC, supra, 567 F.2d at 45. See also Preferred Communications, Inc. v. City of Los Angeles, 754 F.2d at 1404; [ ].

Nor do we discern other attributes of cable television that would justify a standard of review analogous to the more forgiving First Amendment analysis traditionally applied to the broadcast media. We cannot agree, for example, that the mere fact that cable operators require use of a public right of way—typically utility poles—somehow justifies lesser First Amendment scrutiny. [ ] The potential for disruption inherent in stringing coaxial cables above city streets may well warrant some governmental regulation of the process of installing and maintaining the cable system. But hardly does it follow that such regulation could extend to controlling the nature of the programming that is conveyed over that system. No doubt a municipality has some power to control the placement of newspaper vending machines. But any effort to use that power as the basis for dictating what must be placed in such machines would surely be invalid.

Nor, on this record, can we concur in the "natural monopoly characteristics" of cable create economic constraints on competition comparable to the physical constraints imposed by the limited size of the electromagnetic spectrum. [  ] At the outset, the "economic scarcity" argument rests on the entirely unproven—and indeed doubtful—assumption that cable operators are in a position to exact monopolistic charges. [  ] Moreover, the tendency toward monopoly, if present at all, may well be attributable more to governmental action—particularly the municipal franchising process—than to any "natural" economic phenomenon. [  ] In any case, whatever the outcome of the debate over the monopolistic characteristics of cable, the Supreme Court has categorically rejected the suggestion that purely economic constraints on the number of voices available in a given community justify otherwise unwarranted intrusions into First Amendment rights. Miami Herald Publishing Co. v. Tornillo, 418 U.S. 241, 247–256 (1974). While *Miami Herald* involved the conventional press, as this court has had prior occasion to observe, there is no meaningful "distinction between cable television and newspapers on this point." Home Box Office, Inc. v. FCC, 567 F.2d at 46.

Indeed, once one has cleared the conceptual hurdle of recognizing that all forms of television need not be treated as a generic unity for purposes of the First Amendment, the analogy to more traditional media is compelling.  .  .  .

In sum, beyond the obvious parallel that both cable and broadcast television impinge on the senses via a video receiver, the two media differ in constitutionally significant ways. In light of cable's virtually unlimited channel capacity, the standard of First Amendment review reserved for occupants of the physically scarce airwaves is plainly inapplicable. Accordingly, we must look elsewhere to determine the appropriate yardstick against which to measure the constitutionality of the must-carry rules.

### B. *The Appropriateness of Treating the Must-Carry Rules as an Incidental Burden on Speech*

That cable television shares attributes of the more traditional press does not, of course, suggest that the First Amendment interposes an impermeable bulwark against any regulation. As the *Home Box Office* court observed, for cable, no less than for other media, the First Amendment draws a distinction between "incidental" burdens on speech—regulations that evince a governmental interest unrelated to the suppression or protection of a particular set of ideas—and restrictions that are "intended to curtail expression—either directly by banning speech because of . . . its communicative or persuasive effect on its intended audience . . . or indirectly by favoring certain classes of speakers over others . . . ."  567 F.2d at 47–48.

If the regulation falls in the former category, it will be sustained if "it furthers an important or substantial governmental interest . . . and if the incidental restriction on alleged First Amendment freedoms is no greater than is essential to the furtherance of that interest."  United States v. O'Brien, supra, 391 U.S. at 377.  [  ]  If, however, the regulation cannot fairly be understood as a merely incidental restriction on expression, the regulation will be upheld, if at all, only if the government adequately carries a significantly heavier burden of justification.  Indeed, some governmental objectives—"such as a desire to suppress support for a minority party or an unpopular cause, or to exclude the expression of certain points of view from the marketplace of ideas— . . . are so plainly illegitimate" that they are forbidden altogether. [  ]

Thus, the threshold question before us, as before the court in *Home Box Office*, is whether the intrusion worked by the challenged regulations merits treatment as an "incidental" burden on speech.  . . .

In one sense, of course, as is invariably the case, the government can frame the interest served by the must-carry rules in essentially speech-neutral terms.  So framed, the rules' object is to assure that the rise of a potentially monolithic national television industry not undermine the economic vitality of free, locally-controlled broadcasting.

Yet even so understood, the Commission's objective is a far cry from the sort of interests that typically have been viewed as imposing a merely "incidental" burden on speech.  Although not intended to suppress or protect any particular viewpoint, the rules are explicitly designed to "favor certain classes of speakers over others."  Home Box Office, Inc. v. FCC, supra, 567 F.2d at 48.  Their very purpose is to bolster the fortunes of local broadcasters even if the inevitable consequence of implementing that goal is to create an overwhelming competitive advantage over cable programmers.  [  ]  Under the protective aegis of the rules, local broadcasters are guaranteed the right to convey their messages over the cable system while cable programmers must vie for a proportionally diminished number of channels.  In the case of systems saturated with mandatory signals, cable programmers are shut out entirely from the only forum capable of conveying their programming.  Because "the concept that government may restrict the speech of some elements of society in order to enhance the relative voice of others is wholly foreign to the First Amendment," Buckley v. Valeo, 424 U.S. 1, 48–49 (1976), the conclusion that the must-carry rules burden First Amendment rights only incidentally is far from inevitable.

Viewed from the perspective of the cable operator, the entity that delivers a preselected package of channels to paying subscribers, the must-carry rules are equally intrusive.  The rules coerce speech; they require the operator to carry the signals of local broadcasters regardless of their content and irrespective of whether the operator considers them appropriate programming for the community it serves. The difficulty is not so much that the rules force operators to act as a mouthpiece for ideological perspectives they do not share, [   ], although such a result is by no means implausible.[38] The more certain injury stems from the substantial limitations the rules work on the operator's otherwise broad discretion to select the programming it offers its subscribers. See Miami Herald Co. v. Tornillo, supra, 418 U.S. 241 (recognizing First Amendment protection of editorial discretion).

. . .

Indeed, in the context of reviewing the FCC's power to promulgate regulations mandating public access to cable channels, the Supreme Court explicitly acknowledged the breadth of the editorial judgment exercised by cable operators. Midwest II, 440 U.S. at 707–708 n. 17. No less than the access regulations at issue in *Midwest II*, the must-carry rules "significantly compromise" the cable operator's editorial discretion: "Even when not occasioning the displacement of alternative programming, compelling cable operators indiscriminately to accept . . . programming will interfere with their determinations regarding the total service offering to be extended to subscribers." Id. Moreover, unlike access rules, which serve countervailing First Amendment values by providing a forum for public or governmental authorities, the must-carry rules transfer control to local broadcasters who already have a delivery mechanism granted by the government without cost and capable of bypassing the cable system altogether.

That the intrusion into cable operators' editorial autonomy is deep does not, of course, require the conclusion that the rules are inappropriate for analysis under the *O'Brien* test. [   ] Nonetheless, the Supreme Court's prior treatment of other laws and regulations that impinged on the editorial function engenders at least some doubt about the appropriateness of shunting the must-carry rules onto the analytical track reserved for other incidental burdens on expression. . . .

. . .

In short, our examination of the purposes that underlie the must-carry rules, the nature and degree of the intrusions they effect, and prior judicial treatment of analogous regulations leaves us with serious doubts about the propriety of applying the standard of review reserved for incidental burdens on speech. Although the goal of the rules—preserving local broadcasting—can be viewed as unrelated to the suppression or protection of any particular set of ideas, the rules nonetheless profoundly affect values that lie near the heart of the First Amendment. They favor one group of speakers over another. They severely impinge on editorial discretion. And, most importantly, if a system's channel capacity is substantially or completely occupied by mandatory signals, the rules prevent cable programmers from reaching their intended audience even

---

**38.** One operator recently objected to the carriage of the religious programming of a local broadcaster. [   ] The Commission denied the requested waiver.

if that result directly contravenes the preference of cable subscribers. Indeed, as a matter of established regulatory policy, the Commission considers the desires of cable subscribers to be irrelevant to the application of the rules. [ ] This conscious disregard of subscribers' viewing preferences is difficult, if not impossible, to reconcile with the Supreme Court's repeated admonition that the interests of viewers should be considered "paramount" in the First Amendment calculus. Red Lion Broadcasting Co. v. FCC, supra, 395 U.S. at 390. While, of course, viewers of broadcast television also have significant First Amendment interests, we doubt very much that cable subscribers "can[ ] be left out of the equation" entirely. Community Communications Co. v. City of Boulder, 660 F.2d 1370, 1376 n. 5 (10th Cir.1981), certiorari denied, 456 U.S. 1001 (1982).

We need not, however, definitively decide whether a more exacting standard than that announced in *O'Brien* and applied in *Home Box Office* is the correct test for evaluating the constitutionality of the must-carry rules. For even if we assume that the regulations burden speech only incidentally and therefore can pass muster under the First Amendment if they "further[ ] an important or substantial governmental interest" and impose a restriction "no greater than is essential to the furtherance of that interest," Home Box Office, Inc. v. FCC, supra, 567 F.2d at 48, we have concluded that the must-carry regulations, as written, are clearly impermissible.

## III. THE STANDARD APPLIED

### A.  *The Substantiality of the Governmental Interest*

The Commission contends that the must-carry rules serve the interest of preserving free, locally-oriented television. The difficult question whether, taken as an abstract proposition, that interest is sufficiently weighty to warrant the rules' interference with First Amendment rights must await resolution in another case. For even if we accept the common wisdom that the goal of encouraging "localism" qualifies as "important or substantial," United States v. O'Brien, supra, 391 U.S. at 377, we would be unable to find that the FCC has carried its heavy burden of justification.

.   .   .

### I.

In a burst of deregulatory activity unparalleled in its history, the FCC has recently dismantled large portions of the extensive regulatory structure under which both broadcast and cable television have labored for many decades. [ ] Details aside, the thrust of this movement has been the Commission's belief that the public interest in diverse video options is best served by deferring to the marketplace. [ ] As part of this comprehensive endeavor, the Commission has eliminated numerous regulations which, like the must-carry rules, were premised on the desire to protect local broadcasters from competition from the expanding cable industry. [   ] In addition, it has authorized a wide array of new multichannel video competitors to over-the-air broadcast television and exempted them from any obligation to carry local programming. [   ]

. . .

2.

But even if we accept that the Commission's position that it continues to stand by the economic assumptions on which the must-carry rules are premised, we would still be unable to conclude that it has adequately carried its heavy burden of justification. For if the FCC has not repudiated the rules' underlying assumptions, neither has it proved them.

. . .

For many of its cable regulations, the Commission, with admirable vigor and creativity, has met its acknowledged responsibility to move beyond unsubstantiated intuition. For the must-carry rules, however, the Commission's promise "to get the facts" remains unfulfilled. [   ] In the past two decades since the rules' original promulgation, the Commission has never seriously examined any of the admittedly speculative links in the chain of reasoning advanced in support of the rules. In particular, it has never sought support for the assumptions that are the linchpins of its analysis: (1) that without protective regulations cable subscribers would cease to view locally available off-the-air television either because they would disconnect their antennas or because the inconvenience of a switching device would deter them; and (2) that even if some cable subscribers did abandon local television, they would do so in sufficient numbers to affect the economic vitality of local broadcasting. Indeed, as noted above, to the extent the Commission has addressed these issues at all, it has questioned their validity.

In short, here, no less than in *Home Box Office*, the FCC has failed to "put itself in a position to know" whether the problem the rule seeks to cure—the destruction of free, local television—"is a real or merely a fanciful threat." 567 F.2d at 50. That approach, we have concluded, falls far short of the burden the government must affirmatively bear to prove the substantiality of the interest served by the rules. [   ] Although in some instances "complete factual support . . . for the Commission's judgment or prediction is not possible or required," FCC v. National Citizens Committee for Broadcasting, 436 U.S. 775, 814 (1978), as we now explain, the particular circumstances of this constitutional challenge make continued deference to the Commission's concededly unsupported determinations plainly inappropriate.

We note first that, in sharp and unexplained contrast to its defense of the must-carry rules, the Commission itself now applies a far more rigorous standard of proof before crediting the broadcast industry's inevitable refrain that regulation is essential to protect it from the deleterious effects of new video technologies. As a matter of explicit agency policy, the Commission will consider such regulation only if presented with "hard evidence" that the new technology "will have a critically adverse effect on existing broadcast service." [ ] "[S]peculative allegations concerning possible reductions in service from other sources" simply will not do. . . . In light of the Commission's express unwillingness to premise intrusive regulations on unsubstantiated speculation, we find it difficult to sustain the suggestion that we defer to the Commission's admittedly unproven belief that the must-carry rules in fact serve the substantial interest of protecting local broadcasting.

Moreover, this is demonstrably not an instance in which "complete factual support . . . for the Commission's judgment or prediction is not possible . . . ." FCC v. National Citizens Committee for Broadcasting, supra, 436 U.S. at 814. When the FCC first asserted jurisdiction 20 years ago, the cable industry was in its infancy and its impact on local broadcasting could not be gauged with accuracy. In that historical context, courts faced with nonconstitutional claims concerning the breadth of the FCC's jurisdiction consistently and appropriately deferred to the Commission's admittedly speculative fears that the advent of cable television would displace local broadcasting. See, e.g., United States v. Southwestern Cable Co., supra, 392 U.S. at 175. Nearly two decades have now passed, and the Commission has shown itself capable of the most sophisticated analysis of the effects of cable on conventional television. [ ] And yet, even in the context of a serious constitutional challenge, a context in which it must affirmatively bear the burden of proof, [ ], it continues to rely on precisely the kind of "speculative allegations" it expressly refuses to credit elsewhere. [ ] At some point, especially where First Amendment rights are at stake, the Commission must do more than ask us to defer to its "more or less intuitive model" and "collective instinct" to sustain its assertion that a rule is both necessary and important. [ ] Where, as here, the Commission itself has expressly acknowledged that its regulatory promises are susceptible of empirical proof and, in fact, has demanded such proof as a prerequisite of regulation in analogous contexts, we believe that point has passed.

We reiterate that this case has not required us to decide whether, as an abstract proposition, the preservation of free, local television service qualifies as a substantial and important governmental interest. We hold only that in the particular circumstances of this constitutional challenge the Commission has failed adequately to demonstrate that an unregulated cable industry poses a serious threat to local broadcasting and, more particularly, that the must-carry rules in fact serve to alleviate that threat. Should the Commission move beyond its "more or less intuitive model," as it clearly has the capacity to do, we would be extremely hesitant to second-guess its expert judgment. As long as it continues to rely on wholly speculative and unsubstantiated assumptions, however, our powerful inclination to defer to the agency in its area of expertise must be tempered by our duty to assure that the government not infringe First Amendment freedoms unless it has adequately borne its heavy burden of justification. That, we have determined the Commission has not done.

## B. *The Congruence Between Means and Ends*

Even were we to conclude that the Commission adequately demonstrated the substantiality of the interest served by the must-carry rules, we could uphold their validity only if the restriction on activity protected by the First Amendment were "no greater than is essential to the furtherance of that interest." Home Box Office, Inc. v. FCC, supra, 567 F.2d at 48, quoting United States v. O'Brien, supra, 391 U.S. at 377. The task of evaluating the constitutional sufficiency of the congruence between the government's means and its ends is often a delicate one. On the one hand, we must, at the very least, make sure that the challenged regulation not gratuitously impinge on protected activity that poses no threat to the interest the agency is seeking to further. [ ] On the other hand, we must be careful not to lose sight of our proper role in the constitutional scheme. As this court recently had occasion to observe, our duty to police the First Amendment's requirement that intrusive governmental action be narrowly tailored to the evil sought to be corrected does not imply the authority to "finetune" administrative regulations. [ ] An agency typically has broad discretion over the manner in which it endeavors to effect its public interest objectives. Once we have determined that the agency action falls within the wide range of constitutionally permissible regulatory options, our task is at an end.

Fully aware of the breadth of the agency's discretion and the concomitant limits on the scope of our review, our analysis leaves us with no doubt that the must-carry rules, as currently drafted, represent a "fatally overbroad response" to the perceived fear that cable will displace free, local television. [ ] We stress that "[w]e are not quibbling over fine-tuning . . . ." For, as we now show, it is difficult to imagine a less discriminating or more overinclusive means of furthering the Commission's stated objectives.

1.

In the Commission's own words, the must-carry rules are designed to "maintain the availability of local broadcast service to both those who [are] cable subscribers and those who [are] not." [ ] The goal is to assure that "as many communities as possible . . . have the opportunity of enjoying the advantages that derive from having local outlets that will be responsive to local needs." [ ] Thus, and the distinction is critical, the rules seek to protect local broadcast*ing* and not local broadcast*ers*. As the Commission itself acknowledges, it "cannot reject a new [video] service solely because its entry will reduce the revenues or profits of existing licensees. . . . 'Plainly, it is not the purpose of the [Communications] Act to protect a licensee against competition but to protect the public.' " DBS Inquiry, 90 F.C.C.2d at 689, quoting FCC v. Sanders Brothers Radio Station, 309 U.S. 470, 475 (1940). . . .

2.

But, if the goal is to preserve "localism" and not "local broadcast-ers," the must-carry rules are "grossly" overinclusive.  Home Box Office, Inc. v. FCC, supra, 567 F.2d at 50.  The rules indiscriminately protect each and every broadcaster regardless of the quantity of local service available in the community and irrespective of the number of local outlets already carried by the cable operator.  The 18th station is entitled to carriage no less than the first even if its programming is virtually duplicative of the viewing fare already transmitted over the cable system.  Indeed, it is entitled to carriage even if it carries no local programming at all.

We readily acknowledge that it is for the Commission as Congress' delegate and not this court to address the essentially legislative question of the optimal amount of local service or programming in a given community.  But in the context of the must-carry rules the FCC has simply never grappled with this issue.  The rules themselves suggest an implicit determination that "more is better," but in those rare instances in which the Commission has intimated its views it has never taken so absolute a position.  Indeed, in its most recent and comprehensive exposition of its regulatory objectives the Commission suggested that its goal was to preserve "a modicum of local programming," an objective significantly narrower than the undifferentiated sweep the must-carry rules would suggest.  [  ]  It is far from clear to us how a community that already has 17 local broadcast stations carried over the cable systems is not already "enjoying the advantages that derive from having local outlets that will be responsive to local needs."  [  ]

It may well be that in some circumstances requiring carriage of the 18th broadcast station is consistent with the objective of preserving free, community-oriented television.  And we certainly do not mean to imply that there is such a thing as too many communicative outlets in a given community.  It is not the fact of the 18th station that is troubling, but the fact that it is guaranteed a channel even if carriage effectively bumps a cable programmer, regardless of the extent it impinges on the cable operator's editorial autonomy, and irrespective of whether it thwarts viewer preferences.  Given the substantial First Amendment costs implicit in this sweeping guarantee, the Commission must make some effort to move beyond the amorphous in defining the interest served by the must-carry rules.  Until it establishes a baseline for its general objective of preserving free, community-oriented television— measured by the number of local broadcast stations in the community, the amount of local programming, or any other criterion within its discretion to choose—we simply cannot know whether the rules are adequately tailored to pass constitutional muster.  In this circumstance, the Commission has fallen far short of *its* "affirmative obligation" to show the requisite fit between means and ends.  [  ]

3.

In addition to their complete indifference to the quantity of local television already available either over the air or on the cable system itself, the rules' overinclusiveness lies in their indiscriminate protection of every broadcaster regardless of whether or to what degree the affected cable system poses a threat to its economic well-being. Indeed, the Commission has expressly taken the position that the "financial health" of the broadcaster is irrelevant to its absolute right to occupy a channel on the local cable system. [  ] This blanket protection, by sweeping even the most financially secure broadcaster under the rules' beneficent mantle, reaches well beyond the rules' asserted objective of assuring that the advent of cable technology not undermine the financial viability of community-oriented, free television.

Significantly, this complete absence of any effort to analyze the extent to which the must-carry rules further their stated objective is in sharp contrast to the Commission's analysis elsewhere. In the *Economic Inquiry Report,* for example, the Commission found that any cable-induced audience loss suffered by VHF licensees, who already "earn substantially more than a normal return on their tangible investment," takes place "in a context of offsetting factors [such as] [i]ncreases in population and in the level of economic activity," which "result in a fairly steady growth in the demand for advertising exposures and in station revenues." Economic Inquiry Report, 71 F.C.C.2d at 661. If, in fact, "offsetting factors" render VHF broadcasters (or an identifiable subset of that group) relatively immune to the competitive impact of cable, then rules designed to guard against their demise or diminished profitability are clearly pointless. Yet, oblivious to the must-carry rules' primary object of protecting local broadcasters from competitive injury (and thus preserving localism), each and every broadcaster from the struggling UHF educational station to the most profitable VHF network affiliate— no matter how profitable, no matter how invulnerable to significant cable-induced revenue losses—can demand mandatory carriage.

. . . At some point the goal of preserving localism becomes undifferentiated protectionism. Until the Commission makes some effort to demonstrate the contrary, the blunderbuss approach of the rules in their current form makes inescapable the conclusion that that point has been passed.

## IV. CONCLUSION

Regulation of emerging video technologies requires a delicate balancing of competing interests. On the one hand, a regulatory framework that throttles the growth of new media or otherwise limits the number and variety of outlets for expression is likely to run afoul of the First Amendment's central mission of assuring "the widest possible dissemination of information from diverse and antagonistic sources," [  ]. On the other hand, unfettered growth of new video services may well threaten other deeply ingrained societal values. In particular, the complete displacement of expressive outlets attuned to the needs and concerns of the communities they serve not only would contravene a long-standing historical tradition of a locally oriented press but might itself disserve the objective of diversity.

When the Commission strikes this balance in favor of regulations that impinge on rights protected by the First Amendment, it assumes a heavy burden of justification. As the Supreme Court made clear long ago, "Mere . . . preferences or beliefs respecting matters of public convenience may well support regulation directed at other personal activities, but be insufficient to justify such as diminishes the exercise of rights so vital to the maintenance of democratic institutions." [ ] Even where the infringement on protected First Amendment rights is incidental to the pursuit of other legitimate objectives, the government must affirmatively demonstrate that the regulation is narrowly tailored to serve a substantial interest.

After extensive examination of the purposes and effects of the must-carry rules, we have concluded that the Commission has failed to carry this heavy burden. After the passage of nearly two decades, and despite its demonstrated capacity to do so, the Commission has failed entirely to determine whether the evil the rules seek to correct "is a real or merely a fanciful threat." Home Box Office, Inc. v. FCC, supra, 567 F.2d at 50. Moreover, because the must-carry rules indiscriminately sweep into their protective ambit each and every broadcaster, whether or not that protection in fact serves the asserted interest of assuring an adequate amount of local broadcasting in the community, the rules are insufficiently tailored to justify their substantial interference with First Amendment rights.

We stress that we have not found it necessary to decide whether any version of the mandatory carriage rules would contravene the First Amendment. We hold only that in their current form they can no longer stand. . . . Should the Commission wish to recraft the rules in a manner more sensitive to the First Amendment concerns we outline today, it is, of course, free to do so. We would consider the constitutionality of the product of that effort at the appropriate time.

*So Ordered.*

### Notes and Questions

1. After the Commission announced it would not appeal the decision, broadcasters unsuccessfully sought a stay of the court of appeals' decision pending a petition for certiorari. On September 10, 1985, the Commission stopped enforcement of the must-carry rules and dismissed all proceedings resulting from the rules. Meanwhile, the NAB filed a petition for certiorari.

2. In late 1985, the FCC started a new must-carry rulemaking proceeding. The Commission had no specific proposal of its own, but instead asked for comments on proposals made by various private organizations

such as the Association of Independent Television Stations (INTV) and the NAB. These proposals range from more limited forms of the old must-carry rules with smaller cable systems exempted to elimination of the compulsory copyright license for secondary transmissions for any cable system failing to carry all local stations. One major issue is whether any of these proposals would conform to the court of appeals' decision in *Quincy Cable*.

Meanwhile NTIA has proposed abolishing the compulsory copyright license for secondary transmissions. If the compulsory license is not abolished, NTIA favors restricting it to those systems that carry all local television signals.

## D.  FEDERAL v. STATE REGULATION

---

### 1.  PREEMPTION

Cable, unlike broadcasting, is regulated by both state and federal government. As we discussed, state and local jurisdiction was originally based primarily on the cable operator's use of the city streets and other rights of way. Federal jurisdiction grew out of the FCC's jurisdiction over broadcasting. Gradually a conflict arose over where the line between state and federal jurisdiction should be drawn.

The majority of cable operators preferred to have state and local jurisdiction restricted as much as possible. They believed that some cities were making impossible demands in return for their franchises and imposing heavy burdens on the cable operators once the franchises were awarded. There were also serious fears that franchise renewal in cable would not carry the same renewal expectancy that is present in broadcasting (discussed in Chapter IV).

At the same time the FCC was gradually asserting the right to preempt more and more state and local regulation. As these issues reached the courts, the Commission's position was generally being upheld. In mid–1984, the Commission received strong support for its asserted right to preempt in a case in which it was not directly involved.

### CAPITAL CITIES CABLE, INC. v. CRISP
Supreme Court of the United States, 1984.
467 U.S. 691, 104 S.Ct. 2694, 81 L.Ed.2d 580.

[In 1980, the Oklahoma Attorney General decided that the state's ban on the advertising of alcoholic beverages applied to advertisements carried by out-of-state broadcast stations when retransmitted by Oklahoma cable television systems. Because the definition of alcoholic beverages did not include beer, and there was very little, if any, electronic media advertising of hard liquors, the statute was only applied to electronic media advertising of wine. Capital Cities Cable filed a suit seeking a declaratory judgment that application of the law violated the

Supremacy Clause and First Amendment to the Federal Constitution. The district court found the ban a violation of the First Amendment, but the decision was reversed by the court of appeals.]

JUSTICE BRENNAN delivered the opinion of the Court.

The question presented in this case is whether Oklahoma may require cable television operators in that State to delete all advertisements for alcoholic beverages contained in the out-of-state signals that they retransmit by cable to their subscribers. Petitioners contend that Oklahoma's requirement abridges their rights under the First and Fourteenth Amendments and is pre-empted by federal law. Because we conclude that this state regulation is pre-empted, we reverse the judgment of the Court of Appeals for the Tenth Circuit and do not reach the First Amendment question.

. . .

## II

Petitioners and the FCC contend that the federal regulatory scheme for cable television systems administered by the Commission is intended to pre-empt any state regulation of the signals carried by cable system operators. Respondent apparently concedes that enforcement of the Oklahoma statute in this case conflicts with federal law, but argues that because the State's advertising ban was adopted pursuant to the broad powers to regulate the transportation and importation of intoxicating liquor reserved to the States by the Twenty-first Amendment, the statute should prevail notwithstanding the conflict with federal law. . . .

. . . Under the Supremacy Clause, U.S. Const., Art. VI, cl. 2, the enforcement of a state regulation may be pre-empted by federal law in several circumstances: first, when Congress, in enacting a federal statute, has expressed a clear intent to pre-empt state law, [ ]; second, when it is clear despite the absence of explicit pre-emptive language, that Congress has intended, by legislating comprehensively, to occupy an entire field of regulation and has thereby "left no room for the States to supplement" federal law, [ ]; and, finally, when compliance with both state and federal law is impossible, [ ], or when the state law "stands as an obstacle to the accomplishment and execution of the full purposes and objectives of Congress." [ ]

And as we made clear in Fidelity Federal Savings and Loan Ass'n v. De La Cuesta, 458 U.S. 141 (1982):

> "Federal regulations have no less pre-emptive effect than federal statutes. Where Congress has directed an administrator to exercise his discretion, his judgments are subject to judicial review only to determine whether he has exceeded his authority or acted arbitrarily. When the administrator promulgates regulations intended to pre-empt state law, the court's inquiry is similarly limited: 'If [h]is choice represents a reasonable accommodation of conflicting policies that were committed to the agency's care by the statute, we

should not disturb it unless it appears from the statute or its legislative history that the accommodation is not one that Congress would have sanctioned.' " [ ]

The power delegated to the FCC plainly comprises authority to regulate the signals carried by cable television systems. In United States v. Southwestern Cable Co., 392 U.S. 157 (1968), the Court found that the Commission had been given "broad responsibilities" to regulate all aspects of interstate communication by wire or radio by virtue of § 2(a) of the Communications Act of 1934, 47 U.S.C. § 152(a), and that this comprehensive authority included to regulate cable communications systems. [ ] We have since explained that the Commission's authority extends to all regulatory actions "necessary to ensure the achievement of the Commission's statutory responsibilities." FCC v. Midwest Video Corp., 440 U.S. 689, 706 (1979). Accord, United States v. Midwest Video Corp., 406 U.S. 649, 665–667 (1972). Therefore, if the FCC has resolved to pre-empt an area of cable television regulation and if this determination "represents a reasonable accommodation of conflicting policies" that are within the agency's domain, [ ], we must conclude that all conflicting state regulations have been precluded.

A

In contrast to commercial television broadcasters, which transmit video signals to their audience free of charge and derive their income principally from advertising revenues, cable television systems generally operate on the basis of a wholly different entrepreneurial principle. In return for service fees paid by subscribers, cable operators provide their customers with a variety of broadcast and nonbroadcast signals obtained from several sources. Typically, these sources include over-the-air broadcast signals picked up by a master antenna from local and nearby television broadcasting stations, broadcast signals from distant television stations imported by means of communications satellites, and nonbroadcast signals that are not originated by television broadcasting stations, but are instead transmitted specifically for cable systems by satellite or microwave relay. Over the past twenty years, pursuant to its delegated authority under the Communications Act, the FCC has unambiguously expressed its intent to pre-empt any state or local regulation of this entire array of signals carried by cable television systems.

The Commission began its regulation of cable communication in the 1960's. At that time, it was chiefly concerned that unlimited importation of distant broadcast signals into the service areas of local television broadcasting stations might, through competition, "destroy or seriously degrade the service offered by a television broadcaster," and thereby cause a significant reduction in service to households not served by cable systems. . . .

. . . . In marking the boundaries of its jurisdiction, the FCC determined that, in contrast to its regulatory scheme for television broadcasting stations, it would not adopt a system of direct federal licensing for cable systems. Instead, the Commission announced a program of "deliberately structured dualism" in which state and local authorities were given responsibility for granting franchises to cable operators within their communities and for overseeing such local incidents of cable operations as delineating franchise areas, regulating the construction of cable facilities, and maintaining rights of way. [ ] At the same time, the Commission retained exclusive jurisdiction over all operational aspects of cable communication, including signal carriage and technical standards. . . . The Commission has also made clear that its exclusive jurisdiction extends to cable systems' carriage of specialized, nonbroadcast signals. . . . [ ]

Although the FCC has recently relaxed its regulation of importation of distant broadcast signals to permit greater access to this source of programming for cable subscribers, it has by no means forsaken its regulatory power in this area. [ ] Indeed, the Commission's decision to allow unfettered importation of distant broadcast signals rested on its conclusion that "the benefits to existing and potential cable households from permitting the carriage of additional signals are substantial. Millions of households may be afforded not only increased viewing options, but also access to a diversity of services from cable television that presently is unavailable in their communities." 79 F.C.C.2d, at 746. [ ] . . . Clearly, the full accomplishment of such objectives would be jeopardized if state and local authorities were now permitted to restrict the ability of cable operators to provide these diverse services to their subscribers.

Accordingly, to the extent it has been invoked to control the distant broadcast and nonbroadcast signals imported by cable operators, the Oklahoma advertising ban plainly reaches beyond the regulatory authority reserved to local authorities by the Commission's rules, and trespasses into the exclusive domain of the FCC. To be sure, Oklahoma may, under current Commission rules, regulate such local aspects of cable systems as franchisee selection and construction oversight, [ ], but, by requiring cable television operators to delete commercial advertising contained in signals carried pursuant to federal authority, the State has clearly exceeded that limited jurisdiction and interfered with a regulatory area that the Commission has explicitly pre-empted.

## B

Quite apart from this generalized federal pre-emption of state regulation of cable signal carriage, the Oklahoma advertising ban plainly conflicts with specific federal regulations. These conflicts arise in three principal ways. First, the FCC's so-called "must-carry" rules require certain cable television operators to transmit the broadcast signals of any local television broadcasting station that is located within a specified 35-mile zone of the cable operator or that is "significantly viewed" in the community served by the operator. [ ] These "must-carry" rules require many Oklahoma cable operators, including petitioners, to carry signals from broadcast stations located in nearby states such as Missouri and Kansas. [ ] In addition, under Commission regulations, the local broadcast signals that cable operators are required to carry must be carried "in full, without deletion or alteration of any portion. . . ." [ ] Because, in the Commission's view, enforcement of these non-deletion rules serves to "prevent a loss of revenues to local broadcasters sufficient to result in reduced service to the public," they have been applied to commercial advertisements as well as to regular programming. [ ] Consequently, those Oklahoma cable operators required to carry out-of-state broadcast signals in full, including any wine commercials, are subject to criminal prosecution under Oklahoma law as a result of their compliance with federal regulations.

Second, current FCC rulings permit, and indeed encourage, cable television operators to import out-of-state television broadcast signals and retransmit those signals to their subscribers. [ ] For Oklahoma cable operators, this source of cable programming includes signals from television broadcasting stations located in Kansas, Missouri and Texas, as well as the signals from so-called "superstations" in Atlanta and Chicago. [ ] It is undisputed that many of these distant broadcast signals retransmitted by petitioners contain wine commercials that are lawful under federal law and in the states where the programming originates. Nor is it disputed that cable operators who carry such signals are barred by Commission regulations from deleting or altering any portion of those signals, including commercial advertising. [ ] Under Oklahoma's advertising ban, however, these cable operators must either delete the wine commercials or face criminal prosecution. Since the Oklahoma law, by requiring deletion of a portion of these out-of-state signals, compels conduct that federal law forbids, the State ban clearly "stands as an obstacle to the accomplishment and execution of the full purposes and objectives" of the federal regulatory scheme. [ ]

Finally, enforcement of the state advertising ban against Oklahoma cable operators will affect a third source of cable programming over which the Commission has asserted exclusive jurisdiction. Aside from relaying local television broadcasting in accordance with the "must-carry" rules, and distant broadcast signals, cable operators also transmit specialized nonbroadcast cable services to their subscribers. This source of programming . . . includes such advertiser-supported national cable programming as the Cable News Network (CNN) and the Entertainment and Sports Programming Network (ESPN). Although the Commission's "must-carry" and non-deletion rules do not apply to such nonbroadcast cable services, the FCC, as noted earlier, [ ], has explicitly stated that state regulation of these services is completely precluded by federal law.

Petitioners generally receive such signals by antenna, microwave receiver, or by satellite dish and retransmit them by wire to their subscribers. But unlike local television broadcasting stations that transmit only one signal and receive notification from their networks concerning advertisements, cable operators simultaneously receive and channel to their subscribers a variety of signals from many sources without any advance notice about the timing or content of commercial advertisements carried on those signals.  [  ]  As the record of this case indicates, developing the capacity to monitor each signal and delete every wine commercial before it is retransmitted would be a prohibitively burdensome task.  [  ]  . . .  Accordingly, if the state advertising ban is enforced, Oklahoma cable operators will be compelled either to abandon altogether their carriage of both distant broadcast signals and specialized non-broadcast cable services or run the risk of criminal prosecution. As a consequence, the public may well be deprived of the wide variety of programming options that cable systems make possible.

Such a result is wholly at odds with the regulatory goals contemplated by the FCC.  Consistent with its congressionally defined charter to "make available, so far as possible, to all the people of the United States a rapid, efficient, Nation-wide and world-wide wire and radio communication service . . . ,"  47 U.S.C. § 151, the FCC has sought to ensure that "the benefits of cable communications become a reality on a nationwide basis."  [  ]  With that end in mind, the Commission has determined that only federal pre-emption of state and local regulation can assure cable systems the breathing space necessary to expand vigorously and provide a diverse range of program offerings to potential cable subscribers in all parts of the country.  While that judgment may not enjoy universal support, it plainly represents a reasonable accommodation of the competing policies committed to the FCC's care and we see no reason to disturb the agency's judgment.  And, as we have repeatedly explained, when federal officials determine, as the FCC has here, that restrictive regulation of a particular area is not in the public interest, "States are not permitted to use their police power to enact such a regulation."  [  ]

## C

Although the FCC has taken the lead in formulating communications policy with respect to cable television, Congress has considered the impact of this new technology, and has, through the Copyright Revision Act of 1976, 90 Stat. 2541, 17 U.S.C. § 101 et seq., acted to facilitate the cable industry's ability to distribute broadcast programming on a national basis.  Prior to the 1976 revision, the Court has determined that the retransmission of distant broadcast signals by cable systems did not subject cable operators to copyright infringement liability because such retransmissions were not "performances" within the meaning of the 1909 Copyright Act.  [  ]  In revising the Copyright Act, however, Congress concluded that cable operators should be required to pay royalties to the owners of copyrighted programs retransmitted by their systems on pain of liability for copyright infringement.  At the same time, Congress recognized that "it would be impractical and unduly burdensome to require every cable system to negotiate [appropriate royalty payments] with every copyright owner" in order to secure consent for such retransmission. [ ] Section 111 of the 1976 Act codifies the solution devised by Congress. It establishes a program of compulsory copyright licensing that permits cable systems to retransmit distant broadcast signals without securing permission from the copyright owner and, in turn, requires each system to pay royalty fees to a central royalty fund based on a percentage of its gross revenues. To take advantage of this compulsory licensing scheme, a cable operator must satisfy certain reporting requirements, § 111(d)(1) and (2)(A), pay specified royalty fees to a central fund administered by the Register of Copyrights, § 111(d)(2)(B)—(D), and (3), and refrain from deleting or altering commercial advertising on the broadcast signals it transmits, § 111(c)(3). Failure to comply with these conditions results in forfeiture of the protections of the compulsory licensing system.

In devising this system, Congress has clearly sought to further the important public purpose framed in the Copyright Clause, U.S. Const., Art. I, § 8, of rewarding the creators of copyrighted works, and of "promoting broad public availability of literature, music, and the other arts," [ ]. Compulsory licensing not only protects the commercial value of copyrighted works but also enhances the ability of cable systems to retransmit such programs carried on distant broadcast signals, thereby allowing the public to benefit by the wider dissemination of works carried on television broadcast signals. By requiring cable operators to delete commercial advertisements for wine, however, the Oklahoma ban forces these operators to lose the protections of compulsory licensing. Of course, it is possible for cable systems to comply with the Oklahoma ban by simply abandoning their importation of the distant broadcast signals covered by the Copyright Act. But such a loss of viewing options would plainly thwart the policy identified by both Congress and the FCC of facilitating and encouraging the importation of distant broadcast signals.

### III

[Oklahoma argued that even if normal pre-emption analysis invalidated the ban, it was valid because of the Twenty-first Amendment. "States enjoy broad power under § 2 of the Twenty-first Amendment to regulate the importation and use of intoxicating liquor within their borders." The Court decided that the state interest in regulating liquor was outweighed by the substantial "federal objective of ensuring widespread availability of diverse cable services throughout the United States." In reaching this conclusion the Court was heavily influenced by the extremely limited approach that Oklahoma had taken to further its asserted interest. Oklahoma had only banned electronic media advertising of wine. There was no direct regulation of consumption or even a ban on other alcoholic beverage advertising.]

### IV

We conclude that the application of Oklahoma's alcoholic beverage advertising ban to out-of-state signals carried by cable operators in that

State is pre-empted by federal law and that the Twenty-first Amendment does not save the regulation from pre-emption. The judgment of the Court of Appeals is

Reversed.

**Notes and Questions**

1. How does the balance between state and federal regulation set out here differ from the balance established in broadcast regulation? Why have these differences developed? Is either model preferable to the other?

2. By deciding the case on preemption grounds, the Court avoided having to address the First Amendment question concerning regulation of alcoholic beverage advertising. Recall our discussion of this issue in Chapter VII.

## 2.  FRANCHISING

Cable systems operate under franchise authority granted by a municipality, though state agencies also may grant permission to operate. See, e.g., Clear Television Cable Corp. v. Board of Public Utility Commissioners, 85 N.J. 30, 424 A.2d 1151 (1981). A franchise gives the cable operator access to city streets and other rights-of-way within a defined area for specific periods of time. Franchises usually are awarded after competitive bidding by several companies in response to a request for proposals outlining the requirements of the franchising authority. In practice they are almost always exclusive. After a franchise is awarded, a franchise agreement is signed specifying services the system must provide, construction schedules and franchise fees. Many also specify fees the operators may charge subscribers, although much of this rate regulation has now been preempted by the FCC as we will discuss later in this Chapter.

For a while, the competition among cable operators for city franchises was incredibly intense. At the height of the franchising process, operators were willing to promise almost anything to obtain a franchise. For example, in 1981, Denver attracted bids from three firms, one offering a 215-channel system including a 107-channel home network. The three offered basic home services for monthly fees ranging from nothing to $3.95.

Unfortunately, once they had obtained the franchises, some operators discovered that cable wasn't necessarily the goldmine they had anticipated. These operators are now asking cities to renegotiate the franchise agreements and eliminate some of the promised services, or selling the franchises to other operators. One company that found itself in that position, Warner Amex Cable Communications, ended up building a 56-channel system in Milwaukee in lieu of the 108–channel system originally agreed upon. Broadcasting, Oct. 29, 1984 at 10.

From the 1970's into the early 1980's, when franchising competition was at its peak, cities were able to demand far more than large numbers of channels. Access channels, studios, mobile vans, financial contributions to access foundations, and free wiring of public buildings were commonly sought—and offered. In many cities, cable companies ended up providing benefits totally unrelated to cable service. These benefits ranged from building new libraries to planting trees along the roads.

A slightly more subtle approach to winning the franchise competition was a practice known as "rent-a-citizen." Prominent local citizens were given shares in the local subsidiary of a company seeking the franchise. If the company was granted the franchise, these shares suddenly acquired great value. Obviously, this meant that these prominent citizens would exert all their influence towards having that company awarded the franchise.

In addition, the cable company would try to persuade the city that these citizens would provide local ownership, thus guaranteeing that the cable company would always be looking out for the city's best interests. The reality was that these citizens never had a controlling interest in even the local subsidiary. Their influence was minimal. Furthermore, the arrangement between the company and the local stockholders almost always included a buy-back arrangement where after a few years the local citizens would sell the stock back to the company for a healthy profit.

Spurred on by cable industry hype and franchising fever, the cities kept increasing the cost of obtaining franchises. Gradually, the FCC increased its limitations on state and municipal regulation of cable. Among the more important restrictions imposed by the Commission were a prohibition of rate regulation of premium services and a ceiling on franchise fees. Further restrictions were under consideration when the Cable Communications Policy Act of 1984 was enacted.

### a. The 1984 Policy Act

The FCC's increasingly aggressive policy of preemption had already led the National League of Cities (NLC) to pursue legislative relief. However, lengthy negotiations between NLC and the National Cable Television Association (NCTA) had not produced a compromise satisfactory to both constituencies. Perhaps given new impetus by Court decisions such as *Crisp,* a compromise bill was drafted and presented to Congress with the backing of both groups. In late 1984, this bill was enacted into law as the Cable Communications Policy Act of 1984.

*Franchising.* Under the Cable Act, franchising is still the province of state and local governments with certain restrictions. The most important of these is the prohibition on regulating cable service as a common carrier. At the same time, anyone wishing to offer cable service must obtain a franchise. 47 U.S.C. § 621. Franchising authorities are prohibited from specifying video programming or other information services in requests for proposals. 47 U.S.C. § 624.

*Franchise Fees.* Section 622 of the Act prohibits franchising authorities from charging more than five percent of gross revenues as a franchise fee. In the case of existing franchises money used to support community access channels will not be covered by the five percent limit. 47 U.S.C. § 622. The Commission has now eliminated its rule limiting franchise fees to three percent (five percent with a waiver).

*Concentration Rules.* The Cable Act essentially codified existing FCC crossownership restrictions. A television broadcast licensee may not own a cable system within its primary signal coverage area. 47 U.S.C. § 613(a). Similarly, a common-carrier may not own a cable system within its telephone service area. The latter restriction does not apply to rural areas. 47 U.S.C. § 613(b). What is the reason for this exemption?

The Commission is permitted to issue further ownership restrictions, but state regulation is preempted. Some states previously had more restrictive crossownership rules. For example, in Massachusetts, crossownership of cable and a newspaper, daily or weekly, was prohibited.

*Renewals.* One of the great fears of cable operators was nonrenewal. Specific guidelines for franchise renewal are set out in great detail in § 626 of the Communications Act. 47 U.S.C. § 626. A denial of renewal must be based on a finding that the operator failed to comply substantially with the existing franchise agreement; that the quality of the operator's service was unreasonable in light of community needs; that the operator lacks necessary technical, financial or legal ability to fulfill the promises made in its proposal; or that the operator's proposal is not reasonable in terms of meeting the future needs of the community. This appears to create a strong renewal expectancy. The full impact of this section will, of course, not be clear until it has been in effect for several years.

*Rate Regulation.* The new law allows regulation only of rates of basic cable service, and then only in the absence of effective competition. Somewhat more extensive regulation of existing franchises is permitted until December 29, 1986. 47 U.S.C. § 623. This provision is viewed as a major victory for cable operators, who have long argued that rate regulation was unnecessary due to competition from other communication technologies. Opponents of the provision contended that cable is effectively a monopoly and thus, cable rates are not subject to adequate pressure from competition.

The Commission has defined effective competition as the availability of three or more off-the-air television signals in the market. The Commission rejected the suggestion of some parties that the availability of the three major networks be part of the definition. Cable Communications Act Rules, 58 R.R.2d 1 (1985).

The decision in *Quincy Cable* has raised a new problem. Under the Cable Act only basic cable is subject to rate regulation. Premium service is completely excluded. The Commission had defined basic cable in terms of the must-carry channels, so it now has to reconsider the definition.

### b.  Constitutional Questions

During this period, there were no serious challenges to the cities' authority to extract everything possible from the cable companies by running what was, in essence, an auction, with the franchise going to the highest bidder.  Probably, most companies were loathe to start fights with the cities for fear of being denied the franchises.  As a result serious questions remained unanswered.  What is the connection between a city's control of public rights of way and authority over cable programming?  Is awarding a franchise based in part on programming promises a violation of the First Amendment?  If there is room for more than one company's cables, does awarding an exclusive franchise violate the First Amendment?

These issues were raised in Preferred Communications, Inc. v. City of Los Angeles.  The case arose when Preferred requested a cable franchise after refusing to participate in the city's competitive franchising process.  When denied the franchise, Preferred sued, alleging the franchising process violated the First Amendment.  The suit was dismissed for failure to state a claim upon which relief could be granted and Preferred appealed.  [Note: When a suit is dismissed for failure to state a claim upon which relief can be granted, it means that even if every fact in dispute is assumed to be in the plaintiff's favor, the plaintiff would still lose the case.  Thus, on appeal the issue is not should the plaintiff have won the case, but rather, has the plaintiff at least indicated a chance of winning the case.  If the plaintiff wins the appeal, the case will then proceed further.]

## PREFERRED COMMUNICATIONS, INC. v. CITY OF LOS ANGELES

United States Court of Appeals, Ninth Circuit, 1985.
754 F.2d 1396, 57 R.R.2d 1339.

Before SNEED, ANDERSON and FERGUSON, CIRCUIT JUDGES.

SNEED, CIRCUIT JUDGE.

.   .   .

### I.

### STANDARD OF REVIEW

A decision to dismiss a complaint for failure to state a claim upon which relief can be granted is reviewable de novo.  [   ]  In conducting this review, we must accept all material allegations in the complaint as true.  [   ]  All doubts are resolved in favor of the plaintiff.  [   ]  A dismissal cannot be upheld "unless it appears beyond doubt that the plaintiff can prove no set of facts in support of his claim which would entitle him to relief." [  ]  With these principles in mind, we turn to PCI's complaint.

## II.

## THE COMPLAINT

As alleged in PCI's complaint, the pertinent facts appear as follows. PCI is a corporation which was organized for the purpose of operating a cable system in an area of Los Angeles designated by the City as the South Central District.  PCI's intended operation entailed the installation of a network of distribution cables in the region PCI wished to serve. PCI proposed to attach its cable to existing public utility facilities—poles and conduits located on property owned in fee by the utility and on or under easements owned by the utility running over both public and private rights of way.

For a number of years, utilities throughout the State of California have dedicated surplus space on their facilities for similar uses.  The California legislature recognized this dedication, at least with regard to nonmunicipal utilities, when it enacted West's Ann.Cal.Pub.Util.Code § 767.5(b) (West Supp. 1984) (dedicating surplus space and excess capacity on public utility support structures for use by cable television companies).    Accordingly, PCI approached two utilities in the Los Angeles area—the Pacific Telephone and Telegraph Company and the Los Angeles Department of Water and Power—to negotiate a lease of space on those companies' poles and conduits.  Both utilities informed PCI that such an agreement would not be possible until PCI obtained a cable franchise from the City.  PCI then petitioned the City in an attempt to obtain such a franchise.

The City allocates franchises through an auction process.  Franchising or licensing the construction of a cable television system is authorized by West's Ann.Cal.Gov't Code § 53066 (West Supp. 1984).  The City requires companies wishing to participate in the process to submit to a variety of conditions.  A potential bidder must pay a $10,000 filing fee and a $500 good faith deposit and must agree to pay up to an additional $60,000 to reimburse the City for expenses incurred in holding the auction.  It must provide the City with a detailed proposal outlining its intended operations over the succeeding nine years and must demonstrate to the satisfaction of the City that it has a "sound financial base," that its proposed operations constitute "sound business plans," and that it has the proper "character qualifications" and "demonstrated business experience."  The City also requires hopeful bidders to agree to pay the City a percentage of future annual gross revenues and to provide a variety of customer services, including at least 52 channels of video service and interactive (two way) service.

More significantly, the City exacts a commitment to provide various mandatory access and leased access channels.  Bidders must agree to provide, without compensation, two channels for use by the City and by other government entities, two channels for use by educational institutions, and two channels for use by the general public, along with staff and facilities to aid in programming. Bidders must further agree to provide two leased access channels as well. An undertaking to provide portable production facilities and to permit free use by the City of all poles, towers, ducts, and antennas is also required.

Finally, potential cable operators must agree to leave a variety of business decisions to the discretion of the City. Pricing and customer relations are left to the City's control. The operator must form a "cable franchise advisory board," subject to City approval. Lastly, the City reserves the right to inspect the cable operation upon demand and requires a waiver of any right to recover for damages or other injury arising from the cable franchise or its enforcement.

After the submission of bids from companies willing to submit to the foregoing conditions, the City chooses the operator it deems to be "best" for each area. It awards just one franchise in each region. The City refuses PCI's request for a franchise because PCI had failed to participate in the auction process. The City will not permit PCI to operate a cable television system in the South Central District under any circumstances.

. . .

## IV.

## THE FIRST AMENDMENT

PCI's arguments amount to a sweeping attack against the City's cable television franchising process. PCI contends, inter alia, that its right to construct a cable television system and disseminate programming via the cable medium should not be conditioned upon having to participate in an auction procedure or be otherwise subject to the City's discretion. It maintains that the City cannot choose which cable providers may use the City's facilities to install and operate cable systems and cannot condition that use on such requirements as the City has imposed in this case.

These contentions are wide-ranging. Were we to attempt to respond in like measure, we would not escape the charge of rendering advisory opinions poorly disguised as sweeping dicta. On the other hand, we cannot regard this case as one which is either unripe for decision or moot. PCI has sought a franchise from the City which the City to date has refused to grant.

An escape from our dilemma would be to identify a fundamental issue which, if decided in favor of the City, would require affirming the judgment of the district court and which, if decided adversely to the City, would require reversal and redesign by the City of its procedures relating to cable television. We believe such an issue is as follows:

> "Can the City, consistent with the First Amendment, limit access by means of an auction process to a given region of the City to a single cable television company, when the public utility facilities

and other public property in that region necessary to the installation and operation of a cable television system are physically capable of accommodating more than one system?"

We do not decide the validity of any of the specific requirements called for by the City's franchising process. In particular, we do not decide whether the City may validly require cable operators to turn over channels for use by the government, by educational institutions, and by the public and for leased use by others.

.  .  .

We conclude that the question we consider raised by this appeal should be answered negatively. For that reason we reverse the district court's dismissal of PCI's First Amendment claim.

.  .  .

B.  *The Cable Television Medium and the First Amendment*

.  .  .

1.  *Cable Television and Broadcasting Distinguished*

Initially, the City argues that the standards applicable to government regulation of broadcasting also govern the regulation of cable. We disagree. We recognize that the First Amendment allows the government greater latitude in regulating the broadcast medium than it enjoys in regulating other, more traditional media. See Red Lion Broadcasting Co. v. FCC, 395 U.S. 367 (1969); National Broadcasting Co. v. United States, 319 U.S. 190 (1943). And several courts, to a varying extent, have applied the broadcasting standards to the government's efforts to regulate cable. See, e.g., Community Communications Co., 660 F.2d at 1375–1380; Black Hills Video Corp. v. FCC, 399 F.2d 65, 69 (8th Cir.1968); Berkshire Cablevision of Rhode Island v. Burke, 571 F.Supp. 976, 983–88 (D.R.I.1983). We decline to do so. "Each medium of expression .  .  . must be assessed for First Amendment purposes by standards suited to it.  .  .  ." Southeastern Promotions, Ltd. v. Conrad, 420 U.S. 546, 557 (1975). "[D]ifferences in the characteristics of new media justify differences in the First Amendment standards applied to them." Red Lion Broadcasting Co., 395 U.S. at 386. Despite the superficial similarity between broadcasting and cable television, there are significant differences between the two media that have First Amendment consequences.

The Supreme Court's determination to allow greater government intrusion into the affairs of broadcasters rests on the physical scarcity of radiowaves; the electromagnetic spectrum simply is physically incapable of carrying the messages of all who wish to use the medium. [ ] As Justice Frankfurter observed in National Broadcasting Co. v. United States,

> "Unlike other modes of expression, radio inherently is not available to all. That is its unique characteristic, and that is why, unlike other modes of expression, it is subject to governmental

regulation. . . . The right of free speech does not include, however, the right to use the facilities of radio without a license."

319 U.S. 190, 226–27 (1943); [ ]. Without licensing, the broadcast spectrum would be rendered virtually useless to all.

This is not the case under the alleged facts before us. PCI wishes to obtain permission to string its cable from utility poles and through utility conduits. Because of PCI's refusal to comply with the City's auction process, the City has withheld that permission. We cannot accept the City's contention that, because the available space on such facilities is to an undetermined extent physically limited, the First Amendment standards applicable to the regulation of broadcasting permit it to restrict access and allow only a single cable provider to install and operate a cable television system.

Apparently the only case to apply the physical scarcity rationale to cable television in such a direct fashion is Black Hills Video Corp. v. FCC, 399 F.2d 65, 69 (8th Cir.1968). That case involved the FCC's efforts to regulate an early community antenna system that merely retransmitted signals received from broadcasting stations; cable technology, however, has evolved significantly since the time of *Black Hills Video*. [ ] More recent cases have expressly concluded that the physical scarcity rationale does not apply to cable. See, e.g., Omega Satellite Products Co., 694 F.2d at 127 ("[F]requency interference [is] a problem that does not arise with cable television."); Home Box Office, Inc., 567 F.2d at 44–45 ("[A]n essential precondition of [broadcast] theory—physical interference and scarcity requiring an umpiring role for government—is absent.") *Black Hills Video*, therefore, is a doubtful precedent today.

Moreover, PCI has alleged in its complaint that there *is* space available on the City's poles and in its conduits. PCI has alleged that the City had held itself out as a provider of space on its utility poles to cable television companies and state law requires private utilities to make space available for the attachment of television cable. [ ] Because we must accept these allegations as true, we must find that the physical scarcity that could justify increased regulation of cable operations does not exist in this case. We express no opinion on the issue of the manner in which the City should allocate access to poles and conduits to competing cable systems when these structures are incapable of accommodating all those seeking access.

### 2. *Natural Monopoly as a Justification of Governmental Regulation*

The City asserts next that, because cable television is a natural monopoly, economic scarcity justifies government regulation. We need not decide this issue at this time. PCI's complaint alleges that competition for cable services is economically feasible in the Los Angeles area. As we must accept this allegation as true, we must conclude that no natural monopoly exists.

In passing, we note that the Supreme Court rejected an argument that rested a particular government regulation of the press on economic scarcity. In Miami Herald Publishing Co. v. Tornillo, 418 U.S. 241 (1974), the court invalidated a state statute granting political candidates a right to equal space to reply to criticism in newspapers. The court refused to accept the plaintiff's argument that because economic conditions made entry into newspaper markets difficult, the government could impose a limited right of access to the press. Although the court acknowledged that most newspapers enjoy a monopoly in their areas of distribution, it did not conclude that this circumstance gave rise to a duty to provide public access to the press. See id. at 249–58; see also Midwest Video Corp., 571 F.2d at 1056; Home Box Office, Inc., 567 F.2d at 46.

Several cases, however, have concluded that cable's alleged natural monopoly characteristics do provide a basis for some degree of government regulation. See, e.g., Community Communications Co., 660 F.2d at 1379; Berkshire Cablevision of Rhode Island, 571 F.Supp. at 985–86; [ ]. In *Community Communications Co.*, the Tenth Circuit distinguished *Tornillo* by tying the natural monopoly characteristics of cable to the fact that installing and operating a cable system burdens public utility facilities and streets. The court asserted that the economic scarcity present in *Tornillo* "was unrelated to a disruptive use of the public domain requiring a government license." 660 F.2d at 1379. A cable company, by contrast, "must significantly impact the public domain in order to operate; without a license, it cannot engage in cable broadcasting to disseminate information." Id.

This statement is much too broad. It suggests that simply because cable's disruption of the public domain gives rise to a need for licensing, it would also justify the monopoly the City seeks to create by its auction process. We find it necessary, however, to undertake a more detailed inquiry into whether the City's auction process is a permissible governmental response to the burden imposed by cable on public resources.[8] We now turn to that question.

### 3. Disruption of Public Resources as a Justification of Government Regulation

Concluding that cable is not characterized by physical scarcity analogous to that of the broadcast medium or by economic scarcity does not mean that all regulation of cable operations is invalid. See Home Box Office, Inc. v. FCC, 567 F.2d 9, 46 (D.C.Cir.), certiorari denied, 434

8. The Tenth Circuit also suggested that newspapers had enjoyed a long tradition of freedom from government interference, while cable television had not. Community Communications Co., 660 F.2d at 1379; accord Berkshire Cablevision of Rhode Island, 571 F.Supp. at 985. This distinction merely begs the question.

The district court in Berkshire Cablevision offered a more helpful distinction. It asserted that, while a newspaper's natural monopoly did not preclude the public's use of the print medium, cable's natural monopoly did prevent public use of the television medium. See 571 F.Supp. at 986. As a factual matter, however, it is not clear that this is true. [ ] And in reviewing a dismissal, we must resolve all doubts in favor of the plaintiff.

U.S. 829 (1977). The First Amendment does not preclude government regulation of noncommunicative aspects of speech. Id. at 47; [ ].

The Supreme Court articulated a test for assessing the reasonableness of such regulations in United States v. O'Brien:

> "[A] government regulation is sufficiently justified if it is within the constitutional power of the government; if it furthers an important or substantial government interest; if the governmental interest is unrelated to the suppression of free expression; and if the incidental restriction on alleged First Amendment freedoms is no greater than is essential to the furtherance of that interest."

391 U.S. 367, 377 (1968); [ ]. PCI concedes that the City has an interest in minimizing the disruption of the public domain and that this interest is "unrelated to the suppression of free expression." The question presented, then, is whether allowing only the company selected through the franchise auction process to erect and operate a cable system in each region is the least restrictive means available to the City to further its interest in protecting public resources. We hold that under the facts alleged in this case it is not.

Cable television, to repeat, requires the use of public facilities, and this provides a justification for some government regulation. The City has legitimate interests in public safety and in maintaining public thoroughfares. In Community Communications Co., 660 F.2d at 1377, the court recognized that cable entails use of the public domain and that this use constitutes a basis for governmental regulation that is not present in the case of newspapers:

> "A city needs control over the number of times its citizens must bear the inconvenience of having its streets dug up and the best times for it to occur. Thus, government and cable operators are tied in a way that government and newspapers are not."

Id. at 1378; [ ].

Regulating such use and convenience, however, is quite different from restricting access, as the City attempts to do here. It has not been alleged that public utility facilities owned or controlled by the City can only support the use of a single or a few cables. Indeed, PCI has alleged precisely the contrary. A different and more sharply focused response by the City could protect the legitimate interest of the City and its citizens.

Certainly, the mere fact that the burden on public resources creates a need for government regulation does not lead to the conclusion that the First Amendment allows as much government intrusion in the cable area as it does with regard to broadcasting. [ ] Nor do we believe that the City's interest in protecting the public domain justifies its effort to auction off the right to operate a cable television system. The City's interest is not enough to counterbalance the risk that diversity in editorial judgments will be limited by the City's determination to choose the cable providers that it will permit to use the medium. [ ]

### 4. *The Public Forum Doctrine as a Check on Government Regulation*

Our conclusion that the question before us should be answered, "No," is aided by Supreme Court cases shaping the public forum doctrine. What PCI wants, in essence, is a right of access to utility poles and conduits that are either owned or controlled by the City, subject, of course, to reasonable terms designed to compensate the City for the use of those facilities. PCI wishes to disseminate its message to the public. Of course "the First Amendment does not guarantee access to property simply because it is owned or controlled by the government." [   ] Rather, the nature and character of the property at issue fix the conditions under which we must evaluate both PCI's claimed right of access and the limitations imposed by the City on that right.  .  .  .

The Supreme Court has identified three categories of public property. At one extreme are "places which by long tradition or by government fiat have been devoted to assembly and debate. . . ." [   ] This category includes "streets and parks . . . [that] have immemorially been held in trust for the use of the public and, time out of mind, have been used for purposes of assembly, communicating thoughts between citizens, and discussing public questions." [   ] In such places, the First Amendment sharply curtails the government's ability to limit expressive activity. [   ] While the government may not ban communication entirely it may enforce content-neutral regulations of the time, place, and manner of expression that "are narrowly tailored to serve a significant government interest, and leave open ample alternative channels of communication. [   ] To pass constitutional scrutiny, a content-based exclusion of expression must be "necessary to serve a compelling state and interest and . . . narrowly drawn to achieve that end." [   ]

A second category comprises public property that the government has opened for use by the public for expressive activity. [   ] Although the state is not required to retain the open character of its facilities indefinitely, while it does so, the standards applicable to the traditional public forum govern the state's regulatory efforts. [   ] Again, the government is empowered to enforce reasonable time, place, and manner regulations. [   ]

The third and final category is property "which is not by tradition or designation a forum for public communication. . . ." [   ] There, "[i]n addition to time, place, and manner regulations, the State may reserve the forum for its intended purposes, communicative or otherwise, as long as the regulation on speech is reasonable and not an effort to suppress expression merely because public officials oppose the speaker's view." [   ]

### a. *Utility Poles and Conduits are not the Traditional Public Forums*

We reject the contention that merely because utility poles and conduits are located on or under public streets and rights of way, they constitute traditional public forums.  [   ]  The Supreme Court's recent decision in Members of the City Council of Los Angeles v. Taxpayers for Vincent, 104 S.Ct. 2118 (1984), precludes such a conclusion.  There, the Court upheld a municipal ordinance prohibiting the posting of signs on public property—including public utility poles.  Citing O'Brien, the Court concluded that the government had a valid interest in advancing aesthetic values and that the ordinance was no broader than necessary to protect that interest.  See 104 S.Ct. at 2129–32.

The Supreme Court also rejected the plaintiff's contention that the public property covered by the ordinance constituted a public forum or should have been treated as a public forum because of its location on streets and thoroughfares which traditionally were so viewed.  See id. at 2133–34.  The plaintiff had not demonstrated "the existence of a traditional right of access respecting such items as utility poles for purposes of their communication comparable to that recognized for streets and parks. . . ."  Id. at 2134.

### b.  Vincent Distinguished

We do not believe, however, that Vincent governs the issue before us.  .  .  .

.  .  .

Allowing a procedure such as the City's would be akin to allowing the government discretion to grant a permit for the operation of newspaper vending machines located on public streets only to the newspaper that the government believes "best" serves the community, a practice which we find clearly invalid.  [   ]  Instead, the City must content itself with uniformly applying to all applicants regulations tailored to minimize the burden on public resource and granting franchises to all cable operators who are willing to satisfy the City's legitimate conditions.  We repeat, we do not in this opinion address a situation in which the City lacks the facilities to accommodate all who otherwise meet its conditions.

### 5.  Mandatory and Leased Access Channels and the City's Power to Restrict Access to the Cable Medium

Amici suggest that the City's licensing procedure imposes no restriction on PCI's First Amendment rights.  The mandatory access and leased access requirements, amici assert, provide PCI with the opportunity to originate programming and to disseminate its message using the cable medium.  The City would require that PCI use another's wires to transmit its programming.  We disagree.

We reject the contention that the City's access requirements provide complete protection for the exercise of expressive rights.  Arranging programming for an entire cable television system entails engaging in a wide variety of protected activities.[10]  Substituting the chance to share a

---

10.  In addition to originating their own programming, cable television operators ex- ercise considerable editorial discretion regarding what their programming will in-

few mandatory access and leased access channels with others for the right to operate an entire cable system necessarily diminishes PCI's opportunity to engage in such protected activities. A law allowing free expression in public parks only for a few minutes at 6 a.m. hardly provides an adequate replacement for the right to free, untrammeled debate in that forum. By the same reasoning, we believe the City's franchising program does not provide PCI with an adequate substitute for its right to operate a cable system.

Our conclusion can be reached in another way. The cases recognize that an otherwise valid restriction on protected expression may be rendered invalid, if the modes of communication that remain are inadequate. See, e.g., Taxpayers for Vincent, 104 S.Ct. at 2132–33; [ ]. But the reverse is not true. That is, an otherwise invalid restriction on protected activity is not saved by the availability of other means of expression. [ ] The City's argument is hard to distinguish from an assertion that a law prohibiting Mr. X or Mrs. Y from publishing a newspaper is valid, so long as each is provided an adequate space to print his or her message in already existing newspapers. Obviously, such a law would be invalid. We conclude, therefore, that allowing PCI access to another's channels is not the equivalent of providing it access to an audience by means of its own cable.

## CONCLUSION

We repeat the issue we undertook to resolve:

Can the City, consistent with the First Amendment, limit access by means of an auction process to a given region of the City to a single cable television company, when the public utility facilities and other public property in that region necessary to the installation and operation of a cable television system are physically capable of accommodating more than one system?

Our answer is no, the City cannot.

[PCI also alleged that the Los Angeles franchising process violates the antitrust laws. The court of appeals upheld the trial court's dismissal of the antitrust claim, holding that the City was protected by the state's immunity from antitrust liability.]

clude. See FCC v. Midwest Video Corp., 440 U.S. 689, 707 & n. 17 (1979). Editorial judgment is entitled to First Amendment protection. See, e.g., Miami Herald Publishing Co. v. Tornillo, 418 U.S. 241, 257–58 (1974). Undeniably, cable operators do transmit programs produced by others. To the extent an operator does so, however, we believe it would be treated for First Amendment purposes as would be theater owners, booksellers, and concert promoters. Their First Amendment protection is not diminished because they distribute or present works created by others. [ ] And PCI does not lose its First Amendment rights merely because its judgment is tempered by commercial considerations. [ ]; First National Bank of Boston v. Bellotti, 435 U.S. 765, 786 n. 23 (1978) ("It is too late to suggest that the dependence of a communication on the expenditure of money itself operates to introduce a nonspeech element or to reduce the exacting scrutiny required by the First Amendment.") (quoting Buckley v. Valeo, 424 U.S. 1, 16 (1976)).

We reverse the district court's dismissal of PCI's First Amendment claim and affirm its dismissal of the antitrust claims and remand the case for further proceedings.

Affirmed in part, reversed in part, and remanded.

**Notes and Questions**

1.  The City's petition for a rehearing en banc was denied. However, the court of appeals did change a few sentences in the original decision. Some felt the decision was toned down by the changes, but others saw them as inconsequential. The Supreme Court has granted certiorari.

2.  Shortly after the decision in *Preferred* was announced, a similar result was reached in Telecommunications of Key West, Inc. v. United States, 757 F.2d 1330 (D.C.Cir.1985). The case arose when, in 1973, the Air Force solicited bids from various companies to provide cable service to Homestead Air Force Base. After the bids were submitted, a company was chosen, and TCI, which had been providing cable service to the base for 10 years, was ordered to remove its equipment. TCI sought injunctive relief, arguing that the Air Force order violated its First Amendment rights. As in *Preferred*, TCI's action was dismissed for failure to state a claim upon which relief can be granted.

Using much of the same analysis as the court in *Preferred*, the court of appeals held that by alleging "that there were *no* reasons, practical or legal, why two cable television companies could not simultaneously use the cable rights-of-way on Homestead Air Force Base," TCI stated an adequate First Amendment cause of action.

The court also found that TCI had stated an adequate Fifth Amendment cause of action. If there were indeed no reasons for allowing two cable operators to provide service, then the selection of another operator and the exclusion of TCI might constitute a denial of equal protection.

3.  In both *Preferred* and *TCI*, the courts assumed for the purposes of their decisions that there was adequate space on the poles or other rights of way to accommodate all interested cable companies. What if there are more cable companies wishing franchises than can be accommodated? Under the rationale of *Preferred* and *TCI*, what methods of choosing applicants would be constitutional?

4.  Section 621(a)(3) of the Cable Communications Policy Act states:

In awarding a franchise or franchises, a franchising authority shall assure that access to cable service is not denied to any group of potential residential cable subscribers because of the income of the residents of the local area in which such group resides.

Under the rationale of *Preferred*, can a franchising authority require a cable system to offer service to an area that it does not wish to serve as a prerequisite to the right to serve a more attractive area?

5.  PCI's antitrust claim was based on Community Communications Co. v. City of Boulder, 455 U.S. 40 (1982). Community Communications Co., which had a non-exclusive franchise, notified the city that it was going to

expand into other areas of the city. At that time another company also indicated interest in serving those areas of the city. The city quickly enacted an ordinance halting any expansion while a new ordinance was drafted to cover the franchising process. Community then filed an antitrust action against the city.

Boulder centered its defense around an earlier ruling that states have immunity from the antitrust laws. The defense was unsuccessful as the Court ruled that the state-action doctrine was not applicable to cities unless the municipal ordinance being challenged effectuates a "clearly articulated and affirmatively expressed . . . state policy" requiring the anticompetitive restraint.

Initially, there was great concern over the impact of this ruling on the cable franchising process. However, subsequent antitrust rulings having nothing to do with cable franchising have sharply limited the application of the *Boulder* decision. As long as the municipal ordinance was within the legislative intent of the state statute, the city will enjoy antitrust immunity. The statute does not have to expressly authorize the municipal action.

6. A somewhat different antitrust issue was raised by the Houston franchising process. The mayor of Houston asked four potential franchisees to divide the city among themselves. Subsequently, another company was included in the deal. Affiliated Capital Corporation, after being denied a chance to participate along with the other five companies, filed an antitrust suit against one them, Gulf Coast Cable. Affiliated was awarded $6.3 million. Broadcasting, Aug. 13, 1984 at 66.

## E.  CONTENT REGULATION

Because of the early view that cable television was merely an enhancement of broadcast television, many of the same restrictions on content that were developed for broadcasting are applicable to cable. At the same time there are very few cases involving these restrictions.

### 1.  POLITICAL SPEECH

Many of the political access rules have also been applied to origination cablecasting. The equal opportunities provision applicable to cable is essentially identical to that which governs broadcasting. There is also an equivalent lowest-unit-rate provision. 47 C.F.R. § 76.205.

The Commission has also adopted regulations applying the fairness doctrine, including the personal attack and political editorial rules, to origination cablecasting. 47 C.F.R. § 76.209. In 1983, the Commission instituted proceedings aimed at eliminating the fairness doctrine for cable. As of the end of 1985, no action had been taken in these proceedings.

Because the cable operators are not responsible under these rules for secondary transmissions or mandated access channels, and since many of the premium cable channels do not carry any political programming, there have been no real tests of the application of the rules. Also contributing to the lack of cases is the limited size of the audience for many cable programs.

A potential case arose when Cable News Network showed the Carter-Reagan debate sponsored by the League of Women Voters, but using tape delay included answers to each question by John Anderson. By including Anderson's answers, CNN removed the program from the exemption for "on-the-spot coverage of bona fide news events." Other candidates failed to demand equal opportunities. If one had, CNN was prepared to argue that all of its programming was covered by the exemption for "bona fide newscasts." Is there something wrong with the possibility that CNN could incur equal-opportunity obligations by providing an additional candidate with coverage?

## 2. Nonpolitical Speech

Among the restrictions on nonpolitical speech are a prohibition on cablecasting lottery information and a requirement for sponsorship identification. These provisions mirror the broadcasting rules. Also, the ban on cigarette advertising applies to cable.

However, most of the controversy surrounding restrictions on cable programming has involved attempts to ban indecent programs or nudity. The following case is typical of cases involving such restrictions.

### CRUZ v. FERRE

United States Court of Appeals, Eleventh Circuit, 1985.
755 F.2d 1415, 57 R.R.2d 1452.

Before HATCHETT and CLARK, CIRCUIT JUDGES, and STAFFORD, CHIEF DISTRICT JUDGE, Northern District of Florida.

STAFFORD, DISTRICT JUDGE. This cause involves a challenge to the constitutionality of a Miami ordinance regulating the distribution of obscene and indecent material through cable television. . . .

. . .

. . . The relevant portions of this ordinance provide:

"Section 1. No person shall by means of a cable television system knowingly distribute by wire or cable any obscene or indecent material.

"Section 2. The following words have the following meanings:

. . .

"(f) The test of whether or not material is 'obscene' is (i) whether the average person, applying contemporary community standards, would find that the work, taken as a whole, appeals to the prurient interest; (ii) whether the work depicts or describes, in a patently offensive way, sexual conduct specifically defined by the applicable state law; and (iii) whether the work, taken as a whole, lacks serious literary, artistic, political or scientific value.

"(g) 'Indecent material' means material which is a representation or description of a human sexual or excretory organ or function which the average person, applying contemporary community standards, would find to be patently offensive."

. . .

## First Amendment

The United States Supreme Court has long recognized that the First Amendment's prohibition against any "law . . . abridging the freedom of speech" applies to the states and their subdivisions through the Fourteenth Amendment. Gitlow v. New York, 268 U.S. 652 (1925). The Court has recognized only limited categories of speech that fall outside of the First Amendment's protection. . . . In Miller v. California, 413 U.S. 15 (1973), the Court reaffirmed that obscene material is unprotected by the First Amendment and set forth the current permissible limits of regulation. However, the Miller court "acknowledge[d] . . . the inherent dangers of undertaking to regulate any form of expression. State statutes designed to regulate obscene materials must be carefully limited." Id. at 23–24.

Appellees did not challenge the Miami ordinance's definition of "obscene" material or the city's constitutional authority to regulate obscenity on cable television. (The ordinance's definition of obscenity is in fact closely derived from the test set forth in *Miller.*) Rather, appellees challenged the provisions of the ordinance which attempt to regulate "indecent" materials. The ordinance's definition of indecent materials goes beyond the *Miller* definition of obscenity in two significant respects. First the ordinance does not require that the challenged materials, "taken as a whole, appeal to the prurient interest in sex." [ ] Second, the ordinance does not inquire whether the materials, "taken as a whole, do not have serious literary, artistic, political, or scientific value." [ ] Therefore, if materials falling within the ordinance's definition of "indecent" are to be regulated, the city's authority to do so must be found somewhere other than in the Supreme Court's obscenity cases.

Appellant's primary argument on appeal is that authority for the city's regulation is found in the Supreme Court decision FCC v. Pacifica Foundation, 438 U.S. 726 (1978). . . . Five members of the Court concluded that broadcasting of indecency could be regulated by the FCC under certain circumstances. The Court noted that "of all forms of communication, it is broadcasting that has received the most limited First Amendment protection." Id. at 748. The Court found two factors regarding broadcasting to be of particular relevance to the case with which it was presented. First, the Court found relevance in the fact that "the broadcast media have established a uniquely pervasive presence in the lives of all Americans" and that "[p]atently offensive, indecent material presented over the airwaves confronts the citizen, not only in public, but also in the privacy of the home, where the individual's right to be left alone plainly outweighs the First Amendment rights of an intruder." Id. Second, the Court found that "broadcasting is uniquely accessible to children, even those too young to read." Id. at 749. The Court was concerned with "[t]he ease with which children may obtain access to broadcast material," and also recognized "the government's interest in the 'well-being of its youth' and in supporting 'parents' claim to authority in their own household'. . . ." Id. at 749–50 (quoting Ginsberg v. New York, 390 U.S. 629, 639–640 (1968)).

The *Pacifica* Court, however, made a point of "emphasiz[ing] the narrowness of our holding." 438 U.S. at 750. The Court suggested that factors such as the time of day of the broadcast, the content of the program, and the composition of the audience might affect whether a particular broadcast could be regulated. Id. Moreover, the Court wrote that "differences between radio, television, and perhaps closed-circuit transmissions, may also be relevant." Id.

The district court after "a careful consideration of *Pacifica*," found *Pacifica* to be "inapplicable to the facts herein." [ ] After describing the cable television medium, the district court contrasted the cable medium with broadcast television. A cablevision subscriber must make the affirmative decision to bring Cablevision into his home. By using the monthly program guides, the Cablevision subscriber may avoid the unpleasant surprises that sometimes occur in broadcast programming. Additionally, the district court noted, the ability to protect children is provided through the use of a free "lockbox" or "parental key" available from Cablevision. [ ]

.  .  .

Although we recognize the complicated and uncertain area of constitutional interpretation which we are entering and the importance of the interests asserted by the city, we are persuaded that *Pacifica* cannot be extended to cover the particular facts of this case. *Pacifica*, it must be remembered, focused upon broadcasting's "pervasive presence," [ ]. The Court's concern with the pervasiveness of the broadcast media can best be seen in its description of broadcasted material as an "intruder" into the privacy of the home. Cablevision, however, does not "intrude" into the home. The Cablevision subscriber must affirmatively elect to have cable service come into his home. Additionally, the subscriber must make the additional affirmative decision whether to purchase any "extra" programming services, such as HBO. The subscriber must make a monthly decision whether to continue to subscribe to cable, and if dissatisfied with the cable service, he may cancel his subscription. The Supreme Court's reference to "a nuisance rationale," id. at 750, is not applicable to the Cablevision system, where there is no possibility that a non-cable subscriber will be confronted with materials carried only on cable. One of the keys to the very existence of cable television is the fact that cable programming is available only to those who have the cable attached to their television sets.[6]

Probably, the more important justification recognized in *Pacifica* for the FCC's authority to regulate the broadcasting of indecent materials was the accessibility of broadcasting to children. "The ease with which children may obtain access to broadcast material . . . justif[ies] special treatment of indecent broadcasting." Id. at 750. This interest, however, is significantly weaker in the context of cable television because parental manageability of cable television greatly exceeds the ability to manage the broadcast media. Again, parents must decide whether to allow Cablevision into the home. Parents decide whether to select supplementary programming services such as HBO. These services publish programming guides which identify programs containing "vulgarity," "nudity," and "violence." Additionally, parents may obtain a "lockbox" or "parental key" device enabling parents to prevent children from gaining access to "objectionable" channels of programming. Cablevision provides these without charge to subscribers.

*Pacifica* represents a careful balancing of the First Amendment rights of broadcasters and willing adult listeners against the FCC's interests in protecting children and unwilling adults. The Court held that, under the particular facts of *Pacifica*, the balance weighed in favor of the FCC. Because we determine that, under the facts of the instant case the interests of the City of Miami are substantially less strong than those of the FCC in *Pacifica*, we believe that we must hold *Pacifica* to be inapplicable to this case.

. . .

Even if we were to find the rationale of *Pacifica* applicable to this case, we would still be compelled to strike the ordinance as facially overbroad. As the district judge noted, the ordinance "prohibits far too broadly the transmission of indecent materials through cable television. The ordinance's prohibition is wholesale, without regard to the time of day or other variables indispensable to the decision in *Pacifica*." [ ] The ordinance totally fails to account for the variables identified in *Pacifica* : the time of day; the context of the program in which the material appears; the composition of the viewing audience. In ignoring these variables, the ordinance goes far beyond the realm of permissible regulation envisioned by the *Pacifica* Court.

However noble may have been the city's intentions, we are constrained to recognize the limitations imposed by the Constitution and the opinions of the Supreme Court. The city's attempt through the challenged ordinance to regulate indecency on its cable television system exceeds these limitations.

---

**6.** Appellants seem to want to extend Justice Stevens' "pig in the parlor" analogy. See Brief of Appellants at 16 ("it makes no difference whether the pig enters the parlor through the door of broadcast, cable, or amplified speech: government is entitled to keep the pig out of the parlor"). It seems to us, however, that if an individual voluntarily opens his door and allows a pig into his parlor, he is in less of a position to squeal.

[The court also upheld the district court's determination that the enforcement provisions of the ordinance violated due process. These provisions authorized the city manager to initiate complaints, conduct hearings on complaints, determine the admissibility of evidence, and make findings based on the hearing and impose sanctions. "[C]oncentrating the functions of complainant, jury, judge and 'executioner' in one person" created a "risk of arbitrary or capricious governmental action [which] under these circumstances is intolerably high."]

For the reasons stated herein, we hold that the findings of the district court were correct as a matter of law. Accordingly, we affirm.

**Notes and Questions**

1. What is the difference between buying a television set, certainly a prerequisite to bringing broadcast service into the home, and subscribing to cable? What if basic cable service is provided free of charge? Would a statute banning nudity on basic cable then be subject to the *Pacifica* rationale?

2. A similar Utah statute was struck down on similar grounds. Community Television v. Wilkinson, 11 Med.L.Rptr. 2217 (D.Utah 1985). The Cable Television Programming Decency Act authorized the filing of nuisance actions against anyone who continuously and knowingly distributed indecent material over cable television. Material was defined as indecent if it was "presented in a patently offensive way for the time, place and manner, and context in which the material is presented." The court held that the statute was unconstitutionally vague and overbroad.

3. The Cable Communications Policy Act provides that anyone who "transmits over any cable system any matter which is obscene or otherwise unprotected by the Constitution of the United States shall be fined not more than $10,000 or imprisoned not more than two years." 47 U.S.C. § 639. Could someone be prosecuted for indecent programming under this statute? As a result of this provision, the Commission eliminated its regulation banning obscene or indecent cable programming. Cable Communications Act Rules, 58 R.R.2d 1 (1985).

4. The Act also provides that cable operators must, upon request, sell or lease lock-out devices to subscribers. 47 U.S.C. § 624(2)(a).

# Chapter X

## NEW COMMUNICATIONS TECHNOLOGIES

As we discussed in Chapter IX, at one time cable was seen as the ultimate communications technology. At the height of the franchising battles, operators were promising that cable would provide everything to everybody. Not only were those promises unfulfilled, but cable is no longer even the "new" technology. A proliferation of new delivery systems such as multi-point distribution service (MDS), direct broadcast satellites (DBS), and satellite master antenna television (SMATV) are fighting for their share of the communications marketplace.

As each of these services has developed, new regulatory questions have arisen. The FCC does not have complete freedom in developing regulatory frameworks for new technologies. Rather, the Commission must work within the context of the Communications Act. Originally, the Act provided two basic models for regulation. One is the "broadcast" model we studied in Chapters II–VIII. The second is the "common-carrier" model to be discussed below. If a communications technology does not fit either of these models, the authority of the Commission to regulate it is questionable. This was a major issue in the regulation of cable. In *Midwest Video I*, p. 340, supra, the Commission's jurisdiction over cable was upheld as being ancillary to its jurisdiction over broadcasting. However, the exact limits of this jurisdiction were never clear, a problem that has apparently been solved by the Cable Communications Policy Act of 1984.

Common carriers are regulated under Title II of the Communications Act. The key element of common carrier regulation is that the "content is separated from the conduit." In other words, unlike broadcasters, common carriers have no editorial discretion. Instead, they must provide, in a non-discriminatory manner, the facilities for transmission of the customer's message. National Association of Regulatory Utilities Commissioners v. Federal Communications Commission (NARUC I), 525 F.2d 630 (D.C.Cir.), certiorari denied 425 U.S. 992 (1976). Telephone and telegraph companies are examples of common carriers.

There are a number of other important distinctions between broadcasters and common carriers. The federal government has preempted state regulation of broadcasting. In contrast, common carriers are regulated on both the state and federal levels. Interstate service is regulated by the Federal Communications Commission, while intrastate service is regulated by state agencies.

Sometimes, however, the Commission will decide to preempt the states and regulate a service on a strictly federal basis. When the Commission decides to preempt state regulation it does not necessarily imply that the Commission will choose to regulate to the same extent.

Instead, the FCC may choose to "preempt and forbear." This means that the Commission will eliminate the state regulations without substituting any of its own because the Commission believes as a matter of policy that no regulation is the proper regulation for that area.

The regulations most commonly subject to preemption are entry requirements and rate regulation. When a common carrier wishes to provide a service, it is usually required to demonstrate a need for the service. Some states require that, in addition to showing need, an applicant demonstrate that current carriers are either unable to or unwilling to provide the additional needed service. These requirements can effectively bar any new entrants into a given type of service.

Because common carriers often enjoy either a natural or government-created monopoly, they are often subject to rate regulation by either the FCC or appropriate state agencies. Rate regulation is usually eliminated when there is a finding of sufficient effective competition in the services provided.

Traditionally, the Commission has assigned services to the two regulatory models based on the method of transmission. Thus, STV is under the broadcast model while Multipoint Distribution Service (MDS) is a common carrier, because STV is transmitted through the broadcast portion of the spectrum, but MDS utilizes the microwave portion, which has always been viewed as a point-to-point medium. This led to seemingly anomalous results. For example, STV operators leasing their facilities to a movie service would be subject to different regulations than MDS operators leasing their facilities to the same movie service. In fact, a third regulatory scheme would obtain when the same movie service was carried over cable. While many of these anomalies still exist, the Commission has started to take a new approach, imposing regulations based on the service provided as opposed to the method of transmission. In some cases the Commission has even left the initial choice of regulatory model up to the licensee. In other words, licensees can decide for themselves which regulatory model would be most appropriate for the type of service they wish to offer.

Still another major concern for the Commission is that it not favor one service or technology over another. This attempt at regulatory neutrality has come to be called the "level playing field." As we will see, a level playing field can be very difficult to create. Nevertheless, it is an important issue as most of the regulatory battles involving new communications technologies are grounded firmly in economics. While the rhetoric may concentrate on the public interest or even the First Amendment, the real issue in almost every case is which service will gain some competitive advantage.

Obviously, the flood of new communications technologies has presented the FCC with serious problems as it tries to fit them into the traditional regulatory models. Let us now turn to some of these new communication technologies and examine how the Commission has attempted to resolve these problems.

## A.  MULTIPOINT DISTRIBUTION SERVICE (MDS)

MDS transmits microwave signals over super-high frequencies within a range of about 25 miles.  The signal is received by a small microwave antenna, usually located on a rooftop.  The signal can then be converted to a broadcast frequency and shown on a vacant VHF channel. Originally, MDS was intended to be used to transmit data.  However, some operators found that a more profitable use was distribution of video programming to hotels and other multi-unit buildings.  As the cost of converters and antenna systems dropped it even became feasible to distribute programming to single-family dwellings.  In some urban areas in which cable is not available, MDS has been distributing HBO programming.

MDS is regulated as a common carrier because, as we previously discussed, it was viewed by the Commission as a point-to-point service. In a 1977 decision, the Commission preempted state and local regulation that serves to hinder the development of MDS.  Orth-O-Vision, Inc., 69 F.C.C.2d 657, 44 R.R.2d 329 (1978), recon., 82 F.C.C.2d 178, 48 R.R.2d 503 (1980), affirmed sub nom. New York State Commission on Cable Television v. Federal Communications Commission, 669 F.2d 58, 50 R.R.2d 1201 (2d Cir.1982).  In essence, the case preempted state and local government attempts to impose entry restrictions.

In 1983, the FCC reallocated eight of the 28 instructional television fixed service (ITFS) microwave channels to MDS, making multichannel multipoint distribution service (MMDS) available.  ITFS (MDS Reallocation), 54 R.R.2d 107 (1983).  MMDS operators may also obtain extra channel capacity by leasing an ITFS operator's excess capacity.  Utilizing these leased ITFS channels, Premier Communications Networks Inc. is offering five-channel service in San Francisco.  Subscribers receive HBO, superstations WOR and WTBS, CNN, and ESPN.  Four-channel service is available in Washington, D.C., and a similar system is under construction in New York.  Broadcasting, July 1, 1985 at 5.

More ambitious operations are now being proposed in some cities. For example, Argonox Communications has announced plans to offer 21-channel service in Oklahoma City beginning sometime in 1986.  In Milwaukee, Movie Systems, Inc. (MSI) has proposed a 14-channel system. If it is successful, MSI will then construct a similar system in Minneapolis.  Broadcasting, Sept. 16, 1985 at 84.

The Commission decided to use a lottery system to award licenses for the ITFS channels reallocated to MDS.  In July, 1985, the Court of Appeals for the District of Columbia Circuit ordered the FCC either to postpone the MDS lottery scheduled for that time until rulemaking on women's preferences was completed or to protect women applicants until the rulemaking was completed.  The Commission postponed the lottery. The next month the Commission voted to give women no preference in MDS lotteries and rescheduled the lottery.  Broadcasting, Aug. 12, 1985 at 36.  An appeal of the Commission's decision is expected.

## B.  DIRECT BROADCAST SATELLITES (DBS)

DBS is a system of broadcasting directly from studio to home via satellite.  The technology involves the usual transmission to a satellite and the return to earth, where the signal is collected by a receiving dish two or three feet in diameter placed on the roof of the home of the subscriber.

The first communications satellites were not suitable for DBS because their relatively weak signals could only be received by very large, expensive dishes.  By the late 1970's, however, the technology had improved to the point where a commercial DBS system appeared feasible.  It was now possible to build higher-powered satellites, which would allow the use of small, inexpensive dishes for home reception.

At the 1979 World Administrative Radio Conference (WARC–79) the 12 GHz band was allocated to DBS.  Decisions on specific orbital locations and frequency assignments were left for the 1983 Regional Administrative Radio Conference (RARC–83).  In the interim, the Commission opened proceedings on domestic DBS service.  As a result of those proceedings, the Commission decided to adopt interim DBS regulations pending the outcome of RARC–83.  These interim DBS regulations authorizing domestic DBS service were adopted in July, 1982.  Three months later, the Commission granted Satellite Television Corporation's (STC) application to construct an experimental DBS system offering subscription television service to the Eastern portion of the United States.  Both the Interim DBS Regulations and the grant of STC's application were appealed.

### NATIONAL ASSOCIATION OF BROADCASTERS v. FEDERAL COMMUNICATIONS COMMISSION

United States Court of Appeals, District of Columbia Circuit, 1984.
740 F.2d 1190, 56 R.R.2d 1105.

Before TAMM, MIKVA and DAVIS, CIRCUIT JUDGES.

MIKVA, CIRCUIT JUDGE:

Of the technological innovations currently revolutionizing the communications field, the most recent, and potentially the most significant, is direct broadcast satellite service (DBS).  DBS involves the transmission of signals from the earth to highpowered, geostationary satellites which then beam television signals directly to individual homes equipped to receive them.  Use of satellites massively extends the range of a broadcast's voice by freeing it from the atmospheric limitations that traditionally limit terrestrial broadcasters to narrow broadcast areas; a single DBS signal will eventually be capable of reaching the entire continental United States.  For this reason and others, DBS promises several significant advantages over existing television technology: high-quality service to individuals in rural or remote areas where conventional broadcasting is inefficient; the addition of many more channels even in urban areas already receiving several television signals; "narrowcasting" of programs to specialized tastes through the ability to aggregate small, widely dispersed audiences; the development of higher quality visual and audio signals through use of high-definition-television signals; and television transmission of non-entertainment programming, such as medical data and educational information.

The regulatory approach to DBS taken by the Federal Communications Commission . . . is as novel as the technology with which it is concerned.  In essence, the Commission has chosen to deregulate DBS even before the service is born. . . .  We find that, on the whole, the FCC has done a commendable job in assuring that regulation in the communications field not impede new technologies that offer substantial public benefits . . ..  We also find, however, that in its zeal to promote this new technology, the FCC gave short shrift to certain of its statutory obligations, and we therefore vacate part of the Interim DBS regulations; in addition, our approval of other parts is qualified by several guidelines to which the Commission must hew in its continuing oversight of this nascent technology.

. . .

## ANALYSIS

### I. *The FCC's Power to Approve Non-Local Broadcast Service*

DBS technology is inherently unsuitable for the provision of traditional local broadcast service.  The satellites involved cannot presently be located with the requisite precision nor economically equipped with a sufficiently large antenna to provide a spot beam capable of covering only a traditional size local community.  [ ]  Moreover, many of the benefits of DBS—including narrowcasting and provision of service to less densely populated areas—could not practically be realized by a "local" DBS system. . . .

Petitioner NAB argues that the FCC does not have the power to approve a technology that will sever broadcast services from their traditional link to a particular community.  NAB seeks to rest this Luddite argument on section 307(b) of the [Communications Act], which provides:

> the Commission shall make such *distribution of licenses* . . . *among the several States and communities* as to provide a fair, efficient, and equitable distribution of radio service to each of the same.

47 U.S.C. § 307(b) (emphasis added).  NAB reads this provision to require that broadcast licenses indeed *be* "distributed" among the "States" and "communities;" NAB thus concludes that the Act mandates a system of *local* broadcast licensing and service with which STC's authorization, and DBS in general, is "fundamentally irreconcilable."

We do not think it necessary to ascribe to the framers of the Act an intent so shortsighted as to preclude new technology that offers the promise of substantial public benefit.  The plain language of the Act does not compel such impracticable consequences. . . .  The ultimate touchstone for the FCC is . . . the distribution of service, rather than of licenses or of stations; the constituency to be served is people, not municipalities. Moreover, the Commission also has an obligation to "encourage the larger and more effective use of radio in the public interest." 47 U.S.C. § 303(g) . . . . Just as we have held that the Act does not bestow a vested right on any particular *licensee* to retention of its license, [ ], so too we now hold that the Act does not entrench any particular *system* of broadcasting: existing systems, like existing licensees, have no entitlement that permits them to deflect competitive pressure from innovative and effective technology.

In so holding we do not denigrate the importance of local programming to a national broadcasting system that is designed to serve the public interest. [ ] We need not define the outer limits of the Commission's authority to make this country's broadcasting system a regional or national one, however, for two reasons. First, the *DBS Order* does not by its terms eliminate local programming. Second, the Commission explicitly found that DBS will merely supplement the existing local broadcast system, rather than replace it, [ ], and we find no error in that finding. We therefore need not decide how far the Commission may go toward the elimination of local programming to hold that not *every* communications service approved by the Commission need be tied to a local community.

. . .

## II. *Applicability to DBS of Broadcast Restrictions*

The most innovative of the steps taken by the FCC with respect to DBS was the Commission's decision, in the service of a "flexible regulatory approach" designed to stimulate DBS technology, not to apply to DBS the major regulatory restrictions traditionally imposed on broadcasters. Central to this approach was the Commission's refusal to extend the broadcast restrictions of Title III of the [Communications Act] to all DBS systems.

. . .

Among the statutory restraints that broadcasters currently face are section 312(a)(7), which requires that qualified candidates for federal office be provided reasonable access to broadcast facilities, and section 315, which provides that, if one political candidate is allowed to use a station, other qualified candidates must be given an equal opportunity to respond. Because DBS is likely to be a particularly attractive medium at least for presidential candidates, the question of how these broadcast restraints apply to DBS is of great moment.

The *DBS Order* established the following classificatory scheme for purposes of applying the Act's broadcasting rules. Those DBS applicants which propose to provide service (whether in the form of free or pay-TV) direct to homes and to "retain [ ] control over the content of the transmissions" will be treated as broadcasters. A DBS satellite owner can choose instead to operate as a common carrier, in which case satellite transmission services would have to be offered indiscriminately to the public pursuant to tariff under the provisions of Title II of the Act; a satellite owner who chooses the common carrier option will not be treated as a broadcaster. Also not treated as a broadcaster under the *DBS Order* are those who lease satellite space from a DBS common carrier and who use the leased channels to distribute programming via satellite to individual homes. These lessees, who neither own nor operate a DBS satellite, are referred to as "customer-programmers" of DBS common carriers, and it is they who control the content of the programming transmitted by a DBS common carrier.

.   .   .

We recognize the Commission's authority to approve services on an experimental basis in an effort to gather important market data to be used in the completion of a regulatory framework. [ ] Moreover, as other parts of this opinion will confirm, that discretion is particularly capacious when the Commission is dealing with new technologies unforeseen at the time the Communications Act was passed. But that discretion is not boundless: the Commission has no authority to experiment with its statutory obligations. We conclude that the Commission has engaged in precisely such forbidden statutory experimentation in exempting from Title III the customer-programmers of DBS common carriers.

Section 3(*o*) of the Communications Act defines "broadcasting" as "the dissemination of radio communications intended to be received by the public, directly or by the intermediary of relay stations." 47 U.S.C. § 153(*o*). We have previously held that the test for whether a particular activity constitutes broadcasting is whether there is "an intent for *public* distribution" and whether the programming is "of interest to the *general* .   .   . audience." .   .   .

When DBS systems transmit signals directly to homes with the intent that those signals be received by the public, such transmissions rather clearly fit the definition of broadcasting; radio communications are being disseminated with the intent that they be received by the public. That remains true even if a common carrier satellite leases its channels to a customer-programmer who does not own any transmission facilities; in such an arrangement, someone—either the lessee or the satellite owner—is broadcasting. Despite the argument of some intervenors and the suggestion of the government .   .   ., it also remains true regardless of whether a DBS system is advertiser or subscriber funded. .   .   .   While the FCC may be coming increasingly to the view that subscription services are not "broadcasting" [ ], a view not yet passed upon by the courts, the *DBS Order* must rise or fall upon the FCC's articulated policies at the time of the order. And as the *Order* itself recognizes, these policies did not distinguish free-TV from pay-TV for purposes of defining "broadcasting." [ ] The FCC therefore cannot justify its exemption of some DBS systems from broadcast restrictions by pointing to the fact that those systems are subscriber rather than advertiser funded.  [  ]

The irrationality of the Commission's view of the statute, which makes ownership the touchstone of broadcasting, is illustrated by the following example.  If a DBS owner broadcasts programming directly to homes, it is subject to regulation as a broadcaster; if that owner sends its programs via leased channels on another satellite, the very same programming will be immune from broadcast regulation.  Through a general system of cross-leasing, all DBS systems could therefore escape Title III.  Nothing in the statutory definition allows the Commission to elevate form over function in this way nor suggests that the definition of broadcasting turns on whether the provider of the service leases satellite facilities from a common carrier or owns the satellite outright.  .  .  .

.  .  .

Very real practical consequences could therefore follow from the FCC's exemption of common carrier DBS lessees from broadcast restrictions—consequences at odds with the basic objectives of the Communications Act.  Under the *DBS Order*, a federal candidate who wanted access to a DBS system that was operated as a common carrier could not force either the satellite owner or its channel lessees to provide that access, for both would be immune from the Act's broadcast restraints; the candidate would instead have to rely on his or her purchasing power, as well as on the whim of the channel programmer, to receive access and an opportunity to respond to opponents.  It was to avoid this very result, in which a speaker "who could afford the cost" could purchase enough time on a broadcast station operated as a common carrier to dominate American thought and American politics without any regulatory restraints, that Congress imposed restraints such as the equal opportunity rule upon broadcasters.  [  ]

We therefore reject the central rationale upon which the Commission relied to exempt customer-programmers of DBS common carriers from the statutory constraints under which broadcasters must operate: the fact that Congress did not in 1934 contemplate DBS does not give the Commission a blank check to regulate DBS in any way it deems fit.

.  .  .

The Commission's other rationales for its treatment of customer-programmers provide even less persuasive reasons for the Commission's departure from the statute's plain language.  The claim that imposition of Title III obligations on channel lessees "merely would serve to duplicate the more pervasive" common carrier obligations of Title II, [  ], is clearly wrong, as Title II merely requires a carrier to accept all applicants for service on a non-discriminatory basis and thus offers no surrogate for Title III requirements such as reasonable access or equal opportunity.  A common carrier *cannot* guarantee political candidates reasonable access to airtime or an equal opportunity to respond to opponents, for the sine qua non of a common carrier is the obligation to accept applicants on a non-content oriented basis.  [The court also rejected an analogy to MDS. When the Commission decided not to apply broadcast regulations to MDS, it had not contemplated MDS being used to supply subscription television. Since the time the Commission had authorized the use of MDS for subscription television, no court had passed on the validity of exempting MDS programmer-customers from broadcast regulations.]

.  .  .

A final reason for exempting DBS customer-programmers from broadcast regulation, a reason not directly invoked by the FCC but raised by intervenors in the companion case, [    ], must also be rejected. These intervenors argue that the Commission never regulates *programmers* but only station *licensees*; examples of non-regulated programmers are said to be television networks, which provide programming over the facilities of affiliated broadcast stations, subscription television programmers, who perform similar functions on stations of television licensees, and pay television programmers such as Home Box Office, whose services are carried via satellites to cable television systems. However, the Commission previously *has* applied broadcast restraints to programmers and has been upheld in doing so. Columbia Broadcasting System, Inc. v. FCC, 629 F.2d 1, 26 (D.C.Cir.1980) (affirming Commission's authority to apply reasonable access requirements of Section 312(a)(7) to major broadcast networks) [affirmed by the Supreme Court]. The reason the FCC does not *ordinarily* regulate programmers is a simple one: the Commission applies the statute directly to the entities responsible for program selection and transmission—the broadcast licensees. This approach is consistent with the Act's philosophy, for where a programmer operates through a broadcast licensee who must comply with the statute's broadcast restrictions, as is the case with STV programmers, the networks, and cable, the Act's objectives are met. But when both the customer-programmer *and* the common-carrier through which the former's signals are carried are immunized from broadcast regulation, as they are in the *DBS Order*, the statutory scheme is completely negated.

To avoid this result, we vacate that part of the *DBS Order* that exempts customer-programmers of DBS common carriers from the statutory requirements imposed on broadcasters.  .  .  .

We also do not suggest that all uses of DBS constitute broadcasting; activity that would provide non-general interest, point-to-point service, where the format is of interest to only a narrow class of subscribers and does not implicate the broadcasting objectives of the Act, need not be regulated as broadcasting.  .  .  .

.  .  .

### III. *The FCC's Refusal to Apply its Ownership Restrictions to DBS*

In addition to refusing to impose statutory broadcast restrictions on customer-programmers of DBS common carrier, the FCC also declined to apply to DBS Commission regulations that seek to assure that control of the media is lodged in diverse hands. . . .

The interim DBS rules temporarily suspend for DBS both the multiple channel and the cross-ownership rules. . . .

The refusal to apply the cross-ownership rules to DBS is not at issue in this case. However, petitioner NAB argues that it was arbitrary and capricious for the FCC to relax temporarily the multiple-channel rule for DBS while leaving that same rule in place for terrestrial licensees.

At least at this early stage in the development of DBS, we reject that argument: DBS and traditional television broadcasting are not sufficiently similar in their technology, marketability, capitalization requirements, or other relevant factors that identical regulatory treatment of the two is required. Unlike conventional television systems, DBS systems are extraordinarily capital intensive and have high fixed costs; one applicant estimated that preoperational and first year expenditures alone would be $600 million. [ ] Weighing in against these costs are significant risks which the FCC has found to be associated with the new technology: (i) a lengthy delay (approaching five years) between issuance of a construction permit and initiation of service; (ii) reliance on unproven and developing technology; (iii) an uncertain and rapidly changing marketplace; (iv) operational and marketing problems associated with the provision of service and distribution of home receiving equipment over vast geographic areas. [ ]

These differences led several potential applicants to comment that no "responsible business organization" would enter the DBS field "without control over the programming of more than one channel." [ ] Such multiple-channel control allows counter programming, in which a satellite owner can offer movies on one channel, for example, sports on another, and cultural and children's programs on the third—thereby potentially attracting substantially more viewers than would be possible were only a single channel available. Based on the comments of some applicants that the ability to counterprogram was necessary to justify investment in DBS, the FCC concluded that, at least for the time being, it was unwise to impose ownership restrictions comparable to those existing in other areas. However, the FCC expressly reserved the right to impose ownership restrictions if actual operational experience with DBS systems demonstrated the need for increased regulatory intervention.

. . .

In this case, we conclude that the Commission acted within its discretion in suspending the multiple-channel restrictions. . . .

. . .

## CONCLUSION

When technology as novel as DBS confronts a statute as broadly drafted as the Communications Act of 1934, the administering agency has substantial leeway in its efforts to harmonize the two. We conclude that, on the whole, the Commission has exercised this leeway in a reasonable manner. We therefore vacate only that portion of the *DBS Order* that makes broadcast restrictions inapplicable to some DBS systems and, with the caveats noted above, affirm the rest of that Order. We also affirm in its entirety the *STC Decision*.

It is so ordered.

### Notes and Questions

1.  Subsequent to the court of appeals decision, STC attempted to find a partner to help finance its DBS operation. When none of the negotiations proved successful, STC abandoned its DBS plans entirely.

2.  The first DBS system began operating in November, 1983, utilizing medium-powered communications satellites. United Satellite Communications, Inc. (USCI) began five-channel service to central Indiana. The consumer response was far less than USCI had envisioned, and the service was discontinued in mid-1985. The future of DBS is still hard to determine since high-powered satellites allowing inexpensive receiving equipment will not be operational until 1988.

3.  At RARC–83, orbital slots and frequencies were awarded. A frequency band from 12.2 to 12.7 GHz was set aside for DBS. Meanwhile, further questions of satellite use and allocation were negotiated at the 1985 World Administrative Radio Conference, which has become known as Space-WARC, p. 36, supra.

4.  Given the court's opinion in NAB v. FCC, would the Commission's exemption of MDS customer-programmers from broadcast regulation be able to withstand a legal challenge? What distinctions between the new MMDS subscription television systems and DBS might allow a different result?

## C.  SATELLITE MASTER ANTENNA TELEVISION (SMATV)

SMATV involves setting up one or more earth stations on a large building or complex and distributing by wire or cable the various programming received. The distinction between SMATV and cable television is that no city streets or rights of way are used. This prevents cities from subjecting SMATV operators to a franchising process. It also limits SMATV systems to large apartments and hotels where enough subscribers can be reached without crossing city streets.

In some ways SMATV resembles MMDS in that multiple channels are distributed to receiving systems most of which are set up on rooftops. However, there are some distinctions. SMATV uses large expensive earth stations to receive the programming directly from satellites, whereas MMDS receives the satellite feeds at some central location and then redistributes them by microwave to the customer. Since the more expensive satellite receiving equipment must be located at each building served by SMATV, it is only viable for large buildings. In contrast, a single earth station facility allows MMDS to serve all buildings in an approximately 25-mile radius. Because the equipment needed at a customer's location is relatively inexpensive, a small microwave antenna and a converter, MMDS can economically serve single-family homes.

However, SMATV does have some advantages over MMDS. A SMATV system can offer essentially unlimited channels since the transmission from central facility to actual customers is through wires. MMDS is limited to the number of separate microwave channels available. Recall that until two years ago that limit was essentially a single channel.

SMATV's freedom from franchising requirements has long concerned cable operators, who argue that it gives SMATV an unfair competitive advantage. Cable companies must compete through a long and expensive process and often are required to pay franchise fees and make expensive concessions for the right to do business, but SMATV operators can just set up a dish and start delivering service. Furthermore, cable companies are required to offer service to everyone within their franchise areas. SMATV operators are free to choose their customers.

To counter this perceived inequity, cable operators tried to persuade state and local governments to regulate SMATV by imposing strict entry requirements similar to those applied to cable television. In 1983, Earth Satellite Communications, Inc. (ESCOM) was enjoined from constructing a SMATV system in East Orange, New Jersey, for failure to comply with the New Jersey Cable Television Act. ESCOM responded by filing a petition with the FCC asking it to preempt state and local entry regulation of SMATV. In November, 1983, the Commission acted favorably on the ESCOM petition. The FCC's action was then appealed by the New York State Commission on Cable Television.

## NEW YORK STATE COMMISSION ON CABLE TELEVISION v. FEDERAL COMMUNICATIONS COMMISSION

United States Court of Appeals, District of Columbia Circuit, 1984.
749 F.2d 804, 57 R.R.2d 363.

Before TAMM, WILKEY, and EDWARDS, CIRCUIT JUDGES.

TAMM, CIRCUIT JUDGE. . . .

. . .

### II.

. . .

### B. *The Commission's Authority*

. . .

In its preemption order the Commission based its authority over SMATV upon the federal interest in "the unfettered development of interstate transmission of satellite signals." [ ] This development would be frustrated, the Commission found, if each state could impose its own entry restrictions upon systems that were part of the national satellite network.  [   ]  The Commission chose not to impose entry restrictions of its own, believing that open entry policies in the satellite field would create a more diverse and competitive telecommunications environment.  [   ]

Petitioners do not challenge the general authority of the Commission to preempt state and local regulation of cable television in appropriate circumstances.  Rather, they contend that, in this particular instance, because the Commission has failed to show that preemption is necessary "to ensure the achievement of the Commission's statutory responsibilities," FCC v. Midwest Video Corp., 440 U.S. 689, 706 (1979), it has acted beyond its authority.  To support this contention, petitioners advance two closely related arguments.  First, they contend that preemption of state and local regulation of SMATV is a reversal of well-established policy and therefore "presumptively" contrary to the achievement of the Commission's statutory responsibilities.  Second, petitioners contend that the policies underlying the Communications Act cannot be advanced by the Commission's determination to allow SMATV to enter the telecommunications marketplace unregulated.  We reject both of these arguments and conclude that the Commission's action is not only consistent with prior Commission policy, but also a " 'reasonable accommodation of conflicting policies' that are within the agency's domain."  [   ]

1.  The Allocation of Regulatory Responsibilities Between the Commission and State and Local Governments

During the past 12 years, the Commission has given local jurisdictions significant control over the franchising of traditional cable systems. Petitioners contend that the Commission's refusal to give state and local governments the same authority over SMATV as they have over traditional cable is a reversal of well-established policy.  Careful review of Commission precedent, however, reveals that the petitioners' argument ignores the critical distinction the Commission has made between cable television systems that use public rights-of-way and systems, like SMATV, that are operated solely on private property.

The Commission recognized in 1972 that direct federal licensing of the thousands of cable systems operating in large and small communities throughout the country would place "an unmanageable burden on the Commission." . . .  The Commission therefore created a "deliberately structured dualism" whereby local government would be responsible for selecting franchises, pursuant to minimum standards established by the Commission, while the Commission retained exclusive authority over all operational aspects of cable communication, including technical standards and signal carriage.  [   ]

. . .  Although the Commission recognized that "the essentially local service offered by cable television, at least in its formative stages, could best be developed through local participation and enforcement," it cautioned that "the developing duplicative and burdensome overregulation of cable television" was of increasing concern.  [   ]

Following a comprehensive study of the effect of dual regulation upon the cable industry, the Commission in 1975 recognized the need for clarification of local governments' regulatory responsibilities.  .  .  . The Commission made explicit its intention to preempt local regulation whenever necessary "to assure the orderly development of this new technology into the national communications structure." [   ]

Under this dual regulatory framework, the Commission has consistently retained exclusive authority over these elements of cable television that do not involve the use of public rights-of-way.  The Commission has retained exclusive authority over the licensing of the satellites that transmit SMATV signals, [   ], and the earth stations that receive the satellite signals.  [   ]  The Commission has preempted regulation of pay television programming services and rates, [   ], and the carriage of television broadcast signals.  [   ]  As the Supreme Court stated in its unanimous *Crisp* decision, "[o]ver the past twenty years, pursuant to its delegated authority under the Communications Act, the FCC has unambiguously expressed its intent to preempt any state or local regulation of this entire array of signals carried by cable television systems." [   ]

A case similar to this appeal, Orth-O-Vision, Inc., 69 F.C.C.2d 657 (1978), recon., 82 F.C.C.2d 178 (1980), affirmed sub nom. New York State Commission on Cable Television v. FCC, 669 F.2d 58 (2d Cir.1982), clearly demonstrates the Commission's willingness to preempt state regulation of systems that do not involve the use of public rights-of-way.
.  .  .

.  .  .

In affirming the Commission's preemption, the Second Circuit found that by denying franchises, municipalities could curtail the development of MDS.  [   ]  Since the Commission's policy of advancing the development of MDS was within its statutory authority, the Commission properly preempted conflicting state entry regulation. [   ]

.  .  .  The Commission's preemption of a cable system, which, like the system involved in this appeal, does not use public rights-of-way, plainly refutes petitioners' contention that the Commission has arbitrarily reversed well-established policy.

### 2.  Commission Reliance on Market Forces to Regulate SMATV

In a general challenge to the Commission's decision not to impose entry regulations upon SMATV, petitioners contend that the Commission has failed to show that its open entry policy is necessary for the achievement of its statutory responsibilities.  Franchise cable television and SMATV have flourished under local regulation, they claim, and no federal interest would be promoted by allowing SMATV to compete unregulated with traditional cable.

Although the Commission does not have unbridled discretion to use the marketplace to regulate an industry under its control, "the public interest touchstone of the Communications Act, beyond question, permits the FCC to allow the marketplace to substitute for direct Commission regulation in appropriate circumstances." [   ]  Indeed, the Commission has increasingly come to rely upon market forces to regulate the entry and operation of new cable television systems. [   ]

Petitioners advance no credible argument to show that the market is an inappropriate tool for the Commission to choose in this instance to effectuate its statutory mandate.  Competition, petitioner NYSCCT argues, will have a grave impact upon the existing cable franchises.  The Commission's determination that SMATV should be allowed to serve residents of multi-unit dwellings cannot be challenged as contrary to the purposes of the Communications Act merely because some harm will be visited upon existing and developed franchises.  Measuring the public interest standard of the Communications Act with sole reference to the impact Commission action would have upon a developed technology ensures a regulatory regime frozen into maintaining the status quo.  We cannot read into the Communications Act a congressional intent to so prevent innovative technologies from conferring substantial benefits upon the viewing public.  We therefore conclude that the Commission's present reliance on market forces to regulate the entry of SMATV into the cable television marketplace is consistent with its statutory mandate.

.  .  .

## C.   The Reasonableness of the Commission's Exercise of Authority

Having established the preemption of state regulation of SMATV is within the Commission's statutory authority, we now consider whether in exercising its authority the Commission acted arbitrarily or capriciously. [   ]  As this court recently stated in Wold Communications, Inc. v. FCC, 735 F.2d 1465, 1476 (D.C.Cir.1984), the proper inquiry under the arbitrary and capricious standard is "whether a reasonable person, considering the matter on the agency's table, could arrive at the judgment the agency made." [   ]  Our discussion of the Commission's authority forecloses extensive inquiry into the rationality of its decision.  A finding that the Commission has the power to preempt state regulation means that preemption is necessary for the full accomplishment of lawful Commission objectives.  Establishing this logical relationship between the action taken—preemption—and the Commission policy involves, at least to a certain extent, the determination that the Commission has not acted arbitrarily or capriciously.  Furthermore, the nature of this preemption action obviates extensive analysis of the facts upon which the determination was reached: the parties do not so much dispute the factual circumstances surrounding the cable industry as the kind of regulation that should or should not be imposed upon the existing and emerging cable systems.  Yet, if the Commission has chosen rationally among competing policies, we cannot reverse because we would have chosen other means of effectuating the congressional mandate. . . .

Petitioner NYSCCT claims that there is inadequate evidence in the record to justify the Commission's conclusion that state and local regulations actually impede the growth of SMATV. The petitioner's comments to the Commission, however, betray the weakness of its contention. The petitioner argued that "[t]he principal evil of allowing private cable to exist outside the regulatory scheme for cable is the impact upon territorial cable television." [  ] Since the dominant theme of the petitioner's opposition to the preemption order is the alleged need to stifle SMATV development, the Commission rationally determined that federal preemption was necessary to effectuate its policy of enhancing the diversity of cable programming. [  ]

Petitioners contend with only slightly more force that the Commission acted arbitrarily by failing to consider the impact preemption and deregulation would have upon the traditional cable industry. Petitioner NYSCCT estimated that the unregulated entry of SMATV into the New York City marketplace would cost franchise cable systems between $348 million and $793 million over the lifetime of the franchises. To replace the revenue lost from those subscribers who would choose SMATV, the franchise systems would have to increase their rates of their remaining subscribers from $7.00 to $11.00 per month.

The Commission found NYSCCT's analysis unpersuasive for several reasons. First, the Commission stated that it is "not an economic guarantor of competitive communications technologies which may offer similar services to subscribers." [  ] Second, the Commission noted that NYSCCT's arguments had been raised and answered in the Orth-O-Vision proceedings. Finally, the Commission predicted that, in states such as New York where cable franchises have mandatory access to multi-unit dwellings, franchise cable and SMATV could co-exist or at least compete for the same subscribers. [  ]

The Commission's response, while terse, was reasonably commensurate with the persuasive force of the petitioner's argument. Petitioner's "economic analysis" purports to document the degree of SMATV penetration into the cable television marketplace. Instead of doing so, it simply assumes that SMATV will replace franchise cable in every apartment of every multi-unit dwelling. Moreover, the data provided by the petitioner, viewed in the most positive light, merely show what the Commission already recognizes: the unregulated entry of SMATV into the cable television marketplace will have a competitive impact upon franchise cable. Petitioner's argument does not relate to the Commission's evaluation of the *facts*; it merely involves a recharacterization of the petitioner's basic quarrel with the Commission's *policy* of allowing SMATV to compete with franchise cable. We have already determined that the Commission has the statutory authority to adopt the policy of preventing local governments from enforcing entry regulations that have the purpose or the effect of restricting SMATV's competitive position.

Evidence purporting to document the degree of SMATV penetration into the cable television marketplace does nothing to undermine the rationality of this decision.  [   ]

.   .   .

For the foregoing reasons, the Commission's order is affirmed.

**Notes and Questions**

1.  What is the real issue in this case?  Is it the "public interest" or merely which of two competing communication delivery systems will gain a competitive advantage?  Are cable operators—through the New York State Commission on Cable Television—asking to be protected from SMATV in the same way that broadcasters sought protection against cable?

2.  The Commission's stated rationale for preempting state and local regulation of SMATV was to prevent such regulation from inhibiting the development of SMATV service to the public.  Couldn't it be argued, however, that the Commission's action served to give SMATV an unfair regulatory advantage over cable television?  Which is more important, regulatory parity or service to the public?  Would it make a difference if, as a result of SMATV competition, some cable systems failed, leaving many people with no service at all?

## D.  HOME SATELLITE DISHES

In 1979, the Commission decided to eliminate a licensing requirement for receive-only satellite dishes.  Regulation of Domestic Receive-Only Satellite Earth Stations, 74 F.C.C.2d 205, 46 R.R.2d 698 (1979).  Over the next few years, the cost of receive-only satellite dishes dropped from more than $10,000 to under $1,000.  As a result of this deregulation and sudden affordability, a rapidly increasing number of people have bought dishes for their homes.  The dishes give them access to the hundreds of video signals being transmitted by communications satellites.  Among these signals are many of the cable programming services and programming fed by the broadcast networks to their affiliates.  In addition, a lot of unedited video, e.g. news feeds, can be picked up by the dishes.

The dishes became very controversial because the dish owners were paying nothing for the programming.  The cable programming companies argued that the dish owners were pirates, stealing the signals.  The dish owners and their trade association, Society of Private and Commercial Earth Stations (SPACE), claimed that they were willing to pay for the service, but the programming companies refused to sell to them.  From a legal standpoint, it was unclear whether § 605 of the Communications Act, which prohibited unauthorized reception of some signal transmissions, applied to home satellite dishes.

A compromise solution to the controversy was included in the Cable Communications Policy Act of 1984.  Section 605, now redesignated § 705, of the Communications Act was amended to authorize receipt of any non-encrypted signal for private viewing, unless a system for marketing the programming service for private viewing has been established.

Many cable programming services have begun scrambling their signals to prevent any unauthorized reception.   It now appears that all the major programming services will use the same scrambling technology.   This means that home dish owners will have to buy only one decoder.   They will then have to contract for each service they wish to receive.   How many dish owners will be willing to pay $400 for a decoder and then pay a monthly fee for each service they desire is not clear. Meanwhile, SPACE has been lobbying Congress for protection against excessive fees for access to the programming services.

## E.  SUBSIDIARY COMMUNICATION AUTHORIZATIONS

It may seem odd to consider part of an AM or FM radio signal a new communications technology, but due to longstanding Commission restrictions, very few radio stations used their subcarriers prior to the mid-1980's.   A subcarrier is a secondary transmission that can be "piggy-backed" on the primary signal.   These subcarriers can be heard only through the use of special receivers.

Until 1983, use of subcarriers was limited to broadcast-related services such as stereo-enhancement, background music for stores and elevators, foreign language programming, and commodities reports. AM subcarriers could also be used for utility-load management.   In 1983, the Commission authorized FM licensees to use their subcarriers for any purpose they wished.   The new expanded authorization allows for such uses as entertainment programming, data transmission and paging.

At the same time, the Commission increased the width of the FM baseband from 75 to 99 khz, making two subcarriers rather than one possible for each station.   The FCC eliminated a requirement that FM subcarriers be frequency modulated and that subcarriers operate only during the hours when main-channel programming is carried.   The Commission no longer requires a formal application for subcarrier operation.

All of these changes left the Commission with an important question: What regulatory model should be applied to the newly authorized subcarrier services?   When subcarriers were limited to broadcast-related services, it was clear that the broadcast model applied.   But services such as paging and data-transmission had traditionally been regulated as common-carriers.   The Commission took the novel approach of requiring the licensee to determine which regulatory model to apply.   In other words, a licensee wishing to offer a subcarrier service must decide which model is most appropriate for the service in question.

If the licensee plans to provide a fixed service, this determination must be made in accordance with the test laid down in NARUC I, p. 395, supra.   If the licensee plans to provide a land mobile service, the regulatory status will be determined by Section 331(c) of the Communications Act.   47 U.S.C. § 332 (1982).

Most of the controversy surrounding the expanded use of subcarriers focused on the use of subcarriers for paging. Radio Common Carriers (RCCs) had been providing paging services for a number of years and obviously did not welcome the competition. They argued that the Commission was favoring FM broadcasters over RCCs. Meanwhile, broadcasters contended that the Commission was favoring the RCCs.

The controversy provides another good illustration of the difficulty the Commission faces when it attempts to establish regulatory parity between two competing services. The idea of a level playing field is good in theory, but difficult to put into practice. Consider the following facts about RCCs and FM subcarriers.

Due to height and power limitations imposed on RCCs, an RCC cannot serve as large an area as a full-power Class C FM. On the other hand, a full-power Class A FM cannot serve as large an area as an RCC. RCCs can put up multiple towers—an option denied FMs by the duopoly rule—giving them better coverage in large cities because tall buildings can block line-of-sight transmissions. In less populated areas, the extra height of some FM towers gives them a coverage advantage.

The Commission decided on reconsideration to preempt state entry requirements that might hinder the development of subcarrier service. Concern over the needs-showing requirements, p. 396, supra, imposed on paging services by more than 20 states, was the primary motivation for the preemption. FM Subsidiary Communications Authorizations, 55 R.R.2d 1607 (1984). As a result, RCCs are subject to more state regulation. However, for many years RCCs were able to do business without any competition from FM licensees because use of subcarriers for paging was prohibited by the Commission. Thus, the RCCs were able to establish themselves before having to face any competition.

Given these circumstances, how can the FCC establish regulatory parity? It is impossible to make both service providers subject to identical regulations because of the other services offered by FM broadcasters. The duopoly rule cannot be eliminated for subcarriers alone, and forcing RCCs to suddenly divest themselves of all but one transmitter in a market would impose great hardship. Even if it were possible to establish identical regulation, would that be the solution? Does equal regulation translate into regulatory parity? Among other problems, suddenly imposing equal regulation fails to take into account the effect of previous regulation. For example, allowing needs-showing requirements to apply equally to RCCs and FM subcarriers would ignore the effects of the earlier prohibition on FM subcarriers offering paging services. But does preempting the needs-showing requirements for subcarriers really level the playing field? Obviously, this is not an easy question to answer.

In a 1984 decision, the Commission similarly freed AM subcarriers from the limitations placed on their use. AM Carrier Signals, 56 R.R.2d 1292 (1984).

## F.  ELECTRONIC PUBLISHING

Electronic publishing puts pages of information, both text and images, on television sets or other display tubes.  Teletext is a one-way system with signals flowing only from the computer to the screen.  It operates by sending a continuous cycle of information to home television screens during the regular vertical blanking interval (VBI) of a television signal (the black horizontal line that appears when the vertical hold is not properly adjusted).  A user chooses the desired "page" of information from a published index, and instructs the receiver terminal to "grab" the page as it goes by.  When the user is finished, the page is released from the screen.  Teletext can be delivered by either broadcasting or cable.

Another system, called "videotex," is a two-way system in which the computer holds a much larger data base and the user signals which information is sought.  The selected pages are then transmitted to the user.  This system requires telephone lines or cable.

When the Commission authorized teletext service in 1983, several important questions had to be answered.  Teletext Transmission, 53 R.R. 2d 1309 (1983).  Again, it was necessary to determine an appropriate regulatory model.  As in the SCA proceeding, the Commission opted to place the onus on the licensee to decide this based on the nature of the service to be provided.

The Commission also decided that, even in the case of broadcast-related services, teletext would be exempt from content restrictions such as § 315 and the fairness doctrine.  In response to petitions for reconsideration filed by various parties, the Commission reaffirmed its position, Teletext Transmission (Reconsideration), 57 R.R.2d 842 (1985):

14.  .  .  .  First, we dispute the contrary implications of some petitioners and reaffirm our intention to pursue continued enforcement of these content-related broadcast laws, policies and rules until and unless they are altered by ourselves or other competent authority.  This, however, in no way alters or diminishes our authority and responsibility to interpret and apply these as necessary when novel questions and circumstances arise.  This is particularly true as in this situation where new services are being authorized that could not be, or were not, contemplated when Congress passed related statutory provisions nor when this Commission enacted rules and policies designed to give force to these provisions.  Our attention is further focused in this area where the changing nature of the industry due both to competitive and technological flux requires us to give primary concern to the First Amendment implications of our actions.
.  .  .

15.  .  .  .  In this context we view our decision here as no way inconsistent with the court's views in NAB v. FCC, 740 F.2d 1190 (D.C.Cir.1984), for the reasons detailed below.  We consider teletext clearly as an ancillary service not strictly related to the traditional broadcast mode of mass communication.  First, the very definition of teletext confined the service to traditional print and textual data

transmission. [  ] Thus, although these data will be transmitted at some point through the use of the electromagnetic spectrum, its primary and overriding feature will be its historical and cultural connection to the print media, especially books, magazines and newspapers. Users of this medium will not be listening or viewing teletext in any traditional broadcasting sense, but instead will be *reading* it, and thus be able to skip, scan and select the desired material in ways that are incomparable to anything in the history of broadcasting and broadcast regulation. In this light, we believe that the content regulations created for traditional broadcast operations are simply out of place in this new print-related textual data transmission medium.  .  .  .

The Commission continued the analogy to print media by noting that modern newspapers are often written and edited in one location and then transmitted by satellite to other locations for printing. Relying on Miami Herald v. Tornillo, p. 72, supra, the Commission concluded that application of content restrictions to teletext would serve "neither the letter nor the purpose of the First Amendment."

At the time of the Commission's original authorization of teletext service, the most controversial part of the ruling was the decision to allow cable systems to remove the teletext portion of the signal from any broadcast transmissions they carried. The importance of the Commission's failure to mandate carriage of teletext has been reduced, however, by the *Quincy Cable* decision, and the question of mandatory carriage for teletext has now been made a part of the Commission's new must-carry proceeding, p. 367, supra.

Despite the Commission's ruling and *Quincy Cable,* cable operators are not free to remove all teletext from the (VBI) of secondary transmissions of broadcast signals. In WGN Continental Broadcasting Co. v. United Video, Inc., 685 F.2d 218, petition for rehearing denied, 693 F.2d 628 (7th Cir.1982), the court of appeals held that under some circumstances, stripping teletext constitutes a copyright violation. According to the court, main-channel programming and program-related teletext constitute a single, copyrighted work. Deletion of the teletext not only is infringement, but it removes the signal from the protection of the compulsory license normally applicable to secondary transmissions.

The extent of the protection afforded teletext providers by *WGN* is difficult to determine. It is not at all clear what constitutes program-related teletext. Closed-captioning and subtitles are obviously program-related material, as is provision of more detailed information concerning the subject of the main-channel programming, e.g., where to buy an advertised product. What about announcements of upcoming programs? The court thought they were also program-related material.

A second problem with *WGN* is its holding that deletion constitutes infringement. This relatively novel holding was based on a single case, Gilliam v. American Broadcasting Company, 538 F.2d 14 (2d Cir.1976), and the facts in that case were markedly different. *Gilliam* involved a complaint by the British comedy group, Monty Python, that during a broadcast, ABC deleted material from one of their movies in a way that seriously damaged the artistic value of the movie.

Due in part to the limited teletext service available at this time, WGN has yet to be tested further in the courts.

# Chapter XI

## COPYRIGHT AND TRADEMARK

There are several ways to protect a creative work product, but historically this protection was first achieved through copyright law. Copyright and trademark law provide protection for intellectual property—something akin to the protection of a patent for an invention. Copyright protects a literary or artistic creation, such as the script of a television program. Specifically, it protects the *expression* of ideas and facts rather than the *facts* or *ideas* themselves, because it is generally in the public interest to encourage dissemination of the latter. Trademark law, on the other hand, protects words or symbols associated with a company or product, such as the call letters of a broadcasting station or the name of a television show.

The right to own, to control, and to profit from one's creative work is, of course, essential to people who make their living in the communications media.

As we shall see, a great deal of expression is in the *public domain*—not owned by any one owner—and can be used freely by anyone without permission. When one wants to use copyrighted work, however (with some exceptions to be noted later), one needs permission.

The laws of copyright are thus restraints on freedom of expression, but they are not generally condemned for being so.

Article I, § 8, of the Constitution of the United States gives Congress the power "to promote the progress of science and useful arts by securing for limited times to authors and inventors the exclusive right to their respective writings and discoveries . . . ." The very first Congress utilized that authority to adopt copyright legislation, and it has been with us in some form ever since. The framers of the Constitution could hardly have envisioned the wide range of media with which copyright must today be concerned: broadcast, cable, print, computer, videorecording, photocopying, jukeboxes, etc.

The copyright statute is found in Title 17 of the United States Code, §§ 101–118.

## A. THE NATURE OF COPYRIGHT

### 1. BACKGROUND

The origins of copyright are interwoven with the history of English licensing procedures. One technique for controlling the printing press in England was to organize printers into a group that became known as the Stationers Company. The Crown granted to that company a monopoly of all printing, with the power to seek out and suppress material published by non-members who violated the monopoly. The Crown's goal was to thwart seditious libel and other objectionable material. The printers, for their part, seized on the monopoly situation to control reproduction of whatever they printed. The result was the licensed printers' right to control copies based on the censorship of the 16th and 17th centuries. When licensing was discontinued in 1695, the rights of the printers were undermined. They petitioned Parliament to adopt protections resembling what they had had under the licensing schemes. In 1709, Parliament responded with the Statute of Anne, which has set the pattern for copyright legislation both in England and in this country. The Stationers Company remained, but its new role was to register printed material, which would serve to protect that material against unauthorized copying.

The first U.S. Congress adopted a similar procedure: printed matter could be protected by filing a copy with the newly established copyright office, headed by the "Register of Copyrights." The types of writings protected and the period of protection have been expanded since the 1790 statute, which protected only books, maps, and charts for 14 years plus renewal for a second 14-year term.

Under the 1909 statute, published works were protected by federal law while unpublished works were protected under state law. Under the new legislation, all protection is in a single national framework.

In 1976, the copyright statute enacted in 1909 was replaced with new legislation that preserves the basic philosophical strands of copyright law, including the denial of copyright for federal government documents. Changes have been made in legal technicalities or to accommodate media that emerged after 1909 and did not easily fit within the old framework. The new statute went into effect Jan. 1, 1978.

## 2. SUBJECT MATTER

Section 102 of the 1976 copyright statute sets out the basic pattern of protection when it states that protection subsists in "original works of authorship fixed in any tangible medium of expression, now known or later developed, from which they can be perceived, reproduced or otherwise communicated, either directly or with the aid of a machine or device." Such works include:

(1) literary works; (2) musical works, including any accompanying words; (3) dramatic works, including any accompanying music; (4) pantomimes and choreographic works; (5) pictorial, graphic, and sculptural works; (6) motion pictures and other audiovisual works; and (7) sound recordings.

The section then states the other side of the coin:

In no case does copyright protection for an original work of authorship extend to any idea, procedure, process, system, method or operation, concept, principle, or discovery, regardless of the form it which it is described, explained, illustrated, or embodied in such work.

This issue arose in a case involving the explosion and crash of the German dirigible Hindenburg in New Jersey in 1937. The plaintiff author developed the theory that a crew member sabotaged the dirigible to please a Communist girlfriend. Plaintiff sued two others whose versions of the disaster developed a similar explanation. Hoehling v. Universal City Studios, Inc., 618 F.2d 972 (2d Cir.1980), certiorari denied 449 U.S. 841 (1980). The court began its discussion by placing copyright in its broader context:

> A grant of copyright in a published work secures for its author a limited monopoly over the expression it contains. The copyright provides a financial incentive to those who would add to the corpus of existing knowledge by creating original works. Nevertheless, the protection afforded the copyright holder has never extended to history, be it documented fact or explanatory hypothesis. The rationale for this doctrine is that the cause of knowledge is best served when history is the common property of all, and each generation remains free to draw upon the discoveries and insights of the past. Accordingly, the scope of copyright in historical accounts is narrow indeed, embracing no more than the author's original expression of particular facts and theories already in the public domain. As the case before us illustrates, absent wholesale usurpation of another's expression, claims of copyright infringement where works of history are at issue are rarely successful.

The court asserted that although plaintiff had a valid copyright on his book to prove "infringement" he had to prove that defendants had "improperly appropriated" his "expression." Although plaintiff admitted that his idea was not copyrightable, he correctly argued that "his 'expression' of *his* idea is copyrightable." The court analyzed that claim as follows:

> He relies on Learned Hand's opinion in [Sheldon v. Metro-Goldwyn Pictures Corp., 81 F.2d 49 (2d Cir.), certiorari denied 298 U.S. 669 (1936)] holding that *Letty Lynton* infringed *Dishonored Lady* by copying its story of a woman who poisons her lover, and Augustus Hand's analysis in Detective Comics, Inc. v. Bruns Publications, Inc., 111 F.2d 432 (2d Cir.1940), concluding that the exploits of "Wonderman" infringed the copyright held by the creators of "Superman," the original indestructible man. Moreover, Hoehling asserts that, in both these cases, the line between "ideas" and "expression" is drawn, in the first instance, by the fact finder.
>
> *Sheldon* and *Detective Comics*, however, dealt with works of fiction, where the distinction between an idea and its expression is especially elusive. But, where, as here, the idea at issue is an interpretation of an historical event, our cases hold that such interpretations are not copyrightable as matter of law. In Rosemont Enterprises, Inc. v. Random House, Inc., 366 F.2d 303 (2d Cir.1966), cert. denied, 385 U.S. 1009 (1967), we held that the defendant's biography of Howard Hughes did not infringe an earlier biography

of the reclusive alleged billionaire.  Although the plots of the two works were necessarily similar, there could be no infringement because of the "public benefit in encouraging the development of historical and biographical words and their public distribution."  Id. at 307;  accord, Oxford Book Co. v. College Entrance Book Co., 98 F.2d 688 (2d Cir.1938).  To avoid a chilling effect on authors who contemplate tackling an historical issue or event, broad latitude must be granted to subsequent authors who make use of historical subject matter, including theories or plots.  Learned Hand counseled in Myers v. Mail & Express Co., 36 C.O.Bull 487, 479 (S.D.N.Y.1919), "[t]here cannot be any such thing as copyright in the order of presentation of the facts, nor, indeed, in their selection."

The court went further, however, and asserted that it may not even be possible to protect even some fictitious episodes:

> The remainder of Hoehling's claimed similarities relate to random duplications of phrases and sequences of events.  For example, all three works contain a scene in a German beer hall, in which the airship's crew engages in revelry prior to the voyage.  Other claimed similarities concern common German greetings of the period, such as "Heil Hitler," or songs, such as the German National anthem.  These elements, however, are merely *scenes a faire*, that is, "incidents, characters or settings which are as a practical matter indispensable, or at least standard, in the treatment of a given topic."  [  ]  Because it is virtually impossible to write about a particular historical era or fictional theme without employing certain "stock" or standard literary devices, we have held that *scenes a faire* are not copyrightable as a matter of law.  See Reyher v. Children's Television Workshop, 533 F.2d 87, 91 (2d Cir.), cert. denied, 429 U.S. 980 (1976).

Finally, the court brought these several aspects of the case together and recognized that breaking the copyrighted work up into many little parts created a new danger:

> All of Hoehling's allegations of copying, therefore, encompass material that is non-copyrightable as a matter of law, rendering summary judgment entirely appropriate.  We are aware, however, that in distinguishing between themes, facts, and *scenes a faire* on the one hand, and copyrightable expression on the other, courts may lose sight of the forest for the trees.  By factoring out similarities based on non-copyrightable elements, a court runs the risk of overlooking wholesale usurpation of a prior author's expression.  A verbatim reproduction of another work, of course, even in the realm of nonfiction, is actionable as copyright infringement.  See Wainwright Securities, Inc. v. Wall Street Transcript Corp.,  558 F.2d 91 (2d Cir.1977), cert. denied, 434 U.S. 1014 (1978).  Thus, in granting or reviewing a grant of summary judgment for defendants, courts should assure themselves that the works before them are not

virtually identical. In this case, it is clear that all three authors relate the story of the Hindenburg differently.

In works devoted to historical subjects, it is our view that a second author may make significant use of prior work, so long as he does not bodily appropriate the expression of another. Rosemont Enterprises, Inc., supra, 366 F.2d at 310. This principle is justified by the fundamental policy undergirding the copyright laws—the encouragement of contributions to recorded knowledge. The "financial reward guaranteed to the copyright holder is but an incident of this general objective, rather than an act in itself." Berlin v. E.C. Publications, Inc., 329 F.2d 541, 543–44 (2d Cir.), cert. denied, 379 U.S. 822 (1964). Knowledge is expanded as well by granting new authors of historical works a relatively free hand to build upon the work of their predecessors.

### 3. OWNERSHIP OF COPYRIGHT

The authors of a work are the initial copyright owners unless the work is a "work made for hire." This is defined as

(1) a work prepared by an employee within the scope of his or her employment; or

(2) a work specifically ordered or commissioned for use as a contribution to a collective work, as a part of a motion picture or other audiovisual work, as a translation, as a supplementary work, as a compilation, as an instructional text, as a test, as answer material for a test, or as an atlas, if the parties expressly agree in a written instrument signed by them that the work shall be considered a work made for hire.

In the case of a "work made for hire," the original ownership belongs to the employer or person who commissioned the work. As is the case with any property right, ownership of a copyright can be left to the owner's heirs or sold.

### 4. RIGHTS OF COPYRIGHT OWNER(S)

Section 106 states the nature of the protection extended to the copyright owner:

Subject to sections 107 through 118, the owner of copyright under this title has the exclusive right to do and to authorize any of the following:

(1) to reproduce the copyrighted work in copies or phonorecords;

(2) to prepare derivative works based upon the copyrighted work;

(3) to distribute copies or phonorecords of the copyrighted work to the public by sale or other transfer of ownership, or by rental, lease, or lending;

(4) in the case of literary, musical, dramatic, and choreographic works, pantomimes, and motion pictures and other audiovisual works, to perform the copyrighted work publicly; and

(5) in the case of literary, musical, dramatic, and choreographic works, pantomimes, and pictorial, graphic, or scupltural works, including the individual images of a motion picture or other audiovisual work, to display the copyrighted work publicly.

It is also quite possible for a copyright owner to sell some rights and retain others. A famous novelist, for example, might first sell the rights to publish excerpts of his upcoming novel to a national magazine, then sell the rights to publish the hardcover first edition of the book to a publishing house, and then sell rights for publication of a later paperback edition to another publisher.

### 5. Duration of Copyright

Under the 1909 Act, copyright protection lasted for 28 years with the opportunity for one 28-year renewal. Under the 1976 Act, it lasts for the life of the author plus 50 years. With joint authors it is 50 years from the last surviving author's death. Anonymous works, pseudonymous works, and "works made for hire," are protected for 75 years from publication or 100 years from creation, whichever comes first.

### 6. Statutory Formalities

Under the Copyright Act of 1976, any work is protected as soon as it is "fixed in a tangible medium." However, to retain this protection certain statutory formalities must be observed. Every copy must carry notice consisting of the full word copyright, the accepted abbreviation "copr.," or the internationally accepted symbol ©, plus the name of the copyright proprietor. A printed literary, musical, or dramatic work must also have the year of first publication. With maps, works of art, reproductions of works of art, drawings, or plastic works of a scientific or technical character, photographs and prints or pictures, notice may consist of © plus the initials, monogram, mark, or symbol of the proprietor.

Under the 1909 Act failure to follow the notice procedure exactly resulted in the loss of copyright protection. Under the 1976 Act omission or error in placing the notice no longer results in automatic forfeiture of the copyright, as long as the notice has been omitted only from a relatively small number of copies and registration is made within five years after the publication without notice, or a reasonable effort is made to add the notice to all copies distributed to the public in the United States, or the notice has been omitted in violation of an express requirement in writing that, as a condition of the copyright owner's authorization of the public distribution of copies, they bear the prescribed notice.

However, failure to follow the notice procedure can limit the author's remedies in the event of an infringement, because "innocent infringers"—those who innocently infringe a copyright while relying on an unauthorized copy from which the copyright notice has been omitted—incur no liability. The court may, however, allow partial recovery of the infringer's profits.

The other requirement for obtaining full copyright protection is to register the work with the Register of Copyrights. Registration is a prerequisite for filing a copyright infringement suit and involves filling out a form, paying a small fee, and providing a few copies of the work.

Forms and current fee schedules are available from the Copyright Office, Library of Congress, Washington, D.C. 20559.

### 7. PREEMPTION OF STATE LAW

The Copyright Act of 1976 preempted all state law governing rights equivalent to copyright protection. As previously noted, this eliminated common-law copyright protection for unpublished works. It does not, however, mean that other state laws, such as those relating to defamation, cannot be applied to copyrighted works.

Sometimes, however, determining what constitutes a non-equivalent right is not easy. In Chapter XIII, in the discussion of the right of privacy, we will see the Supreme Court decision in Zacchini v. Scripps-Howard Broadcasting Co., which recognized a "right of publicity" for Hugo Zacchini, an entertainer known for his "human cannonball" act. Zacchini's 15-second act at a fair grounds was videotaped by a television station and broadcast on the evening news. The Court held that the broadcast posed a substantial threat to the economic value of the performance and that the performer was entitled to damages in an invasion of privacy suit.

Zacchini's act was not copyrighted. Had he "fixed" it by having it filmed or taped himself, he could have copyrighted it.

Notice the similarities between copyright law and this special application of privacy law in protecting one's right to control one's own creation or performance.

It is difficult to generalize from *Zacchini* because so few entertainers' acts are so short that they can be recorded in substantial portion by news media and because this area of privacy law is so undeveloped.

## B.  ALLEGED OR ACTUAL INFRINGEMENTS

Infringements, real or imagined, can take a variety of forms. In some instances permission to use all or part of the copyrighted material may have been given, but the copyright holder may allege that the user has exceeded the permission. That might happen when the material is disseminated more widely (perhaps in another country) than originally envisioned, when the material used is more extensive than the copyright holder envisioned, or when the purpose of the dissemination or the context in which the material is presented is not what the copyright holder expected.

More frequently, the problem may be that material is used with no permission having been granted at all. In some such instances, the material has been attributed correctly to the copyright holder (which still does not give the user any right to use it without permission); in other instances the material has not been attributed.

In cases involving such literary or artistic creative work as music or dramatic presentation, the problem may involve the question of whether the user's reproduction of the copyright holder's work actually constituted a "performance" of it.

In other cases, such as those in which two writers or two composers have created similar works, juries are sometimes called upon to decide whether the works are two totally independent creations which are coincidentally alike or there is a *substantial similarity* which would lead to the conclusion that there had been a copyright infringement. The plaintiffs in such cases attempt to prove that they own the copyright on their own work, that the defendant had access to the copyrighted work, and that there is substantial similarity between the copyrighted work and the defendant's work.

### 1. FAIR USE AND OTHER DEFENSES

Of the defenses possible in a copyright infringement suit, the most probable is fair use. The 1909 copyright statute was worded in such absolute terms that *any* copying of a copyrighted work, for whatever purpose, appeared to be an infringement. The courts found that to be unrealistically severe, and the judicial doctrine of fair use came to protect book reviewers, journalists, scholars, and others who used parts of a copyrighted work for certain purposes. The 1976 statute incorporates the fair use concept.

It still does not say, nor can it, exactly how many words or how many seconds or minutes of a copyrighted work may be used without permission. That assessment depends on the criteria enumerated below.

### a. Fair Use

The grant of rights to the owner of the copyright is conditioned on a series of limitations expressed in §§ 107–118 of the copyright statute. These include permitting libraries to make one photocopy of an article and permitting persons to make phonograph records of music without permission upon payment of certain royalties. Probably the most important of these limitations is found in § 107, which deals specifically with the problem of fair use:

> Notwithstanding the provisions of section 106, the fair use of a copyrighted work, including such use by reproduction in copies or phonorecords or by any other means specified by that section, for purposes such as criticism, comment, news reporting, teaching (in-

cluding multiple copies for classroom use), scholarship, or research, is not an infringement of copyright. In determining whether the use made of a work in any particular case is a fair use the factors to be considered shall include—

(1) the purpose and character of the use, including whether such use is of a commercial nature or is for non-profit educational purposes;

(2) the nature of the copyrighted work;

(3) the amount and substantiality of the portion used in relation to the copyrighted work as a whole; and

(4) the effect of the use upon the potential market for or value of the copyrighted work.

Most observers have concluded that the statute does not change the previous approach to fair use.

1. The following fair use cases serve as examples:

a. Plaintiff specialized in preparing copyrighted "in-depth analytical reports on approximately 275 industrial, financial, utility and railroad corporations." The reports, up to 40 pages long and involving months of an analyst's time, were used by 900 clients of plaintiff, including banks, insurance companies and mutual funds. Defendant, a weekly financial newspaper, featured a column called "Wall Street Roundup," which consisted almost exclusively of abstracts of institutional research reports, including those of plaintiff. Defendant's advertising promised readers "a fast-reading, pinpointed account of heavyweight reports from the top institutional research firms."

Plaintiff sued for infringement and sought a preliminary injunction. The trial judge granted it and was upheld on appeal. Defendant argued that it was simply covering the financial news. The court disagreed. Although a news event cannot be copyrighted, the expression used by the author may be protected. Here, defendant was found to have copied the manner of expression used by plaintiff's analysts. The court noted that, unlike traditional news coverage, defendant provided no independent analysis or research; it carried no industry comments on the reports and included no criticism or praise of the reports. "Rather, the Transcript appropriated almost verbatim the most creative and original aspects of the reports, the financial analyses and predictions, which represent a substantial investment of time, money and labor." Wainwright Securities, Inc., v. Wall Street Transcript Corp., 558 F.2d 91 (2d Cir. 1977), certiorari denied 434 U.S. 1014 (1978).

b. Defendant wrote a book about Julius and Ethel Rosenberg: their trial, conviction, and execution for conspiring to transmit national defense information to the Soviet Union. The book quoted verbatim from 28 copyrighted letters written by the Rosenbergs while in prison—a total of 1,957 words. The plaintiffs, sons of the Rosenbergs, claimed the copyright in the letters, which had been published as the book *Death*

*House Letters.*  The trial judge dismissed the claim but was reversed on appeal.

The court noted that although the letters represented less than one percent of the defendant's book, they were featured prominently in promotional literature for the book.  Several questions of fact had to be resolved before the fair use question could be answered: the purpose for which the letters were used in the defendant's book, the need for verbatim copying of the letters, and the effect of their use on the future market for *Death House Letters.*  The fact that *Death House Letters* had been out of print for 20 years did not necessarily mean that the letters had no future market.  The possibilities of republication, and sale of motion picture rights, might have been affected by their use in defendant's book.  Meeropol v. Nizer, 560 F.2d 1061 (2d Cir.1977), certiorari denied 434 U.S. 1013 (1978).

c.  In 1977, after an arrest in the famous "Son of Sam" murder hunt, five strips of "Doonesbury" were devoted to commentary on the way a columnist for the *New York Daily News* behaved during the search for the killer.  The *News,* which held the New York City rights to the strip, decided not to use the five strips.  The *New York Post* reported the action of the *News* and, since "censorship is news," the *Post* reprinted the five deleted strips to show its readers what the *News* had refused to carry.  No suit resulted.  Might the copyright owner have successfully sued the *Post?*

d.  When a network televised a parade during which music copyrighted by plaintiff was being played, the court held that the fair use doctrine protected the network.  Italian Book Corp. v. American Broadcasting Companies, Inc., 458 F.Supp. 65 (S.D.N.Y.1978).

2.  The traditional view has been that if the defendant has extensively copied plaintiff's expression and cannot rely on the defense of fair use, the plaintiff would succeed in the infringement action.  But some situations may exist in which, although the defendant's use of the copyrighted material cannot be justified as "fair use," the public's need to have the information is so great that *perhaps* the First Amendment would serve as a defense to an infringement action.  Although such a situation would be rare because one can always make use of facts and simply alter the form of expression, there may be situations in which the form of presentation cannot be paraphrased with the same effect as the original presentation.

The best examples of such circumstances may be photographs, such as the Zapruder photographs of the John Kennedy assassination or the photographs of the MyLai massacre in Vietnam.  The best evidence for the public to have in debating the assassination or the massacre may be all of the actual photographs rather than an intermediary's attempted verbal description of what the photographs purport to show—even though a copier, by using all the photographs, exceeds the bounds of fair use.  This problem may be unique to the visual presentations.  The subject is well discussed, using these examples, in Nimmer, Does Copyright Abridge the First Amendment Guarantees of Free Speech and Press?, 17 U.C.L.A.L.Rev. 1180 (1970).

3.  Another important question—one requiring a balancing of property rights and First Amendment rights—is to what extent a news organization can make unauthorized use of the research and labor of a competitor either by directly copying the work of the competitor or by "appropriating" the facts contained in a competitor's news release. Although the substance of news cannot be protected by copyright, the doctrine of unfair competition has been used to protect the gatherer of news from the direct, unauthorized reproduction of its material for commercial use.  In International News Service v. Associated Press, 248 U.S. 215 (1918), I.N.S. was enjoined from copying news from A.P. bulletin boards and early editions of A.P. member newspapers until "the commercial value" of the news to the complainant and all of its members had passed.  The Court found unfair competition in the taking of material acquired through the expenditure of skill, labor, and money by A.P. for the purpose of diverting "a material portion of the profit" to I.N.S.  Although the Court condemned the "habitual failure" of I.N.S. to give credit to A.P. as the source of its news, the misrepresentation was not considered essential to a finding of unfair competition: "It is something more than the advantage of celebrity of which complainant is being deprived."

This type of protection has been extended to other areas.  Radio stations may not broadcast news items taken verbatim from a local newspaper, and a second publisher may not photograph an existing edition of a book in order to save the cost of setting type, whether or not the first edition was copyrighted.  Where words and ideas are involved, the courts have been quite protective of the initiator, perhaps because of the fragile and ephemeral nature of the finished product.

The doctrine does not inhibit the traditional practice of getting "tips" or "leads" from any source and then going out to research and write the story.  The court in the A.P. case barred only the taking of news "either bodily or in substance, from bulletins issued by [AP], or any of its members, or from editions of their newspapers, 'until its commercial value as news to the complainant and all its members has passed away.'"  The Supreme Court drew a distinction "between the utilization of tips and the bodily appropriation of news matter, either in its original form or after rewriting and without independent investigation and verification . . . ."  See Sullivan, News Piracy: An Interpretation of the Misappropriation Doctrine, 54 Journ.Q. 682 (1977).

4.  A small company named TV News Clips and operated by Carol Duncan monitored videotaped news programs of three network affiliates in Atlanta as well as the Cable News Network and then offered the tapes for sale to interested parties.  The company maintained that its use of the copyrighted news material was "fair use," but Pacific and Southern Company, owner of station WXIA–TV, Atlanta, sued for copyright infringement.  Both the federal district court and the court of appeals

held that the material could not be exempted under "fair use," but for different reasons. The district court had said that a fair use must be inherently productive or creative to be a fair use. But the court of appeals emphasized that all four criteria for determining use must be invoked. It said that the use to which TV News Clips put its tapes was of a "commercial nature" which "militates quite strongly against a finding of fair use." Pacific and Southern Company v. Duncan, 744 F.2d 1490 (11th Cir.1984), certiorari denied, 471 U.S. __ (1985).

5. In March, 1979, when an undisclosed source gave Victor Navasky, editor of *The Nation*, an unauthorized copy of former President Ford's memoirs, Navasky prepared an article comprising quotations from and paraphrases of the manuscript. The article was published in *The Nation* prior to the book publication of President Ford's memoirs by Harper & Row. As a direct result of *The Nation* article, an agreement between Harper & Row and *Time* magazine selling *Time* certain prepublication rights was canceled. *The Nation's* fair use defense was rejected by the trial court. On appeal the Second Circuit Court of Appeals reversed 2–1. Relying on the fact that much of what was discussed in the article was historical fact, the majority concluded that only a small portion of the article constituted copyrightable material. Harper & Row appealed the decision to the Supreme Court.

## HARPER & ROW PUBLISHERS, INC. v. NATION ENTERPRISES

Supreme Court of the United States, 1985.
471 U.S. __, 105 S.Ct. 2218, 85 L.Ed.2d 588.

JUSTICE O'CONNOR delivered the opinion of the Court.

This case requires us to consider to what extent the "fair use" provision of the Copyright Revision Act of 1976, 17 U.S.C. § 107 (hereinafter the Copyright Act), sanctions the unauthorized use of quotations from a public figure's unpublished manuscript. . . . Working directly from the purloined manuscript, an editor of The Nation produced a short piece entitled "The Ford Memoirs—Behind the Nixon Pardon." The piece was timed to "scoop" an article scheduled shortly to appear in Time magazine. Time had agreed to purchase the exclusive right to print prepublication excerpts from the copyright holders . . . .

I

. . . The memoirs were to contain "significant hitherto unpublished material" concerning the Watergate crisis, Mr. Ford's pardon of Former President Nixon and "Mr. Ford's reflections on this period of history, and the morality and personalities involved." . . . In addition to the right to publish the Ford memoirs in book form, the agreement gave petitioners the exclusive right to license prepublication excerpts, known in the trade as "first serial rights." . . . [A]s the memoirs were nearing completion, petitioners negotiated a prepublication licensing agreement with Time, a weekly news magazine. Time agreed to pay $25,000, $12,500 in advance and an additional $12,500 at publication, in exchange for the right to excerpt 7,500 words from Mr. Ford's account of the Nixon pardon. The issue featuring the excerpts was timed to appear approximately one week before shipment of the full length book version to bookstores. Exclusivity was an important consideration; Harper & Row instituted procedures designed to maintain the confidentiality of the manuscript, and Time retained the right to renegotiate the second payment should the material appear in print prior to its release of the excerpts.

[Mr. Navasky received a copy of the manuscript.] Mr. Navasky knew that his possession of the manuscript was not authorized and that the manuscript must be returned to his "source" to avoid discovery. [  ] He hastily put together what he believed was a "real hot news story" composed of quotes, paraphrases and facts drawn exclusively from the manuscript. [  ] Mr. Navasky attempted no independent commentary, research or criticism, in part because of the need for speed if he was to "make news" by "publish[ing] in advance of publication of the Ford book." [  ] The 2,250 word article . . . appeared on April 3, 1979. As a result of The Nation's article, Time canceled its piece and refused to pay the remaining $12,500.

. . .

## II

We agree with the Court of Appeals that copyright is intended to increase and not to impede the harvest of knowledge. But we believe the Second Circuit gave insufficient deference to the scheme established by the Copyright Act for fostering the original works that provide the seed and substance of this harvest. The rights conferred by copyright are designed to assure contributors to the store of knowledge a fair return for their labors. [  ]

. . .

The Nation's appropriation of unoriginal and uncopyrightable elements encroached on the originality embodied in the work as a whole. Especially in the realm of factual narrative, the law is currently unsettled regarding the ways in which uncopyrightable elements combine with the author's original contributions to form protected expression . . . .

We need not reach these issues, however, as the Nation has admitted to lifting verbatim quotes of the author's original language totaling between 300 and 400 words and constituting some 13% of The Nation article. In using generous verbatim excerpts of Mr. Ford's unpublished manuscript to lend authenticity to its account of the forthcoming memoirs, The Nation effectively arrogated to itself the right of first publication, an important marketable subsidiary right. . . . [W]e find that this use of the copyrighted manuscript, even stripped to the verbatim quotes conceded by The Nation as to be copyrightable expression, was not a fair use within the meaning of the Copyright Act.

### III

.   .   .

### B

.   .   . [The Nation advances] the substantial public import of the subject matter of the Ford memoirs as grounds for excusing a use that would ordinarily not pass muster as a fair use—the piracy of verbatim quotations for the purpose of "scooping" the authorized first serialization.   Respondents explain their copying of Mr. Ford's expression as essential to reporting the news story it claims the book itself represents. In respondents' view, not only the facts contained in Mr. Ford's memoirs, but "the precise manner in which [he] expressed himself was as newsworthy as what he had to say."   [   ]   Respondents argue that the public's interest in learning this news as fast as possible outweighs the right of the author to control its first publication.

.   .   .

Respondents' theory .   .   . would expand fair use to effectively destroy any expectation of copyright protection in the work of a public figure.   Absent such protection, there would be little incentive to create or profit in financing such memoirs and the public would be denied an [important] source of significant historical information.   The promise of copyright would be an empty one if it could be avoided merely by dubbing the infringement a fair use "news report" of the book.   [   ]

.   .   .

In our haste to disseminate news, it should not be forgotten that the Framers intended copyright itself to be the engine of free expression.   .   .   .

It is fundamentally at odds with the scheme of copyright to accord lesser rights in those works that are of greatest importance to the public. Such a notion ignores the major premise of copyright and injures author and public alike .   .   .   .

.   .   .

### V

.   .   . Because we find that The Nation's use of these verbatim excerpts from the unpublished manuscript was not a fair use, the judgment of the Court of Appeals is reversed and remanded for further proceedings consistent with this opinion.   .   .   .

Justice Brennan, joined by Justices White and Marshall, wrote a dissenting opinion:

.   .   . Although the Court pursues the laudable goal of protecting "the economic incentive to create and disseminate ideas," .   .   . this zealous defense of the copyright owner's prerogative will, I fear, stifle the broad dissemination of ideas and information copyright is intended to nurture. Protection of the copyright owner's economic interest is achieved in this case through an exceedingly narrow definition of the scope of fair use. The progress of arts and sciences and the robust public debate essential to an enlightened citizenry are ill served by this constricted reading of the fair use doctrine. [   ] I therefore respectfully dissent.

## Notes and Questions

1. Usually, a fair use case involves use *subsequent* to the copyright owner's publication. How much do you think the Court was influenced by by the fact that here *The Nation* published its excerpts first? How much was the Court influenced by the apparent theft of the material?

2. Note that one of the considerations in determining fair use is whether the use is of an educational nature. Clearly, however, the fact that a use is educational does not give one free license to use another's copyrighted property and to infringe on another's ability to profit from his work. Recording of broadcast programming for classroom use presents particular problems which were addressed by a committee composed of representatives from both industry and education. Committee members agreed upon a set of "Guidelines for Off-Air Recording of Broadcast Programming for Educational Purposes."

   1.   The guidelines were developed to apply only to off-air recording by non-profit educational institutions.

   2.   A broadcast program may be recorded off-air simultaneously with broadcast transmission (including simultaneous cable re-transmission) and retained by a non-profit educational institution for a period not to exceed the first forty-five (45) consecutive calendar days after date of recording. Upon conclusion of such retention period, all off-air recordings must be erased or destroyed immediately. "Broadcast programs" are television programs transmitted by television stations for reception by the general public without charge.

   3.   Off-air recordings may be used once by individual teachers in the course of relevant teaching activities, and repeated once only when instructional reinforcement is necessary, in classrooms and similar places devoted to instruction within a single building, cluster or campus, as well as in the homes of students receiving formalized home instruction, during the first ten (10) consecutive school days in the forty-five (45) day calendar day retention period. "School days" are school session days—not counting weekends, holidays, vacations, examination periods, or other scheduled interruptions—within the forty-five (45) calendar day retention period.

   4.   Off-air recordings may be made only at the request of and used by individual teachers, and may not be regularly recorded in anticipation of requests. No broadcast program may be record-

ed in anticipation of requests. No broadcast program may be recorded off-air more than once at the request of the same teacher, regardless of the number of times the program may be broadcast.

5.   A limited number of copies may be reproduced from each off-air recording to meet the legitimate needs of teachers under these guidelines. Each such additional copy shall be subject to all provisions governing the original recording.

6.   After the first ten (10) consecutive school days, off-air recordings may be used up to the end of the forty-five (45) calendar day retention period only for teacher evaluation purposes, i.e., to determine whether or not to include the broadcast program in the teaching curriculum, and may not be used in the recording institution for student exhibition or any other non-evaluation purpose without authorization.

7.   Off-air recordings need not be used in their entirety, but the recorded programs may not be altered from their original content. Off-air recordings may not be physically or electronically combined or merged to constitute teaching anthologies or compilations.

8.   All copies of off-air recordings must include the copyright notice on the broadcast program as recorded. Educational institutions are expected to establish appropriate control procedures to maintain the integrity of these guidelines.

It is too early to tell exactly how these guidelines will be treated by the courts, because they are not part of the Copyright Act. They were, however, entered into the Congressional Record, and they are expected to carry weight with the courts.

### b. Independent Creation

Copyright protection extends only to copying the work in question. If someone independently creates a similar work, there is no copyright infringement. Consequently, an argument for the defense in a copyright infringement case might be that the defendant did not have access to the plaintiff's work, and that what appears to be a "copy" is in fact an independent creation. Note, however, that, as former Beatle George Harrison learned, plaintiff does not have to prove that defendant intentionally or even consciously copied it. Bright Tunes Music Corp. v. Harrisongs Music, Ltd., 420 F.Supp. 177 (S.D.N.Y.1976).

### c. Public Domain

There are instances in which a defendant might successfully argue that the ownership asserted by the plaintiff in fact no longer exists. If the copyright holder has disseminated copies of his material without including the proper copyright notice, or if he has allowed others to use his property without permission and has done nothing about the situation, his work *may* have entered the public domain.  In that case, as indicated above, anyone may use it without permission.

A somewhat similar but different defense would be for the defendant to show that he was unaware that the work was protected by copyright because he relied on a copy of the work which had been disseminated without proper copyright notice.  For general purposes, such a work would not have entered the public domain, but the copyright holder would be precluded from collecting damages for the infringement which resulted from his own error in omitting the copyright notice.

Recall from *Hoehling* that facts and ideas are not copyrightable and thus are always in the public domain.  Norman v. Columbia Broadcasting System, Inc., 333 F.Supp. 788 (S.D.N.Y.1971), involved an alleged copyright infringement by the network in its broadcast of a 1966 television program titled "In Search of Ezra Pound," about the well-known American poet.  Charles Norman, who wrote a 1960 biography of Pound, contended that use of his material—the fact that the poet had been engaged, had awakened a roommate to read poetry to him, had torn up manuscripts, had lived in a particular room, etc.—was a copyright infringement.  The district court dismissed the complaint: "The historical and factual contents of plaintiff's material [in specific instances] are not copyrightable by him."

## 2. REMEDIES AND SANCTIONS

The Copyright Act of 1976 provides numerous remedies for copyright infringement.  Sections 502–503 provide for an injunction against further infringement as well as destruction of all existing infringing materials.  Under § 504, the copyright owner may elect to receive either the damages actually suffered plus any additional profits of the infringer or statutory damages of not less than $250 or more than $10,000.  The court may also at its discretion award costs and attorney's fees.

In the case of willful infringement for commercial advantage or private financial gain, criminal sanctions are also available.  Section 506 provides for fines of up to $50,000 and imprisonment for up to two years, depending on the type of work infringed and the prior record of the defendant.

## C. MUSIC LICENSING

The frequent use of copyrighted musical works by the electronic media requires special treatment.  It would be difficult for individual music composers and performers to police the use of their own works, so performing rights societies have been organized for the protection of copyright holders.  The groups include the American Society of Composers, Authors and Publishers (ASCAP), Broadcast Media, Inc. (BMI) and SESAC, Inc. (formerly the Society of European State Authors and Composers).

Getting permission to use copyrighted music is especially complicated. One must be concerned with both synchronization rights and performance rights. Synchronization rights allow the combining of the copyrighted music with a video to create a single work. Performance rights allow one to show the video work to others.

Whether you need to obtain the performance rights as well as the synchronization rights depends how you intend to use your video piece. If you intend to show it on broadcast television, performance rights are unnecessary. Because of the practical realities of the licensing system, broadcasters have little or no choice but to obtain blanket licenses from the major licensing societies. This means the broadcaster must either pay for a blanket license giving the right to all music licensed by that organization or refrain from using any material licensed by that organization. Even if the material is supplied by a network or syndicator and that supplier has rights to the material, the broadcaster must have the blanket license.

Thus, since the broadcaster has obtained the performing rights for almost any copyrighted piece of music, you will not need to obtain them. If you do the synchronizing, however, you must still obtain these rights.

This licensing scheme has survived several legal challenges, one of them in the case below. Performance and synchronization rights can be obtained either from the individual authors or from music licensing organizations. If you plan to use a record, the label will designate which organization (BMI, ASCAP, or SESAC) licenses that piece of music.

The following case illustrates some of the music licensing problems:

## BUFFALO BROADCASTING COMPANY, INC. v. AMERICAN SOCIETY OF COMPOSERS, AUTHORS AND PUBLISHERS

United States Court of Appeals, Second Circuit, 1984,
744 F.2d 917, certiorari denied 469 U.S. ___ (1985).

JON O. NEWMAN, CIRCUIT JUDGE:

Once again we consider the lawfulness under section 1 of the Sherman Antitrust Act of the blanket license offered by the American Society of Composers, Authors and Publishers (ASCAP) and Broadcast Music, Inc. (BMI). The license permits the licensee to perform publicly any musical composition in the repertory of the licensor. In this litigation the blanket license is challenged by a class of licensees comprising all owners of "local" television stations in the United States, i.e., stations not owned by any of the three major television networks, ABC, CBS, and NBC. After a bench trial . . . the blanket license was held to be an unreasonable restraint of trade. [ ] ASCAP and BMI were enjoined from licensing to local television stations non-dramatic music performing rights for any "syndicated" program. For reasons that follow, we conclude that the evidence was insufficient as a matter of law to show that the blanket license is an unlawful restraint of trade in the legal and factual context in which it currently exists. We therefore reverse the judgment of the District Court.

## Background

### I. The Parties

The five named plaintiffs own and operate one or more local television stations. They represent a class of owners of local television stations in the United States who obtain music performing rights pursuant to license agreements with ASCAP and/or BMI. The class does not include the three major television networks, ABC, CBS, and NBC, each of which owns five television stations. The class includes approximately 450 owners who, because of multiple holdings, own approximately 750 local television stations. . . .

Defendant ASCAP is an unincorporated membership association of composers, authors, and publishers of music, formed in 1914. It has approximately 21,000 writer and 8,000 publisher members. It holds non-exclusive licenses for the non-dramatic performing rights to more than three million musical compositions. BMI is a non-profit corporation organized in 1939 by radio broadcasters. It has approximately 38,000 writer and 22,000 publisher affiliates. Its repertory, for which it holds non-exclusive licenses for non-dramatic performing rights, includes more than one million compositions. The eleven individual defendants represent two classes of defendants that include all persons from whom ASCAP and BMI have obtained the non-exclusive right to license non-dramatic music performing rights to others.

### II. Music, Rights, and Licenses

The subject matter of this litigation is music transmitted by television stations to their viewer-listeners. Television music is classified as either theme, background, or feature. Theme music is played at the start or conclusion of a program and serves to enhance the identification of the program. Background music accompanies portions of the program to heighten interest, underscore the mood, change the pace, or otherwise contribute to the overall effect of the program. Feature music is a principal focus of audience attention, such as a popular song sung on a variety show.

More particularly, we are concerned with the licensing of non-dramatic performing rights to copyrighted music, that is, the right to "perform" the music publicly by transmitting it, whether live or on film or tape, to television audiences.[1] This performance right is created by the Copyright Act as one of the exclusive rights enjoyed by the copyright

---

1. A non-dramatic performing right is the right to perform a musical composition other than in a dramatic performance, which the ASCAP blanket license defines as "a performance of a musical composition on a television program in which there is a definite plot depicted by action and where the performance of the musical composition is woven into and carries forward the plot and its accompanying action." See *3 Nimmer on Copyright* § 10.10[E] (1984).

owner. 17 U.S.C. § 106(4) (1982). Also pertinent to this litigation is the so-called synchronization right, or "synch" right, that is, the right to reproduce the music onto the soundtrack of a film or a videotape in synchronization with the action. The "synch" right is a form of the reproduction right also created by statute as one of the exclusive rights enjoyed by the copyright owner. Id. § 101.

Music performed by local television stations is selected in one of three ways. It may be selected by the station itself, or by the producer of a program that is sold to the station, or by a performer spontaneously. The stations select music for the relatively small portion of the program day devoted to locally produced programs. The vast majority of music aired by television stations is selected by the producers of programs supplied to the stations. In some instances these producers are the major television networks, but this litigation is not concerned with the performing rights to music on programs supplied to the local stations by the major networks because the networks have blanket licenses from ASCAP and BMI and convey performing rights to local stations when they supply network programs. Apart from network-produced programs, the producers of programs for local stations are "syndicators" supplying the stations with "syndicated" programs. Most syndicated programs are feature length movies or one-hour or half-hour films or videotapes produced especially for television viewing by motion picture studios, their television production affiliates, or independent television program producers. However, the definition of "syndicated program" that was stipulated to by the parties also includes live, non-network television programs offered for sale or license to local stations.[2] These syndicated programs are the central focus of this litigation. The third category of selected music, songs chosen spontaneously by a performer, accounts for a very small percentage of the music aired by the stations. These spontaneous selections of music can occur on programs produced either locally or by the networks or by syndicators.

Syndicators wishing to include music in their programs may either select pre-existing music (sometimes called "outside" music) or hire a composer to compose original music (sometimes called "inside" music). Most music on syndicated programs, up to 90% by plaintiffs' estimate, is inside music commissioned through the use of composer-for-hire agreements between the producer and either the composer alone or the composer and a corporation entitled to contract for a loan of the composer's services. Composer-for-hire agreements are normally standard form contracts. The salary paid to the composer, sometimes called "up front money," varies considerably from a few hundred dollars to several thousand dollars. The producer for whom a "work made for hire" was composed is considered by the Act to be the author and, unless the producer and composer have otherwise agreed, owns "all of the

---

2. The stipulation defines "syndicated program" as "a theatrical motion picture, pre-recorded television program or live television program which is offered for sale or license to a television station to be broadcast by that station as a non-network program."

rights comprised in the copyright." [  ] However, composer-for-hire agreements for syndicated television programs typically provide that the producer assigns to the composer and to a music publishing company the performing right to the music composed pursuant to the agreement.[3]

When the producer wishes to use outside music in a film or video-tape program, it must obtain from the copyright producer the "synch" right in order to record the music on the soundtrack of the film or tape. "Synch" rights vary in price, usually within a range of $150 to $500. When the producer wishes to use inside music, as is normally the case, it need not obtain the "synch" right because it already owns this right by virtue of the "work made for hire" provision of the Act.

Whether the producer decides to use outside or inside music, it need not acquire the television performing right since neither the making of the program nor the selling of the program to a television station is a "performance" of the music that would require a performing right. The producer is therefore free either to sell the program without the performing right and leave it to the station to obtain that right, or to obtain the performing right from the copyright proprietor, usually the composer and a publishing company, and convey that music performing right to the station along with the performing rights to all other copyrighted components of the program. If the producer obtains the music performing right from the copyright proprietor and conveys it to the station, the transaction is known as "source licensing" or "clearance at the source." If the station obtains the music right directly from the copyright proprietor, the transaction is known as "direct licensing."

The typical arrangement whereby local television stations acquire music performing rights in syndicated and all other programs is neither source licensing nor direct licensing. Instead, the stations obtain from ASCAP and BMI a blanket license permitting television performance of all of the music in the repertories of these organizations. The license is conveyed for a fee normally set as a percentage of the station's revenue. That fee, after deduction of administrative expenses, is distributed to the copyright proprietors on a basis that roughly reflects the extent of use of the music and the size of the audience for which the station "performed" the music. The royalty distribution is normally divided equally between the composer and the music publishing company.

In addition to offering stations a blanket license, ASCAP and BMI also offer a modified form of the blanket license known as a "program" or "per program" license. The program license conveys to the station the music performing rights to all of the music in the ASCAP or BMI repertory for use on the particular program for which the license is issued. The fee for a program license is a percent of the revenue derived by the station from the particular program, i.e., the advertising dollars paid to sponsor the program.

3. The assignment of performing rights from the producer to the composer and publishing company is typically not an assign-ment of all performing rights, but the exceptions are not pertinent to this litigation.

The blanket license contains a "carve-out" provision exempting from the base on which the license fee is computed the revenue derived by the station from any program presented by motion picture or transcription for which music performing rights have been licensed at the source by the licensor, i.e., ASCAP or BMI. The program license contains a more generous version of this provision, extending the exemption to music performing rights licensed at the source *either* by ASCAP/BMI *or* by the composer and publisher. Thus, for film and videotaped syndicated programs, a station can either obtain a blanket license for all of its music performing rights and reduce its fee for those programs licensed at the source by ASCAP/BMI, or obtain program licenses for each of its programs that use copyrighted music and avoid the fee for those programs licensed at the source by either ASCAP/BMI or by the composers and publishers.

### III. Prior Litigation

[The opinion recounts previous litigation concerning the licensing of music performing rights back to a 1941 antitrust suit brought against ASCAP and BMI. That suit was settled by consent decrees that imposed some limitations on ASCAP and BMI but permitted them to obtain exclusive licenses for music performing rights from their members and affiliates. The consent decree was amended in 1950; there were suits in 1951 and 1961. CBS sued ASCAP in 1969, challenging the legality of blanket licenses taken by local television stations from ASCAP and BMI. The Supreme Court eventually held that the blanket license was not a *per se* violation of section 1 of the Sherman Anti-Trust Act, BMI, Inc. v. CBS, Inc., 441 U.S. 1 (1979). On remand, the United States Court of Appeals for the Second Circuit agreed that the blanket license had not been proven to be a restraint of trade. CBS, Inc. v. ASCAP, 620 F.2d 930 (2d Cir.1980), certiorari denied 450 U.S. 970 (1981). The local stations began this litigation in 1978.]

    . . . We think the initial and, as it turns out, dispositive issue on the merits is whether the blanket licensing of performing rights to the local television stations has been proven to be a restraint of trade. [  ] Arguably the answer is *a fortiori* after the Supreme Court's decision and our decision on remand in the CBS litigation. The Supreme Court noted that "the necessity for and advantages of a blanket license for [television and radio networks] may be far less obvious than is the case when the potential users are individual television or radio stations . . . ." 441 U.S. at 21 [  ]. And on remand we upheld the blanket license against the claim of a network. However, for several reasons, it does not follow that the local stations lose simply because the CBS network lost. First, the Supreme Court's observation concerned the relative pro-competitive effects of the blanket license for a network compared to local stations. Even though the pro-competitive effects may be greater when the licensees are local stations, those pro-competitive effects do not necessarily outweigh the anti-competitive effects. Second, the Supreme Court's comparative statement does not determine the threshold issue of whether the blanket licensing of performing rights to local television stations is a restraint at all. The fact that CBS did not prove that blanket licensing of networks restrained competition does not necessarily mean that blanket licensing of local stations may not be shown to be a restraint. Finally, in *CBS-remand* we reviewed the District Judge's ruling that no restraint had been proved; here, we review a ruling that the local stations proved the existence of a restraint.

.   .   .

In reaching the conclusion that plaintiffs had proven the lack of realistically available alternatives to the blanket license, Judge Gagliardi gave separate consideration to three possibilities: the program license, .   .   . direct licensing, and source licensing. We consider each in turn.

*Program License.* Judge Gagliardi based his conclusion that a program license is not realistically available to the plaintiffs essentially on two circumstances: the cost of a program license and the reporting requirements that such a license imposes on a licensee. "The court therefore concludes that the per program license is too costly and burdensome to be a realistic alternative to the blanket license." [  ] Without rejecting any subsidiary factual finding concerning the availability of a program license, we reject the legal conclusion that it is not a realistic alternative to the blanket license.

.   .   .

.   .   . [T]he only valid test of whether the program license is "too costly" to be a realistic alternative is whether the price for such a license, in an objective sense, is higher than the value of the rights obtained. But plaintiffs presented no evidence that the price of the program license is "high" in terms of value received.   .   .   .

.   .   .

.   .   . The fact that very few stations have elected to take program licenses is not evidence that they are priced beyond an objectively reasonable price range. It may simply reflect, as defendants believe, that the blanket license has virtues of convenience that make it a legitimate object of customer preference.

.   .   .

[The conclusion that the program license is not realistically available because of the burdens of required record-keeping that accompany its use] is similarly flawed by the lack of evidence .   .   .   .

.   .   .

*Direct Licensing.* The District Court concluded that direct licensing is not a realistic alternative to the blanket license without any evidence that any local station ever offered any composer a sum of money in exchange for the performing rights to his music.   .   .   . Judge Gigliardi concluded .   .   . that direct licensing could not occur without the intervention of some agency to broker the numerous transactions .   .   .   . We have no quarrel with [that] proposition.   .   .   .

However, we see no evidentiary support for the . . . proposition
. . . that no one would undertake the brokering function for direct
licensing .   . . .

*Source Licensing.*   As Judge Gagliardi noted, the "current availability and comparative efficiency of source licensing have been the focus of
this lawsuit." [ ] The availability of source licensing is significant to the
inquiry as to whether the blanket license is a restraint because so much
of the stations' programming consists of syndicated programs for which
the producer could, if so inclined, convey music performing rights.   Most
of these syndicated programs use composer-for-hire music.   As to such
music, the producer starts out with the rights of the copyright, including
the performing right, by operation of law, 17 U.S.C. § 201(b), unless the
hiring agreement otherwise provides.   Thus it becomes important to
determine whether the stations can obtain from the producer the music
performing right, along with all of the other rights in a syndicated
program that are conveyed to the stations when the program is licensed.
.  .  .

     .  .  .

Judge Gagliardi properly declined to give any probative weight to
the plaintiffs' transparent effort to assemble in the midst of litigation
evidence that they had seriously tried to obtain source licensing.  .   .   .
Nevertheless the District Court concluded that source was not a realistic
alternative .  .   .  .  [But we conclude that plaintiffs have simply failed
to produce sufficient evidence to support a conclusion that the blanket
license is a restraint of trade.]

     .  .  .

*The Claimed Lack of Necessity.*   Plaintiffs earnestly advance the
argument that the blanket license, as applied to syndicated programming, should be declared unlawful for the basic reason that it is
unnecessary.   In their view, the blanket license is suspect because,
where it is used, no price competition occurs among songs when those
who need performing rights decide which songs to perform.   The resulting absence of price competition, plaintiffs urge, is justifiable only in
some contexts such as night clubs, live and locally produced programming of television stations, and radio stations, which make more spontaneous choices of music than do television stations.

There are two fundamental flaws in this argument.   First, it has not
been shown on this record that the blanket license, even as applied to
syndicated television programs, is not necessary.   If all the plaintiffs
mean is that a judicial ban on blanket licensing for syndicated television
programs would not halt performance of copyrighted music on such
programs and that some arrangement for the purchase of performing
rights would replace the blanket license, we can readily agree.  .   .   .
But a licensing system may be "necessary" in the practical sense that it
is far superior to other alternatives in efficiency .  .   .  .

     .  .  .

. . . Even if the evidence showed that most of the efficiencies of the blanket license could be achieved under source licensing, it would not follow that the blanket license thereby becomes unlawful. . . .

. . . [W]e hold that the local television stations have not presented evidence in this case permitting a conclusion that the blanket license is a restraint of trade in violation of section 1.

The judgment of the District Court is therefore reversed.

[Judge Winter wrote a separate opinion, concurring.]

## Notes and Questions

1. If the court of appeals had upheld the district court ruling that ASCAP and BMI blanket licenses to local television stations constituted an unreasonable restraint of trade under section 1 of the Sherman Anti-Trust Act, the performing societies could have lost $80 million in annual local television performing rights revenues. That represents about 25 percent of the performing rights societies' total annual revenues. The Entertainment and Sports Lawyer, Winter 1985 at 10.

2. Do you agree with the court of appeals' conclusion that there was no violation of the Sherman Act, or would you be more inclined to agree with the district court? Does it seem reasonable to conclude that direct licensing and source licensing are viable alternatives to blanket licensing just because the plaintiffs had been unable to prove that they were not?

3. An All-Industry Television Station Music License Committee advocating source licensing of music has sought to persuade Congress to adopt legislation requiring producers and syndicators to deliver syndicated programming to stations with music performance rights included. Broadcasting, Oct. 7, 1985 at 7. Walter H. Annenberg has said that a bill introduced in the House by Rep. Frederick C. Boucher (D.-Va.) and Rep. Henry J. Hyde (R.-Ill.) "could reduce payments to songwriters for use of their music on television to a pittance." Arguing in favor of the present system, Annenberg called the proposals "unwarranted and unfair." TV Guide, Dec. 28, 1985 at A–1.

4. ASCAP, BMI, and other music licensing organizations negotiate with stores that wish to play music for their customers. Even playing radio stations in commercial establishments can require copyright permission. The key question is whether or not playing the radio constitutes a performance.

In Twentieth Century Music Corp. v. Aiken, 422 U.S. 151 (1975), the owner of a fast-service food shop in Pittsburgh known as "George Aiken's Chicken" was sued for copyright infringement because he played a radio with four ceiling speakers in his shop each day. Included in the broadcasts were copyrighted musical compositions which plaintiffs complained were being "performed." The Supreme Court held that there was no performance:

> The practical unenforceability of a ruling that all of those in Aiken's position are copyright infringers is self-evident. One has

only to consider the countless business establishments in this country with radio or television sets on their premises—bars, beauty shops, cafeterias, car washes, dentists' offices, and drive-ins—to realize the total futility of any evenhanded effort on the part of copyright holders to license even a substantial percentage of them . . . . Secondly, to hold that all in Aiken's position "performed" these musical compositions would be to authorize the sale of an untold number of licenses for what is basically a single public rendition of a copyrighted work. The exaction of such multiple tribute would go far beyond what is required for the economic protection of copyright owners . . . .

By contrast, in Sailor Music v. Gap Stores, Inc., 668 F.2d 84 (2d Cir. 1981), certiorari denied 456 U.S. 945 (1982), it was held that use of music companies' copyrighted works by radio in Gap stores (average size 3,500 square feet) *did* constitute copyright infringement. Because they exceeded the "outer limit" of size, the Gap stores were enjoined from use of the works.

## D.  PROBLEMS OF NEW TECHNOLOGIES

### 1.  PROBLEMS OF CABLE

As we saw in Chapter IX, the 1976 copyright statute, in § 111, has set up a complex, compulsory licensing system to cover the retransmission of broadcast programming over cable systems. The cable operators pay a fee to the Copyright Royalty Tribunal for each station that they retransmit. The fees are then distributed by the CRT to the various copyright claimants.

### 2.  PROBLEMS OF VIDEO TAPE RECORDERS

The increasing use of home video tape recorders to record copyrighted television programs and films produced another difficult copyright question, as demonstrated below.

### SONY CORP. v. UNIVERSAL CITY STUDIOS

Supreme Court of the United States, 1984.
464 U.S. 417, 104 S.Ct. 774, 78 L.Ed.2d 574.

JUSTICE STEVENS delivered the opinion of the Court.

Petitioners manufacture and sell home video tape recorders. Respondents own the copyrights on some of the television programs that are broadcast on the public airwaves. Some members of the general public use video tape recorders sold by petitioners to record some of these broadcasts, as well as a large number of other broadcasts. The question presented is whether the sale of petitioners' copying equipment to the general public violates any of the rights conferred upon respondents by the Copyright Act.

Respondents commenced this copyright infringement action against petitioners in the United States District Court for the Central District of California in 1976. Respondents alleged that some individuals had used Betamax video tape recorders (VTR's) to record some of respondents' copyrighted works which had been exhibited on commercially sponsored television and contended that these individuals had thereby infringed respondents' copyrights. Respondents further maintained that petitioners were liable for the copyright infringement allegedly committed by Betamax consumers because of petitioners' marketing of the Betamax VTR's. Respondents sought no relief against any Betamax consumer. Instead, they sought money damages and an equitable accounting of profits from petitioners, as well as an injunction against the manufacture and marketing of Betamax VTR's.

. . .

An explanation of our rejection of respondents' unprecedented attempt to impose copyright liability upon the distributors of copying equipment requires a quite detailed recitation of the findings of the District Court. In summary, those findings reveal that the average member of the public uses a VTR principally to record a program he cannot view as it is being televised and then watch it once at a later time. This practice, known as "time-shifting," enlarges the television viewing audience. For that reason, a significant amount of television programming may be used in this manner without objection from the owners of the copyrights on the programs. For the same reason, even the two respondents in this case, who do assert objections to time-shifting in this litigation, were unable to prove that the practice has impaired the commercial value of their copyrights or has created any likelihood of future harm. Given these findings, there is no basis in the Copyright Act upon which respondents can hold petitioners liable for distributing VTR's to the general public. The Court of Appeals' holding that respondents are entitled to enjoin the distribution of VTR's, to collect royalties on the sale of such equipment, or to obtain other relief, if affirmed, would enlarge the scope of respondents' statutory monopolies to encompass control over an article of commerce that is not the subject of copyright protection. Such an expansion of the copyright privilege is beyond the limits of the grants authorized by Congress.

. . .

## II

Article I, Sec. 8 of the Constitution provides that:

"The Congress shall have Power . . . to Promote the Progress of Science and useful Arts, by securing for limited Times to Authors and Inventors the exclusive Right to their respective Writings and Discoveries."

The monopoly privileges that Congress may authorize are neither unlimited nor primarily designed to provide a special private benefit. Rather, the limited grant is a means by which an important public purpose may be achieved. It is intended to motivate the creative activity of authors and inventors by the provision of a special reward, and to allow the public access to the products of their genius after the limited period of exclusive control has expired.

"The copyright law, like the patent statute, makes reward to the owner a secondary consideration. In Fox Film Corp. v. Doyal, 286 U.S. 123, 127, Chief Justice Hughes spoke as follows respecting the copyright monopoly granted by Congress. 'The sole interest of the United States and the primary object in conferring the monopoly lie in the general benefits derived by the public from the labors of authors.' It is said that reward to the author or artist serves to induce release to the public of the products of his creative genius."
[  ]

As the text of the Constitution makes plain, it is Congress that has been assigned the task of defining the scope of the limited monopoly that should be granted to authors or to inventors in order to give the public appropriate access to their work product. Because this task involves a difficult balance between the interests of authors and inventors in the control and exploitation of their writings and discoveries on the one hand, and society's competing interest in the free flow of ideas, information, and commerce on the other hand, our patent and copyright statutes have been amended repeatedly.

From its beginning, the law of copyright has developed in response to significant changes in technology. Indeed, it was the invention of a new form of copying equipment—the printing press—that gave rise to the original need for copyright protection. Repeatedly, as new developments have occurred in this country, it has been the Congress that has fashioned the new rules that new technology made unnecessary. Thus, long before the enactment of the Copyright Act of 1909, 35 Stat. 1075, it was settled that the protection given to copyrights is wholly statutory. [  ] The remedies for infringement "are only those prescribed by Congress." [  ]

The judiciary's reluctance to expand the protections afforded by the copyright without explicit legislative guidance is a recurring theme. [  ] Sound policy, as well as history, supports our consistent deference to Congress when major technological innovations alter the market for copyrighted materials. Congress has the constitutional authority and the institutional ability to accommodate fully the varied permutations of competing interests that are inevitably implicated by such new technology.

In a case like this, in which Congress has not plainly marked our course, we must be circumspect in construing the scope of rights created by a legislative enactment which never contemplated such a calculus of interests. In doing so, we are guided by Justice Stewart's exposition of the correct approach to ambiguities in the law of copyright:

"The limited scope of the copyright holder's statutory monopoly, like the limited copyright duration required by the Constitution, reflects a balance of competing claims upon the public interest: Creative work is to be encouraged and rewarded, but private motivation must ultimately serve the cause of promoting broad public availability of literature, music, and the other arts. The immediate effect of our copyright law is to secure a fair return for an 'author's' creative labor. But the ultimate aim is, by this incentive, to stimulate artistic creativity for the general public good. "The sole interest of the United States and the primary object in conferring the monopoly,' this Court has said, 'lie in the general benefits derived by the public from the labors of authors.' [ ] When technological change has rendered its literal teams ambiguous, the Copyright Act must be construed in light of this basic purpose." [ ]

. . .

The two respondents in this case do not seek relief against the Betamax users who have allegedly infringed their copyrights. Moreover, this is not a class action on behalf of all copyright owners who license their works for television broadcast, and respondents have no right to invoke whatever rights other copyright holders may have to bring infringement actions based on Betamax copying of their works. As was made clear by their own evidence, the copying of the respondents' programs represents a small portion of the total use of VTR's. It is, however, the taping of respondents' own copyrighted programs that provides them with standing to charge Sony with contributory infringement. To prevail, they have the burden of proving that users of the Betamax have infringed their copyrights and that Sony should be held responsible for that infringement.

### III

The Copyright Act does not expressly render anyone liable for infringement committed by another. In contrast, the Patent Act expressly brands anyone who "actively induces infringement of a patent" as an infringer, 35 U.S.C. § 271(b), and further imposes liability on certain individuals labeled "contributory" infringers, id., § 271(c). The absence of such express language in the copyright statute does not preclude the imposition of liability for copyright infringements on certain parties who have not themselves engaged in the infringing activity. For vicarious liability is imposed in virtually all areas of the law, and the concept of contributory infringement is merely a species of the broader problem of identifying the circumstances in which it is just to hold one individual accountable for the actions of another.

. . .

If vicarious liability is to be imposed on petitioners in this case, it must rest on the fact that they have sold equipment with constructive knowledge of the fact that their customers may use that equipment to make unauthorized copies of copyrighted material. There is no precedent in the law of copyright for the imposition of vicarious liability on such a theory. The closest analogy is provided by the patent law cases to which it is appropriate to refer because of the historic kinship between patent law and copyright law.

In the Patent Code both the concept of infringement and the concept of contributory infringement are expressly defined by statute. The prohibition against contributory infringement is confined to the knowing sale of a component especially made for use in connection with a particular patent. There is no suggestion in the statute that one patentee may object to the sale of a product that might be used in connection with other patents. Moreover, the Act expressly provides that the sale of a "staple article or commodity of commerce suitable for substantial noninfringing use" is not contributory infringement.

When a charge of contributory infringement is predicated entirely on the sale of an article of commerce that is used by the purchaser to infringe a patent, the public interest in access to that article of commerce is necessarily implicated. A finding of contributory infringement does not, of course, remove the article from the market altogether; it does, however, give the patentee effective control over the sale of that item. Indeed, a finding of contributory infringement is normally the functional equivalent of holding that the disputed article is within the monopoly granted to the patentee.

For that reason, in contributory infringement cases arising under the patent laws the Court has always recognized the critical importance of not allowing the patentee to extend his monopoly beyond the limits of his specific grant. These cases deny the patentee any right to control the distribution of unpatented articles unless they are "unsuited for any commercial noninfringing use." [ ] Unless a commodity "has no use except through practice of the patented method," ibid., the patentee has no right to claim that its distribution constitutes contributory infringement. "To form the basis for contributory infringement the item must almost be uniquely suited as a component of the patented invention." [ ] "[A] sale of an article which though adapted to an infringing use is also adapted to other and lawful uses, is not enough to make the seller a contributory infringer. Such a rule would block the wheels of commerce." [ ]

We recognize there are substantial differences between the patent and copyright laws. But in both areas the contributory infringement doctrine is grounded on the recognition that adequate protection of a monopoly may require the courts to look beyond actual duplication of a device or publication to the products or activities that make such duplication possible. The staple article of commerce doctrine must strike a balance between a copyright holder's legitimate demand for effective— not merely symbolic—protection of the statutory monopoly, and the rights of others freely to engage in substantially unrelated areas of commerce. Accordingly, the sale of copying equipment, like the sale of other articles of commerce, does not constitute contributory infringement if the product is widely used for legitimate, unobjectionable purposes.   Indeed, it need merely be capable of substantial noninfringing uses.

## IV

The question is thus whether the Betamax is capable of commercially significant noninfringing uses.   In order to resolve that question, we need not explore *all* the different potential uses of the machine and determine whether or not they would constitute infringement.   Rather, we need only consider whether on the basis of the facts as found by the district court a significant number of them would be non-infringing. Moreover, in order to resolve this case we need not give precise content to the question of how much use is commercially significant.   For one potential use of the Betamax plainly satisfies this standard, however it is understood: private, noncommercial time-shifting in the home.   It does so both (A) because respondents have no right to prevent other copyright holders from authorizing it for their programs, and (B) because the District Court's factual findings reveal that even the unauthorized home time-shifting of respondents' programs is legitimate fair use.

.   .   .

The District Court's conclusions are buttressed by the fact that to the extent time-shifting expands public access to fairly broadcast television programs, it yields societal benefits.   Earlier this year, in Community Television of Southern California v. Gottfried, 459 U.S. 498, [at] n. 12 (1983), we acknowledged the public interest in making television broadcasting more available.   Concededly, that interest is not unlimited.   But it supports an interpretation of the concept of "fair use" that requires the copyright holder to demonstrate some likelihood of harm before he may condemn a private act of time-shifting as a violation of federal law.

When these factors are all weighed in the "equitable rule of reason" balance, we must conclude that this record amply supports the District Court's conclusion that home time-shifting is fair use.   In light of the findings of the District Court regarding the state of the empirical data, it is clear that the Court of Appeals erred in holding that the statute as presently written bars such conduct.

In summary, the record and findings of the District Court lead us to two conclusions.   First, Sony demonstrated a significant likelihood that substantial numbers of copyright holders who license their works for broadcast on free television would not object to having their broadcasts time-shifted by private viewers.   And second, respondents failed to demonstrate that time-shifting would cause any likelihood of nonminimal harm to the potential market for, or the value of, their copyrighted works.   The Betamax is, therefore, capable of substantial noninfringing uses.   Sony's sale of such equipment to the general public does not constitute contributory infringement of respondent's copyrights.

V

"The direction of Art. I is that *Congress* shall have the power to promote the progress of science and the useful arts. When, as here, the Constitution is permissive, the sign of how far Congress has chosen to go can come only from Congress." Deepsouth Packing Co. v. Laitram Corp., 406 U.S. 518, 530 (1972).

One may search the Copyright Act in vain for any sign that the elected representatives of the millions of people who watch television every day have made it unlawful to copy a program for later viewing at home, or have enacted a flat prohibition against the sale of machines that make such copying possible.

It may well be that Congress will take a fresh look at this new technology, just as it so often has examined other innovations in the past. But it is not our job to apply laws that have not yet been written. Applying the copyright statute, as it now reads, to the facts as they have been developed in this case, the judgment of the Court of Appeals must be reversed.

[Justice Blackmun dissented in an opinion joined by Justices Marshall, Powell and Rehnquist. He believed that Universal had shown substantial harm to "potential markets for" Universal's copyrighted works and thus, taping of broadcast shows could not be considered a fair use. He argued that the majority had incorrectly focused on existing rather than potential markets.

He would have remanded the case for further proceedings on the issue of contributory infringement. In his view the unanswered question to be addressed was the proportion of VTR recording that constitutes infringement.]

### Notes and Questions

1. How does the ease of taping at home affect the market for videotapes of films and television programs? All of the episodes of "Star Trek," for example, are now available for sale. What if viewers at home have "warehoused" the episodes—taped them for their own use?

2. What possible remedies might exist for the copyright holders? A tax on VCR's? A tax on blank tapes? What are the problems with these remedies?

### E. TRADEMARKS

Trademarks, like copyright, protect intellectual property. Instead of protecting an entire movie script, an entire book, or an entire magazine, as a copyright may, trademarks protect "identifying symbols"—words, names, symbols, devices, or, in the instance of broadcast stations, call letters.

Registration of trademarks takes place under Congressional legislation. Unlike copyright and patents, trademarks are not specifically mentioned in the Constitution. The governing statute is the Federal Trademark Act of 1946, known as the Lanham Act after the late Rep. Fritz Garland Lanham. Registrations are filed with the United States Patent and Trademark Office.

Manufacturers, for obvious reasons, want to protect their exclusive right to use names and symbols associated with their products. Sometimes, if they are not sufficiently vigilant in their protection of their trademarks, the trademarks enter the *public domain* and can be used by anyone. Formica is one example. The owners of the registered trademarks Xerox and Kleenex, knowing that people sometimes misuse their trademarks as though they were generic names, are among those which advertise in such magazines as *Editor & Publisher* and *Broadcasting*, emphasizing that their names are protected and should be capitalized.

Trademark owners particularly concerned about the problem emphasize the ® symbol next to their names or go to considerable lengths to emphasize that their names are brand names, as in broadcast commercials referring to "Sanka Brand" coffee.

Groups of letters, even an individual letter, can function as a trademark. If one uses an individual letter, the typestyle or design of the letter must be distinctive.

Broadcasters may, as a result of a 1985 change, protect their stations' call letters by trademark. For years, under an assumption that the government owned the call letters, individuals could not trademark them. The issue arose in an appeal before the Trademark Trial and Appeal Board of the Patent and Trademark Office, U.S. Department of Commerce. WSM, Inc., an AM radio station, had used the call letters "WSM" since 1925 and claimed use of the call letters as a service mark. The Examining Attorney in the Patent and Trademark Office had refused to register the letters as a service mark on the assumption that the station did not own the call letters because they were used only with FCC approval. The Trademark Trial and Appeal Board reversed:

> The Examining Attorney has apparently misunderstood the nature of the relationship between the FCC and applicant. . . . It is clear that the FCC is not the owner of the call letters used by the broadcasters which it regulates. The right to broadcast is not what the agency licenses to broadcasters. . . . In the case at hand the applicant obtained whatever rights it has in its service mark by adopting it and using it to identify its broadcasting services. The FCC neither selected the mark for applicant nor used it to identify any services. . . . [A]s long as applicant uses the mark to identify its services which are lawfully rendered in commerce applicant is the owner of its service mark [and is therefore entitled to register it].

Today, although it is possible to trademark call letters, problems still can arise when two stations have call letters which look or sound similar. An example involves a trademark infringement alleged by station WMEE(FM) of Fort Wayne, Ind., which in 1984 complained after a station in Decatur, Ind., whose signal overlapped with that of WMEE, changed its call letters from WADM to WMCZ(FM). On the request of WMEE, a federal district court judge issued a preliminary injunction prohibiting the new WMCZ from identifying itself by those call letters. Furthermore, the judge ordered WMCZ to air a disclaimer differentiating itself from WMEE. The judge, who said the two calls were "overwhelmingly phonetically and rhythmically similar," said that, "Implicit in the FCC's relinquishment of its role as arbiter of call letter disputes is the conclusion that, when local courts resolve call letter disputes, the law of that local forum and circuit would apply." Broadcasting, Sept. 30, 1984 at 90.

It is also possible to register titles, characters, names, and "other distinctive features" of radio or television programs under § 45 of the Lanham Act. "Mork & Mindy," "The Drifters," and "Johnny Carson" are examples of registered service marks. Section 43(a) of the Lanham Act permits protection of unregistered names of performers or sports teams, etc. Examples include "Monday Night Football," "Dallas Cowboys Cheerleaders," and "Deep Purple."

Cartoon characters and literary characters can also be protected under copyright or trademark, depending on the use. "Superman" and "Tarzan" are examples.

# Chapter XII

# DEFAMATION

In this Chapter and the two that follow we will consider the range of legal arguments for prohibiting certain communications because of their substantive content. In each case we will consider, among other points, the justifications offered for restriction and the value of the communication. The justifications are as diverse as the situations to which they are applied. Arguments for limiting speech and press to protect privacy are unlikely to resemble the arguments based on national security.

Even if the speech is determined to be subject to governmental control, there is the further question of what types of sanctions may be imposed. Among the array are criminal prosecutions, civil damage remedies, and bans on speech imposed by administrative techniques or by court injunction. Again, particular sanctions are used for specific kinds of speech. Even when speech is found to be defamatory, for example, it is regulated after the fact and is not enjoined. On the other hand, speech held to invade privacy has been barred from publication. In sum, the sanctions available are as diverse as the justifications offered to restrict the speech in the first place.

We begin our survey of restraints on communication with the state's interest in granting redress to persons whose reputations have been hurt by false statements. We start with defamation law in part because it was one of the earliest legal actions available against journalists and in part because even today it poses a significant legal danger for broadcasters. It is certainly the most extensively litigated area of media law.

Harm to reputation is one of the earliest injuries recognized by virtually every legal system. Early societies were undoubtedly concerned that the failure to provide legal recourse to those whose reputations had been impugned would lead to breaches of the peace. Although that concern has eased as civilization has advanced, states may still be concerned about the potential for violence. Beyond that, however, traditional values emphasize the importance of an individual's good name. Whatever the justifications, the action for defamation has long had a place in the common law.

English law has redressed and punished attacks on reputation since the feudal days. During the 16th century, the authorities began using the law of defamation to punish political criticism of the government and its officials. These attacks were referred to as seditious libel.

Although it is doubtful that the English law of seditious libel was transplanted in this country, it seems clear that the tort law that provided damage remedies to individuals did cross the Atlantic. After independence, defamation law continued to be enforced. The First

Amendment's statement that "Congress shall make no law . . . abridging the freedom of speech, or of the press . . ." had no apparent impact upon defamation law until the mid-1960's. Since defamation law was a creature of state law—the power to regulate defamation law was not delegated to Congress—the First Amendment had no immediate effect on the states' administration of that law.

Even after it became clear that the First Amendment applied to the states through the Fourteenth Amendment, these provisions were thought inapplicable to false statements that adversely affected an individual's reputation. The Supreme Court did not tie defamation and the First Amendment together until the seminal case of New York Times Co. v. Sullivan, decided in 1964. That case not only brought major change to the law of defamation, but also provided a philosophy that has led to many other recent developments in mass media law. We shall consider the impact of this case on defamation law shortly.

## A. THE STATE LAW OF DEFAMATION

Before we can appreciate the significance of the constitutional developments, however, we must understand the common-law world of defamation. The constitutional developments have not created a totally new legal area; rather they have altered some of the pre-existing state rules and left the remaining ones in place. States remain free to protect reputation in whatever manner they see fit so long as they do so consistently with the First Amendment.

A second reason for inquiring into state law is that state law itself has a significant number of protections for those who are sued for defamation. It is often possible for a defendant to win a defamation case under the state's traditional rules without ever having to rely upon the protection of the First Amendment.

Why might a defendant who could win a case under First Amendment principles try to win that case under state rules? There are several practical explanations. Perhaps the major one is that, as a matter of procedure, the state defenses may permit a defendant to win the case earlier in the litigation (such as on a motion to dismiss, rather than on a motion for summary judgment or perhaps only after a trial is held). It is often faster and cheaper for a media defendant to succeed on state law grounds than to rely exclusively on the more glorious, but perhaps less expeditious, ground of the First and Fourteenth Amendments.

The point is that we must understand the basic operation of traditional state defamation law as well as the Constitution. We turn first to the state law and then to the impact of constitutional law.

1.  THE REPUTATION ELEMENT

*a.  Definition*

The essence of the action for defamation is the claim that defendant has uttered a false statement that has harmed the plaintiff's reputation. The modern view is that a statement is defamatory if it harms the plaintiff's reputation by lowering him in the estimation of the community or by deterring others from associating or dealing with him.  It is easy to think of statements that will fit such a broad definition.  It obviously covers charges that plaintiff committed a crime or that he was inept in his chosen trade or profession.  It is enough that the published statement be of the sort that would lead a segment of the community to think less of the plaintiff.  That segment need not be large.

When the false statement is transmitted by electronic media, obviously, there is usually a large audience, but there need not be.

Most cases have involved charges of volitional behavior by plaintiff—committing a crime, lacking skill, or writing an article.  The broad sweep of the definition, however, extends to accusations that the plaintiff was of illegitimate birth, had been raped, or was in dire financial straits.  Even though the plaintiff cannot be blamed for a condition, the courts have nonetheless bowed to reality and recognized that these kinds of charges may in fact cause others to shun, or refrain from associating with, the plaintiff.  Judges "take the world as we find it" even if the segment of the community that thinks less of the plaintiff can be characterized as "wrong-thinking"—as they would be in the illegitimacy and rape examples.

At the same time, there is a limit to that principle.  Consider, for example, a false charge that the mob's gunman missed his target.  Were the gunman to sue and assert that his reputation had been tarnished among the underworld, it is unlikely that a court would entertain the charge.  Is it appropriate to redress a claim based on an audience segment that is criminal rather than simply wrong-thinking?

*b.  Corporations*

Until now, the discussion has been directed to the question of protecting the reputation of a human being.  Not infrequently, however, defamatory statements are made about corporations.  It is generally held that corporations also have reputations that they may vindicate through actions for defamation.  Generally the corporation must be attacked in a way that affects its credit or, if it is a corporation organized for profit, its profit-making ability.

A non-profit corporation may also be defamed if the charge is one that tends to interfere with its ability to obtain financial support from the public.  A corporation that relies on public donations may be able to sue for defamation if the charge would interfere with its ability to obtain such funds.

### c. Ambiguity

Statements are often ambiguous. In such cases the prevailing rule is to have the judge decide whether any of the statement's possible meanings can reasonably be understood to have a defamatory impact. If the judge decides that at least one of the possible meanings would be defamatory, it then becomes a function of the jury to decide the meaning that was in fact conveyed.

It should be noted here that the Supreme Court in one discussion of ambiguous statements resolved the question itself. The case arose from a tumultuous city council meeting involving the plaintiff, a local real estate developer, in a negotiation with the city council. Members of the audience characterized the plaintiff's bargaining position as "blackmail." The defendant newspaper accurately reported the meeting and included the blackmail charges—sometimes without quotation marks. The state courts granted plaintiff a judgment against the newspaper.

Justice Stewart concluded for the majority that "as a matter of constitutional law, the word 'blackmail' in these circumstances was not" defamatory:

> It is simply impossible to believe that a reader who reached the word "blackmail" in either article would not have understood exactly what was meant; it was Bresler's public and wholly legal negotiating proposals that were being criticized. No reader could have thought that either the speakers at the meeting or the newspaper articles reporting their words were charging Bresler with the commission of a criminal offense. On the contrary, even the most careless reader must have perceived that the word was no more than rhetorical hyperbole . . ..

Justice White dissented. He could not "join the majority claim of superior insight with respect to how the word 'blackmail' would be understood by the ordinary reader in Greenbelt, Maryland." Greenbelt Cooperative Publishing Association v. Bresler, 398 U.S. 6 (1970).

Another problem arises when part of a story has a defamatory impact but another part of the story negates that impact. The lead-in to a story may be defamatory but the story as a whole may be harmless. Normally, courts consider how a reasonable reader would respond.

Statements may be defamatory even though the thrust of the accusations is not clear from the words used. In such indirect defamation cases, plaintiffs' complaints must show the court how the plaintiffs have been defamed. The description of how plaintiffs do this involves the use of three technical words. If the plaintiffs themselves are not directly named, they must show by "colloquium" that the statements were "of and concerning" them. If it is still not clear how the plaintiffs have been defamed, they must plead extrinsic facts that would permit a defamatory meaning to be applied to defendants' words. Such an allegation of extrinsic facts is called the "inducement." Finally we have "innuendo." Where the statements are not clearly defamatory on their face, it is the function of the innuendo to assert the meanings that plaintiffs attach to the passages and any additions by colloquium and inducement. The innuendo is not a fact but is the plaintiffs' assertion of how the passages would be understood by those who heard the defendants' words and knew the additional unstated facts.

An example may help clarify the matter. Let us assume a defendant says, "The man who lives in the house two doors east of my house was the only person in the Smith home between 7 p.m. and 8 p.m. last night." If the plaintiff thinks that this statement defames him and wishes to sue, his pleading must establish how he has been defamed. For colloquium he might allege, "I am the only man who lives in the house two doors east of the speaker's house." This ties the plaintiff to the statement but does not clarify its defamatory nature. The defamation is clarified if the plaintiff alleges as inducement that the Smith house was burglarized between 7 and 8 p.m. that night. The plaintiff will then assert that the innuendo is that he is being accused of the crime of burglary.

### d.   *"Of and Concerning Plaintiff"*

In order for a defamatory statement to affect the plaintiff adversely, the reader must connect that statement with the plaintiff. As we said above, the plaintiff must show that the statement objected to was "of and concerning" him. Sometimes this is a problem because of the ambiguity of the statement or because the plaintiff is only indirectly identified. In those cases our discussion about ambiguous statements will help resolve the case. If readers could plausibly believe that the plaintiff was referred to, then a jury will decide whether the statement was in fact so understood.

### e.   *Groups*

Another aspect of this problem involves statements that attack large groups of people. In such cases is it possible for an individual member of that group to assert that the statement hurt his personal reputation? At the extreme, an attack on all lawyers in the United States or on all clergymen would be held to be such a general broadside that no individual lawyer or clergyman could sue. The same would be true of broadside attacks on racial, religious, or ethnic groups.

At the other extreme it is generally accepted that a charge made against a small group may defame all members of that group. For example, a television newscast may assert that "the officers" of a corporation have embezzled funds. There are only four officers of the corporation. Each of them may be found to have been defamed. Even if the statement had said "one of the officers of the corporation" had embezzled funds, the group is small enough so that all four officials are put under a shadow and can sue.

As the group grows larger the impact of the statement may depend on the number accused.  In one case, a defamatory charge was made against one unidentified member of a 21-member police force.  All 21 sued.  The court dismissed the case.  It feared that allowing the action would permit a suit by an entire baseball team over a report that one member was disciplined for brawling.  Such a result "would chill communication to the marrow."  But suppose the charge had been against "all but one" of the members of that police force.  Such a statement may reflect on each member of the force though the same charge made against only one of the 21 might not.  Arcand v. Evening Call Publishing Co., 567 F.2d 1163 (1st Cir.1977).

All states deny damage actions to large groups, but a few have attempted to use criminal statutes to prevent or punish such charges against racial or ethnic groups as discussed at p. 494, infra.

### *f.  Opinions—A Special Problem*

At common law there was much confusion about whether opinion, as distinguished from fact, could be the basis for a defamation action.  Such a strongly expressed unfavorable opinion could easily lower a person's reputation in the eyes of others, the courts usually held that such a statement could form the basis of a defamation action even though it could not be found to be true or false.  Occasionally, the courts held that although truth was a defense to defamation, that did not mean that a statement could be defamatory only if it could be shown to be false.  Courts held that those sued for publishing defamatory opinions might invoke the defense of fair comment—the privilege of stating opinions that they actually held and did not express solely for the purpose of hurting the object of the attack.  We consider fair comment at p. 463, infra.

Much of this confusion is disappearing, largely as a result of a passage in Gertz v. Robert Welch, Inc., 418 U.S. 323 (1974), reprinted at p. 474, infra: "Under the First Amendment there is no such thing as a false idea.  However pernicious an opinion may seem, we depend for its correction not on the conscience of judges and juries but on the competition of other ideas."  418 U.S. at 339–40.

The states have moved sharply to clarify their own law without waiting for further prodding by the Supreme Court.  In Rinaldi v. Holt, Rinehart & Winston, Inc., 42 N.Y.2d 369, 397 N.Y.S.2d 943, 366 N.E.2d 1299 (1977), certiorari denied 434 U.S. 969 (1977), an author had strongly attacked a judge's decisions and competence.  The court relied on the *Gertz* dictum: "The expression of opinion, even in the form of pejorative rhetoric, relating to fitness for judicial office or to performance while in judicial office, is safeguarded. . . . Plaintiff may not recover from defendants for simply expressing their opinion of his judicial performance, no matter how unreasonable, extreme or erroneous these opinions might be."  In his writing, the author "set forth the basis for his belief that plaintiff is incompetent and should be removed.  Based upon the facts stated and public debate provoked by the statements, each reader may draw his own conclusions as to whether Newfield's views should be supported or challenged."

In cases arising from statements during political campaigns, the courts have concluded that the statements must have been understood by the electorate as opinion. One letter to the editor accused the plaintiff of "contrived public opinion polls, unfounded statements, emphatic denials, committees no one ever heard of, attacks on straw men and a lot of slick, big-time expensive political public relations." It also charged him with an "amateurish job of chicanery."

The court concluded that "distasteful as this letter may have been to Block, it sounds remarkably similar to the usual and ordinary kind of political rhetoric which is all too often composed of equal parts of bombast, hyperbole, and billingsgate." The reader could only conclude that Block was being accused of "being a city slicker who is trying to bamboozle the good citizens of Palm Springs with the old snake-oil routine . . .. As such it is a statement of opinion, not fact." Desert Sun Publishing Co. v. Superior Court, 97 Cal.App.3d 49, 158 Cal.Rptr. 519 (1979).

In Ollman v. Evans, 750 F.2d 970 (D.C.Cir.1984), certiorari denied, 471 U.S. __ (1985), a political science professor who had been nominated to head the University of Maryland's Department of Politics and Government sued nationally-syndicated columnists Evans and Novak after their column characterized him as an "outspoken proponent of political Marxism." The column quoted Professor Bertell Ollman's writings and asked, "What is the true measurement of Ollman's scholarship? Does he intend to use the classroom for indoctrination? Will he indeed be followed by other Marxist professors? Could the department in time be closed to non-Marxists, following the tendency at several English universities?"

The professor sued for defamation, and the defendants sought summary judgment on the ground that the statements were all statements of opinion. The federal district court's granting of summary judgment was first remanded by the court of appeals; on rehearing en banc the court affirmed the granting of the summary judgment in a 6–5 vote, reflecting the lack of consensus on the court.

### g.   Vagueness

Some courts have found language too imprecise to form the basis of a defamation action. An accusation that William F. Buckley, Jr., was a "fellow traveler" of fascist causes was too "loosely definable" and too "variously interpretable" to be actionable as a defamation. The court suggested that there might be a difference between that vague charge and a more specific charge that plaintiff was a member of a particular party or group that subscribed to that type of belief. Buckley v. Littell, 539 F.2d 882 (2d Cir.1976), certiorari denied 429 U.S. 1062 (1977).

Similarly, a charge that a police union's collective bargaining efforts involved the "inroad of communism" was held too vague to support a suit. National Association of Government Employees, Inc. v. Central Broadcasting Corp., 379 Mass. 220, 396 N.E.2d 996 (1979). The court thought it clear from the context and words used that no hearer in the community after even brief reflection would understand the speaker to be charging plaintiff with complicity in the "horrors distinctive of a totalitarian regime."

## 2. LIBEL AND SLANDER—THE DAMAGE QUESTION

So far we have been discussing the general subject of "defamation." Included within defamation are the subcategories of libel and slander. Historically, slanders were oral defamations and were handled by the common-law courts; libels were written defamations that, because of the development of printing, became a major concern of the crown. After the end of the days of the Star Chamber, a criminal court, oral and written defamations were redressed by the common-law courts. Those courts, however, preserved some distinctions between the two that have survived to our day.

The critical distinction relates to what types of damages a plaintiff must show in order to be allowed to bring an action for defamation. Two types of damages are central to this discussion. "Special damages" are specific identifiable losses that the plaintiff can prove he has sustained and can trace to the defendant's defamatory statement. "General damages" are damages to reputation that the plaintiff is presumed or proven to have sustained as a result of the defendant's statement. The jury is permitted to speculate on the extent of injury based on the words used, the medium used, and the predicted response of the community.

The common law courts have treated libel as substantially more serious than slander. The distinction arose when relatively few people could read and the written word inspired awe and thus was more credible. A writing may be given more weight because it requires more thought and planning than a spontaneous oral utterance. Furthermore, the writing is more lasting and is likely to reach a larger audience than most, if not all, slanders. Thus, libels as a class were more likely to cause harm than slanders, and courts declared that plaintiffs in libel cases were able to recover general damages without any showing of special damages. Therefore, a plaintiff proceeding under libel has always been at least as well off as, and often better off than, a plaintiff suing for slander for precisely the same words.

If an action is for slander, plaintiff must prove "special damages" unless the defamatory thrust fits into at least one of four categories. These categories are: the imputation of a serious crime involving moral turpitude; imputation of an existing loathsome disease; a charge that attacks the plaintiff's competence or honesty in business, trade, or profession; or a charge of unchastity in a woman. Such a spoken charge is called "slander per se" and permits an action enabling plaintiff to claim general damages to reputation without proving actual pecuniary harm.  Here the jury may conclude that publication of the charge caused substantial harm in the community, and can measure damages according to the number and identity of those who learned of the charge, and their presumed reaction based on the seriousness and credibility of the charge. If a plaintiff can also establish special damages, these could be recovered in addition to any general damages.

If the slander is not within the four categories, then an action must be supported by proof of special damages, such as losing a job or a business deal.

The distinction between libel and slander has blurred with the development of new modes of communication.  Until this century, it was likely that a written defamation would reach more people than an oral one.  But with the development of radio and then of television, the odds have shifted.  In analyzing new technology should we stick to the traditional oral-written line or should we develop an approach that treats all modes of mass communication as libel and other modes of communication as slander?  In a few states, legislation has resolved the matter. For example, California provides that broadcasting is slander.  In the states that are resolving the question by common law, the tendency has been to treat broadcasting as libel.

The resulting libel-slander rules have sometimes permitted a plaintiff to recover enormous amounts in general damages.  At other times they have barred a plaintiff from recovering anything whatever, because special damages were required but could not be proven although serious general harm seemed likely.

In addition to the critical distinction between general and special damages, two other classifications loom large in defamation law: nominal damages and punitive damages.  Although nominal damages are unimportant in most tort actions, they may be central in defamation cases.  The award of a symbolic amount such as six cents usually shows that the jury found the attack to be false but also found the words not to have hurt, either because the speaker was not credible or the plaintiff's strong reputation blunted the harm (or his reputation was so low nothing could really hurt it).  For an example, see the suit by Quentin Reynolds against the Hearst Corporation and one of its columnists, upholding a jury award of $1 in compensatory damages and $175,000 in punitive damages against the various defendants.  Reynolds v. Pegler, 223 F.2d 429 (2d Cir.), certiorari denied 350 U.S. 846 (1955) (Black, J. dissenting).

A few states declare that punitive damages, which are to punish defendants for serious misbehavior, are never recoverable.  Most states allow them in appropriate cases.

### 3. The Basis for Liability—The Trouble Spot

Before one person is liable in tort law for hurting another, commonly, but not universally, some "fault" must be ascribed to the actor's conduct. For example, a plaintiff cannot win an automobile accident case simply by showing that the defendant's car hit the plaintiff. Instead, plaintiff must show that the defendant driver was "at fault" in his behavior. (It is, of course, different in so-called "no-fault" states, which emphasize the harm to plaintiff rather than the fault of the defendant.)

In defamation, the common law long took the view that fault played no part in the tort. In other words, historically, plaintiffs had only to show that the defendants' statements hurt the plaintiffs' reputations and prove whatever damages were required by the libel-slander rules. It was irrelevant that the defendants did not realize that their statements could hurt the plaintiffs or anyone.

Thus, a newspaper lost a case in which it published a birth announcement that was a hoax—the couple had been married only three months. Those who read the article and who knew the fact of plaintiff's recent marriage would have given the story a meaning the newspaper never intended. Even if the newspaper had tried unsuccessfully to check the story but failed to learn about the hoax, it would not have mattered. The common law asserted that defendants in defamation cases were subject to "strict liability"—a liability that was not based on fault. The peril to free speech is readily apparent today. But the response in earlier times was that the remedy was accuracy and refusal to write about things that were not known first hand.

As we shall see, this troubling aspect of the common law has become the focus of constitutional developments.

For the electronic media, the problem of determining liability can be particularly difficult in instances of near or near-live transmissions. In a Massachusetts case, Pacella v. Milford Radio Corp., a candidate for public office alleged that he had been libeled when the host of a radio talk show failed to take advantage of a seven-second delay to terminate the remarks of an anonymous caller. 18 Mass.App.Ct. 6, 462 N.E.2d 355 (1984), affirmed 394 Mass. 1051, 476 N.E.2d 595 (1985), certiorari denied 474 U.S. ___ (1985). Under the common law, the candidate might have won. The common law tradition was that media were responsible for libelous statements they transmitted, whether they originated them or not, and whether they were careful or not. Several states adopted a model statute giving broadcasters greater protection. As we shall see in the discussion of Constitutional privilege, p. 463, infra, however, a different standard is imposed in cases involving public figures today. Thus, in the Pacella case, the court held that the broadcaster was not responsible because it had not been shown that failure to stop the allegedly libelous statement demonstraated "reckless disregard of truth or falsity," language to which we will return in New York Times v. Sullivan, p. 464, infra.

Traditionally, the plaintiff's action for defamation has been easy to establish.  The plaintiff had to prove the publication to a third person of a statement of and concerning plaintiff that injured his reputation, and then had to meet whatever damage showing was required under the relevant libel-slander rules.  These elements shown, it was up to the defendant to present a defense.

### 4.  COMMON LAW DEFENSES

Several common law libel defenses are typically recognized in state law.  They include truth, the privilege accorded participants in certain official proceedings, the privilege accorded to those who quote accurately from such proceedings, and the privilege of criticism, sometimes called "fair comment."  These defenses were used by libel defendants under strict liability prior to the New York Times v. Sullivan decision.  We will discuss them first and then look at the important constitutional privilege of absence of malice in a separate section.

#### a.  *Truth*

The most obvious defense, but one rarely used, is to prove the essential truth of the defamatory statement.  Most states recognize truth as a complete defense regardless of the speaker's motives.  Because the action is intended to compensate those whose reputations are damaged incorrectly, if the defendant has spoken the truth, the reputational harm is deemed to provide no basis for an action.  A minority of states have required the truth to have been spoken with "good motives" or for "justifiable ends" or both, but in the wake of *New York Times* and its progeny, such requirements may not last.

The defendant need not prove literal truth but must establish the "sting" of his charge.  Thus, if the defendant has charged the plaintiff with stealing $25,000 from a bank, truth will be established even if the actual amount was only $12,000.  If the defendant cannot prove any theft whatever but can prove the plaintiff is a bigamist, this information will not support his defense of truth, but it may help mitigate damages to show that the plaintiff's reputation is already in low esteem for other reasons and, thus he has suffered less harm than might otherwise have occurred.

Truth is little used as a defense because the defense may be very expensive to establish.  A defendant relying on truth almost always bears the legal costs of a full-dress trial as well as the sometimes major expense of investigating the matter and gathering enough evidence to ensure the outcome.

An aspect of the truth defense is the focus of Hepps v. Philadelphia Newspapers, discussed at p. 492, infra.

## b.  State Privileges

Not only were there disadvantages to the defense of truth, there were attractive alternatives.  Over the centuries the law of defamation has developed several privileges to protect those who utter defamations. Some privileges are "absolute" in the sense that if the occasion gives rise to an absolute privilege, there will be no liability even if the speaker deliberately lied about the plaintiff.  The most significant example is the federal and state constitutional privilege afforded legislators who may not be sued for defamation for any statement made during debate.  High executive officials, judges, and participants in judicial proceedings also have an absolute privilege to speak freely on matters relevant to their obligations.  No matter how such a speaker abuses the privilege by lying, no tort liability will flow.  See Barr v. Matteo, 360 U.S. 564 (1959). The main circumstance that gives absolute privilege to the media occurs when broadcasters are required to grant equal opportunity to all candidates for the same office.  If a candidate commits defamation, the broadcaster is not liable for the defamation.  See Farmers Educational & Cooperative Union of America v. WDAY, Inc., 360 U.S. 525 (1959) discussed in Chapter VI.

Most common law privileges serve individuals and do not specifically affect media—with two important exceptions.  The first involves the conditional privilege to make fair and accurate reports of governmental proceedings.  Under general defamation law, one who repeats another's statement is responsible for the truth of what he repeats.  Thus, if X states that "Y told me that Z is a murderer," and Z sues X for defamation, X will be treated as the publisher who is responsible for his own statement.  In order to prevail on the defense of truth, X must prove that Z is in fact a murderer—it is not enough for X to prove that in fact Y told him that Z was a murderer.  The general reason underlying this view is the reluctance to protect gossip.

It was not long, however, before the courts and the legislatures began to realize that sometimes speakers should be encouraged to repeat others' statements.  The federal and state constitutions had already provided that members of the legislative branch could quote others in debate with absolute protection against legal sanctions.

The major example of the value of repetition was found in the reporting of how government was functioning and what government officials were saying.  Thus, observers were to be encouraged to report what legislators said on the floor or in the committee as well as events in court.  It would put reporters in a hopeless situation to be able to report safely only the truthful statements of government officials or of witnesses at a trial.  As a result of these considerations, a privilege developed, sometimes called the privilege of "record libel," under which reports of what occurs in governmental proceedings are privileged even if some of those quoted have spoken falsely—so long as the report is accurate or a fair summary of what transpired.

The second major common law privilege of value to the media was the privilege of fair comment upon matters of public interest. When the privilege was applied in cases of literary and artistic criticism it caused little confusion. Problems raised by such comment are discussed in the classic Cherry v. Des Moines Leader, 114 Iowa 298, 86 N.W. 323 (1901) in which a reviewer scathingly described a performance by the Cherry sisters. But at the turn of the century cases arose in which the privilege of fair comment was claimed with regard to other matters of public interest, including the conduct of politicians. This was not the privilege of reporting what certain public officials were doing in their official capacity. Rather the privilege claimed would permit citizens to criticize and argue about the conduct of their officials, and these cases presented the problem of distinguishing between facts and opinion. In the literary criticism area the application of the privilege could depend upon the accuracy of the "facts" because they were usually readily apparent. When dealing with politics, however, the "facts" were often elusive. This new problem created a judicial split.

Most state courts decided that in order for criticism of government officials and others to be privileged, the facts upon which the comments were based had to be true. A minority of courts, including Coleman v. MacLennan, 78 Kan. 711, 98 P. 281 (1908), disagreed. They decided that facts relating to matters of public interest could not form the basis for a defamation case even if the facts were incorrect, so long as the speaker honestly believed them to be true.

It was from this disagreement among the states that the constitutional developments sprang.

## B.  CONSTITUTIONAL PRIVILEGE

So long as state law controlled, publishers and broadcasters could try to persuade state courts and legislatures to alter the defamation rules. As we have seen, their success varied in different states. Early efforts to gain further protection in defamation cases by invoking federal constitutional law to limit state power did not fare well.

In Near v. Minnesota, 283 U.S. 697 (1931), the case that perhaps first reinforced the protection of the press in this country, the majority observed, "But it is recognized that punishment for the abuse of the liberty accorded to the press is essential to the protection of the public, and that the common-law rules that subject the libeler to responsibility for the public offense, as well as for the private injury, are not abolished by the protection extended in our Constitution."

In Chaplinsky v. New Hampshire, p. 21, supra, the Court said:

There are certain well-defined and narrowly limited classes of speech, the prevention and punishment of which have never been thought to raise any Constitutional problem. These include the lewd and obscene, the profane, the libelous, and the insulting or "fighting" words—those that by their very utterance inflict injury or tend to incite an immediate breach of the peace. It has been well observed that such utterances are no essential part of any exposition of ideas, and are of such slight social value as a step to truth that any benefit that may be derived from them is clearly outweighed by the social interest in order and morality.

This language was often quoted approvingly. Justice Frankfurter, writing for a 5–4 majority in Beauharnais v. Illinois, 343 U.S. 250 (1952), to sustain a state criminal libel law, relied on *Chaplinsky* for the proposition that libelous utterances were not "within the area of constitutionally protected speech."

This sequence set the stage for the following case from Alabama, a state that had long followed the majority rule that there was no privilege for incorrect facts, even in stories of public importance.

## NEW YORK TIMES CO. v. SULLIVAN
### Together with Abernathy v. Sullivan

Supreme Court of the United States, 1964.
376 U.S. 254, 84 S.Ct. 710, 11 L.Ed.2d 686.

[This action was based on a full-page advertisement in *The New York Times* on behalf of several individuals and groups protesting a "wave of terror" against blacks involved in non-violent demonstrations in the South. Plaintiff, one of three elected commissioners of Montgomery, the capital of Alabama, was in charge of the police department. When he demanded a retraction, as state law required, *The Times* instead responded that it failed to see how he was defamed. He then filed suit against *The Times* and four clergymen whose names appeared as sponsors—although they denied having authorized this—in the ad. Plaintiff alleged that the third and the sixth paragraphs of the advertisement libelled him:

> "In Montgomery, Alabama, after students sang 'My Country, 'Tis of Thee' on the State Capitol steps, their leaders were expelled from school, and truckloads of police armed with shotguns and tear-gas ringed the Alabama State College Campus. When the entire student body protested to state authorities by refusing to re-register, their dining hall was padlocked in an attempt to starve them into submission."
>
> . . .
>
> "Again and again the Southern violators have answered Dr. King's peaceful protests with intimidation and violence. They have bombed his home almost killing his wife and child. They have assaulted his person. They have arrested him seven times—for 'speeding,' 'loitering' and similar 'offenses.' And now they have charged him with 'perjury'—a *felony* under which they could imprison him for *ten years*. . . ."

Plaintiff claimed that he was libelled in the third paragraph by the reference to the police, since his responsibilities included supervision of the Montgomery police. He asserted that the paragraph could be read as charging the police with ringing the campus and seeking to starve the students by padlocking the dining hall. As to the sixth paragraph, he contended that the word "they" referred to his departments since arrests are usually made by the police and the paragraph could be read as accusing him of committing the acts charged. Several witnesses testified that they read the statements as referring to plaintiff in his capacity as commissioner.

The defendants admitted several inaccuracies in these two paragraphs; the students sang "The Star Spangled Banner," not "My Country, 'Tis of Thee"; nine students were expelled, not for leading the demonstration, but for demanding service at a lunch counter in the county courthouse; the dining hall was never padlocked; police at no time ringed the campus though they were deployed nearby in large numbers; they were not called to the campus in connection with the demonstration; Dr. King had been arrested only four times; and officers disputed his account of the alleged assault. Plaintiff proved that he had not been commissioner when three of the four arrests occurred and that he had nothing to do with procuring the perjury indictment.

The trial judge charged that the statements were libel per se, that the jury should decide whether they were made "of and concerning" the plaintiff, and, if so, general damages were to be presumed. Although noting that punitive damages required more than carelessness, he refused to charge that they required a finding of actual intent to harm or "gross negligence and recklessness." He also refused to order the jury to separate its award of general and punitive damages. The jury returned a verdict for $500,000—the full amount demanded. The Alabama Supreme Court affirmed, holding that malice could be found in several aspects of *The Times*'s conduct.

The Supreme Court began by disposing of the assertion that the Fourteenth Amendment is directed against State action and not private action, holding that "[t]he test is not the form in which state power has been applied but, whatever the form, whether such power has in fact been exercised." It also rejected the argument that constitutional guarantees were inapplicable because the statements were part of an advertisement.]

JUSTICE BRENNAN delivered the opinion of the Court.

.  .  .

## II.

.  .  .

The question before us is whether [Alabama's] rule of liability, as applied to an action brought by a public official against critics of his official conduct, abridges the freedom of speech and of the press that is guaranteed by the First and Fourteenth Amendments.

Respondent relies heavily, as did the Alabama courts, on statements of this Court to the effect that the Constitution does not protect libelous publications. Those statements do not foreclose our inquiry here. None of the cases sustained the use of libel laws to impose sanctions upon expression critical of the official conduct of public officials. . . . In deciding the question now, we are compelled by neither precedent nor policy to give any more weight to the epithet "libel" than we have to other "mere labels" of state law. NAACP v. Button, 371 U.S. 415, 429 (1963). Like insurrection, contempt, advocacy of unlawful acts, breach of the peace, obscenity, solicitation of legal business, and the various other formulae for the repression of expression that have been challenged in this Court, libel can claim no talismanic immunity from constitutional limitations. It must be measured by standards that satisfy the First Amendment.

The general proposition that freedom of expression upon public questions is secured by the First Amendment has long been settled by our decisions. . . . Mr. Justice Brandeis, in his concurring opinion in Whitney v. California, 274 U.S. 357, 375–376 (1927), gave the principle its classic formulation:

> "Those who won our independence believed . . . that public discussion is a political duty; and that this should be a fundamental principle of the American government. . . . Believing in the power of reason as applied through public discussion, they eschewed silence coerced by law—the argument of force in its worst form. Recognizing the occasional tyrannies of governing majorities, they amended the Constitution so that free speech and assembly should be guaranteed."

Thus we consider this case against the background of a profound national commitment to the principle that debate on public issues should be uninhibited, robust, and wide-open, and that it may well include vehement, caustic, and sometimes unpleasantly sharp attacks on government and public officials. [ ] The present advertisement, as an expression of grievance and protest on one of the major public issues of our time, would seem clearly to qualify for the constitutional protection. The question is whether it forfeits that protection by the falsity of some of its factual statements and by its alleged defamation of respondent.

. . .

Injury to official reputation affords no more warrant for repressing speech that would otherwise be free than does factual error. Where judicial officers are involved, this Court has held that concern for the dignity and reputation of the courts does not justify the punishment as criminal contempt of criticism of the judge or his decision. Bridges v. California, 314 U.S. 252 (1941). . . . There is no force in respondent's argument that the constitutional limitations implicit in the history of the Sedition Act apply only to Congress and not to the States. It is true that the First Amendment was originally addressed only to action by the Federal Government, and that Jefferson, for one, while denying the power of Congress "to control the freedom of the press," recognized such a power in the States. [  ] But this distinction was eliminated with the adoption of the Fourteenth Amendment and the application to the States of the First Amendment's restrictions. [  ]

What a State may not constitutionally bring about by means of a criminal statute is likewise beyond the reach of its civil law of libel . . . . .

[The Court quoted James Madison, suggesting the need for breathing space in public discussion, and the fear that even speakers of the truth will be chilled when the law is too restrictive.]

The constitutional guarantees require, we think, a federal rule that prohibits a public official from recovering damages for a defamatory falsehood relating to his official conduct unless he proves that the statement was made with "actual malice"—that is, with knowledge that it was false or with reckless disregard of whether it was false or not. An oft-cited statement of a like rule, which has been adopted by a number of state courts, is found in the Kansas case of Coleman v. MacLennan, 78 Kan. 711, 98 P. 281 (1908). . . .

Such a privilege for criticism of official conduct is appropriately analogous to the protection accorded a public official when *he* is sued for libel by a private citizen. In Barr v. Matteo, 360 U.S. 564, 575 (1959), this Court held the utterance of a federal official to be absolutely privileged if made "within the outer perimeter" of his duties. The States accord the same immunity to statements of their highest officers, although some differentiate their lesser officials and qualify the privilege they enjoy. But all hold that all officials are protected unless actual malice can be proved. The reason for the official privilege is said to be that the threat of damage suits would otherwise "inhibit the fearless, vigorous, and effective administration of policies of government" and "dampen the ardor of all but the most resolute, or the most irresponsible, in the unflinching discharge of their duties." Barr v. Matteo, supra, 360 U.S., at 571. Analogous considerations support the privilege for the citizen-critic of government. It is as much his duty to criticize as it is the official's duty to administer. . . . .

We conclude that such a privilege is required by the First and Fourteenth Amendments.

## III.

We hold today that the Constitution delimits a State's power to award damages for libel in actions brought by public officials against critics of their official conduct. Since this is such an action, the rule requiring proof of actual malice is applicable. While Alabama law apparently requires proof of actual malice for an award of punitive damages, where general damages are concerned malice is "presumed." Such a presumption is inconsistent with the federal rule. . . . Since the trial judge did not instruct the jury to differentiate between general and punitive damages, it may be that the verdict was wholly an award of one or the other. But it is impossible to know, in view of the general verdict returned. Because of this uncertainty, the judgment must be reversed and the case remanded. [   ]

Since respondent may seek a new trial we deem that considerations of effective judicial administration require us to review the evidence in the present record to determine whether it could constitutionally support a judgment for respondent. . . .

Applying these standards, we consider that the proof presented to show actual malice lacks convincing clarity which the constitutional standard demands, and hence that it would not constitutionally sustain the judgment for respondent under the proper rule of law. The case of the individual petitioners requires little discussion. Even assuming that they could constitutionally be found to have authorized the use of their names on the advertisement, there was no evidence whatever that they were aware of any erroneous statements or were in any way reckless in that regard. The judgment against them is thus without constitutional support.

As to the Times, we similarly conclude that the facts do not support a finding of actual malice. . . .

. . .

We also think the evidence was constitutionally defective in another respect: it was incapable of supporting the jury's finding that the allegedly libelous statements were made "of and concerning" respondent. Respondent relies on the words of the advertisement and the testimony of six witnesses to establish a connection between it and himself. . . . There was no reference to respondent in the advertisement, either by name or official position. . . .

This proposition has disquieting implications for criticism of governmental conduct. For good reason, "no court of last resort in this country has ever held, or even suggested, that prosecutions for libel on government have any place in the American system of jurisprudence." City of Chicago v. Tribune Co., 307 Ill. 595, 601, 139 N.E. 86, 88 (1923). The present proposition would sidestep this obstacle by transmuting criticism of government, however impersonal it may seem on its face, into personal criticism, and hence potential libel, of the officials of whom the government is composed. . . . We hold that such a proposition may not constitutionally be used to establish that an otherwise impersonal attack on governmental operations was a libel of an official responsible for those operations. Since it was relied on exclusively here, and there was no evidence to connect the statements with respondent, the evidence was constitutionally insufficient to support a finding that the statements referred to respondent.

The judgment of the Supreme Court of Alabama is reversed and the case is remanded to that court for further proceedings not inconsistent with this opinion.

Reversed and remanded.

MR. JUSTICE BLACK, with whom MR. JUSTICE DOUGLAS joins, concurring.

I concur in reversing this half-million-dollar judgment against the New York Times Company and the four individual defendants. In reversing the Court holds that "the Constitution delimits a State's power to award damages for libel in actions brought by public officials against critics of their official conduct." I base my vote to reverse on the belief that the First and Fourteenth Amendments not merely "delimit" a State's power to award damages to "public officials against critics of their official conduct" but completely prohibit a State from exercising such a power. The Court goes on to hold that a State can subject such critics to damages if "actual malice" can be proved against them. "Malice," even as defined by the Court, is an elusive, abstract concept, hard to prove and hard to disprove. The requirement that malice be proved provides at best an evanescent protection for the right critically to discuss public affairs and certainly does not measure up to the sturdy safeguard embodied in the First Amendment. Unlike the Court, therefore, I vote to reverse exclusively on the ground that the Times and the individual defendants had an absolute unconstitutional right to publish in the Times advertisement their criticisms of the Montgomery agencies and officials. . . .

. . .

We would, I think, more faithfully interpret the First Amendment by holding that at the very least it leaves the people and the press free to criticize officials and discuss public affairs with impunity. . . . An unconditional right to say what one pleases about public affairs is what I consider to be the minimum guarantee of the First Amendment.[6]

I regret that the Court has stopped short of this holding indispensable to preserve our free press from destruction.

MR. JUSTICE GOLDBERG, with whom MR. JUSTICE DOUGLAS joins, concurring in the result.

. . .

In my view, the First and Fourteenth Amendments to the Constitution afford to the citizen and to the press an absolute, unconditional privilege to criticize official conduct despite the harm which may flow from excesses and abuses. . . .

. . .

. . . It may be urged that deliberately and maliciously false statements have no conceivable value as free speech. That argument, however, is not responsive to the real issue presented by this case, which is whether that freedom of speech which all agree is constitutionally protected can be effectively safeguarded by a rule allowing the imposition of liability upon a jury's evaluation of the speaker's state of mind. If individual citizens may be held liable in damages for strong words,

6. Cf. Meiklejohn, Free Speech and Its Relation to Self-Government (1948).

which a jury finds false and maliciously motivated, there can be little doubt that public debate and advocacy will be constrained. And if newspapers, publishing advertisements dealing with public issues, thereby risk liability, there can also be little doubt that the ability of minority groups to secure publication of their views on public affairs and to seek support for their causes will be greatly diminished.  .  .  .

.  .  .

If the government official should be immune from libel actions so that his ardor to serve the public will be dampened and "fearless, vigorous, and effective administration of policies of government" not be inhibited [    ], then the citizen and the press should likewise be immune from libel actions for their criticism of official conduct.  .  .  .

The conclusion that the Constitution affords the citizen and the press an absolute privilege for criticism of official conduct does not leave the public official without defenses against unsubstantiated opinions or deliberate misstatements. "Under our system of government, counter-argument and education are the weapons available to expose these matters, not abridgment . . . of free speech. . . ." Wood v. Georgia, 370 U.S. 375, 389 (1962). The public official certainly has equal if not greater access than most private citizens to media of communication.  .  .  .

.  .  .

**Notes and Questions**

1.  What is the justification for the majority position?

2.  The majority twice observes that deliberate falsity is used in argument. Why is such behavior not protected here?

3.  Do you consider either of the concurring opinions preferable to the majority approach? Would it be desirable to enable a public official to have a jury assess the truth of charges against him—without seeking damages?

4.  Commenting after the Times case, Professor Kalven speculated on the case's future:

> The closing question, of course, is whether the treatment of seditious libel as the key concept for development of appropriate constitutional doctrine will prove germinal. It is not easy to predict what the Court will see in the *Times* opinion as the years roll by. It may regard the opinion as covering simply one pocket of cases, those dealing with libel of public officials, and not destructive of the earlier notions that are inconsistent only with the large reading of the Court's action. But the invitation to follow a dialectic progression from public official to government policy to public policy to matters in the public domain, like art, seems to me to be overwhelming. If the Court accepts the invitation, it will slowly work out for itself the theory of free speech that Alexander Meiklejohn has been offering us for some fifteen years now.

Kalven, The New York Times Case: A Note on "The Central Meaning of the First Amendment," 1964 Sup.Ct.Rev. 191, 221. Does his prediction seem sound? Keep it in mind as we consider the cases decided since *Times*.

5. The majority in the *New York Times* case did not explicitly condemn the concurring approaches. A few months later, in Garrison v. Louisiana, 379 U.S. 64 (1964), the Court, in an opinion by Justice Brennan, extended the *Times* rule to cases of criminal libel and also held that truth must be a defense in cases brought by public officials. The majority explained its refusal to protect deliberate falsity:

> Although honest utterance, even if inaccurate, may further the fruitful exercise of the right of free speech, it does not follow that the lie, knowingly and deliberately published about a public official, should enjoy a like immunity. At the time the First Amendment was adopted, as today, there were those unscrupulous enough and skillful enough to use the deliberate or reckless falsehood as an effective political tool to unseat the public servant or even topple an administration. [ ] That speech is used as a tool for political ends does not automatically bring it under the protective mantle of the Constitution. For the use of the known lie as a tool is at once at odds with the premises of democratic government and with the orderly manner in which economic, social, or political change is to be effected. Calculated falsehood falls into that class of utterances which "are no essential part of any exposition of ideas, and are of such slight social value as a step to truth that any benefit that may be derived from them is clearly outweighed by the social interest in order and morality. . . ." [ ] Hence the knowingly false statement and the false statement made with reckless disregard of the truth, do not enjoy constitutional protection.

6. The next major case was Rosenblatt v. Baer, 383 U.S. 75 (1966). Plaintiff Baer had been hired to be Supervisor of a public recreation facility owned by Belknap County, N.H. Defendant, in his weekly newspaper column, noted that a year after plaintiff's discharge the facility was doing much better financially. The column could be understood as charging either inefficiency or dishonesty. In reversing plaintiff's state court judgment, the Supreme Court said that the vague language could be read as an attack on government—and that Baer could not sue unless he showed that he had been singled out for attack. Justice Brennan's majority opinion said that it is clear that the public figure designation from *New York Times* applies all the way down the hierarchy of government employees "who have, or appear to the public to have, substantial responsibility for or control over the conduct of governmental affairs." The case was remanded for further proceedings.

7. The Supreme Court next considered two cases together, Curtis Pub. Co. v. Butts, and Associated Press v. Walker, 388 U.S. 130 (1967). In *Butts*, the defendant magazine had accused the plaintiff athletic director of disclosing his game plan to an opposing coach before their game.

Although he was on the staff of a state university, Butts was paid by a private alumni organization.  In *Walker,* the defendant news service reported that the plaintiff, a former United States Army general who resigned to engage in political activity, had personally led students in an attack on federal marshals who were enforcing a desegregation order at the University of Mississippi.

In both cases, lower courts had affirmed substantial jury awards against the defendants and had refused to apply the *Times* doctrine on the ground that public officials were not involved.  The Supreme Court divided several ways on several issues, affirming *Butts,* 5–4, and reversing *Walker,* 9–0.  Chief Justice Warren wrote the pivotal opinion in which he concluded that both men were "public figures" and that the standard developed in *New York Times* should apply to "public figures" as well:

> To me, differentiation between "public figures" and "public officials" and adoption of separate standards of proof for each has no basis in law, logic, or First Amendment policy.  Increasingly in this country, the distinctions between governmental and private sectors are blurred. . . . [A]lthough they are not subject to the restraints of the political process, "public figures," like "public officials," often play an influential role in ordering society.  And surely as a class these "public figures" have as ready access as "public officials" to mass media of communication, both to influence policy and to counter criticism of their views and activities.  Our citizenry has a legitimate and substantial interest in the conduct of such persons, and freedom of the press to engage in uninhibited debate about their involvement in public issues and events is as crucial as it is in the case of "public officials."  The fact that they are not amenable to the restraints of the political process only underscores the legitimate and substantial nature of the interest, since it means that public opinion may be the only instrument by which society can attempt to influence their conduct.

He found that on the merits the standard had not been met in *Walker.* In *Butts,* he found that defendant's counsel had deliberately waived the *Times* doctrine and he also found evidence establishing reckless behavior.  He thus voted to reverse *Walker* and affirm *Butts.*

Justices Brennan and White agreed with the Chief Justice in *Walker* but found no waiver in *Butts* and would have reversed both cases.  They agreed with the Chief Justice that *Butts* had presented enough evidence to come within the *Times* standard but thought that errors in the charge required a new trial.

Justices Black and Douglas adhered to their position, urged that the *Times* rule was too weak, and voted to reverse both cases.

Four dissenters, led by Justice Harlan, argued that the *Times* standard should not apply to public figures because criticism of government was not involved:

We consider and would hold that a "public figure" who is not a public official may also recover damages for a defamatory falsehood whose substance makes substantial danger to reputation apparent, on a showing of highly unreasonable conduct constituting an extreme departure from the standards of investigation and reporting ordinarily adhered to by responsible publishers. . . .

Applying that standard Justice Harlan concluded that Walker had failed to establish a case, but that Butts had shown that the *Saturday Evening Post* ignored elementary precautions in preparing a potentially damaging story. Together with the Chief Justice's vote, there were five votes to affirm *Butts*.

8. In St. Amant v. Thompson, 390 U.S. 727 (1968), the defendant, a candidate for public office, read on television a series of statements he had received from Mr. Albin, a member of a Teamsters' Union local. The statements, made under oath, falsely implied that the plaintiff, a deputy sheriff, had taken bribes. The defendant had not checked the facts stated by Albin, nor had he investigated Albin's reputation for veracity. The state court ruled that these failures to inquire further sufficed to meet the required standard of reckless disregard for the truth. The Supreme Court reversed and concluded that the standard of "reckless disregard" had not been met. It recognized that the term could receive no single "infallible definition" and that its outer limits would have to be developed in "case-to-case adjudication, as is true with so many legal standards for judging concrete cases, whether the standard is provided by the Constitution, statutes or case law." There "must be sufficient evidence to permit the conclusion that the defendant in fact entertained serious doubts as to the truth of his publication" in order for recklessness to be found.

9. Next the Court unanimously extended the *Times* rationale to candidates because "it can hardly be doubted that the constitutional guarantee has its fullest and most urgent application precisely to the conduct of campaigns for political office." Monitor Patriot Co. v. Roy, 401 U.S. 265 (1971) and Ocala Star-Banner Co. v. Damron, 401 U.S. 295 (1971).

10. A plurality of the Court took the next step in Rosenbloom v. Metromedia, Inc., 403 U.S. 29 (1971), involving a broadcaster's charge that a magazine distributor sold obscene material and was arrested in a police raid. Justice Brennan, joined by Chief Justice Burger and Justice Blackmun, held that the *Times* standard should be extended to "all discussion and communication involving matters of public or general concern, without regard to whether the persons involved are famous or anonymous." The arrest and the distributor's subsequent claims against the police were thought to fit this category, and the *Times* standard was applied. In reaching that position, Justice Brennan concluded that the focus on the plaintiff's status begun in the *Times* case bore "little relationship either to the values protected by the First Amendment or to the nature of our society. . . . Thus, the idea that certain 'public' figures have voluntarily exposed their entire lives to public inspection,

while private individuals have kept theirs carefully shrouded from public view is, at best, a legal fiction." Discussion of a matter of public concern must be protected even when it involves an unknown person. If the states fear that private citizens will be unable to respond to adverse publicity, "the solution lies in the direction of ensuring their ability to respond, rather than in stifling public discussion of matters of public concern," a reference to possible use of a right for people attacked in the media to reply. 403 U.S. at 47.

Justice White concurred on the narrow ground that the press is privileged to report "upon the official actions of public servants in full detail." Justice Black provided the fifth vote against liability for the reasons stated in his earlier opinions. Justices Harlan, Stewart, and Marshall dissented on various grounds, but they agreed that the private plaintiff should be required to prove no more than negligence in this case. Justice Douglas did not participate.

Because there was no majority opinion from the Court in *Rosenbloom*, the case provided little guidance for future defamation cases. Three years later, in Gertz v. Robert Welch, Inc., the Court handed down a major libel decision, considered by many to be the most important since *Sullivan*. As you will see, *Gertz* attempts to clarify the difference between public and private figure libel plaintiffs. It also lifts from many private figure plaintiffs—depending on the state in which they sue—the burden of proving "actual malice" to collect compensatory damages.

## GERTZ v. ROBERT WELCH, INC.

Supreme Court of the United States, 1974.
418 U.S. 323, 94 S.Ct. 2997, 41 L.Ed.2d 789.

[Plaintiff, an attorney, was retained to represent the family of a youth killed by Nuccio, a Chicago policeman. In that capacity, plaintiff attended the coroner's inquest and filed an action for damages but played no part in a criminal proceeding in which Nuccio was convicted of second degree murder. Respondent publishes *American Opinion*, a monthly outlet for the views of the John Birch Society. As part of its efforts to alert the public to an alleged nationwide conspiracy to discredit local police, the magazine's editor engaged a regular contributor to write about the Nuccio episode. The article that appeared charged a frame-up against Nuccio and portrayed plaintiff as a "major architect" of the plot. It also falsely asserted that he had a long police record, was an official of the Marxist League for Industrial Democracy, and was a "Leninist" and a "Communist-fronter." The editor made no effort to verify the story.

Gertz filed an action for libel in District Court because of the diversity of citizenship. The trial judge first ruled that Gertz was not a public official or public figure and that under Illinois law there was no defense. The jury awarded $50,000. On further reflection, the judge decided that since a matter of public concern was being discussed, the *Times* rule should apply, and he granted the defendant judgment notwithstanding the jury's verdict. He thus anticipated the plurality's approach in Rosenbloom v. Metromedia, Inc. The court of appeals, relying on the intervening decision in *Rosenbloom*, affirmed because of the absence of "clear and convincing" evidence of "actual malice." Gertz appealed.]

MR. JUSTICE POWELL delivered the opinion of the Court.

. . .

## II

The principal issue in this case is whether a newspaper or broadcaster that publishes defamatory falsehoods about an individual who is neither a public official nor a public figure may claim a constitutional privilege against liability for the injury inflicted by those statements. The Court considered this question on the rather different set of facts presented in Rosenbloom v. Metromedia, Inc., 403 U.S. 29 (1971). . . .

. . .

In his opinion for the plurality in Rosenbloom v. Metromedia, Inc., [ ], Mr. Justice Brennan took the *New York Times* privilege one step further. He concluded that its protection should extend to defamatory falsehoods relating to private persons if the statements concerned matters of general or public interest. . . .

. . .

## III

We begin with the common ground. Under the First Amendment there is no such thing as a false idea. However pernicious an opinion may seem, we depend for its correction not on the conscience of judges and juries but on the competition of other ideas. But there is no constitutional value in false statements of fact. Neither the intentional lie nor the careless error materially advances society's interest in "uninhibited, robust, and wide-open" debate on public issues. . . .

Although the erroneous statement of fact is not worthy of constitutional protection, it is nevertheless inevitable in free debate. . . . And punishment of error runs the risk of inducing a cautious and restrictive exercise of the constitutionally guaranteed freedoms of speech and press. Our decisions recognize that a rule of strict liability that compels a publisher or broadcaster to guarantee the accuracy of his factual assertions may lead to intolerable self-censorship. Allowing the media to avoid liability only by proving the truth of all injurious statements does not accord adequate protection to First Amendment liberties. . . . The First Amendment requires that we protect some falsehood in order to protect speech that matters.

The need to avoid self-censorship by the news media is, however, not the only societal value at issue. If it were, this Court would have embraced long ago the view that publishers and broadcasters enjoy an unconditional and indefeasible immunity from liability for defamation.

The legitimate state interest underlying the law of libel is the compensation of individuals for the harm inflicted on them by defamatory falsehood. . . . Some tension necessarily exists between the need for a vigorous and uninhibited press and the legitimate interest in redressing wrongful injury. . . .

The *New York Times* standard defines the level of a constitutional protection appropriate to the context of defamation of a public person. Those who, by reason of the notoriety of their achievements or the vigor and success with which they seek the public's attention, are properly classed as public figures and those who hold governmental office may recover for injury to reputation only on clear and convincing proof that the defamatory falsehood was made with knowledge of its falsity or with reckless disregard for the truth. This standard administers an extremely powerful antidote to the inducement to media self-censorship of the common-law rule of strict liability for libel and slander. And it exacts a correspondingly high price from the victims of defamatory falsehood. Plainly many deserving plaintiffs, including some intentionally subjected to injury, will be unable to surmount the barrier of the *New York Times* test. Despite this substantial abridgment of the state law right to compensation for wrongful hurt to one's reputation, the Court has concluded that the protection of the *New York Times* privilege should be available to publishers and broadcasters of defamatory falsehood concerning public officials and public figures. [ ] We think that these decisions are correct, but we do not find their holdings justified solely by reference to the interest of the the press and broadcast media in immunity from liability. Rather, we believe that the *New York Times* rule states an accommodation between this concern and the limited state interest present in the context of libel actions brought by public persons. For the reasons stated below, we conclude that the state interest in compensating injury to the reputation of private individuals requires that a different rule should obtain with respect to them.

Theoretically, of course, the balance between the needs of the press and the individual's claim to compensation for wrongful injury might be struck on a case-by-case basis. As Mr. Justice Harlan hypothesized, "it might seem, purely as an abstract matter, that the most utilitarian approach would be to scrutinize carefully every jury verdict in every libel case, in order to ascertain whether the final judgment leaves fully protected whatever First Amendment values transcend the legitimate state interest in protecting the particular plaintiff who prevailed." Rosenbloom v. Metromedia, Inc., 403 U.S., at 63 (footnote omitted). But this approach would lead to unpredictable results and uncertain expectations, and it could render our duty to supervise the lower courts unmanageable. Because an *ad hoc* resolution of the competing interests at stake in each particular case is not feasible, we must lay down broad rules of general application. Such rules necessarily treat alike various cases involving differences as well as similarities. Thus it is often true that not all of the considerations which justify adoption of a given rule will obtain in each particular case decided under its authority.

With that caveat we have no difficulty in distinguishing among defamation plaintiffs. The first remedy of any victim of defamation is self-help—using available opportunities to contradict the lie or correct the error and thereby to minimize its adverse impact on reputation. Public officials and public figures usually enjoy significantly greater access to the channels of effective communication and hence have a more realistic opportunity to counteract false statements than private individuals normally enjoy.[9] Private individuals are therefore more vulnerable to injury, and the state interest in protecting them is correspondingly greater.

More important than the likelihood that private individuals will lack effective opportunities for rebuttal, there is a compelling normative consideration underlying the distinction between public and private defamation plaintiffs. An individual who decides to seek governmental office must accept certain necessary consequences of that involvement in public affairs. He runs the risk of closer public scrutiny than might otherwise be the case. And society's interest in the officers of government is not strictly limited to the formal discharge of official duties. As the Court pointed out in Garrison v. Louisiana, 379 U.S., at 77, the public's interest extends to "anything which might touch on an official's fitness for office . . . . Few personal attributes are more germane to fitness for office than dishonesty, malfeasance, or improper motivation, even though these characteristics may also affect the official's private character."

Those classed as public figures stand in a similar position. Hypothetically, it may be possible for someone to become a public figure through no purposeful action of his own, but the instances of truly involuntary public figures must be exceedingly rare. For the most part those who attain this status have assumed roles of especial prominence in the affairs of society. Some occupy positions of such persuasive power and influence that they are deemed public figures for all purposes. More commonly, those classed as public figures have thrust themselves to the forefront of particular public controversies in order to influence the resolution of the issues involved. In either event, they invite attention and comment.

Even if the foregoing generalities do not obtain in every instance, the communications media are entitled to act on the assumption that the public officials and public figures have voluntarily exposed themselves to increased risk of injury from defamatory falsehood concerning them. No such assumption is justified with respect to a private individual . . . . Thus, private individuals are not only more vulnerable to injury than public officials and public figures; they are also more deserving of recovery.

---

9. Of course, an opportunity for rebuttal seldom suffices to undo harm of defamatory falsehood. Indeed, the law of defamation is rooted in our experience that the truth rarely catches up with a lie. But the fact that the self-help remedy of rebuttal, standing alone, is inadequate to its task does not mean that it is irrelevant to our inquiry.

For these reasons we conclude that the States should retain substantial latitude in their efforts to enforce a legal remedy for defamatory falsehood injurious to the reputation of a private individual. The extension of the *New York Times* test proposed by the *Rosenbloom* plurality would abridge this legitimate state interest to a degree that we find unacceptable. And it would occasion the additional difficulty of forcing state and federal judges to decide on an *ad hoc* basis which publications address issues of "general or public interest" and which do not—to determine, in the words of Mr. Justice Marshall, "what information is relevant to self-government." Rosenbloom v. Metromedia, Inc., 403 U.S., at 79. We doubt the wisdom of committing this task to the conscience of judges. . . .

We hold that, so long as they do not impose liability without fault, the States may define for themselves the appropriate standard of liability for a publisher or broadcaster of defamatory falsehood injurious to a private individual. This approach provides a more equitable boundary between the competing concerns involved here. It recognizes the strength of the legitimate state interest in compensating private individuals for wrongful injury to reputation, yet shields the press and broadcast media from the rigors of strict liability for defamation. . . .

## IV

Our accommodation of the competing values at stake in defamation suits by private individuals allows the States to impose liability on the publisher or broadcaster of defamatory falsehood on a less demanding showing than that required by *New York Times.* This conclusion is not based on a belief that the considerations which prompted the adoption of the *New York Times* privilege for defamation of public officials and its extension to public figures are wholly inapplicable to the context of private individuals. Rather, we endorse this approach in recognition of the strong and legitimate state interest in compensating private individuals for injury to reputation. But this countervailing state interest extends no further than compensation for actual injury. For the reasons stated below, we hold that the States may not permit recovery of presumed or punitive damages, at least when liability is not based on a showing of knowledge of falsity or reckless disregard for the truth.

The common law of defamation is an oddity of tort law, for it allows recovery of purportedly compensatory damages without evidence of actual loss. Under the traditional rules pertaining to actions for libel the existence of injury is presumed from the fact of publication. Juries may award substantial sums as compensation for supposed damage to reputation without any proof that such harm actually occurred. The largely uncontrolled discretion of juries to award damages where there is no loss unnecessarily compounds the potential of any system of liability for defamatory falsehood to inhibit the vigorous exercise of First Amendment freedoms. Additionally, the doctrine of presumed damages invites juries to punish unpopular opinion rather than to compensate individuals for injury sustained by the publication of a false fact. More to the point, the States have no substantial interest in securing for plaintiffs such as this petitioner gratuitous awards of money damages far in excess of any actual injury.

We would not, of course, invalidate state law simply because we doubt its wisdom, but here we are attempting to reconcile state law with a competing interest grounded in the constitutional command of the First Amendment. It is therefore appropriate to require that state remedies for defamatory falsehood reach no farther than is necessary to protect the legitimate interest involved. It is necessary to restrict defamation plaintiffs who do not prove knowledge of falsity or reckless disregard for the truth to compensation for actual injury. We need not define "actual injury," as trial courts have wide experience in framing appropriate jury instructions in tort actions. Suffice it to say that actual injury is not limited to out-of-pocket loss. Indeed, the more customary types of actual harm inflicted by defamatory falsehood include impairment of reputation and standing in the community, personal humiliation, and mental anguish and suffering. Of course, juries must be limited by appropriate instructions, and all awards must be supported by competent evidence concerning the injury, although there need be no evidence which assigns an actual dollar value to the injury.

We also find no justification for allowing awards of punitive damages against publishers and broadcasters held liable under state-defined standards of liability for defamation. In most jurisdictions jury discretion over the amounts awarded is limited only by the gentle rule that they not be excessive. Consequently, juries assess punitive damages in wholly unpredictable amounts bearing no necessary relation to the actual harm caused. And they remain free to use their discretion selectively to punish expressions of unpopular views. Like the doctrine of presumed damages, jury discretion to award punitive damages unnecessarily exacerbates the danger of media self-censorship, but, unlike the former rule, punitive damages are wholly irrelevant to the state interest that justifies a negligence standard for private defamation actions. They are not compensation for injury. Instead, they are private fines levied by civil juries to punish reprehensible conduct and to deter its future occurrence. In short, the private defamation plaintiff who establishes liability under a less demanding standard than that stated by *New York Times* may recover only such damages as are sufficient to compensate him for actual injury.

V

Notwithstanding our refusal to extend the *New York Times* privilege to defamation of private individuals, respondent contends that we should affirm the judgment below on the ground that petitioner is either a public official or a public figure. There is little basis for the former assumption. Several years prior to the present incident, petitioner had served briefly on housing committees appointed by the mayor of Chicago, but at the time of publication he had never held any remunerative governmental position. Respondent admits this but argues that petitioner's appearance at the coroner's inquest rendered him a "de facto public official." Our cases recognize no such concept. Respondent's suggestion would sweep all lawyers under the *New York Times* rule as officers of the court and distort the plain meaning of the "public official" category beyond all recognition. We decline to follow it.

Respondent's characterization of petitioner as a public figure raises a different question. That designation may rest on either of two alternative bases. In some instances an individual may achieve such pervasive fame or notoriety that he becomes a public figure for all purposes in all contexts. More commonly, an individual voluntarily injects himself or is drawn into a particular public controversy and thereby becomes a public figure for a limited range of issues. In either case such persons assume special prominence in the resolution of public questions.

Petitioner has long been active in community and professional affairs. He has served as an officer of local civic groups and of various professional organizations, and he has published several books and articles on legal subjects. Although petitioner was consequently well known in some circles, he had achieved no general fame or notoriety in the community. None of the prospective jurors called at the trial had ever heard of petitioner prior to this litigation, and respondent offered no proof that this response was atypical of the local population. We would not lightly assume that a citizen's participation in community and professional affairs rendered him a public figure for all purposes. Absent clear evidence of general fame or notoriety in the community, and pervasive involvement in the affairs of society, an individual should not be deemed a public personality for all aspects of his life. It is preferable to reduce the public-figure question to a more meaningful context by looking to the nature and extent of an individual's participation in the particular controversy giving rise to the defamation.

In this context it is plain that petitioner was not a public figure. He played a minimal role at the coroner's inquest, and his participation related solely to his representation of a private client. He took no part in the criminal prosecution of Officer Nuccio. Moreover, he never discussed either the criminal or civil litigation with the press and was never quoted as having done so. He plainly did not thrust himself into the vortex of this public issue, nor did he engage the public's attention in an attempt to influence its outcome. We are persuaded that the trial court did not err in refusing to characterize petitioner as a public figure for the purpose of this litigation.

We therefore conclude that the *New York Times* standard is inapplicable to this case and that the trial court erred in entering judgment for respondent. Because the jury was allowed to impose liability without fault and was permitted to presume damages without proof of injury, a new trial is necessary. We reverse and remand for further proceedings in accord with this opinion.

It is so ordered.

MR. JUSTICE BLACKMUN, concurring.

[Although I joined the *Rosenbloom* plurality opinion,] I am willing to join, and do join, the Court's opinion and its judgment for two reasons:

1. By removing the specters of presumed and punitive damages in the absence of *New York Times* malice, the Court eliminates significant and powerful motives for self-censorship that otherwise are present in the traditional libel action. By so doing, the Court leaves what should prove to be sufficient and adequate breathing space for a vigorous press. What the Court has done, I believe, will have little, if any, practical effect on the functioning of responsible journalism

2. The Court was sadly fractionated in *Rosenbloom*. A result of that kind inevitably leads to uncertainty. I feel that it is of profound importance for the court to come to rest in the defamation area and to have a clearly defined majority position that eliminates the unsureness engendered by *Rosenbloom*'s diversity. If my vote were not needed to create a majority, I would adhere to my prior view. A definitive ruling, however, is paramount. [  ]

For these reasons, I join the opinion and the judgment of the Court.

MR. CHIEF JUSTICE BURGER, dissenting.

. . .

Agreement or disagreement with the law as it has evolved to this time does not alter the fact that it has been orderly development with a consistent basic rationale. In today's opinion the Court abandons the traditional thread so far as the ordinary private citizen is concerned and introduces the concept that the media will be liable for negligence in publishing defamatory statements with respect to such persons. Although I agree with much of what Mr. Justice White states, I do not read the Court's new doctrinal approach in quite the way he does. I am frank to say I do not know the parameters of a "negligence" doctrine as applied to the news media. Conceivably this new doctrine could inhibit some editors, as the dissents of Mr. Justice Douglas and Mr. Justice Brennan suggest. But I would prefer to allow this area of law to continue to evolve as it has up to now with respect to private citizens rather than embark on a new doctrinal theory which has no jurisprudential ancestry.

The petitioner here was performing a professional representative role as an advocate in the highest tradition of the law, and under that tradition the advocate is not to be invidiously identified with his client. The important public policy which underlies this tradition—the right to counsel—would be gravely jeopardized if every lawyer who takes an "unpopular" case, civil or criminal, would automatically become fair game for irresponsible reporters and editors who might, for example, describe the lawyer as a "mob mouthpiece" for representing a client with a serious prior criminal record, or as an "ambulance chaser" for representing a claimant in a personal injury action.

I would reverse the judgment of the Court of Appeals and remand for reinstatement of the verdict of the jury and the entry of an appropriate judgment on that verdict.

MR. JUSTICE DOUGLAS, dissenting.

. . .

. . . The standard announced today leaves the States free to "define for themselves the appropriate standard of liability for a publisher or broadcaster" in the circumstances of this case. This of course leaves the simple negligence standard as an option with the jury free to impose damages upon a finding that the publisher failed to act as "a reasonable man." With such continued erosion of First Amendment protection, I fear that it may well be the reasonable man who refrains from speaking.

Since in my view the First and Fourteenth Amendments prohibit the imposition of damages upon respondent for this discussion of public affairs, I would affirm the judgment below.

MR. JUSTICE BRENNAN, dissenting.

I agree with the conclusion, expressed in Part V of the Court's opinion, that, at the time of publication of respondent's article, petitioner could not properly have been viewed as either a "public official" or "public figure"; instead, respondent's article, dealing with an alleged conspiracy to discredit local police forces, concerned petitioner's purported involvement in "an event of public or general interest." . . .

. . .

[Justice Brennan restated the views he expressed in *Rosenbloom.* ]

. . . Under a reasonable-care regime, publishers and broadcasters will have to make pre-publication judgments about juror assessment of such diverse considerations as the size, operating procedures, and financial condition of the newsgathering system, as well as the relative costs and benefits of instituting less frequent and more costly reporting at a higher level of accuracy. [ ] Moreover, in contrast to proof by clear and convincing evidence required under the *Times* test, the burden of proof for reasonable care will doubtless be the preponderance of the evidence. . . .

The Court does not discount altogether the danger that jurors will punish for the expression of unpopular opinions. This probability accounts for the Court's limitation that "the States may not permit recovery of presumed or punitive damages, at least when liability is not based on a showing of knowledge of falsity or reckless disregard for the truth." [ ] But plainly a jury's latitude to impose liability for want of due care poses a far greater threat of suppressing unpopular views than does a possible recovery of presumed or punitive damages. Moreover, the Court's broad-ranging examples of "actual injury," including impairment of reputation and standing in the community, as well as personal humiliation, and mental anguish and suffering, inevitably allow a jury bent on punishing expression of unpopular views a formidable weapon for doing so.   Finally, even a limitation of recovery to "actual injury"— however much it reduces the size or frequency of recoveries—will not provide the necessary elbowroom for First Amendment expression.   .   .   .

.   .   .

MR. JUSTICE WHITE, dissenting.

.   .   .

The impact of today's decision on the traditional view of libel is immediately obvious and indisputable.   No longer will the plaintiff be able to rest his case with proof of a libel defamatory on its face or proof of a slander historically actionable *per se*.   In addition, he must prove some further degree of culpable conduct on the part of the publisher, such as intentional or reckless falsehood or negligence.   And if he succeeds in this respect, he faces still another obstacle: recovery for loss of reputation will be conditioned upon "competent" proof of actual injury to his standing in the community.   This will be true regardless of the nature of the defamation and even though it is one of those particularly reprehensible statements that have traditionally made slanderous words actionable without proof of fault by the publisher or of the damaging impact of his publication.   The Court rejects the judgment of experience that some publications are inherently capable of injury, and actual injury so difficult to prove, that the risk of falsehood should be borne by the publisher, not the victim.   .   .   .

.   .   .

These are radical changes in the law and severe invasions of the prerogatives of the States.   .   .   .

.   .   .

The central meaning of *New York Times*, and for me the First Amendment as it relates to libel laws, is that seditious libel—criticism of government and public officials—falls beyond the police power of the State.   .   .   .

.   .   .

The Court evinces a deep-seated antipathy to "liability without fault."   But this catch-phrase has no talismanic significance and is almost meaningless in this context where the Court appears to be addressing those libels and slanders that are defamatory on their face and where the publisher is no doubt aware from the nature of the material that it would be inherently damaging to reputation.   He publishes notwithstanding, knowing that he will inflict injury.   With this knowledge, he must intend to inflict that injury, his excuse being that he is privileged to do so—that he has published the truth.   But as it turns out, what he has circulated to the public is a very damaging falsehood.   Is he nevertheless "faultless?"   Perhaps it can be said that the mistake about his defense was made in good faith, but the fact remains that it is he who launched the publication knowing that it could ruin a reputation.

In these circumstances, the law has heretofore put the risk of falsehood on the publisher where the victim is a private citizen and no grounds of special privilege are invoked. The Court would now shift this risk to the victim, even though he has done nothing to invite the calumny, is wholly innocent of fault, and is helpless to avoid his injury. I doubt that jurisprudential resistance to liability without fault is sufficient ground for employing the First Amendment to revolutionize the law of libel, and in my view, that body of legal rules poses no realistic threat to the press and its service to the public. The press today is vigorous and robust. To me, it is quite incredible to suggest that threats of libel suits from private citizens are causing the press to refrain from publishing the truth. I know of no hard facts to support that proposition, and the Court furnishes none.

The communications industry has increasingly become concentrated in a few powerful hands operating very lucrative businesses reaching across the Nation and into almost every home. Neither the industry as a whole nor its individual components are easily intimidated, and we are fortunate that they are not. Requiring them to pay for the occasional damage they do to private reputation will play no substantial part in their future performance or their existence.

In any event, if the Court's principal concern is to protect the communications industry from large libel judgments, it would appear that its new requirements with respect to general and punitive damages would be ample protection.

.   .   .

For the foregoing reasons, I would reverse the judgment of the Court of Appeals and reinstate the jury's verdict.

### Notes and Questions

1. Why did the majority adhere to the *Times* rule for public officials? Public figures? Some have argued that *Gertz* was a public figure and that the case should have been analyzed along the lines of *Butts* and *Walker*.

2. Why does the majority in *Gertz* prefer its approach to the plurality's approach in *Rosenbloom* ?

3. What criteria might be relevant in deciding whether a broadcaster has been at fault in broadcasting a false statement?

4. If a private citizen proves fault, why can he not recover traditional damages for defamation?

5. The Supreme Court has not decided finally whether libel plaintiffs may recover punitive damages, but *Dun & Bradstreet* (see note 12 below) indicates that some can.

6. The first significant application of *Gertz* occurred in Time, Inc. v. Firestone, 424 U.S 448 (1976), in which *Time* magazine reported, perhaps incorrectly, that a member of "one of America's wealthier families" had received a divorce because of his wife's adultery. The divorce decree

was probably based on either "extreme cruelty" or "lack of domestication" but the judge was not explicit. The state court upheld the wife's defamation award of $100,000. *Time* argued that the "actual malice" standard should apply for two reasons. First, it asserted that the plaintiff was a public figure, but the majority disagreed: "Respondent did not assume any role of especial prominence in the affairs of society, other than perhaps Palm Beach society, and she did not thrust herself to the forefront of any particular public controversy in order to influence the resolution of the issues involved in it." The Court rejected the argument that because the case was of great public interest, the respondent must have been a public figure: "Dissolution of a marriage through judicial proceedings is not the sort of 'public controversy, referred to in *Gertz*, even though the marital difficulties of extremely wealthy individuals may be of interest to some portion of the reading public." Moreover, plaintiff was compelled to go to court to seek relief in a marital dispute and her involvement was not voluntary. The fact that she held "a few" press conferences during the case did not change her otherwise private status. She did not attempt to use them to influence the outcome of the trial or to thrust herself into an unrelated dispute.

The second claim was that negligent errors in the reporting of judicial proceedings should never lead to liability. Justice Rehnquist's opinion for the Court rejected the contention:

> It may be that all reports of judicial proceedings contain some informational value implicating the First Amendment, but recognizing this is little different from labeling all judicial proceedings matters of "public or general interest," as that phrase was used by the plurality in *Rosenbloom*. Whatever their general validity, use of such subject matter classifications to determine the extent of constitutional protection afforded defamatory falsehoods may too often result in an improper balance between the competing interests in this area.

Plaintiff had withdrawn her claim of damages to reputation before trial, but the Court held that the award could be sustained on proof of anxiety and concern over the impact of the adultery charge on her young son. The Court vacated the judgment for lack of consideration of fault by either the jury or any of the state courts. Justices Powell and Stewart, though joining the majority, asserted that the grounds of divorce were so unclear in this "bizarre case" that there was "substantial evidence" that *Time* was not negligent. Justice White, believing that the state courts had found negligence, would have affirmed the award. Justice Brennan dissented on the ground that reports of judicial proceedings should not lead to liability unless the errors are deliberate or reckless. He also thought the damage limits of *Gertz* had been "subverted" by the recovery allowed here with no showing of reputational harm. Justice Marshall, dissenting, thought that plaintiff was a public figure; he also doubted the existence of negligence. Justice Stevens took no part.

The Florida Supreme Court ordered a new trial, but plaintiff dropped the case, saying that she had been vindicated.

Recall that under the common law "record libel" privilege, reports of governmental proceedings were privileged if they were fair and accurate reports of what had happened—even if the speaker being quoted had committed a defamation. Under the common law privilege, *Time*'s report, if incorrectly reporting the basis of the divorce decree, would not have been protected. For this reason *Time* had to assert a constitutional privilege.

7. In Wolston v. Reader's Digest Association, 443 U.S. 157 (1979), defendant published a book in 1974 that included plaintiff's name on a list of "Soviet agents identified in the United States." A footnote said that the list consisted of agents "who were convicted of espionage or falsifying information or perjury and/or contempt charges following espionage indictments or who fled to the Soviet bloc to avoid prosecution."

Plaintiff had been convicted of contempt of court in 1958 for failing to appear before a grand jury investigating Soviet espionage. He was never indicted for any of the listed offenses. At the time, plaintiff did not attempt to debate the propriety of his behavior. During the six weeks between his failure to appear and his sentencing, plaintiff's case was the subject of 15 stories in Washington and New York newspapers. "This flurry of publicity subsided" following the sentencing and plaintiff "succeeded for the most part in returning to the private life he had led" prior to the subpoena.

When plaintiff sued for libel, the lower courts held that in both 1958 and 1974 he was a public figure and that summary judgment was properly granted against him because he had presented no evidence of actual malice. (In the Supreme Court, plaintiff abandoned the argument that even if he was a public figure in 1958, he was no longer in 1974.)

The Supreme Court reversed. For the majority, Justice Rehnquist reviewed the "self-help" and the "assumption of risk" explanations developed in *Gertz* to support the public-private distinction, and concluded that the second was the more important.

Justice Rehnquist concluded that plaintiff had neither "voluntarily thrust" nor "injected" himself into the forefront of the controversy surrounding the investigation of Soviet espionage in the United States:

> It would be more accurate to say that petitioner was dragged unwillingly into the controversy. The government pursued him in its investigation. . . .
>
> Petitioner's failure to appear before the grand jury and citation for contempt no doubt were "newsworthy," but the simple fact that these events attracted media attention also is not conclusive of the public figure issue. A private individual is not automatically transformed into a public figure just by becoming involved in or associated with a matter that attracts public attention. . . .

Nor do we think that petitioner engaged the attention of the public in an attempt to influence the resolution of the issues involved. . . . He did not in any way seek to arouse public sentiment in his favor and against the investigation. Thus, this case is not a case where a defendant invites a citation for contempt in order to use the contempt citation as a fulcrum to create public discussion about the methods being used in connection with an investigation or prosecution. . . . In short, we find no basis whatsoever for concluding that petitioner relinquished, to any degree, his interest in the protection of his own name.

This reasoning leads us to reject the further contention of respondents that any person who engages in criminal conduct automatically becomes a public figure for purposes of comment on a limited range of issues relating to his conviction. [    ] We declined to accept a similar argument in Time, Inc. v. Firestone.

Justice Rehnquist concluded that, "[t]o hold otherwise would create an 'open season' for all who sought to defame persons convicted of a crime."

Justice Blackmun, joined by Justice Marshall, concurred in the result. He would hold that even if plaintiff had acquired public figure status in 1958, "he clearly had lost that distinction" by 1974. Although plaintiff had not pressed that argument in the Supreme Court, Justice Blackmun, noting that the lower courts had decided the point, thought it still open as a basis for decision.

Justice Blackmun recognized that his view put a more difficult burden on historians than on contemporary commentators:

This analysis implies, of course, that one may be a public figure for purposes of contemporaneous reporting of a controversial event, yet not be a public figure for purposes of historical commentary on the same occurrence. Historians, consequently, may well run a greater risk of liability for defamation. Yet this result, in my view, does no violence to First Amendment values. While historical analysis is no less vital to the marketplace of ideas than reporting current events, historians work under different conditions than do their media counterparts.

Justice Brennan dissented. He thought plaintiff a public figure for the limited purpose of comment on his connection with espionage in the 1940's and 1950's. He remained a public figure in 1974 because the issue of Soviet espionage "continues to be a legitimate topic of debate today . . . ." But he found enough evidence of "actual malice" to warrant a trial under the *Times* standard.

The next case was decided on the same day as *Wolston.*

8.  Hutchinson v. Proxmire, 443 U.S. 111 (1979), arose from Senator Proxmire's awarding of one of his Golden Fleece awards—made to government agencies that he believed engaged in wasteful spending. In this case he awarded it to agencies that had funded the plaintiff-

scientist's research work on aggression in animals. The Senator had uttered the alleged defamation in several forums, including a speech prepared for delivery on the Senate floor; advance press releases; a newsletter sent to 100,000 people; and a television interview program. The Court first decided that in this case Article I, Section 6 of the Constitution—the so-called Speech or Debate Clause—protected only a speech delivered on the floor.

The Court then turned to the First Amendment issue. Chief Justice Burger concluded that neither the fact that plaintiff had successfully applied for federal funds nor that he had access to media after Senator Proxmire's charges, "demonstrates that Hutchinson was a public figure prior to the controversy . . . ."

On this record Hutchinson's activities and public profile are much like those of countless members of his profession. His published writings reach a relatively small category of professionals concerned with research in human behavior. To the extent the subject of his published writings became a matter of controversy, it was a consequence of the Golden Fleece Award. Clearly those charged with defamation cannot, by their own conduct, create their own defense by making the claimant a public figure. See Wolston v. Reader's Digest, Inc., [ ].

Hutchinson did not thrust himself or his views into public controversy to influence others. Respondents have not identified such a particular controversy; at most, they point to concern about general public expenditures. But that concern is shared by most and relates to most public expenditures; it is not sufficient to make Hutchinson a public figure. . . .

. . .

In a footnote, the Chief Justice observed that "The Court has not provided precise boundaries for the category of 'public official'; it cannot be thought to include all public employees, however."

Justice Brennan was the sole dissenter. He believed that "public criticism by legislators of unnecessary governmental expenditures, whatever its form, is a legislative act shielded by the Speech and Debate Clause." He did not reach the public figure question.

Senator Proxmire subsequently made a public retraction, before television cameras, of his comments about Hutchinson.

9. One case on proving "actual malice" raised the issue of what types of questions the plaintiff could ask the media defendants during the pretrial effort to obtain evidence for the trial. The normal rule in civil cases is that any evidence that would be admissible at the trial may be obtained by "discovery" beforehand—usually either by deposition (oral testimony given by a prospective witness with only the lawyers for the sides present) or by interrogatories (written answers to written questions). This exchange of information allows the parties to know the strengths and weaknesses of their cases and avoids surprises at trial.

In Herbert v. Lando, 441 U.S. 153 (1979), the plaintiff, an admitted public figure, sued the producer and reporter of the television program "60 Minutes" and the CBS network for remarks on the program about his behavior while in military service in Vietnam. During his deposition, Lando, the producer, generally responded, but he refused to answer some questions about why he made certain investigations and not others, what he concluded about the honesty of certain people he interviewed for the program, and about conversations he had with Mike Wallace, the reporter, in preparation for the segment. Lando contended that these thought processes and internal editorial discussions were protected from disclosure by the First Amendment. The Supreme Court disagreed.

Justice White, for the Court, understood the defendants to be arguing that "the defendant's reckless disregard of truth, a critical element, could not be shown by direct evidence through inquiry into the thoughts, opinions, and conclusions of the publisher but could be proved only by objective evidence from which the ultimate fact could be inferred." This was a barrier of some substance "particularly when defendants themselves are prone to assert their good-faith belief in the truth of their publications, and libel plaintiffs are required to prove knowing or reckless falsehood with 'convincing clarity.'"

Justice White concluded that permitting plaintiffs "to prove their cases by direct as well as indirect evidence is consistent with the balance struck by our prior decisions." He "found it difficult to believe that error-avoiding procedures will be terminated or stifled simply because there is liability for culpable error and because the editorial process will itself be examined in the tiny percentage of instances in which error is claimed and litigation ensues."

Justice Powell concurred in the opinion of the Court but wrote separately to emphasize that trial judges must consider First Amendment interests as well as the private interests of plaintiffs in deciding how much pretrial discovery to allow.

Three justices dissented in separate opinions.

This case indirectly suggests problems when a reporter is asked to identify the source of a story. That subject is discussed at length in Chapter XIV.

In January, 1986, Colonel Herbert's $44 million libel suit was dismissed by the court of appeals, which said that CBS had presented sufficient evidence to defend its overall view of him and that a libel action cannot be based on minor subsidiary statements that merely support the story's overall conclusion. New York Times Jan. 16, 1986 at A1.

10. In Bose Corp. v. Consumers Union, 466 U.S. 485 (1984), the Supreme Court held in favor of the publisher of *Consumer Reports* magazine in a product disparagement suit filed by the manufacturer of loudspeakers criticized in the magazine. The magazine said that Bose 901 speakers produced sounds that "tended to wander about the room"

and that a violin "appeared to be 10 feet wide and a piano stretched from wall to wall."

The Supreme Court held that appeals courts, when reviewing findings of actual malice in libel cases and other cases governed by New York Times v. Sullivan, must exercise their own judgment in determining whether actual malice was shown with convincing clarity. Thus, the court of appeals decision in favor of Consumers Union was affirmed.

11. One federal case suggests the possibility of a First Amendment privilege that differs from the *Times-Gertz* variety. In the case, Edwards v. Audubon Society, Inc., 556 F.2d 113 (2d Cir.1977), certiorari denied sub nom. Edwards v. New York Times Co., 434 U.S. 1002 (1977), Devlin, a *Times* nature reporter, was following the continuing dispute between the Audubon Society and the chemical industry over the impact of various pesticides on birds. Based in part on the fact that annual bird counts conducted by the Audubon Society showed increasing numbers, some scientists retained by the industry argued that pesticides were not harmful. The Society believed that the higher numbers were due to more watchers with more skill using better observation areas.

An editorial in a Society publication asserted that whenever members heard a scientist use the bird count in an argument "you are in the presence of someone who is being paid to lie, or is parroting something he knows little about." The reporter called the Society and, the jury found, was told the names of five scientists that Society officials had in mind. The reporter then wrote a story accurately reporting the dispute and stating that a Society official had said that the scientists referred to in the editorial included five the reporter then named. In a suit by the scientists, the court held that an accurate report of this nature could not constitutionally lead to a libel judgment against the newspaper.

> At stake in this case is a fundamental principle. Succinctly stated, when a responsible, prominent organization like the National Audubon Society makes serious charges against a public figure, the First Amendment protects the accurate and disinterested reporting of those charges, regardless of the reporter's private views regarding their validity. [ ] What is newsworthy about such accusations is that they were made. We do not believe that the press may be required under the First Amendment to suppress newsworthy statements merely because it has serious doubts regarding their truth. Nor must the press take up cudgels against dubious charges in order to publish them without fear of liability for defamation. [ ] The public interest in being fully informed about controversies that often rage around sensitive issues demands that the press be afforded the freedom to report such charges without assuming responsibility for them.

> . . .

> It is clear here, that Devlin reported Audubon's charges fairly and accurately. He did not in any way espouse the Society's accusations: indeed, Devlin published the maligned scientists' out-

raged reactions in the same article that contained the Society's attack. The *Times* article, in short, was the exemplar of fair and dispassionate reporting of an unfortunate but newsworthy contretemps. Accordingly, we hold that it was privileged under the First Amendment.

What are the limits of the *Edwards* principle? Are there times when the public should be informed of charges that are not made by a "responsible, prominent organization"? What is the test for whether a report of a particular charge is "newsworthy"? What level of error in the report, if any, should deprive the reporter of the privilege? Should it be restricted to public figures?

Some courts have rejected the neutral reportage defense as inconsistent with *St. Amant*, since *Edwards* would allow one who reports a story that he knows to be false or has serious doubts about, to be protected from liability.

One can only conjecture about whether the neutral reportage privilege retains much vitality. In the 1970's and 1980's, some courts adopted the standard and some flatly rejected it. An example of the former is Barry v. Time, Inc., 584 F.Supp. 1110 (N.D.Cal.1984). An example of the latter is Postill v. Booth Newspapers, Inc., 118 Mich.App. 608, 325 N.W.2d 511, 518 (1982).

Note that the record libel privilege discussed earlier is a state privilege that can be limited by state statutes and decisions. In New York, for example, the relevant statute requires "official proceedings" before a privilege comes into play—and the New York courts have not expanded that privilege. Thus, in *Edwards*, the state statute did not apply.

12. Dun & Bradstreet, Inc. v. Greenmoss Builders, Inc., 472 U.S. ___ (1985), dealt with an erroneous report on the financial condition of Greenmoss Builders based on information supplied by a teenage part-time employee of Dun & Bradstreet, a national credit reporting agency. The report said Greenmoss, a construction contractor, had filed a voluntary petition for bankruptcy. Five subscribers had received the confidential report. Despite considerable speculation that the Supreme Court would decide the case by distinguishing it from defamation cases involving media defendants, the Court affirmed the judgment against Dun & Bradstreet on other grounds. Justice Powell announced the judgment of the Court, but only Justices Rehnquist and O'Connor joined his plurality opinion.

In deciding whether *Gertz* applied to Greenmoss, Justice Powell wrote, ". . . *Gertz* involved expression on a matter of undoubted public concern. . . . We have never considered whether the *Gertz* balance obtains when the defamatory statements involve no issue of public concern. . . . [In this case, the factors of content, form, and context] indicate that petitioner's credit report concerns no public issue. [ ] It was speech solely in the individual interest of the speaker and its specific business audience. [ ] This particular interest warrants no special protection when—as in this case—the speech is wholly false and clearly damaging to the victim's business reputation. . . . We conclude that permitting recovery of presumed and punitive damages in defamation cases absent a showing of 'actual malice' does not violate the First Amendment when the defamatory statements do not involve matters of public concern . . . ."

Chief Justice Burger and Justice White concurred in the judgment. Justices Blackmun, Brennan, Marshall, and Stevens dissented.

13. The Supreme Court agreed in June, 1985, to hear Hepps v. Philadelphia Newspapers, 506 Pa. 304, 485 A.2d 374 (1984), probable jurisdiction noted 492 U.S. __ (1985). Central to the case is the issue of whether a state can place the burden of proving the truth of allegedly libelous statements on libel defendants. *The Philadelphia Inquirer,* which published five articles in 1975–76 alleging ties among organized crime, a former state senator, and the Thrifty Beverage Chain, was sued by Thrifty's principal stockholder. The newspaper argued in its petition to the Supreme Court that Pennsylvania law is unconstitutional because it would permit a plaintiff to recover damages without proving the publisher disseminated false information. The paper's lawyers said the party who has the burden of proving fault must also prove falsity.

## C. REMEDIES FOR DEFAMATION

### 1. INJUNCTIONS

Injunctions are generally unavailable for reasons discussed in Chafee's Government and Mass Communication 91–92 (1947): "One man's judgment is not to be trusted to determine what people can read. . . . So our law thinks it better to let the defamed plaintiff take his damages for what they are worth than to intrust a single judge (or even a jury) with the power to put a sharp check on the spread of possible truth." Furthermore, there are gradations of partial truth that are too subtle for a blanket injunction.

### 2. REPLY

If the plaintiff completes the obstacle course we have described, damages are the only available remedy of any importance. The right of reply mentioned by Justice Brennan in *Rosenbloom* and *Gertz* would allow the victim of the defamation to respond in his own words in the offending publication, but states rarely require this, and such a requirement now appears to have constitutional problems. See Miami Herald Pub. Co. v. Tornillo, p. 72, supra. As to the role of reply in broadcasting, see Chapters III and VI.

### 3.  Retraction

The common law itself had some rules that tended to reduce the amount of damages recoverable in defamation.  They were called "partial" defenses since they did not defeat liability but only reduced the size of the award.  At common law if the defendant voluntarily retracted the statement, that fact was admissible to show that the plaintiff had not been damaged as badly as he claimed.  It might also show that the defendant had not acted maliciously in the first place.  Some states have enacted retraction statutes that grant further protection to mass media defendants.  These apply only to media because of the requirement that the retraction be published promptly and with the same prominence as the defamation.  It would be meaningless to make the retraction privilege available to media such as books and motion pictures, and the effectiveness of retraction varies even among those media that are covered in most states.  It is generally thought, for example, that a retraction in the same space in a newspaper or magazine is more likely to reach the audience that read the original defamation than would most retractions over radio or television of an electronic media defamation.

The statutes vary in covering those who defame innocently, carelessly, or maliciously.  What they have in common is a requirement that the prospective plaintiff demand a retraction shortly after the defamation.  If the publisher complies within a similar period of time, then the plaintiff may recover only his special damages, and no general damages.  If the retraction is not published within the time limit, the plaintiff may recover whatever damages the common law allowed—subject now to the damage limitations of *Gertz*.

Some "retractions," of course, result in something far less than a full withdrawal of an allegation or an apology.  In General William Westmoreland's 1984 libel suit against CBS, for example, the joint statement that was part of the litigants' out-of-court settlement was subject to varied interpretations.  Westmoreland's supporters tried to claim at least partial victory from CBS's statement that it never intended to suggest that the general was unpatriotic.  Media advocates, on the other hand, stressed the fact that CBS stood by its original program.

## D.  CRIMINAL LIBEL AND GROUP LIBEL

### 1.  Criminal Libel

Criminal libel is not generally available although it is part of the law in most states.  The New York State Constitution, for example, provides that, "In all criminal prosecutions or indictments for libels, the truth may be given in evidence to the jury; and if it shall appear to the jury that the matter charged as libelous is true, and was published with good motives and for justifiable ends, the party shall be acquitted; and the jury shall have the right to determine the law and the fact." McKinney's Const. Art. 1, § 8.

Criminal libel had already fallen into disuse before *Garrison*, p. 471, supra. The strictures placed on the action in that case diminished still further its usefulness. The role of the action is even more doubtful when it is used by prosecutors in behalf of famous or powerful persons who do not wish to bring a civil action themselves. This was the situation in 1976 when a state court declared the California criminal libel law unconstitutional because of its limitations on the defense of truth and its presumption of malice. Since other states have taken the same path, criminal libel no longer appears to be a serious risk to the media.

### 2.  GROUP LIBEL STATUTES

The main concern in the debate over group libel has been the hazards of unrestricted hate propaganda. Curbs on group defamation have been advocated to reduce friction among racial, religious, and ethnic groups. As early as 1917 some states enacted criminal group libel laws for that purpose. The Nazi defamation of minority groups, and conspicuous racial tensions in the United States, brought renewed attention to group libel laws in the 1940's and 1950's.

The most common method of confronting group libel has been the enactment of criminal laws directed specifically at the problem. Such laws typically prohibit communications that are abusive or offensive toward a group or that tend to arouse hatred, contempt, or ridicule of the group. Penalties have ranged from a fine of $50 or 30 days imprisonment, to $10,000 or two years in prison.

Beauharnais v. Illinois, 343 U.S. 250 (1952), is the only Supreme Court decision to review the constitutionality of group libel legislation. The Court, 5–4, affirmed a conviction under Illinois's 1917 group libel statute. The law prohibited publications portraying "depravity, criminality, unchastity, or lack of virtue of a class of citizens, of any race, color, creed, or religion" that subjected those described to "contempt, derision, or obloquy or which is productive of breach of the peace or riots." Beauharnais, the president of an organization called the "White Circle League," had distributed leaflets calling on the Mayor and City Council to halt the "further encroachment, harassment and invasion of white people, their property, neighborhoods and persons, by the Negro."

Justice Frankfurter's opinion for the Court treated the statute as "a form of criminal libel law" and accepted the dictum of Chaplinsky v. New Hampshire, 315 U.S. 568 (1942), that libel was one of those "well-defined and narrowly limited classes of speech, the prevention and punishment of which has never been thought to raise any constitutional problem." He traced the history of violent and destructive racial tension in Illinois and concluded that it would "deny experience" to say that the statute was without reason. He disposed of the First Amendment question in a single paragraph near the end of his opinion.

Libelous utterances not being within the area of constitutionally protected speech, it is unnecessary, either for us or for the State courts, to consider the issue behind the phrase "clear and present danger." Certainly no one would contend that obscene speech, for example, may be punished only upon a showing of such circumstances. Libel, as we have seen, is in the same class.

Of the four dissenters, only Justices Black and Douglas addressed the First Amendment problems that the majority had cast aside by excluding the whole area of libel from First Amendment protection. Justice Black analyzed the decision as extending the scope of the law of criminal libel from "the narrowest of areas" involving "purely private feuds" to "discussions of matters of public concern." This was an invasion of the First Amendment's absolute prohibition of laws infringing the freedom of public discussion. Justice Douglas concurred in Justice Black's opinion and wrote separately to emphasize that he would have required a demonstration that the "peril of speech" was "clear and present." He agreed with Justice Black that allowing a legislature to regulate "within reasonable limits" the right of free speech was "an ominous and alarming trend." Only a half-dozen states retain group defamation statutes.

Group libel statutes also raise practical objections. Group libel prosecutions normally involve issues on which the community is sharply divided. The incidence as well as the outcome of prosecutions may thus depend on which segments of the community are represented in the office of the prosecuting attorney and on the jury. Moreover, a defendant could use the trial to promote his views and might well benefit regardless of the result: an acquittal would validate his viewpoint, while a conviction would make him a martyr whose civil liberties have been violated. These difficulties have led most commentators and many representatives of minority groups to oppose group libel litigation.

## E.  PRACTICAL CONSIDERATIONS FOR MEDIA DEFENDANTS

### 1.  MEGAVERDICTS

Much has been written in the 1980's about the dollar size of libel suits and about jury verdicts for millions of dollars sometimes characterized as "megaverdicts" or "monster verdicts." To some extent the media play into the hands of plaintiffs seeking publicity through multimillion dollar suits, because such amounts are the stuff of which headlines are made. Among the suits receiving extraordinary attention were actress Carol Burnett's suit against the *National Enquirer* and Army General William Westmoreland's suit against CBS. A jury awarded Carol Burnett $1.6 million in damages. Westmoreland sued CBS for $120 million. These cases are hardly typical, but large damage awards are not imaginary either. What press headlines usually fail to point out is how many of these large damage awards are reversed or reduced by appellate courts. Apparently, $550,000 is the largest damage award yet upheld on appeal.

Most of those that claimed big headlines have subsequently been reduced. In the Carol Burnett case, for example, the original award was reduced to $200,000. With the possibility of a new trial on the damage amount, Burnett and *National Enquirer* settled out of court for an undisclosed amount rumored to be about $400,000—still only one-fourth the amount of the original award. The Westmoreland case, on the other hand, ended with no money changing hands between the litigants (but with each side reportedly having incurred millions of dollars in legal fees). Even though we have not yet seen multi-million dollar verdicts sustained by appellate courts, the publicity surrounding them may encourage libel plaintiffs to file more and larger libel suits, and there may be a chilling effect both on large media organizations, who may fear that they will be the targets of such suits because of their "deep pockets," and on smaller organizations that seldom consult their legal counsel and sometimes are afraid to publish because they fear the kinds of immobilizing libel suits they read about.

## 2. LIBEL INSURANCE

When a court awards damages against a media defendant in a libel suit, it is legally irrelevant whether that defendant carries libel insurance. As a practical matter, of course, it is extremely important. Media employers are often reluctant to be candid about their insurance, even with their own employees. Certainly no employer wants his employees to take unnecessary risks, and media employers typically value their reputations for accuracy so they do not want to lose libel suits even if they do carry insurance. Media libel insurance policies typically provide for a deductible amount that is paid by the insured before the insurance coverage comes into play. The higher the deductible, the lower the premiums that the employer pays for the insurance. Media employers who could afford to sustain losses of $50,000 or $100,000 on each damage award against them or who can afford the legal expenses might elect to be "self-insured" for those amounts and to carry insurance policies with the $50,000 or $100,000 deductible clause to cover them for any awards or expenses greater than those amounts. The increasing size of trial court awards for libel damages has, inevitably, led to an increase in libel insurance premiums; that increase in the premiums in turn has a negative effect on virtually every insured media organization—not just those that are sued.

Libel insurance policies sometimes are offered through trade associations like the National Association of Broadcasters.

## 3. DEFENSE COSTS

Even the media defendants who win their cases in trial or appellate courts may spend large sums of money defending themselves. In major cases some defendants have spent several million dollars defending themselves. While vindication in court may seem ideal, the cost of lawyers and the cost in terms of one's own employees' time may make it tempting to settle out of court with the plaintiff—even where there is a substantial likelihood that the defendant would ultimately prevail should the case be decided by an appellate court. A media defendant who developed the reputation of settling out of court too easily could become a target for nuisance suits brought by plaintiffs who do not really expect to win but hope defendants will buy them off by settling out of court without ever going to trial. Some major media organizations have adopted the position of never settling out of court for just that reason, but such a posture is difficult to maintain in an instance where the media organization really did publish a false statement, particularly where the plaintiff is a private figure who does not need to prove actual malice and who has real damages. The defendant's own insurance carrier may apply pressure to settle, and the size of the verdicts of recent years makes the risk of going to trial all the greater and increases the temptation to settle out of court.

### 4.  EVIDENCE AND WITNESSES

Attorneys representing media clients sometimes have a difficult choice to make: if they scare the journalists too much about possible libel suits, they may create their own chilling effect; but if they ignore the subject, the journalists may fall into traps that can make the defense of a libel suit more troubling. Plaintiffs who are public officials or public figures will, of course, be seeking evidence that the defendant published with knowledge of falsity or with a high degree of awareness of probable falsity. Internal memos or margin notes written on copy expressing doubts about the facts in a story can be just the kind of evidence the plaintiff will seek. Newsroom conversations about doubts—even doubts in one's own mind—may be discoverable (see discussion of Herbert v. Lando at p. 565, infra).

In an age in which libel litigation is common, journalists publishing material that may damage a person's reputation would be wise to think of the story subject as a potential plaintiff and to be as sure of their facts as possible. Just as such nationally-known journalists as Dan Rather and Mike Wallace have been called to discuss their stories from the witness stand, younger journalists may have to do the same and should be unafraid to do so if they have followed accepted journalistic practices. (The latter can present interesting questions, because professional standards in journalism vary. Codes of ethics—like the code of The Society of Professional Journalists, Sigma Delta Chi—may be of some use. Principles such as getting at least two independent sources before disseminating damaging information may be widely followed but still are not provably a part of a universally accepted code of conduct for the journalist.)

# Chapter XIII

## PRIVACY

Defamation, which we discussed in the last Chapter, and invasion of privacy, which we discuss in this one, are sometimes treated together in law courses as related rights to protect one's dignity. In defamation, we balance the right of freedom of expression against the right of individuals to protect their reputations. In privacy, we balance the right of freedom of expression against the right of individuals to be let alone. Although many people tend to think of privacy as a basic human right and many assume that it is constitutional, the word privacy never appears in the Constitution. Compared to defamation, privacy is a relatively new legal concept with many facets.

Concerns for privacy in the 1980's are diverse—involving such varied issues as the dissemination of personal credit information via computerized systems, electronic eavesdropping, the protection of newsrooms from police searches, release of personal information about individuals by government, and a right to know what is in one's own academic records. Some of these issues we will address elsewhere in this book, because they are related to other topics; the protection of newsrooms from police searches, for example, is dealt with in Chapter XIV because the "privacy" of the newsroom is directly related to the confidentiality of journalists' sources and their notes.

In this Chapter we will be concerned primarily with invasion of privacy as a tort—a civil wrong or injury. Although the recognition of privacy torts varies from state to state, scholars generally have recognized four different torts or branches of invasion of privacy. One of these relates to the newsgathering stage of the communications process: intruding on the plaintiff's physical solitude. It is akin to the tort of trespass. The other three torts or branches of invasion of privacy relate to the publication stage of the communications process. They are publication of embarrassing private (true) facts; putting the plaintiff in a false light in the public eye; and appropriation of another's name or likeness for commercial or trade purposes. Of the four branches, the "false-light" tort comes closest to the tort of defamation, because it is the only one that involves falsity.

Because of the similarities between defamation and false-light invasion of privacy, some of the traditional defenses in defamation are sometimes applicable to this branch of invasion of privacy—including truth. Truth is not, obviously, a defense for publication of embarrassing private facts, because the fact that an embarrassing publication is true just makes it all the more embarrassing. Because the applicability of defenses varies with the branch of invasion of privacy being considered, we shall touch on defenses at several different points in this Chapter.

## A.  INTRUSION ON THE PLAINTIFF'S PHYSICAL SOLITUDE

As indicated above, intrusion on the plaintiff's physical solitude is the only one of the four branches of privacy that comes up in the context of *newsgathering* rather than in the context of dissemination.  In the absence of any Supreme Court decision involving such an invasion of privacy by the mass media, we will look here at some cases decided by the lower courts as examples.

The major divisions of this branch of invasion of privacy reflect the type of consent problem involved.  Within each subsection we consider the types of invasions that plaintiff may complain about.  The most traditional are trespass (unpermitted entry) on land and theft of personal property.  The claim is that the physical zone of privacy that surrounds each of us has been intruded upon—usually in an effort to obtain information that would otherwise not be available.

### 1.  Intrusions Without Express Consent

-----

#### *a. Trespass*

For centuries, the act of intentionally entering the land of another without consent has made the entrant liable for trespass.  The civil damages include any actual harm done to the property and some damages for the symbolic invasion of the owner's or occupier's legal interest.  If accompanied by ill will or spite or a desire to harm the owner, perhaps punitive damages as well are awarded.  Comparable rules apply to a person who legally enters land but then remains on it against the wishes of the owner or occupier of the land.

In one clear case, the plaintiff alleged that his wife had committed suicide during the day; that when he returned to the house that evening he discovered that the screen over the kitchen window had been cut and that a photograph of his wife that had been on a table in the living room that morning had been taken.  Although the plaintiff failed to prove that the defendant's reporters had committed the trespass, the court indicated that the only problem in the case was one of identification.  The trespass and theft could not be defended even if there had been great public interest in the photograph.  Metter v. Los Angeles Examiner, 35 Cal. App.2d 304, 95 P.2d 491 (1939).

Sometimes the reporter may claim that he has authority to enter the property even though the owner has not expressly consented.  Two Florida cases present examples.

In Florida Publishing Co. v. Fletcher, 340 So.2d 914 (Fla.1976), the plaintiff alleged that after she had left town on a trip, a fire broke out in her house that killed her 17-year-old daughter; that after the daughter's body was removed from the floor a silhouette was revealed; that defendant newspaper's photographer took a photograph of the silhouette; and that plaintiff first learned of the tragedy by reading the story in a newspaper and seeing the accompanying photographs. In her claim for trespass, the depositions revealed that police and fire officials, as was their standard practice, invited press photographers and reporters to enter the house; that the media representatives entered through an open door without objection; and that they entered quietly and did no damage to the property. The fire marshal wanted a clear picture of the silhouette to show that the body had been on the floor before the heat of the fire damaged the room. After the official took one picture, he ran out of film and asked the newspaper photographer to take pictures for the official investigation. He did so and also made copies for his own paper, which published them.

The defendant moved for summary judgment on the trespass claims. Affidavits from various government and media sources stated that entering private property and inviting the press in this type of situation was common practice. Plaintiff filed only her own affidavit and none from media or other experts. She conceded that it was proper for the police and fire officials to enter and also admitted that no one had objected to the entry of the press. The trial judge granted summary judgment because the affidavits "attest to the fact that it is common usage, custom, and practice for news media to enter private premises and homes to report on matters of public interest or a public event."

The Florida Supreme Court agreed that implied consent covered the case. Research showed that implied consent by custom and usage "do not rest upon the previous nonobjection to entry by the particular owner of the property in question but rest upon custom and practice generally." In addition to the fact that here the press entered in response to an express invitation from public officials, the court stressed that this was the first case presenting the question. "This, in itself, tends to indicate that the practice has been accepted by the general public since it is a widespread practice of longstanding." One judge dissented on jurisdictional grounds. The Supreme Court denied certiorari, 431 U.S. 930 (1977).

Compare Green Valley School Inc. v. Cowles Florida Broadcasting, Inc., 327 So.2d 810 (Fla.App.1976). State officials planned a midnight raid, under a properly issued warrant, to search the premises of a controversial local private boarding school. The head of the party of 50 raiders invited reporters and photographers from several local media organizations to accompany the party. The defendant television station presented an extensive report of the raid on the evening news the following night, suggesting that the raid had turned up evidence of mistreatment of the students, rampant sexual misbehavior, and use of drugs. The school sued the station for defamation and trespass.

The trial judge granted summary judgment to the station on the trespass claim. The court of appeals reversed, addressing the question entirely in the following passage.

To uphold appellees' assertion that their entry upon appellant's property at the time, manner, and circumstances as reflected by this record was as a *matter of law* sanctioned by "the request of and with the consent of the State Attorney" and with the "common usage and custom in Florida" could well bring to the citizenry of this state the hobnail boots of a Nazi stormtrooper equipped with glaring lights invading a couple's bedroom at midnight with the wife hovering in her nightgown in an attempt to shield herself from the scanning TV camera. In this jurisdiction, a law enforcement officer is not as a *matter of law* endowed with the right or authority to invite people of his choosing to invade private property and participate in a midnight raid of the premises.

On the same day that it decided *Fletcher*, the Florida Supreme Court dismissed an appeal in the Green Valley case, indicating that it found no conflict between the results in the two cases. Can they be reconciled?

As soon as we move from private residential property to premises that are usually open to the public for some purpose, the questions get more difficult.

In Le Mistral v. Columbia Broadcasting System, 61 App.Div.2d 491, 402 N.Y.S.2d 815 (1978), CBS, as owner and operator of WCBS–TV in New York City, directed reporter Rich and a camera crew to visit restaurants that had been cited for health code variations. Plaintiff was on the list. The crew entered plaintiff's restaurant with cameras "rolling" and using bright lights that were necessary to get the pictures. The jury found CBS liable for trespass and awarded plaintiff $1,200 in compensatory damages and $250,000 in punitive damages. After the verdict (in a passage approved on appeal), the trial judge stated:

> The instructions given to the crew, whether specific to this event or as standing operating procedure, were to avoid seeking an appointment or permission to enter any of the premises where a story was sought, but to enter unannounced catching the occupants by surprise; "with cameras rolling" in the words of CBS' principal witness, Rich. From the evidence the jury was entitled to conclude that following this procedure the defendant's employees burst into plaintiff's restaurant in noisy and obtrusive fashion and following the loud commands of the reporter, Rich, to photograph the patrons dining, turned their lights and camera upon the dining room. Consternation, the jury was informed, followed. Patrons waiting to be seated left the restaurant. Others, who had finished eating, left without waiting for their checks. Still others hid their faces behind napkins or table cloths or hid themselves beneath tables. (The reluctance of the plaintiff's clientele to be video taped was never explained, and need not be. Patronizing a restaurant does not carry with it an obligation to appear on television). [The] president of the plaintiff and manager of its operations, refused to be interviewed, and as the camera continued to "roll" he pushed the protesting Miss Rich and her crew from the premises. All told, the CBS personnel were in the restaurant not more than ten minutes, perhaps as little as one minute, depending on the testimony the jury chose to credit.

The jury by its verdict clearly found the defendant guilty of trespass and from the admissions of CBS' own employees they were guilty of trespass. The witness Rich sought to justify her crew's entry into the restaurant by calling it, on a number of occasions, a "place of public accommodation", but, as she acknowledges, they did not seek to avail themselves of the plaintiff's "accommodation"; they had no intention of purchasing food or drink.

The trial judge upheld the determination of liability but set aside both damage awards because he had erroneously barred a defense witness from testifying as to CBS's motive and purpose in entering the premises. On appeal, the court held that its review of the record "demonstrates an adequate basis to justify the compensatory damage award rendered by the jury and, accordingly, such award must stand." As to punitive damages, the court agreed that the judge had erred in excluding the testimony because all "circumstances immediately connected with the transaction tending to exhibit or explain the motive of the defendant are admissible." One judge thought it clear that the defendants were "not motivated by actual malice or such an intentional disregard of plaintiff's rights as would justify the imposition of punitive damages. [ ] The defendant was merely pursuing a newsworthy item in the overly aggressive but good faith manner that characterizes the operation of the news media today. . . . In this sensitive and evolving First Amendment area, I would permit this precedent-setting opinion to stand as a warning to all news gatherers that future trespasses may well be met with an award of punitive damages."

CBS, dissatisfied with the decision, sought to appeal to New York's highest court to argue that no trespass had been committed and also that, in any event, punitive damages were improper. That court ultimately refused to hear the case for jurisdictional reasons.

The case is complicated by the disruptive presence of the television cameras. If newspaper reporters had entered the restaurant, would they have been trespassers from the moment they entered—or only from the moment they refused to leave? If, while the newspaper reporters were leaving, they continued watching the scene and making mental notes of what they saw, would that be improper? If the court is suggesting that the premises were open only to those seriously considering purchasing food or drink, why should it matter whether the entry was disruptive?

Under traditional law, the owner could prevent entry by posting a notice on the front door stating that no reporters are permitted on the premises. But today it is possible that the courts of New York would develop a special rule allowing reporters to enter "newsworthy" premises—at least so long as they are not disruptive. Further, the courts might develop some First Amendment privilege to allow reporters to enter certain types of "private" premises—at least until they are explicitly asked to leave. All of this is most unclear. See Watkins, Private

Property vs. Reporter Rights—A Problem in Newsgathering. 54 Journ. Q. 690 (1977).

In order for plaintiffs to claim damages for trespass or theft of property, they must own or occupy the property. If the property has been abandoned—the former owners have indicated a desire to relinquish their control over it—then no civil damages can be brought. An example of this situation may have occurred in 1975 when it was revealed that a reporter had been sifting through the garbage cans outside the house of Secretary of State Kissinger. A reporter who went on the land to reach the garbage cans would have been a trespasser. If the cans were on the public sidewalk, the only claim would be interference with personal property—the garbage. But if, as seems likely, the property has been abandoned, no civil liability would be possible. Commenting on the episode in an editorial, *Editor & Publisher* (July 19, 1975 at 6) attacked the practice: "Pawing through someone else's garbage is a revolting exercise and doing it in the name of journalism makes it none the less so." Do you agree?

### b.   Other Intrusions Without Consent

We turn now to alleged invasions of privacy that do not fit into the trespass mold. These involve issues of how far persons may use cameras or high-technology equipment to obtain information about a subject; wiretapping; and secretly recording conversations to which the person is a party.

Galella v. Onassis, 487 F.2d 986 (2d Cir.1973), involved aggressive efforts by a "paparazzo" photographer to obtain photographs of the widow and children of President Kennedy. Among his actions, Galella brought his power boat close to Mrs. Onassis as she was swimming; jumped out of bushes as she was walking past; jumped into her son's path to take a photograph of him riding his bicycle; and invaded the children's private schools. Those acts that reasonably put the subject in fear of personal safety would create tort liability under longstanding rules. But those that involved annoyance presented harder questions.

Mrs. Onassis claimed that when she went through the streets to go shopping or to visit a friend, or walked alone in Central Park, she was engaged in private activities that should not be the subject of any unwanted photography. The court disagreed. Mrs. Onassis was "a public figure and thus subject to news coverage" although the First Amendment provided no "wall of immunity protecting newsmen" from liability for torts committed while gathering news. The court balanced Mrs. Onassis's concern about intrusion with the legitimate interests of photography by ordering Galella to stay 25 feet from Mrs. Onassis at all times; not to block her movement in public places; and not to do "any act foreseeably or reasonably calculated" to place Mrs. Onassis in jeopardy or frighten her. Any further restriction on his taking and selling photographs of her would be improper.

Galella was subsequently charged with criminal contempt for violating the order, but he avoided paying a $120,000 fine for contempt by agreeing not to take any more pictures of Mrs. Onassis.

In 1979, a TV camera crew trailed a man as he was trying to pay a ransom to persons who had kidnapped his wife. Despite his pleas, the crew followed the man, apparently along public ways. The episode attracted much press discussion after the FBI said the action had "put that woman's life in danger." An editorial in *Editor & Publisher*, July 28, 1979 at 6, asserted that although the TV crew might have considered its actions "enterprising reporting . . . it was more like sheer stupidity. . . . It is this sort of arrogance and brashness that gets media in trouble with the public."

After the woman was released, the couple sued the station for endangering the woman's life. Since no harm actually occurred in the case the suit might be difficult. Should the husband be able to sue for mental anguish he suffered as a result of the crew's actions? Criminal liability might be possible if it was shown that the crew learned of the man's movements by making unauthorized interceptions of messages on a nonbroadcast frequency in violation of what was then § 605 of the Communications Act (now § 705). Should the law impose a sanction against reporters whose gathering efforts in fact lead to harm because kidnappers panic or get angry because their instructions apparently are not being followed?

Where solitude is invaded, the courts speak of the subject's reasonable expectations of privacy as the guide to available protection. Thus, one who leaves his curtains open, knowing that persons in the building across the street can look inside his apartment, can claim no reasonable expectation of privacy. But if the only vantage point from which the inside of the apartment can be seen is a hilltop two miles away, a court might well find that a reporter who set up a powerful telescope on that hill and looked through the open window has invaded privacy.

Similarly, a person inside a dwelling can make no reasonable claim of invasion of privacy if he shouts at his spouse and is overheard by others outside. But if he speaks in a normal or hushed voice—and is overheard because a highly sensitive microphone in the next apartment or across the street has picked up the communication, a court would probably find an invasion.

Wiretapping and other forms of intercepting messages frequently have been involved in litigation. For a thorough discussion of the issue, see Middleton, "Journalists and Tape Recorders: Does Participant Monitoring Invade Privacy?" 2 Comm/Ent L.J. 287 (Winter 1979–80). Although some early cases did impose tort liability in these cases, the major development occurred when Congress passed The Omnibus Crime Control and Safe Streets Act of 1968, 18 U.S.C. §§ 2510–2520. The basic provision subjects to criminal liability "any person" who without a warrant "willfully intercepts" any "wire or oral communication." Section 2520 provides that violators are liable for compensatory and punitive damages.  Some exclusions apply, but none specially to reporters.

Two television cases exemplify more recent litigation.  In one, a woman who was alleged to have traded sexual favors for a light sentence by an Ohio judge agreed to be interviewed by ABC in her home, but she refused to appear on camera.  The network made surreptitious video and voice recordings, and she sued.  Although the court held that there was no criminal or tortious purpose, it held that the plaintiff was entitled to try to prove in court that ABC intended to injure her.  Boddie v. American Broadcasting Companies, 731 F.2d 333 (6th Cir.1984).  In the other, ABC had surreptitiously recorded a meeting between congressional investigators and a cancer insurance salesman—with the consent of the investigators.  The court ruled that ABC must show that its *only* purpose was to aid Congress or that it must demonstrate that it had no injurious purpose in secretly recording the encounter.  Benford v. American Broadcasting Companies, 502 F.Supp. 1159 (D.Md.1980), affirmed 661 F.2d 917 (4th Cir.1981), certiorari denied 454 U.S. 1060 (1981).  For discussion of such problems, see Spellman, "Tort Liability of the News Media for Surreptitious Recording," Journalism Quarterly, Summer 1985 at 289.

For a recent example of a state case, see Ribas v. Clark, 38 Cal.3d 355, 212 Cal.Rptr. 143, 696 P.2d 637 (1985), in which a woman with marital difficulties had a friend listen in on a telephone call with her husband, the court awarded no common law damages, but there was a statutory penalty.  The court quoted a law review comment:

> There is a qualitative as well as a quantitative difference between secondhand repetition by the listener and simultaneous dissemination to a second auditor, whether that auditor be a tape recorder or a third party.  In the former situation the speaker retains control over the extent of his immediate audience.  Even though that audience may republish his words, it will be done secondhand, after the fact, probably not in entirety, and the impact will depend upon the credibility of the teller.  Where electronic monitoring is involved, however, the speaker is deprived of the right to control the extent of his own firsthand dissemination. . . .  In this regard participant monitoring closely resembles third-party surveillance;  both practices deny the speaker a most important aspect of privacy of communication—the right to control the extent of first instance dissemination of his statements.

Florida has a statute that reaches participant monitoring by barring persons "not acting under color of law" from intercepting a wire or oral communication unless all parties to the communication had given their prior consent.  An important lawsuit arose from a general attack on the statute by reporters who claimed that the use of concealed recording equipment was essential to investigative reporting for three reasons:  it aided accuracy of reporting;  persons being interviewed would not be candid if they knew they were being recorded; and the recording provided corroboration in case of suit for defamation.

The Florida Supreme Court upheld the statute's constitutionality. The statute allows "each party to a conversation to have an expectation of privacy from interception by another party to the conversation. It does not exclude any source from the press, intrude upon the activities of the news media in contacting sources, prevent the parties to the communication from consenting to the recording, or restrict the publication of any information gained from the communication. First Amendment rights do not include a constitutional right to corroborate news gathering activities when the legislature has statutorily recognized the private rights of individuals."

In response to the argument that secret recording may be the only way to get credible information about crime, the court stated that protection against intrusion might protect even a person "reasonably suspected of committing a crime." Shevin v. Sunbeam Television Corp., 351 So.2d 723 (Fla.1977).

Based on the briefs and without argument, the Supreme Court dismissed the appeal by the press for want of a substantial federal question, 435 U.S. 920 (1978). Three justices dissented.

The Florida court had relied to some extent on the case of Dietemann v. Time, Inc., 449 F.2d 245 (9th Cir.1971). In that case, two reporters obtained access to plaintiff's home to find out whether he was a medical quack. While plaintiff was diagnosing the alleged ailment of one reporter, the other secretly took photographs with a hidden camera. The entire conversation was transmitted to confederates outside by means of a transmitter hidden in one reporter's purse. In this part of the case, the court concluded that California would impose liability for invasion of privacy:

> [One who invites others to his home] does not and should not be required to take the risk that what is heard and seen will be transmitted by photograph or recording, or in our modern world, in full living color and hi-fi to the public at large or to any segment of it that the visitor may select. A different rule could have a most pernicious effect upon the dignity of man and it would surely lead to guarded conversations and conduct where candor is most valued, e.g., in the case of doctors and lawyers.

> The defendant claims that the First Amendment immunizes it from liability for invading plaintiff's den with a hidden camera and its concealed electronic instruments because its employees were gathering news and its instrumentalities "are indispensable tools of investigative reporting." We agree that newsgathering is an integral part of news dissemination. We strongly disagree, however, that the hidden mechanical contrivances are "indispensable tools" of newsgathering. Investigative reporting is an ancient art; its successful practice long antecedes the invention of miniature cameras and electronic devices. The First Amendment has never been con-

strued to accord newsmen immunity from torts or crimes committed during the course of newsgathering. The First Amendment is not a license to trespass, to steal, or to intrude by electronic means in the precincts of another's home or office. It does not become such a license simply because the person subjected to the intrusion is reasonably suspected of committing a crime.

Defendant relies upon the line of cases commencing with New York Times Co. v. Sullivan, 376 U.S. 254 (1964) . . . to sustain its contentions that (1) publication of news, however tortiously gathered, insulates defendant from liability for the antecedent tort . . . . .

As we previously observed, publication is not an essential element of plaintiff's cause of action. Moreover, it is not the foundation for the invocation of a privilege. Privilege concepts developed in defamation cases and to some extent in privacy actions in which publication is an essential component are not relevant in determining liability for intrusion conduct antedating publication. [ ] Nothing in *New York Times* or its progeny suggests anything to the contrary. Indeed, the Court strongly indicates that there is no First Amendment interest in protecting news media from calculated misdeeds. [ ]

## 2. Consent Has Been Obtained

We turn now to cases in which the reporter contends that what might otherwise be a tort is not because the plaintiff consented to the conduct in question. The basic legal principle is not in doubt. Occasionally, the cases involve such neat situations as a plaintiff who signs a written consent. Usually, the cases are more complex.

In Cassidy v. American Broadcasting Companies, 60 Ill.App.3d 831, 17 Ill.Dec. 936, 377 N.E.2d 126 (1978), an undercover policeman was sent to a massage parlor. After paying $30 he was escorted to a room to watch "de-luxe lingerie modeling." On entering the warm room he observed camera lights. He asked, "What are we on, TV?" The model replied, "Yes, we're making a movie." As plaintiff reclined on the bed watching the model change her lingerie several times, he made suggestive remarks and advances. He then arrested the model for solicitation. The entire scene was in fact being photographed from an adjacent room by a local television station through a two-way mirror. The manager of the parlor had asked the defendant to film the episode to show that police were harassing him.

Plaintiff's suit failed because, among other reasons, the plaintiff apparently did not intend his conduct to be private because he knew that someone might be making a movie of his conduct. He testified his actions were in the line of duty as an officer and that if the model wished to sell him a completed film he would use it as evidence in his investigation. Plaintiff had no expectation of privacy.

Although plaintiff had not explicitly consented to being filmed, his conduct after being informed that a film was being made amounted to consent. But should the same rule apply if a jury could reasonably find that the model made her statement jokingly or sardonically so that a reasonable person in plaintiff's position would not have believed what she said?

The most common problems reporters face in consent cases appear to involve consents that are obtained by some type of misrepresentation. Since reporters often investigate alleged misdeeds they are unlikely to get consent to do interviews, go to certain places or record interviews if they identify themselves as reporters. In such cases, what is the role of consent?

In *Dietemann*, the reporters posed as a couple seeking medical advice from the plaintiff, who lived a quiet life and did not advertise or even have a telephone. They went to his gate and rang the bell. When plaintiff appeared, the reporters falsely said that they had been sent by a certain person and wanted to see plaintiff because the female visitor had a lump in her breast that she wanted diagnosed. Plaintiff admitted the pair to his den and made his diagnosis. On this part of the case the court observed:

> Plaintiff's den was a sphere from which he could reasonably expect to exclude eavesdropping newsmen. He invited two of defendant's employees to the den. One who invites another to his home or office takes a risk that the visitor may not be what he seems, and that the visitor may repeat all he hears and observes when he leaves. But he does not and should not be required to take the risk that what is heard and seen will be transmitted by photograph or recording . . ..

Why does plaintiff take the risk that a vistor may not be who he claims to be, or that a visitor may repeat what he hears inside, but not take the risk that secret recordings and photographs are being made? Is it that the plaintiff does in fact intend to deal with the persons who are standing before him—whatever names they give or whatever reasons they give for coming?

Courts generally rule that consent to enter one section of land does not authorize entering any other part; and that consent to do one thing, such as reading the gas meter, does not authorize removal of the gas meter. In these cases, it is apparent that the actor has exceeded the consent. In *Dietemann*, however, the plaintiff gave consent to enter the land and come to the den—and that is precisely what the reporters did. His misunderstanding about identity did not lead him to consent to one thing but to be hit with another. (A person who wants legal protection against someone who is told a secret and then reveals it may obtain it by entering into a contract in which the recipient makes legally enforceable promises about his future behavior.)

If misrepresenting identity doesn't raise major legal problems, it does raise ethical questions that are much discussed among journalists.

The matter is reviewed at length in Zimmerman, By Any Other Name
. . ., Washington Journalism Review (Nov./Dec. 1979) at 32.

The matter received much attention in 1979 when the Pulitzer prize
for local investigative reporting was denied to a newspaper that uncovered massive official corruption after it bought and ran a bar in Chicago
under a false name.   At about the same time, a reporter posed as a
Congressman to obtain a seat at the signing of the Egyptian-Israeli
peace treaty.   The reporter said that the episode involved telling "only
one lie."   *Editor & Publisher*, June 9, 1979 at 6, responded, "But *how
many lies* are too many?   Are we getting back to the no-holds-barred
philosophy that the story should be gotten at any cost?"   Noting that the
press complains loudly when someone impersonates a newsman, the
editorial continued, "We believe that newsmen's impersonations of
others in order to get a story [are] equally damaging to their believabili-
ty and should be scrupulously avoided."   Some have suggested that if
reporters will lie to get a story, readers may believe that they would also
lie in writing the story if they thought the matter important enough.

The argument the other way, of course, stresses that uncovering
crime or other misbehavior is very hard—that it would have been
virtually impossible to have demonstrated the corruption in Chicago
without setting up the fake business.   A recent example involved a
reporter who got a job as a guard at the Three Mile Island nuclear plant
after the malfunctioning and then took photographs while on the job.
His goal was to show how easy it was to get a job—his asserted
background and references were never checked—and to show how lax
security was inside the plant.   Are there other ways to obtain this
information?   How important is it to obtain the information?   Does such
behavior damage the credibility of the press?

For a former *New York Times* reporter's analysis of some of these
ethical issues, see Goldstein, *News At Any Cost: How Journalists
Compromise Their Ethics to Shape the News*, 1985.

Although civil actions by persons deceived in these cases may not be
likely, some of the cases may well involve potential criminal liability—
particularly cases involving impersonation of government officials or
lying to government officials.

Should different principles apply if reporters knowingly accept material improperly obtained by others?   In one case, aides to a United States
Senator removed numerous documents from his files, copied them, and
passed the copies to columnists who knew how they had been obtained.
The court held that the columnists had committed no tort:

> If we were to hold appellants liable for invasion of privacy on these
> facts, we would establish the proposition that no one who receives
> information from an intruder, knowing it has been obtained by
> improper intrusion, is guilty of a tort.   In an untried and developing
> area of tort law, we are not prepared to go so far.   A person
> approached by an eavesdropper with an offer to share in the
> information gathered through the eavesdropping would perhaps play

the nobler part should he spurn the offer and shut his ears. However, it seems to us that at this point it would place too great a strain on human weakness to hold one liable in damages who merely succumbs to temptation and listens. Pearson v. Dodd, 410 F.2d 701 (D.C.Cir.) certiorari denied 395 U.S. 947 (1969). Should the result change if a reporter had said to the aide "I'd sure love to see your file on" a particular matter—and three days later the aide presented the file?

*Defenses.* As discussed above, consent (if not exceeded) can be a defense for a suit for an intrusion on physical solitude. Such defamation defenses as truth and absence of malice have no relevance because neither falsity nor its cause is part of an intrusion suit. It should be noted specifically that newsworthiness is *not* a defense for intrusion: the fact that the public wants news is no justification for violating another's rights in order to obtain it.

### 3.  CRIMINAL LIABILITY

At several points during the foregoing discussion of civil liability, we have had occasion to touch on related criminal sanctions. In this section we draw together the likely sources of criminal liability that may confront newsgatherers.

At the outset, federal and state governments have statutes punishing such acts as the theft of government property and the concealment or removal of official records and documents. See, e.g., 18 U.S.C. §§ 641, 2071. In addition, conspiracy to commit criminal acts is also a crime. Other statutes directly relate to property or information in specific areas, such as national security or nuclear energy. Knowingly receiving stolen property may also be criminal even though the recipient had nothing to do with the original theft.

Other crimes involving direct harm to government may include impersonating an officer, not obeying a lawful order of a police officer, or bribing a government employee. The latter was involved when a news photographer paid a prison guard to take secret photographs of the accused killer known as "Son of Sam."

The government also uses criminal legislation to support the civil law in protecting individual property and privacy. We have seen some in operation already, such as the criminal punishment for intercepting communications whether by wiretapping or otherwise. Breaking into a home and stealing a photograph from the table would involve several criminal offenses as well as tort liability. Other protections are available. In one episode, a publisher was charged with extortion by allegedly threatening to write untrue stories about people in the community unless they supplied information for forthcoming stories or agreed to advertise in the paper.

In one case, reporters covering a demonstration at a construction site for a nuclear plant in Oklahoma were convicted of trespassing on

private property.  The utility, Public Service Company of Oklahoma
(PSO), did not want extensive coverage of the marchers—as had occurred at an earlier demonstration.  This time, PSO warned all reporters
that they would be arrested if they entered the fenced property at any
point not permitted by PSO.  PSO then set up a viewing area that
reporters might use on its otherwise closed property.  It was not clear in
advance whether the demonstration or any confrontation would be visible
from that point.

Several reporters used the viewing area.  Others followed the demonstrators and entered the land when the demonstrators went through
the fence.  These reporters were the ones convicted of trespass.  Each
was fined $25.

The Oklahoma Court of Criminal Appeals held that the First Amendment does not shield newspersons from state criminal prosecution in
their newsgathering function and affirmed the convictions.  Stahl v.
State, 665 P.2d 839 (Okl.Crim.1983), certiorari denied 464 U.S. 1069
(1984).

## B.  INVASION OF PRIVACY BY PUBLICATION

As indicated above, there are several ways the media may invade
privacy through the publication or dissemination of information rather
than through its gathering.

The idea that a right of privacy from the media should be legally
protected can be traced to a law review article by Louis D. Brandeis and
his law partner, Samuel D. Warren, The Right to Privacy, 4 Harv.L.Rev.
193 (1890), often considered the most influential law review article ever
published.  The authors, reacting to the editorial practices of Boston
newspapers, made clear their concerns:

> The press is overstepping in every direction the obvious bounds
> of propriety and of decency.  Gossip is no longer the resource of the
> idle and of the vicious, but has become a trade, which is pursued
> with industry as well as effrontery.  To satisfy a prurient taste the
> details of sexual relations are spread broadcast in the columns of the
> daily papers.  To occupy the indolent, column upon column is filled
> with idle gossip, which can only be procured by intrusion upon the
> domestic circle.

Working with a variety of rather remote precedents from other
areas of law, the authors developed an argument that courts should
recognize an action for invasion of privacy by media publication.

The theory was rejected in the first major case to consider it.  In
Roberson v. Rochester Folding Box Co., 171 N.Y. 538, 64 N.E. 442 (1902),
the defendants, a flour company and a box company, obtained a good
likeness of the plaintiff, a pretty girl, and reproduced it on their advertising posters.  Plaintiff said she was humiliated and suffered great
distress.  The court, 4–3, rejected a common law privacy action on
grounds that suggested concern about innovating after so many centu-

ries; an inability to see how the doctrine, once accepted, could be judicially limited to appropriate situations; and skepticism about finding liability for behavior that might actually please some potential "victims." The Warren and Brandeis article was discussed at length, but the court concluded that the precedents relied upon were too remote to sustain the proposed rights.

The outcry was immediate. At its next session, the New York legislature created a statutory right of privacy (New York Civil Rights Law, §§ 50 and 51). The basic provision was that "a person, firm or corporation that uses for advertising purposes, or the purposes of trade, the name, portrait or picture of any living person without having first obtained the written consent of such person, or if a minor or his or her parent or guardian, is guilty of a misdemeanor." The other section provided for an injunction and created an action for compensatory and punitive damages. The meaning of "advertising purposes" was clear, but the phrase "purposes of trade" was not self-explanatory. Eventually it came to mean that an accurate story carried as editorial (non-advertising) content did not violate the statute.

Other states, perhaps learning from the New York experience, slowly began to develop a common law right to privacy that was not influenced by statutory language and not limited to advertising invasions. In addition to an action for commercial use of one's name, the courts also developed actions for truthful uses of plaintiff's name that were thought to be outside the areas of legitimate public concern. The action for invasion of privacy by publication of true editorial material began to take hold during the 1920's and early 1930's.

Courts in the late 1930's became more attentive to the Supreme Court's expanding protection of expression. Operating on a common law level, they tended to expand protection for the media by taking a narrow view of what were legitimately private areas.

For the embarrassing private facts tort, the courts allowed a defense of newsworthiness to be expanded, because they were reluctant to impose normative standards of what should be newsworthy. Instead, they leaned toward a descriptive definition of newsworthiness that protected whatever editors had decided would interest their readers. By the 1960's some doubted whether the action for invasion of privacy had any remaining vitality.

It was precisely, during the last part of the 1960's and the beginning of the 1970's, however, that privacy as a general social value was perceived to be threatened in different ways by the encroachment of computers, data banks, and electronic devices, as well as the media. The concept of privacy also expanded as the Supreme Court dealt with birth control, abortion, and other problems in the context of a right of privacy. This was bound to have an impact on the media aspects of privacy as well.

One result of the new thinking was to broaden the area of privacy protection.

### 1.  Putting the Plaintiff in a False Light

As indicated earlier, the tort of putting the plaintiff in a false light in the public eye is the privacy tort closest to defamation, because both involve publication of falsity.  There is a critical difference between the two, however: the publication that results in a successful defamation action is *harmful* as well as false.  The publication that results in a successful false light invasion of privacy action may not be harmful in the sense of harming the plaintiff's reputation.  It may be just the opposite—a publication that falsely portrays the plaintiff to be better than he is in real life (i.e., a hero) or simply *different* than he is in real life.

In one example, a group used the plaintiff's name without authorization on a petition to the governor to veto a bill.  Although falsely stating that plaintiff had signed the petition would not be defamatory, the court found the situation actionable because it cast plaintiff in a false light.

The first two Supreme Court decisions involving alleged invasions of privacy by the mass media both happened to be false light cases.  They were Time, Inc. v. Hill, 385 U.S. 374 (1967) and Cantrell v. Forest City Publishing Co., 419 U.S. 245 (1974).

In 1952, James Hill and his family were held hostage in their Pennsylvania home for 19 hours by escaped convicts who apparently treated them decently.  The incident received nationwide coverage.  Thereafter the Hills moved to Connecticut, sought seclusion, and refused to make public appearances.  A novel—*The Desperate Hours*—modeled partially on the event was published the following year.  In 1955, *Life* magazine in a short article announced that a play and motion picture were being made from the novel, which they said was "inspired" by the Hill episode.  The play, "a heartstopping account of how a family rose to heroism in a crisis," would enable the public to see the Hill story "re-enacted."  Photographs showed actors performing scenes from the play at the house at which the original events had occurred.  The Hills claimed the story was inaccurate because the novel and play showed convicts committing violence on the father and uttering a "verbal sexual insult" at the daughter.

Suit was brought under the New York statute requiring plaintiff to show the article was being used for advertising purposes or purposes of trade.  A truthful article, no matter how unpleasant for the Hills, would not have been actionable.  The state courts had previously indicated that falsity would show that the article was really for the purposes of trade and not for public enlightenment.  The state courts allowed recovery after lengthy litigation.

The Supreme Court, by a fragile majority, decided that the privilege to comment on matters of public interest had constitutional protection and could not be lost by the introduction of falsity unless actual malice could be proved.  Thus, the Hill family lost.

The decision should be viewed in the context of what was happening in the court's defamation decisions in the same period. This was only three years after the Court had decided, in New York Times v. Sullivan, that public officials would be required to prove actual malice in defamation cases. By 1967 thinking, the members of the Hill family were public figures—having become so involuntarily as the result of having been part of a newsworthy event. And 1967 was the same year in which the Court extended the actual malice rule of Times v. Sullivan to public figures like Wally Butts and former Army General Edwin Walker.

One should not miss the irony that the attorney who represented the Hill family before the Supreme Court was a man with a strong sense of privacy and considerable distaste for the media: then former Vice President, not-yet-President Richard M. Nixon.

The next false-light privacy case decided by the Supreme Court was Cantrell v. Forest City Publishing Co. A reporter for *The Cleveland Plain Dealer* had written a prize-winning story about a bridge collapse that had killed 44 people, including Melvin Cantrell. Some months later the reporter returned to the Cantrell home for a follow-up on how the family coped with the disaster. Although Mrs. Cantrell was not present, her children were. The reporter's story failed to make clear that Mrs. Cantrell had been absent, and a reader presumably would have concluded just the opposite from the story, which said she "will talk neither about what happened nor about how they are doing. She wears the same mask of non-expression she wore at the funeral. She is a proud woman. Her world has changed. She says that after it happened, the people in town offered to help them out with money and they refused to take it." The family sought damages on a false-light privacy theory.

The Court, in an opinion by Justice Stewart, held that the First Amendment did not protect deliberate or reckless falsity. He also observed that because the actual malice standard was met in this case, it was not an appropriate case in which to consider the hypothetical question of whether private figure plaintiffs like the Cantrells *had* to prove actual malice or might merely be asked to prove simple negligence. As Justice Stewart put it, it was not an appropriate occasion to "consider whether a State may constitutionally apply a more relaxed standard of liability for a publisher . . . of false statements injurious to a private individual under a false-light theory of privacy, or whether the constitutional standard announced in Time, Inc. v. Hill applies to all false-light cases."

Justice Douglas was the sole dissenter in *Cantrell*: "Those who write the current news seldom have the objective, dispassionate point of view—or the time—of scientific analysts. They deal in fast-moving events and the need for 'spot reporting.' . . .. [I]n matters of public import such as the present news reporting, there must be freedom from damages lest the press be frightened into playing a more ignoble role than the Framers visualized."

The stories which resulted in the *Cantrell* and *Hill* cases purported to tell the truth. A different sort of false light problem arises in the context of "docudramas" and which openly mix fact and fiction. Actress Elizabeth Taylor held a nationally-publicized news conference to say she would sue ABC if it dared to broadcast a docudrama based on her life. Taylor v. ABC, 82 Civ. 6977, S.D.N.Y. The network cancelled the docudrama.

However, in Hicks v. Casablanca Records, 464 F.Supp. 426 (S.D.N.Y.1978), a motion picture and novel about an incident in the life of mystery-writer Agatha Christie was held to be protected under the First Amendment so long as it was not presented to be taken as true.

A particular problem for broadcasters is contextual false light, in which something truthful becomes misleading because of the context in which it is used. Broadcasters must be especially careful of using old file footage which viewers may mistake as current.

*Defenses.* Many of the same defenses that can be used by media defendants in defamation cases might also be argued to have application in a false-light privacy case. *Truth* would be a strong defense. Qualified privilege might be offered as a defense if one had quoted accurately from a record of an official proceeding. Privileged criticism or fair comment might work as a defense if the publication alleged to put the plaintiff in a false light was actually a statement of opinion rather than a statement of fact. If the plaintiff is a public official or public figure, absence of malice could be a strong defense. To a large extent, the applicability of the libel defenses in privacy cases is yet to be determined in the courts.

## 2.  PUBLICATION OF EMBARRASSING PRIVATE FACTS

Publication of embarrassing private facts (which we address in this section) and appropriation of another's name or likeness for commercial or trade purposes (which we address in the next section) are the two branches of invasion of privacy that have to do with truthful publication—either by electronic media or by print—that interferes with someone's right to be let alone. The former is of greater importance to journalism students; the latter is of greater importance to advertising and public relations students. Redundant though it may seem, it may be helpful to think of the former as publication of embarrassing private *true* facts.

### a.  *Categories*

The cases of publication of embarrassing private facts fall into a small number of categories—those dealing with sexual matters, commission of crime, poverty, idiosyncratic qualities, and other embarrassing stories.

The important point is not whether the state cases are decided "correctly." The area is so new and unformed that the cases do not fit into a neat pattern—except that plaintiffs rarely win. The results are given in capsule form at the end of each case, without reasons, simply to satisfy curiosity—not to suggest the proper resolution. Below, we will explore approaches to this very troublesome area. The law aside, prospective reporters and news directors should consider how the facts of each story should be handled.

*Sexual Matters.* 1. In a study of official misconduct at a county home, a newspaper reported that among the misconduct was the involuntary sterilization of a named 18-year-old young woman seven years earlier. Howard v. Des Moines Register and Tribune Co., 283 N.W.2d 289 (Iowa 1979), certiorari denied 445 U.S. 904 (1980) (case dismissed).

2. Television cameras went to the scene of a report that a man was threatening harm to his housekeeper's sister. The crew arrived and began filming as police led the stark-naked man from the house. In a news report the following evening, plaintiff's "buttocks and genitals were visible to television viewers for a time period of approximately eight-to-nine-tenths of one second." Taylor v. KTVB Inc., 96 Idaho 202, 525 P.2d 984 (1974) (case remanded to determine defendant's reasons for using the film; settled out of court).

3. A television station reported the identity of a deceased rape victim. Cox Broadcasting Corp. v. Cohn, 420 U.S. 469 (1975) (case is reported at p. 522, infra).

4. Plaintiff was kidnapped by her estranged husband and taken to an apartment. He forced her to disrobe and then beat her. Police came. Following the suicide of the husband, police hurried plaintiff from the apartment nude "save for a mere towel." Photographers on the scene took photographs and turned them over to defendant newspaper, which ran several of them. Cape Publications, Inc. v. Bridges, 423 So.2d 426 (Fla.App.1982), certiorari denied 464 U.S. 893 (1983) (judgment for $10,000 reversed on appeal and case dismissed).

5. A group of Pittsburgh Steeler fans urged a photographer from *Sports Illustrated* to take pictures of them. The photographer did so. From among many photographs available for use, the editors chose one that showed the plaintiff with his fly open. Neff v. Time, Inc., 406 F.Supp. 858 (W.D.Pa.1976) (case dismissed).

6. A newspaper columnist included the following item: "More education stuff: The students at the College of Alameda will be surprised to learn that their student body president, Toni Diaz, is no lady, but is in fact a man whose real name is Antonio.

"Now I realize, that in these times, such a matter is no big deal, but I suspect his female classmates in P.E. 97 may wish to make other showering arrangements." The plaintiff, who had had sex change surgery, won a $775,000 judgment at the trial court, which thought the amount was not excessive. Diaz v. Oakland Tribune, Inc., 139 Cal.App. 3d 118, 188 Cal.Rptr. 762 (1983) (reversed on appeal and remanded for new trial; parties settled).

7. During an assassination attempt on President Ford in San Francisco, Oliver Sipple knocked the arm of the assailant as she sought to aim a second shot at the President. Sipple was the object of extensive media attention, including stories that identified him as homosexual. Sipple, asserting that relatives who lived in the Midwest did not know of his orientation, sued the *San Francisco Chronicle*. The newspaper defended in part on the argument that privacy was not involved because Sipple had marched in gay parades and had acknowledged that at least 100 to 500 people in San Francisco knew he was homosexual. The newspaper argued that his sexual orientation was relevant to the story because, although some stereotyped gays as sissies, Sipple was an ex-marine who acted heroically. The court held that the newspaper articles' references to Sipple's homosexuality did not constitute unlawful public disclosure of private facts, because Sipple's sexual orientation was well known and the articles about him were of legitimate public interest. Sipple v. Chronicle Publishing, 154 Cal.App.3d 1040, 201 Cal.Rptr. 665 (1984).

*Prison and Criminal Behavior.*    8. Plaintiff was arrested for drunk driving. At the police station, he was "hitting and banging on his cell door, hollering and cursing from the time of his arrest" until five hours later. A local broadcaster taped some of the noise and played excerpts from it on the radio. Holman v. Central Arkansas Broadcasting Co., 610 F.2d 542 (8th Cir.1979) (case dismissed).

9. A newspaper reproduced the front page of a 1952 edition as part of its regular feature called "Page from Our Past." The page contained an article about the cattle theft trial of three brothers who asserted that the 25-year-old matter was no longer of public concern and that they had been law-abiding and hard working citizens of the community, and had ultimately received full pardons. Roshto v. Hebert, 439 So.2d 428 (La. 1983). (Judgment for plaintiffs reversed on appeal and case dismissed.)

*Poverty.*    10. A newspaper article included a front-page photograph of the plaintiff's home. The photograph was one of a series on the newspaper's hometown and its environs. The caption read, "one of Crowley's stately homes, a bit weatherworn and unkempt, stands in the shadow of a spreading oak." Jaubert v. Crowley Post-Signal, Inc., 375 So.2d 1386 (La.1979) (case dismissed).

*Idiosyncrasies.*    11. *The New Yorker* magazine did one of its extensive profiles on a man who, 27 years earlier, had been an 11-year-old child prodigy who had lectured to mathematicians. For the last 20 years, however, he had lived as unobtrusively as possible. The profile reported that the plaintiff was living in a hall bedroom in Boston's "shabby south end," that his room was untidy, that he had a curious laugh, that he collected street car transfers, and that he was interested at the moment in the lore of the Okamakammessett Indians. The article was "merciless in its dissection of intimate details of its subject's personal life" and a "ruthless exposure of a once public character who has since sought and has now been deprived of the seclusion of private

life." Sidis v. F–R Publishing Corp., 113 F.2d 806 (2d Cir.1940), certiorari denied 311 U.S. 711 (1940) (case dismissed).

12. *Sports Illustrated* planned an article about a California beach
reputed to be the world's most dangerous site for body surfing. Plaintiff, known as the most daring surfer at the site, was interviewed and
was referred to in the story as one who extinguished cigarettes in his
mouth, ate spiders and other insects, dove head first down a flight of
stairs, had never learned to read, and was perceived by other surfers as
"abnormal." (Although plaintiff had once consented to be interviewed,
he withdrew the consent when he learned the shape the story would
take. The court rejected the defense of consent.) Virgil v. Time, Inc.,
527 F.2d 1122 (9th Cir.1975), certiorari denied 425 U.S. 998 (1976)
(affirming denial of summary judgment, two justices dissenting).

*Embarrassment or Ridicule.* 13. A newspaper article reported
that the basketball team at the state university was in trouble because
four named players, of the eight who were returning, "are on academic
probation and in danger of flunking." Bilney v. Evening Star Newspaper Co., 43 Md.App. 560, 406 A.2d 652 (1979) (case dismissed).

14. Plaintiff was a janitor who found $240,000 that had fallen from
an armored car. He returned it (and received a reward of $10,000), to
the scorn of his neighbors and his children's friends. When their hostile
reaction was reported, he received many congratulatory messages, including one from President Kennedy. The full story was reported in a
periodical and reprinted in a college English textbook. Johnson v.
Harcourt, Brace, Jovanovich, Inc., 43 Cal.App.3d 880, 118 Cal.Rptr. 370
(1974) (case dismissed).

### b. Legal Analysis

As the law has been developing, the plaintiff must show that the
information made public was in fact "private," that the disclosure would
be "highly offensive to a reasonable person," and that the revelation was
not newsworthy. We look at each element in turn.

*Private Information.* The courts have not been very attentive to
this aspect of the matter—perhaps because in most cases the information
is clearly something that the plaintiff has held closely and did not want
bandied about. Our examples ranged from one extreme to the other.
The plaintiff in the sex-change case had not publicized the surgery. On
the other hand, private facts are unlikely to exist as to the exterior of a
home, when someone at a football game with his fly open poses for a
professional photographer, or when someone at a police station shouts so
loudly that others cannot help but hear what is said.

Between these extremes we have cases like that of Oliver Sipple,
whose sexual orientation was not a secret among his friends and his
immediate community, and who was willing to march in gay parades, but
who wanted the information kept inside San Francisco. Although some
cases should be eliminated on the ground that the information published

had not been "private" at the time of the publication, most do seem to involve matters that most people would attempt to keep secret.

*"Highly Offensive to a Reasonable Person."* This formulation has received much more attention. Although the specific language is taken from the Restatement of Torts (Second) § 652D, similar expressions have been used in the cases during this tort's development. The single most important consideration appears to be the substance of the statement. In some cases it appears difficult to argue that the revelation would be highly offensive to a reasonable person—as in the case of the janitor who returned the money he found, even though some members of plaintiff's community criticized his behavior. It would also apply to the "weather-worn and unkempt" house. Perhaps a similar analysis would apply to the cases involving idiosyncrasies—the body surfer and the child prodigy. Even though the article about the prodigy was described as "merciless in its dissection of intimate details of its subject's personal life," perhaps what was revealed would not be highly offensive to a reasonable person. That some people may wish to keep private some of their quirks is not the same as saying that reasonable people would find the revelation of that information to be highly offensive.

It is no coincidence that the cases commonly involve sexual, health, and financial topics that are generally thought to involve the most intimate matters. Another area has involved revelations about rehabilitated criminals. As we shall see, simply showing that the revelation would be highly offensive to a reasonable person does not guarantee that the defendant will be held liable for an invasion of privacy. It is, however, an essential first step.

Note that no complex damage rules, such as exist in defamation, have emerged in privacy. The plaintiff who can successfully demonstrate an invasion of privacy will recover damages measured by the emotional harm suffered. Obviously, damages here cannot rehabilitate the plaintiff in the way that damages in defamation might pay for the reputational harm caused by the false statement.

*"Newsworthiness"* or *"Legitimate Concern" Defense.* In addition to requiring that the publicized matter be private and "highly offensive to a reasonable person," the courts demand that the matter be "not of legitimate concern to the public." Most litigation has revolved around this or similar phrases, such as claims that the article in question was "newsworthy" or that it was of "general or public concern." It should be emphasized at the outset that this requirement exists under state common law and has been applied with greater or lesser rigor in every major state case in which a privacy claim has been raised.

As noted in the introduction to this section, there was a period in which the courts seemed to treat "newsworthy" or "of legitimate concern" as descriptive terms. Any article appearing in a newspaper would meet that requirement because if an editor chose to include it, it must be newsworthy. Such an approach would soon eliminate the privacy action. More recently, the courts have shifted and now attempt to develop normative guidelines to determine when the information might be of "legitimate concern to the public."

Although the public figure definitions in libel are not used in privacy, an important distinction here too is between voluntary and involuntary public figures. It should not be surprising that those who seek the public limelight should be thought to have a lesser claim to privacy protection than those brought into the glare of publicity simply because they are either the unfortunate victims of an accident or crime or are otherwise swept up in an event. But even involuntary subjects are not immune. As a comment to the Restatement puts it:

> These persons are regarded as properly subject to the public interest, and publishers are permitted to satisfy the curiosity of the public as to its heroes, leaders, villains and victims, and those who are closely associated with them. As in the case of the voluntary public figure, the authorized publicity is not limited to the event that itself arouses the public interest, and to some extent includes publicity given to facts about the individual that would otherwise be purely private.

One should note the categorization of voluntary and involuntary public figures and private figures in post-*Gertz* libel law. In libel one assumes that one *must* be voluntary to be public; in privacy, however, one can be involuntarily drawn into the public eye.

Our examples include a variety of plaintiffs. The body surfer has voluntarily brought himself into the public eye by his prowess, his continued attendance at a particular beach, and his engaging in a particular type of activity. Sidis, who may have been a voluntary public figure at age 11 and in his teens, later sought obscurity—but the public has a legitimate concern with what happens to prodigies in later life. Is there a similar concern with criminals? Others "voluntarily" become public figures on the spur of the moment—as when Sipple knocked the arm of the President's assailant or when Johnson returned the money he found in the street. Most of our examples, however, involved involuntary public figures—those who wished to keep their sterilization private, and in no other way had been voluntarily in the public spotlight.

Although courts sometimes suggest that the distinction is relevant to the decision, the difference is at most a matter of degree and more often may control the question of whether the editor will choose to name the person in the story. As a practical matter, a voluntary public figure who is involved in an accident or other misfortune is much more likely to be named in any story that results from the episode than is a previously anonymous person. Those who seek the limelight risk having their names used in unwanted contexts. But this does not mean that every aspect of their lives, or that no aspects of the lives of involuntary figures, may be revealed. The Restatement seeks to draw a line in the following comment:

> Permissible publicity to information concerning either voluntary or involuntary public figures is not limited to the particular events

that arouse the interest of the public. That interest, once aroused by the event, may legitimately extend, to some reasonable degree, to further information concerning the individual and to facts about him, which are not public and which, in the case of one who had not become a public figure, would be regarded as an invasion of his purely private life. Thus the life history of one accused of murder, together with such heretofore private facts as may throw some light upon what kind of person he is, his possible guilt or innocence, or his reasons for committing the crime, are a matter of legitimate public interest. . . . On the same basis the home life and daily habits of a motion picture actress may be of legitimate and reasonable interest to the public that sees her on the screen.

The extent of the authority to make public private facts is not, however, unlimited. There may be some intimate details of her life, such as sexual relations, which even the actress is entitled to keep to herself. In determining what is a matter of legitimate public interest, account must be taken of the customs and conventions of the community; and in the last analysis what is proper becomes a matter of the community mores. The line is to be drawn when the publicity ceases to be the giving of information to which the public is entitled, and becomes a morbid and sensational prying into private lives for its own sake, with which a reasonable member of the public, with decent standards, would say that he had no concern. The limitations, in other words, are those of common decency, having due regard to the freedom of the press and its reasonable leeway to choose what it will tell the public, but also due regard to the feelings of the individual and the harm that will be done to him by the exposure. Some reasonable proportion is also to be maintained between the event or activity that makes the individual a public figure and the private facts to which publicity is given. Revelations that may properly be made concerning a murderer or the President of the United States would not be privileged if they were to be made concerning one who is merely injured in an automobile accident.

### c. Constitutional Privilege Defense

The Supreme Court of the United States has not been called upon frequently in this area because the state courts, operating at common law, have tended to protect the press. Because they have prevailed under state law, the media defendants rarely have needed recourse to the Supreme Court to assert constitutional rights. In *Cox*, the case of the naming of a deceased rape victim, however, the state court ruled that the plaintiffs were entitled to a judgment. The broadcaster's appeal led to the first, and still the only, Supreme Court decision in this area.

## COX BROADCASTING CORP. v. COHN
Supreme Court of the United States, 1975.
420 U.S. 469, 95 S.Ct. 1029, 43 L.Ed.2d 328.

[Mr. Cohn's 17-year-old daughter was raped in Georgia and did not survive the occurrence. In Georgia it was a misdemeanor for "any news media or any other person to print and publish, broadcast, televise or disseminate through any other medium of public dissemination . . . the name or identity of any female who may have been raped. . . ." Ga. Code Ann. § 26–9901. Similar statutes exist in a few other states. The girl was not identified at the time. Eight months later, appellant's reporter, Wassell, also an appellant, attended a hearing for the six youths charged with the rape and murder. He learned the girl's name by inspecting the indictment in the courtroom. His report naming the girl was telecast.

The Georgia Supreme Court held that the complaint stated a common law action for damages for invasion of the father's own privacy. Defendant's First Amendment argument was rejected on the ground that the statute was an authoritative declaration that Georgia considered a rape victim's name not to be a matter of public concern. The court could discern "no public interest or general concern about the identity of the victim of such a crime as will make the right to disclose the identity of the victim rise to the level of First Amendment protection."

On appeal, the Supreme Court first decided that the decision below was a "final" judgment so as to give the court jurisdiction. The Court then turned to the First Amendment issue.]

MR. JUSTICE WHITE delivered the opinion of the Court.

. . .

Georgia stoutly defends both § 26–9901 and the State's common-law privacy action challenged here. Her claims are not without force, for powerful arguments can be made, and have been made, that however it may be ultimately defined, there *is* a zone of privacy surrounding every individual, a zone within which the State may protect him from intrusion by the press, with all its attendant publicity. Indeed, the central thesis of the root article by Warren and Brandeis, The Right to Privacy, 4 Harv.L.Rev. 193, 196 (1890), was that the press was overstepping its prerogatives by publishing essentially private information and that there should be a remedy for the alleged abuses.

More compellingly, the century has experienced a strong tide running in favor of the so-called right of privacy. . . .

. . . Because the gravamen of the claimed injury is the publication of information, whether true or not, the dissemination of what is embarrassing or otherwise painful to an individual, it is here that claims of privacy most directly confront the constitutional freedoms of speech and press. The face-off is apparent, and the appellants urge upon us the broad holding that the press may not be made criminally or civilly liable for publishing information that is neither false nor misleading but absolutely accurate, however damaging it may be to reputation or individual sensibilities.

. . .

Rather than address the broader question whether truthful publications may ever be subjected to civil or criminal liability consistently with the First and Fourteenth Amendments, or to put it another way, whether the State may ever define and, protect an area of privacy free from unwanted publicity in the press, it is appropriate to focus on the narrower interface between press and privacy that this case presents, namely, whether the State may impose sanctions on the accurate publication of the name of a rape victim obtained from public records—more specifically, from judicial records which are maintained in connection with a public prosecution and which themselves are open to public inspection. We are convinced that the State may not do so.

In the first place, in a society in which each individual has but limited time and resources with which to observe at first hand the operations of his government, he relies necessarily upon the press to bring to him in convenient form the facts of those operations. Great responsibility is accordingly placed upon the news media to report fully and accurately the proceedings of government, and official records and documents open to the public are the basic data of governmental operations. Without the information provided by the press most of us and many of our representatives would be unable to vote intelligently or to register opinions on the administration of government generally. With respect to judicial proceedings in particular, the function of the press serves to guarantee the fairness of trials and to bring to bear the beneficial effects of public scrutiny upon the administration of justice. See Sheppard v. Maxwell, 384 U.S. 333, 350 (1966).

Appellee has claimed in this litigation that the efforts of the press have infringed his right to privacy by broadcasting to the world the fact that his daughter was a rape victim. The commission of crime, prosecutions resulting from it, and judicial proceedings arising from the prosecution, however, are without question events of legitimate concern to the public and consequently fall within the responsibility of the press to report the operations of government.

The special protected nature of accurate reports of judicial proceedings has repeatedly been recognized. This Court, in an opinion written by Mr. Justice Douglas, has said:

"A trial is a public event. What transpires in the court room is public property. If a transcript of the court proceedings had been published, we suppose none would claim that the judge could punish the publisher for contempt. And we can see no difference though the conduct of the attorneys, of the jury, or even of the judge himself, may have reflected on the court. *Those who see and hear what transpired can report it with impunity.* There is no special perquisite of the judiciary which enables it, as distinguished from other institutions of democratic government, to suppress, edit, or censor events which transpire in proceedings before it." Craig v. Harney, 331 U.S. 367, 374 (1947) (emphasis added).

. . .

The developing law surrounding the tort of invasion of privacy recognizes a privilege in the press to report the events of judicial proceedings. The Warren and Brandeis article, supra, noted that the proposed new right would be limited in the same manner as actions for libel and slander where such a publication was a privileged communication: "the right to privacy is not invaded by any publication made in a court of justice . . . and (at least in many jurisdictions) reports of any such proceedings would in some measure be accorded a like privilege."

. . .

Thus, even the prevailing law of invasion of privacy generally recognizes that the interests in privacy fade when the information involved already appears on the public record. The conclusion is compelling when viewed in terms of the First and Fourteenth Amendments and in light of the public interest in a vigorous press. The Georgia cause of action for invasion of privacy through public disclosure of the name of a rape victim imposes sanctions on pure expression—the content of a publication—and not conduct or a combination of speech and non-speech elements that might otherwise be open to regulation or prohibition. See United States v. O'Brien, 391 U.S. 367, 376–377 (1968). The publication of truthful information available on the public record contains none of the indicia of those limited categories of expression, such as "fighting" words, which "are no essential part of any exposition of ideas, and are of such slight social value as a step to truth that any benefit that may be derived from them is clearly outweighed by the social interest in order and morality." Chaplinsky v. New Hampshire, 315 U.S. 568, 572 (1942) (footnote omitted).

By placing the information in the public domain on official court records, the State must be presumed to have concluded that the public interest was thereby being served. Public records by their very nature are of interest to those concerned with the administration of government, and a public benefit is performed by the reporting of the true contents of the records by the media. The freedom of the press to publish that information appears to us to be of critical importance to our type of government in which the citizenry is the final judge of the proper conduct of public business. In preserving that form of government the First and Fourteenth Amendments command nothing less than that the States may not impose sanctions on the publication of truthful information contained in official court records open to public inspection.

We are reluctant to embark on a course that would make public records generally available to the media but forbid their publication if offensive to the sensibilities of the supposed reasonable man. Such a rule would make it very difficult for the media to inform citizens about the public business and yet stay within the law. The rule would invite timidity and self-censorship and very likely lead to the suppression of many items that would otherwise be published and that should be made available to the public. At the very least, the First and Fourteenth Amendments will not allow exposing the press to liability for truthfully publishing information released to the public in official court records. If there are privacy interests to be protected in judicial proceedings, the States must respond by means which avoid public documentation or other exposure of private information. Their political institutions must weigh the interests in privacy with the interests of the public to know and of the press to publish.[26] Once true information is disclosed in public court documents open to public inspection, the press cannot be sanctioned for publishing it. In this instance as in others reliance must rest upon the judgment of those who decide what to publish or broadcast. See Miami Herald Pub. Co. v. Tornillo, 418 U.S., at 258.

Appellant Wassell based his televised report upon notes taken during the court proceedings and obtained the name of the victim from the indictments handed to him at his request during a recess in the hearing. Appellee has not contended that the name was obtained in an improper fashion or that it was not on an official court document open to public inspection. Under these circumstances, the protection of freedom of the press provided by the First and Fourteenth Amendments bars the State of Georgia from making appellants' broadcast the basis of civil liability.[27]

Reversed.

MR. CHIEF JUSTICE BURGER concurs in the judgment.

MR. JUSTICE POWELL, concurring.

. . .

MR. JUSTICE DOUGLAS, concurring.

On the merits, . . . there is no power on the part of the government to suppress or penalize the publication of "news of the day."

MR. JUSTICE REHNQUIST, dissenting.

Because I am of the opinion that the decision which is the subject of this appeal is not a [reviewable] "final" judgment or decree, . . . I would dismiss this appeal for want of jurisdiction.

### Notes and Questions

1. What issues does the majority opinion avoid deciding? Why do you think the majority took the approach it did?

26. We mean to imply nothing about any constitutional questions which might arise from a state policy not allowing access by the public and press to various kinds of official records, such as records of juvenile court proceedings.

27. Appellants have contended that whether they derived the information in question from public records or instead through their own investigation, the First and Fourteenth Amendments bar any sanctions from being imposed by the State because of the publication. Because appellants have prevailed on more limited grounds, we need not address this broader challenge to the validity of § 26–9901 and of Georgia's right of action for public disclosure.

2.  On the importance of the passage of time, consider this comment to Restatement, Second § 652D:

> The fact that there has been a lapse of time, even of considerable length, since the event that has made the plaintiff a public figure, does not of itself defeat the authority to give him publicity or to renew publicity when it has formerly been given.  Past events and activities may still be of legitimate interest to the public, and a narrative reviving recollection of what has happened even many years ago may be both interesting and valuable for purposes of information and education.  Such a lapse of time is, however, a factor to be considered, with other facts, in determining whether the publicity goes to unreasonable lengths in revealing facts about one who has resumed the private, lawful and unexciting life led by the great bulk of the community . . ..  Again the question is to be determined upon the basis of community standards and mores.  Although lapse of time may not impair the authority to give publicity to a public record, the pointing out of the present location and identity of the individual raises a quite different problem.

Is this passage consistent with the Cox case?  Does it help analyze the problem of Sidis, the child prodigy?  Consider *Roshto*, p. 517, supra.

3.  The principal opinion in *Howard*, the involuntary sterilization case, p. 516, supra, responded to the argument that plaintiff's name was unnecessary as follows:

> Here the disclosure of plaintiff's involuntary sterilization was closely related to the subject matter of the news story.  It documented the article's theme of maladministration and patient abuses at the Jasper County Home. . . .

> In the sense of serving an appropriate news function, the disclosure contributed constructively to the impact of the article.  It offered a personalized frame of reference to which the reader could relate, fostering perception and understanding.  Moreover, it lent specificity and credibility to the report.

> In this way the disclosure served as an effective means of accomplishing the intended news function.  It had positive communicative value in attracting the reader's attention to the article's subject matter and in supporting expression of the underlying theme.

> Examined in the light of the first amendment, we do not believe the disclosure could reasonably be held to be devoid of news value. [   ]

> Assuming, as plaintiff argues, the newspaper had a right to print an article that documented extrastatutory involuntary sterilizations at the Jasper County Home, the editors also had a right to buttress the force of their evidence by naming names.  We do not say it was necessary for them to do so, but we are certain they had a

right to treat the identity of victims of involuntary sterilizations as matters of legitimate public concern.  .  .  .

This is a far cry from embarrassing people by exposing their medical conditions or treatment when identity can add nothing to the probity of the account. [  ]

The disclosure of plaintiff's identity in this case could not reasonably be viewed as the spreading of gossip solely for its own sake.  .  .  .

Would *Cox* reach the same result?

4.  In Virgil v. Time, Inc., involving the body surfer, the publisher, citing *Cox*, argued in its brief that the First Amendment protected almost all true statements from liability:

> A press which must depend upon a governmental determination as to what facts are of 'public interest' in order to avoid liability for their truthful publication is not free at all.  .  .  .  A constitutional rule can be fashioned which protects all the interests involved. This goal is achieved by providing a privilege for truthful publications which is defeasible only when the court concludes as a matter of law that the truthful publication complained of constitutes a clear abuse of the editor's constitutional discretion to publish and discuss subjects and facts which in his judgment are matters of public interest.

The court rejected the argument and adopted the view of the Restatement (Second) of Torts, that liability may be imposed if the matter published is "not of legitimate concern to the public." Then the court relied on a passage from the Restatement that was quoted earlier in this section—that "in the last analysis what is proper becomes a matter of the community mores."

In libel and obscenity cases juries utilize community standards, and the court thought they should do so here, too, "subject to close judicial scrutiny to ensure that the jury resolutions comport with First Amendment principles." What is the difference between *Time's* position and that adopted by the court? Is the court's view consistent with *Cox*? Over the dissents of Justices Brennan and Stewart, the Supreme Court denied certiorari in *Virgil*. 425 U.S. 998 (1976). The case was remanded for trial.

On remand, the trial judge held that the magazine was entitled to summary judgment. First, the judge concluded that the facts revealed were not "highly offensive." Even if they were, the facts were "included as a legitimate journalistic attempt to explain Virgil's extremely daring and dangerous style of body surfing at the Wedge. There is no possibility that a juror would conclude that the personal facts were included for any inherent morbid, sensational, or curiosity appeal they might have." Virgil v. Sports Illustrated, 424 F.Supp. 1286 (S.D.Cal 1976).

5.  Although the courts have tended to take this area case-by-case, editors complain that such an approach breeds intolerable uncertainty.

An editor must decide today what might happen in court in several years—and the standards are said to be vague. What will be found "highly offensive to a reasonable person" or to violate "community standards and mores"? Juries given these questions may punish unpopular broadcasters and publishers.

Compare this situation with that confronting an editor in the defamation area. There the editor, with advice from lawyers, must decide whether the *Times* or *Gertz* rule applies and then decide whether the publication's conduct meets that standard. And truth is always a defense. Do you see a sharp difference between the editor's position there and where the case involves privacy?

6. The 1980's have seen some embarrassing private facts cases brought under the principle of infliction of emotional distress or "outrage." An example is Hyde v. City of Columbia, 637 S.W.2d 251 (Mo.App.1982), certiorari denied 459 U.S. 1226 (1983), in which the complaining witness in an abduction sued reporters, newspapers, and the municipality after being identified in the press and then terrorized by the criminal defendant. A dismissal of the claim was reversed by the appellate court.

### d. *Enjoining Violations of Privacy*

Many commentators have observed that damages in defamation are a more adequate remedy than in truthful invasion of privacy cases. In defamation the award of damages, especially special damages, may compensate the plaintiff for a loss of reputation that has in fact injured him financially. Even a judgment for nominal damages may have a vital symbolic function. In privacy, however, once the invasion has occurred the embarrassing truth is out and a judgment or an award of money does not resurrect a sullied reputation or undo other harm caused by the publication. Counterattack and counterspeech are not useful here.

Thus, courts have looked more seriously at alternatives in privacy suits and have been somewhat more responsive to a plea for an injunction to prevent the utterance of the invasion in the first place. Often the plaintiff learns about the invasion only after actual broadcast or publication, but in some situations prevention is feasible. Because the privacy action is so recent in origin, it lacks a long history like that of defamation. In the latter, the injunction came to be totally rejected in actions for private defamations.

The Supreme Court has never passed on the constitutionality of injunctions in this area. Despite three cases taken on appeal, the Court has yet to come to grips with the issue. In the first, a famous baseball player persuaded the New York courts to enjoin the publication of an unauthorized biography that contained false dialogue. Spahn v. Julian Messner, Inc., 21 N.Y.2d 124, 286 N.Y.S.2d 832, 233 N.E.2d 840 (1967). The defendants compromised and settled their dispute while it was being appealed to the Supreme Court.

The second chance came in a case involving a motion picture about conditions in a Massachusetts institution for the criminally insane. The state court barred showing of the picture except to selected groups because of the producer's invasion of the privacy of the inmates, assertedly in violation of an agreement he signed in order to get permission to make the film. Commonwealth v. Wiseman, 356 Mass. 251, 249 N.E.2d 610 (1969). The Supreme Court denied certiorari to Wiseman, the producer, 398 U.S. 960 (1969), over the lengthy dissent of Justice Harlan, joined by Justices Douglas and Brennan:

> Petitioners seek review in this Court of a decision of the Massachusetts Supreme Judicial Court enjoining the commercial distribution to general audiences of the film "Titticut Follies." Petitioners' film is a "documentary" of life in Bridgewater State Hospital for the criminally insane. Its stark portrayal of patient routine and treatment of the inmates is at once a scathing indictment of the inhumane conditions that prevailed at the time of the film and an undeniable infringement of the privacy of the inmates filmed, who are shown nude and engaged in acts that would unquestionably embarrass an individual of normal sensitivity. . . .

> The balance between these two interests, that of the individual's privacy and the public's right to know about conditions in public institutions, is not one that is easily struck, particularly in a case like that before us where the importance of the issue is matched by the extent of the invasion of privacy. . . .

The third Supreme Court case involved a claim by a former patient trying to enjoin her analyst from publishing a book the analyst had written about the patient's treatment. Although names and other facts were changed in the book, plaintiff alleged that she and her family were easily identifiable. The state courts granted a preliminary injunction enjoining all distribution until the litigation concluded. The defendants, including the book's publisher, sought certiorari, claiming that the injunction against publishing concededly true statements of medical and scientific importance violated the First Amendment. The Court granted certiorari, Roe v. Doe, 417 U.S. 907 (1974), and heard oral arguments. It then decided not to decide the case by dismissing the writ of certiorari as having been "improvidently granted." 420 U.S. 307 (1975). The complication of the confidential relationship between the parties and the murky record caused by the use of Does and Roes might have dissuaded the Court from deciding the case.

The case then went to trial on the merits. The trial judge found that the plaintiff was entitled to a remedy because of defendant's violation of an implied agreement to treat the plaintiff in confidence. He awarded damages for the harm plaintiff suffered from the release of 220 copies of the book before the preliminary injunction was issued. He also permanently enjoined distribution of the remaining stock. Doe v. Roe, 93 Misc. 2d 201, 400 N.Y.S.2d 668 (1977). By subsequent order, the remaining volumes were destroyed.

In 1976, a television crew entered an institution for the care of neglected children and filmed some of the children.  Questions "which could fairly be described as leading or suggestive were directed to the children with respect to drugs, assaults, etc. to which the children responded."  The institutions director sought to enjoin the televising of the film.  The trial judge denied a preliminary injunction and vacated his temporary restraining order, but granted a stay pending appeal.  The appellate court concluded after viewing the film that they were "not persuaded that its sole or even its chief object is to provide information which could lead to a correction of the conditions it claims exists." Nonetheless, nothing in the film warranted a ban on its showing.  If appropriate, the defendants could be "called to account" after the fact. Quinn v. Johnson, 51 A.D.2d 391, 381 N.Y.S.2d 875 (1976).  At this point, the case was resolved when the broadcaster decided that it could blur the faces of the children to make them unrecognizable.  One newspaper noted, "Here was a case where the large principle against prior restraint or censorship was upheld; and yet, where a humane judgment could be made at the same time.  Nothing in the First Amendment prevents the exercise of good taste and compassion."  New York Times, May 10, 1976 at 26.

How might one analyze the competing interests in these invasion of privacy cases when the issue becomes one of a remedy for a true statement that is adjudged an invasion?  How do these cases square with concern about prior restraint?

### 3.  APPROPRIATION

The fourth branch of invasion of privacy is appropriation of another's name or likeness for commercial or trade purposes.  Its major impact is on the field of advertising, because news reports have generally been held not to be "for commercial or trade purposes."  But see Zacchini v. Scripps-Howard Broadcasting, infra.  As is the case with other branches of invasion of privacy, truth is not a defense.  A manufacturer who advertises that John Smith uses his product may not be able to defend himself merely by proving that John Smith does use his product, although that is important for other reasons.

What must be demonstrated to avoid a successful appropriation action is consent.  This usually comes in the form of a written "release" since many states require that consent to appropriation be written. Indeed, it is common for advertising agencies and even news organizations to have standard release forms available for use.  Many release forms are limited in that they restrict the uses that can be made of a particular name or likeness or the period of time during which the use will be permitted.  Numerous appropriation cases have been the result of using a picture in a manner not covered by the original release.

Determining what constitutes commercial or trade purposes has not always proved easy for the courts.  In one case, a television station that telephoned a couple during the program "Dialing for Dollars," and aired the ensuing conversation found itself liable for appropriation. Does the following case offer any guidance?

### ZACCHINI v. SCRIPPS–HOWARD BROADCASTING CO.

Supreme Court of the United States, 1977.
433 U.S. 562, 97 S.Ct. 2849, 53 L.Ed.2d 965.

Mr. Justice White delivered the opinion of the Court.

Petitioner, Hugo Zacchini, is an entertainer. He performs a "human cannonball" act in which he is shot from a cannon into a net some 200 feet away. Each performance occupies some 15 seconds. In August and September 1972, petitioner was engaged to perform his act on a regular basis at the Geauga County Fair in Burton, Ohio. He performed in a fenced area, surrounded by grandstands, at the fair grounds. Members of the public attending the fair were not charged a separate admission fee to observe his act.

On August 2, a freelance reporter for Scripps-Howard Broadcasting Co., the operator of a television broadcasting station and respondent in this case, attended the fair. He carried a small movie camera. Petitioner noticed the reporter and asked him not to film the performance. The reporter did not do so on that day; but on the instructions of the producer of respondent's daily newscast, he returned the following day and videotaped the entire act. This film clip, approximately 15 seconds in length, was shown on the 11 o'clock news program that night, together with favorable commentary.[1]

Petitioner then brought this action for damages, alleging that he is "engaged in the entertainment business," that the act he performs is one "invented by his father and  .  .  .  performed only by his family for the last fifty years," that respondent "showed and commercialized the film of his act without his consent," and that such conduct was an "unlawful appropriation of plaintiff's professional property." App. 4–5. Respondent answered and moved for summary judgment, which was granted by the trial court.

.   .   .

.   .   .   Insofar as the Ohio Supreme Court held that the First and Fourteenth Amendments of the United States Constitution required judgment for respondent, we reverse the judgment of that court.

.   .   .

Even if the judgment in favor of respondent must nevertheless be understood as ultimately resting on Ohio law, it appears that at the very least the Ohio court felt compelled by what it understood to be federal

---

1. The script of the commentary accompanying the film clip read as follows: [Indent] "This .  .  . now .  .  . is the story of a *true spectator* sport .  .  . the sport of human cannonballing .  .  . in fact, the great *Zacchini* is about the only human cannonball around, these days .  .  . just happens that, *where* he is, is the Great Geauga County Fair, in Burton .  .  . and believe me, although it's not a *long* act, it's a thriller .  .  . and you really need to see it *in person* .  .  . to appreciate it. .  .  ." (Emphasis in original.)

constitutional considerations to construe and apply its own law in the manner it did.  In this event, we have jurisdiction and should decide the federal issue;  for if the state court erred in its understanding of our cases and of the First and Fourteenth Amendments we should so declare, leaving the state court free to decide the privilege issue solely as a matter of Ohio law.  [   ]  If the Supreme Court of Ohio "held as it did because it felt under compulsion of federal law as enunciated by this Court so to hold, it should be relieved of that compulsion.  It should be freed to decide . . . these suits according to its own local law."  [   ]

The Ohio Supreme Court relied heavily on Time, Inc. v. Hill, 385 U.S. 374 (1967), but that case does not mandate a media privilege to televise a performer's entire act without his consent.  Involved in Time, Inc. v. Hill was a claim under the New York "Right of Privacy" statute that Life Magazine, in the course of reviewing a new play, had connected the play with a long-past incident involving petitioner and his family and had falsely described their experience and conduct at that time.  The complaint sought damages for humiliation and suffering flowing from these nondefamatory falsehoods that allegedly invaded Hill's privacy.  The Court held, however, that the opening of a new play linked to an actual incident was a matter of public interest and that Hill could not recover without showing that the Life report was knowingly false or was published with reckless disregard for the truth—the same rigorous standard that had been applied in New York Times Co. v. Sullivan [   ].

Time, Inc. v. Hill, which was hotly contested and decided by a divided Court, involved an entirely different tort from the "right of publicity" recognized by the Ohio Supreme Court. . . .

The differences between these two torts are important.  First, the State's interests in providing a cause of action in each instance are different.  "The interest protected" in permitting recovery for placing the plaintiff in a false light "is clearly that of reputation, with the same overtones of mental distress as in defamation."  Prosser, supra, 48 Calif. L.Rev., at 400.  By contrast, the State's interest in permitting a "right of publicity" is in protecting the proprietary interest of the individual in his act in part to encourage such entertainment.  As we later note, the State's interest is closely analogous to the goals of patent and copyright law, focusing on the right of the individual to reap the reward of his endeavors and having little to do with protecting feelings or reputation. Second, the two torts differ in the degree to which they intrude on dissemination of information to the public.  In "false light" cases the only way to protect the interests involved is to attempt to minimize the publication of the damaging matter, while in "right of publicity" cases the only question is who gets to do the publishing.  An entertainer such as petitioner usually has no objection to the widespread publication of his act as long as he gets the commercial benefit of such publication. Indeed, in the present case petititoner did not seek to enjoin the broadcast of his act; he simply sought compensation for the broadcast in the form of damages.

. . .

Moreover, *Time, Inc. v. Hill, New York Times, Metromedia, Gertz*, and *Firestone* all involved the reporting of events; in none of them was there an attempt to broadcast or publish an entire act for which the performer ordinarily gets paid. It is evident, and there is no claim here to the contrary, that petititoner's state-law right of publicity would not serve to prevent respondent from reporting the newsworthy facts about petitioner's act. Wherever the line in particular situations is to be drawn between media reports that are protected and those that are not, we are quite sure that the First and Fourteenth Amendments do not immunize the media when they broadcast a performer's entire act without his consent. The Constitution no more prevents a State from requiring respondent to compensate petitioner for broadcasting his act on television than it would privilege respondent to film and broadcast a copyrighted dramatic work without liability to the copyright owner, [  ], or to film and broadcast a prize fight, [  ], or a baseball game, [  ], where the promoters or the participants had other plans for publicizing the event. There are ample reasons for reaching this conclusion.

The broadcast of a film of petitioner's entire act poses a substantial threat to the economic value of that performance. As the Ohio court recognized, this act is the product of petitioner's own talents and energy, the end result of much time, effort, and expense. Much of its economic value lies in the "right of exclusive control over the publicity given to his performance"; if the public can see the act free on television, it will be less willing to pay to see it at the fair.[12] The effect of a public broadcast of the performance is similar to preventing petitioner from charging an admission fee. . . . Moreover, the broadcast of petitioner's entire performance, unlike the unauthorized use of another's name for purposes of trade or the incidental use of a name or picture by the press, goes to the heart of petitioner's ability to earn a living as an entertainer. Thus, in this case, Ohio has recognized what may be the strongest case for a "right of publicity"—involving, not the appropriation of an entertainer's reputation to enhance the attractiveness of a commercial product, but the appropriation of the very activity by which the entertainer acquired his reputation in the first place.

Of course, Ohio's decision to protect petitioner's right of publicity here rests on more than a desire to compensate the performer for the time and effort invested in his act; the protection provides an economic incentive for him to make the investment required to produce a performance of interest to the public. This same consideration underlies the patent and copyright laws long enforced by this Court. . . .

12. It is possible, of course, that respondent's news broadcast increased the value of petitioner's performance by stimulating the public's interest in seeing the act live. In these circumstances, petitioner would not be able to prove damages and thus would not recover. But petitioner has alleged that the broadcast injured him to the extent of $25,000, App. 5, and we think the State should be allowed to authorize compensation of this injury if proved.

There is no doubt that entertainment, as well as news, enjoys First Amendment protection. It is also true that entertainment itself can be important news. Time, Inc. v. Hill. But it is important to note that neither the public nor respondent will be deprived of the benefit of petitioner's performance as long as his commercial stake in his act is appropriately recognized. Petitioner does not seek to enjoin the broadcast of his performance; he simply wants to be paid for it. Nor do we think that a state-law damages remedy against respondent would represent a species of liability without fault contrary to the letter or spirit of Gertz v. Robert Welch, Inc., [  ]. Respondent knew exactly that petitioner objected to televising his act but nevertheless displayed the entire film.

We conclude that although the State of Ohio may as a matter of its own law privilege the press in the circumstances of this case, the First and Fourteenth Amendments do not require it to do so.

Reversed.

MR. JUSTICE POWELL, with whom MR. JUSTICE BRENNAN and MR. JUSTICE MARSHALL join, dissenting.

Disclaiming any attempt to do more than decide the narrow case before us, the Court reverses the decision of the Supreme Court of Ohio based on repeated incantation of a single formula: "a performer's entire act." The holding today is summed up in one sentence:

> "Wherever the line in particular situations is to be drawn between media reports that are protected and those that are not, we are quite sure that the First and Fourteenth Amendments do not immunize the media when they broadcast a performer's entire act without his consent."

I doubt that this formula provides a standard clear enough even for resolution in this case.[1] In any event, I am not persuaded that the Court's opinion is appropriately sensitive to the First Amendment values at stake, and I therefore dissent.

Although the Court would draw no distinction, I do not view respondent's action as comparable to unauthorized commercial broadcasts of sporting events, theatrical performances, and the like where the broadcaster keeps the profits. There is no suggestion here that respondent made any such use of the film. Instead, it simply reported on what petitioner concedes to be a newsworthy event, in a way hardly surprising

---

1. Although the record is not explicit, it is unlikely that the "act" commenced abruptly with the explosion that launched petitioner on his way, ending with the landing in the net a few seconds later. One may assume that the actual firing was preceded by some fanfare, possibly stretching over several minutes, to heighten the audience's anticipation: introduction of the performer, description of the uniqueness and danger, last-minute checking of the apparatus, and entry into the cannon, all accompanied by suitably ominous commentary from the master of ceremonies. If this is found to be the case on remand, then respondent could not be said to have appropriated the "entire act" in its 15-second newsclip—and the Court's opinion then would afford no guidance for resolution of the case. Moreover, in future cases involving different performances, similar difficulties in determining just what constitutes the "entire act" are inevitable.

for a television station—by means of film coverage. The report was part of an ordinary daily news program, consuming a total of 15 seconds. It is a routine example of the press fulfilling the informing function so vital to our system.

The Court's holding that the station's ordinary news report may give rise to substantial liability has disturbing implications, for the decision could lead to a degree of media self-censorship. [   ] Hereafter whenever a television news editor is unsure whether certain film footage received from a camera crew might be held to portray an "entire act," he may decline coverage—even of clearly newsworthy events—or confine the broadcast to watered-down verbal reporting, perhaps with an occasional still picture. The public is then the loser. This is hardly the kind of news reportage that the First Amendment is meant to foster. [   ]

In my view the First Amendment commands a different analytical starting point from the one selected by the Court. Rather than begin with a quantitative analysis of the performer's behavior—is this or is this not his entire act?—we should direct initial attention to the actions of the news media: what use did the station make of the film footage? When a film is used, as here, for a routine portion of a regular news program, I would hold that the First Amendment protects the station from a "right of publicity" or "appropriation" suit, absent a strong showing by the plaintiff that the news broadcast was a subterfuge or cover for private or commercial exploitation.[4]

. . . In a suit like the one before us, however, the plaintiff does not complain about the fact of exposure to the public, but rather about its timing or manner. He welcomes some publicity, but seeks to retain control over means and manner as a way to maximize for himself the monetary benefits that flow from such publication. But having made the matter public—having chosen, in essence, to make it newsworthy—he cannot, consistent with the First Amendment, complain of routine news reportage. Cf. Gertz v. Robert Welch, Inc., [   ] (clarifying the different liability standards appropriate in defamation suits, depending on whether or not the plaintiff is a public figure).

Since the filmclip here was undeniably treated as news and since there is no claim that the use was subterfuge, respondent's actions were constitutionally privileged. I would affirm.

[Mr. Justice Stevens dissented on the ground that he could not tell whether the Ohio Supreme Court had relied on federal constitutional issues in deciding the case. He would have remanded the case to that court "for clarification of its holding before deciding the federal constitutional issue."]

---

4. This case requires no detailed specification of the standards for identifying a subterfuge, since there is no claim here that respondent's news use was anything but bona fide. [   ] I would point out, however, that selling time during a news broadcast to advertisers in the customary fashion does not make for "commercial exploitation" in the sense intended here. [   ]

On remand, the Ohio Supreme Court took advantage of the opportunity afforded by the majority opinion and decided that nothing in the Ohio Constitution protected the behavior of the media defendant. The case was remanded for trial. Zacchini v. Scripps-Howard Broadcasting Co., 54 Ohio St.2d 286, 376 N.E.2d 582 (1978).

**Notes and Questions**

1.  How important is it that the majority treats the 15 seconds as the "entire act"?

2.  Does this case involve an aspect of "privacy"? Does it resemble the Cox Broadcasting case in that both involved lawfully obtained information of interest or concern to the public? Can you explain why the defendant in *Cox Broadcasting* did not have to pay while the defendant in *Zacchini* might have to pay?

3.  After *Zacchini*, what would happen in a case in which a street artist who survives on contributions from passersby—a mime, an accordionist, a dancer—is photographed by the local television station and shown in a story about summer diversions on the streets of the city? Is the street artist's claim as strong as Zacchini's?

4.  *Right of publicity.* The Zacchini case is an example of an offshoot of appropriation known as right of publicity. This particular right was once defined as follows:

> The distinctive aspect of the common-law right of publicity is that it recognizes the commercial value of the picture or representation of a prominent person or performer and protects his proprietary interest in the profitability of his public reputation or persona. Ali v. Playgirl, Inc., 447 F.Supp. 723 (S.D.N.Y.1978).

Unlike the traditional tort of appropriation, right of publicity is exclusively the province of well-known individuals. Also, whereas the original tort was at least partially rooted in the concept of the right to be let alone and not to be exploited for commercial or trade purposes, this new variation seems only concerned with who should reap the financial benefits. In essence it is a property right, as opposed to a personal right. Thus, Johnny Carson was able to sue a manufacturer of portable toilets that were marketed under the name, "Here's Johnny." Carson v. Here's Johnny Portable Toilets, Inc., 698 F.2d 831 (6th Cir.1983), reversing 498 F.Supp. 71 (E.D.Mich.1980). Similarly, the estate of Elvis Presley won a claim against the producers of THE BIG EL SHOW, an imitation of Presley's performances. Estate of Presley v. Russen, 513 F.Supp. 1339 (D.N.J.1981).

In some cases it is not even the true name or likeness of a person, but rather some character or role that is at issue. In Groucho Marx Productions v. Day and Night Co., 523 F.Supp. 485 (S.D.N.Y.1981), reversed on other grounds 689 F.2d 317 (2d Cir.1982), the court held that the play, "A Day in Hollywood, a Night in the Ukraine," appropriated the Marx brothers' characters. In this context, a suit for appropriation has become a new method of protecting creative work—even characters created by comedians. Is this a right equivalent to copyright? Should it be preempted by the federal copyright statute, especially in this context? How does it differ from copyright?

5.   In a more recent case, Stephano v. News Group Publications, 11 Med. L.Rptr. 1303 (1984), a model sued for invasion of privacy under New York State's statute prohibiting appropriation for "advertising or trade purposes." The model had posed in a "bomber jacket" for a 1981 article on men's fall fashions for *New York* magazine. Contending that he had agreed to model for one article only, he sued, claiming a breach of his "right of publicity" because one of the photos was used in a "Best Bets" magazine column, giving an approximate price for the jacket and listing several stores at which it would be available. The New York Court of Appeals held that the magazine's use of the photo in the "Best Bets" column was of general public interest and that it was not used for advertising or trade purposes as defined by New York law. Despite the unusual result in *Zacchini,* the principle seems clear that the media will usually win such cases unless their claims of newsworthiness or public interest are exceptionally weak. Stephano's suit was *not,* of course, a copyright action, but the similarities to copyright—attempting to control or profit from what one perceives as one's property—are worth noting.

6.   *Descendability.* Personal rights such as those protected by defamation and invasion of privacy law terminate at death. Thus, for example, one can publish defamatory statements about deceased individuals with impunity (unless the same statement also defames people who are still alive). Because the right of publicity is a property right, a great controversy has developed as to whether it survives the death of its creator. Currently, there seem to be three distinct approaches being taken by various courts. One is that the right terminates upon death. Under this view as soon as people die, their names, likenesses and characterizations are available for anyone to use without legal liability. At the other extreme is the position that death has no effect on the right of publicity. In jurisdictions that adhere to this view, the consent of whoever owns the right of publicity in question (perhaps the individual's heirs or someone who has purchased the right) is always necessary. Finally, there is an intermediate approach that holds the right of publicity to survive death only if it was commercially exploited during the person's lifetime. With this approach the right of publicity is a property right only if the individual treated it as such.

# Chapter XIV

# SPECIAL PROBLEMS OF ELECTRONIC MEDIA JOURNALISTS

Whereas defamation and invasion of privacy problems can arise in the context of entertainment programming on the electronic media (as well as in the context of electronic journalism), the special problems we consider in this Chapter are ones that are typically limited to news and documentary programming. Among the problems are protection of government secrets, news coverage of the administration of justice, journalist's privilege, and newsgathering from public sources.

## A. THE PROTECTION OF GOVERNMENT INTERESTS

In the discussion in Chapter I of abridgment of freedom of the press, we examined the question of prior restraint on dissemination of messages. In Near v. Minnesota, we saw an example of a restraint imposed on a publication that had, in part, accused public officials in Minneapolis of involvement in bootlegging and gambling. In New York Times v. United States, we saw the federal government's Vietnam era attempt to restrain publication of the "Pentagon Papers," the secret study of U.S. decision-making in Southeast Asia. Recall that the Supreme Court found that the heavy burden of showing justification for the imposition of a prior restraint was met in neither case. In U.S. v. The Progressive, we saw the federal government's attempt to stop dissemination of the "secret of the H-bomb." That case, recall, ended with publication of the "secret" in publications other than *The Progressive,* and the case never reached the Supreme Court.

There are a variety of other contexts in which the government may want to use prior restraint or some other means to discourage or stop dissemination of messages that may present problems for the government, its officials, or its citizens.

For example, a 1972 case exemplifies the problems of authors who have had access to national security information. United States v. Marchetti, 466 F.2d 1309 (4th Cir.1972), involved an injunction obtained by the government against publication of Marchetti's book about the Central Intelligence Agency, his former employer. At the time Marchetti joined, he promised not to divulge any classified information unless specifically authorized in writing by the director, and when he resigned from the CIA he signed a loyalty oath. The court upheld the restraint, and the Supreme Court denied certiorari, 409 U.S. 1063 (1972).

Sometimes the government's interest is with the protection of the private rights of its citizens—as in an instance in which a judge may seek to restrain dissemination of information in order to protect the fair trial rights of an accused individual. In 1976, for example, in Nebraska Press

Association v. Stuart, 427 U.S. 539 (1976), the Supreme Court held that the heavy burden imposed as a condition for a prior restraint was not met when broadcasters and publishers were restrained from disseminating material "strongly implicative" of the accused in a widely reported murder of six persons. (This case and others in which the state interest is a "fair trial" interest are discussed in the next section of this Chapter.)

Recall also from Chapter I the discussion of Landmark Communications, Inc. v. Virginia and Smith v. Daily Mail Publishing Co., both of which involved attempts to protect a state or public interest through discouraging or restraining publication of facts that most electronic media journalists would certainly consider to be news.

Our long legal tradition against censorship and the difficulty of justifying such a restraint in court discourage most attempts to protect public or private interests through such restraints. Instead, as we have seen in defamation and privacy, we usually rely on the ability of persons who are damaged to sue *after* the dissemination has taken place.

## B.  PRESS COVERAGE OF THE ADMINISTRATION OF JUSTICE

Press coverage of the administration of justice poses special problems both for the press and for the courts. It is easy to generalize about the openness of the judicial system and about Americans' distaste for secret courts, and it is easy to generalize about our proud tradition of protecting the fairness of civil and criminal trials. The generalizations too often ignore the reality: the First Amendment right to freedom of the press and the Sixth Amendment right to a fair trial sometimes appear to give rise to conflict.

As journalists tell the story of a crime or arrest prior to trial, they inevitably influence opinions in the area, and it can be difficult—perhaps even impossible—to find jurors who can ignore press reports and come to a fair verdict based solely on evidence presented in court. On the other hand, if judges try to shape or stop news coverage of the administration of justice, they may be interfering with the First Amendment rights of journalists.

### 1.  BACKGROUND

The judicial branch has been the object of considerable litigation as to which of its functions are to be open to public scrutiny. A specific constitutional provision, held to be solely for the benefit of the accused and not addressed to the press, is basic to our discussion. The Sixth Amendment to the United States Constitution provides: "In all criminal prosecutions, the accused shall enjoy the right to a speedy and public trial, by an impartial jury of the State and district wherein the crime shall have been committed. . . ."

Problems arise primarily in the context of press and public interest in dramatic criminal cases involving either sensational crimes or prominent persons, and less frequently in the context of highly-publicized civil lawsuits like General William Westmoreland's against CBS. The resulting problems between journalists and lawyers/judges over pre-trial and trial news accounts have been referred to as "fair trial-free press" by the bar and "free press-fair trial" by the press.

In several Supreme Court cases of the 1960's, criminal convictions were reversed because the Court found that prejudicial press coverage had resulted in possible unfairness. Judges, realizing their responsibilities to protect defendants from such unfairness, reached for means of protection—ordering the press not to report certain information, closing pre-trial hearings to the press, keeping cameras out of the courtrooms, closing trials, etc. The press viewed such steps as intrusions on First Amendment rights. The Supreme Court decided cases involving these issues in the 1970's and 1980's.

The Supreme Court's first confrontation with the problem in constitutional dimension was in Irvin v. Dowd, 366 U.S. 717 (1961). Defendant Leslie Irvin had been arrested in Indiana following a series of murders attributed to the "Mad Dog Killer." He was convicted and sentenced to death; his appeal included 46 exhibits indicating that, as Justice Clark put it, ". . . a barrage of newspaper headlines, articles, cartoons and pictures were unleashed against him during the six or seven months preceding his trial."

Typically in such appeals, newspaper headlines and stories receive greater emphasis than broadcast news accounts because of the easier availability of the former. The majority opinion in *Irvin* did, however, note that in the area "radio and TV stations . . . also carried extensive newscasts covering the same incidents."

Prominent in the telling evidence of trouble at the trial was the fact that the panel of potential jurors included 430 persons, of whom 268 were excused by the court itself as having fixed opinions as to the guilt of Irvin. At least 370 of the prospective jurors entertained some opinion as to Irvin's guilt. Finding a "pattern of deep and bitter prejudice," the Court vacated the conviction and remanded the case for retrial, at which Irvin was convicted again.

Another troubling case occurred when Wilbert Rideau was arrested in Louisiana for bank robbery, kidnapping, and murder. The sheriff invited a film crew from the local television station to film the sheriff's "interview" with Rideau. During the 20-minute interrogation, Rideau confessed to the crimes. The station showed the interview three times. After a requested change of venue was denied, Rideau was convicted and sentenced to death. The Supreme Court overturned the conviction, noting that after drawing a jury from people who could have been exposed to the confession, any "court proceedings . . . could be but a hollow formality." The Court implied that nothing could have overcome the effects of the television film and that specific proof of juror prejudice was not necessary under such circumstances. Rideau v. Louisiana, 373 U.S. 723 (1963). (Rideau was ultimately retried and convicted a second time.)

Perhaps the most famous of the 1960's cases in this area was Sheppard v. Maxwell, 384 U.S. 333 (1966).  Dr. Sam Sheppard was accused of the 1954 murder of his pregnant wife, Marilyn, and tried in the light of national publicity.  He was convicted and spent a number of years in prison before his attorney, a young, relatively unknown F. Lee Bailey, successfully carried Sheppard's appeal to the Supreme Court. Mr. Justice Clark delivered the opinion of the Court:

> Much of the material printed or broadcast during the trial was never heard from the witness stand, such as the charges that Sheppard had purposely impeded the murder investigation and must be guilty since he had hired a prominent criminal lawyer; that Sheppard was a perjurer; that he had sexual relations with numerous women; that his wife had characterized him as a "Jekyll-Hyde"; that he was "a bare-faced liar" because of his testimony as to police treatment; and finally, that a woman convict claimed Sheppard to be the father of her illegitimate child.  As the trial progressed, the newspapers summarized and interpreted the evidence, devoting particular attention to the material that incriminated Sheppard, and often drew unwarranted inferences from testimony.  At one point, a front-page picture of Mrs. Sheppard's blood-stained pillow was published after being "doctored" to show more clearly an alleged imprint of a surgical instrument.

> Nor is there doubt that this deluge of publicity reached at least some of the jury.  On the only occasion that the jury was queried, two jurors admitted in open court to hearing the highly inflammatory charge that a prison inmate claimed Sheppard as the father of her illegitimate child.  Despite the extent and nature of the publicity to which the jury was exposed during trial, the judge refused defense counsel's other requests that the jurors be asked whether they had read or heard specific prejudicial comment about the case, including the incidents we have previously summarized.  In these circumstances, we can assume that some of this material reached members of the jury.  [   ]

>               .  .  .

> The carnival atmosphere at trial could easily have been avoided since the courtroom and courthouse premises are subject to the control of the court.  .  .  .

Concluding that the trial court judge had failed to protect the defendant's rights adequately, the Court ordered Sheppard released unless the state gave him a new trial.  Ohio retried him, and Sheppard (unlike Irvin or Rideau) was acquitted at the second trial.

Some would argue that the overturned convictions of Irvin, Rideau, and Sheppard reflected the strong protection of defendants' rights by the Warren Court.  A 1975 case, Murphy v. Florida, 421 U.S. 794 (1975), in which a criminal conviction was upheld, could be seen simply as reflecting the Court's changing attitudes toward defendants, but that analysis would fail to recognize that the circumstances of *Murphy* were quite

different from those of the earlier cases. In *Murphy* the jurors in
defendant's robbery trial had learned through news stories about some
or all of Jack "Murph the Surf" Murphy's earlier convictions for murder,
securities theft, and for the 1964 theft of the Star of India sapphire from
a New York museum. The majority stated that qualified jurors need not
be totally ignorant of the facts surrounding the case. The Court found
in the *voir dire*—the examination of the potential jurors—no showing of
hostility to the defendant. Four of the six jurors volunteered that
defendant's past was irrelevant. Only 20 of the 78 persons examined
were excused because of an opinion of guilt. (Note that this is quite
unlike *Irvin*.) "This may indeed be 20 more than would occur in the trial
of a totally obscure person, but it by no means suggests a community
with sentiment so poisoned against the petitioner as to impeach the
indifference of jurors who displayed no animus of their own." Only
Justice Brennan dissented.

### 2.  So–Called Remedies for the Fair Trial–Free Press Problem

#### a.  The Standard Remedies

Although the judge's failure to maintain proper decorum during the
trial was viewed as his major error in *Sheppard,* the Court devoted
extensive consideration to the behavior of the media and suggested
techniques by which the judge might better have insulated the trial.
Some of those suggestions are included below. Note that most of the
"remedies" have limitations or drawbacks that preclude their being used
widely.

*Cautioning Police, Prosecutors, etc.* Cutting off information at its
source is an obvious way of trying to curtail dissemination by the news
media, and prosecutors sometimes are the sources of news stories about
confessions and probable guilt, but gags on police and attorneys may be
challenged by those gagged on the ground that they interfere with the
First Amendment rights of the police and attorneys to express themselves. Furthermore, to the extent that the process of newsgathering
may be protected by the First Amendment (see discussion of *Richmond
Newspapers* later in this section), such restrictive orders may be unconstitutional.

*Shielding Witnesses.* Shielding witnesses from the press similarly
may interfere with the witnesses' own First Amendment rights and may
interfere with a press right to gather news. On the other hand, of
course, witnesses are under no obligation to answer questions from
journalists.

*Granting a Continuance.* Postponing ("continuing,") the trial until
publicity dies down may interfere with the defendant's right to a *speedy*
trial. Also, when the trial finally *does* take place, it becomes a news
event all over again.

*Cautioning Journalists.* If the court cautions journalists in advance of publication of prejudicial information, the warning can seem to imply a threat of punishment by the contempt powers and may smack of an unconstitutional form of prior restraint (see Chapter I). If the warning is made after prejudicial information has already been revealed, the warning is likely to be ineffective.

*Encouraging the Use of Voluntary Guidelines.* In the 1960's, the American Bar Association responded to the fair trial-free press concern by creating a committee that came to be known as the Reardon Committee to recommend guidelines for pre-trial and trial news coverage. The committee recommended that, prior to trial, lawyers release no extrajudicial statements relating to (1) prior criminal record of the accused, (2) existence or contents of any confession, (3) performance of any examinations or tests or the defendant's refusal to undergo them, (4) identity, testimony, or credibility of prospective witnesses, (5) possibility of a guilty plea to the charge or a lesser offense, or (6) any opinion as to the accused's guilt or innocence. Other recommendations dealt with other facets of the fair trial-free press issue. Many journalists resented what they viewed as an attempt by the legal profession to tell them how to do their jobs and ignored the Reardon Committee's recommendations.

Guidelines of state bench-bar-press organizations may have fared somewhat better because they were generally adopted by joint committees of members of the journalism and legal professions. These guidelines typically suggest that journalists *think carefully* before revealing information that the Reardon Committee cautioned against, but they also express recognition of a right of the journalist to access to information about the criminal justice system.

The effectiveness of the guidelines is directly related to their voluntariness. Even in states in which the guidelines are followed with some regularity in routine cases, they tend to lose their effectiveness when sensational crimes are committed. There is also some danger that courts may use the guidelines in ways the journalists never envisioned; see Nebraska Press Association v. Stuart and Federated Publications v. Swedberg later in this Chapter.

*Granting Change of Venue.* Where news accounts in an area may have created a situation in which it is unlikely that the accused can obtain a fair trial, a judge can transfer a trial to another area less touched by the publicity. A constitutional problem may arise in some instances, because the Sixth Amendment provides for one's trial "by an impartial jury of the State and district wherein the crime shall have been committed." Furthermore, such changes of venue are costly and bothersome to both the prosecution and the defense. If news accounts have already been state-wide or national, the change is unlikely to do much to mitigate the damage. Even if the new site of the trial has been untouched by earlier news accounts, the scheduling of the trial there becomes a news event in that area, and the problem may begin anew, though with less attention because the victim(s) are not local people.

*Granting Change of Venire.* Rather than moving the trial, it is theoretically possible to import a panel of jurors—or veniremen—from another area where they are less likely to have formed opinions about the case. In practice, this is extremely rare, and it raises questions as to whether the jurors from the remote area are really the accused's peers.

*Relying on the Voir Dire.* During the *voir dire*, the process under which the prospective jurors are screened, attempts are made to exclude from the jury those people whose previously formed opinions will preclude their reaching a fair verdict based on the evidence presented during the trial. The *voir dire* may be successful in keeping truly biased people off a jury, but it is less successful when potential jurors have heard a specific piece of information. Also, the criticism is made that it can tend to eliminate from the jury those potential jurors who follow the news in their community most closely and who form intelligent opinions based on what they read or hear.

*Cautioning Jurors.* The Court in *Sheppard* was critical of the trial judge for failing to give the jurors sufficient instruction about not reading media accounts of the trial or listening to comment outside the courtroom. Despite the fact that most judges today can be expected to give careful instructions, and most have faith in jurors to follow those instructions, there are undoubtedly instances in which jurors fail to heed those instructions and do see prejudicial news accounts outside the courtroom.

*Sequestering the Jury.* Sequestering the jury—keeping them in a hotel during the trial—greatly reduces the risk of improper exposure to media accounts of the trial. Because the public reads about sequestration in some highly publicized cases, it seems to perceive sequestration as a more common practice than it is. Its high cost precludes its use in all but a few cases, and defense attorneys are sometimes reluctant even to suggest it because of uncertainty about the effect on the jury. As some say, a juror who is unhappy about being confined for the duration of a trial cannot take out his frustrations on the judge and just may take them out on the accused.

### b.   *Restraints on Publication*

Because the First Amendment has traditionally been seen as a protection for the freedom to publish, restraints on the publication of information are undoubtedly the least desirable and most constitutionally suspect of the theoretically-available remedies for the fair trial-free press problem. Two cases that illustrate the problem are United States v. Dickinson, 465 F.2d 496 (5th Cir.1972), and Nebraska Press Association v. Stuart, 427 U.S. 539 (1976).

The press calls them gag orders; lawyers and judges call them restrictive orders or protective orders. By whatever name, such an order directs the press (and often others) not to disseminate information a judge thinks may prejudice jurors in a forthcoming or present trial. Violating such an order can result in a citation for contempt.

In *Dickinson*, a federal judge ordered the media not to publish any testimony taken at a hearing for fear it might prejudice an upcoming state trial. Two reporters violated the order, were cited for criminal contempt, and were fined $300 each. On appeal, the court of appeals held the order unconstitutional, but ruled that it had to be obeyed until overturned on appeal. The court held that such orders must be followed unless there is "a showing of 'transparent invalidity' or patent frivolity surrounding the order . . .." The Supreme Court denied certiorari. 414 U.S. 979 (1973).

States need not follow *Dickinson*, though they may. In jurisdictions that do follow *Dickinson*, a critical question is how rapidly a trial court's injunction can be "stayed" or "vacated" by an appellate court or judge. A "stay" involves delaying the effect of the lower court's order until later appellate review. "Vacate" is more drastic and occurs when the lower court's error is clear on cursory inspection.

In State v. Coe, 101 Wash.2d 364, 679 P.2d 353 (1984), a trial judge's order holding a broadcaster in contempt for playing tapes that had been played in open court was reversed on appeal. The judge had ordered that the tapes not be played on the air because the defendant might be suicidal. The appellate court majority held that the state permitted those cited for contempt to violate the order and then challenge it if the order was "patently invalid or 'void' as outside the court's power."

A major case involving a restrictive order faced the Supreme Court in Nebraska Press Association v. Stuart, 427 U.S. 539 (1976). Six members of the Kellie family were found murdered in their rural home in 1975. A neighbor, Erwin Charles Simants, was an immediate suspect, and the crime attracted widespread news coverage by electronic and print media. Three days after the crime, the prosecutor and the defense attorney joined in asking the trial court to enter a restrictive order relating to "matters that may or may not be publicly reported or disclosed to the public" because of the "mass coverage of news media" and the "reasonable likelihood of prejudicial news which would make difficult, if not impossible, the impaneling of an impartial jury and tend to prevent a fair trial."

The county court entered such an order, also requiring the members of the press to observe the Nebraska Bar-Press Guidelines, a set of voluntary guidelines of the type mentioned above. Attempts by the media to get the restrictive order lifted were unsuccessful. Simants was convicted, but the case brought by the Nebraska Press Association and other media organizations continued to the Supreme Court.

Chief Justice Burger, writing for the majority, said that in order to determine whether the danger posed by the media justified the restrictive order, "we must examine the evidence before the trial judge when the order was entered to determine (a) the nature and extent of pretrial news coverage; (b) whether other measures would be likely to mitigate the effects of unrestrained pretrial publicity; (c) how effectively a restraining order would operate to prevent the threatened danger." Finding that the trial judge's conclusion as to the impact of publicity on prospective jurors was "of necessity speculative" because he was dealing with "factors unknown and unknowable," the Court concluded that "the heavy burden imposed as a condition to securing a prior restraint was not met . . . ." The judgment of the Nebraska Supreme Court was therefore reversed.

If a trial judge waits until unrestrained pretrial news accounts seem dangerous enough to justify a restraint, would such an order then be unacceptable because it would be largely ineffective?

In Goldblum v. National Broadcasting Co., 584 F.2d 904 (9th Cir. 1978), plaintiff, former executive officer of Equity Funding Corp., was serving a sentence for fraudulent activity in connection with the corporation's insolvency. NBC produced a "docudrama" based on the case, using the names of plaintiff and the corporation. Plaintiff, alleging that the program was inaccurate, sought an injunction against the showing of the program on the ground that it might inflame public opinion against him, jeopardize his release on parole, and adversely affect jury selection in any future criminal or civil cases arising out of the episode.

The district judge ordered NBC to produce the movie for review the day its presentation was scheduled. When NBC refused, the judge ordered counsel for the network imprisoned until the film was produced. A few hours later, a panel of the court of appeals granted an application for relief and freed the attorney. In a subsequent opinion, the court said that it found "no authority which is even a remote justification" for issuing a prior restraint on the theory that parole officials might become inflamed or that jury selection in some "wholly speculative criminal prosecution" might be adversely affected. The order to produce and the imprisonment were invalid.

*Gag Orders on Litigants.* A special problem arises when the media are themselves parties to litigation and want to report on the case. Part of the problem, in fact, is that the courts treat the press like any other litigant. In Seattle Times v. Rhinehart, 467 U.S. 20 (1984), the Supreme Court held that a protective order by a trial court in the state of Washington did not violate the First Amendment even though it prohibited the *Seattle Times* newspaper from publishing certain information related to a libel case against them. The information in question had been obtained by the newspaper as part of the discovery process prior to the libel trial, and the Court reasoned that there was a sufficient showing of good cause for the order and that the rights of a litigant do not necessarily include the right to disseminate information obtained through the "legislative grace" of the discovery process. Although most journalists and attorneys representing media clients consider it a disturbing trend, lower courts in other cases have also affirmed orders gagging litigants or trial participants.

### c.  Denials of Access to the Courtroom and Conditional Access

As judges faced the reality that other means of solving the fair trial-free press problems were either undesirable or ineffective, some turned to excluding the press and public from the courtroom during pretrial hearings or during trials themselves, or granted access to the courtroom only on the acceptance of conditions.

*Pretrial Proceedings.* Journalists, of course, are also members of the public. But more, they see themselves as the eyes and ears of the public—surrogates for those who cannot attend a hearing or trial. They brought the first major challenge to closed pretrial hearings.

Gannett Co. v. DePasquale, 443 U.S. 368 (1979), presented the question of whether members of the public are constitutionally entitled to attend a pretrial hearing. The issue arose out of a murder prosecution in upstate New York. The murder victim disappeared in 1976 after last having been seen fishing with two men. The victim's truck was found in Michigan, and the two young men were arrested there. Newspapers in New York State reported the arrest and police theories of the crime. Brought back to New York, the two men moved to suppress statements they had made to Michigan police, claiming the statements were given involuntarily. They also moved to suppress the gun that had been found as a result of the confession in Michigan.

The motions came before Judge Daniel DePasquale, and defense counsel asked the judge to close the hearing because "the unabated buildup of adverse publicity" had jeopardized the ability of the defendants to receive a fair trial. Neither the prosecutor nor the Gannett reporter in the courtroom objected. The judge removed press and public from the courtroom. The next day the reporter complained to the judge, but the hearing had concluded and the judge refused to release a transcript. Three days later counsel for Gannett appeared and asked that the ruling be vacated and that a transcript of the hearing be provided. The judge refused, the New York Court of Appeals upheld the judge's action, and the Supreme Court affirmed, 5–4, in an opinion by Justice Stewart.

Justice Stewart concluded that the Sixth Amendment's provision that "the accused shall enjoy the right to a speedy and public trial by an impartial jury" extended no rights whatever to the public. He said the right to a public trial is a personal right of the accused. He also said that any First and Fourteenth Amendment rights of Gannett to attend a criminal trial were not violated because the trial judge made an appraisal of the situation and concluded that, under the circumstances of this particular case, any right to attend the proceeding was outweighed by the defendants' right to a fair trial.

Four dissenters—Justices Brennan, White, Marshall, and Blackmun—all joined in a dissent emphasizing their belief (1) that the Sixth Amendment should be read to define trials as including suppression hearings because of the critical importance of such hearings, and (2) that the Sixth Amendment guarantee of a public trial extended to the public as well as to the accused.

After the *Gannett* decision, many thought the matter was left to each state. The decision caused considerable confusion, with its references to both pretrial hearings and trials, and there was considerable speculation that the majority opinion had been drafted as a dissenting opinion before one of the justices was persuaded to join it as the majority opinion.

Following the decision, news directors, editors, and professional associations circulated "Gannett cards" among their reporters. The cards, worded so that a reporter can read them on the spot should a judge be considering a closure, ask that such a decision be delayed until the reporter's media employer has an opportunity to be represented by legal counsel to argue on behalf of the right of the media and public to observe the proceedings.

*Trials.* After the announcement of the Supreme Court's decision in *Gannett*, a trial judge in Hanover County, Va., closed a trial—setting the stage for Richmond Newspapers, Inc. v. Virginia, 448 U.S. 555 (1980).

The trial was a murder trial. The defendant had been convicted of second-degree murder, and his conviction had been overturned on appeal because improper evidence had been admitted. The second and third trials resulted in mistrials. At the start of the fourth trial, defense counsel moved to exclude the press and public from the courtroom. He did not want witnesses to compare stories or information to leak out and be learned by the jurors, who had not been sequestered. The prosecutor offered no objection, and the judge closed the courtroom.

The newspaper appealed the reporter's exclusion, and the Supreme Court eventually held that the trial should have been open. The vote was 7–1, but the reasoning behind the decision is difficult to explain because the seven justices in the majority wrote six opinions and there was no majority opinion. Chief Justice Burger wrote the plurality opinion, stressing that *Gannett* had involved "pretrial" proceedings while this case involved a trial. He traced at length the history of public trials that ran back at least to the 13th century in England, mentioning as reasons for openness the greater likelihood that witnesses would tell the truth, the therapeutic value of having open criminal trials as an outlet for community concern, hostility, and emotion, and the opportunity for understanding the system and its workings in a particular case.

The Chief Justice then recognized a First Amendment right to attend criminal trials. Writing that it was not crucial whether the right be called a "right of access" or a "right to gather information," he said "The explicit, guaranteed rights to speak and to publish concerning what takes place at a trial would lose much meaning if access to observe the trial could, as it was here, be foreclosed arbitrarily." This recognition of a right to gather information is significant because the far more traditional view of the First Amendment had been that it protected one's right to disseminate information one had already obtained, not one's right to obtain information.

Although some confusion about closures of either pretrial hearings or trials remained after *Richmond,* many fewer judges closed courtrooms, but in Globe Newspaper Co. v. Norfolk County Superior Court, 457 U.S. 596 (1982), the Supreme Court had to examine *The Boston Globe's* challenge to a state statute that provided for automatic closure of rape and other sexual assault trials during the testimony of minors who are victims. Justice Brennan wrote for the six-member majority, "We agree with respondent that the first interest—safe-guarding the physical and psychological well-being of a minor—is a compelling one. But as compelling as that interest is, it does not justify a mandatory-closure rule, for it is clear that the circumstances of the particular case may affect the significance of the interest. A trial court can determine on a case-by-case basis whether closure is necessary to protect the welfare of a minor victim. . . ."

In such closure decisions, the First Amendment requires that any such restriction on access to criminal trials be necessitated by compelling state interest and be narrowly tailored to serve that interest

In Press-Enterprise Co. v. Superior Court, 464 U.S. 501 (1984), the Supreme Court dealt with the issue of the closing of the *voir dire* examination of potential jurors. Holding that such proceedings in criminal trials are presumptively open to the public, the Court said that closure would be justified only where there is an overriding interest, where the closure is narrowly tailored, and where alternatives to closure have been considered. The court found no support for the trial court's conclusion that an open proceeding would have threatened the prospective jurors' interests in privacy in this case. (The problem was compounded, from the press's point of view, by the fact that the trial court had refused to release the transcript of the *voir dire* as well.)

In Waller v. Georgia, 467 U.S. 39 (1984), the Supreme Court addressed the problem of a closure of pretrial suppression hearings over the objection of the defendant. The case involved allegations of racketeering and gambling, and a pretrial hearing was held to consider suppression of wiretaps and evidence seized during searches at the defendants' homes. The hearing was closed when the prosecution moved for closure alleging that unnecessary "publication" of information obtained under the wiretaps would render the information inadmissible as evidence, and that the wiretap evidence would "involve" the privacy interests of some persons who were indicted but were not then on trial, and some who were not then indicted. Citing *Press-Enterprise,* the court held the closure of the suppression hearing was unjustified, noting that the entire seven-day hearing had been closed even though the tapes were played for less than 2½ hours.

*Conditional Access.* With a variety of precedents holding that trial court judges should not gag journalists and should not keep them or other members of the public out of the courtroom, it was perhaps inevitable that trial judges would seek another way of trying to solve fair trial-free press problems. A trial court judge in the State of Washington decided to use the voluntary bench-bar-media guidelines adopted in that state as a basis for granting access to his courtroom, allowing only reporters who agreed to abide by the guidelines into the room.

The Washington Supreme Court upheld the trial judge's order in Federated Publications v. Swedberg, 96 Wash.2d 13, 633 P.2d 74 (1981), certiorari denied 456 U.S. 984 (1982). Critics of bench-bar-press guidelines said that one of the envisioned dangers of such guidelines—their misuse by the courts—had become a reality. Early predictions of a trend toward such conditions on access to courtrooms proved premature, however. Adoption of amendments to state bench-bar-press guidelines, specifically precluding their use by courts for any purpose, lessened the likelihood that the guidelines, which media representatives had adopted in good faith, might be used against them in this way.

Conditional access also arises in juvenile proceedings. In many states, hearings in juvenile cases are confidential on the ground that they are primarily to rehabilitate and are clinical rather than punitive. The Supreme Court has said that a state may "continue, if it deems it appropriate, to provide and to improve provision for the confidentiality of records of police contracts and court action relating to juveniles." In re Gault, 387 U.S. 1, 25 (1967). Judges in many states will permit reporters to attend juvenile proceedings on the condition that they agree not to identify the juveniles involved.

### d.  Denials of Access to Court Records

Although there is a tradition of openness of court records, there are instances in which courts have withheld certain information during and sometimes after trials. Judges may bar release of the names of jurors in notorious cases to protect their privacy and impartiality. Or, as in *Press-Enterprise*, supra, part or all of a transcript may be withheld.

In one case, a trial court judge in Iowa, concerned about retaliation against jurors, ordered reporters not to print the names, addresses, or phone numbers of jurors in a murder trial involving the widow of a slain motorcycle gang member. The judge also barred photographs of the jurors entering and leaving the courthouse. The press appealed the order, and it was overturned in light of *Nebraska Press*. Des Moines Register & Tribune Co. v. Osmundson, 248 N.W.2d 493 (Iowa 1976).

If a judge cannot prevent the press from reporting the names of jurors that have become public, the next step might be to try to prevent the names from becoming public in a state in which jurors' names are not public property. This was approved in a criminal prosecution of major narcotics suspects in New York City. The trial judge gave prospective jurors numbers and never released their names and addresses. After conviction, defendants appealed, asserting, as one ground, that the lack of names and addresses meant the defendants could not question neighbors and learn on their own about the prospective jurors. The court affirmed the convictions. United States v. Barnes, 604 F.2d 121 (2d Cir. 1979), certiorari denied 446 U.S. 907 (1980). The court, in a decision called disturbing by *The New York Times* and others, said if an anonymous juror feels less pressure as the result of anonymity "this is as it should be—a factor contributing to his impartiality."

### e.  Use of the Contempt Power

Courts have long been concerned about efforts by the parties and press to influence judges to decide pending cases in a certain way. The traditional approach was that such efforts either influenced the judge or appeared to influence the judge—and that either view seriously impaired the functioning of the judicial branch. The technique for handling the problem was to hold the perpetrator in contempt of court and impose appropriate sanctions.

Contempt of court involves a variety of actions that obstruct the administration of justice. These include disturbance of a judicial proceeding by shouting in the courtroom, willful refusal to obey a court order to pay alimony, and refusal to answer a grand jury question after a judge has ordered the witness to do so. If a court were to punish a member of the press for contempt, it would be more likely to be for disobeying an order of the court (not to bring equipment into the courtroom, for instance), for interfering with the administration of justice by broadcasting or publishing something prejudicial (the power is generally *not* used in such instances but might be) or for refusing to answer a question about a secret source or secret notes. (See discussion of confidentiality in the next section of this chapter).

### f.  Restrictions on Cameras and Other Equipment

For most of the last half century, cameras and sound-recording equipment have been kept out of courtrooms—partially because of the canons of ethics of judges, partially because of Supreme Court decisions, and partially because of tradition. During those years, electronic equipment has become less and less obtrusive, and television has become commonplace in most other places in which newsworthy events are taking place. Experimentation with cameras in the last 10 years has led to changes in the rules in many states, but some others still forbid them. To understand the situation, one must look at its history.

When Bruno Hauptmann was brought to trial for kidnapping and slaying the son of famous aviator Charles Lindbergh in 1932, journalists and photographers packed the courtroom. Hauptmann, found guilty and sentenced to death, may not have gotten a fair trial because of the adverse publicity. In response, the American Bar Association adopted Canon 35, banning radio and television broadcasting and still cameras from courtrooms, in 1937. The canon's successor, Canon 3A(7), was amended in 1982, reflecting changing state practices. The canon now says a judge should prohibit broadcasting, reporting, and photographing, except when they are authorized by supervising appellate courts or other authorities and are consistent with fair trial rights—being unobtrusive, not distracting, and not interfering with the administration of justice.

In a Supreme Court case, Estes v. Texas, 381 U.S. 532 (1965), defendant had been indicted in the Texas state courts for "swindling"— inducing farmers to buy nonexistent fertilizer tanks and then to deliver to him mortgages on the property. The nature of the charges and the large sums of money involved attracted national interest. Texas was one of two states that then permitted televised trials (the other, Colorado, required the defendant's permission). Over Estes's objection, the trial judge permitted televising of a two-day hearing before trial.

Estes was convicted, but the Supreme Court eventually reversed the conviction, 5–4. In his majority opinion Justice Clark concluded that the use of television at the trial involved "such a probability that prejudice will result that it is deemed inherently lacking in due process" even without any showing of specific prejudices. He was concerned about the impact on jurors, judges, parties, witnesses, and lawyers.

Justice Harlan, who provided the crucial fifth vote for reversal, joined the majority opinion only to the extent that it applied to televised coverage of "courtroom proceedings of a criminal trial of widespread public interest," "a criminal trial of great notoriety," and "a heavily publicized and highly sensational affair." In such cases he was worried about the impact on jurors.

Despite the fact that there had not been five votes on the court for the notion that cameras were inherently unfair, the *Estes* decision was frequently and erroneously cited as standing for that principle during the years when cameras were almost universally banned from courtrooms. When some states began experimenting again with cameras, it was inevitable that the Supreme Court would again face this issue. The Court did so in Chandler v. Florida, 449 U.S. 560 (1981), unanimously rejecting the view that televising a criminal trial over the objections of the defendant *automatically* rendered the trial unfair. (In Florida, only the consent of the trial judge is required to allow the trial to be televised.) The defendants had argued that the impact of television on the participants introduced potentially prejudicial, but unidentifiable, aspects into the trial. The majority, in an opinion by Chief Justice Burger, first concluded that *Estes* did not stand for the proposition that broadcasting was barred "in all cases and under all circumstances." Because of Justice Harlan's narrow views in that case, the ruling of *Estes* should apply only to cases of widespread interest. (On this point, two Justices insisted that *Chandler* overruled *Estes* and should say so.)

Then, Chief Justice Burger continued that the risk of prejudice from press coverage of a trial was not limited to broadcasting. "The risk of juror prejudice in some cases does not justify an absolute ban on news coverage of trials by the printed media; so also the risk of such prejudice does not warrant an absolute constitutional ban on all broadcast coverage." A case attracts attention because of its intrinsic interest to the public. The "appropriate safeguard" against prejudice in such cases "is the defendant's right to demonstrate that the media's coverage of his case—be it printed or broadcast—compromised the ability of the particular jury that heard the case to adjudicate fairly." The Court also observed that the changes in technology since *Estes* supported the state's argument that it now be permitted to allow television in the courtroom.

Since the defendants in *Chandler*—two former city policemen accused of burglarizing a restaurant—showed no adverse impact from the televising, the convictions were upheld.

Notice that this case involved criminal defendants attacking their convictions. It did *not* involve a First Amendment claim by broadcasters to bring their equipment into the courtroom in a state that barred such entry. The Court did not discuss the impact of *Richmond Newspapers* or other First Amendment cases. As of the time *Chandler* was decided, over half the states were permitting television in the courtroom either on an experimental basis or on a permanent basis after a successful experiment had ended. In many of these states, the consent of a criminal defendant was required before entry could be allowed. Many states that barred entry or required consent of a party before entry have continued their practices after *Chandler*. Cameras are not permitted in federal courts, and Chief Justice Burger has been outspoken in his distaste for them. Special attempts for permission have thus far failed. The Supreme Court denied certiorari in the attempt to get the Westmoreland libel trial televised in 1984. By 1985, more than 40 states were admitting cameras to courtrooms.

Among the arguments in favor of cameras in courtrooms are educational value, the opportunity to let more people see the administration of justice, the "neutral" way the camera views the scene without necessity of human narration, the possibility that witnesses will testify more truthfully because others who know the truth may be watching, the creation of a video record for appellate purposes, and the possibility of closed circuit viewing by spectators elsewhere in the courthouse.

Among arguments against cameras in courtrooms are the danger that excerpts of trials will be used sensationally, threats to the privacy or safety of the jurors, the possibility that participants (judge, lawyers, witnesses) may behave differently with cameras present, the fear that camera angles and choices of shots will influence viewers' perceptions of the scene, and the creation of disruption in the courtroom.

*Courtroom Sketching.* Where television has not been permitted in courtrooms, television news directors have resorted to sketching of the courtroom scene to provide a visual dimension to their reports of judicial proceedings. That practice came under attack during the pretrial proceedings involving the trial of the "Gainesville Eight," who were charged with conspiring to disrupt the 1972 Republican National Convention. The trial judge decreed that no sketches be drawn in the courtroom. On appeal, the court refused to accept "a sweeping prohibition of in-court sketching where there has been no showing whatsoever that sketching is any way obtrusive or disruptive." United States v. Columbia Broadcasting System, Inc., 497 F.2d 102 (5th Cir.1974).

*The Nixon Tapes in the Courts.*  As we will see later, the saga of the Nixon tapes reached its first significant stage when the Supreme Court ordered the then President to honor a subpoena from the Watergate special prosecutor to deliver tapes of a large group of conversations for use in the so-called Watergate trial.  United States v. Nixon, 418 U.S. 683 (1974).  In 1974, Congress passed the Presidential Recordings and Materials Preservation Act, directing the Administrator of General Services to take custody of the former President's tapes and documents.  The Administrator was directed to submit to Congress regulations governing access to Presidential materials of historical value.  The act was upheld in Nixon v. Administrator of General Services, 433 U.S. 425 (1977).  That was chapter two.

The third episode took shape during the Watergate trial.  The tape reels obtained from the President were played in the judge's chambers before trial.  Some conversations were declared irrelevant or privileged and were not reproduced.  The other conversations were rerecorded on new tapes designated Copy A for the district court and Copy B for the special prosecutor.  Some, but not all, of the conversations on Copy A were admitted into evidence.  Some, but not all, of these were played to the jury.  Some were played in full; others only in part.  "Deletions were effected not by modifying the exhibit itself, but by skipping deleted portions on the tape or by interrupting the sound transmission to the jurors' headphones."  Written transcripts of the conversations being played to the jurors were provided to the jurors and others in the court—all of whom heard the tapes over headphones.

During the trial, broadcasters approached Judge Sirica to obtain copies of the 22 hours of tapes played to the jury.  After extensive proceedings, he denied the request for immediate access to the tapes on the ground that the convicted defendants had appeals pending, and release of the tapes might prejudice their rights.

The court of appeals reversed, relying on the importance of the common law privilege of inspecting and copying judicial records.  The fear of prejudice to the defendants did not outweigh the public's right to access.

The Supreme Court reversed the court of appeals.  Nixon v. Warner Communications, Inc., 435 U.S. 589 (1978).  Justice Powell, writing for the majority, began by discussing the asserted common law right to inspect judicial records.  Although he found some case support, the right was not absolute.  "Every court has supervisory power over its own records and files and access has been denied where court files might have become a vehicle for improper purposes."  Common law rights to inspect had given way in cases in which the record might be used to "gratify private spite or promote public scandal" as in divorce cases; where the record contained libelous statements; and where the record contained "business information that might harm a litigant's competitive standing."  Although he thought the cases showed that the decision was "one best left to the sound discretion of the trial court," Justice Powell was willing to assume that some right to inspect the tapes existed.

The Court then reviewed Nixon's arguments against disclosure. First, he argued that he had a property interest in his voice that the broadcasters should not be allowed to exploit for commercial gain. Second, he asserted a right of privacy. (The court of appeals had rejected that argument on the grounds that the passage of the Presidential Recordings Act contemplated release of the tapes at some time, and that presidential documents are not subject to ordinary privacy claims. The broadcasters added that the privacy claim was overridden by the fact that the tapes, with the nuances and inflections, would provide added understanding. Nixon disagreed on the ground that out of 22 hours of tapes, broadcasters and record makers would use fractions, necessarily taken out of context.) Third, Nixon argued that United States v. Nixon authorized use of the tapes only for the trial since they were obtained from a third party. Finally, he argued that it would be unseemly for the courts to "facilitate the commercialization" of the tapes for presentation "at cocktail parties" or in "comedy acts or dramatic productions." Justice Powell continued:

> At this point, we normally would be faced with the task of weighing the interests advanced by the parties in light of the public interest and the duty of the courts.[14] On respondents' side of the scales is the incremental gain in public understanding of an immensely important historical occurrence that arguably would flow from the release of aural copies of these tapes, a gain said to be not inconsequential despite the already widespread dissemination of printed transcripts. Also on respondents' side of the scales is the presumption—however gauged—in favor of public access to judicial records. On petitioner's side are the arguments identified above, which must be assessed in the context of court custody of the tapes. Underlying each of petitioner's arguments is the crucial fact that respondents require a court's cooperation in furthering their commercial plans. The court—as custodian of tapes obtained by subpoena over the opposition of a sitting President, solely to satisfy "fundamental demands of due process of law in the fair administration of criminal justice," United States v. Nixon, 418 U.S., at 713— has a responsibility to exercise an informed discretion as to release of the tapes, with a sensitive appreciation of the circumstances that led to their production. This responsibility does not permit copying upon demand. Otherwise, there would exist a danger that the court could become a partner in the use of the subpoenaed material "to gratify private spite or promote public scandal." [ ], with no corresponding assurance of public benefit.

Having set the stage, Justice Powell announced that the Court need not decide the case because of a "unique element that was neither

14. Judge Sirica's principal reason for refusing to release the tapes—fairness to the defendants, who were appealing their convictions—is no longer a consideration. All appeals have been resolved.

advanced by the parties nor given appropriate consideration by the courts below." Although the parties argued that the Presidential Recordings Act did not cover these tapes, the Court found a Congressional intent to create an administrative procedure for processing all the Nixon documents, including these recordings. (Why might each party have argued against the Act's relevance?) "The presence of an alternative means of public access tips the scales in favor of denying release." Questions concerning the regulations prepared by the Administrator of General Services were reserved "for future consideration in appropriate proceedings."

The broadcasters argued that even the presence of the Act could not destroy their constitutional claims to inspect the documents. First, the broadcasters relied on Cox Broadcasting Corp. v. Cohn, 420 U.S. 469 (1975), p. 522, supra, which barred damage liability against a broadcaster that named a rape victim whose name was obtained from official court records. The broadcasters argued that this gave them a right to copy anything displayed in open court. Justice Powell disagreed: the case gave the press only the right to copy records "open to the public." Here, reporters heard the tapes and were given transcripts, and could comment on each. *Cox Broadcasting* did not require that copies of the tapes "to which the public has never had *physical* access" be made available for copying. "The First Amendment generally grants the press no right to information about a trial superior to that of the general public."

In their second constitutional argument, the broadcasters relied on the Sixth Amendment's guarantee of a public trial, asserting that public understanding of the trial is incomplete if the public cannot hear the tapes that the jury heard. Justice Powell thought this proved too much—because it would require recording testimony of live witnesses at trials. Also, the guarantee is to avoid the use of "courts as instruments of persecution" and confers no special benefit on the press. Finally, the right to public trial does not require that the trial be broadcast or recorded for the public. The requirement "is satisfied by the opportunity of members of the public and the press to attend the trial and to report what they have observed. [ ] That opportunity abundantly existed here."

Although the lower court decision favoring the broadcasters was reversed, the Court did not decide how the district court should dispose of the tapes. Justices White and Brennan dissented in part on the reading of the Recordings Act and would have ordered the tapes delivered immediately to the Administrator. Justices Marshall and Stevens, in separate opinions, would have affirmed the court of appeals.

During 1980, a federal investigation of corruption among Congressmen (Abscam) produced several cases in which Congressmen took bribes from FBI agents posing as wealthy Arabs. The meetings were videotaped secretly and provided strong evidence at the trials—at which several Congressmen were convicted. After one early trial, the networks sought, and obtained, permission to make copies of the tapes for showing on television. The argument against the showing was that this might prejudice trials still to come or retrials of those convicted if their appeals should succeed. The tapes were shown.

## C. CONFIDENTIALITY IN NEWSGATHERING

The administration of justice depends upon access to information relevant to court disputes. When the only apparent way to obtain such information is by asking a journalist to reveal a confidential source or turn over unpublished notes, documents, or outtakes, problems between the media and the courts can occur. Constitutional guarantees of a fair trial are meant to allow the parties a complete, objective hearing on the issues. What if a journalist refuses to divulge certain information? What about tapes in a television station's newsroom that shed light on an incident being considered by a court?

Journalists traditionally have sought recognition of a special privilege not to have to reveal their confidential sources, even when the identity of the source is part of the evidence sought by a court, a grand jury, or a legislative committee; but confidential sources are just part of a larger problem. In addition to being asked to reveal sources, journalists have been asked for their notes, for documents and other evidence that they obtained in the course of newsgathering, for unpublished materials (negatives of photos not used and outtakes of television productions), and for testimony as to their thoughts during the newsgathering and editing processes. In addition, there have been attempts to gather evidence by police searches of newsrooms or by obtaining reporters' travel records or telephone records in an attempt to deduce their sources.

### 1. THE ROLE OF CONFIDENTIALITY

#### a. Background

It has been generally accepted that persons thought to have relevant information may be subpoenaed to testify as witnesses at certain governmental proceedings. Nevertheless, some relationships have been held to give rise to "privileges" permitting a party to withhold information he has learned in a confidential relationship. The most venerable of these relationships have been those of physician and patient, lawyer and client, and priest and penitent. In each of these the recipient may be prevented by the source from testifying as to information learned in confidence in that professional capacity.

Under common law, an assertion by journalists of a similar privilege from testifying was generally rejected. Critics of a privilege for journalists sometimes point out that professionals in medicine and law typically must meet certain educational requirements, be certified to practice, and be subject to disciplinary action if they fail to adhere to professional standards.  Journalists, on the other hand, have no minimum educational requirements, require no certification or license to be journalists, and are not subject to the same kinds of peer review to which doctors and lawyers are subject.  So long as freedom of press belongs to everyone, not just to a few licensed to be journalists, professional standards are difficult to police.  Although one likes to believe that the vast majority of journalists are ethical and truthful, such incidents as that involving the Janet Cooke Pulitzer Prize-winning story on the juvenile heroin addict (who turned out not to be a real child) in *The Washington Post* attract public attention and are sometimes pointed to by critics of a privilege for journalists.

Despite the rejection of the privilege at common law, it has made headway as a statutory protection.  Since the first reporter's privilege statute was enacted in Maryland in 1896, half the states have enacted so-called "shield" laws.  As we shall see, these statutes may have limited utility in certain situations.

In states without privilege statutes, reporters tried, with little success, to claim such a privilege under common law.  Then, in 1958, columnist Marie Torre tried a different approach.  She had reported that a CBS executive had made certain disparaging remarks about entertainer Judy Garland.  Garland sued CBS for defamation and sought by deposition to get Torre to identify the executive.  Torre attacked the effort as a threat to freedom of the press, refused to answer the question, and asserted that the First Amendment protected her refusal.  The court, though seeing some constitutional implications, held that even if the First Amendment were to provide some protection, the reporter must testify when the information sought goes to the "heart" of the plaintiff's claim.  Garland v. Torre, 259 F.2d 545 (2d Cir.1958), certiorari denied 358 U.S. 910 (1958).  Torre ultimately served 10 days in jail for criminal contempt.

After *Garland,* reporters continued to assert First Amendment claims, still with little success.  In the late 1960's, the situation became more serious as the federal government began to serve subpoenas on reporters more frequently.  The media asserted that this made previously willing sources of information unwilling because of fear that the courts would not protect the reporter or the source, and reporters would violate confidences when pressed by the government.

### b.  The Supreme Court Considers the Privilege

The first Supreme Court case to consider whether the First Amendment supports privileges claimed by reporters involved grand jury testimony.  A grand jury is a group of citizens who receive evidence of alleged crimes brought to them by a prosecutor.  If the grand jury believes that this evidence, uncontroverted by the accused, would justify conviction, it will return an "indictment"—a formal accusation of crime.  This will set the criminal prosecution in operation.  The Fifth Amendment to the United States Constitution provides that no one be brought to trial for "a capital, or otherwise infamous crime" unless first indicted by a grand jury. States need not, and some do not, use grand juries. (Where the grand jury is not used, the prosecutor instead files an "information" against the accused to get the case started.) Grand juries are able to subpoena witnesses, and all testimony before grand juries is supposed to be kept secret. In part, this confidentiality requirement is to prevent a stigma from attaching to those whom the grand jury refuses to indict.

The Supreme Court's decision in Branzburg v. Hayes, 408 U.S. 665 (1972) was actually a decision in three cases, one of which involved a television reporter, Paul Pappas. Pappas recorded and photographed statements of Massachusetts Black Panther Party officials during a period of racial turmoil. He was allowed to enter the Party's headquarters to cover an expected police raid in return for his promise to disclose nothing he observed within. He stayed three hours, no raid occurred, and he wrote no story. He was summoned before the county grand jury but refused to answer any questions about what had taken place while he was there. When he was called a second time, he moved to quash the second summons. The motion was denied by the trial judge, who noted the absence of a statutory journalist's privilege in Massachusetts and denied the existence of a constitutional privilege. The Supreme Judicial Court of Massachusetts affirmed, and the case was appealed to the Supreme Court of the United States.

(The other two cases considered with *Pappas* involved print reporters. Paul Branzburg, a Kentucky newspaper reporter, had been called before a grand jury and directed to identify two individuals mentioned in an article he wrote about marijuana and hashish. Earl Caldwell, a *New York Times* reporter, had been subpoenaed to appear before a federal grand jury in California investigating the Black Panthers and to bring with him notes and tape recordings of interviews given to him for publication by the Panthers.)

The Supreme Court split 5–4. Justice White's opinion for the Court said, "The sole issue before us is the obligation of reporters to respond to grand jury subpoenas as other citizens do and to answer questions relevant to an investigation into the commission of a crime. . . . It is clear that the First Amendment does not invalidate every incidental burdening of the press that may result from the enforcement of civil or criminal statutes of general applicability. . . . A number of States have provided newsmen a statutory privilege of varying breadth, but the majority have not done so, and none has been provided by federal statute. Until now the only testimonial privilege for unofficial witnesses that is rooted in the Federal Constitution is the Fifth Amendment privilege against compelled self-incrimination. We are asked to create another by interpreting the First Amendment to grant newsmen a testimonial privilege that other citizens do not enjoy. This we decline to do. . . . The argument that the flow of news will be diminished by compelling reporters to aid the grand jury in a criminal investigation is not irrational, nor are the records before us silent on the matter. But we remain unclear how often and to what extent informers are actually deterred from furnishing information when newsmen are forced to testify before a grand jury. . . ."

The opinion invited legislative action: "At the federal level, Congress has freedom to determine whether a statutory newsman's privilege is necessary and desirable and to fashion standards and rules as narrow or broad as deemed necessary to deal with the evil discerned and, equally important, to refashion those rules as experience from time to time may dictate. There is also merit in leaving state legislatures free, within First Amendment limits, to fashion their own standards . . . ."

Accordingly, the Court affirmed the decision that Pappas must appear before the grand jury and made similar decisions in the cases of the print reporters.

Justice Powell wrote a concurring opinion:

I add this brief statement to emphasize what seems to me to be the limited nature of the Court's holding. The Court does not hold that newsmen, subpoenaed to testify before a grand jury, are without constitutional rights with respect to the gathering of news or in safeguarding their sources. Certainly, we do not hold, as suggested in Mr. Justice Stewart's dissenting opinion, that state and federal authorities are free to "annex" the news media as "an investigative arm of government." The solicitude repeatedly shown by this Court for First Amendment freedoms should be sufficient assurance against any such effort, even if one seriously believed that the media—properly free and untrammeled in the fullest sense of these terms—were not able to protect themselves.

. . . [T]he Court states that no harassment of newsmen will be tolerated. If a newsman believes that the grand jury investigation is not being conducted in good faith he is not without remedy. Indeed, if the newsman is called upon to give information bearing only a remote and tenuous relationship to the subject of the investigation, or if he has some other reason to believe that his testimony implicates confidential source relationships without a legitimate need of law enforcement, he will have access to the court on a motion to quash and an appropriate protective order may be entered. The asserted claim to privilege should be judged on its facts by the striking of a proper balance between freedom of the press and the obligation of all citizens to give relevant testimony with respect to criminal conduct. The balance of these vital constitutional and societal interests on a case-by-case basis accords with the tried and traditional way of adjudicating such questions . . . .

In short, the courts will be available to newsmen under circumstances where legitimate First Amendment interest require protection.

Justice Stewart, dissenting, wrote that "The Court's crabbed view of the First Amendment reflects a disturbing insensitivity to the critical role of an independent press in our society. . . . The right to gather news implies, in turn, a right to a confidential relationship between a reporter and his source."

Justice Stewart's dissent suggested three possible qualifications that might be incorporated into a qualified privilege for journalists: "[W]hen a reporter is asked to appear before a grand jury and reveal confidences, I would hold that the government must (1) show that there is probable cause to believe that the newsman had information that is clearly relevant to a specific probable violation of law; (2) demonstrate that the information sought cannot be obtained by alternative means less destructive of First Amendment rights; and (3) demonstrate a compelling and overriding interest in the information."

*Outtakes.* The problem of reporter's privilege arises most frequently in the context of material that has been published without attribution to a source, but the electronic media (and, less frequently, the print media) also face problems with "outtakes," parts of film or videotape that have been cut and not transmitted. The term might also refer to notes taken by a reporter that are not used in a story or even to perceptions or observations not even written down. Are government efforts to obtain this unpublished or unrecorded information different from the more conventional effort to get a reporter to identify a source of published information? Outtakes are essential when the goal is to try to judge the fairness of what was actually presented. This was the situation when a committee of the House of Representatives sought outtakes from a CBS documentary, "The Selling of the Pentagon," during the Vietnam War.

*Unsolicited information.* The courts are even less sympathetic when unsolicited information has been thrust on the reporter. See Lewis v. United States, 517 F.2d 236 (9th Cir.1975), upholding the contempt conviction of a manager of a radio station for refusing to produce the original of a "communique" he received from an underground group t:hat claimed responsibility for a bombing. Does this situation differ greatly from those presented in *Branzburg*?

*State Shield Laws.* Although there is still no federal shield law, about half of the states now have shield laws. Journalists might have been more effective in lobbying for such shield laws had they been in agreement about whether to lobby for absolute shield laws (that would be "airtight" but difficult to "sell" to legislators) or for qualified shield laws (that would be easier to sell but would be considerably weakened by the qualifications built into them). Some journalists, believing that the First Amendment should automatically protect confidentiality despite the Supreme Court decision in *Branzburg*, maintained that seeking shield laws from legislatures would be an inappropriate recognition of the legislators' right to pass such laws. Shield laws vary in detail but generally are statutory attempts to exempt journalists from divulging certain information—usually confidential sources or the information itself.

### c.  After Branzburg:  Other Contexts

*Criminal Trials and Shield Laws.*  The conflict between the Sixth Amendment rights of defendants in criminal trials and First Amendment claims to testimonial privilege is well illustrated in the Farber case.

Myron Farber, a reporter for *The New York Times*, began investigating a series of mysterious deaths that had occurred several years earlier at a hospital in New Jersey.  His investigations led to a series of articles and to murder indictments against a physician.  During the six-month-long murder trial, the defendant's attorney had subpoenas served on the reporter and the newspaper demanding that they produce certain documents relating to interviews with witnesses at the trial.  Motions to quash the subpoenas were denied, but the trial judge did order that the documents be delivered to him for *in camera* inspection.  Farber and the *Times* refused.  Efforts to stay the order pending appeals were denied by the state appellate courts and Justices White and Marshall.

Farber and the *Times* refused to comply and were held in civil and criminal contempt.  The civil contempt involved a fine of $5,000 per day on the *Times* and a flat $1,000 on Farber, who was sentenced to jail until he complied.  The criminal penalties were $100,000 on the newspaper, and $1,000 on Farber plus six months in jail.  On review, the New Jersey Supreme Court affirmed, 5–2.  Matter of Farber, 78 N.J. 259, 394 A.2d 330 (1978).

The court rejected the argument that the First Amendment protected Farber's refusal because of the need to keep newsgathering and dissemination from being substantially impaired.  It concluded that *Branzburg* "squarely held that no such First Amendment right exists." "Thus we do no weighing or balancing of societal interest in reaching our determination that the First Amendment does not afford appellants the privilege they claim."

The court held that the state constitutional provision affording a criminal defendant the right to compel witnesses to produce documents prevailed over the shield law.  There is also a Sixth Amendment right under the U.S. Constitution to compulsory process.  The Supreme Court of the United States denied certiorari sub nom. New York Times Co. v. New Jersey, 439 U.S. 997 (1978).  Justice Brennan took no part in the decision.

Farber spent a total of 40 days in jail, and the *Times* was fined $285,000.  The physician was acquitted.  The New Jersey Legislature subsequently strengthened its shield law.

In most confidentiality cases, it is the plaintiff or the prosecutor who seeks additional information from the journalist.  *Farber* was unusual in that it was the defendant—a murder defendant at that—seeking the information.  Under the Sixth Amendment, the defendant is entitled to compulsory process to seeks information.

C.B.S., Inc. v. Superior Court, 85 Cal.App.3d 241, 149 Cal.Rptr. 421 (1978), involved an arrangement between CBS and the Santa Clara County sheriff's department under which CBS was permitted to photograph meetings between undercover agents and two men.  The meetings led to the arrest of both men for selling controlled substances, and CBS showed the arrest sequence on its program "60 Minutes."  Before the criminal trial, the attorney for one defendant sought the CBS outtakes.  CBS refused.  The trial judge ordered the outtakes turned over to the defense.

On appeal, the court concluded that under state law, "where a criminal defendant has demonstrated a *reasonable possibility* that evidence sought to be discovered might result in his exoneration, he is entitled to its discovery."  The court ordered the judge to conduct a preliminary screening of the film and to consider whether delivery of voice clips alone would satisfy the defendant's needs.

On remand, the tapes were made available to the parties.  As a result, the prosecutor dropped the charges against the defendant who had sought the film.  The defendant's attorney is reported to have said that the film clips showed that although the defendant was present, "he didn't participate" in the transaction, contrary to the officers' version.  San Francisco Chronicle, Feb. 24, 1979 at 4.

*Civil cases.*  When we turn to civil cases the justifications change for insisting on a reporter's testimony.  Since the case is not criminal, society's interest may be less direct, and no one's freedom or life is at stake.  Instead, a private person or group is suing for injury to person, property, privacy, or reputation.

A qualified privilege was found in Democratic National Committee v. McCord, 356 F.Supp. 1394 (D.D.C.1973).  The Committee for the Reelection of the President (President Nixon's reelection committee) was defending several suits arising out of the Watergate break-in.  To obtain evidence for use in the trials, the Committee caused subpoenas to be issued against a number of journalists.  On motions to quash the subpoenas, a federal court held that since all other means had not been used to obtain the material before requesting it from reporters, and since the Committee had not shown clearly that the material was relevant to the trials, the subpoenas should not be issued.  In so ruling, the court discussed "the right of the press to gather and publish, and that of the public to receive, news from .  .  . ofttimes confidential sources."  The court also noted that the suits in question were civil, not criminal, and that the media were not parties to the suits.

The courts thus adapted to civil cases the thrust of Justice Stewart's dissent in *Branzburg*, in which he contended that three conditions be met before a journalist is forced to testify or submit material: "the government must (1) show that there is probable cause to believe that the newsman has information that is clearly relevant to a specific probable violation of law; (2) demonstrate that the information sought cannot be obtained by alternative means less destructive of First Amendment rights; and (3) demonstrate a compelling and overriding interest in the information." A number of federal cases involving subpoenas to reporters in civil suits have followed the *McCord* approach.

*The Reporter as Plaintiff.* What if the reporter *is* a party in the case? Syndicated columnist Jack Anderson sued several officials of the Nixon administration for trying to harass him. The defendants asserted that the statute of limitations had run and denied the merits of the claims. As part of their defense, they asked plaintiff when and how he learned about the alleged harassment and also sought information on other aspects of his claims. Several of these questions required disclosure of confidential sources, but plaintiff refused to reveal them. The judge ordered Anderson to reveal the sources on the ground that they were central to the defenses being raised:

> Here the newsman is not being obliged to disclose his sources. Plaintiff's pledge of confidentiality would have remained unchallenged had he not invoked the aid of the Court seeking compensatory and punitive damages based on his claim of conspiracy. Plaintiff is attempting to use the First Amendment simultaneously as a sword and a shield. He believes he was wronged by a conspiracy that sought to retaliate against the sources and to undermine his reliability and professional standing before the public because what he said was unpopular with the conspirators. But when those he accuses seek to defend by attempting to discover who his sources were, so that they may find out what the sources knew, their version of what they told him and how they were hurt, plaintiff says this is off limits—a forbidden area of inquiry. He cannot have it both ways. Plaintiff is not a bystander in the process but a principal. He cannot ask for justice and deny it to those he accuses.

The judge rejected plaintiff's claim that the conflicting claims should be "balanced." This was "most unrealistic. Having chosen to become a litigant, the newsman is not exempt from those obligations imposed by the rule of law on all litigants. . . ." The choice was plaintiff's: reveal the sources or have the case dismissed. Anderson v. Nixon, 444 F.Supp. 1195 (D.D.C.1978). The case was subsequently dismissed.

*Press as Defamation Defendant.* One complex question that cuts across several areas we have discussed is whether media defendants in defamation cases are privileged to refuse to identify confidential sources who gave them allegedly defamatory information. The philosophy of New York Times v. Sullivan counsels that debate should be open and robust—but that the press should be liable for defamations that are deliberately or recklessly false. What if the public figure plaintiff must know the source of the story to prove that the falsehood was deliberate or reckless? On the other hand, if the plaintiff can expose confidential sources simply by the expedient of suing for libel, such sources may disappear. Is *Branzburg* relevant on this aspect of reporters' privilege?

Several courts struggled with this matter in the 1970's. (Recall that in the Judy Garland case, the newspaper was not sued.) In 1979, Herbert v. Lando, p. 489, supra, shed some light on the question. Recall that the Supreme Court held that the First Amendment did not protect a journalist from having to testify about his thoughts, opinions and conclusions as he was researching and preparing a story, and about his intra-office communications with others working on the story. The Court stressed that a plaintiff operating under the *New York Times* standard had a difficult task and should be able to seek direct evidence of constitutional malice.

The Court's suggestion that relevant evidence should be available to the plaintiff would suggest that confidential sources not be protected. On the other hand, the Herbert case involved little or no potential for chilling confidential sources, because it involved only the professional journalist's thoughts and communications. The compelled revelation of confidential sources would raise a different question.

These cases present two different questions. The first is when many courts order journalists to reveal confidential sources. It is highly unlikely that any court will allow a person to sue a newspaper for libel and then immediately learn all the confidential sources that were involved in the creation of the story. Much more likely, whether under state law or the First Amendment, courts will require the plaintiff to show his need for the information. The role the source played in the story's development and the article will be crucial.

The second question is what sanction should be imposed on a defendant who refuses to obey an order to disclose the identity of its confidential sources. Since Herbert v. Lando, a few state and lower federal courts have begun to address both questions. The results in these cases appear to permit the defendant who refuses to obey an order still to prevail on the truth-falsity issue, or to prove that the damages claimed were not caused by the defamation. State shield laws may affect this question if they directly create a testimonial privilege for reporters that extends to cases where the reporter is a party.

*Identifying Violators of Judicial Orders.* Another issue of privilege arises when a judge or grand jury wants to learn who told a reporter information that was supposed to be secret. The problem is illustrated by the case of William Farr, a newspaper reporter covering the lurid Manson trial in Los Angeles. To reduce potentially prejudicial publicity in that case, the trial judge ordered the attorneys and certain others not to speak about specific phases of the case. Farr reported certain facts that he could only have learned from a person covered by the judge's order. The judge demanded that Farr identify his source despite the California privilege statute: "A publisher, editor, reporter . . . . cannot be adjudged in contempt by a court . . . . for refusing to disclose the source of any information procured for publication and published in a newspaper . . . ." Farr stated that the information had come from forbidden sources including two of the six attorneys. Each attorney denied having been a source. The judge again asked Farr to identify the individuals. Farr refused and was held in contempt.

The statute was held inapplicable because the legislature had no power to prohibit the court from seeking to preserve the integrity of its own operations. The legislature's efforts to immunize persons from punishment for violation of court orders violated the separation of powers. To immunize Farr "would severely impair the trial court's discharge of a constitutionally compelled duty to control its own officers. The trial court was enjoined by controlling precedent of the United States Supreme Court to take reasonable action to protect the defendants in the Manson case from the effects of prejudicial publicity." Farr v. Superior Court, 22 Cal.App.3d 60, 99 Cal.Rptr. 342 (1971). The Supreme Court of California denied a hearing and the Supreme Court of the United States denied certiorari 409 U.S. 1011 (1972).

In a later proceeding, Farr argued that a contempt citation upon him was essentially a sentence of imprisonment for life because he clearly would not comply. The court noted that an order committing a person until he complies with a court order is "coercive and not penal in nature." The purpose of this sanction is not to punish but to obtain compliance with the order. Where an individual demonstrates conclusively that the coercion will fail, the contempt power becomes penal and comes within a five-day maximum sentence set by California statute. The case was remanded to determine whether coercion could be justified. In re Farr, 36 Cal.App.3d 577, 111 Cal.Rptr. 649 (1974). Farr was released.

*Disclosing Information to Other Bodies.* Not only do courts ask journalists for information, so do legislatures and administrative agencies. In 1971, the House of Representatives Commerce Committee subpoenaed then-CBS president Frank Stanton, ordering him to produce portions of film shot for, but not shown on, the documentary, "The Selling of the Pentagon." When Stanton refused to give the outtakes to the Committee, it voted 25–13 to recommend that Congress issue a contempt citation. The House refused to do so.

Later, Daniel Schorr, a former CBS journalist, obtained a copy of a "secret" report of the House Intelligence Committee concerning the Central Intelligence Agency. He gave the report to the *Village Voice*, which published it in 1976. When asked by the House Ethics Committee to name the person from whom he received the report, Schorr declined. The Committee did not vote to ask for a contempt citation.

The Justice Department in July, 1985, subpoenaed the three major television networks, the Cable News Network, and the national news magazines to turn over all video and audio tapes and photographs (including outtakes) of the 17-day hostage crisis at Beirut International Airport. Government lawyers said the evidence they hoped to gather would be used for presentation to a grand jury that would be asked to indict the hijackers. Despite protests that the request amounted to a "fishing expedition," most of the media turned over copies of at least some of their tapes and photographs.

## 2.  USE OF SEARCH WARRANTS AGAINST THE PRESS

Basically, law enforcement officials may choose from among three methods for obtaining relevant evidence.  The first is simply to ask the person who probably has it to turn it over.  The lack of formality simplifies and expedites the process.  The drawback is that if the possessor of the information decides not to cooperate he may legally destroy or transfer possession of the material after learning that the police want it.

The second procedure is the subpoena, discussed above.  Prosecutorial officials ask either the court or grand jury for authority to issue a subpoena for evidence sought in connection with an investigation, or act under delegated authority.  The recipient may not legally destroy the material after being served with the subpoena.  A recipient who thinks the subpoena asks something illegal may challenge it.  If the recipient claims not to have the material or information being sought, he makes a statement to that effect under oath.  It may be difficult to prove whether the person illegally destroyed the material after receiving the subpoena.

The third method, the search warrant, plays the central role in a case involving *The Stanford Daily*, the campus newspaper at Stanford University.  A magistrate must decide whether a police request for a search warrant establishes probable cause to believe that the material sought is at the named location.  If the magistrate is persuaded, the police may execute the warrant by appearing at the specified location without prior notice and may search the premises until they find the identified material.

Police believed that *Stanford Daily* photographers had taken photographs that would aid in identifying persons who had assaulted policemen during a violent demonstration.  The police obtained a search warrant and served it on the *Daily*.  After the search, the *Daily* brought an action against the chief of police and other local officials, and the case, Zurcher v. Stanford Daily, 436 U.S. 547 (1978), eventually reached the Supreme Court.  Justice White wrote for the majority that valid warrants may be issued to search *any* property, and that even though the Fourth Amendment may protect the materials sought to be seized, nothing in the First Amendment bars searches of newspaper offices.

After the decision, a few states enacted bans on the issuance of search warrants against the media, and Congress passed the Privacy Protection Act of 1980, making it unlawful for an official of any government to search or seize "any work product material possessed by a person reasonably believed to have a purpose to disseminate to the public a newspaper, book, broadcast, or other similar form of public communication, in or affecting interstate or foreign commerce," except in special circumstances.

*Telephone Records.*  The government may learn about reporters' sources or activities in ways that do not involve search warrants or subpoenas. Reporters Committee for Freedom of the Press v. American Telephone & Telegraph Co., 593 F.2d 1030 (D.C.Cir.1978), involved government requests for records of long distance calls charged to (but perhaps not made to or from) certain telephone numbers. Reporters charged that the First and Fourteenth Amendments required that subscribers be given notice before AT&T honored the government's request for toll-call records. The court, 2–1, concluded that balancing was not appropriate because "Government access to third-party evidence in the course of a good faith felony investigation in no sense 'abridges' plaintiffs' information-gathering activities." The possibility of bad-faith investigations (to harass reporters) did not warrant prior judicial intervention unless the reporter could establish "a clear and imminent threat of such future misconduct." The dissenter would have afforded reporters the opportunity to have prior judicial decisions made on such requests on a case-by-case basis. Certiorari was denied, 440 U.S. 949 (1979), Brennan, Marshall and Stewart, JJ., dissenting.

*Department of Justice Guidelines.* After *Branzburg*, the Attorney General of the United States, in 1973, adopted guidelines to regulate the issuance of subpoenas to members of the news media. The main point was that, except for cooperating reporters, no subpoena could be issued to any member of the news media "without the express authorization of the Attorney General." In requesting such authorization, subordinates were told to do so in criminal cases only if there is reasonable ground to believe that a crime has occurred and that the information sought is essential to a successful investigation, particularly with respect to guilt or innocence, and only after efforts to obtain the information from alternative nonmedia sources have failed. In civil cases, the litigation must be "of substantial importance." Even subpoena authorization requests for publicly disclosed information "should be treated with care to avoid claims of harassment." All requests should be directed at limited subject matter, should cover a limited period of time, and "should avoid requiring production of a large volume of unpublished material."

After the Department of Justice, in 1979, obtained records of a reporter's toll calls from the local telephone company, the press urged government attention to the problem. The result was the promulgation, in November, 1980, of amendments to the subpoena guidelines to provide that discussions with the reporter should precede any subpoena to the telephone company where the appropriate Assistant Attorney General concludes that such disclosure would not jeopardize the investigation. Before any subpoena is issued, the "express authorization of the Attorney General" is required. Such authorization should not be requested from the Attorney General unless there is reason to believe a crime has been committed, the need is clear, and alternative investigation steps have been unsuccessfully explored. The reporter should be informed within 45 days (though that may be delayed another 45 days) and the information obtained shall be closely held to prevent unauthorized persons from learning what the records reveal. The amended guidelines, which may be altered by any successor Attorney General, are in 45

Fed.Reg. 76,436 (Nov. 19, 1980), are codified in 28 C.F.R. § 50.10, and are reprinted in 6 Med.L.Rptr. 2153 (1980).

### 3.  IMPLICATIONS FOR JOURNALISTS

No journalist would want to go through his career in constant fear of a subpoena or a jail term; that sort of "chill" would seriously damage the newsgathering process and the free flow of information to the public. On the other hand, journalists handling sensitive material or dealing with confidences would be foolish not to make themselves aware of the shield law protection or lack thereof in the state(s) in which they work. Journalists sometimes will find that their sources, particularly those in official positions who are experienced at dealing with the press, are themselves familiar with the state shield laws.

Legalities aside, identifiable sources and attributable quotes strengthen good news stories. That is enough reason not to promise confidentiality to every source who asks for such a promise. Even in those instances in which reporters believe pledges of confidentiality are the only way they can get information from a source, they should be certain they have authorization from their employers before making such promises. As we have seen from the cases, reporters and their employer publications or stations are often "in it together" when a court seeks evidence in their hands. News organizations are well advised to be sure that news directors, editors, reporters, and others are aware of the organization's policy on confidential sources and information before promises are made or subpoenas are served.

Although journalists can reasonably expect their employers to be supportive when subpoena problems arise, legal problems can create stress. When reporters' notes are subpoenaed, who owns the notes—the reporters or their employers? Absent any formal understanding to the contrary, employers may assert that they have "bought" them as part of the reporters' work product when the reporters endorsed their pay checks, even though the employers do not normally ask for the notes. Journalists may be more likely to feel they have "sold" only their finished stories and that the notes are still their personal property. Should it make any difference whether the reporters have taken notes in notebooks from their employers' supply rooms or in notebooks they bought themselves?

Obviously, where sensitive material is concerned, journalists should be careful about what materials they create and where they store them. Generating photocopies of confidential materials or writing memos within the news organization that might reveal or tend to reveal confidential information are examples of creating additional pieces of paper that could be subject to subpoena and should therefore not be done unnecessarily. Despite the protection against newsroom searches afforded by 1980 Congressional action, journalists may prefer to keep their most confidential notes or documents away from their offices—even away from their homes—in safe deposit boxes, for instance. This is not to suggest that paranoia should be the order of the day, and most reporters will never face such problems, but caution is in order for those handling the most sensitive information.

Computers also raise questions. If the confidential information is stored in the computer, can the journalist be compelled to create a print-out? In the event of a newsroom search, could the journalist be compelled to give law enforcement agents the password?

Even where there is no subpoena or search, journalists will some-times find themselves having to make difficult decisions about the release of unpublished (not necessarily confidential) information. Sup-pose, for example, a television newsperson takes several minutes of videotape at the scene of a fatal auto accident, but only a few seconds are used on the air. An insurance company, involved in subsequent litigation, asks the television station if it can buy the complete tape, because it believes the tape will show some details of the accident scene better than the official police photos. Should the station turn over the tape? Would doing so be a harmless extension of the station's usual role in disseminating the truth about events. Would the fact that the station last week turned over unaired tapes of a children's Halloween party play any part in the decision? Would accident victims or other news subjects be less cooperative with television cameramen if they thought the latter might give or sell tapes for non-journalistic purposes, including use in litigation?

These questions and others relating to the confidentiality problems are difficult to answer. Although it may at first be easy for journalists to say they would go to jail rather than to reveal a source or break a confidence, that becomes more difficult when relatives, neighbors, and friends outside of journalism ask how journalists think they are "above the law" and not subject to the same obligations that other citizens have. And, although a few journalists have briefly become famous by going to jail and have written about the experience, the fact is that the experience is inconvenient and disruptive at the least and quite difficult at the worst.

## D.  NEWSGATHERING FROM PUBLIC SOURCES

Journalists obtain news from government sources and government-controlled places the same way they obtain news of other kinds—by cultivating sources, making phone calls, asking questions, observing. Sometimes government and the people in it are reluctant sources, and the journalist can use legal help in obtaining access to the information. The recognition by the Supreme Court in Richmond Newspapers v. Virginia, p. 548, supra, of a First Amendment right of the public to attend trials is still an unusual recognition of a constitutional protection for newsgathering; more typically, the First Amendment has been recognized only as a right to publish news that one already possesses. Because a constitutional right of newsgathering was far from clearly established, journalists and others interested in observing the workings of government lobbied successfully in the 1960's and later for legislation at both the federal and state levels to provide access to government information.

In this section we consider access to public records, access to public meetings, and access to public places. Refer to the related discussion at p. 546, supra, on access to courtrooms and to Chapter XIII for discussion of access to private places.

### 1.   ACCESS TO PUBLIC RECORDS

#### a.   *Freedom of Information Act*

As long as legislatures were the preeminent lawmakers in the country, persons concerned with government actions could follow the process. With the New Deal, however, vast numbers of administrative agencies and organizations emerged. Congress empowered most of them to promulgate their own internal rules, to issue substantive regulations, to enforce laws, to adjudicate some controversies, and take other action of great importance to citizens. The sheer number of regulations and orders being promulgated made it difficult to keep track of the process. In addition, some of the agencies were not open about their operations.

In 1946, Congress passed the Administrative Procedure Act to require all administrative agencies to follow certain procedures in the adoption of regulations and in their adjudicative hearings. Congress also sought to make the internal rules and procedures of agencies more readily available to the public.

For a variety of reasons, this first effort at openness was not notably successful. In 1967, Congress responded to growing criticism by adopting the first version of the Freedom of Information Act. The FOIA was amended in 1974 to expand its scope. 5 U.S.C. § 552.

The FOIA applies to all federal government agencies except Congress, the courts, the government of the District of Columbia, and courts martial or the military during wartime. The Act requires each agency to publish in the Federal Register a description of its organization and a list of its personnel through whom the public can obtain information. Each agency must also explain the procedures by which it will furnish information. Each agency must make available to the public staff manuals and internal instructions that affect members of the public, final opinions in adjudicated cases, and current indexes.

Agencies may set reasonable fees for finding and copying material requested by the public. These fees are to be waived when the information will be of benefit to the general public.

Agencies are supposed to respond quickly to requests for information. Should an agency not comply with the FOIA, a member of the public may ask a federal district court to enforce the act. The court may review in private the material the agency wishes to withhold, but it is the agency that bears the burden of showing that the material may be withheld under one of the exemptions to the Act discussed below. If the court decides the information should be released, it can order the government to pay all costs associated with the court action. Additionally, the agency employee who authorized the improper withholding of the information may be punished.

The FOIA contains nine exemptions—categories of material that need not be made available to the public. Several of these exemptions were amended in 1974 to require more material to be given to the public. The exemptions are:

(b) This section does not apply to matters that are—

(1)(A) specifically authorized under criteria established by an Executive order to be kept secret in the interest of national defense or foreign policy and (B) are in fact properly classified pursuant to such Executive order;

(2) related solely to the internal personnel rules and practices of an agency;

(3) specifically exempted from disclosure by statute (other than [the Privacy Act], provided that such statute (A) requires that the matters be withheld from the public in such a manner as to leave no discretion on the issue, or (B) establishes particular criteria for withholding or refers to particular types of matters to be withheld;

(4) trade secrets and commercial or financial information obtained from a person and privileged or confidential;

(5) inter-agency or intra-agency memorandums or letters which would not be available by law to a party other than an agency in litigation with the agency;

(6) personnel and medical files and similar files the disclosure of which would constitute a clearly unwarranted invasion of personal privacy;

(7) investigatory records compiled for law enforcement purposes, but only to the extent that the production of such records would (A) interfere with enforcement proceedings, (B) deprive a person of a right to a fair trial or an impartial adjudication, (C) constitute an unwarranted invasion of personal privacy, (D) disclose the identity of a confidential source and, in the case of a record compiled by a criminal law enforcement authority in the course of a criminal investigation, or by an agency conducting a lawful national security intelligence investigation, confidential information furnished only by the confidential source, (E) disclose investigative techniques and procedures, or (F) endanger the life or physical safety of law enforcement personnel;

(8) contained in or related to examination, operating, or condition reports prepared by, on behalf of, or for the use of an agency

responsible for the regulation or supervision of financial institutions; or

(9) geological and geophysical information and data, including maps, concerning wells.

[Any reasonably segregable portion of a record must be provided to any person requesting such record after deletion of the portions that are exempt under this subsection.]

### Notes and Questions

1. Notice that nothing in the Act gives any special rights to the press as opposed to the public generally. Is that surprising?

2. What appear to be the crucial limitations of the Act?

3. Each exemption has produced its share of litigation. Those causing the most difficulty appear to be the first, third, fifth, and seventh exemptions. In some cases amendments have already altered interpretations when Congress disagreed with a judicial interpretation. The procedures under the Act can get quite complicated. The Reporters Committee for Freedom of the Press and other organizations have prepared publications on how to use the Act.

The Supreme Court has had occasion to pass on several cases interpreting the Act. These are often technical in nature and not particularly useful for our purposes.

4. Critics of the Act argue that compliance with it costs the government and the taxpayers too much money, that it endangers some law enforcement personnel and informants, and that it is an example of too much government, but the Act appears to have weathered most of the attempts to weaken it.

### b.   The Privacy Act

The movement toward openness in government has been tempered by growing concern about the dangers to individual privacy resulting from the growing number of records and federal agencies keeping records. In response to these concerns, Congress passed the Privacy Act of 1974. 5 U.S.C. § 522a. One major part of the Act permits subjects of records to see their files, obtain copies, and correct inaccuracies. Individuals are not required to give the agencies any reasons for wanting to see their files. Civil actions may be brought for improper refusals to provide the file and for improper refusals to make corrections.

The part of the Act of most interest to the press, however, is the part that restricts disclosure of the contents of records unless certain conditions are met:

(b) Conditions of disclosure.—No agency shall disclose any record which is contained in a system of records by any means of communication to any person, or to another agency, except pursuant to a written request by, or with the prior written consent of, the individual to whom the record pertains, unless disclosure of the record would be—

(1) to those officers and employees of the agency which maintains the record who have a need for the record in the performance of their duties;

(2) required under section 552 of this title [FOIA];

(3) for a routine use as defined . . .;

(4) to the Bureau of the Census for purposes of planning or carrying out a census or survey or related activity . . .;

(5) to a recipient who has provided the agency with advance adequate written assurance that the record will be used solely as a statistical research or reporting record, and the record is to be transferred in a form that is not individually identifiable;

(6) to the National Archives of the United States as a record which has sufficient historical or other value to warrant its continued preservation by the United States Government, or for evaluation by the Administrator of General Services or his designee to determine whether the record has such value;

(7) to another agency or to an instrumentality of any governmental jurisdiction within or under the control of the United States for a civil or criminal law enforcement activity if the activity is authorized by law, and if the head of the agency or instrumentality has made a written request to the agency which maintains the record specifying the particular portion desired and the law enforcement activity for which the record is sought;

(8) to a person pursuant to a showing of compelling circumstances affecting the health or safety of an individual if upon such disclosure notification is transmitted to the last known address of such individual;

(9) to either House of Congress, or, to the extent of matter within its jurisdiction, any committee or subcommittee thereof, any joint committee of Congress or subcommittee of any such joint committee;

(10) to the Comptroller General, or any of his authorized representatives, in the course of the performance of the duties of the General Accounting Office; or

(11) pursuant to the order of a court of competent jurisdiction.

### c. State Open Records Statutes

Although they vary a great deal, state access to information statutes exist in every state and they are frequently parallel to the federal statute by beginning with a premise that all government records should be publicly available and then listing a series of exceptions or exemptions. These statutes are generally still new enough that they are subject to frequent amendment, and journalists are well advised to obtain copies of their open records statutes for their states to see just what is available.

### d.   Using the Statutes

Freedom of information legislation can sometimes be helpful to a journalist—or, for that matter, any other member of the public seeking information—but that is not to say that it is frequently relied upon by the average journalist covering government. Establishing a good relationship with friendly sources inside government is a much more common way of obtaining information than using the statutes. When, however, the information would otherwise be unavailable, the reporter needs to know how to use the statute.

Freedom of information requests often have to be put into writing. Persons requesting information are advised to make their requests as simple as possible, specify the records wanted as specifically as possible, cite the statute under which the records are sought, ask to whom an appeal should be addressed should access to the records be denied, and either put a dollar limit on the amount they are willing to pay or ask to be advised of the cost before the request is filled.

Even with attempts to strengthen the federal statute in 1974 and the state statutes in other years, a number of problems remain. Among those most frequently cited are (1) charging excessive fees for the records, (2) delaying the filling of requests, (3) demanding unreasonable specificity in identifying the records sought, (4) contaminating otherwise releasable records by filing them with classified information, and (5) applying the exemptions too broadly.

Regrettable though it may be, it is a fact of life that the level of compliance with the state statutes is sometimes a factor of the level of government from which information is sought. Small town officials are still heard to deny access to information and to respond to mention of their states' freedom of information laws by saying, "That's just some law passed in the state capital. What are they going to do to me about it?" With few penalties built into the state laws for non-compliance and enforcement, the freedom of information legislation still has a long way to go before it becomes very helpful from the journalists' point of view.

From government's viewpoint, one problem with freedom of information legislation has been so-called "reverse FOIA" lawsuits. At issue was whether the exemptions in the statute are mandatory or discretionary. The Supreme Court held in Chrysler Corporation v. Brown, 441 U.S. 281 (1979), that FOIA does *not* create a private right of action to stop an agency from releasing documents covered by exemptions. A submitter of confidential business information, however, might attempt to stop disclosure by asserting that release would constitute an abuse of an agency's discretion under the Trade Secrets Act, 18 U.S.C. § 1905.

## 2.  ACCESS TO PUBLIC MEETINGS

Guidelines for access to meetings of Congress or its committees and access to information about Congressional proceedings are prescribed initially in the Constitution.  (Art. I, § 5):

> Each House may determine the Rules of its Proceedings.
> . . .  Each House shall keep a Journal of its Proceedings, and from time to time publish the same, excepting such Parts as may in their Judgment require Secrecy;  and the Yeas and Nays of the Members of either House on any question shall, at the Desire of one fifth of those Present, be entered on the Journal.

From the earliest days, sessions of the full House or Senate have usually been open to the public.  Senate sessions were occasionally closed for discussion of treaties or nominations, and in the 30 years between 1945 and 1975, the Senate held 17 closed sessions, devoted usually to foreign relations or defense questions.  Guide to the Congress of the United States 73 (2d ed. 1976).

Although most sessions of the full House and Senate have been open, most committee meetings were closed unless hearings were being held.  Since 1970, there has been a sharp increase in open committee meetings, extending first to mark-up sessions (in which a pending bill may be approved, amended or rewritten), and later to conference committee meetings in which representatives of the two houses try to reconcile two different versions of proposed legislation.  In 1975, the House and Senate voted to require open conferences unless a majority of conferees from either chamber vote in public to close a session.  Can such negotiations be conducted effectively in open sessions?  Should all meetings of all committees and subcommittees be open?

A different problem arises out of the conduct of Congressional investigations.  The power to legislate implies the power to inquire into subjects that may require legislation, and allows Congress to conduct investigations and hold hearings.  Congress may compel the attendance of witnesses and the production of documents at these hearings under threat of citation for contempt.  The arguments against open hearings do not involve national security or the inhibiting effect of publicity on legislative compromise.  Rather they reflect a concern for the privacy of witnesses and those whose behavior is under scrutiny.  The advent of television coverage of some Congressional hearings has made this concern more significant.

### a.  *The "Sunshine Act"*

At the urging of Congressmen and Senators from Florida, which had had good experience with its "Sunshine Law," Congress in 1976 passed a federal "Government in the Sunshine Act."  5 U.S.C. § 552b.  The statement of purpose accompanying the Act declares that "the public is entitled to the fullest practicable information regarding the decision-making processes of the Federal Government." The Act seeks to "provide the public with such information while protecting the rights of individuals and the ability of the Government to carry out its responsibilities."

Essentially, the Act provides that all federal agencies headed by boards of two or more persons appointed by the President—approximately 50 agencies—must hold "every portion of every meeting" open to the public unless there is a valid reason for closure. Adequate advance notice must be given of each meeting. If a meeting is closed because it falls within one of the 10 exemptions to be noted, the agency must make public a transcript or minutes of all parts of the meeting that do not contain exempt material. Meetings may be closed only after a publicly recorded vote of a majority of the full membership of the agency.

The exemptions apply where the agency "properly determines" that a portion of the meeting "is likely to" result in the disclosure of specified information. The exemptions include verbatim copies of several FOIA exemptions—(1) involving national defense or foreign policy; (2) involving internal rules and practices of the agency; (3) matters specifically exempted from disclosure by another statute; (4) trade secrets; (7) law enforcement investigatory records; and (8) involving financial institutions. In addition, another exemption tracks closely the "clearly unwarranted invasion of personal privacy" language of the sixth exemption of the FOIA. Given the similar goals of the two statutes, it is not surprising that they contain similar exemptions.

In addition, the Sunshine Act contains the following summarized exemptions not found in the FOIA:

(5) disclosures that "involve accusing any person of a crime, or formally censuring any person;"

(9) "premature disclosures" involving agencies that regulate currencies, securities, commodities, or financial institutions, where the disclosure would be likely to (i) lead to "significant financial speculation" in these items or (ii) "significantly endanger the financial stability of any financial institution" or where the disclosure would be likely to "significantly frustrate implementation of a proposed agency action."

(10) information concerning an agency's issuance of a subpoena or its participation in a civil action or proceeding.

### b. State Open Meetings Statutes

Clearly, less governmental business is conducted by the state legislature than by the multitude of agencies created by the legislature or by the executive branch under legislative authorization. In an effort to bring these agencies and their decision-making processes under public scrutiny many state legislatures have adopted "open meeting" or "sunshine" laws. These statutes and their enforcement provisions vary greatly. Some statutes provide that actions improperly taken in closed meetings can be declared null and void. Journalists generally favor fines or other penalties for public officials who disregard the open meetings statutes.

### 3. ACCESS TO PUBLIC PLACES

In addition to keeping records and holding meetings, governments also control access to their own buildings and grounds and sometimes to privately-owned property as well. No general legislation covers these situations. Instead, each has been handled under regulations issued by the person in control or by specific governmental departments such as the Bureau of Prisons.

For example, in 1974, President Ford excluded all reporters from mingling with guests at White House receptions. In 1975, he announced new rules under which a small pool of reporters, carrying only note-books, might circulate at such events "with the understanding that the pool reporters will respect the privacy of personal communications be-tween myself or Mrs. Ford and our guests." Editor & Publisher, Sept. 13, 1975 at 15.

In 1979, when President Carter took a steamer trip down the Mississippi River, he set rules for reporters who wished to accompany him: that the White House must approve all photographs, that no photos be bought from tourists, and that national organizations not distribute photos taken by local photographers along the way. As a result, several organizations refused to send their staffs on the trip. New York Times, Aug. 15, 1979 at A18.

*Access and Terrorism.* Terrorist activity has shown the tension between the efforts of the press to gather news and the desire of law enforcement officials to isolate the terrorists and to prevent them from learning in advance what action the police are planning to take. The problem is, of course, aggravated if the terrorists have taken hostages whose lives are now in danger. Some have suggested that reporters covering such events receive training in psychology so that they under-stand the impact their coverage may have on the situation itself. Some police officials have proposed guidelines for handling future episodes, such as requiring that broadcast journalists be kept farther from the scene than are print reporters so that officials could brief the print press without risking the possibility that important information would reach the terrorists prematurely.

Many reporters have objected, obviously, to plans to keep them from the scene. They urge that the matter be left to the sense of responsibili-ty of the reporters. One journalist has said that "suppressing news of terrorism would be a denial of democracy that could take more lives than it saves. It is unworkable and philosophically unthinkable." The Quill (Dec. 1977) at 23.

*Access to Police and Fire Scenes.* As for local situations, almost all states have statutes that authorize police to bar access and provide that failure to obey an order to remain outside is punishable as failing to obey lawful police orders. Press passes that frequently permit journalists to cross police or fire lines at the scene of an accident, crime, or tragedy are typically subject to the control of the police and do not give the reporter a privilege to disregard police orders directed to them.

*Access to Prisons.* In 1974, the Supreme Court decided two companion cases involving efforts to obtain information from inmates confined in prisons. Pell v. Procunier, 417 U.S. 817 (1974), involved a ban on press interviews with named inmates in the California prison system. Saxbe v. Washington Post Co., 417 U.S. 843 (1974) involved a similar ban in the federal prison system. The Court concluded in *Pell* that the security and penological considerations of incarceration were sufficient to justify rejection of the inmates' claims that the interview ban violated their First Amendment rights.

Justice Stewart, writing for the Court in *Pell* and in *Saxbe*, then turned to the claims raised by the press. He noted that "this regulation is not part of an attempt by the State to conceal the conditions in its prisons or to frustrate the press' investigation and reporting of those conditions." Reporters could visit the institutions and "speak about any subject to any inmates whom they might encounter." Interviews with inmates selected at random were also permitted and both the press and public could take tours through the prisons. "In short, members of the press enjoy access to California prisons that is not available to other members of the public." Indeed, the only apparent restriction was the one being challenged.

Relying in part on the logic of *Branzburg*, Justice Stewart said that ". . . [N]ewsmen have no constitutional right of access to prisons or their inmates beyond that afforded the general public." Four justices dissented.

A few years later the Supreme Court returned to the prison question in a slightly different context in Houchins v. KQED, Inc., 438 U.S. 1 (1978). A suicide had occurred at a jail in Santa Rita, Calif. KQED, licensee of a television station in San Francisco, reported the story and quoted a psychiatrist as saying that conditions at part of the jail were responsible for the illnesses of some prisoners there. Earlier, a federal judge had ruled that conditions at part of the jail constituted cruel and unusual punishment. Houchins, the county sheriff, refused to admit a KQED camera crew to the jail, and no public tours of the jail were permitted.

KQED and the NAACP filed suit under 42 U.S.C. § 1983 claiming violation of their First Amendment rights. The NAACP claimed that information about the jail was essential to permit public debate on jail conditions in the county. After the suit was filed, the sheriff permitted monthly tours. Although he barred cameras and tape recorders, he allowed several reporters, including one from KQED, to tour. Tour members "were not permitted to interview inmates and inmates were generally removed from view."

KQED argued that the tours were unsatisfactory because advance scheduling prevented timely access and because photography and interviewing were barred. The sheriff defended his policy on grounds of "inmate privacy," the danger of creating "jail celebrities," and the concern that there would be a disruption of jail operations.

Chief Justice Burger announced the judgment of the Supreme Court and delivered an opinion joined by Justices White and Rehnquist. In it, he wrote, "The media are not a substitute for or an adjunct of government, and like the courts, they are 'ill-equipped' to deal with problems of prison administration. . . . The public importance of conditions in penal facilities and the media's role of providing information afford no basis for reading into the Constitution a right of the public or the media to enter these institutions, with camera equipment, and take moving and still pictures of inmates for broadcast purposes. This Court has never intimated a First Amendment guarantee of a right of access to all sources of information within government control . . . ."

Justices Marshall and Blackmun took no part in the case. Justice Stewart concurred in the judgment but thought KQED was entitled to more limited injunctive relief. Justices Stevens, Brennan, and Powell dissented.

Does the Supreme Court's decision in Richmond Newspapers v. Virginia, supra, have implications for any future cases in which journalists might seek access to prisons for the purpose of newsgathering?

### 4. DISCRIMINATORY ACCESS TO INFORMATION

Our focus has been on the question of whether any statute or constitutional provision requires unwilling government officials to reveal information or to permit the press or public to gather information from government files, meetings, or areas under government control. (Occasionally, a statute like the Privacy Act bars willing officials from supplying information.) In such a situation, government officials want nobody to learn certain information.

A quite different question arises when government officials are willing to part with information that they are not required to divulge—but want to discriminate among the prospective gatherers. The government's interest in this situation is no longer that the material should remain confidential or that secrecy is needed, because the official is quite prepared to divulge the information. The claim of government secrecy has been replaced by the desire of a government official to play favorites in the disclosure process, either for personal or political reasons.

Reporters have no right to force unwilling private persons to reveal information. If the private sources do decide to speak, there is no reason why they cannot sell their stories to the highest bidders or give them first to reporters who are close friends. But government traditionally must not behave in a discriminatory fashion. Even though government officials may not be required by statute or constitution to reveal certain information, they do not have unlimited control over the method of dissemination.

The starting point in general is that unless an official can demonstrate some reason for treating two apparently similar persons differently, the one who is being treated less well is not receiving equal protection of the laws. Notice that this constitutional protection in the Fourteenth Amendment applies broadly to all government action. If a government welfare program were arbitrarily to pay more money to redheads than to other recipients, the others would be able to claim a denial of equal protection.

Not all distinctions are invidious. When press cards must be limited for some reasons, some government agencies may prefer media organizations that regularly cover the situations in which the cards will be needed. For example, if media representatives need press cards to get through police lines at emergencies, the police might give cards to media that regularly cover such events but not give cards to specialized newspapers or magazines that do not. Drawing these lines is sometimes difficult. The situation is explored in Los Angeles Free Press, Inc. v. City of Los Angeles, 9 Cal.App.3d 448, 88 Cal.Rptr. 605 (1970), certiorari denied 401 U.S. 982 (1971), Justices Black, Douglas, and Brennan dissenting.

Sometimes gender differences between reporters have been asserted to justify unequal treatment. The question of admitting women sports reporters to men's locker rooms went to court when the New York Yankees refused to allow them in after games. (This is not a case of private discrimination because Yankee Stadium was located on property owned by the city and thus involved governmental action.) The judge ordered that the women be admitted when the men were admitted. The players' privacy could be protected in less restrictive ways than by totally excluding women reporters. "The other two interests asserted by defendants, maintaining the status of baseball as a family sport and conforming to traditional notions of decency and propriety, are clearly too insubstantial to merit serious consideration." Ludtke v. Kuhn, 461 F.Supp. 86 (S.D.N.Y.1978).

Sometimes different treatment may be based on characteristics of the individual. For example, in Sherrill v. Knight, 569 F.2d 124 (D.C.Cir. 1977), Sherrill, Washington correspondent for *The Nation*, had credentials for the House and Senate press galleries but was denied a White House press pass because of Secret Service objections. He was said to be a security risk because he had assaulted the press secretary to the governor of Florida and also faced assault charges in Texas.

The Secret Service had been ordered by the trial court to formulate "narrow and specific" standards for deciding who posed a sufficient danger to the President to be denied a press card.  Security officials were the appellants in the court of appeals.

The court recognized that the safety of a President was a compelling, indeed overwhelming, interest that would justify restrictions on a reporter's access to the White House.  But simply telling the reporter that he was barred "for reasons of security" did not meet the procedural safeguards that were required in this case.  The court ordered the Secret Service to "publish or otherwise make publicly known the actual standard employed in determining whether an otherwise eligible journalist will obtain a White House pass."  This did not lend itself to the narrow specifications required by the trial judge.  It is enough if the Service is guided by the standard of whether the applicant "presents a potential source of physical danger .  .  . so serious as to justify his exclusion."  In addition, a reporter who is barred must get notice of the facts the Service is relying on and have a chance to rebut them.

Occasionally, the basis for the different treatment is to be found in the nature of the media involved.  Some states have barred journalists with tape recorders from legislative chambers, though they have allowed reporters to use pencil and pad.  These limits, which have rarely been challenged, have usually been upheld.

Television has presented special problems.  Earlier in this Chapter, we considered the question of television cameras in courtrooms.  Television has also raised questions in connection with the coverage of executions.  In Garrett v. Estelle, 556 F.2d 1274 (5th Cir.1977), certiorari denied 438 U.S. 914 (1978), the court upheld Texas's refusal to allow cameras or tape recorders into the execution chamber.  The state was willing to allow press pool reporters into the chamber and to permit other reporters to view the events over simultaneous closed-circuit television.  The court held, following *Pell* and *Saxbe*, that "the first amendment does not accompany the press where the public may not go."  There was no public right to entry or to film the event.

The final argument was that Texas had already chosen to make executions public by televising them over a closed circuit.  Texas responded that legislation closing executions had already been upheld, Holden v. Minnesota, 137 U.S. 483 (1890), and that the limited televising of the execution should not be equated with making the event public.  The court agreed that the closed circuit television was for those allowed to be present and should not be used to justify opening the event to the public.

*Televising Congress.*  In early 1979, the House of Representatives began television coverage of its proceedings.  The House decided to maintain control over the cameras and allow broadcasters to use whatever footage they wanted.  The entire proceedings are available to subscribers to a special cable network.  An early dispute involved the practice of blacking out the picture during votes.  At these times the screen shows only the ongoing tally.  Speaker O'Neill explained that since members may change their votes at the end of the 15-minute voting period only by "going to the well" and informing the clerk, they may be reluctant to do that with the cameras focused on them.  Attempts to introduce cameras in the Senate have thus far failed.

# Appendix A

# THE CONSTITUTION OF THE UNITED STATES OF AMERICA

We the People of the United States, in Order to form a more perfect Union, establish Justice, insure domestic Tranquility, provide for the common defence, promote the general Welfare, and secure the Blessings of Liberty to ourselves and our Posterity, do ordain and establish this Constitution for the United States of America.

## ARTICLE I.

SECTION 1.   All legislative Powers herein granted shall be vested in a Congress of the United States, which shall consist of a Senate and House of Representatives.

SECTION 2.   The House of Representatives shall be composed of Members chosen every second Year by the People of the several States, and the Electors in each State shall have the Qualifications requisite for Electors of the most numerous Branch of the State Legislature.

No Person shall be a Representative who shall not have attained to the Age of twenty five Years, and been seven Years a Citizen of the United States, and who shall not, when elected, be an inhabitant of that State in which he shall be chosen.

Representatives and direct Taxes shall be apportioned among the several States which may be included within this Union, according to their respective Numbers, which shall be determined by adding to the whole Number of free Persons, including those bound to Service for a Term of Years, and excluding Indians not taxed, three fifths of all other Persons.   The actual Enumeration shall be made within three Years after the first Meeting of the Congress of the United States, and within every subsequent Term of ten Years, in such Manner as they shall by Law direct.   The Number of Representatives shall not exceed one for every thirty Thousand, but each State shall have at Least one Representative; and until such enumeration shall be made, the State of New Hampshire shall be entitled to chuse three, Massachusetts eight, Rhode Island and Providence Plantations one, Connecticut five, New York six, New Jersey four, Pennsylvania eight, Delaware one, Maryland six, Virginia ten, North Carolina five, South Carolina five, and Georgia three.

When vacancies happen in the Representation from any State, the Executive Authority thereof shall issue Writs of Election to fill such Vacancies.

The House of Representatives shall chuse their Speaker and other Officers; and shall have the sole Power of Impeachment.

SECTION 3. The Senate of the United States shall be composed of two Senators from each State, chosen by the Legislature thereof, for six Years; and each Senator shall have one Vote.

Immediately after they shall be assembled in Consequence of the first Election, they shall be divided as equally as may be into three Classes. The Seats of the Senators of the first Class shall be vacated at the Expiration of the second Year, of the second Class at the Expiration of the fourth Year, and of the third Class at the Expiration of the sixth Year, so that one third may be chosen every second Year; and if Vacancies happen by Resignation, or otherwise, during the Recess of the Legislature of any State, the Executive thereof may make temporary Appointments until the next Meeting of the Legislature, which shall then fill such Vacancies.

No Person shall be a Senator who shall not have attained to the Age of thirty Years, and been nine Years a Citizen of the United States, and who shall not, when elected, be an Inhabitant of that State for which he shall be chosen.

The Vice President of the United States shall be President of the Senate, but shall have no Vote, unless they be equally divided.

The Senate shall chuse their other Officers, and also a President pro tempore, in the Absence of the Vice President, or when he shall exercise the Office of President of the United States.

The Senate shall have the sole Power to try all Impeachments. When sitting for that Purpose, they shall be on Oath or Affirmation. When the President of the United States is tried the Chief Justice shall preside: And no Person shall be convicted without the Concurrence of two thirds of the Members present.

Judgment in Cases of Impeachment shall not extend further than to removal from Office, and disqualification to hold and enjoy any Office of honor, Trust, or Profit under the United States: but the Party convicted shall nevertheless be liable and subject to Indictment, Trial, Judgment, and Punishment, according to Law.

SECTION 4. The Times, Places and Manner of holding Elections for Senators and Representatives, shall be prescribed in each State by the Legislature thereof; but the Congress may at any time by Law make or alter such Regulations, except as to the Places of chusing Senators.

The Congress shall assemble at least once in every Year, and such Meeting shall be on the first Monday in December, unless they shall by Law appoint a different Day.

SECTION 5. Each House shall be the Judge of the Elections, Returns, and Qualifications of its own Members, and a Majority of each shall constitute a Quorum to do Business; but a smaller Number may adjourn from day to day, and may be authorized to compel the Attendance of absent Members, in such Manner, and under such Penalties as each House may provide.

Each House may determine the Rules of its Proceedings, punish its Members for disorderly Behaviour, and, with the Concurrence of two thirds, expel a Member.

Each House shall keep a Journal of its Proceedings, and from time to time publish the same, excepting such Parts as may in their Judgment require Secrecy; and the Yeas and Nays of the Members of either House on any question shall, at the Desire of one fifth of those Present, be entered on the Journal.

Neither House, during the Session of Congress, shall, without the Consent of the other, adjourn for more than three days, nor to any other Place than that in which the two Houses shall be sitting.

SECTION 6.  The Senators and Representatives shall receive a Compensation for their Services, to be ascertained by Law, and paid out of the Treasury of the United States.  They shall in all Cases, except Treason, Felony and Breach of the Peace, be privileged from Arrest during their Attendance at the Session of their respective Houses, and in going to and returning from the same; and for any Speech or Debate in either House, they shall not be questioned in any other Place.

No Senator or Representative shall, during the Time for which he was elected, be appointed to any civil Office under the Authority of the United States, which shall have been created, or the Emoluments whereof shall have been encreased during such time; and no Person holding any Office under the United States, shall be a Member of either House during his Continuance in Office.

SECTION 7.  All Bills for raising Revenue shall originate in the House of Representatives; but the Senate may propose or concur with amendments as on other Bills.

Every Bill which shall have passed the House of Representatives and the Senate, shall, before it becomes a Law, be presented to the President of the United States; If he approve he shall sign it, but if not he shall return it, with his Objections to that House in which it shall have originated, who shall enter the Objections at large on their Journal, and proceed to reconsider it.  If after such Reconsideration two thirds of that House shall agree to pass the Bill, it shall be sent, together with the Objections, to the other House, by which it shall likewise be reconsidered, and if approved by two thirds of that House, it shall become a Law. But in all such Cases the Votes of both Houses shall be determined by Yeas and Nays, and the Names of the Persons voting for and against the Bill shall be entered on the Journal of each House respectively.  If any Bill shall not be returned by the President within ten Days (Sunday excepted) after it shall have been presented to him, the Same shall be a Law, in like Manner as if he had signed it, unless the Congress by their Adjournment prevent its Return, in which Case it shall not be a Law.

Every Order, Resolution, or Vote to which the Concurrence of the Senate and House of Representatives may be necessary (except on a question of Adjournment) shall be presented to the President of the

United States; and before the Same shall take Effect, shall be approved by him, or being disapproved by him, shall be repassed by two thirds of the Senate and House of Representatives, according to the Rules and Limitations prescribed in the Case of a Bill.

SECTION 8. The Congress shall have Power To lay and collect Taxes, Duties, Imposts and Excises, to pay the Debts and provide for the common Defence and general Welfare of the United States; but all Duties, Imposts and Excises shall be uniform throughout the United States;

To borrow Money on the credit of the United States;

To regulate Commerce with foreign Nations, and among the several States, and with the Indian Tribes;

To establish an uniform Rule of Naturalization, and uniform Laws on the subject of Bankruptcies throughout the United States;

To coin Money, regulate the Value thereof, and of foreign Coin, and fix the Standard of Weights and Measures;

To provide for the Punishment of counterfeiting the Securities and current Coin of the United States;

To establish Post Offices and post Roads;

To promote the Progress of Science and useful Arts, by securing for limited Times to Authors and Inventors the exclusive Right to their respective Writings and Discoveries;

To constitute Tribunals inferior to the supreme Court;

To define and punish Piracies and Felonies committed on the high Seas, and Offences against the Law of Nations;

To declare War, grant Letters of Marque and Reprisal, and make Rules concerning Captures on Land and Water;

To raise and support Armies, but no Appropriation of Money to that Use shall be for a longer Term than two Years;

To provide and maintain a Navy;

To make Rules for the Government and Regulation of the land and naval Forces;

To provide for calling forth the Militia to execute the Laws of the Union, suppress Insurrections and repel Invasions;

To provide for organizing, arming, and disciplining, the Militia, and for governing such Part of them as may be employed in the Service of the United States, reserving to the States respectively, the Appointment of the Officers, and the Authority of training the Militia according to the discipline prescribed by Congress;

To exercise exclusive Legislation in all Cases whatsoever, over such District (not exceeding ten Miles square) as may, by Cession of particular States, and the Acceptance of Congress, become the Seat of the Government of the United States, and to exercise like Authority over all Places purchased by the Consent of the Legislature of the State in which the

Same shall be, for the Erection of Forts, Magazines, Arsenals, dock-Yards, and other needful Buildings;—And

To make all Laws which shall be necessary and proper for carrying into Execution the foregoing Powers, and all other Powers vested by this Constitution in the Government of the United States, or in any Department or Officer thereof.

SECTION 9.  The Migration or Importation of such Persons as any of the States now existing shall think proper to admit, shall not be prohibited by the Congress prior to the Year one thousand eight hundred and eight, but a Tax or duty may be imposed on such Importation, not exceeding ten dollars for each Person.

The Privilege of the Writ of Habeas Corpus shall not be suspended, unless when in Cases of Rebellion or Invasion the public Safety may require it.

No Bill of Attainder or ex post facto Law shall be passed.

No Capitation, or other direct, Tax shall be laid, unless in Proportion to the Census or Enumeration herein before directed to be taken.

No Tax or Duty shall be laid on Articles exported from any State.

No Preference shall be given by any Regulation of Commerce or Revenue to the Ports of one State over those of another; nor shall Vessels bound to, or from, one State, be obliged to enter, clear, or pay Duties in another.

No Money shall be drawn from the Treasury, but in Consequence of Appropriations made by Law; and a regular Statement and Account of the Receipts and Expenditures of all public Money shall be published from time to time.

No Title of Nobility shall be granted by the United States: And no Person holding any Office of Profit or Trust under them, shall, without the Consent of the Congress, accept of any present, Emolument, Office, or Title, of any kind whatever, from any King, Prince or foreign State.

SECTION 10.  No State shall enter into any Treaty, Alliance, or Confederation; grant Letters of Marque and Reprisal; coin Money; emit Bills of Credit; make any Thing but gold and silver Coin a Tender in Payment of Debts; pass any Bill of Attainder, ex post facto Law, or Law impairing the Obligation of Contracts, or grant any Title of Nobility.

No State shall, without the Consent of the Congress, lay any Imposts or Duties on Imports or Exports, except what may be absolutely necessary for executing its inspection Laws: and the net Produce of all Duties and Imposts, laid by any State on Imports or Exports, shall be for the Use of the Treasury of the United States; and all such Laws shall be subject to the Revision and Controul of the Congress.

No State shall, without the Consent of Congress, lay any Duty of Tonnage, keep Troops, or Ships of War in time of Peace, enter into any Agreement or Compact with another State, or with a foreign Power, or engage in War, unless actually invaded, or in such imminent Danger as will not admit of delay.

## ARTICLE II.

SECTION 1.  The executive Power shall be vested in a President of the United States of America.  He shall hold his Office during the Term of four Years, and, together with the Vice President, chosen for the same Term, be elected, as follows

Each State shall appoint, in such Manner as the Legislature thereof may direct, a Number of Electors, equal to the whole Number of Senators and Representatives to which the State may be entitled in the Congress: but no Senator or Representative, or Person holding an Office of Trust or Profit under the United States, shall be appointed an Elector.

The Electors shall meet in their respective States, and vote by Ballot for two Persons, of whom one at least shall not be an Inhabitant of the same State with themselves.  And they shall make a List of all the Persons voted for, and of the Number of Votes for each; which List they shall sign and certify, and transmit sealed to the Seat of the Government of the United States, directed to the President of the Senate.  The President of the Senate shall, in the Presence of the Senate and House of Representatives, open all the Certificates, and the Votes shall then be counted.  The Person having the greatest Number of Votes shall be the President, if such Number be a Majority of the whole Number of Electors appointed;  and if there be more than one who have such Majority, and have an equal Number of Votes, then the House of Representatives shall immediately chuse by Ballot one of them for President;  and if no Person have a Majority, then from the five highest on the List the said House shall in like Manner chuse the President.  But in chusing the President, the Votes shall be taken by States, the Representation from each State having one Vote;  a quorum for this Purpose shall consist of a Member or Members from two thirds of the States, and a Majority of all the States shall be necessary to a Choice. In every Case, after the Choice of the President, the Person having the greatest Number of Votes of the Electors shall be the Vice President. But if there should remain two or more who have equal Votes, the Senate shall chuse from them by Ballot the Vice President.

The Congress may determine the Time of chusing the Electors, and the Day on which they shall give their Votes; which Day shall be the same throughout the United States.

No Person except a natural born Citizen, or a Citizen of the United States, at the time of the Adoption of this Constitution, shall be eligible to the Office of President; neither shall any Person be eligible to that Office who shall not have attained to the Age of thirty five Years, and been fourteen Years a Resident within the United States.

In Case of the Removal of the President from Office, or of his Death, Resignation, or Inability to discharge the Powers and Duties of the said Office, the Same shall devolve on the Vice President, and the

Congress may by Law provide for the Case of Removal, Death, Resignation or Inability, both of the President and Vice President, declaring what Officer shall then act as President, and such Officer shall act accordingly, until the Disability be removed, or a President shall be elected.

The President shall, at stated Times, receive for his Services, a Compensation, which shall neither be encreased nor diminished during the Period for which he shall have been elected, and he shall not receive within that Period any other Emolument from the United States, or any of them.

Before he enter on the Execution of his Office, he shall take the following Oath or Affirmation:—"I do solemnly swear (or affirm) that I will faithfully execute the Office of President of the United States, and will to the best of my Ability, preserve, protect and defend the Constitution of the United States."

SECTION 2.   The President shall be Commander in Chief of the Army and Navy of the United States, and of the Militia of the several States, when called into the actual Service of the United States; he may require the Opinion, in writing, of the principal Officer in each of the executive Departments, upon any Subject relating to the Duties of their respective Offices, and he shall have Power to grant Reprieves and Pardons for Offences against the United States, except in Cases of Impeachment.

He shall have Power, by and with the Advice and Consent of the Senate, to make Treaties, provided two thirds of the Senators present concur; and he shall nominate, and by and with the Advice and Consent of the Senate, shall appoint Ambassadors, other public Ministers and Consuls, Judges of the supreme Court, and all other Officers of the United States, whose Appointments are not herein otherwise provided for, and which shall be established by Law: but the Congress may by Law vest the Appointment of such inferior Officers, as they think proper, in the President alone, in the Courts of Law, or in the Heads of Departments.

The President shall have Power to fill up all Vacancies that may happen during the Recess of the Senate, by granting Commissions which shall expire at the End of their next Session.

SECTION 3.   He shall from time to time give to the Congress Information of the State of the Union, and recommend to their Consideration such Measures as he shall judge necessary and expedient; he may, on extraordinary Occasions, convene both Houses, or either of them, and in Case of Disagreement between them, with Respect to the Time of Adjournment, he may adjourn them to such Time as he shall think proper; he shall receive Ambassadors and other public Ministers; he shall take Care that the Laws be faithfully executed, and shall Commission all the Officers of the United States.

SECTION 4. The President, Vice President and all civil Officers of the United States, shall be removed from Office on Impeachment for, and Conviction of, Treason, Bribery, or other high Crimes and Misdemeanors.

## ARTICLE III.

SECTION 1. The judicial Power of the United States, shall be vested in one supreme Court, and in such inferior Courts as the Congress may from time to time ordain and establish. The Judges, both of the supreme and inferior Courts, shall hold their Offices during good Behaviour, and shall, at stated Times, receive for their Services, a Compensation, which shall not be diminished during their Continuance in Office.

SECTION 2. The judicial Power shall extend to all Cases, in Law and Equity, arising under this Constitution, the Laws of the United States, and Treaties made, or which shall be made, under their Authority;—to all Cases affecting Ambassadors, other public Ministers and Consuls;—to all Cases of admiralty and maritime Jurisdiction;—to Controversies to which the United States shall be a Party;—to Controversies between two or more States;—between a State and Citizens of another State;—between Citizens of different States;—between Citizens of the same State claiming Lands under Grants of different States, and between a State, or the Citizens thereof, and foreign States, Citizens or Subjects.

In all Cases affecting Ambassadors, other public Ministers and Consuls, and those in which a State shall be Party, the supreme Court shall have original Jurisdiction. In all the other Cases before mentioned, the supreme Court shall have appellate Jurisdiction, both as to Law and Fact, with such Exceptions, and under such Regulations as the Congress shall make.

The Trial of all Crimes, except in Cases of Impeachment, shall be by Jury; and such Trial shall be held in the State where the said Crimes shall have been committed; but when not committed within any State, the Trial shall be at such Place or Places as the Congress may by Law have directed.

SECTION 3. Treason against the United States, shall consist only in levying War against them, or in adhering to their Enemies, giving them Aid and Comfort. No Person shall be convicted of Treason unless on the Testimony of two Witnesses to the same overt Act, or on Confession in open Court.

The Congress shall have Power to declare the Punishment of Treason, but no Attainder of Treason shall work Corruption of Blood, or Forfeiture except during the Life of the Person attainted.

## ARTICLE IV.

SECTION 1. Full Faith and Credit shall be given in each State to the public Acts, Records, and judicial Proceedings of every other State.

And the Congress may by general Laws prescribe the Manner in which such Acts, Records and Proceedings shall be proved, and the Effect thereof.

SECTION 2. The Citizens of each State shall be entitled to all Privileges and Immunities of Citizens in the several States.

A Person charged in any State with Treason, Felony, or other Crime, who shall flee from Justice, and be found in another State, shall on Demand of the executive Authority of the State from which he fled, be delivered up, to be removed to the State having Jurisdiction of the Crime.

No Person held to Service or Labour in one State, under the Laws thereof, escaping into another, shall, in Consequence of any Law or Regulation therein, be discharged from such Service or Labour, but shall be delivered up on Claim of the Party to whom such Service or Labour may be due.

SECTION 3. New States may be admitted by the Congress into this Union; but no new State shall be formed or erected within the Jurisdiction of any other State; nor any State be formed by the Junction of two or more States, or Parts of States, without the Consent of the Legislatures of the States concerned as well as of the Congress.

The Congress shall have Power to dispose of and make all needful Rules and Regulations respecting the Territory or other Property belonging to the United States; and nothing in this Constitution shall be so construed as to Prejudice any Claims of the United States, or of any particular State.

SECTION 4. The United States shall guarantee to every State in this Union a Republican Form of Government, and shall protect each of them against Invasion; and on Application of the Legislature, or of the Executive (when the Legislature cannot be convened) against domestic Violence.


## ARTICLE V.

The Congress, whenever two thirds of both Houses shall deem it necessary, shall propose Amendments to this Constitution, or, on the Application of the Legislature of two thirds of the several States, shall call a Convention for proposing Amendments, which, in either Case, shall be valid to all Intents and Purposes, as Part of this Constitution, when ratified by the Legislatures of three fourths of the several States, or by Conventions in three fourths thereof, as the one or the other Mode of Ratification may be proposed by the Congress; Provided that no Amendment which may be made prior to the Year One thousand eight hundred and eight shall in any Manner affect the first and fourth Clauses in the Ninth Section of the first Article; and that no State, without its Consent, shall be deprived of its equal Suffrage in the Senate.

## ARTICLE VI.

All Debts contracted and Engagements entered into, before the Adoption of this Constitution, shall be as valid against the United States under this Constitution, as under the Confederation.

This Constitution, and the Laws of the United States which shall be made in Pursuance thereof; and all Treaties made, or which shall be made, under the Authority of the United States, shall be the supreme Law of the Land; and the Judges in every State shall be bound thereby, any Thing in the Constitution or Laws of any State to the Contrary notwithstanding.

The Senators and Representatives before mentioned, and the Members of the several State Legislatures, and all executive and judicial Officers, both of the United States and of the several States, shall be bound by Oath or Affirmation, to support this Constitution; but no religious Test shall ever be required as a Qualification to any Office or public Trust under the United States.

## ARTICLE VII.

The Ratification of the Conventions of nine States, shall be sufficient for the establishment of this Constitution between the States so ratifying the Same.

. . .

## ARTICLES IN ADDITION TO, AND AMENDMENTS OF, THE CONSTITUTION OF THE UNITED STATES OF AMERICA, PROPOSED BY CONGRESS, AND RATIFIED BY THE SEVERAL STATES, PURSUANT TO THE FIFTH ARTICLE OF THE ORIGINAL CONSTITUTION.

### AMENDMENT I [1791]

Congress shall make no law respecting an establishment of religion, or prohibiting the free exercise thereof; or abridging the freedom of speech, or of the press; or the right of the people peaceably to assemble, and to petition the Government for a redress of grievances.

### AMENDMENT II [1791]

A well regulated Militia, being necessary to the security of a free State, the right of the people to keep and bear Arms, shall not be infringed.

### AMENDMENT III [1791]

No Soldier shall, in time of peace be quartered in any house, without the consent of the Owner, nor in time of war, but in a manner to be prescribed by law.

## AMENDMENT IV [1791]

The right of the people to be secure in their persons, houses, papers, and effects, against unreasonable searches and seizures, shall not be violated, and no Warrants shall issue, but upon probable cause, supported by Oath or affirmation, and particularly describing the place to be searched, and the persons or things to be seized.

## AMENDMENT V [1791]

No person shall be held to answer for a capital, or otherwise infamous crime, unless on a presentment or indictment of a Grand Jury, except in cases arising in the land or naval forces, or in the Militia, when in actual service in time of War or public danger; nor shall any person be subject for the same offence to be twice put in jeopardy of life or limb; nor shall be compelled in any criminal case to be a witness against himself, nor be deprived of life, liberty, or property, without due process of law; nor shall private property be taken for public use, without just compensation.

## AMENDMENT VI [1791]

In all criminal prosecutions, the accused shall enjoy the right to a speedy and public trial, by an impartial jury of the State and district wherein the crime shall have been committed, which district shall have been previously ascertained by law, and to be informed of the nature and cause of the accusation; to be confronted with the witnesses against him; to have compulsory process for obtaining Witnesses in his favor, and to have the Assistance of Counsel for his defence.

## AMENDMENT VII [1791]

In Suits at common law, where the value in controversy shall exceed twenty dollars, the right of trial by jury shall be preserved, and no fact tried by a jury be otherwise re-examined in any Court of the United States, than according to the rules of the common law.

## AMENDMENT VIII [1791]

Excessive bail shall not be required, nor excessive fines imposed, nor cruel and unusual punishments inflicted.

## AMENDMENT IX [1791]

The enumeration in the Constitution, of certain rights, shall not be construed to deny or disparage others retained by the people.

## AMENDMENT X [1791]

The powers not delegated to the United States by the Constitution, nor prohibited by it to the States, are reserved to the States respectively, or to the people.

## AMENDMENT XI [1798]

The Judicial power of the United States shall not be construed to extend to any suit in law or equity, commenced or prosecuted against one of the United States by Citizens of another State, or by Citizens or Subjects of any Foreign State.

## AMENDMENT XII [1804]

The Electors shall meet in their respective states and vote by ballot for President and Vice-President, one of whom, at least, shall not be an inhabitant of the same state with themselves; they shall name in their ballots the person voted for as President, and in distinct ballots the person voted for as Vice-President, and they shall make distinct lists of all persons voted for as President, and of all persons voted for as Vice-President, and of the number of votes for each, which lists they shall sign and certify, and transmit sealed to the seat of the government of the United States, directed to the President of the Senate;—The President of the Senate shall, in the presence of the Senate and House of Representatives, open all the certificates and the votes shall then be counted;—The person having the greatest number of votes for President, shall be the President, if such number be a majority of the whole number of Electors appointed; and if no person have such majority, then from the persons having the highest numbers not exceeding three on the list of those voted for as President, the House of Representatives shall choose immediately, by ballot, the President. But in choosing the President, the votes shall be taken by states, the representation from each state having one vote; a quorum for this purpose shall consist of a member or members from two-thirds of the states, and a majority of all the states shall be necessary to a choice. And if the House of Representatives shall not choose a President whenever the right of choice shall devolve upon them, before the fourth day of March next following, then the Vice-President shall act as President, as in the case of the death or other constitutional disability of the President—The person having the greatest number of votes as Vice-President, shall be the Vice-President, if such number be a majority of the whole number of Electors appointed, and if no person have a majority, then from the two highest numbers on the list, the Senate shall choose the Vice-President; a quorum for the purpose shall consist of two-thirds of the whole number of Senators, and a majority of the whole number shall be necessary to a choice. But no person constitutionally ineligible to the office of President shall be eligible to that of Vice-President of the United States.

## AMENDMENT XIII [1865]

SECTION 1.  Neither slavery no involuntary servitude, except as a punishment for crime whereof the party shall have been duly convicted, shall exist within the United States, or any place subject to their jurisdiction.

SECTION 2.  Congress shall have power to enforce this article by appropriate legislation.

## AMENDMENT XIV [1868]

SECTION 1.  All persons born or naturalized in the United States and subject to the jurisdiction thereof, are citizens of the United States and of the State wherein they reside.  No State shall make or enforce any law which shall abridge the privileges or immunities of citizens of the United States; nor shall any State deprive any person of life, liberty, or property, without due process of law;  nor deny to any person within its jurisdiction the equal protection of the laws.

SECTION 2.  Representatives shall be apportioned among the several States according to their respective numbers, counting the whole number of persons in each State, excluding Indians not taxed.  But when the right to vote at any election for the choice of electors for President and Vice President of the United States, Representatives in Congress, the Executive and Judicial officers of a State, or the members of the Legislature thereof, is denied to any of the male inhabitants of such State, being twenty-one years of age, and citizens of the United States, or in any way abridged, except for participation in rebellion, or other crime, the basis of representation therein shall be reduced in the proportion which the number of such male citizens shall bear to the whole number of male citizens twenty-one years of age in such State.

SECTION 3.  No person shall be a Senator or Representative in Congress, or elector of President and Vice President, or hold any office, civil or military, under the United States, or under any State, who, having previously taken an oath, as a member of Congress, or as a member of any State legislature, or as an executive or judicial officer of any State, to support the Constitution of the United States, shall have engaged in insurrection or rebellion against the same, or given aid or comfort to the enemies thereof.  But Congress may by a vote of two-thirds of each House, remove such disability.

SECTION 4.  The validity of the public debt of the United States, authorized by law, including debts incurred for payment of pensions and bounties for services in suppressing insurrection or rebellion, shall not be questioned.  But neither the United States nor any State shall assume or pay any debt or obligation incurred in aid of insurrection or rebellion against the United States, or any claim for the loss or emancipation of any slave;  but all such debts, obligations and claims shall be held illegal and void.

SECTION 5. The Congress shall have power to enforce, by appropriate legislation, the provisions of this article.

## AMENDMENT XV [1870]

SECTION 1. The right of citizens of the United States to vote shall not be denied or abridged by the United States or by any State on account of race, color, or previous condition of servitude.

SECTION 2. The Congress shall have power to enforce this article by appropriate legislation.

## AMENDMENT XVI [1913]

The Congress shall have power to lay and collect taxes on incomes, from whatever source derived, without apportionment among the several States, and without regard to any census or enumeration.

## AMENDMENT XVII [1913]

The Senate of the United States shall be composed of two Senators from each State, elected by the people thereof, for six years; and each Senator shall have one vote. The electors in each State shall have the qualifications requisite for electors of the most numerous branch of the State legislatures.

When vacancies happen in the representation of any State in the Senate, the executive authority of such State shall issue writs of election to fill such vacancies: *Provided,* That the legislature of any State may empower the executive thereof to make temporary appointments until the people fill the vacancies by election as the legislature may direct.

This amendment shall not be so construed as to affect the election or term of any Senator chosen before it becomes valid as part of the Constitution.

## AMENDMENT XVIII [1919]

SECTION 1. After one year from the ratification of this article the manufacture, sale, or transportation of intoxicating liquors within, the importation thereof into, or the exportation thereof from the United States and all territory subject to the jurisdiction thereof for beverage purposes is hereby prohibited.

SECTION 2. The Congress and the several States shall have concurrent power to enforce this article by appropriate legislation.

SECTION 3. This article shall be inoperative unless it shall have been ratified as an amendment to the Constitution by the legislatures of the several States, as provided in the Constitution, within seven years from the date of the submission hereof to the States by the Congress.

## AMENDMENT XIX [1920]

The right of citizens of the United States to vote shall not be denied or abridged by the United States or by any State on account of sex.

Congress shall have power to enforce this article by appropriate legislation.

## AMENDMENT XX [1933]

SECTION 1.  The terms of the President and Vice President shall end at noon on the 20th day of January, and the terms of Senators and Representatives at noon on the 3d day of January, of the years in which such terms would have ended if this article had not been ratified; and the terms of their successors shall then begin.

SECTION 2.  The Congress shall assemble at least once in every year, and such meeting shall begin at noon on the 3d day of January, unless they shall by law appoint a different day.

SECTION 3.  If, at the time fixed for the beginning of the term of the President, the President elect shall have died, the Vice President elect shall become President.  If a President shall not have been chosen before the time fixed for the beginning of his term, or if the President elect shall have failed to qualify, then the Vice President elect shall act as President until a President shall have qualified; and the Congress may by law provide for the case wherein neither a President elect nor a Vice President elect shall have qualified, declaring who shall then act as President, or the manner in which one who is to act shall be selected, and such person shall act accordingly until a President or Vice President shall have qualified.

SECTION 4.  The Congress may by law provide for the case of the death of any of the persons from whom the House of Representatives may choose a President whenever the right of choice shall have devolved upon them, and for the case of the death of any of the persons from whom the Senate may choose a Vice President whenever the right of choice shall have devolved upon them.

SECTION 5.  Sections 1 and 2 shall take effect on the 15th day of October following the ratification of this article.

SECTION 6.  This article shall be inoperative unless it shall have been ratified as an amendment to the Constitution by the legislatures of three-fourths of the several States within seven years from the date of its submission.

## AMENDMENT XXI [1933]

SECTION 1.  The eighteenth article of amendment to the Constitution of the United States is hereby repealed.

SECTION 2.  The transportation or importation into any State, Territory, or possession of the United States for delivery or use therein of intoxicating liquors, in violation of the laws thereof, is hereby prohibited.

SECTION 3. This article shall be inoperative unless it shall have been ratified as an amendment to the Constitution by conventions in the several States, as provided in the Constitution, within seven years from the date of the submission hereof to the States by the Congress.

## AMENDMENT XXII [1951]

SECTION 1. No person shall be elected to the office of the President more than twice, and no person who has held the office of President, or acted as President, for more than two years of a term to which some other person was elected President shall be elected to the office of the President more than once. But this Aritcle shall not apply to any person holding the office of President when this Article was proposed by the Congress, and shall not prevent any person who may be holding the office of President, or acting as President, during the term within which this Article becomes operative from holding the office of President or acting as President during the remainder of such term.

SECTION 2. This article shall be inoperative unless it shall have been ratified as an amendment to the Constitution by the legislatures of three-fourths of the several States within seven years from the date of its submission to the States by the Congress.

## AMENDMENT XXIII [1961]

SECTION 1. The District constituting the seat of Government of the United States shall appoint in such manner as the Congress may direct:

A number of electors of President and Vice President equal to the whole number of Senators and Representatives in Congress to which the District would be entitled if it were a State, but in no event more than the least populous State; they shall be in addition to those appointed by the States, but they shall be considered, for the purposes of the election of President and Vice President, to be electors appointed by a State; and they shall meet in the District and perform such duties as provided by the twelfth article of amendment.

SECTION 2. The Congress shall have power to enforce this article by appropriate legislation.

## AMENDMENT XXIV [1964]

SECTION 1. The right of citizens of the United States to vote in any primary or other election for President or Vice President, for electors for President or Vice President, or for Senator or Representative in Congress, shall not be denied or abridged by the United States or any State by reason of failure to pay any poll or other tax.

SECTION 2. The Congress shall have power to enforce this article by appropriate legislation.

## AMENDMENT XXV [1967]

SECTION 1. In case of the removal of the President from office or of his death or resignation, the Vice President shall become President.

SECTION 2. Whenever there is a vacancy in the office of the Vice President, the President shall nominate a Vice President who shall take office upon confirmation by a majority vote of both Houses of Congress.

SECTION 3. Whenever the President transmits to the President pro tempore of the Senate and the Speaker of the House of Representatives his written declaration that he is unable to discharge the powers and duties of his office, and until he transmits to them a written declaration to the contrary, such powers and duties shall be discharged by the Vice President as Acting President.

SECTION 4. Whenever the Vice President and a majority of either the principal officers of the executive department or of such other body as Congress may by law provide, transmit to the President pro tempore of the Senate and the Speaker of the House of Representatives their written declaration that the President is unable to discharge the powers and duties of his office, the Vice President shall immediately assume the powers and duties of the office as Acting President.

Thereafter, when the President transmits to the President pro tempore of the Senate and the Speaker of the House of Representatives his written declaration that no inability exists, he shall resume the powers and duties of his office unless the Vice President and a majority of either the principal officers of the executive department or of such other body as Congress may by law provide, transmit within four days to the President pro tempore of the Senate and the Speaker of the House of Representatives their written declaration that the President is unable to discharge the powers and duties of his office. Thereupon Congress shall decide the issue, assembling within forty-eight hours for that purpose if not in session. If the Congress, within twenty-one days after receipt of the latter written declaration, or, if Congress is not in session, within twenty-one days after Congress is required to assemble, determines by two-thirds vote of both Houses that the President is unable to discharge the powers and duties of his office, the Vice President shall continue to discharge the same as Acting President; otherwise, the President shall resume the powers and duties of his office.

## AMENDMENT XXVI [1971]

SECTION 1. The right of citizens of the United States, who are eighteen years of age or older, to vote shall not be denied or abridged by the United States or by any State on account of age.

SECTION 2. The Congress shall have power to enforce this article by appropriate legislation.

# Appendix B

# COMMUNICATIONS ACT OF 1934

48 Stat. 1064 (1934), as amended, 47 U.S.C.A. § 151 et seq.

---

## TITLE I—GENERAL PROVISIONS

### PURPOSES OF ACT; CREATION OF FEDERAL COMMUNICATIONS COMMISSION

**Sec. 1. [47 U.S.C.A. § 151.]**

For the purpose of regulating interstate and foreign commerce in communication by wire and radio so as to make available, so far as possible, to all the people of the United States a rapid, efficient, Nation-wide, and world-wide wire and radio communication service with adequate facilities at reasonable charges, for the purpose of the national defense, for the purpose of promoting safety of life and property through the use of wire and radio communication, and for the purpose of securing a more effective execution of this policy by centralizing authority heretofore granted by law to several agencies and by granting additional authority with respect to interstate and foreign commerce in wire and radio communication, there is hereby created a commission to be known as the "Federal Communications Commission," which shall be constituted as hereinafter provided, and which shall execute and enforce the provisions of this Act.

.    .    .

### APPLICATION OF ACT

**Sec. 2. [47 U.S.C.A. § 152.]**

(a) The provisions of this Act shall apply to all interstate and foreign communication by wire or radio and all interstate and foreign transmission of energy by radio, which originates and/or is received within the United States, and to all persons engaged within the United States in such communication or such transmission of energy by radio, and to the licensing and regulating of all radio stations as hereinafter provided .  .  .  . The provisions of this Act shall apply with respect to cable service to all persons engaged within the United States in providing such service, and to the facilities of cable operators which relate to such service as provided in title VI.

.    .    .

## TITLE III—PROVISIONS RELATING TO RADIO

### LICENSE FOR RADIO COMMUNICATION OR TRANSMISSION OF ENERGY

**Sec. 301.  [47 U.S.C.A. § 301.]**

It is the purpose of this Act, among other things, to maintain the control of the United States over all the channels of interstate and foreign radio transmission; and to provide for the use of such channels, but not the ownership thereof, by persons for limited periods of time, under licenses granted by Federal authority, and no such license shall be construed to create any right, beyond the terms, conditions, and periods of the license.  No person shall use or operate any apparatus for the transmission of energy or communications or signals by radio (a) from one place in any Territory or possession of the United States or in the District of Columbia to another place in the same Territory, possession, or district;  or (b) from any State, Territory, or possession of the United States, or from the District of Columbia to any other State, Territory, or possession of the United States;  or (c) from any place in any State, Territory, or possession of the United States, or in the District of Columbia, to any place in any foreign country or to any vessel;  or (d) within any State when the effects of such use extend beyond the borders of said State, or when interference is caused by such use or operation with the transmission of such energy, communications, or signals from within said State to any place beyond its borders, or from any place beyond its borders to any place within said State, or with the transmission or reception of such energy, communications, or signals from and/or to places beyond the borders of said State;  or (e) upon any vessel or aircraft of the United States;  or (f) upon any other mobile stations within the jurisdiction of the United States, except under and in accordance with this Act and with a license in that behalf granted under the provisions of this Act.

.   .   .

### GENERAL POWERS OF THE COMMISSION

**Sec. 303.  [47 U.S.C.A. § 303.]**

Except as otherwise provided in this Act, the Commission from time to time, as public convenience, interest, or necessity requires shall:

(a) Classify radio stations;

(b) Prescribe the nature of the service to be rendered by each class of licensed stations and each station within any class;

(c) Assign bands of frequencies to the various classes of stations, and assign frequencies for each individual station and determine the power which each station shall use and the time during which it may operate;

(d) Determine the location of classes of stations or individual stations;

(e) Regulate the kind of apparatus to be used with respect to its external effects and the purity and sharpness of the emissions from each station and from the apparatus therein;

(f) Make such regulations not inconsistent with law as it may deem necessary to prevent interference between stations and to carry out the provisions of this Act: *Provided, however,* That changes in the frequencies, authorized power, or in the times of operation of any station, shall not be made without the consent of the station licensee unless, after a public hearing, the Commission shall determine that such changes will promote public convenience or interest or will serve public necessity, or the provisions of this Act will be more fully complied with;

(g) Study new uses for radio, provide for experimental uses of frequencies, and generally encourage the larger and more effective use of radio in the public interest;

(h) Have authority to establish areas or zones to be served by any station;

(i) Have authority to make special regulations applicable to radio stations engaged in chain broadcasting;

(j) Have authority to make general rules and regulations requiring stations to keep such records of programs, transmissions of energy, communications, or signals as it may deem desirable;

. . .

(m)(1) Have authority to suspend the license of any operator upon proof sufficient to satisfy the Commission that the licensee—

(A) has violated any provision of any Act, treaty, or convention binding on the United States, which the Commission is authorized to administer, or any regulation made by the Commission under any such Act, treaty, or convention; or

. . .

(D) has transmitted superfluous radio communications or signals or communications containing profane or obscene words, language, or meaning. . . .

. . .

(r) Make such rules and regulations and prescribe such restrictions and conditions, not inconsistent with law, as may be necessary to carry out the provisions of this Act, or any international radio or wire communications treaty or convention, or regulations annexed thereto, including any treaty or convention insofar as it relates to the use of radio, to which the United States is or may hereafter become a party.

(s) Have authority to require that apparatus designed to receive television pictures broadcast simultaneously with sound be capable of adequately receiving all frequencies allocated by the Commission to television broadcasting when such apparatus is shipped in inter- state commerce, or is imported from any foreign country into the United States, for sale or resale to the public.

.  .  .

## ALLOCATION OF FACILITIES; TERM OF LICENSES

**Sec. 307.  [47 U.S.C.A. § 307.]**

(a) The Commission, if public convenience, interest, or necessity will be served thereby, subject to the limitations of this Act, shall grant to any applicant therefor a station license provided for by this Act.

(b) In considering applications for licenses, and modifications and renewals thereof, when and insofar as there is demand for the same, the Commission shall make such distribution of licenses, frequencies, hours of operation, and of power among the several States and communities as to provide a fair, efficient, and equitable distribution of radio service to each of the same.

.  .  .

(d) No license granted for the operation of a television broadcasting station shall be for a term longer than five years .  .  . and any license granted may be revoked as hereinafter provided.  Each license granted for the operation of a radio broadcasting station shall be for a term of not to exceed seven years.  Upon the expiration of any license, upon application therefor, a renewal of such license may be granted from time to time for a term of not to exceed five years in the case of television broadcasting licenses, for a term of not to exceed seven years in the case of radio broadcasting station licenses, and for a term of not to exceed five years in the case of other licenses, if the Commission finds that public interest, convenience, and necessity would be served thereby.

.  .  .

(e) No renewal of an existing station license in the broadcast or the common carrier services shall be granted more than thirty days prior to the expiration of the original license.

## APPLICATIONS FOR LICENSES .  .  .

**Sec. 308.  [47 U.S.C.A. § 308.]**

.  .  .

(b) All applications for station licenses, or modifications or renewals thereof, shall set forth such facts as the Commission by regulation may prescribe as to the citizenship, character, and financial, technical, and other qualifications of the applicant to operate the station;  the owner- ship and location of the proposed station and of the stations, if any, with which it is proposed to communicate;  the frequencies and the power desired to be used;  the hours of the day or other periods of time during which it is proposed to operate the station;  the purposes for which the

station is to be used; and such other information as it may require.
. . .
. . .

## ACTION UPON APPLICATIONS; FORM OF AND CONDITIONS ATTACHED TO LICENSES

**Sec. 309.** [47 U.S.C.A. § 309.]

(a) Subject to the provisions of this section, the Commission shall determine, in the case of each application filed with it to which section 308 applies, whether the public interest, convenience, and necessity will be served by the granting of such application, and, if the Commission, upon examination of such application and upon consideration of such other matters as the Commission may officially notice, shall find that public interest, convenience, and necessity would be served by the granting thereof, it shall grant such application.
. . .

(d)(1) Any party in interest may file with the Commission a petition to deny any application. . . .

(2) If the Commission finds on the basis of the application, the pleadings filed, or other matters which it may officially notice that there are no substantial and material questions of fact and that a grant of the application would be consistent with subsection (a), it shall make the grant, deny the petition, and issue a concise statement of the reasons for denying the petition, which statement shall dispose of all substantial issues raised by the petition. If a substantial and material question of fact is presented or if the Commission for any reason is unable to find that grant of the application would be consistent with subsection (a), it shall proceed as provided in subsection (e).

(e) If, in the case of any application to which subsection (a) of this section applies, a substantial and material question of fact is presented or the Commission for any reason is unable to make the finding specified in such subsection, it shall formally designate the application for hearing on the ground or reasons then obtaining and shall forthwith notify the applicant and all other known parties in interest of such action and the grounds and reasons therefor, specifying with particularity the matters and things in issue but not including issues or requirements phrased generally. . . .
. . .

(h) Such station licenses as the Commission may grant shall be in such general form as it may prescribe, but each license shall contain, in addition to other provisions, a statement of the following conditions to which such license shall be subject: (1) The station license shall not vest in the licensee any right to operate the station nor any right in the use of the frequencies designated in the license beyond the term thereof nor in any other manner than authorized therein; (2) neither the license nor the right granted thereunder shall be assigned or otherwise transferred in violation of this Act; (3) every license issued under this Act shall be subject in terms to the right of use or control conferred by section 606 of this Act.*

.    .    .

## LIMITATION ON HOLDING AND TRANSFER OF LICENSES

**Sec. 310.  [47 U.S.C.A. § 310.]**

(a) The station license required hereby shall not be granted to or held by any foreign government or representative thereof.

(b) No broadcast or common carrier .   .   . license shall be granted to or held by—

(1) Any alien or the representative of any alien;

(2) Any corporation organized under the laws of any foreign government;

.    .    .

(d) No construction permit or station license, or any rights thereunder, shall be transferred, assigned, or disposed of in any manner, voluntarily or involuntarily, directly or indirectly, or by transfer of control of any corporation holding such permit or license, to any person except upon application to the Commission and upon finding by the Commission that the public interest, convenience, and necessity will be served thereby.  Any such application shall be disposed of as if the proposed transferee or assignee were making application under section 308 for the permit or license in question;  but in acting thereon the Commission may not consider whether the public interest, convenience, and necessity might be served by the transfer, assignment, or disposal of the permit or license to a person other than the proposed transferee or assignee.

## SPECIAL REQUIREMENTS WITH RESPECT TO CERTAIN APPLICATIONS IN THE BROADCASTING SERVICE

**Sec. 311.  [47 U.S.C.A. § 311.]**

.    .    .

(c)(1) If there are pending before the Commission two or more applications for a permit for construction of a broadcasting station, only one of which can be granted, it shall be unlawful, without approval of the Commission, for the applicants or any of them to effectuate an agreement whereby one or more of such applicants withdraws his or their application or applications.

(2) The request for Commission approval in any such case shall be made in writing jointly by all the parties to the agreement.  Such request shall contain or be accompanied by full information with

---

* [Section 606 grants substantial powers to the President to utilize communications facilities during wartime or a national emergency.]

respect to the agreement, set forth in such detail, form, and manner as the Commission shall by rule require.

(3) The Commission shall approve the agreement only if it determines (A) that the agreement is consistent with the public interest, convenience, or necessity; and (B) no party to the agreement filed its application for the purpose of reaching or carrying out such agreement. If the agreement does not contemplate a merger, but contemplates the making of any direct or indirect payment to any party thereto in consideration of his withdrawal of his application, the Commission may determine the agreement to be consistent with the public interest, convenience, or necessity only if the amount or value of such payment, as determined by the Commission, is not in excess of the aggregate amount determined by the Commission to have been legitimately and prudently expended and to be expended by such applicant in connection with preparing, filing, and advocating the granting of his application.

. . .

## ADMINISTRATIVE SANCTIONS

**Sec. 312. [47 U.S.C.A. § 312.]**

(a) The Commission may revoke any station license or construction permit—

(1) for false statements knowingly made either in the application or in any statement of fact which may be required pursuant to section 308;

(2) because of conditions coming to the attention of the Commission which would warrant it in refusing to grant a license or permit on an original application;

(3) for willful or repeated failure to operate substantially as set forth in the license;

(4) for willful or repeated violation of, or willful or repeated failure to observe any provision of this Act or any rule or regulation of the Commission authorized by this Act or by a treaty ratified by the United States;

(5) for violation of or failure to observe any final cease and desist order issued by the Commission under this section;

(6) for violation of section 1304, 1343, or 1464 of title 18 of the United States Code; * or

* [Relevant provisions read as follows:

§ 1304. Broadcasting lottery information

Whoever broadcasts by means of any radio station for which a license is required by any law of the United States, or whoever, operating any such station, knowingly permits the broadcasting of, any advertisement of or information concerning any lottery, gift enterprise, or similar scheme, offering prizes dependent in whole or in part upon lot or chance, or any list of the prizes drawn or awarded by means of any such lottery, gift enterprise, or scheme, whether said list contains any part or all of such prizes, shall be fined not more than $1,000 or imprisoned not more than one year, or both.

(7) for willful or repeated failure to allow reasonable access to or to permit purchase of reasonable amounts of time for the use of a broadcasting station by a legally qualified candidate for Federal elective office on behalf of his candidacy.

(b) Where any person (1) has failed to operate substantially as set forth in a license, (2) has violated or failed to observe any of the provisions of this Act, or section 1304, 1343, or 1464 of title 18 of the United States Code, or (3) has violated or failed to observe any rule or regulation of the Commission authorized by this Act or by a treaty ratified by the United States, the Commission may order such person to cease and desist from such action.

(c) Before revoking a license or permit pursuant to subsection (a), or issuing a cease and desist order pursuant to subsection (b), the Commission shall serve upon the licensee, permittee, or person involved an order to show cause [at a hearing] why an order of revocation or a cease and desist order should not be issued. . . .

(d) In any case where a hearing is conducted pursuant to the provisions of this section, both the burden of proceeding with the introduction of evidence and the burden of proof shall be upon the Commission.

. . .

## APPLICATION OF ANTITRUST LAWS; REFUSAL OF LICENSES AND PERMITS IN CERTAIN CASES

### Sec. 313. [47 U.S.C.A. § 313.]

(a) All laws of the United States relating to unlawful restraints and monopolies and to combinations, contracts, or agreements in restraint of trade are hereby declared to be applicable to the manufacture and sale of and to trade in radio apparatus and devices entering into or affecting interstate or foreign commerce and to interstate or foreign radio commu-

Each day's broadcasting shall constitute a separate offense.

§ 1343. Fraud by wire, radio, or television

Whoever, having devised or intending to devise any scheme or artifice to defraud, or for obtaining money or property by means of false or fraudulent pretenses, representations, or promises, transmits or causes to be transmitted by means of wire, radio, or television communication in interstate or foreign commerce, any writings, signs, signals, pictures, or sounds for the purpose of executing such scheme or artifice, shall be fined not more than $1,000 or imprisoned not more than five years, or both.

§ 1464. Broadcasting obscene language

Whoever utters any obscene, indecent, or profane language by means of radio communications shall be fined not more than $10,000 or imprisoned not more than two years, or both.

§ 1307. State-conducted lotteries

(a) The provisions of sections 1301, 1302, 1303, and 1304 shall not apply to an advertisement, list of prizes, or information concerning a lottery conducted by a State acting under the authority of State law—

(1) contained in a newspaper published in that State, or

(2) broadcast by a radio or television station licensed to a location in that State or an adjacent State which conducts such a lottery. . . .]

nications. Whenever in any suit, action, or proceeding, civil or criminal, brought under the provisions of any of said laws or in any proceedings brought to enforce or to review findings and orders of the Federal Trade Commission or other governmental agency in respect of any matters as to which said Commission or other governmental agency is by law authorized to act, any licensee shall be found guilty of the violation of the provisions of such laws or any of them, the court, in addition to the penalties imposed by said laws, may adjudge, order, and/or decree that the license of such licensee shall, as of the date the decree or judgment becomes finally effective or as of such other date as the said decree shall fix, be revoked and that all rights under such license shall thereupon cease: *Provided, however,* That such licensee shall have the same right of appeal or review, as is provided by law in respect of other decrees and judgments of said court.

(b) The Commission is hereby directed to refuse a station license and/or the permit hereinafter required for the construction of a station to any person (or to any person directly or indirectly controlled by such person) whose license has been revoked by a court under this section.

. . .

## FACILITIES FOR CANDIDATES FOR PUBLIC OFFICE

**Sec. 315. [47 U.S.C.A. § 315.]**

(a) If any licensee shall permit any person who is a legally qualified candidate for any public office to use a broadcasting station, he shall afford equal opportunities to all other such candidates for that office in the use of such broadcasting station: *Provided,* That such licensee shall have no power of censorship over the material broadcast under the provisions of this section. No obligation is imposed under this subsection upon any licensee to allow the use of its station by any such candidate. Appearance by a legally qualified candidate on any—

(1) Bona fide newscast,

(2) Bona fide news interview,

(3) Bona fide news documentary (if the appearance of the candidate is incidental to the presentation of the subject or subjects covered by the news documentary), or

(4) On-the-spot coverage of bona fide news events (included but not limited to political conventions and activities incidental thereto), shall not be deemed to be use of a broadcasting station within the meaning of this subsection. Nothing in the foregoing sentence shall be construed as relieving broadcasters, in connection with the presentation of newscasts, news interviews, news documentaries, and on-the-spot coverage of news events, from the obligation imposed upon them under this Act to operate in the public interest and to afford reasonable opportunity for the discussion of conflicting views on issues of public importance.

(b) The charges made for the use of any broadcast station by any person who is a legally qualified candidate for any public office in connection with his campaign for nomination for election, or election, to such office shall not exceed—

(1) During the 45 days preceding the date of a primary or primary runoff election and during the 60 days preceding the date of a general or special election in which such person is a candidate, the lowest unit charge of the station for the same class and amount of time for the same period; and

(2) At any other time, the charges made for comparable use of such station by other users thereof.

(c) For the purposes of this section:

(1) The term "broadcasting station" includes a community antenna television system.

(2) The terms "licensee" and "station licensee" when used with respect to a community antenna television system, mean the operator of such system.

(d) The Commission shall prescribe appropriate rules and regulations to carry out the provisions of this section.

## MODIFICATION BY COMMISSION OF CONSTRUCTION PERMITS OR LICENSES

**Sec. 316.  [47 U.S.C.A. § 316.]**

(a) Any station license or construction permit may be modified by the Commission either for a limited time or for the duration of the term thereof, if in the judgment of the Commission such action will promote the public interest, convenience, and necessity, or the provisions of this Act or of any treaty ratified by the United States will be more fully complied with.  No such order of modification shall become final until the holder of the license or permit shall have been notified in writing of the proposed action and the grounds and reasons therefor, and shall have been given reasonable opportunity, in no event less than thirty days, to show cause by public hearing, if requested, why such order of modification should not issue.  . . .

(b) In any case where a hearing is conducted pursuant to the provisions of this section, both the burden of proceeding with the introduction of evidence and the burden of proof shall be upon the Commission.

## ANNOUNCEMENT WITH RESPECT TO CERTAIN MATTER BROADCAST

**Sec. 317.  [47 U.S.C.A. § 317.]**

(a)(1) All matter broadcast by any radio station for which any money, service or other valuable consideration is directly or indirectly paid, or promised to or charged or accepted by, the station so broadcasting, from any person, shall, at the time the same is so broadcast, be announced as paid for or furnished, as the case may be, by such person: *Provided,* That "service or other valuable consideration" shall not include any service or property furnished without charge or at a nominal charge for use on, or in connection with, a broadcast unless it is so furnished in consideration for an identification in a broadcast of any person, product, service, trademark, or brand name beyond an identification which is reasonably related to the use of such service or property on the broadcast.

. . .

## FALSE DISTRESS SIGNALS; REBROADCASTING . . .

**Sec. 325. [47 U.S.C.A. § 325.]**

(a) No person within the jurisdiction of the United States shall knowingly utter or transmit, or cause to be uttered or transmitted, any false or fraudulent signal of distress, or communication relating thereto, nor shall any broadcasting station rebroadcast the program or any part thereof of another broadcasting station without the express authority of the originating station.

. . .

## CENSORSHIP . . .

**Sec. 326. [47 U.S.C.A. § 326.]**

Nothing in this Act shall be understood or construed to give the Commission the power of censorship over the radio communications or signals transmitted by any radio station, and no regulation or condition shall be promulgated or fixed by the Commission which shall interfere with the right of free speech by means of radio communication.

## PROHIBITION AGAINST SHIPMENT OF CERTAIN TELEVISION RECEIVERS

**Sec. 330. [47 U.S.C.A. § 330.]**

(a) No person shall ship in interstate commerce, or import from any foreign country into the United States, for sale or resale to the public, apparatus described in paragraph (s) of section 303 unless it complies with rules prescribed by the Commission pursuant to the authority granted by that paragraph: *Provided,* That this section shall not apply to carriers transporting such apparatus without trading in it.

. . .

## TITLE V—PENAL PROVISIONS—FORFEITURES

### FORFEITURES

**Sec. 503.   [47 U.S.C.A. § 503.]**

. . .

(b)(1) Any person who is determined by the Commission, in accordance with paragraph (3) or (4) of this subsection, to have—

(A) willfully or repeatedly failed to comply substantially with the terms and conditions of any license, permit, certificate, or other instrument or authorization issued by the Commission;

(B) willfully or repeatedly failed to comply with any of the provisions of this Act or of any rule, regulation, or order issued by the Commission under this Act or under any treaty convention, or other agreement to which the United States is a party and which is binding upon the United States;

(C) violated any provision of section 317(c) or 509(a) of this Act; or

(D) violated any provision of sections 1304, 1343, or 1464 of Title 18, United States Code;

shall be liable to the United States for a forfeiture penalty. A forfeiture penalty under this subsection shall be in addition to any other penalty provided for by this Act; except that this subsection shall not apply to any conduct which is subject to forfeiture under . . . section 507 of this Act.

(2) The amount of any forfeiture penalty determined under this subsection shall not exceed $2,000 for each violation. Each day of a continuing violation shall constitute a separate offense, but the total forfeiture penalty which may be imposed under this subsection, for acts or omissions described in paragraph (1) of this subsection and set forth in the notice or the notice of apparent liability issued under this subsection, shall not exceed:

(A) $20,000, if the violator is (i) a common carrier subject to the provisions of this Act, (ii) a broadcast station licensee or permittee, or (iii) a cable television operator; or

(B) $5,000, in any case not covered by subparagraph (A).

The amount of such forfeiture penalty shall be assessed by the Commission, or its designee, by written notice. In determining the amount of such a forfeiture penalty, the Commission or its designee shall take into account the nature, circumstances, extent, and gravity of the prohibited acts committed and, with respect to the violator, the degree of culpability, any history of prior offenses, ability to pay, and such other matters as justice may require.

. . .

## PROHIBITED PRACTICES IN CASES OF CONTESTS OF INTELLECTUAL KNOWLEDGE, INTELLECTUAL SKILL OR CHANCE

**Sec. 509. [47 U.S.C.A. § 509.]**

(a) It shall be unlawful for any person, with intent to deceive the listening or viewing public—

(1) To supply to any contestant in a purportedly bona fide contest of intellectual knowledge or intellectual skill any special and secret assistance whereby the outcome of such contest will be in whole or in part prearranged or predetermined.

(2) By means of persuasion, bribery, intimidation, or otherwise, to induce or cause any contestant in a purportedly bona fide contest of intellectual knowledge or intellectual skill to refrain in any manner from using or displaying his knowledge or skill in such contest, whereby the outcome thereof will be in whole or in part prearranged or predetermined.

.  .  .

## TITLE VI—CABLE COMMUNICATIONS

### PURPOSES

**Sec. 601. [47 U.S.C.A. § 601.]**

The purposes of this title are to

(1) establish a national policy concerning cable communications;

(2) establish franchise procedures and standards which encourage the growth and development of cable systems and which assure that cable systems are responsive to the needs and interests of the local community;

(3) establish guidelines for the exercise of Federal, State, and local authority with respect to the regulation of cable systems;

(4) assure and encourage that cable communications provide and are encouraged to provide the widest possible diversity of information sources and services to the public.

(5) establish an orderly process for franchise renewal which protects cable operators against unfair denials of renewal where the operator's past performance and proposal for future performance meet the standards established by this title; and

(6) promote competition in cable communications and minimize unnecessary regulation that would impose an undue economic burden on cable systems.

.  .  .

[Until 1984, Sec. 605 dealt with unauthorized publication or use of communications. For the current provisions, see Sec. 705.]

## CABLE CHANNELS FOR PUBLIC, EDUCATIONAL OR GOVERNMENTAL USE

**Sec. 611. [47 U.S.C.A. § 611.]**

(a) A franchising authority may establish requirements in a franchise with respect to the designation or use of channel capacity for public, educational, or governmental use only to the extent provided in this section.

(b) A franchising authority may in its request for proposals require as part of a franchise, and may require as part of a cable operator's proposal for a franchise renewal, subject to section 626, that channel capacity be designated for public, educational, or governmental use,

. . .

(c) A franchising authority may enforce any requirement in any franchise regarding the providing or use of such channel capacity. Such enforcement authority includes the authority to enforce any provisions of the franchise for services, facilities, or equipment proposed by the cable operator, which relate to public, educational, or governmental use of channel capacity, whether or not required by the franchising authority pursuant to subsection (b).

. . .

(e) Subject to section 624(d), a cable operator shall not exercise any editorial control over any public, educational, or governmental use of channel capacity provided pursuant to this section.

. . .

## GENERAL FRANCHISE REQUIREMENTS

**Sec. 621. [47 U.S.C.A. § 621.]**

(a)(1) A franchising authority may award, in accordance with the provisions of this title, one or more franchises within its jurisdiction.

. . .

(3) In awarding a franchise or franchises, a franchising authority shall assure that access to cable service is not denied to any group of potential residential cable subscribers because of the income of the residents of the local area in which such group resides.

. . .

(c) Any cable system shall not be subject to regulation as a common carrier or utility by reason of providing any cable service.

. . .

## FRANCHISE FEES

**Sec. 622. [47 U.S.C.A. § 622.]**

(a) Subject to the limitation of subsection (b), any cable operator may be required under the terms of any franchise to pay a franchise fee.

(b) For any 12-month period, the franchise fees paid by a cable operator with respect to any cable system shall not exceed 5 percent of such cable operator's gross revenues derived in such period from the operation of the cable system.

. . .

## REGULATION OF RATES

**Sec. 623.   [47 U.S.C.A. § 623.]**

(a) Any Federal agency or State may not regulate the rates for the provision of cable service except to cable subscribers only to the extent provided under this section.   Any franchising authority may regulate the rates for the provision of cable service or any other communications service provided over a cable system to cable subscribers, but only to the extent provided under this section.

(b)(1) Within 180 days after the date of the enactment of this title, the Commission shall prescribe and make effective regulations which authorize a franchising authority to regulate rates for the provision of basic cable service in circumstances in which a cable system is not subject to effective competition.   Such regulations may apply to any franchise granted after the effective date of such regulations.   Such regulations shall not apply to any rate while such rate is subject to the provisions of subsection (c).

(2) For purposes of rate regulation under this subsection, such regulations shall—

(A) define the circumstances in which a cable system is not subject to effective competition;  and

(B) establish standards for such rate regulation.

. . .

(c) In the case of any cable system for which a franchise has been granted on or before the effective date of this title, until the end of the 2-year period beginning on such effective date, the franchising authority may, to the extent provided in a franchise—

(1) regulate the rates for the provision of basic cable service, including multiple tiers of basic cable service;

(2) require the provision of any service tier provided without charge (disregarding any installation or rental charge for equipment necessary for receipt of such tier);  or

(3) regulate rates for the initial installation or the rental of one set of the minimum equipment which is necessary for the subscriber's receipt of basic cable service.

. . .

RENEWAL

**Sec. 626. [47 U.S.C.A. § 626.]**

(a) During the 6-month period which begins with the 36th month before the franchise expiration, the franchising authority may on its own initiative, and shall at the request of the cable operator, commence proceedings which afford the public in the franchise area appropriate notice and participation for the purpose of—

(1) identifying the future cable-related community needs and interests; and

(2) reviewing the performance of the cable operator under the franchise during the then current franchise term.

(b)(1) Upon completion of a proceeding under subsection (a), a cable operator seeking renewal of a franchise may, on its own initiative or at the request of a franchising authority, submit a proposal for renewal.

(2) Subject to section 624, any such proposal shall contain such material as the franchising authority may require, including proposals for an upgrade of the cable system.

(3) The franchising authority may establish a date by which such proposals shall be submitted.

(c)(1) Upon submittal by a cable operator of a proposal to the franchising authority for the renewal of a franchise, the franchising authority shall provide prompt public notice of such proposal and, during the 4-month period which begins on the completion of any proceedings under subsection (a), renew the franchise or, issue a preliminary assessment that the franchise should not be renewed and, at the request of the operator or on its own initiative, commence an administrative proceeding after providing prompt public notice of such proceeding in accordance with paragraph (2) to consider whether—

(A) the cable operator has substantially complied with the material terms of the existing franchise and with applicable law;

(B) the quality of the operator's service including signal quality, response to consumer complaints, and billing practices, but without regard to the mix, quality, or level of cable services or other services provided over the system, has been reasonable in light of community needs;

(C) the operator has the financial, legal, and technical ability to provide the services, facilities, and equipment as set forth in the operator's proposal; and

(D) the operator's proposal is reasonable to meet the future cable-related community needs and interests, taking into account the cost of meeting such needs and interests.

. . .

(3) At the completion of a proceeding under this subsection, the franchising authority shall issue a written decision granting or

denying the proposal for renewal based upon the record of such proceeding, and transmit a copy of such decision to the cable operator. Such decision shall state the reasons therefor.

(d) Any denial of a proposal for renewal shall be based on one or more adverse findings made with respect to the factors described in subparagraphs (A) through (D) of subsection (c)(1) . . . . .

. . .

## OBSCENE PROGRAMMING

### Sec. 639. [47 U.S.C.A. § 639.]

Whoever transmits over any cable system any matter which is obscene or otherwise unprotected by the Constitution of the United States shall be fined not more than $10,000 or imprisoned not more than two years, or both.

## UNAUTHORIZED PUBLICATION OR USE OF COMMUNICATIONS

### Sec. 705. [47 U.S.C.A. § 705.]

(a) Except as authorized by Chapter 119, Title 18, no person receiving, assisting in receiving, transmitting, or assisting in transmitting, any interstate or foreign communication by wire or radio shall divulge or publish the existence, contents, substance, purport, effect, or meaning thereof, except through authorized channels of transmission or reception, (1) to any person other than the addressee, his agent, or attorney, (2) to a person employed or authorized to forward such communication to its destination, (3) to proper accounting or distributing officers of the various communicating centers over which the communication may be passed, (4) to the master of a ship under whom he is serving, (5) in response to a subpoena issued by a court of competent jurisdiction, or (6) on demand of other lawful authority. No person not being authorized by the sender shall intercept any radio communication and divulge or publish the existence, contents, substance, purport, effect, or meaning of such intercepted communication to any person. No person not being entitled thereto shall receive or assist in receiving any interstate or foreign communication by radio and use such communication (or any information therein contained) for his own benefit or for the benefit of another not entitled thereto. No person having received any intercepted radio communication or having become acquainted with the contents, substance, purport, effect, or meaning of such communication (or any part thereof) knowing that such communication was intercepted, shall divulge or publish the existence, contents, substance, purport, effect, or meaning of such communication (or any part thereof) or use such communication (or any information therein contained) for his own benefit or for the benefit of another not entitled thereto. This section shall not apply to the receiving, divulging, publishing, or utilizing the contents of any radio communication which is transmitted by any station for the use of the general public, which relates to ships, aircraft, vehicles or persons in distress, or which is transmitted by an amateur radio station operator or by a citizens band radio operator.

(b) The provisions of subsection (a) shall not apply to the interception or receipt by any individual, or the assisting (including the manufacture or sale) of such interception or receipt, of any satellite cable programming for private viewing if—

(1) the programming involved is not encrypted;  and

(2)(A) a marketing system is not established under which—

(i) an agent or agents have been lawfully designated for the purpose of authorizing private viewing by individuals, and

(ii) such authorization is available to the individual involved from the appropriate agent or agents;  or

(B) a marketing system described in subparagraph (A) is established and the individuals receiving such programming have obtained authorization for private viewing under that system.

(c) For purposes of this section—

(1) the term "satellite cable programming" means video programming which is transmitted via satellite and which is primarily intended for the direct receipt by cable operators for their retransmission to cable subscribers;

(2) the term "agent," with respect to any person, includes an employee of such person;

(3) the term "encrypt," when used with respect to satellite cable programming, means to transmit such programming in a form whereby the aural and visual characteristics (or both) are modified or altered for the purpose of preventing the unauthorized receipt of such programming by persons without authorized equipment which is designed to eliminate the effects of such modification or alteration;

(4) the term "private viewing" means the viewing for private use in an individual's dwelling unit by means of equipment, owned or operated by such individual, capable of receiving satellite cable programming directly from a satellite;  and

(5) the term "private financial gain" shall not include the gain resulting to any individual for the private use in such individual's dwelling unit of any programming for which the individual has not obtained authorization for that use.

(d)(1) Any person who willfully violates subsection (a) shall be fined not more than $1,000 or imprisoned for not more than 6 months or both.

(2) Any person who violates subsection (a) willfully and for purposes of direct or indirect commercial advantage or private financial gain shall be fined not more than $25,000 or imprisoned for not more than 1 year, or both, for the first such conviction and shall

be fined not more than $50,000 or imprisoned for not more than 2 years, or both, for any subsequent conviction.

(3)(A) Any person aggrieved by any violation of subsection (a) may bring a civil action in a United States district court or in any other court of competent jurisdiction.

(B) The court may—

(i) grant temporary and final injunctions on such terms as it may deem reasonable to prevent or restrain violations of subsection (a);

(ii) award damages as described in subparagraph (C); and

(iii) direct the recovery of full costs, including awarding reasonable attorneys' fees to an aggrieved party who prevails.

(C)(i) Damages awarded by any court under this section shall be computed, at the election of the aggrieved party, in accordance with either of the following subclauses;

(I) the party aggrieved may recover the actual damages suffered by him as a result of the violation and any profits of the violator that are attributable to the violation which are not taken into account in computing the actual damages; in determining the violator's profits, the party aggrieved shall be required to prove only the violator's gross revenue, and the violator shall be required to prove his deductible expenses and the elements of profit attributable to factors other than the violation; or

(II) the party aggrieved may recover an award of statutory damages for each violation involved in the action in a sum of not less than $250 or more than $10,000, as the court considers just.

(ii) In any case in which the court finds that the violation was committed willfully and for purposes of direct or indirect commercial advantage or private financial gain, the court in its discretion may increase the award of damages, whether actual or statutory, by an amount of not more than $50,000.

(iii) In any case where the court finds that the violator was not aware and had no reason to believe that his acts constituted a violation of this section, the court in its discretion may reduce the award of damages to a sum of not less than $100.

(4) The importation, manufacture, sale, or distribution of equipment by any person with the intent of its use to assist in any activity prohibited by subsection (a) shall be subject to penalties and remedies under this subsection to the same extent and in the same manner as a person who has engaged in such prohibited activity.

(5) The penalties under this subsection shall be in addition to those prescribed under any other provision of this title.

(6) Nothing in this subsection shall prevent any State, or political subdivision thereof, from enacting or enforcing any laws with respect to the importation, sale, manufacture, or distribution of equipment by any person with the intent of its use to assist in the interception or receipt of radio communications prohibited by subsection (a).

(e) Nothing in this section shall affect any right, obligation, or liability under Title 17, United States Code, any rule, regulation, or order thereunder, or any other applicable Federal, State, or local law.

# Appendix C

# FEDERAL COMMUNICATIONS COMMISSION

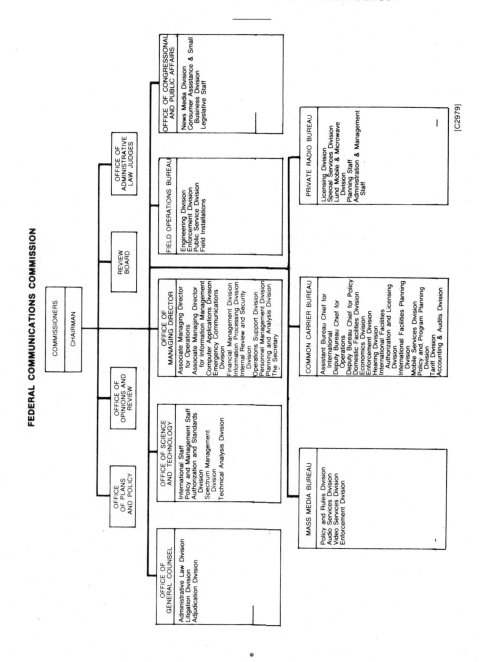

FEDERAL COMMUNICATIONS COMMISSION

COMMISSIONERS

CHAIRMAN

OFFICE OF PLANS AND POLICY

OFFICE OF OPINIONS AND REVIEW

REVIEW BOARD

OFFICE OF ADMINISTRATIVE LAW JUDGES

**OFFICE OF GENERAL COUNSEL**
Administrative Law Division
Litigation Division
Adjudication Division

**OFFICE OF SCIENCE AND TECHNOLOGY**
International Staff
Policy and Management Staff
Authorization and Standards Division
Spectrum Management Division
Technical Analysis Division

**OFFICE OF MANAGING DIRECTOR**
Associate Managing Director for Operations
Associate Managing Director for Information Management
Computer Applications Division
Emergency Communications Division
Financial Management Division
Information Processing Division
Internal Review and Security Division
Operations Support Division
Personnel Management Division
Planning and Analysis Division
The Secretary

**FIELD OPERATIONS BUREAU**
Engineering Division
Enforcement Division
Public Service Division
Field Installations

**OFFICE OF CONGRESSIONAL AND PUBLIC AFFAIRS**
News Media Division
Consumer Assistance & Small Business Division
Legislative Staff

**MASS MEDIA BUREAU**
Policy and Rules Division
Audio Services Division
Video Services Division
Enforcement Division

**COMMON CARRIER BUREAU**
Assistant Bureau Chief for International
Deputy Bureau Chief for Operations
Deputy Bureau Chief for Policy
Domestic Facilities Division
Economics Division
Enforcement Division
Hearing Division
International Facilities Authorization and Licensing Division
International Facilities Planning Division
Mobile Services Division
Policy and Program Planning Division
Tariff Division
Accounting & Audits Division

**PRIVATE RADIO BUREAU**
Licensing Division
Special Services Division
Lund Mobile & Microwave Division
Planning Staff
Administration & Management Staff

[C2979]

\*

621

# INDEX

References are to Pages

†